THE ROUTLEDGE COMPANION TO DIRECTORS' SHAKESPEARE

The Routledge Companion to Directors' Shakespeare is a major collaborative book about plays in performance. Thirty-one authoritative accounts describe in illuminating detail how some of theatre's most talented directors have brought Shakespeare's texts to the stage. Each chapter has a revealing story to tell as it presents new and revitalising approaches to the most familiar works in the English language.

A must-have work of reference for students of both Shakespeare and theatre, this book presents some of the most acclaimed productions of the last hundred years in a variety of cultural and political contexts. Each entry describes a director's own theatrical vision and methods of rehearsal and production. These studies chart the extraordinary feats of interpretation and innovation that have given Shakespeare's plays enduring life in the theatre.

Notable entries include: Ingmar Bergman, Peter Brook, Declan Donnellan, Tyrone Guthrie, Peter Hall, Fritz Kortner, Robert Lepage, Joan Littlewood, Ninagawa Yukio, Joseph Papp, Roger Planchon, Max Reinhardt, Giorgio Strehler, Deborah Warner, Orson Welles and Franco Zeffirelli.

John Russell Brown is Visiting Professor of Theatre at Middlesex University. For fifteen years he was Associate Director of the Royal National Theatre, and he has also chaired the Drama Panel of the Arts Council of Great Britain. He is author of numerous works on Shakespeare, including *New Sites for Shakespeare* (Routledge 1999) and *Shakespeare and the Theatrical Event* (2002), and is editor of *The Oxford Illustrated History of Theatre* (1995) and Routledge's new Theatres of the World series.

THE ROUTLEDGE COMPANION TO DIRECTORS' SHAKESPEARE

Edited by John Russell Brown

LONDON AND NEW YORK

First published 2008
by Routledge
2 Park Square, Milton Park, Abingdon, Oxon OX14 4RN

Simultaneously published in the USA and Canada
by Routledge
270 Madison Ave, New York, NY 10016

Routledge is an imprint of the Taylor & Francis Group, an informa business

Typeset in Sabon by
RefineCatch Limited, Bungay, Suffolk
Printed and bound in Great Britain by
TJ International, Padstow, Cornwall

British Library Cataloguing in Publication Data
A catalogue record for this book is available from the British Library

Library of Congress Cataloging-in-Publication Data
The Routledge companion to directors' Shakespear/edited by John Russell Brown.
p. cm.
Includes bibliographical references and index.
1. Shakespeare, William 1564–1616 – Dramatic production. 2. Shakespeare, William, 1564–1616 – Stage history – 1950-I. Brown, John Russell.
PR3100.R68 2008
792.9'5–cd22

2007028261

ISBN10: 0–415–40044–9 (hbk)
ISBN10: 0–203–93252–8 (ebk)

ISBN13: 978–0–415–40044–2 (hbk)
ISBN13: 978–0–203–93252–0 (ebk)

CONTENTS

ACKNOWLEDGEMENTS

Many conversations with colleagues and associates have contributed to planning this book, and new contacts were made during its commissioning. I am most grateful for this good fellowship that has greatly enhanced the value of the book while lightening my task, compensating for my limitations and helping me to decide which directors to include and which authors to enlist. While 'directors' Shakespeare' has been the topic of more conversations and exchanges of information than I can possibly remember, I know very well that over the course of several years the book has greatly benefited from these interactions. For help with more specific issues, I am especially indebted to those who became contributors and, among those who were not free to join as authors, to Arnold Aronson, John Bradby, Graham Bradshaw, Yuli Dubov, Paul Edmondson, Maik Hamburg, Alex Huang, Barbara Hodgdon, Wilhelm Hortmann, Dennis Kennedy, Ric Knowles, Wilmar Sauter, Robert Smallwood, Uchino Tadashi, Kate Wallis, Stanley Wells and Hersh Zeifman. Once the writing was in hand, discussions with contributors covered not only the content and presentation of their individual entries but also larger questions about the nature of directing and performance, and about the functions of textual and interpretative criticism. Our frequent communication also established the form of individual entries and of their chronologies and bibliographies. I am especially grateful for all the help the contributors have given.

At the publisher's, Talia Rodgers has supported and guided the project from the start and, during the past few years, Minh-Ha Duong has fielded questions and handled the copy promptly and efficiently. As the typescripts moved towards becoming a book, I was most grateful for the expertise and patient, willing care of Liz O'Donnell and Katie Young.

JOHN RUSSELL BROWN
June 2007

INTRODUCTION

This Companion is a new resource for students of both Shakespeare and theatre. Close and detailed accounts of leading directors at work show how varied productions of Shakespeare have been and how theatre has met the challenges of new times and new technology. The concentration on Shakespeare's plays, especially those most frequently produced, brings contrasting intentions and methods into clear focus. Although the directors have worked in very different contexts and over the course of many years, their opportunities and problems will have had much in common so that their achievements are more comparable than if the whole range of their productions were being considered. As an individual's work changes over the years, a reader may discover what the directors have learned from working on Shakespeare and some of the inherent and enduring qualities of the texts. Attention is repeatedly drawn to dramatic structure and development, to theatre's visual, physical, temporal and aural elements and to opportunities in the text for actors to heighten or control an audience's awareness – all elements of performance which are not immediately apparent on the page or readily understood without the test of rehearsal and performance.

Directors, as they are known today, had no role in theatre before the end of the nineteenth century, but as they learnt how to draw a complicated production towards completion they became key persons in its creation: its instigators, inspiration and leaders. They are persons who meet a text head-on in all its many characteristics, both the obvious and those that are hidden until the dialogue becomes part of a performance. This book contains stories about how each of its thirty-one directors have brought the texts to life on stage, the difficulties they have overcome or avoided, their growth in ability, understanding, control and confidence, and the additions, omissions, special emphases and interpretations that have served personal visions and the time and place of performance. And so, besides being a work of reference, this book is also a collection of theatre stories that can be read either from cover to cover or starting wherever interest is caught.

Directors have an unusually complete view of a play, and, when working with actors, they can study the dialogue with exceptional thoroughness. Many of them look for suggestions and implications in a text as well as its explicit meanings, for implied movement, action, tension, emphasis, for variations of tempo, rhythm and mood, for the building of expectation and development of feelings or understanding – all the many subtextual possibilities that are not readily apparent to a reader. In rehearsal, directors discover how action relates to speech and sometimes supplements or contradicts it, and, in following their insights, they discover the play's structure and how it unfolds in time for the pleasure and understanding of audiences. When their productions are studied in sequence, imaginative and experienced directors can serve as uniquely informed critics of Shakespeare's plays, as well as artists who explore and extend the possibilities of theatre in their time. This Companion presents the results of their work in accessible form.

By bringing together the practical requirements of language, speech, acting and stagecraft, and by considering the plays both on the page and in the theatre, this book makes connections and contrasts that are seldom possible in works of reference with narrower briefs or in historical and critical studies that give a wider view of a single career or play-text. When directors work against the surface meanings of a text to satisfy their own creative impulse, they carry with them actors, stage action and the impact of an entire play so that reference to the text will show the bias and needs of the production and how words have been omitted or their meaning or effect twisted in order to give new life to the play's characters, themes and narrative. Numerous consequences and further possibilities will come to mind as a reader moves from one entry to another, raising questions about a director's opportunities and responsibilities and yielding an unusually wide and theatrical view of Shakespeare's imagination.

To give sufficient detail of what is unique in any theatrical event – context, occasion, play-text, personnel, production, stage, performance, audience – space could be found for only thirty-one directors if this book was to be easily handled and affordable. Three criteria governed the difficult choices that had to be made. A director's work should be innovative in its time, a requirement that tended to tell against inclusion of some who worked within an already established tradition, for example at Stratford Ontario or Stratford-upon-Avon, England, and the many theatres under their influence. A director's Shakespeare productions also had to span a number of years in order to show change, reappraisal or sustained development, a criterion that meant no room could be found for innovators as remarkable as Buzz Goodbody, whose career was cut short as her small-scale *Hamlet* opened, or Ariane Mnouchkine, whose group of related Shakespeare productions spanned only a few years, or Yury Lyubimov, whose *Hamlet* could be seen over several years but had no Shakespearian successor. Third, the productions had to influence other directors or the expectations of later audiences, a requirement that caused directors of the most recent generation to fall out of the net.

If the work of two directors satisfied all three criteria but had much in common, space could be found for only one of them, and a choice had to be made that was often difficult and not entirely satisfactory. For instance, Peter Hall is included rather than John Barton on the grounds of a longer and more varied career, even though clear differences are to be found in their careers. Either Michael Bogdanov or Barry Rutter might have found a place because the popular and politically radical productions of them both have been innovative; in this case, the consistent North Country dialect and a more constant company membership gave preference to the latter. The loss of one of such pairs had to be borne in order to include other directors whose careers explore other possibilities and have very different achievements. Regrettably, certain other directors are not included because they satisfied only two of the three criteria. A very few are missing through exigency or misfortune in my editorial handling, which I very much regret and for which I can, at this stage, only apologise. Some of these omissions time may remedy if, as I hope, a second volume of *The Routledge Companion to Directors' Shakespeare* can follow that would feature these directors and others who are now too young to be contestants. The criteria might then be broadened to include directors, such as Suzuki Tadashi or Heiner Müller, who have used Shakespeare's plays as the basis or starting point for their own plays.

While exploring the plays' further possibilities and the work of other directors, a second volume would not have to go back in time, as this one does, to show the origins of the profession and how it grew in scope and power until it influenced every aspect of theatre-making. Because numerous histories and studies of directing have been published, and still more are to be found in general theatre histories, this book does not attempt a consecutive history or a wide survey of what has been achieved. Essential here is a close look and 'thick' description applied to a comparatively small number of productions of Shakespeare's plays that have been undertaken by a chosen few of the directors who have made major contributions to the development of the the theatre's response to the plays. No excuse is offered for these limitations because only by investigating a director's hands-on work with specific texts can what is significant be described, and only in a limited number of these close encounters can change be adequately understood and assessed.

The choice of authors to write the entries was not so difficult. Among them are active dramaturgs, translators, reviewers, critics and theatre historians who know the plays well in rehearsal and performance. A number have first-hand experience of directing (two being former assistants to the director they write about), two are actors and three others have formerly been actors. Some authors specialise in Shakespeare scholarship and criticism; others usually write about theatre history or theatre practice rather than play-texts and dramatists. Only a few of the persons asked to contribute found that they had earlier commitments that could not be put aside and declined the invitation with regret. It was an unusual brief for theatre specialists because books on directors commonly have to cover a whole career and tend to be exclusively about productions; here was an opportunity to write about both plays and directors while concentrating on comparatively few theatrical events. For Shakespeare scholars who had the necessary experience, this was an opportunity to write about the plays in a fully theatrical context. A decade or more previously, few would have been able to write with authority on both theatre practice and play-texts but recently, chiefly in the UK but also in the USA, a greater rapport has developed between university departments of literature (for a long time the sole home of Shakespeare studies) and departments of theatre (that must cover the entire range of theatre practice and theatre history). More and more scholars, teachers and students are moving from one of these two encampments to the other, and in some universities the old barriers and prejudices have all but disappeared and, with them, some of the difficulties of studying Shakespeare. This book is part of an accelerating and seismic development.

No two entries have the same emphasis, and few make use of the same kinds of evidence although all, except those dealing with productions of long ago, have included attendance at performances or rehearsals or a careful viewing of videos. Programme notes and talks to the company before rehearsals, begin are often quoted and, sometimes, accounts or recordings of the director's discussions with stage designer, composer or other colleagues. Interviews with the director were often given and recorded especially for inclusion in this book. Based on a great deal of diverse material and written by an eclectic band of authors, the individual entries are very different from each other in form, style and basis for judgement, and so this Companion has become a compendium of ways in which theatre directing can be studied and analysed.

The indices add a further dimension to this book. A reader can compare different attitudes towards set design, voice-production, verse-speaking, music and dance (both period and modern), lighting, sound effects, projections, computers, and high-tech equipment. The actor-training that a broad range of directors have recommended or instigated, the research undertaken or commissioned into a play's political and cultural context, either now or in the past, the casting processes and the regimes established for rehearsals – all this and more comes within the scope of this book. Shakespeare's plays are the defining and leading subject of attention, but very much more can be studied in this Companion which has relevance to all aspects of theatre production and the enjoyment of audiences.

Entries are not arranged chronologically because the beginning of a life or career is not always a crucial or meaningful date in a series of Shakespeare productions. The alphabetical order adopted here allows any entry to be found easily, and the indices assist comparisons between directors and productions of specific plays. Relationships between directors and comparisons of their productions can be sought in the Index of Directors (including those without an entry in this book), and an Index of Plays provides a way of tracing the changing fortunes of a particular text over the course of time or in different countries and contexts.

For each director, three or four productions have been chosen for extended treatment so that scope can be found for any aspect of the theatrical event at its first performance and for a wide range of the techniques and choices which were involved. The previous work of director, designer, theatre company or individual actor is sometimes given sustained attention and, often, the policies, successes or failures of the production's producer. For several directors, little division exists between the work of producer and director, and in some cases they are inseparable; for Joe Papp and Mark Rylance, producing was the more effective and influential means of fulfilling a vision of what the plays can become in performance. In these two entries and numerous others, the architecture, size and location of a theatre is given prime attention as well as the shape, size and technical resources of its stage and auditorium.

To keep the price of the book within limits, a choice had to be made between fewer pages or shorter entries and the reproduction of visual evidence. One photograph for a single production would have been quite inadequate as an indication of a director's work and would leave two or three productions entirely without visual representation. Reluctantly, a decision was made to forgo illustrations in favour of a greater number of directors and of giving space for a full verbal description of each production featured. By forgoing visual means, this book may more effectively encourage debate about the work of individual directors and contribute to a verbal understanding or theorisation of the practice of this art and profession.

1
INGMAR BERGMAN

Rikard Loman

For most people, Ingmar Bergman (1918–2007) was a film-maker, an *auteur du cinéma*, but he was also a writer and a theatre director. The stage was, in fact, his creative base for more than sixty years. He made some fifty films, but he produced twice as many plays. In an often-quoted passage, he called the cinema his mistress and the theatre his faithful wife. As a theatre director he is known primarily as an interpreter of the classics, mainly a handful of plays by Strindberg, Ibsen, Molière – and Shakespeare.

Shakespeare seems to have been a lifelong concern. Bergman, however, produced his plays on surprisingly few occasions considering his long career and Shakespeare's standing in Swedish theatre: *The Merchant of Venice* once, in 1940; *Macbeth* in 1940, 1944 and 1948; *A Midsummer Night's Dream*, 1941 and 1942; *Twelfth Night* in 1975; *King Lear* in 1984; *Hamlet* in 1986, and, finally, *The Winter's Tale* in 1994. These productions fall into two periods, the first in the 1940s when he was still learning the craft of directing; only two of these, *Macbeth* in 1944 and 1948, were produced on professional stages, the city theatres in Helsingborg and Göteborg. The second group premiered between 1984 and 1994, when Bergman was an established and celebrated artist.

Bergman's career stretches over six decades and is framed by the Second World War and the tearing down of the Berlin Wall. Birgitta Steene's massive *Ingmar Bergman: A Reference Guide* (2005) offers a notion of his productivity, which is intimately related to, and obliquely inspired by, the Cold War during which Sweden insisted on adopting a neutral stance between two superpowers.

The foreign policy of twentieth-century Sweden has avoided direct involvement in the conflicts that gave the century its horrific singularity. While neither fighting nor supporting any of the countries involved in war, Sweden has developed into a welfare state, but this neutrality has significantly affected the self-image and perception of the nation. In some sense, Bergman's entire œuvre reflects the rapid social transformation of Sweden from a rural to an urban society and the rather slow spiritual transformation of a Lutheran society into one in which there is no God and no ethical guidelines. Contemporary man, in his view, lives in a metaphysical void, and this coloured most of his work.

One might say that an aesthetic equivalent to Sweden's reluctance to engage in conflicts abroad is an unwillingness to deal with social and ideological conflicts in art. The Nordic countries seem to have had a lot in common in this respect. Over 100 years ago, in his inaugural lecture in 1871, Georg Brandes (1842–1927), one of the most influential of nineteenth-century Scandinavian scholars, said about his native Denmark:

> [I]t has been the fate of our little, out-of-the-way country not to have given birth to any important European movement. Nor have we given any support to the great changes that have taken place; we have simply gone through them, that is, if we have been affected by them at all. [. . .] Our literature is like a little chapel in a big church: it has an altar, but the main altar is somewhere else.
>
> (Brandes 1990: 384–5)

Brandes wanted artists to 'submit problems to debate' (Brandes 1990: 388) and was disturbed by the fact that a disproportionate number of the men who set the taste of the times had been clergymen, the sons of clergymen, or students of theology, who feared reality and chose to express themselves in abstract ideals only: 'because of this spirit', he said, 'far too many of the great events of this century were wasted on us' (Brandes 1990: 393).

Brandes described a mental attitude common in Swedish twentieth-century culture, not only in Danish literature. Many of the great events of the twentieth century did not seem to register on Bergman: his works were characterised by a reluctance to deal with the big events of this world. He would never allow that outer reality to distract attention from the inner drama and hidden tensions he sought to bring closer to the audience. The world-view that he developed at an early age was probably typical of people who grew up in an out-of-the-way country and felt that their life was shaped by circumstances beyond their control.

Bergman was the son of a clergyman and so belongs to the group of artists who, according to Brandes, choose to express themselves in abstractions only. An inclination to shape existence according to clear-cut oppositions – in particular the opposition between good and evil – was, indeed, one of Bergman's trademarks as an artist. He was born in Uppsala in 1918 but grew up in Stockholm, where his father held a position in the Lutheran state church and later served as chaplain at the Swedish Court and adviser to the Queen. The moral and religious concerns that were common in the Bergman household were no longer those of mainstream Swedish society. His entire life was regulated by a set of authoritative rules dictated by parents and teachers: children were taught obedience to authority, and society was, as Bergman would later recall, structured so that people could humiliate each other.

Young Bergman found an outlet for his imagination in puppetry, which began simply as play and, in his teens, developed into a serious hobby. His experience as an amateur puppeteer, whose performers were marionettes, appears as a metaphor for an early deterministic view of life. This Shakespearian conception of the world as a stage proved to be one of the governing ideas in Bergman's imagination. He was always anxious to make visible the destructive forces in life and prove the existence of what he called, 'virulent evil' within human nature.

Both his parents were socially ambitious people, but in marriage they were mismatched: Bergman's mother belonged to a cultured, genteel family, whereas his father's origins were humble. His childhood was overshadowed by a crisis in their marriage that affected his view of human relations and, late in his career, he scrutinised their marriage with renewed intensity. The notions of 'family' and the 'past' are important for understanding Bergman as an artist. In his own narratives and in the plays that most appealed to him, the main characters are confronted with their youth and traumatic recollections.

Macbeth in Helsingborg in 1944

Bergman earned the epithet 'demon director' at an early stage when still engaged in amateur and semi-professional theatre in Stockholm. He distinguished himself from the start by his discipline and work-pace, his visual ingenuity and expressiveness, and so, in 1944 at the age of 26, he was appointed Head of the City Theatre in Helsingborg in southern Sweden, only a few miles from occupied Denmark. The technical resources of the theatre were limited, and Bergman had to rely on a group of enthusiastic but inexperienced actors: the average age of this little-known company was 23. Critics were soon noting that the new artistic director did not bow to tradition but showed a true passion for the theatre.

In his first season at Helsingborg, Bergman presented nine productions, including *Macbeth*. He called his interpretation an 'anti-Nazi drama' and 'a furious attack on a murderer and war criminal'. World events did give the production an eerie resonance, but Bergman did not attempt to modernise Shakespeare's play, and the parallels to current political reality were not forced upon the audience. In her study of Swedish *Macbeth* productions, Ann Fridén points out that the young director was less anxious to 'present the anatomy of Nazi tyranny' than to 'explore the psychology of a Fascist-like tyrant' (1986: 178). Bergman's Macbeth was not a Hitler, but rather the personification of those fascist qualities that had infected so many of his own childhood tormentors.

Looking back in January 2006, Bergman described Shakespeare's shortest play as powerful and straightforward but said that he would give the Lady much more prominence if he were to direct the play again. In an English interview from the late 1950s, Bergman said that the main difficulties were staging the witches, creating sympathy for the title character and finding the right young couple to convey the sexual passion between Macbeth and his Lady (*The Times*, 4 May 1959). In 1944, Bergman did, in fact, emphasise the erotic tension between the quite young couple. They seemed obsessed with each other, and their crime was planned in or near their bed. Sture Ericson's Macbeth was emotionally and sexually dependent on Ingrid Luterkort's Lady, and she dominated the first half of the play. As a colourful and sensuous queen, dressed in red with blood-red lips and fingernails, she seemed at first to be a cold-hearted cynic but, as the performance progressed, she was transformed and eventually seemed to be freed from the power of evil. Sture Ericson's Macbeth, by contrast, gradually moved beyond redemption. Initially, he made a weak impression and was not at all warrior-like; the descriptions of his achievements on the battlefield sounded like propaganda. It was Lady Macbeth who convinced him to kill Duncan but, as he transformed into a tyrant, he scared even her away and was eventually isolated.

As Macbeth changed, so did the atmosphere of the production. The first half gave the impression of a medieval ballad. It started in complete darkness as the three witches mourned the dead soldiers on the battlefield. Their roles had been shortened and rearranged; they were ordinary women but one of them (called a 'Sibyl' in the programme) had the gift of prophecy. She was given more lines than the others and remained on stage in silence for much of the performance. Her anguished wailing was heard before each crime. The second half of the production was a long nightmare reaching a climax in Act V, Scene 3 that was directed as an orgy of despair and ended with the actors dancing out one by one through a cone of red light, as if in a *danse macabre*. Red light was repeatedly used for special effects. The music was atonal and very simple, increasing the fateful atmosphere. Banquo's ghost and the witches' apparitions in the final act were clearly projections of Macbeth's bad conscience.

Macbeth in Göteborg in 1948

In 1946, Bergman moved from the small provincial stage in Helsingborg to the City Theatre in Göteborg, a major metropolitan stage on the Swedish west coast and one of the most technically advanced stages in Europe. He also moved from a situation where he had been in complete control to a position as a junior member working under some of Sweden's foremost directors, scenographers and actors.

Now Macbeth's psychology became secondary to the moral issues of the play. The Second World War had ended, and Bergman's family had given their support to the losing side. Revelation of crimes committed during the war came as a shock to Bergman, who, as a consequence, claims to have lost interest in politics. He had no intentions whatsoever to relate his second professional *Macbeth* in 1948 to current events. At a press conference prior to the opening night, Bergman explained that this time he wanted to go back to the sources in order to give his production a historical touch that would bring the play closer to Shakespeare's own time.

Carl-Johan Ström's complex and claustrophobic set design functioned somewhat like an English sixteenth-century theatre. It was constructed with several playing areas on different levels with Macbeth's castle built on the centre-stage lift just 3 metres within the proscenium and completely filling its width. The ceiling of its ground floor was supported by massive pillars, between which was the 'inner stage' with Macbeth's fur-covered bed. Its back wall was hung with a curtain painted with pictures copied from the Bayeux Tapestry. This visual reference was used in costumes and colours throughout the production. The stage was framed by a watchtower – from which Macbeth would look out over Birnam Wood – and by the ominous silhouette of an old oak tree. Four hanged men dangled from branches near the trunk of the tree, and the witches sat there, remaining present in almost every scene as silent witnesses to events.

Bergman divided the play into three acts, each ending violently, the first act with the discovery of Duncan's murder, the second with the killing of the Macduffs, and the final act with the fights in which young Siward and Macbeth are killed. This structure increased the atmosphere of evil and emphasised the ruthlessness of the protagonist. Although the porter's scene was treated as comic relief, and the English scene with Macduff and Malcolm offered a glimpse of a new and happier world, there were few moments of brightness in this production.

The main problem of this *Macbeth* was Bergman's inability to handle the strong conflicting personalities involved in the production. The experienced actors were not ready to subordinate themselves to the young director's intuitive approach. Bergman later explained that he and the strong-willed Anders Ek held diametrically opposing views of Macbeth's character. Ek was a Stanislavsky-trained and physically expressive actor, who related Macbeth's emotions to his own experiences and political interests. According to him,

Macbeth was a victim, innocent from first to last, a sensitive mind driven to crimes by a feudal society. Macbeth was no warrior by nature, but society forced this profession on him, and he was encouraged by the witches to commit his first murder; the root of evil lay in the world around him. To Bergman, on the other hand, the root of evil was *in* him. In his view, Macbeth gradually disintegrated morally and embodied the presence of 'virulent evil' in human nature. In the end, Ek's interpretation prevailed, and his Macbeth dominated the production. Karin Kavli's Lady came across as a loving wife. She did incite Macbeth to murder Duncan, but she had no demonic power and lost every hold over her husband after the murder.

Nobody was pleased with the result. The shortcomings of the, at this stage, quite intuitive approach of the young director were obvious, and Bergman was accused of paying insufficient attention to the text. He later blamed his failure on lack of preparation. Never again would he try to force actors to work against their will; instead, he would prepare analytically and try to persuade them to cooperate. He came to rely increasingly on his actors to carry a production, and his sets became more and more sparse.

In Göteborg, Bergman was eager to exploit the technical possibilities of a well-equipped, modern stage. The bright sky of its cyclorama set off morbid, surrealistic silhouettes to great effect, but the setting violated a more realistic style prevalent at the time. According to the critics, the stage machinery, a centre-stage lift in particular, drew attention away from Macbeth and his Lady. From this point on, only the costumes would be opulent, especially in productions of the classics. His next Shakespeare play – *Twelfth Night* at the Royal Dramatic Theatre (Dramaten) in Stockholm – was performed on a simple platform. Stage properties – chairs, screens, a bench – were carried on and off by stagehands while the actors stood in full view of the audience, awaiting their entrances. The explicit eroticism and sensuousness of this production, as well as its obvious theatricality, stressed that the play was a love game of make-believe. Young love was opposed to ageing. The Fool, for example, was old, becoming increasingly cynical as he coughed his way around the stage. His song of the wind and rain was to reappear years later in the film *Fanny and Alexander*, and the Fool in *King Lear* would sing it on the heath in Bergman's production at Dramaten in 1984.

Bergman's formative years

Bergman did not direct Shakespeare between 1948 and 1975, but his international breakthrough as a film director and in the theatre came when he was the artistic director at the Malmö City Theatre in southern Sweden from 1952 to 1958. This period is important for several reasons. During these years, Bergman established his own stable of actors who were to follow him throughout his career – Bibi Andersson, Max von Sydow, Gunnel Lindblom, Ingrid Thulin and Harriet Andersson – and it was now that he consolidated his basic ideas about theatre-directing. He would, for instance, build his *mise-en-scène* and structure the movements of the actors around a 'focal point of energy' on stage, a 'magnetic point', defined as 'the point where the actor is best and most effectively located' (Marker and Marker 1992: 16–17) and which changes from stage to stage.

During the 1950s, critics flocked to see his productions of plays by Strindberg, Molière and Ibsen. The conspicuous absence of Shakespeare in both the 1950s and 1960s, the decades in which Bergman produced his most famous films, might have something to do with a new direction in Bergman's work, in particular the abandonment of broadly orchestrated stories and development of an ascetic concept. Both film and stage work moved towards the individual psyche and one intense situation that involves only a few people. Bergman has used Strindberg's concept of the 'chamber play' to describe his new artistic formula: the presentation of a small group of characters confined to a single locale. Dramatic structure is like that of a musical chamber piece, with variations on a leitmotif for a few instruments. Clearly, Shakespeare's richly orchestrated plays do not fit into this narrow frame. Bergman has, for example, compared *King Lear* to a five-movement symphony for orchestra, soloists and instrumental groups. He did not direct Shakespeare again until he had turned towards a more lavish style. By then he had gained access to the stage and ensemble at Dramaten, where all four of his last Shakespeare productions were staged.

Bergman set increasing store by his role as an interpreter and in the late 1950s stopped writing plays. He was anxious to allow the text to come forth on its own terms, but his own personal response to the play would be essential to the experience. While most people expected to find his trademarks as film-maker in his stage work, he was eager to promote the image of himself as an interpreter who is faithful to the play and playwright he produces. During his entire career, he maintained that he never deliberately imposed an idea or an artistic formula upon a play, or produced a play against the intentions of the author (Sjögren 1968: 293).

Bergman's creativity was founded on his belief in the artist's function as a therapeutic stand-in for his public, but that status was questioned in the 1960s and 1970s, as the cultural and ideological climate in Sweden changed fundamentally. Traditional theatre was suddenly challenged by radical group theatres that introduced new ways of working and new political ideals. Attitudes to Bergman changed completely, and he was regarded now as a symbol of undemocratic working methods, conservative ideas and élitist institutions.

This hostility climaxed in 1976, when he was charged with tax evasion and arrested during rehearsals of Strindberg's *The Dance of Death* at Dramaten, an incident that led to mental collapse and subsequent hospitalisation. Bergman was eventually acquitted but decided to leave Sweden and settle in Munich, where he worked as a director at the city's Residenztheater. His return to the Swedish stage in 1984 marked the beginning of a remarkably productive period. He finished his last film, the five-and-a-half-hour-long *Fanny and Alexander* (1982), directed opera, wrote novels and television plays and published his memoirs, *The Magic Lantern* (*Laterna magica*, 1987) and *Images: My Life in Film* (1994). During the next twenty years he staged, on average, one play per year at Dramaten.

The film *Fanny and Alexander* testifies to Bergman's renewed interest in Shakespeare by making playful references to *Hamlet*; a television play, *Larmar och gör sig till* (1997) alludes to Macbeth's 'Sound and Fury' soliloquy. Bergman's career after his exile culminated on the national stage with a cycle of Shakespeare productions: *King Lear* in 1984, *Hamlet* in 1986 and *The Winter's Tale* in 1994. All three toured to a number of theatres abroad so that non-Swedish audiences became familiar with Bergman's stagecraft.

King Lear at Dramaten in 1984

King Lear was Bergman's first production at Dramaten after his exile. He had been inspired by Georg Brandes' study of Shakespeare (1896 trans. 1902) and was struck by his view of *King Lear* as a play about security that is suddenly shattered and replaced by chaos. Bergman chose to stage this play as he returned to the country where his own everyday life had been suddenly shattered in 1976.

In Bergman's vision, the play seemed like a slice of eternity, part of an endless cycle of violence and humiliation, a never-ending struggle for power. This Beckett-like atmosphere was reinforced by Gunilla Palmstierna-Weiss's non-referential, black and red set design. The forces of destructiveness were unleashed as Lear resigned, in fact even before he resigned. A silent wall of black warriors ominously awaited the beginning of the play. At the end, a waiting crowd surged forward after Lear's corpse had been carried out, and a sword fight for the crown broke out: Lear's crown and the rolled map of his kingdom had been left on stage throughout the entire performance. The performance ended with an apocalyptic big bang as the stage world itself collapsed, exposing the theatrical machinery before everything disappeared into darkness.

Jarl Kulle's Lear suffered a series of humiliations. He was not so much an aged monarch as an aged actor with expansive gestures and a pompous public appearance: appearance was everything to him. This Lear was not concerned that his daughters should love him but, rather, that they should make other people think that they did. When Lena Olin's Cordelia refused to do just that, it was lack of respect that wore him down at first, and it was lack of power that plunged him into despair: his self-image was founded on the submission of others. Kulle's Lear was in desperate need of the self-knowledge he would eventually gain on his journey through anger, infirmity and madness towards some sort of sanity. He seemed to be ageing already in the first act when he met Kent in disguise and asked, 'Dost thou know me?', the question an expression of his own bewilderment.

The Fool was the only person whom Lear dared trust. One of Sweden's foremost actors, Jan-Olof Strandberg played the role, and this casting stressed the significance of their relationship. The Fool's strangely staccato monologue on the heath (Act III, Scene 2) ended the first act and marked the beginning of a much more sinister climate. The emotional culmination of the production was Lear's last meeting with Cordelia, their reconciliation and Lear's recovery. Olin's Cordelia was a silently watching presence throughout the performance as if she were imprisoned in Lear's nightmare, forced to witness her father's mental breakdown and watch as the blinded Gloucester was led to the non-existent cliff.

In this production, Bergman used formations of actors and stagehands instead of props. Human figures, for instance, assumed the shape of logs when Gloucester was put in the stocks. Later, a line of people was used to divide Dramaten's main stage into two separate playing areas so that action could criss-cross between the fields near Dover and the French and British camps. The production was marked and clarified by sharp contrasts; loud, unpleasant sound followed by sudden silence, crowded scenes by intimate ones. Righteous and wronged persons were clearly separated from the trouble-makers. Those who deliberately caused havoc were sexually and psychologically attracted to each other, because, as Albany points out, 'Filths savour but themselves'. They were easily identified by their maliciousness, their dreadful costumes and their unnatural way of speaking; they trusted each other, because they were all reliably villainous. Those who could be trusted and depended upon – Börje Ahlstedt's Kent, Jan-Olof Strandberg's Fool, Per Myrberg's Gloucester and Mathias Henrikson's Edgar – were also easy to recognise because of their unmistakably good characters. In this hostile environment, loyalty to the right group of people was essential for survival, as was the ability to tell the difference between true nature and outward appearance, what people are and what they seem to be.

Hamlet at Dramaten in 1986

Bergman wanted to produce *Hamlet* for two reasons: he did not want to leave the theatre without having made *his* interpretation of the play, and he thought that Peter Stormare would be an ideal Hamlet.

Hamlet's inner journey and the wilful struggle for power were presented against a grey and black cyclorama. Göran Wassberg's non-referential setting was 'an exteriorization of mood and feeling' (Marker and Marker 1992: 262) and not a specific place: stage space was carved out of darkness, the atmosphere was uninviting, and most of the characters were corrupt or disreputable. The first view of the Danish court showed Börje Ahlstedt's Claudius mounting Gertrude from behind, observed by an applauding crowd of bewigged counsellors. In the final scene, Fortinbras and his storm troopers invaded the stage on roaring motorbikes accompanied by punk music. They dragged Horatio off to be gunned down in the wings; the bodies of Gertrude and Claudius were thrown into Ophelia's grave, and then Fortinbras paid tribute to the safely dead Hamlet and used his corpse to promote himself in a carefully staged media event.

In a rare desire to update Shakespeare, Bergman mixed costume styles from different time epochs. Once again, black and red was the dominant colour scheme, while everything else was a disharmonious mixture of clashing styles. Fortinbras's army was at first dressed in First World War uniforms and then reappeared in full SAS gear; Polonius wore an Edwardian morning coat; Rosencrantz and Guildenstern were dandies; the Gravedigger was dressed like a clown with a red nose and a black bowler. He was accompanied by a pair of masked Pierrots as he popped up from Ophelia's grave, looking at first like Polonius's ghost because he was played by the same actor.

The production was deliberately unattractive and crude. Even though Peter Stormare's Hamlet stood out in his environment – pale and lean and dressed in a black raincoat, a black turtleneck sweater and dark glasses – he was certainly not a noble mind, not the physically and intellectually attractive Danish prince to whom we have become accustomed. He looked anything but relaxed and comfortable as he sat at the edge of the stage facing the audience, first paralysed by anger and then exploding into physical convulsions during his first soliloquy. He seemed to take delight in Ophelia's humiliation and the repeated stabbing of Polonius, and he was somewhat monotonous in his anguish and self-loathing.

At times, Stormare's Hamlet wore young Bergman's clothing insignia – a seaman's jacket and rubber boots – and he was obviously intended to be the director's alter ego. At first, he behaved like a disillusioned and frustrated rebel without a cause, and then the ghost appeared to justify and direct his anger. This ghost was strangely real and eager to plead his case: he set the whole revenge process in motion and reappeared at the end as a silent witness to his son's duel with Laertes.

Hamlet and Ophelia were both outsiders in Claudius' lusty court, but Pernilla Östergren's Ophelia was set distinctly apart from the destructive forces in her light-blue dress. Her vulnerable, barefooted figure was present on stage throughout the performance, even in those scenes that followed her death. She was somehow both inside and outside the action, both a participant and an observer. One critic compared her to Agnes, Indra's daughter in Strindberg's *A Dream Play*. She watched in silence, as Hamlet calmly finished her father off with his knife in the closet scene. She even watched her own funeral.

The Players established a breathing space when they arrived in this oppressive atmosphere. They came to represent sincerity and natural behaviour, and Hamlet, who was desperately seeking to be himself, was strongly attracted to them. His famous 'To be or not to be' soliloquy was shifted to the scene where he instructs the actors on how to pretend in a natural way.

Bergman has called *Hamlet* his angriest work and it was, in a postmodern way, difficult to come to terms with. It was the least attended of Dramaten's productions during the 1986 season. To some spectators, this *Hamlet* was a character study or tragedy about Hamlet, but Ophelia's presence also made it her tragedy and with her it was much easier to identify. To others, it was primarily a stylistic parody, a blend of a dream play and an ethical, political and sexual nightmare enacted in a cold rehearsal light.

The Winter's Tale at Dramaten in 1994

Bergman's production of *Vintersagan* was based on a new Swedish translation by Britt G. Hallqvist and Claes Schaar. Most of the lines were shortened, and the language appeared as only slightly stylised. By reducing the text and the number of scenes, Bergman made room for the visual images, song and dance that he added to the play. The most radical change was a new frame: all the events took place in the hunting castle in which the nineteenth-century Swedish writer C. J. L. Almqvist (1793–1866) placed his tales and adventures. Some fifty festively dressed actors entered the stage ten minutes before the performance was to start and incarnated Almqvist's nineteenth-century characters, who then as amateur players assumed the parts of the characters in *The Winter's Tale*. Shakespeare's sheep-shearing feast was replaced with a Midsummer celebration, the most eminently Swedish of feasts. The province of Dalecarlia, where the director had spent his childhood summer holidays, was to be his Arcadia and substituted for Shakespeare's kingdom of Bohemia. Throughout the performance, the actors at Dramaten slipped back and forth between Almqvist's Sweden and Shakespeare's Sicily and Bohemia. The unchanging setting served to keep the strands of the straying story together, and, in interludes between scenes, the songs that Almqvist wrote to accompany his fiction were used as a means to tie the plot together.

In Shakespeare's *The Winter's Tale*, there is no villain, no Iago, trying actively to provoke Leontes' unfounded jealousy, and no clear psychological development ending in the King's extreme jealousy. In the first act of *Vintersagan*, however, all the actors were employed to prove good reasons for the King's jealousy. Actors in the background were used to direct the audience's attention and to emphasise crucial moments in the foreground. Hermione (Pernilla August) and Polixenes (Krister Henriksson) had a suspiciously intimate relationship, and the courtier Camillo was made to act as the villain. As a consequence, Leontes' (Börje Ahlstedt) actions became understandable, if not excusable.

The *mise-en-scène* was clearly structured around the 'magnetic point' on stage and stage props marked the 'focal point of energy' to bring out the true meaning of Leontes' words and his hidden intentions. In the first scene, Leontes, Hermione and Polixenes were sitting together on a big sofa and seemed to enjoy each other's company, but as soon as Leontes had been left alone on the big sofa, it was obvious that he felt abandoned. In the trial scene, a big table was used as a small stage set upon the big stage in order to intensify interactions between Leontes and Hermione.

Bergman paid equal attention to Hermione and Leontes, Pernilla August's Queen eventually appearing as a kind of Nora, a wife confined within a suffocating marriage to an incapable husband. The strange, stage-managed resurrection bestowed on Hermione was not the perfect restorative ending but was slightly skewed so as to be in better correspondence with the moral of the prodcution: that the love between people diminishes the chaos of the world and lack of it spreads more chaos.

Prince Mamillius is a minor character in Shakespeare's play, but his presence marked the first half of *Vintersagan*, and his absence characterised the second. He was presented as author of the play, the person who conjured up the story the audience saw enacted on the stage. He sat playing on the forestage before the play-within-the-play began. Hermione and Leontes acted out his nightmare, and he was hit hard by the conflict between his parents.

In Sweden, there is no living Shakespeare tradition. *Macbeth*, for instance, was only produced five times in the first half of the twentieth century, and *King Lear* had not been performed on the national stage since 1929 when Bergman decided to direct the play. This is probably why he has had considerable freedom to cut, add to and rearrange the plays. He commissioned new translations for all of his last three Shakespeares, engaging the well-known

Swedish translator Britt G. Hallqvist on each occasion. Although he was obviously content with her work, he still omitted about one-third of *King Lear* and *Hamlet* and almost half of *The Winter's Tale*. Bergman's attitude to the classics was always highly pragmatic in this respect: words were never allowed to get in the way of the protagonists and the overall vision, which, according to Bergman, makes sense of the play.

The last three Shakespeare productions had a lot in common. In all of them great attention was given to psychological development and interaction between the main characters. Movement on stage was choreographed and the rhythms carefully monitored, especially in the opening scenes. Designs were simple and the main characters few, even though Bergman often crowded the stage with people. Nor did his approach to the plays change much: in all of them, he tried to uncover a clear-cut opposition between good and evil and between youth and age. As all three plays laid stress on the clash between generations, Bergman seemed to draw on his own painful memories and life experiences. As a spectator, one felt very strongly that the director had used the blindness of the main characters to see things more clearly himself; Mamillius' experiences seemed copied on his own childhood memories.

The conflicts in these productions were never ideological, and violence was unrelated to a specific place. As Marker and Marker pointed out in the introduction to Bergman's *A Project for the Theatre* (1983), Bergman's Hell is 'not a place but a condition engendered by the deliberate malice that human beings are uniquely capable of inflicting upon another' (1983: 2, 1–18) People create 'private hells of their own devising, trapped in relationships that are defined and deformed by a litany of recurrent rituals – role playing and demasking [. . .] oppression and retaliatory humiliation' (Marker and Marker 1983: 2). Outer reality was never allowed to interfere with the inner feelings he tried to externalise and bring closer to the audience. Like Jarl Kulle's King Lear and Peter Stormare's Hamlet, Börje Ahlstedt's Leontes moved from an outer reality to an inner nightmare: mental collapse coincided with political chaos, but a chaos cut off from the world of familiar reality. *Macbeth, King Lear* and the bewilderingly eclectic *Hamlet* were surrounded on all sides by darkness, *The Winter's Tale* by layers of fiction.

Bergman seemed at ease with Shakespeare's rarely staged *The Winter's Tale*. Several critics compared it to *Fanny and Alexander*, in which good and evil, the small world of the family and the threatening outside world, are subtly intertwined. The first part of Bergman's production was very dark, the pastoral scenes were full of life, and it ended on a positive note. Hermione and Perdita were reunited, and the family left the stage together, while Time – an old woman in this production – crossed the stage, singing a solemn Almqvist song about the passing of time. She left an alarm clock on stage, and it kept ticking as the lights faded away. On the whole, women came to represent hope in all Bergman's productions. Lena Olin's Cordelia, and Pernilla Östergren's Ophelia and Hermione were allotted dominant roles. They were mature women, who learned to cope with the self-centredness of men. Cordelia and Ophelia seemed to be witnesses against their will, but Hermione's ability to survive abuse and to return to her former state of mind after long suffering offered some redemption in a dark world. If there is a remedy to human suffering in Bergman's universe, it is in the hands of women.

Chronology

1918	Born in Uppsala, Sweden
1938–42	Work on amateur and semi-professional stages in Stockholm
1944–46	Artistic Director at Helsingborg City Theatre
1944	*Macbeth* at Helsingborg City Theatre
1946–50	Artistic Director at Göteborg City Theatre
1948	*Macbeth* at Göteborg City Theatre
1952–58	Artistic Director at Malmö City Theatre
1956	International recognition of *Smiles of a Summer Night* at the Cannes Film Festival.
1963–66	Head of the Royal Dramatic Theatre (Dramaten) in Stockholm
1973	*Scenes from a Marriage*, Bergman's popular breakthrough in Sweden
1975	*Twelfth Night* at Dramaten, Stockholm
1976–81	Director at Residenztheater in Munich, Germany
1982	Bergman's last film, *Fanny and Alexander*
1984	*King Lear* at Dramaten, Stockholm
1986	*Hamlet* at Dramaten, Stockholm
1987	The memoirs *The Magic Lantern*
1990	The memoirs *Images: My Life in Film*
1994	*The Winter's Tale* at Dramaten, Stockholm

Bibliography

Bergman, Ingmar (1994) *Images: My Life in Film*, trans. Marianne Ruuth, London: Arcade.

Brandes, Georg (1902) *William Shakespeare: A Critical Study*, trans. William Archer, London: Heinemann.

Brandes, Georg (1990) 'Inaugural Lecture, 1871', in Eric Bentley (ed.), *The Theory of the Modern Stage*, Evans, Evert Sprinchorn, London: Penguin: 383–97.

Fridén, Ann (1986) *Macbeth in the Swedish Theatre, 1838–1986*, Stockholm: Liber.

Marker, Lise-Lone (1983) 'The Magic Triangle: Ingmar Bergman's Implied Philosophy of Theatrical Communication', *Modern Drama* 26 (3, September): 251–61.

Marker, Lise-Lone and Frederick J. Marker (1983) 'Introduction', in Ingmar Bergman, *A Project for the Theatre*, New York: Ungar: 1–18.
—— (1982) *Ingmar Bergman: A Life in the Theatre*, Cambridge: Cambridge University Press.
Sjögren, Henrik (1968) *Ingmar Bergman på teatern*, Stockholm: Almqvist & Wiksell.
Sorelius, Gunnar (2003) 'Bergman's Shakespeare: Some Observations', *Studia Neophilologica*, 85 (2): 119–125.
Steene, Birgitta (2005) *Ingmar Bergman: A Reference Guide*, Amsterdam: Amsterdam University Press.
Törnqvist, Egil (1995) *Between Stage and Screen*, Amsterdam: Amsterdam University Press.

About the author

Rikard Loman works as a theatre critic for the Swedish daily *Dagens Nyheter* and teaches theatre history and theory at the University of Lund. His Ph.D. thesis, 'Foreign-Familiar: Ingmar Bergman's Vintersagan at Dramaten' (1995), analyses Bergman's translation of Shakespeare's late play from page to stage and from one culture to another. He is currently working on a research project which will expand his material and develop his work into a study of all Bergman's Shakespeare productions, scattered over six decades, as a key to his development as a director and interpreter.

2
PETER BROOK
Maria Shevtsova

At the youthful age of 30 in 1955, with five Shakespeare productions already behind him, Peter Brook staged *Titus Andronicus* at the Shakespeare Memorial Theatre in Stratford-upon-Avon. Earlier generations of directors had thought the play's atrocities unstageable, but Brook, undaunted by conventional attitudes, openly embraced its carnage and, according to *The Times*, successfully created 'an atmosphere in which the horrors can take hold of us' (17 August 1955). Apart from directing the play from a clearly defined viewpoint, Brook aimed for cohesion between action and atmosphere by designing the sets and writing the music as well – a precocious desire for total control that he was to temper subsequently by commitment to ensemble work. Indeed, the horrors sustained by this unitary atmosphere could 'take hold' because Brook, instead of portraying them literally, had stylised them in the manner of Chinese and other Asian theatre. Thus, Vivien Leigh as Lavinia, whose hands had been severed by her enemies, appeared in a star-studded cast including Laurence Olivier and Anthony Quale with red ribbons hanging from her wrists for blood. Her mouth covered with red silk indicated that Lavinia's tongue had been cut out.

Visual ellipses like these would become part of the figurative stage vocabulary prominent in Brook's work after 1970, the period of central importance for this essay. In the meantime, they surfaced here and there in the relatively unadorned and not always compelling Shakespeare productions that followed: *Hamlet* (1955), *The Tempest* (1957), *King Lear* (1962), *The Tempest* again (1968), a film of *King Lear* (1969) with Paul Scofield, Brook's stage Lear and Hamlet, in the title role and *A Midsummer Night's Dream* (1970). *A Midsummer Night's Dream*'s spectacular success at home and on tour in 1971 and 1973 considerably enhanced Brook's already illustrious international career. It went as far afield as Australia, Japan and North America, blazing a trail for young people of the calibre of Canadian Robert Lepage who took their cue from it for their own pioneering endeavours.

Brook, who had never wanted to be exclusively a 'Shakespeare director' – regardless of his lifelong conviction that there was 'nothing as rich, powerful, complex, and challenging as the achievement of the Shakespearian theatre' (Croyden 2003: 36) – covered a wide range of material. There was, then, alongside his Shakespeare productions, such diverse works as *A View from the Bridge* (1956), *Irma la douce* (1959), Genet's *The Screens* (1964), Weiss's *The Marat/Sade* (1964) and the devised, purportedly anti-Vietnam War piece *US* (1966). By the end of *US*, the Theatre of Cruelty project Brook had initiated with Charles Marowitz for the Royal Shakespeare Company in 1964 had run its course. Its closely knit group of actors had brought together Artaud's visceral theatre (much of it via Jerzy Grotowski, who had led several workshops) and, paradoxically, Brecht's more intellectual show-and-tell narrative concerns. By the time of *A Midsummer Night's Dream*, Brook was quite certain that texts and their contents were best served non-verbally, by the spatial and corporeal means – gestural, kinetic, dynamic – that were properly *of* the theatre.

A Midsummer Night's Dream had not come about without tensions and confusions among the actors, as David Selbourne points out in his frequently acerbic account of Brook's rehearsals. Yet, the problems, whatever their dimension, must surely have arisen from what looked like an irreconcilable opposition between the 'truth' Brook believed was 'hidden in every particle and syllable of the printed word' (Selbourne 1982: 67), which he probed persistently, and his search for the vital energy of theatre-making which would encompass words but surpass them, nevertheless. This seeming contradiction produced fairies on trapezes flying through the air, lovers tangled in coiled wires, Puck whirling his magic flower on a spinning juggler's plate, swings, stilts, ladders, songs, cymbals, bells and drums, all of it accentuating the movement of bodies in a white box constructed within the stage, lit by bright lights and vivid plain costumes – a circus and a magician's box of tricks in one. All of it made light of words, yet all was deeply connected to speech and so to the meanings, whether explicit or covert, conveyed by dialogue. Brook may well not have achieved the fusion between scenic invention and the 'printed word' that he had envisaged. For Marowitz, for example, it was a 'kind of twin-channel entertainment', one knob giving 'brilliant theatrical effects taking place in outer-space' and the other 'Shakespeare's narrative played in a purely terrestrial style' (Williams 1992: 161). Even so, it was clear that *A Midsummer Night's Dream* had pushed beyond the psychological realism that had long dominated the British stage.

The various aspects of what might be termed the first half of Brook's working life, when he was based in Britain, open a perspective on the second half in France. Brook was no stranger to this country, having directed a number of productions in Paris, starting with *Cat on a Hot Tin Roof* in 1956. He had been invited by the celebrated actor and director Jean-Louis Barrault to stage a Shakespeare play for his Théâtre des Nations festival in 1968 but set up a workshop on *The Tempest* with an international group of actors instead. On the strength of this experience, he and his agent and producer Micheline Rozan established the Centre International de Recherche Théâtrale (CIRT) in 1970, after he had embarked on *A Midsummer Night's Dream* with a nucleus of Royal Shakespeare Company actors.

Having secured the necessary funds with Rozan to make the CIRT viable, Brook was free to explore fully the nature of acting, its connection to the life-spirit of actors, its play in space and its relation, through the very process of performance, to spectators. Three years of intense research in these interconnected areas saw, first of all, *Orghast* (1971) for the Shiraz Festival at Persepolis, a fantasia in a combination of 'dead' languages (Greek, Latin and Avesta) and a 'language' invented by poet Ted Hughes. Its purpose, apart from ritual incantation, was to develop the actors' use of breath, voice and sound coming from their innermost being. Brook's assumption was that something unforced, caught at the quick – 'true' as Brook would call it – would communicate sense, regardless of its lack of semantic meaning.

The second phase of the research was the famous journey to Africa between December 1972 and February 1973 documented by John Heilpern (1977). Here, the CIRT improvised shows on a carpet they put down in villages to define a playing space – shows that were essentially simple, funny stories enacted in a highly physical way. These events confirmed, for Brook, his idea that engagement between people through immediate, directly communicated and directly felt performance overrode their social, cultural, ethnic and other differences. (This is Brook's 'universal' theatre [Brook 1987: 154, 132–33.]) The last phase involved travels across the USA where the group devised fast and sharp political sketches with the Teatro Campesino, learned songs from the Native American Theatre Ensemble, gave workshops and performed *The Conference of the Birds*, a kind of synthesis of its multiple experiments in outdoor as well as indoor spaces.

Brook wanted to consolidate these accumulated experiences, social as much as theatrical, but without the responsibility of a permanent ensemble company. In 1974, he and Rozan came upon the Bouffes du Nord, an unused theatre in disrepair in Paris. The Bouffes was a lucky find and, in this gutted horseshoe space, reminiscent, Brook imagined, of the Shakespearian stage, Brook was to transform the discoveries of his journeys into productions. The laboratory character of the work was to endure as it took form in finished compositions shown not on the fringe but as an alternative theatre within the established framework. And it would be maintained by loosely constituted groups whose individuals came and went but from whom a small core would gradually emerge. Brook's change of term, at this time, from *recherche* to *créations* for the activities to be generated at the Bouffes du Nord – thus the Centre International de Créations Théâtrales (CICT) – unambiguously signalled his shift of emphasis.

Four Shakespeare productions have contributed to the Bouffes's particular identity and world fame and are the focus of this study: *Timon of Athens* (1974), *Measure for Measure* (1978), *The Tempest* (1990) and *The Tragedy of Hamlet* in two versions, like the heads and tails of the same piece (2000 and 2002). A fifth, *Who Is There?* (*Qui est là?*) in 1995, which is tangentially related to *Hamlet*, draws on texts by Artaud, Brecht, Craig, Meyerhold, Stanislavky and Zeami. This pantheon of Brook's masters (its tone, to my mind, verging on the supercilious) is best described as a theatre manifesto and is not included in my discussion.

This brief introduction situates *Timon of Athens*, which inaugurated the Bouffes, its 'battered grey-black walls performing the same supporting-ground function . . . as the rock-cut walls of the tomb of Artaxerxes [a site for *Orghast*]' (Lecat and Todd 2003: 54). Benches were built on the same level as the playing area, allowing spectators to gather around it in an intimate way. Two holes broken into the side walls facilitated rapid entrances and exits, as did a staircase descending into a pit behind the central area. Timon made his first appearance after his ruin from this staircase and disappeared down it in his last to suggest his descent into his grave. An iron gallery across the high back wall going up to a cupola – the whole providing 'an Elizabethan sense of verticality' (Brook quoted in Lecatt and Todd 2003: 39) – took action upwards. Play began with the Poet and the Painter in dialogue on it. Alcibiades later hurled his imprecations against Athens from it. Space also expanded outwards as actors walked in and out through the audience, some, notably the Lords of Athens, speaking, grouped together, among the spectators. These, because of the unspecified, 'abstract' nature of the space, momentarily represented the citizens of virtually any city in the world.

Brook's aim to create, through this space-in-the-round, the sensation of an open-air space recalling his itinerant group's performance spaces abroad was sustained by his use of unchanging light that fell on both players and spectators. This was a shared light of day, so to speak, holding everybody in that union which Brook has repeatedly claimed, and particularly after his three-year research, was the very reason for existence of the theatre. The actors frequently sat on the floor in a circle, notably in *Timon*'s two banquet scenes. This was the holy or magic circle of communion that had become emblematic of Brook's work as a whole – a practice he had begun to cultivate during the later 1960s before carrying it through to the very first 'training' sessions of the

CIRT in Paris and the daily meetings and exercises of the travelling group in Africa. When the company settled into the Bouffes, its circle practice – by now well and truly a second nature – incorporated the rehearsal processes, most of them beginning with a warm-up in the circle, sitting or standing, for 'technique' and, simultaneously, for the inner preparation of each individual as well as group bonding. Both aspects – the physical and the spiritual – were, to Brook's mind, inseparable (his affinity with Grotowski on this point is unmistakable), providing the source from which play could develop, not according to a 'method' (since the process was too fluid to be regularised or routinised), but in harmony with something like organic growth.

The idea of growth evoked here explains why Brook insisted that what he wanted from actors was not a 'matter of acting' (Smith 1972: 76). His goal, as can be interpreted from his various declarations, was seamless continuity between internal wholeness and that communicating outward action to which the term 'acting' refers. It could be argued that, fundamentally, this is a matter of *being*, or, putting it differently, of being in the performance process rather than performing as such. The latter can only be a superficial manifestation. The former plumbs not only existential, but also metaphysical depths.

It has to be acknowledged that Brook's approach was (and continues to be) steeped in his personal spiritual quest, following the teachings of Georgi Gurdjieff (Kustow 2006: 202, 246–52, 290–1). But there was also a dose of Romanticism in his desire to play among the ruins, albeit with the Bouffes's rubble removed. It was still there in his efforts to preserve the theatre's ruin-like appearance when such renovations over the years as painting its walls ochre-red modified its character, giving it a touch of warmth lacking previously. This might be viewed as affectation, but the point, for Brook, was to construct a space that embodied one of his main principles: 'Emptiness in the theatre allows the imagination to fill the gaps' (Brook 1995: 27). Furthermore, such a space was in total harmony with Shakespeare:

> During our travels to Africa and other parts of the world, all we would take with us was a small carpet that defined the area on which we would work. It was through this that we experienced the technical basis of Shakespearean theatre. We saw that the best way to study Shakespeare was not to examine reconstructions of Elizabethan theatres, but simply to do improvisations around a carpet. We realised that it was possible to begin a scene standing, end it by sitting down, and in standing up again find oneself in another country, at another time, without losing the tempo of the story. In Shakespeare, there are scenes where two people are walking in an enclosed space and suddenly find themselves in the open without any noticeable break.

> One part of the scene is indoors, another outdoors, without any indication of the point at which the transition occurs.
>
> (Brook 1995: 28–9)

The symbiosis between the 'technical basis' of Shakespeare and that of the carpet shows is so striking as to suggest that Shakespeare nurtures the whole range of Brook's work at the Bouffes, announced by *Timon of Athens*. Shakespeare had been his model, even in his most radical experiments during the 1960s: 'In Shakespeare there is epic theatre, social analysis, ritual, cruelty, introspection. There is no synthesis, no complicity. They sit contradictorily, side by side, coexisting, unreconciled' (Brook 1987: 55). Such a Shakespeare proved to be his reference for his Shakespeare at the Bouffes.

Timon's multi-dimensional space operated in tandem with the condensed spatiality of the symbolic 'carpet' area in which there was nothing but a few sacks and cushions thrown casually on the floor. There was no scenery to interfere with the imagination and little in the way of costumes. A number of loose robes, revealing the actors' everyday clothes beneath them (shirts, jackets, ties), indicated situations and social relations. Timon wore a white suit, which appeared in a reverse image as white tatters when he was bankrupt and abandoned. But this crystalline image also implied Timon's spiritual disintegration: torn to rags by his loss of faith in humanity, Timon loses his own humanity. In the first banquet scene, his false friends were draped in brightly coloured or gold fabrics, blazons of glitter, like cheap materials sold in a bazaar. In the second, they were in the clothes beneath. Alcibiades wore an undefinable buttoned-up uniform, with medals attached to its front and a dashing red cape to one shoulder, this outfit faintly suggesting a parody of military status. All these garments, while resonant with Shakespeare's text, allowed ease of movement as the actors changed time and place in exactly the way Brook describes above.

Scenes flowed quickly, one into the next, led by the unaffected, only occasionally emphatic style of performance of the actors, as occurs, for instance, when four women pour out of the pit for the first banquet, calling, singing and dancing with such verve as to suggest a whole crowd. Dialogue was in simple, natural speech devoid of 'actorly' inflections, no more so than in François Marthouret's restrained, even conversational, delivery of Timon's misanthropic tirades. The language was French, the mother tongue of three-quarters of the actors, and, according to *Le Figaro*, carried its weight so that 'even the foreign actors who had difficulty in expressing themselves fluently in French gave words their full power' (21 October 1974; all translations are mine). Language, in my memory of the production, was rather like a soundscape, giving free reign to the actors' work on their voices – an impression corroborated by *Le Monde*'s reference to *Timon of Athens*' play of vocal harmony, song-like tonalities and accents (22 October 1974). The critic takes these sonorities, not least the undisguised foreign ones alluded to by her 'accents', to be a necessary part of Brook's 'never explanatory . . . transparent' *mise-en-scène*.

The 'transparency' at issue was achieved, first, through the long physical-spiritual preparation of the actors and then through group immersion in a plethora of exercises (including martial arts) and experiments (including those of a textual-interpretative nature) that gradually shaped the production. Brook's directorial role in this open but collectively galvanised enterprise was to coax from the actors a wide range of impulses that were unique to them and, as such, capable of firing the emotions appropriate both to them and the characters they were slowly exploring. Such 'facilitation', for want of a better term, allowed actors to have an individual sense of their role. Brook helped this sense along as, in the words of Vincent Le Texier some twenty years later, he saw 'into people' and knew 'exactly what each one of them [could] give fully' (in interview with Shevtsova 1994: 366). He was thus able to 'modify his work according to them' (Shevtsova 1994: 366). Le Texier was to describe what they gave fully as a paradoxical development of 'enrichment and simplification' (Shevtsova 1994: 371) by which the complexity reached through experimentation was pulled back to prevent overdone, caricatural representation.

The critics' references to 'accents' were generally benign since they were fully aware that Timon's multinational and multi-racial cast was the outcome of what Brook describes as the CIRT's 'working without contexts' (Brook 1987: 124). He had previously worked 'within a context . . . either geographical, cultural or linguistic' and so within a 'system of reference' (Brook 1987: 124). However, while Brook minimises the problems posed by a lack of context, it is clear that a new challenge was thrust upon him once he was at the Bouffes. The theatre-making he had erected into his *own* system of reference *sui generis* – for that is exactly what it is – was circumscribed by a society whose language had to be acquired for performance purposes, at some workable level, by many of his actors; and this was nothing if not a 'context'. The issue was complicated by the fact that *Timon of Athens* was definitely not *Orghast* and so could not rely on paralinguistic sound effects for communication. More important still, Shakespeare's language entails particular difficulties wherever it is performed, not excluding England. It is 'archaic', as Brook puts it in an interview for an afterword to the published Bouffes text in French of *Timon of Athens*, and this is something he had noticed very much when preparing to film *King Lear* (Brook, in Shakespeare 1974: 107).

The first problem concerning 'context' was an ongoing linguistic one, and it had to be accommodated intelligently by the shared theatre 'language' specific to the CICT. The second involved translation and was attacked head-on by Brook and his long-term collaborator Jean-Claude Carrière. Carrière translated Shakespeare's language into colloquial French, full of current rhythms and expressions – modern, street French that stripped back Shakespeare's dense, metaphoric constructions but caught their fundamental meaning. Some of Carrière's passages captured the tone and intention of Shakespeare's text by a plain, literal translation. Take, for example, the opening scene cited earlier between the Poet and the Painter. Shakespeare's text reads:

POET: Good day, sir.
PAINTER: I am glad y're well.
POET: I have not seen you long; how goes the world?
PAINTER: It wears, sir, as it grows.
(Shakespeare 1969: 3)

Carrière's translation reads:

POÈTE: *Bonjour, Monsieur.*
PEINTRE: *Je suis content de vous voir*
POÈTE: *Je ne vous ai vu de longtemps. Comment va le monde?*
PEINTRE: *Il s'use, monsieur, à mesure qu'il grandit.*
(Shakespeare 1974: 13)

Little could catch the tone of everyday life more than 'Bonjour, Monsieur' and Carrière's rendition of the Painter's 'I am glad y'are well' as 'Je suis content de vous voir', which is exactly what would normally be said in reply. In addition, the Painter's first line, 'I am glad to see you', anticipates the idea of seeing in the Poet's response. This, too, facilitates the easy, spoken quality of their exchange.

Its contemporary flavour continues when the Merchant and the Jeweller enter the conversation. Thus, to Shakespeare's

MERCHANT: O, 'tis a worthy lord.
JEWELLER: Nay, that's most fix'd.

Carrière gives

MARCHAND: *Ah, c'est un digne seigneur.*
JOAILLIER: *Oh oui! Sûr et certain.*

Note Carrière's 'Oh, Oui!' (with an exclamation mark for emphasis) against Shakespeare's 'Nay'. 'Sûr et certain', an idiomatic expression, instantly conveys the familiarity of the Jeweller's speech. Its translation back into English would be 'That's for sure'.

Let us now take one of Timon's long speeches in Act IV, Scene 3. Timon has discovered gold in the forest and now digs for roots to eat. The speech begins with 'That nature, being sick of man's unkindness / Should yet be hungry!' and eventually ends with

> . . . O, a root; dear thanks!
> Dry up thy marrows, vines and plough-torn leas,
> Whereof ingrateful man, with liquorish draughts
> And morsels unctuous, greases his pure mind,
> That from it all consideration slips –
> *Enter Apemantus*
> More man? Plague, plague!
> (Shakespeare 1969: 101–2)

Carrière's translation of Timon's opening gambit as 'Et moi, écoeuré par l'ingratitude des hommes, dire que j'ai faim!' personalises it by replacing 'nature' with 'I' (*moi*). The speech ends:

> *Ah, une racine . . . Mille fois merci. Sèche tes sources, tes praires et tes vignes d'où l'homme ingrat tire ses boissons délicieuses, ces mets onctueuex qui encrassent son esprit, d'où toute réflexion s'échappe.*
> *Encore de l'humain . . . Epidémie! Epidémie!*
> (Shakespeare 1974: 68)

Here, as is consistent with his whole translation, Carrière turns Shakespeare's verse into prose, which, of course, involves changes in texture, trope, colour, rhythm and pace. Note how he omits 'Plough-torn leas' and translates 'liquorish draughts' into 'boissons délicieuses'. This phrase, when translated back, gives 'delicious drinks'. 'Greases', whose subject in Shakespeare is 'ungrateful man', is replaced by 'encrassent', from the verb 'to dirty', whose subject is 'mets' ('morsels').

It is also important to note that Carrière deletes all stage directions (in this instance, 'Enter Apemantus') as well as the divisions into acts and scenes of modern editions of Shakespeare. The effect of his return to pre-edited Shakespeare is a continuous flow of thought, without interruption. In other words, Carrière organises his text in tandem with Brook's organisation of his *mise-en-scène*, which flows in one long movement, its points of transition barely visible so as not to lose the 'tempo of the story' (Brook, in Shakespeare 1974: 108). Carrière renames Timon's steward 'Flavius' and gives him various lines that belong to other servants whom he cuts out of the narrative altogether. He also deletes the Page and the Fool and, consequently, their scene in Act II. These cuts are minor, but the script for Brook's production gains in concision from them.

These few details show how Carrière and Brook had Shakespeare speak to the times. But why did Brook choose to open his new theatre with *Timon of Athens*, not the best-known of Shakespeare's plays and virtually not known at all in France? Its 'novelty' may have influenced him, making this a work to be reinvented. Brook simply says he liked the play (Brook, in Shakespeare 1974: 108). Yet, there were other reasons. For all his wariness of 'contexts', Brook has never been wrapped up in an aesthetic cocoon. Theatre, for him, is about life, and all his writing and most of his interviews reiterate this point in one way or another.

'Life', where *Timon* was concerned, involved the early 1970s, as Brook indicated when observing that 'certain themes are closer to us at certain times' (ibid). The play revolved around the themes of money, credit and wasteful consumption; and Timon thought he 'could buy joy by living beyond his means' and, when confronted by his critical situation, he 'created mirages' rather than face it (ibid). To explain, Brook draws a comparison between Timon and the attitude of most Western countries to the petrol crisis of 1973–4, on which there was an enormous amount of discussion in France, in the media as well as among people going about their daily business. Brook's production was by no means blatantly topical, but spectators with half an eye on the news could have inferred from its tale of 'conspicuous consumption' (the then current phrase for affluence), greed, ruin and disillusion something connected to their quotidian reality.

Timon of Athens was a demonstration of how much richness could be achieved in a production by an economy of means. Fired by his experience of Shakespeare in translation and, as well, by more acclaim for *The Ik* (1975) and *Ubu aux Bouffes* (1977), both also adapted by Carrière, Brook turned *to Measure for Measure* in 1978, with Carrière once again by his side. Publicity for the production quoted Brook as saying

> I have been against adaptations of Shakespeare for a long time. For an Englishman, you know, this would be sacrilege. Well, I am revising my judgement. At home, a Shakespeare play is a cultural event. Its language is fixed in its archaic state, and the spectator guesses more than he understands. In an adaptation, by contrast, the actors use current words; the text has a direct, actual resonance.
>
> (*L'Aurore*, 28–9 October 1978)

Twenty years later, he was to affirm that the 'mysterious power' of Shakespeare 'is there even in translation' (Brook 1999: 35), and even in French, 'the language which is perhaps fartherst removed from English, it's a completely different way of thought and expression' (Brook 1999: 36). Be this as it may (and leaving aside the debatable 'cultural event'), Carrière's translation of *Measure for Measure* was an exercise in sensitivity to the nuances of Shakespeare's text.

Brook's production did not come off quite as well, despite, in the words of *Le Monde*, his 'miraculously clear' treatment of the play's 'complex plot' (10 November 1978). The questions it was asking were also clear: What was order? What was the right course between liberal order, which risked degenerating into laxity, and rigid order, which could lead to dictatorship? However, they appeared detached, suspended above the interaction of the characters; and this despite some remarkable performances. *Le Monde*, for instance, praised Marthouret, who had played Timon, for his 'cerebral' Duke who was also a 'perverse dandy'. The critic was similarly impressed by Bruce Meyer – an enduring CICT core member, unlike Marthouret – who performed Angelo as a 'sincere fanatic' (10 November 1978). Much in the *mise-en-scène* recalled *Timon of Athens*: no décor or props; extensive use of the floor for sitting and reclining, which accentuated horizontal space (much less use was made of the vertical, by contrast with *Timon of Athens*); straightforward presentation of characters, rather than representing or 'becoming' them; objective delineation of events, and so forth. But what was pulsating simplicity in *Timon of Athens* seemed dry austerity in *Measure for Measure*.

Not so *The Tempest* twelve years later. Brook's return to Shakespeare after such a long absence followed *The Mahabharata*, a nine-hour epic based on the Hindu holy book, which premiered at the Avignon Festival in 1985 and toured the world for some three years. A short piece *Woza Albert!* (1989) immediately preceded *The Tempest*. It was a 'township' play by two black South African actors, Percy Mtwa and Mbongeni Ngema, working with Simon Barney, a white South African playwright. Brook chose two of his actors from *The Mahabharata* for it: Mamadou Dioum from Senegal and Bakary Sangaré from Mali, both former French colonies. What he admired in these two actors

> was not just the suppleness of their bodies, the directness of their contact with an audience; it was what he called 'transparency', an openness and simplicity, the ability to slip in and out of character, a playfulness whose source was laughter, no matter how grim the story told, the circumstances revealed.
>
> (Kustow 2006: 270)

Plasticity of this kind was invaluable for *The Tempest*, and Sangaré, a tall, powerfully built, bass baritone actor, was to take the role of Ariel. The tall and lean Sotigui Kouyaté, a *griot* (storyteller) from Burkina Faso, who had played Bhishima in *The Mahabharata*, was to play Prospero. Theirs was a partnership of paradoxical physiques in relation to each other, which also highlighted the incongruity between them and their roles – for instance, between Sanagré's imposing presence as Ariel, or between the all-but-ethereal Kouyaté as the master-magician Prospero. Contradiction, which Brook had increasingly relished as a director since *A Midsummer Night's Dream* (also a world of spirits), is embodied in *The Tempest* with a facility unmatched by any of his Shakespeare productions at the Bouffes, *Hamlet* included.

Woza Albert!, with its comic-grim story, had no direct bearing on *The Tempest*, unlike *The Mahabharata*, which did. *The Tempest* echoes its themes of violence (blood in *The Mahabharata* flowed in ribbons of red, as had Lavinia's in 1955), betrayal, reconciliation between human beings and reconciliation between human beings, gods, spirits and nature. Above all, its suggestiveness, vitality, grand play with the elements – earth, air, fire and water – and poetic elisions, allusions and associations washed over into *The Tempest* as if they were part of the same spiritual and imaginative surge. It is no wonder that Brook should have recalled his workshop *Tempest* under the auspices of the Théâtre des Nations in his preface to Carrière's translation. The former was his 'first attempt to bring together actors from different parts of the world . . . to explore how one might rediscover Shakespeare in the light of different cultures' (Brook, in Shakespeare 1990: 3).

His 1990 *Tempest* was, to a great extent, the fruit of that project. For the first time, he was able to reach the 'ancient beliefs' that had 'survived' in 'Shakespeare's England' (Brook, in Shakespeare 1990: 3). Western actors excelled in psychological introspection, sexual suffering and other earthy aspects of Shakespeare, but they could not easily find scenic images for his invisible world. This sheds light on the significance, for Brook, of African actors and of Kouyaté, in particular, who was close to the traditional rituals of his culture. Thus, Brook notes, 'for an actor bought up in a climate of ceremony and ritual, the way leading to the invisible world is often direct and natural' (Brook, in Shakespeare 1990: 4).

Brook was also concerned with interweaving the supernatural of 'ancient beliefs' into the 'essential theme of the play' which is 'not theatrical illusion, or the stage, but life itself'; or rather – Brook immediately qualifies it – the 'illusions of life' that Shakespeare explores with compassion and the 'lightest of touches' in a 'whole network of charades and games' (ibid). Brook may have been asserting his difference from interpretations inspired by Giorgio Strehler's 1978 *The Tempest*, an extraordinarily beautiful vision of the power of illusion created by the stage; he may, in fact, have seen the production in

Paris in 1983. He was possibly marking his distance, as well, from the post-colonial view of *The Tempest*, which saw the Prospero–Caliban relationship as one between coloniser and colonised. This perception was taking hold in the late 1980s, indeed in the wake of the controversies surrounding *The Mahabharata*, Brook's fiercest adversaries attacking its alleged imperialism (Williams 1991). Brook's own view homes in on the word 'free', which, Carrière had noticed, recurs throughout the play and closes it. And the word, Brook points out, means different things to different characters, including Prospero, for whom 'freedom is undefinable: it is what he is searching for throughout the play' (Brook, in Shakespeare 1990: 5). Brook may here be suggesting that 'life itself', the core subject of his *Tempest*, is a search for freedom, however defined.

With this having been said, it would be difficult to argue that Brook frees us from the colonial master–servant paradigm by inverting it with colour-blind casting: a black Prospero, a black Ariel and a white Caliban. His relativist notion of freedom leads him to a production that has more to do with initiation rites, with rites of passage, one might say, into individual freedom, than with large-scale political issues concerning collective feeedom. Caliban, as played by the diminutive German actor David Bennant, is an innocent rather than monstrous creature ('this thing of darkness' translated by Carrière as 'cette chose d'obscurité'). His is the darkness/obscurity of ignorance and, once he has been initiated into the struggle for freedom, he claims it as his right. Miranda and Ferdinand find the freedom of youth and love. Ariel/Sangaré, set free, shuffles off, a figure almost of pathos in his awareness that another rite of passage, his own independence, is before him. Prospero comes to the end of a long journey through which he has learned forgiveness, the condition of being free. Kouyaté utters his last words, 'set me free', quietly, more to himself than to the audience. He ends the production alone. The inference to be drawn from this image of resilient aloneness is that freedom can only be an individual affair, which, from a political point of view (not entertained by Brook) is a terrifying prospect in our world of famines, dictators and wars, all involving collectivities.

The very first images of *The Tempest* anticipate its direction. The side walls of the Bouffes are green, the rest daubed with white in a radical transformation of its shell for this production. The floor is covered with red earth, surmounted by a rectangle of sand. A large rock sits at centre back. The sand will be raked at the end of the performance, like the pebbles of a Zen garden, to suggest a new beginning. This is the island designed with her customary ingenuity by Chloé Obolensky, Brook's set and costume designer since *The Cherry Orchard* in 1981. A huge Persian carpet covered the floor of that production, serving a functional purpose while holding symbolically everything that had been invested in the much smaller carpet of the carpet shows

– community, communion, free bodies, open spirits and so forth. The rectangle of sand in *The Tempest* is another type of carpet, symbolising the same values. Obolensky was also the mind behind the tonnes of red earth trucked into the Bouffes for *The Tragedy of Carmen,* Brook's chamber version of Bizet's opera. It was she who dressed the actors of *The Mahabharta* in robes, kaftans, throws and shawls in vibrant colours or iridescent white. Something of that Indian world returns, in muted tones, in *The Tempest.*

Enter Ariel in silence with a long tube on his head which, held and tilted, makes strange rustling sounds, evoking the wind and the sea. This is the tempest, and the spell is cast. The motif will be repeated later, when Ariel returns with, on his head, a model ship all the more startling for Bakaré's solid physique. Actors run in, metaphors for the rolling ship. Later, they play spirits helping Prospero to accomplish his magic. Bamboo sticks serve as mast and breaking hull and prow. Later, they form a frame – a mirror in which Ariel observes Trinculo admiring himself in one of many laughter-filled moments of the production. Or else, carried by an actor-spirit, they hold a white lace shawl for Miranda that drops, as if by magic, onto her shoulders. Branches with luxuriant leaves manipulated by the actors like puppets conjure up the vegetation of the island, with a butterfly here and there, appearing out of nowhere. The enchantment of the island filters through the air to the sounds of two musicians playing dulcimers and percussion instruments in full view of the audience. There are masked fragments, mime and dance, all delicately reinforcing the corporeal dimensions of the work. Caliban lives in a rotting cardboard box, a humorous sign of mundane reality among the dreams and illusions inhabiting the inhabitants of the island. The whole is an exquisite piece of storytelling, the basis of Brook's theatre-making.

The Tempest shows that Brook did not have a formula for directing Shakespeare, any more than he had a fixed vision of any given Shakespeare play, or a totalising one of the Shakespeare canon. The poetic *Tempest* is far removed from the no-frills *Timon of Athens* and the brittle *Measure for Measure.* And it is light years away from his two attempts at *The Tempest* decades before. What transpires from these different productions placed side by side is that Brook approaches Shakespeare from within his concerns at any one period of time. Any spill-over effect from one production to another, as happens from *The Mahabharata* to *The Tempest*, indicates that some of these concerns are not easily exhausted. By the same token, Brook's recurrent 'tools' – carpet or its simulacrum, ribbons, bamboo sticks and so on – are not gadgets to fall back on for want of a better idea but icons of a lifetime's work which are re-explored as Brook continues to live and work. At 82 in 2007, retirement from the theatre is not, for him, an option.

How, then, was *The Tragedy of Hamlet*, first performed at the Bouffes in

2000, in English, contrary to his usual practice? *Hamlet* followed in French in 2002. Adrian Lester, Rosalind in Declan Donnellan's 1991 *As You Like It*, which was hosted by the Bouffes, plays Hamlet in English. William Nadylam, Donnellan's 1998 titular hero in Corneille's *Le Cid*, takes the role in French. Brook himself adapted the text to his needs, letting it flow without acts and scenes, as he and Carrière had done for *Timon of Athens* (but not for *Measure for Measure* and *The Tempest*, where they were written in). The translation was by Carrière, joined, this time, by Marie-Hélène Estienne, Brook's long-term assistant.

Brook's clue is in his title, which echoes *La Tragédie de Carmen*, and he told *Le Figaro* that he was working with the 'quintessence of the play', as he had done with the opera (30 September 2000). What, precisely, 'quintessence' refers to is not revealed until Brook's preface to his French adaptation: 'The real tragedy of *Hamlet* is the individual confronting his destiny, which becomes more and more intense and leads him inexorably towards a death that he must face in a very particular way' (Brook, in Shakespeare 2003: 5).

'Quintessence', 'tragedy', 'destiny' and 'death' go together, are even collocations of each other, and, if they sum up Brook's production of *Hamlet*, they apply equally well to his streamlined *Carmen*. Hamlet, we could say, is Carmen's male double and, like her, the epicentre of Brook's drama. To focus on Hamlet meant pruning the text so as to 'rediscover Shakespeare' (Croyden 2003: 262) and destroy people's preconceptions of the play, allowing them to 'receive it as a new experience' (Croyden 2003: 256). 'Modernising', Brook was adamant, 'is not bringing in gimmicks; it is digging deeply into the text to find the level where one touches the fibres that have been buried through the years' (Croyden 2003: 263).

Getting to the 'fibres' involved excisions far more radical than any for the preceding Shakespeares at the Bouffes. Brook deleted about one-third of the text, reducing a potentially four-hour performance to two-and-a-half hours. Most of Act I was cut, as were Polonius's advice to Laertes, Hamlet's advice to the Players, numerous speeches of Rozencrantz and Guildenstern, the second Gravedigger and Fortinbras, with whom the broader political dimensions of the play disappeared. Brook justified this particular excision by arguing that everything related to Fortinbras belonged to a subplot of no real interest to Shakespeare. Shakespeare simply followed the Elizabethan convention of plot and subplot, in which somebody always 'puts the whole country back in order' (Croyden 2003: 260). To his mind, neither the convention nor the political resolution offered by it was relevant to the present day.

There were also three textual switches, equally bold. The play's opening line 'Who's there?' is said only at the end, and by Horatio, after the carnage. Hamlet's 'To be, or nor to be' is moved from Act III, Scene 1 to Act III, Scene

4, after Hamlet kills Polonius. Laertes does not appear as a character until Act IV, Scene 5, in time to witness Ophelia's madness. Reasons for these alterations can be gleaned from the production. Brook could have removed 'Who's there?' altogether, since he had excised most of Act I anyway. However, by inserting it at the end, he was able to give the last word to the play's metaphysical dimension, to which Hamlet's father's ghost ('Ghost' in Brook's playscript) and Hamlet's reflections on the after life are key. This is why the dead arise in the closing scene. Horatio unostentatiously asks, 'Who's there?' and all look upwards towards the same fixed point. Brook could not have been more explicit about the metaphysical/religious significance of their gaze. Nor could it have been missed in the high walls and dome of the Bouffes. By contrast, in the squat space of the Young Vic in London, where the production was performed in 2001, this invocation looked indeterminate, even vaguely sentimental.

The second switch, 'To be or not to be' after Polonius' murder, provides Hamlet with an immediate reason for thinking about life and death; and both Lester and Nadylam speak this most hackneyed of soliloquies in a conversational manner. Lester risks gestural clichés by examining his arm and wrist as he speaks, as if he were momentarily contemplating suicide. Nadylam's attention goes outwards to an imaginary interlocutor – perhaps the Ghost. Either way, the actors avoid turning it into a set speech. Brook's third change, Laertes' late appearance, is bound up with his desire to contrast Hamlet with Laertes. Hamlet, in Brook's words, is 'enormously talented . . . full of energy and passion and observation and self-doubt, like every human being should be' while Laertes is a 'fine young man, who asks no questions' and rushes into revenge (Croyden 2003: 261). Brook presumably had to give the actor time to establish Hamlet's qualities so that they were incontestable when up against Laertes' negative energy. The 'tragedy' of such a human being, going on Brook's description of Hamlet, is his unfulfilled potential.

The structure, then, of the English and French versions is the same, although there are subtle differences in pace, colour, mood and feeling between them. These come from the personal qualities of the actors playing Hamlet, which greatly influence the group dynamics of each version. Lester, like a sharp knife, speeds his way through the performance. Nadylam, a softer though no less vigorous Hamlet, infuses it with a sense of pain. Both versions exploit humour to the utmost. Myers, for instance, playing in English, is a boisterous, busy-body Polonius and surpasses himself as a prattling Irish Gravedigger, impervious to his surroundings as he digs away behind four grey cushions masquerading as a grave. Kouyaté, in the French version, is funny as a quiet Polonius, bemused by his own pedantry.

Natasha Parry, Brook's wife and a founding member of the CICT, is more self-effacing as Gertrude in English than Lilo Baur, formerly with Simon

McBurney's Theatre de Complicite, is in French. Both, however, whether an insecure woman (Parry) or a dithering one (Baur) are easily bullied by Hamlet. Ophelia does not fare much better. Shantala Shivalingappa (Brook's Miranda) in the role of Ophelia in English and Véronique Sacri in French are sweet and appealing but are muscled out of the field by a mesmerising central character. All in all, none of the women have much of a role to play in what is very much a man's *Hamlet*.

Brook's reductive approach nevertheless generates a good deal of theatrical invention. The Ghost, when he speaks to Hamlet, is always in the same space, close to him – in fact, nearly walks over him when he first appears. And he is always visible. Thus, the invisible is rendered visible not only to Hamlet for dramatic purposes, but also to spectators as a material presence, an affirmation of the reality of the supernatural world. Brook has the Ghost in scenes not assigned by Shakespeare for him. He is there, for instance, during the Players' performance, sitting on a stool beside Hamlet, who is on the floor. Here, as elsewhere, he tempers Hamlet's behaviour, to all intents and purposes Hamlet's guide rather than an avenging force. Play, as in this instance, is frequently close to the ground, a feature not unique to Brook' direction of Shakespeare since it part of the performance 'language' of the Bouffes. It refers, among other things, to the idea of being rooted in the earth, which is of primary importance for Brook and his company.

Proximity between characters, pronounced in the case of Hamlet and the Ghost, is typical of the production. Gertrude is usually beside Claudius, her hand on his shoulder when he is sitting, thereby evoking a family portrait of a *pater familias* and his subservient wife. When Hamlet places himself between them, the duo becomes a tight trio, made tighter still as a quartet when the Ghost enters the scene. In such moments, the Ghost is a clever device for a dual intention: it proves to Gertrude, who cannot see it, that her son is mad; at the same time, it tells the audience, who *can* see it, that he is not. Polonius is continually close to his interlocutors. Ophelia, although detached in her manner, is never detached spatially. The intimacy created through this spatial arrangement is reinforced by the continual presence of the actors, who when not involved in the action, stay on the sides or slightly to the back, looking on and ready to walk on, simply, when a scene requires their active participation.

This is one of the most interesting features of the production for, if it draws attention to Hamlet's network of relations, which also attracts the gaze to him, it is nevertheless a mechanism of inclusion: it keeps other characters within the circle of attention, despite the reduction of their importance for the production as a whole. To put it differently: the other characters are shown to be indispensable for the purposes of the story as a matter of plot, events and sequences but are not altogether central for the substance that the story carries other than the 'tragedy' of the individual, Hamlet. The scene of Claudius praying, shown prostrate and facing the audience, is a momentary exception to Brook's outward display of the story in that it conveys Claudius's repressed, yet genuine, remorse. In doing so, it shifts perception from Hamlet's perspective, which is monological, to a dialogical one.

A similar process occurs in Ophelia's flower scene, which, if not moving, has the advantage of being crystal clear. Brook, in directing the scene, assiduously avoided setting Ophelia up as a poignant, mad heroine. This Ophelia, whether played by Shivalingappa or Sacri, is an ordinary girl who deals with a situation beyond her ken and control with the unquestioning filial duty she showed Polonius. Equally, she holds herself with the same youthful dignity. She keeps her flowers close to her body as she addresses the audience, selecting her flowers according to their message ('rue for you'), each adding a distinct note to Ophelia's 'voice' in the continuo to Hamlet's solo instrument.

The virtuosity of this instrument is indisputable. Hamlet/Lester (Paris performance) uttters 'Words, words, words' (Shakepeare 1982: 247) decisively, as he sits on his knees with his nose in the pages of a book. Others, torn out, are scattered about him. Something of the same confidence, now mixed with street-gang toughness, bites into his dialogue with Rozencrantz and Guildenstern on the purpose of their visit. His actions match his belligerent voice on 'What a piece of work is a man' (Shakespeare 1982: 253) as he swiftly pulls down Rozencrantz's jacket and pulls at his braces – a humorous gesture of derision that lightens the speech. This skittish note returns in his exchange with Ophelia, when he lies on his belly facing her and suggests lying on her lap. It turns into cruel taunting when, on 'country matters' (Shakespeare 1982: 295), he imitates fornication, still lying on the floor. Strong, energetic and feisty as ever, he appears in the graveyard scene and selects one of four skulls on sticks, using it like a ventriloquist. Details such as these add up to a powerful but non-heroic image. Meanwhile Ophelia's dead body is represented both metaphorically and metonymically by the long white scarf she wore. Earlier, when Polonius died, a red scarf on the floor worked in a similar way.

This is the barest of Hamlets. A square red-orange carpet, two low rectangular stools covered in red cloth and several cushions in red, yellow, purple and green lie symmetrically on the floor. It could be the interior of a modern home. Obolensky dresses the characters in simple garments of fine cloth with a classical line and an Eastern touch. Hamlet, for instance is in a black tunic and trousers, Ophelia in a long, white, Indian-style dress and Gertrude in deep purple silk. Two small carpets are put on the larger one and four candles are on its perimeter for the Players to perform their scene. Cushions are stood up on their sides to form Ophelia's grave, and a bamboo stick is the Gravedigger's spade. Music is played on a variety of instruments, many of them unfamiliar, by Toshi Tsuchitori, Brook's collaborator from the early days of the Bouffes. In this environment, warm like *The Tempest*, but much more mundane, Brook demonstrates that an act of the theatre might well be a minimalist affair concerning one person doing something (in *Hamlet* they are eight) while the other watches – here evoking Brook's similarly worded claim in 1973 (video, 1975). Shakespeare, in the process, is reconstituted. Brook would say, as he has done consistently, that Shakespeare is rediscovered.

Selected chronology

Productions of Shakespeare in England

1946 *Love's Labour's Lost*, Stratford-upon-Avon
1947 *Romeo and Juliet*, Stratford-upon-Avon
Appointed Director of the Royal Opera House, Covent Garden, London
1950 *Measure for Measure*, Stratford-upon-Avon
1951 *The Winter's Tale*, Phoenix Theatre, London
1955 *Titus Andronicus*, Stratford-upon-Avon
Hamlet, Moscow Art Theatre, Moscow; Phoenix Theatre, London
1957 *The Tempest*, Stratford-upon-Avon
1962 *King Lear*, Stratford-upon-Avon; Aldwych Theatre, London; New York
Appointed Co-Director of the Royal Shakespeare Company (RSC)
1968 *The Tempest*, RSC, The Round House, London
1969 Film: *King Lear*
1970 *A Midsummer Night's Dream*, Stratford-upon-Avon
1978 *Antony and Cleopatra*, Royal Shakespeare Theatre, Stratford-upon-Avon

Productions of Shakespeare at the Bouffes du Nord in Paris

1974 Beginning of the International Centre for Theatre Creation in Paris (CICT)
Opening of the Bouffes du Nord Theatre, Paris
Timon d'Athènes (*Timon of Athens*), William Shakespeare
1978 *Mesure pour mesure* (*Measure for Measure*), William Shakespeare
1990 *La Tempête* (*The Tempest*), William Shakespeare
2000 *The Tragedy of Hamlet*, William Shakespeare (in English)
2002 *La Mort de Krishna*
TV film: *The Tragedy of Hamlet*

Bibliography

Brook, Peter (1972) *The Empty Space*, Harmondsworth: Penguin.
—— (1974) Afterword to *Timon d'Athènes* adapted by Jean-Claude Carrière, Paris: Centre International de Créâtions Théâtrales, pp. 105–9.
—— (1987) *The Shifting Point: Forty Years of Theatrical Exploration 1946–1987*, New York: Harper & Row.
—— (1990) 'Une Enigme', preface to *La Tempête* adapted by Jean-Claude Carrière, Paris: Centre International de Créâtions Théâtrales, pp. 3–6.
—— (1995) *There Are No Secrets: Thoughts on Acting and Theatre*, London: Methuen.
—— (1998) *Threads of Time: A Memoir,* London: Methuen.
—— (1999) *Evoking Shakespeare*, London: Nick Hern.
—— (2003) Preface to *La Tragédie d'Hamlet*, adapted by Peter Brook and French text by Jean-Claude Carrière and Marie-Hélène Estienne, Paris: Actes Sud-Papiers, pp. 5–7.
Croyden, Margaret (2003) *Conversations with Peter Brook 1970–2000*, New York and London: Faber & Faber.
Heilpern, John (1977) *Conference of the Birds: The Story of Peter Brook in Africa*, London: Faber & Faber.
Helfer, Richard and Glenn Loney (eds) (1998) *Peter Brook: From Oxford to Orghast*, Amsterdam: Harwood Academic Publishers.
Hunt, Albert and Geoffrey Reeves (1995) *Peter Brook: Directors in Perspective*, Cambridge: Cambridge University Press.
Kustow, Michael (2006) *Peter Brook: A Biography*, London: Bloomsbury.
Lecat, Jean-Guy and Andrew Todd (2003) *The Open Circle: Peter Brook's Theatrical Environments*, London: Faber & Faber.
Moffitt, Dale (ed.) (2000) *Between Two Silences: Talking With Peter Brook*, London: Methuen.
Selbourne, David (1982) *The Making of A Midsummer Night's Dream: An Eye-witness Account of Peter Brook's Production from First Rehearsal to First Night*, London: Methuen.
Shakespeare, William (1969) *Timon of Athens*, London: Methuen.
—— (1974) *Timon d'Athènes*, adapted by Jean-Claude Carrièe, Paris: CICT.
—— (1982) *Hamlet*, London: Methuen.
Shevtsova, Maria (1994) 'The Art of Stillness: Brook's *Impressions de Pelléas*' (with an interview with Vincent Le Texier), *New Theatre Quarterly* 10 (40): 358–71.
Smith, A.C.H. (1972) *Orghast at Persepolis, An Account of the Experiment in Theatre Directed by Peter Brook and Written by Ted Hughes*, London: Methuen.
Trewin, J.C. (1971) *Peter Brook: A Biography*, London: Macdonald.
Williams, David (ed.) (1991) *Peter Brook and The Mahabharata: Critical Perspectives*, London: Routledge.
—— (ed.) (1992) *Peter Brook: A Theatrical Casebook*, London: Methuen.

Videography

Brook, Peter (1970) *King Lear*, Columbia/Filmways-Laterna.
Brook, Peter (1975) *The Empty Space*, Paris: Seven Valleys Entertainment Ltd and Centre International de Rechereche Théâtrale.
Brook, Peter (1989) *The Mahabharata*, Paris: Les Productions du 3ème Étage.
Brook, Peter (2001) *Hamlet*, London: BBC.

About the author

Maria Shevtsova is Professor of Drama and Theatre Arts at Goldsmiths College, University of London. She has held Chairs at the Universities of Connecticut and Lancaster, and was Director of European Studies at the University of Sydney. She studied at the Institut d'Etudes Théâtrales, University of Paris III and at the École des Hautes Études en Sciences Sociales (EHESS) in Paris. It is during this period that she began her interdisciplinary work, notably developing the field of the sociology of the theatre. She also focuses on European theatre, drawing on the work of directors with actors and other collaborators and on her fluency in Russian, French and Italian. She has published many articles in such journals as *Théâtre/Public, Alternatives théâtrales, Theatre Forum, Performing Arts Journal, Theatre Research International* and *Australasian Drama Studies*. Her books include *Theatre and Cultural Interaction* (1993), *Dodin and the Maly Drama Theatre: Process to Performance* (2004), *Robert Wilson* (2007), *Fifty Key Theatre Directors*, (co-editor and contributor) (2005) and *Jean Genet: Performance and Politics*, (co-editor and contributor) (2006). She has edited and contributed to the focus issues *Theatre and Interdisciplinarity* for *Theatre Research International* (2001) and *The Sociology of the Theatre* for *Contemporary Theatre Review* (2002). She is co-editor of *New Theatre Quarterly*.

3
GLEN BYAM SHAW
Nick Walton

Glen Byam Shaw's direction was commonly perceived as being 'assured and unobtrusive', 'blessedly straightforward', 'a model of sensitive presentation', and above all 'sympathetic to the players and the play'. His direction was also said to possess a 'Mozartian quality', 'a radiance' and an 'unobtrusive charm'. The superlatives 'enchanting', 'splendid', 'subtle', 'vivid', 'astonishing' and 'sublime' often appeared in descriptions of Shaw's work, and perhaps the greatest compliment paid to this director was the frequency with which critics concurred that he 'allowed Shakespeare to speak for himself'. Shaw's notes, letters and character sketches paint a picture of a deeply sensitive reader of Shakespeare's works, a man who had little difficulty in empathising with Shakespeare's characters and who was open to the variety of interpretations that this dramatist's works allow.

Glencairn Alexander Byam Shaw (1904–86) began his career in the theatre as an actor. During the 1920s and 1930s he gained stage experience, acting alongside John Gielgud, Laurence Olivier, Edith Evans and Peggy Ashcroft, all of whom he would direct later in his career. Shaw believed that the very finest actors are needed to do justice to Shakespeare's works; in his own words, 'Shakespeare calls for stars that sound the trumpets and make the air vibrate' (Addenbrooke 1974: 19). Biographical accounts suggest that he never much enjoyed being on stage, but his experience as a performer certainly contributed to his success as a director. Shaw's formative experiences heightened his awareness of the craftsmanship involved in a performance. Due to his early experience, and later his work as an actor-trainer, theatre administrator and producer, Shaw came to be regarded as a 'actor's director'. He privileged actors' performances above any theoretical ideas of his own, and his sensitivity to their craft allowed them the freedom to experiment.

Shaw's acting career ended when he became an officer in the Royal Scots in 1940. He served his country in Burma from 1942, suffering a terrible wound to his leg for which he had to spend eight months recovering in an army hospital. Shaw's brother was admitted to the same hospital, and during their convalescence he suggested that Glen plan a production of one of Shakespeare's plays. He began to prepare notes towards a production of *Antony and Cleopatra*, making detailed observations about characters, settings and timings of scenes. In conceiving this production, he outlined some of the tenets of his approach to Shakespeare that remained fundamental to his directorial vision. Among his notes, he wrote that, 'It seems difficult to cut any scene without interrupting the flow of the play', and added that 'the chief point which arises from my study is that one does not want a BIG production' (Shaw 1946). Throughout his career, Shaw presented Shakespeare's works free from structural emendation or directorial exhibitionism. His aim was to be faithful to Shakespeare's text and to create an environment in which the play's spirit could be conveyed most clearly.

In preparation for this production, Shaw wrote detailed character sketches for all of the roles. He continued this practice over time, building an archive of insightful character criticism, which served as a starting point for rehearsals. He was familiar with the character criticism of both Harley Granville Barker and A.C. Bradley, and their combined influence is evident in these notes, which he prepared for the role of Antony:

> The man is great. That is the first and foremost thing that must be got over to the audience. If this is not achieved by the actor, then the whole characterisation falls to the ground and probably the play with it. Of course it is easy enough to say 'You must be great' to an actor, but how is it done? I'm sure this is a case where the 'star' is essential [. . .] Antony is a great leader. A dashing cavalry officer. A tremendous personality. A sensualist. He has a wonderful physique. He can drink all night and fight all the next day and win the battle! He is simple minded, easily influenced: quick tempered but kind and honest. The sort of officer who is enormously popular with his troops but not so popular with his Generals. He is in his early 40s, but past his best, and definitely on the decline. He has become slightly Egyptian looking. When he gets back to Rome he looks unusual, almost like a foreigner, and feels out of place.
>
> (Shaw 1946)

Shaw's military experience influenced his reading of Shakespeare's soldiers, and it also helped fashion his approach to direction; like a general he brought a sense of discipline to the rehearsal room; he had a strategy and led his company by example, from the front.

On his return to England, Shaw was able to put his theories into practice when he produced *Antony and Cleopatra* at the Piccadilly Theatre in 1946, with the pre-war film stars Edith Evans and Godfrey Tearle in the principal roles. Consistent with Shaw's desire to avoid a 'big' production, his design team 'Motley' favoured a permanent set, which in theory would allow the action to proceed uninterrupted and at great speed. However, despite Shaw's desire to imitate the conventions of the Elizabethan playhouse and present Shakespeare's scenes in unbroken succession, his production proved ponderous. George Rylands complained that:

> The setting of *Antony and Cleopatra* was so pretentious and uncomfortable that the tragedy never had a chance, from the great processional opening which was muddled away to nothing until the hauling up of the hero with pulleys and a fishing net on to the platform surrounding what appeared to be an air-raid shelter or an elevator with sliding doors. The stage was so cluttered with permanent solids that the essential contrast of the juxtaposed scenes in Rome and Alexandria was quite lost.
>
> (Rylands 1948: 105)

Shaw's development as a director is marked by his desire to address the criticisms levelled at this production. He worked to create practical sets that freed the stage from clutter, and, ultimately, Motley's delicate designs brought distinction to his productions.

The 1946 production was hampered by the mannered acting style of Shaw's principal performers, which was in conflict with his desire for speed and fluidity of performance. Over time, Shaw began to establish a modern acting style, which, though observed from life, could adapt to the speed and rhythms of Shakespeare's texts. From 1947 until 1951, Shaw joined Michel Saint-Denis and George Devine to run the Old Vic Centre in London, which housed The Old Vic Dramatic School, and the Young Vic Company. The aim behind the Dramatic School was to train actors, directors and designers who would create productions for new audiences and whose work could feed into the main stage work of the Old Vic Company. Shaw helped to shape and influence the next generation of theatre practitioners, some of whom he would work with again when he moved to the Stratford Memorial Theatre in 1952. Notable graduates include Keith Mitchell, Derek Godfrey, Joan Plowright, Patrick Wymark and Denis Quilley.

The actor-training at the theatre school covered three broad categories of style: Shakespearian, Restoration and Modern. As Audrey Williamson records:

> The training included much that is usual in serious schools, especially

> schools with elements of group outlook sympathetic to the Russian Arts theatre and the French Vieux Colombier and Compagnie des Quinze [. . .]. There was an emphasis on improvisation, classes in mime and make-up, some use of comic masks, fencing lessons, voice production, and in addition lectures on the history of Literature, drama and design.
>
> (Williamson 1957: 71)

A concentration upon individual characterisation became a defining feature of Shaw's approach to actor-training. He would begin each new course by casting students in a Shakespeare play and proceeded to direct them as if they were fully developed actors.

Having prepared his detailed notes, he would work out the actor's movements using a collection of model soldiers. To clarify the three-dimensional image of his vision, he worked in a model box using figures made from pipe-cleaners, which could sit, kneel and walk upstairs. He arrived in the rehearsal room with the play's moves mapped in his mind, and as he rehearsed, he would gradually withdraw, leaving the actors the freedom to explore a scene's dynamics for themselves.

Shaw approached direction as a business undertaking, and actors valued the meticulous preparation that he put into his productions. At the beginning of rehearsals for the first of the Young Vic's productions in 1948, Shaw expressed his philosophy to his young company:

> Our strength should be in the fact that we are determined to do this play better than it has ever been done, and we can only achieve that if we work on every aspect of the production as well as we possibly can. It must be 'alive' from the beginning.
>
> (Shaw 1948)

Fundamental to Shaw's directorial approach was his desire to encourage actors and audiences to engage more directly with the text itself.

Shaw's growing desire to bring a contemporary relevance to his productions was reflected in his decision to stage *Henry V* at The Old Vic in 1951. His own wartime experience and his sensitivity to London's post-war sensibility helped fashion this production, which differed markedly in its presentation of patriotism from Laurence Olivier's popular 1944 film. Aware that audiences had become disillusioned with the supposed glories of war, Shaw explored the play from the perspective of a quiet, saintly king who fights only because he is convinced of the justice of his cause, not out of a desire for the glories of battle. The battle at Agincourt became one stage in a protracted campaign rather than the climax of patriotic warmongering, an unfortunate necessity. Alec Clunes's King Henry, like the audiences of 1951, had few illusions about the nature of a prolonged military campaign.

Despite Shaw's original contention that, 'it seems difficult to cut any scene without interrupting the flow of the play' (1946), the text of *Henry V* was cut dramatically, encouraging a more sympathetic understanding of Henry's plight and character. A high proportion of the 857 lines omitted made reference to Henry's youthful unruliness and to his ambitions in France. Breaking with tradition, Shaw shortened Henry's reply to the Dauphin's insult; he omitted the King's admission of the 'barbarous licence' he had enjoyed as a young man (Act I, Scene 2, lines 269–72), and he silenced his bloody desire to 'dazzle all the eyes of France, / Yea strike the Dauphin blind to look on us' (Act I, Scene 2, lines 278–80). Henry's reputation was also enhanced significantly by the omission of his command 'Then every soldier kill his prisoners' (Act IV, Scene 6, line 37). Shaw removed some prominent references to the fatalities of war, softening Shakespeare's raw remembrance of the dead; he cut Henry's poignant speech 'A many of our bodies shall no doubt / Find native graves' (Act IV, Scene 3, lines 96–108) and erased the names of the fallen French (Act IV, Scene 8, lines 91–101).

Shaw's textual alterations gave Clunes the freedom to foreground Henry's benevolence in his performance. At first, he appeared remote as if feeling his way into kingship behind a façade of regality. He attained full stature when he rose with dignity to the Dauphin's insult and continued to convey the King's sense of responsibility throughout the production. Shaw's concentration on subtle characterisation can be appreciated from Richard David's description of Clunes's delivery of Henry's lines:

> Just because it began so quietly, so informally, "We few, we happy few, we band of brothers" gathered irresistible power as it proceeded, so that the climax was overwhelming; and in the speech on Commodity Clunes carried us with him through each turn of the King's thought. We were thus brought close to a Harry who was very much more than a heroic figure in a painted cloth.
>
> (David 1952: 126)

Further sympathy for Henry was evoked through Shaw's depiction of the French court. For this post-war audience, Paul Rogers's Dauphin evoked Hitler through the vicious and hysterical delivery of his lines. This vocal intemperance was matched with physical violence; as Exeter departed in Act II, Scene 4, the Dauphin spun round in fury and struck a tray of metal goblets from the hands of an attendant. Later, before his entrance in Act III,

Scene 7, the screams of a peasant girl could be heard offstage implying a cruel lecherous side to the Dauphin's character. Shaw's interpretation of the drama anticipated Ian Holm's portrayal of Henry in John Barton and Peter Hall's 1964 RSC production, which also presented a king with no relish for war.

Great emphasis was placed upon the role of the Chorus played by Roger Livesey; his casual delivery of the Chorus's lines endeared him to the audience, winning him both sympathy and loyalty. Dressed in an open-collared white shirt and black trousers, the Chorus contrasted effectively with the other players, costumed in rich but subdued historical splendour. There was a bareness to Shaw's stage. The Chorus spoke his opening lines in front of six tall flagpoles arranged symmetrically on either side of the stage. Flags and banners were unfurled to indicate movement between the English and French courts; the mastheads of two ships (positioned upstage) towered over the actors before Henry's embarkation for France, and a couple of cannons and provision wagons represented the battlefield as Henry motivated his troops before Agincourt. Shaw successfully blended the bare-stage conventions of Shakespeare's Globe with the new stagecraft's emphasis upon suggestive lighting, and his approach was praised for the demands it put upon the audiences' 'imaginary forces'.

Running the Old Vic Centre developed Shaw's organisational and managerial skills while exploring Shakespeare's works on stage and in the rehearsal room. His administrative and diplomatic skills were of importance when he joined Antony Quayle at the Shakespeare Memorial Theatre in 1952, eventually becoming Head of the Company himself in 1957. Quayle and Shaw shared a vision for Shakespeare at Stratford; they looked to assemble a large company, led by distinguished actors, who could present a small repertoire of plays performed to West End standards. Shaw helped transform the Memorial Theatre from a small provincial theatre into an international showcase for some of the best of British talent. In eight years, he arranged four London seasons, sent tours overseas to thirteen countries and produced twelve plays himself.

Shaw's approach to staging Shakespeare satisfied the diverse expectations of Stratford's post-war audiences. Ivor Brown notes that:

> The producer of Shakespeare at Stratford has always to face one dilemma. His public is a double one. Small, but vocal, is that section which, knowing Shakespeare and theatrical practice intimately, wants novelty of approach and favours experiment even to the verge of the fantastic. The much larger public, with no pretensions to special knowledge, wants to see the play. If there are stars in the sky, so much the better.
>
> (Brown 1959: 11)

In 1953, Shaw chose to return to *Antony and Cleopatra*, which had not been performed in Stratford for eight years. His production boasted West End stars in Michael Redgrave and Peggy Ashcroft, investing the principal roles with instant 'star quality'. Shaw's opening address to his company reveals his approach to directing works for the second time:

> I want to tell you at once that I have produced this play before. It would be silly if I didn't confess it [. . .] I say 'confess it' because I think that if someone has done a thing before there is always a fear that they will want to do it again in exactly the same way or will be led into doing it differently just for the sake of being different. Personally I am always slightly worried when I know an actor has played a part in another production if he is going to play the same part in a production of mine. I can only ask you to believe me when I say that I have tried to eliminate from my mind the memories of that other production and aim to do it fresh. On the other hand I have refused to change my feeling about the play in order to try and be different.
>
> (Shaw 1953)

Shaw stressed at the beginning of rehearsals that 'one of the most important things in the production will be to make a clear differentiation between the atmosphere in Egypt and the atmosphere in Rome' (1953). He associated Egypt with warmth, luxury, colour, disorder and passion, while he perceived Rome as being cold and hard and characterised by ruthless determination. Motley's sparse design attracted praise for its minimalist quality:

> The play is not hampered by unnecessary décor. Both scenery and costumes have been designed by Motley, and yet in the strict sense there is no set scenery. The stage, save for a couple of slender pillars, is as bare as possible. Almost all the rest is 'props'. A simple sail let down from above, with the addition of some sparse ship's furniture, suffices for Pompey's galley. One set for Cleopatra's monument is a simple piece of cracked masonry with gigantic Egyptian wall figures, released hydraulically from below. But during most of these tense three hours the stage is bare except for a flight of shallow steps, and sometimes a simple figure or two figures at parley are sharply etched against the sky. Though it was long before we had the deep unclouded blaze of Egyptian noonday, the lighting was never without its significance in the mood of the play.
>
> (*Scotsman*, 30 April 1953)

Shaw's father John had been a painter and illustrator, and his son evidently inherited his father's scenic eye, varying lighting to suggest changes in space, time and atmosphere. The sultry warmth of the Mediterranean sun faded from the cyclorama upstage whenever action moved to Rome; the lighting changed from balmy, brilliant yellows into cold blue-greys.

By varying the pacing and momentum of the opening scenes, Shaw associated Egypt with heightened and turbulent emotions. The production opened with great energy as Antony and Cleopatra 'whirled in a flurry of passion unsatisfied down the long steps bathed in a hot, sandy light' (Fleming, *Spectator*, 8 May 1953). This opening vigour soon subsided into languor with Antony's departure for Rome. In contrast with her first entrance, Cleopatra was carried onto the stage for Act I, Scene 5 on a litter by four slaves, who, having lowered their queen to the floor, adopted slothful poses: some stretched out on the floor; others leaned against the pillars. Throughout, Cleopatra moved effortlessly about the stage: 'Here is a woman who is all woman with a natural grace and effortless dignity and no need for seductive art' (Ellis, *Stratford-on-Avon Herald*, 1 May 1953).

The atmosphere in Caesar's camp was crisper than in Egypt; Caesar's guards stood before a drape depicting an eagle, flanking their leader, always alert. Scenes in Rome were largely static, and it was not until Caesar's army marched across the forestage in Act III, Scene 6, that action came to be associated with this camp. Shaw introduced two intervals. The first interval came after Act III, Scene 3 with Cleopatra awaiting Antony's return after his marriage to Octavia, and the second after Act IV, Scene 9, concluding with Enobarbus' death. Reviewers praised the production's 'admirable rhythm, the flow of small scenes into the full tide' (Ellis, *Stratford-upon-Avon Herald*, 1 May 1953), and it was commonly asserted that Shaw's 'magnificence consists in avoiding magnificence for the sake of allowing the 42 scenes to follow each other in rapid sequence' (*The Times*, 29 April 1953).

At 6 foot 2 inches, Redgrave towered above Ashcroft, and his powerful physique matched Shakespeare's description of 'the triple pillar of the world' (Act I, Scene 1, line 12). His richly textured voice captured both Antony's nobility and ruin:

> Although he could boom with rage and defiance ("when I cried, Ho! . . . kings would start forth" [Act III; Scene 13, lines 90–1]), there was exquisite music in his voice, and the effect of "unarm, Eros" [Act IV, Scene 15, line 35] was all the more memorable for its delivery by a man who had been, so credibly, "the greatest soldier in the world" [Act I, Scene 3, line 38], the figure in Cleopatra's dream.
>
> (Findlater 1956: 129)

A subtle development in Shaw's reading of Antony can be seen in the differences between the notes that he prepared for Michael Redgrave and those that he wrote while in Burma in 1942. When Shaw approached the play for the first time, he was eager to convey Antony's greatness, yet in 1953 he looked to reveal Antony's failings from the start of the drama. He described Antony as still having 'a dash and courage but his judgement is dangerously affected by his relationship with Cleopatra and her influence over him'. He noted that, 'To him she is like a drug. He knows she is destroying him, but the excitement of being with her is impossible to give up' (Shaw 1953). In line with Shaw's reading, Redgrave's Antony gradually acquired nobility during the course of the play; his swaggering soldier of the opening scenes transformed into a commanding general. Shaw steered Antony's portrayal towards greatness rather than plotting Antony's progressive decline through the drama.

The casting of Ashcroft was controversial. Audiences had come to expect voluptuous performances of the role, yet Ashcroft subtly emphasised Cleopatra's intelligence and innate dignity above her sexual allure. Cleopatra's tigress quality emerged through Ashcroft's appearance; she sported a flame-red wig and wore vibrant orange and purple robes: 'The clash of colours was blinding, but strongly effective. Wilfulness and witchery were in her clothes as much as in her tantrums' (Dick, *Daily Herald*, 27 April 1953). Ashcroft's speed of movement across the bare stage reflected her alternating frenzies of passion and frustration. During the course of the play, she competed with Antony for ascendancy on the upstage steps, which served quite literally as a platform upon which the highs and lows of their relationship were played out. Ashcroft punctuated Cleopatra's early speeches with soft laughter, but this lightness gradually disappeared. Cleopatra's fury was accentuated by her attendants' horror at her actions; it took a scream from Charmian to prevent this Cleopatra from murdering the messenger in Act II, Scene 5. The presentation of Cleopatra's final moments was calm and dignified, in sharp contrast with the energy and passion that characterised the rest of the production: 'In the Monument scene and especially when taking the asp to her bosom, Miss Ashcroft rode the tragedy to a superb climax, calm and lofty, with what might be called a classic detachment' (T.C.K, *Birmingham Post*, 30 April 1953).

Shaw's casting of star actors became a feature of his directorial policy during his time at Stratford. While he looked to nurture young performers such as Diana Rigg, Ian Holm, Vanessa Redgrave and Ian Bannen, the polished quality of his productions was due in part to the remarkable talents of the star actors he employed; stars of the Stratford stage during the 1950s included John Gielgud, Antony Quayle, Charles Laughton, Harry Andrews, Peggy Ashcroft, Michael Redgrave, Laurence Olivier and Vivien Leigh. In 1955,

Shaw cast Olivier and Leigh in *Macbeth*, producing what has become a landmark in that play's stage history. Kenneth Tynan championed the pacing of Olivier's performance:

> [Olivier] begins in a perilously low key, the reason for which is soon revealed. This Macbeth is paralysed with guilt before the curtain rises, having already killed Duncan time and again in his mind. Far from recoiling and popping his eyes, he greets the air-drawn dagger with sad familiarity; it is a fixture in the crooked furniture of his brain. Uxoriousness leads him to the act, which unexpectedly purges him of remorse. Now the portrait swells; seeking security, he is seized with fits of desperate bewilderment as the prize is snatched out of reach. There was true agony in "I had else been perfect"; Banquo's ghost was received with horrific torment as if Macbeth should shriek "I've been robbed!", and the phrase about the dead rising to "push us from our stools" was accompanied with a convulsive shoving gesture which few other actors would have risked.
>
> (Tynan, *Sunday Observer*, 12 June 1955)

Olivier's depiction of Macbeth's psychology was universally acclaimed, and Shaw's concentration upon the inherent rhythms within the drama brought distinction to this production.

Shaw returned three times to *As You Like It*. His sensitivity to its structure became a defining quality of his productions. In 1949, with the Young Vic Company, the theatrical experience was light and romantic. Shaw saw the drama as a 'fairy story' that could be told in three parts. The first would contain, 'drama, action, and description', the second 'freedom, open air, and love', and the third would be concerned with 'the winding up of the story, the pairing off of the couples, and the happy ending' (Shaw 1948). He drew up a list of ten things he felt that audiences needed to be made to believe:

1 That Oliver intends to kill his brother.
2 That Charles is a superb wrestler.
3 That Rosalind is banished.
4 That the forest is a forest.
5 That Adam is dying for want of food and shelter.
6 That it is the sort of forest where one may meet a lion or a snake or a goat.
7 That Orlando is not sure Rosalind is Ganymede or not.
8 That Oliver can marry Celia and that they will both be happy for ever after.
9 That the same can apply to Silvius and Phebe.

10 That Jacques de Boys can bring such extraordinary news just at the right moment.

(Shaw 1948)

While Shaw's first production was not judged a success, his initial impressions were influential for his approach in future years. By 1952, he had come to interpret the play, and the musicality of its characters as follows:

> The theme of this play is love, and there are four main variations on the theme – first Rosalind and Orlando, second Celia and Oliver, third Touchstone and Audrey, fourth Silvius and Phebe. It is of course essential that the true and right balance should be found between these four pairs of lovers for it is on that that the construction of the play hangs. It is like a piece of music, and I, personally think of Mozart because to me it has something of the same charm, gaiety, freshness, youth and vitality of Mozart's music. To explain how I imagine the differences between the four pairs of lovers I shall put it like this: to me Rosalind and Orlando are like the violins. Exciting, exquisite, brilliant and emotional. The top of poetic feeling. Celia and Oliver are the violas. Calmer, warmer and with a certain dramatic feeling which of course comes from Oliver. Not so brilliant as the violins, but with a beauty of their own, and full of heart. Touchstone and Audrey are like the bassoons. Fantastic, humorous, earthy, crude and unexpected. Also with a lush, succulent feeling about them. Silvius and Phebe are the flutes. Light, gay, saucy, and very young and fresh but intermittently touching.
>
> (Shaw 1952)

Experience had taught him that 'if the play becomes heavy handed or middle aged then it is hopeless' (Shaw 1952). For Shaw the lightness of tone was connected to the play's French setting. For his Stratford production he broke with the tradition of giving the play an English setting and worked with his designers to create a stage world reminiscent of the reign of Louis XIII and of the paintings of Van Dyke. The design contrasted exquisite courtly costumes with more romantic rustic attire worn in the forest. Shaw's intentions at the beginning of the rehearsal period were clear; he aimed to produce a theatrical experience that would make 'every old and middle aged person in the audience long to be young again, and every young person in the audience feel how good it is not to be old' (Shaw 1952).

The key to Shaw's staging, and his greatest innovation, was to present the action as unfolding in time with the changing of the seasons. The winter setting of the opening scenes gave way to spring with the awakening of Orlando and Rosalind's love. Audiences were accustomed to seeing this romantic comedy set in high summer, but Shaw's decision to open the play in winter heightened audience awareness to the lack of warmth and fruitfulness in the opening scenes. Some reviewers expressed shock at seeing snow in Arden, yet as Robert Smallwood notes, 'a few productions later, and an Arden that did not progress from winter to summer would be hard to find' (Smallwood 2003: 47).

With Rosalind's entrance into Arden, the lighting warmed to reflect the budding relationships in the forest. By the time that Orlando arrived to hang his verses, the lighting reflected a clear spring morning, and the dull, dreary, low-spirited atmosphere of the opening scenes was banished. As the winter lighting disappeared so too did the sound of whistling wind that underscored the opening scenes. The pastoral sound of bells and bleating goats offstage underscored the second and third movements, bringing a vivid, but knowingly comical sense of location.

Shaw's production was energised by Margaret Leighton's spirited portrayal of Rosalind. On her first entrance, she appeared isolated and lonely; as a courtly procession passed across the stage she appeared at its tail and stood staring dejectedly at the throne. Rosalind's spirit appeared crushed in these opening scenes; her words of remonstrance to the Duke against her banishment (Act I, Scene 3, lines 45–50 and Act I, Scene 2, lines 59–63) were cut, allowing the Duke to dominate the action. On entering Arden, Rosalind acquired a tomboyish quality, and Shaw conveyed the fragility of her posturing through inserting some contrived business at the close of her first interview with Orlando in Act III, Scene 2. Here, Rosalind as Ganymede crossed in front of her companions to leave the stage, but Laurence Harvey's Orlando caught her by the seat of her trousers and pulled her back to allow Celia to go first. As he left the stage, Harvey's Orlando good-humouredly pulled Rosalind's cap over her eyes. Through this gesture, Shaw invited a range of alternative interpretations, centring on whether Ganymede's true identity had been revealed at this point.

While life in the Duke's court was presented as spirit stifling, life in Shaw's Arden was evidently more relaxed and free, if not somewhat fantastical. Motley's greenwood design consisted of a spread of scaffold thin leafless trees, giving the forest both austerity and charm. With the arrival of spring, the forest adopted a tropical exuberance, boasting cacti and a prominent palm tree set between less exotic flora and fauna. Despite the snow on the ground, Shaw's foresters lay around the stage eating fruit; their relaxed poses were in sharp contrast to the formal procession witnessed in Duke Frederick's court in Act I, Scene 2.

Alongside the tender revelations shared between Orlando and Rosalind, Shaw staged moments of vaudevillian slapstick and provided colour to the characterisations of the play's supporting cast. To the audience's delight, Sir Oliver Martext, startled by the sound of a goat, fell backwards into the pond having married Touchstone and Audrey, and later two pageboys sat sniggering as Touchstone and Audrey kissed at the beginning of Act V, Scene 3. Shaw had a gift for eliciting well-conceived portraits from his small-part actors. Barry Warren, who played the goat in this production, received the following detailed directorial note:

> The goat is a very fierce animal that terrifies Sir Oliver Martext. In the forest there are birds, sheep and goats. I want the sounds of all these to be made by the company and not by recordings which are never any good. But they must be done very well. This theatre is in the country, not in London, and audiences here really do know how birds sing and sheep and goats baa and bleat.
>
> (Shaw 1952)

Shaw altered Shakespeare's stagecraft in the final scene by cutting the appearance of Hymen. As in a fairy tale, Rosalind appeared upstage, dressed in her woman's weeds, and the onstage audience turned to watch in disbelief as Rosalind, followed by Celia made their way to the front of the stage. In stark contrast to the low-spirited beginning of this production, the closing dance ended the production in a festive mood.

Shaw directed *As You Like It* at Stratford for the final time five years later in 1957. Since his first production in 1949, he had developed a deep understanding of the play's potential to charm audiences, concluding that 'psychology is not important in this play, compared with the expression of human emotion and relationships' (Shaw 1957). He looked to make his final production 'lighter, fresher and more French in feeling' (Shaw 1957). He achieved this ambition through a combination of inspired casting, redesign and reformulation of some key moments in the play.

The freshness of the production owed much to the casting of Peggy Ashcroft as Rosalind; as J.C. Trewin stated, 'we have to like Rosalind the moment she appears; if we have so much as a shadow of doubt, the play can waver. Dame Peggy can inspire more immediate affection than any actress on the stage' (Trewin, *Illustrated London News*, 13 April 1957). Though at 48 years of age, Ashcroft was more mature than Shakespeare's Rosalind, the actress was able to convey the character's disarming charm. Ashcroft brought a sense of spontaneity to Rosalind's words and actions; the stillness of movement in the court scenes gave way to a fluidity of motion once in the forest; 'Dame Peggy, in her crimson jacket, is essential Ganymede–Rosalind; she is fathoms deep in love, and when she spins round in sudden ecstasy at "But what talk we of fathers when there is such a man as Orlando?", there is no more to add' (Trewin, *Illustrated London News*, 13 April 1957). In Peggy Ashcroft, Shaw cast an actress who 'can be very sad or very gay, and can switch from one mood to another in a surprisingly short space of time. She has enormous energy and vitality and is highly temperamental. She is restless and full of imaginative feeling' (Shaw 1957).

Shaw retained his notion of the play's seasonality for this production and Motley's design duly reflected a progression in the play's action from March to April, though the severity of the winter setting for the opening was moderated somewhat. Shaw's continuing desire to approach the play as a fairy tale was reflected in Motley's new abstract design for Arden which was presented as 'a never-never land where people with real emotions play hide and seek in dappled vistas of unreality' (Fleming, *Spectator*, 26 April 1957). The delicate designs for the forest locations brought a spaciousness to the stage that had been lacking for the production in 1952. Motley's sparse stylised design of tall spindly trees against a clear sky focused attention upon striking stage tableaux. As Jaques concluded his speech on the seven ages of man, he offered his stool to the ailing Adam, who, in his weary condition, personified Shakespeare's description of the seventh age; Shaw's marrying of word with movement brought touches of visual poetry to his production and highlighted the sensual craftsmanship underlying Shakespeare's shaping of this and other moments in the drama.

Shaw respected Shakespeare's structuring of the final scene for this production and included the appearance of Hymen having omitted it five years earlier. He had concluded that, 'whether he is really a God or someone impersonating the God we don't have to worry about. He is accepted as a Deity by everyone including the Duke, and as it is an enchanted Forest I, personally, think that he is the real Hymen' (Shaw 1957). Hymen took to the stage on a rustic wagon pulled by the two pageboys; he shared the wagon with Corin and William who accompanied him on fiddle and pipe as he sang. Shaw avoided ostentatious display at this moment and focused attention upon the heightened emotions provoked by Hymen's words. Muriel St Clare Byrne wrote that, 'a trust in his author and his actors, in straight playing and in a direct and uncomplicated approach to character seems to me the fundamental virtue in Mr Glen Byam Shaw's work as a producer' (Byrne 1957: 481).

Shaw became sole Director of the Memorial Theatre following Antony Quayle's resignation in 1956. Between 1957 and 1959, Shaw oversaw sixteen productions. In his first season, he directed *As You Like It* and *Julius Caesar*, while Douglas Searle, Peter Hall and Peter Brook respectively directed productions of *King John*, *Cymbeline* and *The Tempest*. The range of plays encouraged challenging cross-casting; Alec Clunes, for example, was cast in the roles of Philip Falconbridge, Brutus and Caliban, while Richard Johnson moved between Orlando and Marc Antony. Shaw's final year at Stratford coincided with the theatre's 100th season, for which he designed a star-studded programme. Tony Richardson's *Othello*, starring Paul Robeson and Sam Wanamaker opened the season and was followed by Tyrone Guthrie's Victorian-costumed *All's Well that Ends Well*. Star-casting in the shape of Charles Laughton and Laurence Olivier contributed to the success of Peter Hall's productions of *A Midsummer Night's Dream* and *Coriolanus*, yet Laughton's portrayal of King Lear for Shaw's farewell production proved a disappointment. Failing health limited Laughton's performance, and his lack of authority robbed the play of stature: 'At his best, he sounds like the wind in the willows rather than the brass section of the music of the spheres. At his worst, he mumbles and groans with the thread-bare moan of an old violin' (Brien 1959: 223).

Until his own departure in 1959, to pursue a career as an opera director, Shaw continued to promote a clear approach to presentation. His championing of fresh talent and his commitment to bringing a contemporary edge to his productions became the bedrock of Peter Hall's vision for the RSC. Shaw's influence upon Peter Hall and upon many of the actors who helped create the face of the new company can be seen behind the RSC's founding principle, which was to present Shakespeare in a contemporary fashion and to emphasise the relevance of his plays to the modern world.

For Shaw, it was the potential that an actor has to hold an audience entranced with his or her voice, body and presence, combined with Shakespeare's words, that represented the magic and mystery of theatre. It was his role as director to focus audience attention onto the craftsmanship of the performers on stage and not to distract eyes, ears or minds with anything superfluous to the experience of the performance as it unfolded in time. It is unlikely that Shaw would have labelled himself a theatrical innovator; he regarded Peter Brook and Tyrone Guthrie as innovative and judged his own work to be steeped in traditionalism. However, for audiences of the late 1940s and throughout the 1950s, Shaw's productions appeared innovative because they privileged Shakespeare's texts above any directorial intervention or conception. One reviewer spoke for many when he wrote in 1956 that, 'the supreme virtue of a Byam Shaw production is that Shakespeare is its hero' (Findlater 1956: 127).

Chronology

1946 *Antony and Cleopatra*, Piccadilly Theatre, London
1947 Appointed Director of Old Vic Centre
1949 *As You Like It*, Old Vic Theatre, London
1950 *Merchant of Venice*, Old Vic Theatre, London
1951 *Henry V*, Old Vic Theatre, London
1952 *As You Like It*, Shakespeare Memorial Theatre, Stratford-upon-Avon
Appointed Co-Director of the Shakespeare Memorial Theatre
Coriolanus, Shakespeare Memorial Theatre, Stratford-upon-Avon
1953 *Richard III*, Shakespeare Memorial Theatre, Stratford-upon-Avon
Antony and Cleopatra, Shakespeare Memorial Theatre, Stratford-upon-Avon
1954 *Troilus and Cressida*, Shakespeare Memorial Theatre, Stratford-upon-Avon
1955 *Macbeth*, Shakespeare Memorial Theatre, Stratford-upon-Avon
1956 *The Merry Wives of Windsor*, Shakespeare Memorial Theatre, Stratford-upon-Avon
Othello, Shakespeare Memorial Theatre, Stratford-upon-Avon
1957 Appointed Director of the Shakespeare Memorial Theatre
As You Like It, Shakespeare Memorial Theatre, Stratford-upon-Avon
Julius Caesar, Shakespeare Memorial Theatre, Stratford-upon-Avon
1958 *Romeo and Juliet*, Shakespeare Memorial Theatre, Stratford-upon-Avon
Hamlet, Shakespeare Memorial Theatre, Stratford-upon-Avon
1959 *King Lear*, Shakespeare Memorial Theatre, Stratford-upon-Avon
1962 Appointed Director of Productions at Sadler's Wells Theatre

Bibliography

The Shakespeare Centre Library in Stratford-upon-Avon holds an archive of the promptbooks and notebooks that Glen Byam Shaw used for his work at the Shakespeare Memorial Theatre. The archive also includes recorded interviews with Shaw and photographs of his Stratford productions. The notebooks referred to in this chapter are housed in this archive.

Addenbrooke, David (1974) *The Royal Shakespeare Company: The Peter Hall Years*, London: Kimber.
Bate, Jonathan and Russell Jackson (eds) (1996) *Shakespeare: An Illustrated Stage History*, Oxford: Oxford University Press.
Beauman, Sally (1982) *The Royal Shakespeare Company: A History of Ten Decades*, Oxford: Oxford University Press.
Brien, Alan (1959) 'Simulation in the Fields', *Spectator*, 203: 223–4.
Brown, Ivor (1959) *Shakespeare Memorial Theatre 1957–59*, London: Reinhardt.

Byrne, Muriel St Clare (1957) 'The Shakespeare Season at the Old Vic, 1956–57 and Stratford-upon-Avon, 1957', *Shakespeare Quarterly*, 8(3): 461–92.
David, Richard (1952) 'Shakespeare in the Waterloo Road', *Shakespeare Survey*, 5: 120–9.
Findlater, Richard (1956) *Michael Redgrave: Actor*, London: Heinemann.
Hall, Peter (1993) *Making an Exhibition of Myself*, London: Sinclair-Stevenson.
Madelaine, Richard (1998) *Shakespeare in Production: Antony and Cleopatra*, Cambridge: Cambridge University Press.
Mullin, Michael (ed.) (1976) *'Macbeth' Onstage: An Annotated Facsimile of Glen Byam Shaw's Promptbook*, Columbia, Miss.: University of Missouri Press.
—— (1996) *Design by Motley*, Newark, Del. and London:
Rylands, George (1948) 'London Productions', *Shakespeare Survey*, 1: 103–5.
Shaw, Glen Byam (1946) *Production Notebook for Antony and Cleopatra.*
—— (1948) Production Notebook for *As You Like It.*
—— (1952) *Production Notebook for As You Like It.*
—— (1953) *Production Notebook for Antony and Cleopatra.*
—— (1957) *Production Notebook for As You Like It.*
Smallwood, Robert (2003) *Shakespeare at Stratford: As You Like It*, London: Arden.
Williamson, Audrey (1957) *Old Vic Drama 1947–57*, London: Rockliff.

About the author

Nick Walton is Lecturer in Shakespeare Studies at the Shakespeare Birthplace Trust, Stratford-upon-Avon. He has served as the Executive Secretary of the International Shakespeare Association since 2003. He received his MA and Ph.D. from the Shakespeare Institute, University of Birmingham, and he has lectured on Shakespeare in performance at the University of Warwick and as a guest lecturer for the RSC. His Introduction to the New Penguin edition of *Timon of Athens* was published in 2005, and he also contributed a section on the play in performance for the revised New Penguin edition of *Love's Labour's Lost*. Nick regularly interviews actors and directors about their work and reviews productions for academic journals. He has performed in Shakespeare's plays on stage and screen.

4
DEGUCHI NORIO

Mika Eglinton

In the history of Shakespeare productions in Japan, the achievements of Deguchi Norio (1940–), as the founder-director of 'the Shakespeare Theatre', are outstanding. It was the first Japanese theatre company whose *raison d'être* was to perform the complete works of Shakespeare. In May 1975, monthly productions began at a small underground theatre called 'JeanJean' in Shibuya, a young and trendy district in Tokyo. Gaining recognition and popularity for 'Shakespeare in Jeans and T-shirts', the company completed Shakespeare's entire thirty-seven works by June 1981.

While this seminal 'JeanJean' period set a precedent in Japanese theatre history, for Deguchi it represents just the first part of an ongoing journey spanning almost half a century. In October 2005, the Shakespeare Theatre celebrated its thirtieth anniversary with revivals of its most iconic productions, *A Midsummer Night's Dream* and *Twelfth Night*, along with a new adaptation play titled *Shakespeare Rehearsal*. Looking back at the company's journey in a personal interview with Deguchi in 2005, he recognised equal amounts of upheaval and success in four eight-year cycles. His theatre practice has been influenced at times by key sociocultural changes in Japanese politics and society, and yet despite undergoing radical changes, the consistency and continuity of his unrelenting belief in Shakespeare's plays has cemented the company's credibility and survival. Deguchi's unique personality and his strict, sober and even humble approach to the plays is a rare resistance against the profitable and consumerist Shakespeare industry in contemporary theatre.

He grew up in the rural Shimane prefecture and had his first encounter with theatre at university. In 1959, he was involved in left-wing theatre activities in the University of Tokyo at the beginning of a turbulent political era when student movements against the American military regime and the US–Japan Security Treaty were gaining momentum. Amidst the growing counter-culture of the 1960s, Shingeki (New Drama), a form of theatre performing Western drama in translation, was condemned as the epitome of the establishment and challenged by the emerging avant-garde Shogekijou Undo (Little Theatre Movement) and Angura Engeki (Underground Theatre). Contesting the pseudo-Western realism of Shingeki as old-fashioned, these experimental and ideological initiatives created alternative performance methods and aesthetics, exploring unusual theatre spaces such as deserted houses and outdoor tents. Among the leaders of this era were practitioners such as Juro Kara, Makoto Sato, Tadashi Suzuki and Yukio Ninagawa.

Five years later, Deguchi had become disillusioned with the unrealistic student movement and sceptical of socialist theatre and had begun to form a deeper connection with Shingeki. In 1965, upon graduation, he became an assistant-director for a prestigious Shingeki company, Bungaku-za, while he did not regard Shingeki as the establishment but was not satisfied with the orthodox Shakespeare productions of the 1950s and 1960s; particularly the grand sets, period costumes, make-up to appear Caucasian, overacting and decorative proscenium theatres.

Deguchi's Shakespeare productions for the Bungaku-za were distinctive alternatives to the prevailing style. In 1968, he directed selected scenes from *Hamlet* for a trial production at the Bungaku-za's fifty-seat studio space, mixing the existing translation of Tsuneari Fukuda, a distinguished scholar and theatre practitioner, with a new translation by Yushi Odashima who worked as a dramaturg with the company at that time. Due to limited financial means, the scenes were presented in an empty rehearsal room with a set consisting of just three boxes and some everyday clothes. This simple stage allowed for a powerful emphasis on language and actor presence, which became a leitmotif for his directing style throughout the JeanJean era and beyond (Deguchi 1988: 94–122).

In 1971, Deguchi directed *Twelfth Night* for Bungaku-za, which opened with a naked Orsino taking a bath. This image derived from his personal experience and cultural observation that bathing for Japanese people tends to be a source of relief from personal problems. The script, based on some existing translations, was changed to sound down-to-earth, employing fashionable television idioms, slang and popular jokes. While the production followed the conventions of pseudo-Elizabethan costume, the bold visual and linguistic reframing of the play challenged the stereotype of antiquated Shakespeare in Japan, and it appealed to a wide range of audiences (see Kishi 2005: 92).

After directing a full version of *Hamlet* for the Shakespeare Festival at the Bungaku-za studio in 1972, Deguchi left the company due to an internal conflict. The young and self-assertive Deguchi then joined the Shiki, another mainstream theatre company where he directed *Much Ado about Nothing* in 1973. The following year, he directed *Shakespeare in the 12th year of the Tempo* written by Hisashi Inoue at the commercial Seibu Theatre, part of the

Seibu-Saison Group (renamed the Parco Theatre in 1985). However, unsatisfied with his own directing, Deguchi decided to break from major cultural institutions and to restart from zero.

In April 1974, he opened a drama school in a tiny space in Ogikubo, Tokyo. It specialised in Shakespeare and was attended by approximately seventy inexperienced, young actors. Given that the space measured only 20 square metres, more attention had to be paid to elocution than movement. Subsequently, 'speak then move' and 'speed and flexibility' became the school's mottos and reflected Japan's rapid economic growth at the time. In October of the same year, the chance arose to use the JeanJean space for free on the proviso that Deguchi would produce Shakespeare's complete works on a monthly basis and integrate live popular music in the productions. With selected members of his drama school, Deguchi founded the Shakespeare Theatre and inaugurated the enterprise with a production of *Twelfth Night*, a show that he had already experienced and felt confident in directing.

Yushi Odashima's translations of Shakespeare's complete works, published from 1973 to 1980, coincided with the JeanJean era and were a significant influence on the acting style of the Shakespeare Theatre. In contrast to his predecessors who used Shakespeare for lofty literary appreciation and political propaganda, Odashima, as a keen theatregoer, tailored his new translations to audience-conscious, lively, entertaining performance. His clear, colloquial and contemporary style, exuberant in puns, wordplay and rhymes, made the texts more accessible and subsequently became standard for Shakespeare productions in Japan. Although Deguchi found Odashima's translations oversimplified and weak at first, the style suited the speedy delivery and energetic movement of the young troupe. Deguchi eventually came to believe that Odashima's rhythmical translation was the embodiment of the Shakespearian spirit in Japanese language. He thus became more reluctant to alter the translations, although occasional modifications and cuts were made to suit Japanese audiences and to reduce running time.

Having little budget, Deguchi adopted an economical approach: no set, no costumes. Paradoxically, the 'Shakespeare in Jeans and T-shirts', caused by a lack of resources, turned out to be abundant in creative potential. He insisted on the intensity and diversity of Shakespearian language as well as the simplicity and intimacy of space:

> The real charm of Shakespeare's plays is in the evolving diversity of linguistic images. Our fundamental aim, therefore, is to present the maximum allure and energy of his words on stage. In order to realise this aim, we must avoid decorative elements by simplifying stage set and costumes as much as possible.

> [. . .] In order to express the magnetism of Shakespeare's words, his exquisite brushwork that fuses rhyming poems and daily prose, large-scale theatres, where actors strain their voices, are not appropriate. It is in the small theatres that Shakespearean worlds can best be expressed through words.
>
> (Deguchi 1976: 73)

Deguchi's directing developed in small rehearsal rooms and was then applied to the JeanJean stage: a black L-shaped laboratory with only 130 seats. For *Twelfth Night*, a single chair was used on a bare stage, and the ensemble of semi-professional actors, dressed in plain clothes, moved to the sound of live rock-and-roll music. The limited acting skills and the lack of star actors worked beneficially in familiarising young audiences with the 'classical' plays. The distinction between the passionate actors and lively spectators, which on the final night of five runs numbered 280, including standees, was often blurred. By bringing a sense of community and contemporaneity, the productions embodied ideas from Jan Kott's *Shakespeare is Our Contemporary* and Peter Brook's *The Empty Space*, books that were widely read at that time.

The company's productions also benefited from Deguchi's innovative reading and bold reframing of the texts. One of the most notable examples was *A Midsummer Night's Dream*, first performed in October 1975. Derived from Deguchi's personal belief that love affairs and alcohol are intrinsically connected, he converted the JeanJean into a modern bar called 'The Forest of Athens' by using just tables and chairs. In front of the customer-spectators, the landlord/Oberon causes a disturbance with his wife Titania. Later on in the play, the bartender/Puck dances in rhythm to an intoxicating tune sung by the fairy/bargirls, whilst mixing the aphrodisiac cocktail named 'love-in-idleness'. By drinking the cocktail, the customers/actors are transformed into the characters of the play within the play. While drunken male customers (Lysander and Demetrius) suddenly start pestering a girl (Helena), a worker (Bottom) enters under the scrutiny of the fairy/bargirls. The scene builds into a frenzy and becomes another layer in the overall meta-theatrical structure of the play (see Deguchi 1988: 17–26).

Some conservative theatre critics and academics complained about the actors' inaudible delivery, excessive and inexperienced acting and odd textual interpretations. This divided reaction to the Shakespeare Theatre reflected the changes in the contemporary Japanese economy and culture. The fast developing economy of the 1970s promoted an influx of capital into art industries in order to satisfy the intellectual and materialistic needs of consumers. For example, the department stores in Shibuya, such as the aforementioned Seibu and Tokyu chains, furnished theatres and museums which particularly appealed to the younger generation. In contrast to previous generations, this urban youth neither rejected the so-called high arts nor indulged in political agitation but veered towards entertainment and the Shakespeare Theatre, and the fashionable powerhouse of Shibuya catered to their demand.

Riding on the unexpected wave of popularity of the first year, the company continued the monthly production marathon for a further six years. Alongside this, in 1977 the company started organising performances for high-school theatre programmes and other occasions upon request. Since then, this education and outreach programme has continued to develop and offers opportunities for the actors to communicate with a wider array of audiences in non-theatrical spaces and to raise funds for the company as well.

During the JeanJean era, ten out of thirty-seven Shakespeare works were produced as Japanese premieres along with the rarely performed History plays. The *Henry VI* trilogy, performed in one day, won the Kinokuniya Prize for Drama in 1981; however, upon completion of the entire canon with *Antony and Cleopatra* in May 1981, the company reached an inevitable point of change.

In phasing out the JeanJean era, Deguchi was no longer able to exploit intimate and empty spaces with the actors in ordinary clothes. Furthermore, Deguchi's rigorous speech training resulted in actors rebelling against him; the majority left Deguchi, often setting up their own companies or joining other established theatres. While he dealt with this by recruiting young actors from his drama school and asking ex-members to do guest appearances, he had to radically revise his directorial approach. The Shakespeare Theatre began looking for new venues and hired several black-box theatres with about 300 seats in Tokyo, such as the Haiyu-za in Roppongi and the Honda Gekijou in Shimokitazawa, all of which demanded a new directorial style.

Working by trial and error, Deguchi came to believe that his attempt at modernising his plays in accordance with the atmosphere of the time had been too superficial to be close to the 'essence' of Shakespeare plays which he found in the themes of 'love and power'. Moreover, he claimed that no other playwright depicted the destructive force of power relationships as Shakespeare had done. As a result, Deguchi came to reject any political reading of Shakespeare from contemporary perspectives and treated him as a classic author. He also started to believe in the paradox that as one draws nearer to the essence of Shakespeare, his works become updated and reflect the present day with more clarity, but never vice versa (see Deguchi 1999: 134–6).

The company's shift from everyday Shakespeare in a small theatre to Shakespeare as universal classic in middle-sized theatres occurred around the time of Japan's economic bubble. In contrast to the 1970s, more capital was poured into constructing cultural institutions, and a number of new theatres opened in cities one after another; one of which was the Aoyama Enkei Gekijou, a 376-seat amphitheatre in central Tokyo. In 1985, Deguchi was invited to direct four Shakespeare plays to celebrate its opening. Rising to the occasion, he demonstrated a command of in-the-round space for the first time, exploiting the use of half-masks.

In the 1987 *Comedy of Errors*, all the characters wore *commedia dell'arte* half-masks, which made the confusion caused by the identical twin brothers and their servants seem all the more inevitable. Imaginative props such as a white-painted basketball also became a prominent feature on stage. In the opening scene, the basketball is highlighted at centre stage and used as a point of focus for Egeon's explanation of his impasse to the Duke, becoming symbolic of his desperate search for order, harmony and peace. As the ball is bounced and passed among the characters, it represents money, time as a bald man, the locked gate, fat Nell and a spinning globe. Drawing on his personal experience of playing basketball as a youth, Deguchi used the technique of offence and defence to instil a rhythmic contrast between the movement and stillness of the characters on stage. For example, after a series of frantic chases involving the Antipholus twins, there comes a moment of calm in which the Lady Abbess recognises her bound husband and removes his mask; as a result of this, other characters take off their masks to reveal the 'true' faces/identities of the actors beneath. The final recognition of the long-lost family becomes all the more powerful due to in contrast with previous frantic scenes and without the use of masks (see Deguchi 1988: 48–51).

This engaging production was staged again at another newly opened theatre, the Tokyo Globe. This is a modern version of Shakespeare's second Globe Theatre with thrust stage surrounded by three-story seating. Having begun as a by-product of land development driven by the 'bubble economy', this theatre radically changed post-war staging of Shakespeare both in quality and quantity. It opened with five major British companies visiting in 1988 and continued to invite numerous overseas companies from many parts of the world until its closure during the economic recession in 2002. The influx of other international Shakespeare productions gave the impression that England no longer had a monopoly over his works and that any culture and language had the right to localise and make them their own. It also offered an opportunity for Japanese practitioners to reform their inferior complex towards 'the authenticity of the Western canon'. As a result, Japanese-made and Japanised Shakespeare, which had been subjugated to the binary of East and West and the authority of English Shakespeare for a century, began to diversify and flourish in the 1990s with a sense of liberation. Shakespeare was to be interpreted by almost all Japanese theatre forms from traditional versions such as Kabuki, Noh and Kyogen, to post-modern adaptations (see Suematsu 2006).

The Globe Theatre actively cooperated with several domestic companies including the Shakespeare Theatre to produce a variety of plays and formed its own company called the Tokyo Globe Company in 1989. Its intercultural productions were promoted through collaborations with national and international directors and actors, pushing cultural negotiation and fusion further. As one of its associate directors, Deguchi directed the company's first two productions in 1991, *Pericles* and *Two Gentlemen of Verona*, using an amalgamation of actors from genres such as Shingeki and Shogekijou, along with elaborate modern costumes.

Deguchi was rather sceptical about Japanised Shakespeare produced by traditional theatre practitioners and forms and Orientalised Shakespeare looked at from foreign viewpoints. Although he is aware that Kabuki actors had performed Shakespeare plays for the first time in Japan, he believes that the two methods are different and hence should not be mixed. Furthermore, his continuous focus since his earlier productions has been on Shakespeare's language rather than visual artifice, making his primary goal as director to nurture the actors' elocution skills and to bring Odashima's translations alive in performance. Based on this vision, Deguchi wanted to train Shakespearian specialist actors in Japan of the present time rather than assimilate techniques and conventions from existing Japanese theatres. He tried to persuade the Tokyo Globe Theatre to establish a Shakespeare academy for Japanese actors and to tap into the funding that was usually allocated for inviting overseas companies and directors, but this ambition never materialised.

Nonetheless, his own drama school has played a key role in nurturing Shakespearian specialist actors, to the extent that ex-company members promote his speech skills through their own work and teaching and prove its validity on a wide range of stages. Examples are the work of Kotaro Yoshida who founded the Rhyming Theatre Company in 1984 and subsequently gained attention as a Shakespearian actor in Japan and Kaoru Edo who founded the Tokyo Shakespeare Company in 1990 that has continued ever since.

Deguchi's activities at the Globe Theatre culminated in three consecutive versions of *A Midsummer Night's Dream*, produced over the course of one month, in commemoration of the Shakespeare Theatre Company's twentieth anniversary. These three productions, set in different contexts with almost the same cast of actors, allowed the company to assess its past and to clear the way forward. In cross-referencing each other, the series showed the trajectory of the director from an adventuous newcomer in the 1970s to an experienced veteran in the 1990s.

The first version, set in a modern and elegant bar before opening hours and reminiscent of the 1975 JeanJean production opens with an invented prologue scene: adorned in revealing black dresses, several bar-hostesses sit at a table fixing their make-up when a young bartender enters, absorbed in reading a script while practising a dance. Soon after, a novice hostess in a demure white dress appears and is mocked by her co-workers; she later changes into a black dress to become the Fairy in Act II Scene 1. Bottom was played as a quiet construction worker in overalls while the other mechanicals' occupations were changed to fit a Japanese working context such as a newspaper delivery man and a rice-shop owner. Bottom sits alone at a table, in contrast to the rowdy group of mechanicals who receive a warm greeting from the hostesses. As the bar becomes more and more lively, two young couples dressed like university students enter. One of the women clings to one of the men but, quite coldly, he pushes her to the floor. She rushes out in distress; the two men then compete for the attention of the other woman. Suddenly, a black-clad man and woman, who appear to be the owners of the bar, enter fighting; she accuses him of being unfaithful, but he attacks her back, both verbally and physically. Amid the mêlée, the bartender attempts to intervene but is sent flying and knocked unconscious over a table. A long silence ensues, whilst the novice hostess crosses the room under a spotlight. She hands the awoken bartender his script, *A Midsummer Night's Dream*, and as he opens the text his dream begins to unfold, starting with the bar owner speaking Theseus' lines. Taking their cue from the actor/bartender – who has become Puck and watches over the actors' like an alcoholic stage manager – the young couple stand up from the table as Lysander and Hermia and are summoned to kneel before Theseus. The Athenian courtiers are contrasted with the hostesses and male customers who continue serving and drinking while watching the other actors' actions until they start performing their roles as fairies and mechanicals.

In this prologue scene, Deguchi provided a twisted contemporary analogy to the gender politics embedded in the Elizabethan text. The male control over women was emphasised in the hierarchical relationships between the hostesses and customers, which paralleled that of the owner/Theseus/Oberon and his wife/Hippolyta/Titania. In the frame of the bar, since a great deal of alcohol is being consumed on top of the aphrodisiac cocktail 'love-in-idleness', male sexual aggressiveness becomes more vulgar. The mechanicals' rehearsal turns out to be like an obscene drinking party where the timid and isolated Bottom becomes drunk enough to take liberties with a hostess. The same misogynistic treatment is applied to the younger couples. Lysander takes off his shirt and begs Hermia for sex. Demetrius humiliates Helena in pouring a drink on her head and unbuttons his trousers with the intention of raping her.

In a later scene, both boys again become naked and stalk Helena. Against this violence, Hermia and Helena vehemently resist. However, the female bond among the hostess-fairies is not noticeable except for when they sing a lullaby to the inebriated Titania and cast a sympathetic gaze at the reconciled couples. In contrast to the bartender/Puck who is exercising theatrical control, the hostess-fairies tend to be passive, even when faced with animalistic intercourse between Titania and Bottom. The omnipresent yet wordless female workers blur the border between the humans and the fairies; reality and fantasy are presented as a sexual dream or the ambition of the actor/bartender who wants to play the role of Puck. In the bar filled with disco music and lurid red lights, the drunken excess reaches a climax with Oberon's last words and the hostesses' sexy dance. This wild denouement suddenly cuts to a brief repetition of the prologue scene; in the darkness, the actor/barman wakes up and is handed his script by the young hostess.

The second version, first performed in 1990 to celebrate the opening of the Theatre Cocoon, a 747-seat theatre inside the Tokyu department store in Shibuya, is played out as the dream of a desperate theatre director. Set in an abandoned school in a remote village of post-war Japan, it was one of Deguchi's most personalised works to date. The play opens with a director, arguably an autobiographical allusion to Deguchi himself, dwelling over a set-design model box while the figures of his wife and daughter are seen leaving for good in the distance. Doubly distressed by the lack of creativity in his work and discord with his family, the director lies down, and then a boy suddenly appears behind him. The boy is dressed in school uniform, plimsolls and cap with white wings sprouting from the schoolbag on his back. The boy walks around the man, hugs him and then leads him running in a circle accompanied by Felliniesque festive music. After they exit, the boy returns to the centre stage bringing the man and his wife with him; when the man starts speaking as Theseus, the world of Shakespeare's play begins. As the backdrop of a classroom with wooden desks and chairs and a white chalk circle on the ground become visible, Theseus and Hippolyta are seen as white-winged schoolmaster-fairies. The boy becomes Puck, and his female schoolmates become fairies.

Reflecting Deguchi's nostalgia for his childhood and ambivalence towards the American occupation and modernisation of Japan from the late 1940s onwards, there are several historical twists in the portrayal of the characters. Although sexual connotation is more subtle than in the bar version, a meaningful discrepancy is found between the innocent and rural Puck and the Westernised and urban fairies in schoolgirl blouses, miniskirts and loud red stockings. For example, while Puck boyishly responds to his master Oberon's instruction to go in search of the 'little western flower' and is reprimanded for his mischief, the fairies exhibit sexual playfulness in dancing to a swing tune. Their sexual promiscuity is particularly obvious when they entertain Bottom as an ass who is dressed as a 'Yamiya' (returnee war veterans working on the black market) and sings to the melody of 'Aoi Sanmyaku' ('Green Mountains', the theme song of the film based on Yojiro Ishizaka's popular adolescent novel); in this setting, the fairies become associated with post-war prostitutes. The analogy is repeated in the mechanicals' interlude. Bottom, as Pyramus, has changed out of the Yamiya outfit and is dressed as a GI; he sings a rock and enka (Japanese popular ballad) style song for Flute-Thisbe who looks like a Japanese prostitute.

After the whole cast has performed a ring-dance to Felliniesque carnival music and left the stage, the dream comes to an end. As the music fades away, Puck leads Oberon to the centre of the moon-like white-lined circle, and they shake hands. The rapport between boy/director and fairy/wife runs parallel to that of Theseus/Oberon and Titania/Hippolyta who unite at the end. The boy gently removes Oberon's wings and disappears. The awoken director finds himself sitting alone onstage and contemplates what he has seen. All of a sudden, the whole cast run to the circle, whooping and bringing on the stage model. Does this mean the director's dream is still continued or through this kaleidoscopic dream-play? Does he experience a cerebric rehearsal as well as a spiritual journey of self-discovery and empowerment? The play ends with the image of Puck standing, 'If we shadows have offended'.

The final version was a recreation of the half-mask production at the Aoyama Enkei Gekijou in 1985. Instead of the devised frame and stage sets of the other two productions, this was played on a bare stage exploring the possibilities of masks and stylisation. The three groups of characters are clearly differentiated by masks and stylish contemporary costumes; the Athenian lords wore modern suits and white masks, the fairies frilly dresses and black masks, and the mechanicals were dressed in working clothes without masks. This production with choreographed group dances and synthesised songs for the fairies became part of the company's repertoire and has been frequently performed since then (see Minami et al. 1998; Deguchi 2000: 8–12; Suematsu 2001: 109–10).

Deguchi used personal experience and meta-theatrical frameworks that evoke particular Japanese socio-historical contexts in his productions of *A Midsummer Night's Dream*, yet he notes that his intention is never to make the productions categorically or stereotypically Japanese. However, the border between Deguchi's localisation of Shakespeare in the Japanese context and the Japanised Shakespeare that he rejects remains contestable:

> Shakespeare was becoming increasingly remote from our contemporary

> social reality. So I got the idea of pulling it back to our daily reality by returning Shakespeare to the level of my personal history. For me, making it 'Japanese' is not the ultimate aim. The important thing is to find a place where the text and I can converge. I also know that you can't cross borders by 'Japanization'. 'Making it Japanese' is already about marking a border where exoticism begins. But I think exoticism is partly due to the ignorance of other nations. If there were no such ignorance, mysteriousness would not exist. Once you know that, it becomes an ordinary matter. When people prostrated themselves before British productions, they were worshiping exoticism. For that reason, I don't think we should emphasize our 'Japaneseness.' The images most people have of Japan at the present time derive from the period when we were an agricultural society: that is, old Japan, the 'so-called Japan'.
>
> However, today's Japan is only partly traditional Japan. It is difficult to give an exact definition; nobody can say, 'this is Japan'. But it is also true that if we presented Japan in all its ambiguity, foreigners would not understand. It means that 'Japanese Shakespeare' production cannot be recognized unless we simplify our Japaneseness. I don't think that is universalization; Japanization is simply a particularization.
>
> (Deguchi 2001: 190)

These remarks make clear that Deguchi resists explicit and elaborate self-Japonism such as that found in Ninagawa's productions. On the other hand, it is still possible to see a peculiarity common to Deguchi and Ninagawa, because while remaining faithful to the text, both directors visually reframe Shakespeare in Japanese contexts, and both have been representative revisionists and popularisers of Shakespeare in urbanised Japan since the 1970s.

Deguchi's indifference to exotic spectacle is related to his target audience. Directing Shakespeare solely for Japanese audiences, he does not have to overcome language barriers by resorting to visual effects. In contrast to Ninagawa and Suzuki, who toured extensively overseas from the 1980s onwards, the Shakespeare Company had still not been seen abroad. Even if it were seen in England, Deguchi has speculated that his production in modern suits and dress would garner little attention because it avoids an expected Japanese spectacle.

In addition to this aesthetic disparity, there is an economic disproportion between Deguchi and Ninagawa who left the low-budget Angura Engeki for highly commercial theatre from 1974 onwards. Deguchi has had far less resources always feeling a sense of struggle as 'a tiny penniless company' after he left mainstream theatre in 1974. Even after the company started to receive funding, its survival has often been precarious; the actors have struggled with the upkeep of rehearsal space and have had to take on administrative duties while supporting their own lives through part-time jobs. One of the major financial upheavals was the 'New Place' affair. The company opened their own 100-seat theatre in Koenji, Tokyo in 1999 and produced a number of successful shows, including the award-winning *Hamlet* of 2001, but the architect's plans turned out to be in breach of local-government construction laws; the quarrel turned into a court case, and the theatre was forced to close after only a few years.

In spite of financial pressure and occasional stagnation, particularly during the Japanese economic recession of the mid-1990s, Deguchi's constant and resolute quest for the 'essence' of Shakespeare has kept him going, and the Shakespeare Theatre survived. Around the turn of the new millennium, the company entered another new cycle, which Deguchi has recognised as the most fruitful to date, with actors committed to training and development despite the uncertainty of the future.

Thanks to more stable arts funding after 2003, the Shakespeare Theatre ran yearly productions in spring and autumn of two or three plays at the Haiyu-za. The generation of young actors from the drama school had reached maturity, and the company formed an ensemble that required far less recourse to ex-members. Although the theatre rarely ran at full capacity, the productions appealed to various age groups, ranging from Deguchi's loyal followers of more than three decades to young students who had encountered Shakespeare through the company's high school theatre-in-education programme.

The company had started to produce non-Shakespearian works from 2002 onwards with adaptations of the Japanese wartime novelist Dazai Osamu's *Shin Hamlet* (*New Hamlet*) and contemporary novelist Kiyoshi Shigematsu's *Ebisu-kun* (*Mr Ebisu*). According to Deguchi, this new work offers actors a chance to rediscover both the uniqueness and universality of Shakespeare through different dramaturgical and narrative approaches (see Deguchi 2006).

In October 2005, as part of a triple bill for its thirtieth anniversary, the Shakespeare Theatre produced another adaptation, *Shakespeare Rehearsal*, inspired by Fellini's *Orchestra Rehearsal* and written by Deguchi himself. Highly meta-theatrical and based on actual events from the company's rehearsal process, this production portrayed the daily struggle and frustration of the actors as well as the ambition and failures of the director. The tense rehearsals were comically reproduced on stage, incorporating many citations of Shakespeare's works. Anecdotes from company members were used to portray relationships between the director and actors; these included aspects of their personal lives such as love relationships, part-time jobs and even excuses for leaving the company.

The performance began with a rehearsal of *Macbeth*, Act I, Scene 4. Following the stage manager's call, the actors, wearing casual sports clothes, enter from the wings, and Duncan calls out: 'Rippana miuchi wo motte ureshiizo' ('O worthiest cousin!'). The actor imitating Director Deguchi sits on a chair and repeatedly corrects Duncan's intonation. In spite of all the efforts of the actor (who constantly struggles with his rising intonation in real rehearsals), he cannot repeat after the director and conquer the subtle differences of elocution. While the actor repeats the same line over and over again, the other actors become uncomfortable. The frustrated director makes cutting remarks such as 'O worthiest actor!' 'How can you carry on like this after thirty years?' until he finally shouts 'Stop! Have a break!' He then falls asleep, and during this break, seven scenes unfold. In the fifth scene, entitled 'Reasons to Get Separated', three actors explain in monologues why they have to leave the company; the reasons are sickness of a family member, pregnancy and uncertainty of the future.

For audience members who know how strict and sarcastic Deguchi can be during rehearsals and how many actors had left Deguchi thus far, this self-parody production came as a shock. As reality and fiction, action and imitation were intertwined and exposed on stage, Deguchi's intention to show the pathos and absurdity of actors, with little talent and money, still willing to tackle Shakespeare caused great audience laughter. The final scene of the play suggests that the company's struggle has no ending. The director awakes to the stage manager's call ' 'Tis time', which overlaps with the last scene of *The Winter's Tale*, and then the rehearsal of *Macbeth* begins again. Despite his best efforts, Duncan still cannot say 'Rippana', and the director patiently responds by giving him 'one more chance'.

The following note on the programme also demonstrates how directing Shakespeare has been Deguchi's lifelong work and however difficult it is to achieve his goals, the journey no doubt continues:

> After directing Shakespeare for thirty years, I have the impression that Shakespeare is getting into my 'insides'. I don't think this is because I'm doing something special, rather it has just happened to me. Even so I cannot recite Shakespearean words from memory. I just feel my insides respond when I hear, see and read Shakespearean words. I respond to them viscerally. I consider this feeling to be a precious gift, though I still don't know who the sender is.
>
> My life hereafter exists solely to continue directing Shakespeare. I'm

keen to just keep on going until I get somewhere. But at the same time, I feel a sense of lacuna in this quest; that I will probably never get there.

(Deguchi 2005a)

Chronology

1940 Deguchi Norio born in Shimane Prefecture

1963 Graduated from the University of Tokyo and joined Bungaku-za as a trainee director; directed *Twelfth Night* in 1971, co-directed *Troilus and Cressida* with Jeffrey Leavis, and directed *Hamlet* in 1972

1972 Left Bungaku-za and joined Theatre Company Shiki and directed *Much Ado about Nothing* in 1973

1974 Directed *Shakespeare in the 12 year of the Tempo* at the Seibu Gekijou, left the mainstream theatre and started his own acting school

1975 Established the Shakespeare Theatre Company and began monthly productions of Shakespeare's plays at the JeanJean, a small theatre in the basement of a church in Shibuya, Tokyo

1977 The Company started a theatre in education programme to perform (upon request) their repertoire in Japanese high schools, community centres and city halls

1981 The Company finished staging thirty-seven plays by Shakespeare and received the Kinokuniya Drama Award

1982 The Company opened a new studio in Koenji

1984 Tenth anniversary of the Shakespeare Theatre

1985 The Company produced *A Midsummer Night's Dream, The Taming of the Shrew* and *Twelfth Night* for the opening of the Aoyama Enkei Gekijou

1990 Deguchi directed the School Version of *A Midsummer Night's Dream* for the Theatre Cocoon in Shibuya as the first production of 'the project of *A Midsummer Night's Dream* at Theatre Cocoon' in which the play was produced for five consecutive years with a different director each year

1994 The twentieth anniversary of the Shakespeare Theatre. Deguchi staged three consecutive versions of *A Midsummer Night's Dream* at the Tokyo Globe Theatre

1999 The Company opened a small theatre in Koenji with *The Comedy of Errors*

2005 The thirtieth anniversary of the Shakespeare Theatre

Bibliography

Deguchi Norio (1976) 'Shakespeare, Soshite Shakespeare Theatre' (Shakespeare and the Shakespeare Theatre), *Shingeki* 277: 68–78.

—— (1988) *Shakespeare wa Tomaranai* (*There's No Way of Stopping Shakespeare*), Tokyo: Kodansha.

—— (1999) Interview, *Shakespeare ga Wakaru* (Understanding Shakespeare), Tokyo: Asahi Shinbunsya, pp. 134–6.

—— (ed.) (2000) *Shakespeare Sakuhin Guide 37* (The Guide to Shakespeare Works 37), Tokyo: Seibido.

—— (2001) 'Interview with Deguchi Norio', 'Performing Shakespeare in Japan', in Minami Ryuta, Ian Carruthers and John Gillies (eds), *Performing Shakespeare in Japan*, Cambridge: Cambridge University Press, pp. 183–95.

—— (2005a) Director's Note. *Shakespeare Theatre News* 13 (October).

—— (2005b) Interview with the present author, 14 October.

—— (2006) Introduction to the official website of the Shakespeare Theatre, http://www2.odn.ne.jp/shkspr-thr/ (accessed 10 November 2006).

Kishi Tetsuo and Graham Bradshaw (2005) *Shakespeare in Japan*, London: Continuum.

Minami Ryuta, Ian Carruthers and John Gillies (eds) (1998) *Shakespeare in Japan: Deguchi Norio*, Melbourne: La Trobe University. <http://sia.stanford.edu/japan/homepage.htm> (accessed 10 September 2006).

Suematsu Michiko (1998) 'Innovation and Continuity: Two Decades of Deguchi Norio's Shakespeare Theatre', in Minami Ryuta, Ian Carruthers and John Gillies (eds) *Performing Shakespeare in Japan*, Cambridge: Cambridge University Press, pp. 101–11.

—— (2006) 'The Tokyo Globe Years 1988–2002', Seminar Brave Old Worlds: Shakespeare Production and Reception in East Asia. VIII Shakespeare World Congress. Brisbane, 17 July.

About the author

Mika Eglinton is a fellow of the Japan Society for the Promotion of Science researching at the University of Tokyo and University of London. She is also actively involved in the creation of theatre as a translator, dramaturg and critic. Her recent works include the Japanese translations of Sulayman Al-Bassam's *Al-Hamlet Summit* (Tokyo International Festival [TIF], 2004) and *Kalila wa Dimna: The Mirror for Princes* (TIF, 2006); and her work as a translator-dramaturg on the Japanese version of *Cardenio Project* (initiated by Steven Greenblatt). She has published in various journals including *Performing Arts* and *Performance Paradigms*.

5
DECLAN DONNELLAN

Paul Prescott

The director is neurotic, authoritarian and nurtures fantasies of omnipotence. He begins the process with a clear, governing idea of the artistic, affective and moral outcomes. He is pushing his theatre away from the actor and towards spectacle. He robs cast members of their agency, marionettes them around the stage space, and checks their libertarian streaks with threats, magic and mind-games. But despite his control freakery, the spontaneous creativity of the individual breaks out in song, dance and rebellious laughter. Chastened by the experience, the director is finally forced to renounce his quest for absolute authority.

Anyone who has seen Cheek by Jowl's work over the past quarter century will know that the foregoing parable is not an account of the working methods or personality of the company's director, Declan Donnellan. Rather, it is my reading of Timothy Walker's portrayal of Prospero in Donnellan's 1988 production of *The Tempest*. At the opening of that show, Walker was alone on stage while the rest of cast entered from the auditorium where they had been chatting with audience members, establishing that easy and generous actor–audience rapport that is one of the hallmarks of this company. Walker's Prospero used the play's first word ('Boatswain!') as a casting device, directing it to an actor who immediately recognised his servitude: 'Here, master. What cheer?' This apparently ad-lib casting continued until the entire company was frantically engaged in creating the storm-tossed boat. The promptbook reads: 'Prospero builds the storm to a deafening crescendo. Is this the end of the play? Cecilia [an actress] decides to change the story and give the Storm-maker a daughter.'

It was a telling opening and choice of characterisation for the figure in Shakespeare who most resembles what we have since come to call the Director. As Donnellan relates:

> Prospero [is] obsessed by his power, his rough magic and his art. The

> narrative line of the play is often crushed under Prospero's erratic creative energy, as, for example, when he aborts the masque. We felt it would be a withering imposition to strangle the play with a narrative control, e.g. by setting it in a specific period, on a specific island. We had to find a way to match Shakespeare's outrageous inventiveness and breathtaking disregard for any theatrical tradition.
>
> (Berry 1989: 196)

This *Tempest* offered a meta-theatrical parable: matching Shakespeare, going with him cheek by jowl, demands a leap into the void, a recognition of the limits of control, a surrender to contingency and ever-shifting targets; 'The thing you've got to realise about directing is that you are not controlling the evening and that's one thing I've learnt over the last fifteen years as a director: to control less and less' (Delgado and Heritage 1996: 90).

When we talk about Shakespeare, we are always talking about ourselves; Donnellan's characterisation of a Shakespeare blessed with 'outrageous inventiveness and breathtaking disregard for theatrical tradition' might double as a description of the qualities of his own company's work. Cheek by Jowl's Shakespearian productions have achieved an outstanding level of invention and originality by pursuing some core axioms: that the art of the theatre is above all the art of the actor; that the director's primary job is to nurture the health of the ensemble; that the story and the text are not the same thing and that in the case of a clash, the former must prevail; that every single line must be new-minted; that the emotionally unblocked actor needs less physical blocking; that scenery and props should never obtrude between the actor and the audience; that rehearsals and the process of discovery continue until the final performance; that there must always be something at stake.

Cheek by Jowl was formed in 1981 by director Declan Donnellan and designer Nick Ormerod. The partnership is one of the most enduring and productive in recent theatrical history. While it will be convenient in this piece to isolate Donnellan's name and foreground his directorial work, it should be remembered throughout that the division of creative labour is not clear-cut and that Ormerod's contribution extends beyond set and costume design to matters of casting, characterisation and concept. If the company's name tells us anything, it is the symbiotic indivisibility of Ormerod and Donnellan's creative partnership. (That partnership has also been bolstered and enriched by the contributions of other long-term company collaborators including composer Paddy Cuneen, movement expert Jane Gibson and administrator Barbara Matthews.) Donnellan and Ormerod met as undergraduates at Cambridge in the early 1970s. Ormerod studied law, a subject to which Donnellan transferred after two years of an English degree. On leaving Cambridge, they were both called to the Bar (i.e., as would-be barristers, they were granted permission to plead cases before the high courts). Ormerod parachuted out of the legal profession immediately; Donnellan gave his pupillage six months before dedicating himself to forging a career in theatre.

In 1981, Cheek by Jowl's inaugural production of *The Country Wife* hit the road in a van crammed with cast, crew and set; except for a 'sabbatical' break (1998–2002), the company has travelled restlessly ever since. The mid- to late-1980s witnessed a period of giddy ascendance, a rise clearly charted in a hat-trick of Olivier awards. In 1986, a trio of productions made Cheek by Jowl the 'Most Promising Newcomer' on the theatrical scene; a year later, Donnellan was the Best Director (for *Macbeth, Twelfth Night* and *The Cid*); and by 1990, the company was honoured with the award 'For Outstanding Achievement'. This hyper-maturation from promise to achievement turned the erstwhile *enfants terribles* into perhaps the most influential British theatre company of the 1980s. In the 1990s, this reputation was consolidated by a string of revelatory productions including the widely seen and celebrated all-male *As You Like It*. Towards the end of the decade, Donnellan and Ormerod put the company on hold as they pursued projects as diverse as a West End *Hay Fever*, a Bolshoi Ballet *Romeo and Juliet* and a Salzburg *Falstaff*. Increasingly, their work took them to Russia and collaborations with companies from the Maly Theatre and the Chekhov International Theatre Festival, companies they collectively and affectionately dub as 'Cheek by Jowlski'. In 1999, Donnellan was the first foreigner to be nominated for Best Director at Russia's 'Golden Masks' awards; his *The Winter's Tale* was judged the Best Production. Cheek by Jowl itself resumed normal service in 2002 since when it has fruitfully coexisted with its Russian counterparts.

Although the focus of this account is on Shakespeare, it should be stressed that the majority of Donnellan and Ormerod's output has been of non-Shakespearian plays and ranges widely from Wycherley to Sondheim, Racine to Kushner, from Lope de Vega to Ostrovsky. And yet, from the company's inception, Shakespeare has been central to the repertoire, the home key to which its music insistently returns. Almost half of Cheek by Jowl's twenty-nine productions to date have been of 'the best living playwright we have' (Donnellan, *Observer*, 19 April 1987). The first act of interpretation a Shakespearian director makes is in his choice of play. Donnellan has shown a marked preference so far for those plays in the canon that foreground the following themes: sexual identity and the confusion of desire; the chasm between men and women, husbands and wives; the power and pleasures of the imagination. The thematic leitmotif is the desire human beings have for each other rather than those we have for metaphysical abstracts such as the crown, Rome or 'this England'. In 2007, the company completed its cycle of Romances but had yet to produce an English history play.

The First Folio was addressed to the 'great variety of readers'; Cheek by Jowl's work has addressed and entertained the great variety of spectators. Before 2006 (when it agreed on a three-year summer residence at the Barbican Theatre), the company had no permanent base in the UK. In its first decade alone, Cheek by Jowl visited 257 towns in thirty-four different countries. The effect of such Periclean voyaging on the quality and texture of their work should not be underestimated. Main-house, long-run Shakespeare productions have a tendency to ossify very quickly as familiarity with the material, the building and the audience demographic can shade into contempt and ennui. On tour, however, actors 'have no relationship with the building, with dressing rooms, the loos, the front of house staff. All they have is those people in the audience, so they're launched into this relationship of love and terror every night. It's nerve-shredding for the actors, but it keeps the thing alive' (Donnellan in the *Birmingham Post*, 22 February 1988).

The company has a rich history of love and terror with its great variety of viewers. One week it might play to a matinee audience of 'completely uncontrollable' schoolchildren in Karachi and be forced to abandon the show after 'a passionate call for order' failed to stem the flow of eggs and paper aeroplanes from the auditorium. (On the same *Dream* tour of Pakistan, the British Council advised cutting 'not only the giant phallus from the first act but all kissing, and even the popping of a champagne cork' lest the show offended its Muslim audiences [Archive].) Another week, it might be straining hard to warm up a far more inhibited English audience; as the stage manager reported to the creative team after a quiet night in a town that will remain anonymous: 'am I glad you weren't here tonight. Depressing is too good a word for the boring old farts we had in tonight. I must say, I'm not sorry to be leaving B________' (Archive). After a performance of *The Tempest* in Bucharest, a woman jumped on stage and begged an actor to marry her so she could leave the country. A cooler post-show response came from Sister Andrew of the Convent of the Blessed Sacrament, Steyning, who had taken sixty of her students to an 'extremely offensive' *Macbeth* at the University of Sussex and wrote: '"Cheek by Jowl" is obviously a company of much talent [. . .] but I feel pressure must be brought to bear upon it, to take into account the youthfulness of matinee audiences, and to cut out all that is bruising and harmful to young people' (23 October 1987, Archive).

Such vivid responses are more likely to find their way into the archives than the typical audience reaction to this company, which, wherever the location, is one of warm and grateful appreciation. Playing to a new audience each week requires a company to extend a hand of invitation, to meet its new collaborators halfway, to make contact. A pseudo-naturalistic, self-enclosed, arm's-length Shakespeare is far less feasible in these conditions. Without the patronage of the British Council, it is inconceivable that the company could have toured as extensively as it has, but the Council has always appreciated the fact that Cheek by Jowl 'does the classics (for which there is a great demand), but in a way that is "not safe, not grand, not propaganda" (in one Council man's view),' (*Observer*, 19 April 1987). International audiences have welcomed a Shakespeare that is communal, democratic and demotic. And one that actually seeks to represent a multi-racial Britain. One of the profound innovations of this company is that is has challenged the assumption that only a handful of Shakespeare's characters should be played by non-Caucasian actors. Long before it became standard at the RSC or the National, Cheek by Jowl firmly and without fanfare adopted the practice of colour-blind casting. To date, black and Asian actors have taken the parts of Miranda, Hero, Claudio (in both *Much Ado about Nothing* and *Measure by Measure*), Mariana/Mistress Overdone, Rosalind, Jacques and Lear. 'You have to do a lot of really quite desperate things to make Shakespeare appear to support the status quo' claims Donnellan (*Guardian*, 15 June 1994). In its approach to casting, as in so much else, Cheek by Jowl has challenged and therefore changed the status quo of Shakespearian performance.

'Bea. free to roam': Cheek by Jowl's shifting Shakes-space

Cheek by Jowl's promptbooks make for intriguing reading. A theatre historian wishing to reconstruct the broad geometry, let alone the minutiae of a production's blocking would soon be frustrated. Most of the company's promptbooks consist of a photocopied Penguin text on which cuts and small rewrites are handwritten and lighting and sound cues precisely tagged to lines. But, as a rule, the annotation of blocking and stage action is sparse, bordering on the gnomic. Why? A detailed promptbook is a necessity if (a) a director leaves a production soon after its opening and hands it on to an assistant for whom the promptbook serves as a scored, perhaps stern reminder of original intentions; and/or (b) the actors (or their subsequent replacements) need precise guidance as to where to stand for 'specials' or where not to be for elaborate, potentially hazardous changes of scenery. (A heavily scored promptbook, it might be argued, is the textual apotheosis of Directors' Theatre.) Neither (a) nor (b) pertains to Cheek by Jowl. Donnellan and Ormerod stay with a production throughout its life on tour; no matter how far-flung the location, they are invariably there for the all-important get-in (the day or so in which a production adjusts its blocking, lighting and dynamics to its new host space). Furthermore, Ormerod's sets, as we shall see, are spare and uncluttered. But the light annotation in the company's promptbooks is also testimony to the amount of freedom the direction bestows on the actors. In the opening scene of *Much Ado about Nothing* (1998), for example, the promptbook simply reads: 'Bea[trice] free to roam here'. And roam Saskia Reeves' Beatrice did. If approaches to direction run a gamut from dictatorship to collectivism, from battery-farming to free-range rearing, Donnellan pushes his actors towards the latter ends, towards freedom with responsibility. When the imagination of the actors is engaged, conventional blocking becomes impertinent:

> directing a scene between two people, for example, when it's going very well needs very few laws. You don't need to tell them where to stand, you need to make sure that they know what's happening in the scene, and then wonderful things will happen out of the scene because none of us has overburdened it with laws.
>
> (Delgado and Heritage 1996: 90)

'Be free to roam' is an injunction to the mind and body of the Shakespearian actor. Other archive documents speak as eloquently of the company's aesthetic. Over five and a half months in 1994, *Measure for Measure* toured to eighteen venues on four continents, beginning at the Warwick Arts Centre and closing at the Teatro Principal, Almagro, Spain after a tour that had taken in Perth, Tokyo, Montevideo, Darlington and the Moscow Arts Theatre. Each of these very different venues received a letter describing the ideal space that Cheek by Jowl would like to find on arrival:

> STAGE
> Minimum pros. Arch width: 10m. Minimum stage depth: 12m. If there is a forestage we would like to use it.
> We require a BLACK floor, which should extend to the rear wall of the stage and all the way into both wings. There is no fixed set or scenery.
> We do not require any masking.
> The stage should be completely open and clear of any spare debris.
> House tabs are not required.
> There are several AUDITORIUM ENTRANCES so if the stage is raised we require treads both stage left and right.
>
> (Archive)

When it arrived, the company brought with it all that was needed to create 'Vienna': one large desk, six chairs and two red strips of cloth. In his 1930 *Preface* to *Hamlet*, Harley Granville Barker identified a 'perennial' struggle in Shakespearian production between man and machine, character and pageantry, actor and designer; 'all great drama', he concluded, 'tends to concentrate upon character' (1968: 7). If that struggle is indeed still with us, it is clear on which side Cheek by Jowl is fighting. In establishing as its default aesthetic a character/actor-based minimalism, it defiantly resisted the technophiliac high materialism that came to dominate set design in the 1980s. A simple point: the more elaborate a production's design, the more time and labour is required in its construction. In a theatrical system in which six-week rehearsal periods are the norm, set and costume manufacturing is likely to require as much time as the rehearsals themselves. At the RSC, for example, the set design is typically more or less fixed *before* a first cast meeting (at which the designer will often present his model to the nervous initiates). Thus, typically, the people who are actually obliged to work in the set – the actors – have had no influence on its genesis. In contrast to this, Ormerod has no model at the beginning of the rehearsal period; a full *three weeks* into *Much Ado about Nothing* rehearsals a production meeting agenda item read: 'Set: Design report from Nick (model?)' (Archive). The set is a *tabula rasa* on day one of rehearsals and generally stays that way – each object added needs to earn its right to share the space with the actors. As Ormerod comments:

> It is a cliché to say that Shakespeare paints his own scenes and that he doesn't require scenery, but it is true that the word does it in most plays we deal with. Nothing more is needed really than the actor and, say, something to sit on – not even that sometimes. So you start off with an advantage that you don't actually need anything. The essence of theatre is paring down to the essentials of what you actually need.
>
> (Delgado and Heritage 1996: 86)

In the company's early history, this aesthetic ideal was heavily encouraged by fiscal reality. To appreciate the tight financial discipline demanded of the company in its early years, one has only to look at the budget for its first Shakespeare production. The expenditure for the 1982 *Othello* totalled £31,581.44; the income (including c. £15K from the Arts Council of Great Britain and other regional arts councils) was £30,079.64. Thus, the company made a sustainable loss of £1.80. These very slim margins of error combined with the logistical demands of touring and transportation have led to a succession of spare, uncluttered and elegantly functional settings. For *Pericles*, two boxes with rope handles (morphing as occasion demanded from throne to port to brothel bed to coffin to Diana's chapel) backed by a set of wooden frames filled with the musical instruments and thunder sheets that would underscore much of the production. For *As You Like It*, the trademark monochrome empty space hosted both court and forest until the interval; 'Well, this is the Forest of Arden' was even more dryly delivered than usual, given that the stage was as bare as (and the lighting state almost identical to) the opening moments in court. Only after Orlando hung his verses and spring awoke did a pair of silky green banners descend and the lighting designer (Judith Greenwood, aptly) dapple the cyclorama with sylvan shades. For *Othello* (2004), the set consisted only of five rectangular, coffin-like trunks strewn in no particular pattern on a black floor, backed by a white cyclorama. (Five, if one includes Brabantio's offstage demise, is the body count of this play.) Only in the final scene were four of the trunks rearranged to form the bridal death-bed and a small table placed stage right for rosary and candle.

Within these clean spaces, costumes, hand-held props and mobile furniture acquire a semiotic virtuosity. In *As You Like It*, a black duvet placed centre stage with a couple of books, instantly evoked the cosy, sheltered interior of Celia and Rosalind's pre-exilic world. In *A Midsummer Night's Dream*, Miss Flute's 'RELAX' T-shirt spoke volumes of the desperate attempt to associate herself with the hip subversion of the banned single of that name by Frankie Goes to Hollywood. The company's props are often transit-friendly or easily picked up locally, whether in Hong Kong or High Wycombe. In *Twelfth Night* (1986), the puritan Malvolio could be observed sneaking a guilty peek at a trashy tabloid, *The People*, during his lunch break. In the (very Russian) below-stairs piss-up of the second *Twelfth Night*, Sir Toby lovingly produced one – two – three – *four!* bottles of vodka from a plastic bag that was almost as inured to booze as its owner. Cigarettes are a cost-effective prop for a company that can be no stranger to the Duty Free. In *Othello* (1982), Othello's 'flaming minister' was his cigarette lighter, a flame more easily restored than Desdemona's. A second after the strangulation, an upstage Emilia, made to wait 'outside' the bedroom, tapped her foot and lit a cigarette, chillingly underscoring the distinction. In *Twelfth Night* (2003), Olivia was so entranced by Cesario's description of the willow cabin that she forgot to smoke. Cesario obligingly fetched an ash-tray and Olivia saved face with a pert flick of the teetering ash and the louche observation 'You might do much' (Act I, Scene 5, line 266).

Cheek by Jowl's strong preference for minimalist scenography and personal props helps keep their Shakespeare limber, light on its feet and, above all, focused on the actors. From an early point in the company's history, Donnellan has developed a set of staging devices that further italicise the primacy of the ensemble. Most productions begin with a physical epigraph in which the ensemble enters more or less simultaneously; each actor weaves purposefully to his mark until all stand facing out, mirroring and intensifying the audience's expectation. The actors are neither in nor out of character but in a limbo. This gentle confrontation locates the labour and the pleasure of the evening to come in the actors' bodies, presence and their attentiveness to us, their audience. Often the silent initiation will be broken by a verbal epigraph. *Twelfth Night* (1986) began with one actor announcing 'Twelfth Night, or what you will', with each of the other nine cast members successively repeating 'or what you will' to a rapidly enfranchised audience. (In the 2003, the repeated epigraph was the more plaintive, enigmatic 'my father'.) *Hamlet*'s epigraph drew attention to the strolling-player peripatetic nature of the company: 'For us and for our tragedy, / Here stooping to your clemency, / We beg your hearing patiently' (Act III, Scene 2, lines 142–4). *As You Like It* opened with 'All the world's a stage, and all the men' [pause: all except two move stage right] and women [remaining pair of men move stage left: they'll be playing the girls tonight] merely players'.

Cheek by Jowl's epigraphs establish the primacy of the ensemble, but they also prepare the audience for the arbitrariness of role-play and the possibility of doubling. Especially in its first decade, the company of actors was small and doubling/trebling, as on the Shakespearian stage, was a necessity that mothered invention. A cast of seven actors performed *Pericles* and *Othello*, ten played *Twelfth Night* and *A Midsummer Night's Dream*, and twelve embodied the *personae* of *Macbeth*, *Hamlet* and *The Tempest*. In *Othello* (1982), Amanda Harris suggestively doubled as Desdemona and Bianca. In *Dream* (1985), the cast size not only led to relatively conventional doublings (Theseus and Oberon, Hippolita and Titania) but also to Egeus and Bottom. Furthermore, the number of mechanicals shrank to three, an ecclesiast am-dram Bottom and two stage-struck ladies of the parish. The need for fairies led to a creative trick whereby the female duo became possessed by spirits, with Misses Flute and Quince 'starting to do very indecent things with Mr Bottom' (Ormerod) as if the repressed provincial veneer masked feral desires. 'That was something we discovered through poverty. If we'd been able to have the extra six actors we wouldn't have come to that solution. There are certain things which are positive about not having huge resources' (Donnellan in Reade 1991: 90).

In a number of productions, the ensemble has remained onstage throughout. This is hardly original or unique, of course, but nor has it ever been merely sophomoric or theoretical. Rather, it offers 'a deliberate focus for the audience, who [share] the generously absorbed attentiveness of the actors' (Reade 1991: 64). The technique is at its most effective, however, when these 'offstage' characters are made actively present. In *Measure for Measure*, for example, Angelo scratched away at paperwork throughout Act I, Scene 3 and Claudio's seated presence upstage from the end of Act I, Scene 2 until his meeting with the Duke in Act III, Scene 1 would not let us forget the incarcerated body at the centre of the play's plot. In *Much Ado about Nothing*, the first ninety lines of exposition between Beatrice and her uncle were regularly punctuated by a scrum of eight soldiers freezing in and out of tableaux of homosocial horseplay: this was the tight-knit laddish culture that was about to wash up in Messina. In *Twelfth Night* (2003), the straitjackete Malvolio did not leave the stage after the Sir Topaz scene (Act IV, Scene 2) and a topless, post-coital Sebastian danced around and past him as he celebrated the consummation of which Malvolio had always dreamt. In *Othello* (2004), Donnellan's characters had no life offstage: the central quintet (the two couples and Cassio) rarely left our sight, their presences serving not only to illustrate and enrich the action but also to remind the audience of the touching impotence of the slandered. Cassio and Desdemona were onstage throughout the great interchanges between Othello and Iago in which their reputations are so painfully corrupted. They mostly sat frozen with their backs to the audience but, on one memorable occasion, became unwilling and active embodiments of Othello's phobia. They lay down, 'asleep', on either side of the stage during Iago's relation of his bed-sharing with Cassio. Iago cued Cassio to speak his own lines: 'Sweet Desdemona / Let us be wary, let us hide our loves' (Act III, Scene 3, lines 421–2). As Cassio mimed placing his leg over Iago's thigh, across the stage Desdemona groaned, her back arching in sexual climax. It was not subtle, but then again nor is Othello's fear-desire to see his wife and lieutenant 'hot as monkeys' (Act III, Scene 3, line 406).

If the presence of 'offstage' characters adds intensity and clarity to Cheek by Jowl's storytelling, another recurrent device – 'headlining' – ensures a remarkable fluidity between scenes. After the penultimate line of scene A, the first line of scene B is pitched across the playing space. The last line of scene A then prompts whatever scene change needs to take place – a lighting shift, a relocated chair, a reconfiguration of bodies – with no loss of tension before scene B continues. Here, for example, is how the end of *Hamlet* Act I, Scene 2 (with cuts from Hamlet's final lines) sounded:

HAMLET: My father's spirit in arms.
LAERTES: My necessaries are embarked.
HAMLET: All is not well.
LAERTES: Farewell.

That editing cleverly conjoined the detached echoes in Shakespeare's script (My/My; not well/Farewell) to produce a sense of simultaneity and unceasing momentum. It is in this fluid, up-tempo and contrapuntal atmosphere that Cheek by Jowl's actors move, breathe and invent character.

The shifting target and the war against cliché

In Cheek by Jowl's programmes, the cast and crew are typically photographed in an urban playground, informally arranged on a children's climbing frame. There can be no play without structure. Like that playground and frame, Ormerod's designs and Donnellan's stylistic tropes provide the context and the scaffolding for the main business of the company: to celebrate and further the art of the actor through the exploration of character. At the outset of a production that means inducting the actors in the war against cliché, forcing them

> to scrape away at all the accretions of the years, the tricks actors rely on, the remembrances of past productions they've seen, the sentimental view of the big lines in the play [. . .] We go on, and on, until every single line is as if it has been made up for the first time.
>
> (*Independent*, 11 January 1989)

In contrast to the practice of many Shakespearian directors, the first rehearsal does not necessarily begin with a read-through, that inaugurating genuflection to the text. It is as likely to start with exercises in movement, character work and storytelling, exercises with which, Donnellan claims, Russian actors feel more comfortable than their text-reared British counterparts: 'If I say, "We're not going to start on the book, we're going to start moving in the space and discovering relationships and finding out what this world is," Russian actors say, "Of course." It saves a lot of time' (*Independent*, 14 October 2004). It could be argued that Donnellan's work in Russia has not only furthered his exploration of movement as a vehicle for storytelling, but it has also increased the crispness of his direction. Cheek by Jowl is accustomed to communicating across language barriers to non-anglophone audiences. That barrier is higher, however, when Shakespeare is toured in Russian translation. 'Cheek by Jowlski' productions are high-definition, passionate affairs; Donnellan's choreography of emotional and physical contrast has found renewed inspiration in the bold ensemble-playing and supreme commitment of the Russian actor.

Donnellan is 'more interested in training the actor than in imposing specific interpretations on a play' (*Independent*, 4 May 1999). To that end, he published *The Actor and the Target* (2002), an uncommonly useful guide to stimulating the imagination and creativity of the actor. The book repeatedly warns against the quest for certainty and definitiveness in characterisation: 'When we try to capture the essence of someone we are being sentimental. Sentimentality is the refusal to accept ambivalence. Certainty is sentimental [. . .] Pronouncing a character to be either good or evil will block the actor'

(Donnellan 2002: 107). The question 'What do I want?' is unhelpful because it presupposes the possibility of a fixed, definitive answer. 'Wanting' also lowers the stakes: it is more useful to ask what the characters *needs* and to accept that our needs, like Claudius's sorrows, come not as single spies but in battalions. These needs will not be found 'in' the character but will be discovered by seeing through the character's eyes to the succession of 'targets' – external stimuli – presented to the character in the course of the action. Seeing the target means seeing double, perceiving the ambivalence that is at the heart of all human desire. If the actress is looking through Juliet's eyes, hope and fear will be embodied in and generated by the target: 'I see a Romeo who wants to run away with me, **and** I see a Romeo who doesn't want to run away with me', 'I see a Romeo I want to run away with, **and** I see a Romeo I don't want to run away with'.

A concrete example of how this might work in practice: in *Othello*, Emilia's first words on discovering Desdemona's body are 'Help, help, ho, help' (Act V, Scene 2, line 130). These are invariably played as a loud appeal for outside assistance. In 2004, however, Jaye Griffith's Emilia spoke the words softly and imploringly to Othello. She knew that she spoke to a murderer but seemed to be offering him the chance of immediate redemption. The effect was both chilling and heart-wrenching. But how did the actress find this counter-intuitive, unnervingly original reading of the line? 'The stakes are specific and they must come in perfectly paired twos' (Donnellan 2002: 51): Emilia sees an Othello that has killed Desdemona *and therefore also* an Othello that can save Desdemona. The truth is never pure and seldom simple.

Donnellan repeatedly inspires his actors to read against the grain in this fashion. What first shocks and later haunts the viewer is the psychological acuity of these counter-intuitive moments. For example, we may think we know who Malvolio is; we may also 'know' that the scene in which he is gulled is light entertainment bordering on farce. But Malvolio as played by Dmitry Shcherbina (on the 2006 UK tour) confounded such received wisdom. This Malvolio allowed himself to angle for approximately one laugh: a quick glance up at the skies to see whether a passing pigeon might have dropped 'Olivia's' letter. As a rule, though, Shcherbina looked through Malvolio's eyes and what he saw were some very high stakes indeed. On deciding to open the letter, he suddenly ripped off his jacket and squatted down to pick it up. This was the turning point – even so quickly can one catch the plague. The enigmas of the unravelling letter whipped him up into an unbuttoning, tie-loosening frenzy. By the end of the letter and convinced that Olivia loved him, he was on his knees, weeping real, hot, childish tears. It was an astonishing piece of acting – the antithesis of Donald Sinden's playing of the scene for a series of ever-rising and quantifiable comic peaks (see Brockbank 1985). Shcherbina played what it was actually like to have one's deepest fantasies fulfilled – to be perched on the threshold of a future of easeful power, endless midday sex and the awed respect of one's immediate community. The half ended with Toby's line 'he must run mad' (a diagnosis, not a prediction) and Malvolio's uncontrollable sobbing. A blackout finally delivered us from this highly disquieting spectacle.

In eliciting this performance and many others like it, Donnellan has sought to disrupt the Shakespearian status quo, to mount an assault on the deadly theatre that gives us the beautiful or serene or patriotic or gently funny or Golden Mean Shakespeare we have all endured and many of us have silently loathed:

> What strikes me as always being so perverse is when we try to stereotype the living characters of Shakespeare – that Juliet must be pretty, that Romeo must be unimaginative – because it's in those moments of strangeness, oddness, weirdness and lunacy that we most connect with them, and that we most feel connected to humanity.
>
> (Donnellan 2003: 164)

In his early Shakespeare productions, Donnellan's desire to subvert stereotype led to some notably iconoclastic and irreverent decisions. Such choices, at least in the first decade of the company's history, provoked a decidedly mixed critical reception, with many reviewers accusing Donnellan of over-cleverness, gimmickry and wilful perversity. In *A Midsummer Night's Dream*, Theseus and Hippolyta were played as Prince Charles and Lady Diana, the lovers as Sloane rangers. This topical strain re-emerged in *The Tempest*: Alonsa, Queen of Naples, was a Margaret Thatcher *doppelgänger* whose cult of the individual had trickled down to the clowns who sang 'There's no such thing as society!'. To at least one disgruntled reviewer of *Twelfth Night* (1986), 'Illyria resembles San Francisco in its heyday: Belch and Aguecheek have apparently been sexual buddies, Aguecheek and Feste the clown vamp and paw each other, [and] Feste and Antonio finally pair off at the play's climax, to general jubilation' (*Independent*, 17 January 1987). In *Macbeth*, Anne White's Glaswegian Porter – Tartan shawl, moth-eaten scarf, fingerless gloves – began 'Fuck off! Here's a fucking knocking, indeed! If youz Porter of fucking Hell Gate, you should grow old turning the fucking key.' The non-Shakespearian intensifier recurred at least fifteen more times in the remainder of a stand-up routine that also incorporated topical swipes at politicians. The *Daily Mirror* reported the minor furore caused by the scene under the headline 'SHOCKSPEARE!'

In the two decades since those early shocks to the Shakespearian system,

Donnellan has refined his approach. The results now seem more organic, less open to the charge of gimmickry. It is hard, for example, to think of a director who pays such sensitive attention to the weird vicissitudes of Shakespearian friendships and the complexity of desire. In *Much Ado about Nothing*, when Claudio revealed to Benedick his intent to 'turn husband' (Act I, Scene 1, lines 183–5), a long, painful pause ensued before Matthew Macfayden could bring himself to the hoarse reproach 'Is't come to this?' (186). In *As You Like It*, Celia's irritation with her friend falling in love was only the visible tip of an iceberg of grief and jealousy. Celia can easily be a superfluous presence during Orlando and Ganymede's wooing games; here, Donnellan had her down-staging the action, sitting on the lip of the stage, silently radiating loss, as behind, her oldest and only friend irreversibly transferred her affections. In *Much Ado about Nothing* and *As You Like It*, same-sex friendship was given its full weight, and in both cases it was the unhappy but inevitable victim of an economy of desire.

With Donnellan's ambivalent double vision, no emotion is pure, no mood unalloyed. The stakes are always rising, and each minute forces a choice that the next might reverse. Nowhere is this more apparent than in the startling climaxes the company has discovered in (and devised from) Shakespeare's endings. In the closing moments of both *As You Like It* and the second *Twelfth Night*, we were confronted with the possibility of tragedy being snatched from the jaws of comedy. On Rosalind's re-entrance 'as herself', her 'To you I give myself, for I am yours' (Act V, Scene 4, line 115) was met not with joy but pained consternation as Orlando struggled to process the lies and betrayal that had set up this revelation. He twice flinched from her outstretched hand and finally turned his back to her. She waited briefly, then, resigned, dropped her bouquet and turned to be comforted by her father. Perhaps prompted by the 'feminine' tears Rosalind wept onto her father's shoulder, Orlando's 'If there be truth in sight, you are my Rosalind' (117) saved the day. As with the exploration of desire and sexuality throughout the production, the presentation of ambivalence in these final moments allowed for a variety of interpretations (see Rutter 2005 and Bulman 2004). Some critics saw a sexuality at work that was beyond gender, some saw a celebration of distinct sexualities (gay, bi-, hetero-), some saw a clear queer political intervention against the rise of homophobia in wider society (Bulman 2004). Few productions of *As You Like It* can ever have so intensely embodied the spectatorly openness of the play's title.

The dramatic pay-off from this moment was so great that Donnellan effectively cashed in again in his Russian *Twelfth Night*. There, he had Viola return to the stage in her woman's weeds, an appearance not sanctioned by the text but one demanded by the story this production wanted to tell. The re-entrance clearly introduced a new distance between Viola and Orsino. She was needy, if dignified, in her quiet desire to be desired. All eyes were on them. He offered his hands, she took them. He flinched and recoiled. She retreated a pace or two. It could all be over. He saw a stranger, not the thing he fell in love with. They were caught in a vertigo of unrecognition, shocked by the suddenly experimental nature of their desires. Eventually, Orsino stepped towards her, picked away a lingering fleck of false moustache, caressed her face and kissed her. Such an ending was consonant with what Donnellan has called the 'warts and all' glory of marriage celebrated by the comedies: 'If you look at any of the three marriages which line up on the stage at the end of *Twelfth Night* [. . .] they are rather peculiar marriages, and that makes them like marriages in real life [. . .] You reduce the play if you say that in a space of a caesura, Orsino becomes "cured" of his homosexuality and suddenly sees through to the femaleness of Viola' (Reade 1991: 94). But there was time for one more twist in this *Twelfth Night*: as the various couples – now improbably including Feste and Antonio – revelled, Malvolio re-entered, dapper again after his incarceration, and dispensed champagne with a reconciliatory smile. As the cream-linened celebrants clinked glasses upstage, he stood downstage centre, a rectangle of black with its back to the audience. Suddenly, he turned on his heels to face us. A block of light picked him out, his features now rigid with determination: 'I'll be revenged on the pack of you'. Blackout.

If the closing minutes of *As You Like It* and *Twelfth Night* mined the deep confusion and potential for unhappiness at the heart of Shakespeare's middle comedies, the close of *The Winter's Tale* (1997) shaded the joy of reconciliation with an unforgettable image of the irrecoverable. Immediately after Hermoine had implored the gods to look down and pour their graces upon her daughter's head (Act V, Scene 3, lines 122–4), the scene of reunion froze. No further words were spoken. Mamillius entered, guided by the young woman who personified Time. They wove their way around the statuesque bodies like after-hours trespassers at Madame Tussaud's. Finally, inevitably, they stopped next to the kneeling Leontes, the father whose mania had destroyed this son. The boy briefly placed a hand upon his father's head before leaving the stage as silently as he entered it.

Mamillius' spectral re-entry was unscripted, non-verbal and its effect overwhelmingly emotional. Like much great theatre, like much of life, the moment hovered on the margins of the articulable:

> When I talk to actors I generalise because I'm using words. But [the actors have] this wonderful canvas (like Nick has, or I might have when I'm doing some staging) where you can do something that's

> non-verbal, that's non-intellectual, and something which couldn't be as well-expressed if you wrote an essay about it. If you could write an essay about it, it wouldn't be a piece of theatre, would it?
>
> (Reade 1991: 97)

This short history of Cheek by Jowl's Shakespeare was an essay, an attempt to say something about the theatre-making of a remarkable company. But words don't work. Performance resists linguistic re-presentation and the experience of reading about theatre is generally a poor surrogate for the act of theatregoing. At the time of this account, the company was in rude health, but it is impossible to predict either its life span or the long-term influence Donnellan and Ormerod's work will have on Shakespearian production. It is a safe bet, however, that Cheek by Jowl's informal, fluid and ludic Shakespeare will continue to influence and inspire other practitioners well into the twenty-first century, long after the company has disbanded and all that remains are archives, photographs, memories and mere words.

Chronology

1981 Cheek by Jowl founded
1982 *Othello*
1984 *Pericles*
1985 *A Midsummer Night's Dream*
1986 *Twelfth Night; Romeo and Juliet*, Regent's Park
1987 *Macbeth; Macbeth*, National Theatre of Finland
1988 *The Tempest*
1990 *Hamlet*
1991 *As You Like It*
1994 *Measure for Measure; As You Like It* revival
1997 *The Winter's Tale*, Maly Dramatic Theatre, St Petersburg
1998 *Much Ado about Nothing*
2002 *King Lear*, RSC Academy
2003 *Twelfth Night*, Chekhov International Theatre Festival; UK tour 2006
2004 *Othello*
2007 *Cymbeline*

Bibliography

Archive. Cheek by Jowl company archive, Theatre Museum, London.

Berry, Ralph (1989) *On Directing Shakespeare: Interviews with Contemporary Directors*, London: Hamish Hamilton.

Brockbank, Philip ed. (1985) *Players of Shakespeare: Essays in Shakespearean Performance by Twelve Players with the Royal Shakespeare Company*. Cambridge: Cambridge University Press.

Bulman, James C. (2004) 'Bringing Cheek by Jowl's *As You Like It* Out of the Closet: The Politics of Gay Theater', *Shakespeare Bulletin* 22 (3): 31–46.

Delgado, Maria M. and Paul Heritage (eds) (1996) *In Contact with the Gods? Directors Talk Theatre*, Manchester: Manchester University Press.

Donnellan, Declan (2002) *The Actor and the Target*, London: Nick Hern.

—— (2003) 'Directing Shakespeare's Comedies: In Conversation with Peter Holland', *Shakespeare Survey* 56: 161–6.

Granville Barker, Harley (1968) *Prefaces to Shakespeare: Hamlet* (1930), London: B.T. Batsford.

Reade, Simon (1991) *Cheek by Jowl: Ten Years of Celebration*, Bath: Absolute Classics.

Rutter, Carol Chillington (2005) 'Maverick Shakespeare', in Barbara Hodgdon and W.B. Worthen (eds) *A Companion to Shakespeare and Performance*, Oxford: Blackwell, pp. 335–58.

About the author

Paul Prescott is Capital Centre Lecturer in English at the University of Warwick. He has acted and taught Shakespeare in Britain, America, Japan and Australia, most recently as Associate Artist (actor-director) with the Palm Beach Shakespeare Festival, Florida. He writes on arts criticism, theatre history and contemporary Shakespearian performance and his publications include *Richard III* (Palgrave Shakespeare Handbooks), introductions to the New Penguin *Coriolanus* and *Hamlet*, and articles on theatre reviewing in *Shakespeare Survey 57* and the *Blackwell Companion to Shakespeare and Performance*. Forthcoming projects include *Shakespeare and the Director* (with Dennis Kennedy; Oxford Shakespeare Topics) and chapters on Sam Wanamaker (*Great Shakespeareans*) and Shakespeare and Popular Culture (*Cambridge Companion to Shakespeare*).

6
PETER GILL
John Burgess

> Trying to be faithful and alive. That's what the adventure has been.
>
> (Peter Gill)

> All Sublimity is founded on Minute Discrimination.
>
> (William Blake)

The first impression was that these were the most interesting people in the world. The things they said were so remarkable, the relationships between them so involving. There was no sense that these were actors, or that the story had been told before. Somewhere in the background there were memories. The proper names – Orlando, Rosalind, Jacques, Celia – seemed familiar; so did the story – the exiled Duke, the lovers in the forest, the girl dressed as a boy: but the predominant feeling was one of freshness, of something being created for the first time there and then and of being immediately and effortlessly inside the characters' thoughts.

This was Peter Gill's 1975 production of *As You Like It*, revived a year later for a single performance as part of the opening weekend at Riverside Studios in West London. The space was a large square hangar; the audience sat on a single bank of raised seating. The stage was wide and shallow, running the full width of the room. There were no wings or masking of any kind. Audience and performers were not separated from each other. The back wall was bare brick and the set a few wooden chairs and a wooden table. The men wore jeans and the women had dresses in period silhouette made out of denim – pale blue figures moving in clear even light against a grey-brown floor.

Gill's first encounter with Shakespeare had been when he was growing up in Cardiff after the war:

> My experience of Shakespeare as an actor started . . . I don't know

> how this happened . . . when I was about eight at this Catholic school taught by the De LaSalle brothers. An undistinguished young brother called Brother Ambrose for some reason got me and John James, who's now a poet, to do the Arthur/Hubert scene in *King John*. We never did anything like that before, again, you know, but it was a very vivid experience. I remember learning it. We did it in the classroom and we learned it off by heart. I suppose we were quite verbally advanced – you know, we could read aloud. We were the kind of boys that went round to other classes to show off our reading.

After leaving school, Gill went to study at the Welsh College of Drama but left after a year to take a job as acting ASM with the company in Nottingham run by Val May and Frank Dunlop. Here he appeared as the Boy in *Henry V*. Like John Dexter, who was slightly older, Gill was one of the few British directors (in the second half of the twentieth century at least) not to have gone to university. His experience of theatre from the beginning was that of a maker, a professional:

> I started from inside the theatre, I think that's the difference. It's much talked about, but the university experience of theatre is a different one. My luck was that I started right inside working as an ASM and as a young actor in the new form of subsidised rep, that wasn't just commercial, and it's a different experience to one that's merely an aristocratic overview. You get to see how things work in a different way. And you learn things sharpish. If you're in a small part on stage every night and you're interested in directing you get to hear the whole of the tent scene in *Henry V*. It gives you another way of sensing things. And all the amusing and desperate side of theatre – in *Three Sisters*, I was Fedotik, and you've just changed the set and you've got go on again, and you have to rush to change into your uniform, and you're only on for a second, waving goodbye at the beginning of the last act. You get a more altar-boy view of theatre, of the sacred mysteries.

From this derives Gill's special feeling for actors and for the life of the theatre. Asked to talk about his productions, the first thing he is likely to do is go through the cast list. Actors' abilities (and foibles) are evoked again and again in his conversation: performers are valued for their skill but also for their history, which is in itself a kind of skill. John Nettleton, for example, who played the part of George Booth in Gill's 2006 production of *The Voysey Inheritance*, was taught by Esme Percy who had in turned learned from Sarah Bernhardt. Pat Hayes, whom Gill cast as Maria in *Twelfth Night* in 1974, had played Moth at Stratford in 1935 and had then gone on to make a successful career as a comic actress in variety.

> She was delightful to have and had an effect on the production, aerating it. And because she'd worked with every comedian, difficult, good, the notion of Nicol (Williamson, who played Malvolio) being a problem to her was not in her repertoire; she didn't understand what that meant [. . .] And I remember at one point we had a very difficult thing to unravel between Belch and one of the other actors, and I thought Pat'll know how this is meant to go because she's been in hundreds of these comic, classic, situations, things like this.

It's sometimes easy to talk (and write) as if Shakespeare productions were made up of ideas, but of course they are also realisations and cannot happen without actors. Gill watches a lot of television, and his casting is never snobbish: he is just as likely to take a performer from a sitcom, a soap, a classic serial, a popular comedy or a commercial as from the straight theatre. '*The thing about acting is it's not a fantasised abstraction.* It's what you can do plus who you are. It isn't true that everyone can do everything. Anything interesting that's not stuck-on comes from the living medium of the actors.'

The Sleepers' Den, Gill's first play, was staged at the Royal Court Theatre in 1965, several months before he directed his first production – making him an actor first, a writer second, and only then a director. His writing has continued alongside his directing: his latest play, *Original Sin*, was produced by the Crucible Theatre Sheffield in 2002. Writing plays is something Gill shares with Roger Planchon and Harley Granville Barker, and it gives him a very particular way of approaching a text:

> One of the things is that if you write plays, or you do new plays with the desire of making the play work, as opposed to making jumping off points for yourself, then of course you don't have the same need as other directors. And if you don't have a particularly lit.-crit., philosopher's-stone bent you end up having the same discussion with a classical piece that you have with any new play. That's what you're interested in – the play, working out *how* it's mean to be done. If you've done a new play, and if you've written a play, you don't obviously have – you *do* have – some of the same needs, but they're not so desperate, I suppose, as to have the authorship that certain directors might want to have.

One of Gill's most important influences was the Royal Court Theatre, where he worked in a variety of roles – as understudy, assistant director, casting director, director and writer – at different times between 1959 and 1972. The special alchemy that occurs when good writing and good acting come together was something the Royal Court was known for: Robert Stephens as George Dillon, Laurence Olivier as Archie Rice, Joan Plowright in *Roots*, Nicol Williamson in *Inadmissible Evidence*, Judy Parfitt in *The Daughter in Law*, the whole cast of *The Changing Room* by David Storey (the list could go on).

George Devine's Royal Court was important because it was an attempt to found a serious art theatre on the European model, along the lines of the Moscow Art Theatre or Antoine's Théâtre Libre. The early success of John Osborne's *Look Back in Anger* gave the project a new inflection, putting the writer at the centre of the work and, alongside the writer, those actors best qualified to realise the playwright's vision. The enterprise also had a wider aspect. The theatre's allegiance was, first and foremost, to the writer but also – beyond and through the writer – to that area of contemporary experience that he or she was endeavouring to describe.

Over the years, Royal Court practice became codified in a number of sayings. There was George Devine's remark, 'You should treat every new play as it if were a classic and every classic as if it were a new play'. Another formulation went, 'Where the continental theatre has dramaturgy, the British theatre has casting instead'. This comes about because doing new work and having a permanent company are contradictory. There is no guarantee that a company will have the range of actors to allow a new play to be cast with any accuracy. Casting a play might mean meeting and auditioning ten, twenty or sometimes more actors for each part. The play is filtered through the imaginations of dozens of performers, each of whom will illuminate it in a unique way. Given a basic technical ability, what is it in the individual performer's temperament or history or class background that they can use to understand the role and bring it to life? How does the particular fusion of role and imagination challenge and extend their technical ability?

This runs counter to a certain kind of European theatre, where in a permanent company not all roles in all the plays can be cast accurately – or even (sometimes) approximately; yet a way of doing the play has to be found. Director and actors are not in a position to embody the play as the author wrote it and are driven to extrapolating some aspect of it, which is singled out and presented as the whole. Or they stage a commentary on the play, or an idea of the play, instead of the play itself. These are standing temptations for anyone approaching a classic but resistance to this manner of working is deeply embedded in the Royal Court tradition, where the fusion of acting and writing to the benefit of the play was the sought-after ideal.

The Royal Court in the 1960s was not, as it later became, exclusively a new writing theatre. It also undertook to explore the world of Shakespeare and his contemporaries, seeing this as part of what a serious British theatre should be trying to do. Not all these experiments were equally successful, but they represent an attempt at a way of doing things that was different – both in casting and design – from the prevailing ethos of the post-war period. The list of these Royal Court productions runs as follows: *The Changeling* directed by Tony Richardson and designed by Jocelyn Herbert 1961; *Twelfth Night*, a Sunday night production directed by George Devine, 1962; *A Midsummer Night's Dream* directed by Tony Richardson and designed by Jocelyn Herbert, 1962; *Julius Caesar* directed by Lindsay Anderson and designed by Jocelyn Herbert, 1964 (Gill worked on this production as Assistant Director); *Twelfth Night* directed by Jane Howell, with Patrick Procktor's set of a Bellini painting on the back wall, 1968.

Particularly important were three productions directed by Gill's Royal Court colleague Bill Gaskill, two of them at Stratford: *Richard III*, designed by Jocelyn Herbert in 1961; *Cymbeline*, designed by René Allio in 1962; and one at the Royal Court in 1966, *Macbeth*, set in a sandpaper-coloured box designed by Christopher Morley. This work, described by Gill as 'Edith Evans meets Bertolt Brecht', was an attempt to create a specifically English style that was open to influences from the European theatre without being subservient to them. René Allio, for example, was Roger Planchon's designer at the Théâtre de la Cité Villeurbanne, where he designed famous productions of *Henry IV Parts I and II*, *Georges Dandin*, *Dead Souls* and *Tartuffe*.

The two directors, Gill and Gaskill talked over the problems of staging Shakespeare a lot during this time. They travelled together to Berlin for the first night of the Berliner Ensemble production of *Coriolan*; Gill appeared as an actor in Gaskill's 1962 production of *The Caucasian Chalk Circle* at the Aldwych; and they were colleagues at the Royal Court in the mid-1960s, when Gaskill was Artistic Director at the time when Gill was establishing his reputation with his famous production of the D.H. Lawrence trilogy. Both shared a relish for acting and for the English acting tradition as embodied in such figures as Gwen Frangcon Davies, Edith Evans and Arthur Lowe, as well as younger talents such as Vanessa Redgrave, Sheila Hancock, Gordon Jackson, Anthony Hopkins, Nicol Williamson and Victor Henry.

Gill's 1974 production of *Twelfth Night* was set in a beautiful shallow ochre box with walls about 12 feet high. The benefit of a box like that is that the performers are held in the colour: the audience upstairs see them against the colour of the floor, the audience downstairs against the colour of the walls. The world is complete and without interruption. The centre part of the upstage wall could truck downstage, opening up two upstage entrances like those in an Elizabethan playhouse. The fact that the sides and back were not too tall helped to keep the focus on the human figure of the actor. The colour had a lot of nuance to it – saffron, sand, ochre, almost every shade of yellow, with bands of purpley blue, indigo and russet running round, a little like a tide mark, at about head height. It was a glowing golden world that held the action of the play and reflected something of its emotional iridescence. Written on the walls, very faintly, were two lines from the Sonnets – 'O learn to read what silent love hath writ' and 'O know sweet love, I always write of you':

> I wanted to let the whole autumnal, whatever we call it, melancholy side of the play spring from a more sunny disposition, to make sure that the comedy, the pure comedy of it, motored the play and the melancholy, if you like, and the sadness, sprang out of the play instead of being an awful fungus over it. We used that in the colour where it was all golden and ochre and sand-coloured in a slightly abstract way, like a series of shapes and bands of colour. I'd been to Stratford a lot, and that stage needs broadening, I think, so we tried to make it look wider by putting two panels one on each side of the stage. We were going to have two images from the *Spartan Youths Exercising* by Degas – the girls on one side and the boys on the other – and on the back, Bill (Dudley, the designer) had found this image, a Victorian painting of Narcissus. But the interesting thing is that the better paintings didn't work – we cut them right at the end – whereas the heavy-duty Victorian image had an illustrative poster quality that suited. The others, the Degas, were too good in this case. So we were eclectic, but we set it in the period, though through Deirdre Clancy's extraordinary refraction – very beautiful tailoring, and a lot of white was used. Viola was in white in her boy's costume, and we worked fantastically hard with the haircuts so that you could hardly tell the difference between them.

The beauty of the placing and the extreme freedom and suppleness of the movement were evidence of Gill's long-standing interest in dance, both classical and modern:

> My friend from seven years old, Michael, one day decided to go to the Royal Ballet when they came on tour, and he just had a good time, and he used to go and see things, and so we went together. I saw *Symphonic Variations* with the original cast I think and I remember at fourteen

> thinking it was an amazing work, a piece of incredible beauty. They didn't bring the whole repertoire. We saw Acts of things and there was the Picasso set for the *Three Cornered Hat*, though I didn't much like the work, and *Les Sylphides*. And then at the Court we would go to the ballet or modern dance. And Merce Cunningham became . . . we went when it was at Sadlers Wells in its first season, and there was this remarkable piece of modern, American . . . absolutely the American thing that was not native to us, you know . . . cool, confident; and this attempt at abstraction with an amazing design by Robert Rauschenberg, who was a painter I loved. And there was a piece designed by Andy Warhol – a beautiful thing with a whole lot of silver helium balloons on the stage. So, there was a combination of sound, this apparently aleatory connection and Cage and all that – it was amazing. And again the understanding of the dynamic of space and then the breaking of the rules which he did.

This interest in dance was something Gill shared with the other directors at the Royal Court, to such a degree it was sometimes said that it was impossible to understand that theatre's production style without reference to the ballets of Frederick Ashton and to *La Fille mal gardée* in particular.

The impulse behind the production of *Twelfth Night* was not primarily aesthetic, however, but emotional: to realise Shakespeare's play in its variety of moods as fully as possible. To this end, the most scrupulous attention was paid to the speaking of the text. To take one small example, the dialogue between Viola and Olivia in Act I, Scene 5, lines 237 onwards:

VIOLA: Good madam let me see your face.
OLIVIA: Have you any commission from your lord to negotiate with my face? You are now out of your text: but we will draw the curtain and show you the picture. Looks you sir, such a one I was as this presents; is't not well done?
VIOLA: Excellently done, if God did all.

Gill concentrated here on the rhythmic contrast between the passionate iambics spoken by Viola, already in love with Orsino, and the lighter suppler prose, that looks forward to Restoration comedy, spoken by Olivia, whose heart is still untouched. Her tone in the scene is made quizzical by the fact that so many of her lines are questions. The pivotal moment comes when Olivia is drawn away from her witty prose to answer Viola in verse. The emotional turbulence has begun:

OLIVIA: How does he love me?
VIOLA: With adorations, with fertile tears
With groans that thunder love, with sighs of fire.
OLIVIA: Your lord does know my mind, I cannot love him . . .

The comedy and the feeling in the scene are inseparable from the writing that embodies them.

'Being faithful to the text' is easily said, but it involves a lot of the sheer hard work attending to grammar, cadence, rhythm, the whole way that a sentence unfolds itself in time. There is a paradox involved: that speaking which is artificial (in terms of enhanced clarity and musicality) produces an effect of extreme naturalness. In a 1966 interview, Sir Lewis Casson and Dame Sybil Thorndike explored this paradox in relation to Harley Granville Barker's method of 'analysing the text and interpreting it through definite stylised music':

Lewis Casson: I saw how Barker was applying to modern plays the method of [William] Poel for Shakespearean speech. Barker showed me at once how he was using that method to translate all emotion and all thought into the actual music of speech.

Sybil Thorndike: It always came out as something more natural, and much richer and truer. People were thinking that it was the most natural speech they'd heard; and yet it was so very carefully stylised [. . .]

Lewis Casson: [. . .] He would prefer, if he had the time, to spend a good half of the period of rehearsal learning the music which was interpreting the thought. The actual acting of the actors themselves could be developed in their own minds. [. . .] after the framework of the music of the play had been fixed.

Sybil Thorndike: When I first met Lewis, I went and saw one of his productions in which he was playing. And his own speech sounded the most natural, ordinary, everyday speech, and yet every thought was so clear, meticulously clear, that you were inside his mind immediately, and inside his personality.

Lewis Casson describes how, working with Barker, once the music of the play had been fixed, the performer's imagination was then left free. Gill releases his actors' intuition in a similar way, using similar means. This contributes enormously to the panache, emotional fullness and suppleness of the playing. Audiences have an intuitive ability of their own, and one of Gill's gifts is to put the intuition of the audience in direct touch with the intuition of the actors on the stage. This is the polar opposite of conceptual theatre, where the idea of a production is flagged up in an emblematic way as a substitute for a real experience of the play, creating theatre of a kind reviewers like (the separated-out ideas are easy to write about) but which often leaves the audience disappointed.

One of the qualities Gill admires in the speaking of Shakespeare is fleetness, achieving a performance that is, as he puts it, 'new minted but ahead of you.' This style of playing corresponds to that springing, forward-leaning, quality in the writing which doesn't just carry the action forward but also catches up everything – feelings, memories, thoughts, reflections – in its movement:

> What it is, is the single impulse, it seems to me, exfoliating, pushing through tributaries, arteries – whatever the word is we have for variegated expression stemming from a single source. *That's* what it's like, Shakespeare, I think. And it goes through what would first appear to be character, but it can go through any actor or anyone who has the competence or sensitivity to express it. And the outpouring of this impulse I think is what you try to achieve. But it's always particular and varied and so your conscience is provoked by the fact that it's realistic and the fact that it's this fanciful compacted language but it's just – that's what I think it must be – it's a sort of expression of the *gush* of the Pierian spring, the wellspring, into all these manifestations of life and flowering.

The 1975 Nottingham/Edinburgh *As You Like It* shared many of the same qualities as the Stratford *Twelfth Night* from the previous year, as it shared many of the same personnel – designer, costume designer, leading actors. Both productions are best seen as extensions of the Royal Court ethos, both in design, casting and general approach. This time, the onstage box was coloured rich moss green and constructed in such a way that actors could enter from anywhere. Suspended above it was a narrow screen divided into rotating panels, so that the image could switch instantly from an Elizabethan cityscape for the scenes at court to an effect that suggested sunlight falling in a clearing for the forest scenes. Like *Twelfth Night*, the production seemed effortless, unfussed. Silvius and Phoebe were powerfully, painfully romantic; the little litany, 'Why blame you me to love you?', given its full weight, was one of the most memorable parts of the evening; Jacques' melancholy had its place but without eccentricity. The Oliver Martext scene was a particular delight, thanks to the skill of an old vaudevillian, Lesley Sarony, whose brilliant yet almost imperceptible drunk acting was the fruit of many years experience of music hall and would have been instantly recognisable to Will Kemp or Richard Tarleton:

> Leslie played Sir Oliver Martext and Old Adam: and there was an old music hall artist called Leslie Sarony, who I'd seen; and an awful bitter, cynical man who'd been in the first production of *Showboat* and in music hall and variety where he did comedy songs. He was a bit Victorian as Adam, but he was absolutely brilliant as Sir Oliver Martext. It was nothing to do with me but there again going back to the Pat Hayes thing . . . what they did was they knew how *simply* to play it. And I've seen that scene done – I've seen him fly, I've seen him drown, I've seen his umbrella turn inside out . . . And Leslie just understood the nature of the scene, this traditional sort of comic *lazzo* written down, and it went wonderfully well because it was so simple and he got a huge round every night. He just did it. It was so *light*.

At the production's heart was the Rosalind of Jane Lapotaire, whose quick-silver thought processes and sense of (sometimes perilous) self-invention made her seem like Hamlet's female cousin.

The productions of Shakespeare that Gill has directed span a period of forty years and have taken place in a variety of institutional and cultural contexts. First came three international productions between 1969 and 1972, one in the USA, one in Canada, one in Switzerland, done as a visiting director at two festivals and at a German repertory house with a permanent company. Interspersed with these was the radical experiment of John Webster's *The Duchess of Malfi* at Gill's home base, the Royal Court Theatre, in 1971. This was an attempt to go beyond the Brecht–Edith Evans mix by drawing on influences from performance art and the American avant-garde. The Webster was markedly more experimental both in its look and in the treatment of the text than any of Gill's Shakespeare productions, either before or since, but its extreme radicalism continues to exercise a gravitational pull on much of his subsequent work:

> This is the period in which we were trying also, while doing D.H. Lawrence, to be interested in the excitement of the modern visual world. So, I went off on this adventure with the designer, Bill Dudley, who was still relatively young. We had to ditch a lot of our original ideas both because of money and because I got . . . That was when the crisis occurred for me, where certain visual imagistic notions of drowning, of cupboards opening and lift shafts inside them, bodies, you know a sort of modern Gothic . . . had to go. Partly because I couldn't sacrifice the play.
>
> My old, my classic Royal Court 'the play, the play' kept banging up against my more freewheeling 'let's do what we like' desire.

So, we resolved it, I often think in a rather cowardly way, with Bill making an image of doors up and downstage either side. The Duchess says in Act IV 'Death hath ten thousand several doors'. He took ordinary doors from building sites and St Thomas's Hospital, which was being rebuilt. We had the Court stage bare, and then he made collages of Renaissance paintings mixed with all kinds of modern images which were suspended up and downstage and across the back. Below it at the back was just the Court Theatre untreated wall, not even beautiful and brick or anything, just as it was. And then all we had were some kitchen chairs and a kitchen table. And then he made shapes for the principals in period – just simply shapes – dresses and doublets which were in ochre drill. And then he bought a lot of things for the younger members of the company from a kitchen supplier – chef's outfits – and he dyed them ochre. I devised it in such a way that there were eight principals, who never did anything but play their parts, and eight young men who could do all the things necessary – playing tiny parts, supporting the action, being women – at will. And I did a lot of physical work, not physical in the sense of jumps, but making living statues, all kinds of visual imagery. And we had a group called the Gentle Fire which was an avant-garde classical music group to do the music, which was rather Cagean, and they wrote some sounds for the actors to make occasionally. We did lots of things we cut. Images I remember all the people who died in the play were brought on and dumped over the Duchess of Malfi and the child had to come and try and get his mother out of it and things like that.

Now I don't think I've found a play, or a way of working – except possibly my own work or perhaps with a bit of *As I Lay Dying* [1984] – where I could let my hair down to that extent since. I tried it in *Macbeth* [1971], but it didn't work because it didn't seem to suit the play or the circumstances I was in. And a bit in *Julius Caesar* [1980], I suppose. Webster seems to give you permission to do this kind of thing in a way that Shakespeare doesn't.

Gill's mastery of the plays at the level of the sentence is paralleled by his skill at animating (and holding in balance) their larger structure – and, in particular, by his ability to bring out the architectural and emotional power of Shakespeare's fourth and fifth Acts:

I think Shakespeare's Act IVs would make a marvellous book if someone would care to write it, because they're fascinating, because usually very interesting and delightful things happen in them. But occasionally he gets in trouble instead of it being beautiful; so the English scene in *Macbeth* is in Act IV and that's a very hard scene whichever way you look at it. There's room for images and another different character – it's always a lovely moment in Shakespeare but it's also very hard because you have to get the audience there and you have to let them rest without losing the momentum; and then if he's given you a great Act V like *Macbeth* or *Twelfth Night* then you're home and dry. In *Measure for Measure*, it's a bit difficult, because round about Barnadine the play gets into trouble and you have to keep your eye on it.

Making Act IV come right requires both patience and confidence to allow the lyric, reflective quality of the writing its due space. Pacing is, of course, part of the larger architecture of a production: it helps if Acts I–III have not been fussy or overdriven or crushed by overemphasis. Gill understands the place of these different Act IVs in the wider structure and his unobtrusive but persistent work on these scenes is part of what gives his productions their special atmosphere:

> It's about taking delight in the complication of structure, the waywardness, and yet it having a narrative enjoyment and a sort of narrative sense. The problem with the theatre is that it isn't music, but it *is* musical – and so you can take this more formal look at it, how it's all made, and how you'd better look after Act IV or you'll regret it in Act V, and looking after Act IV you have to have some sense of that in the beginning. I think I got that from the fact that I studied so many new productions at the Court with so many dismal, half-baked Sunday night productions with people lumbering about in the dark and these frail plays looking frailer – that the good directors always know where the flow lies, which is in the joints, which is how you get from scene to scene – not scene changes, but how you get from one episode to the next in the story. A lot of people from the rep tradition rehearse the scene; they don't rehearse the moments between, so it has no flow, no musicality.

Act V in Gill's production of *Measure for Measure* (1979) at Riverside Studios was handled in such a way that the audience were led step by step through the complicated moral argument that was simultaneously an education in ethical feeling. The desire for vengeance or for some simple 'eye for an eye' solution was held in check, altered by degrees and refined into something more grown-up and more humane. The effect was very grand and luminous, and moving in its acceptance of human frailty.

> MARIANA: Hold up your hands, say nothing, I'll speak all.
> They say best men are moulded out of faults,
> And for the most, become much more the better
> For being a little bad.

The effect of being somehow inside the writer's mind and of being led through the complex argument inexorably step by step was achieved by meticulous pacing and attention to detail:

> It's whether you have any desire to unstitch the puzzle, or whether you want to use the puzzle as an excuse for you to do something else. It's exactly like the staging of the scene with Banquo's ghost. If you want to find out what the trick is, then it will have luminosity automatically if the writer's any good. Well, Shakespeare is good, so without going into, you know, doing it like a masque or any other pose – it's like the end of *Cymbeline* when Bill Gaskill did it – that was the scene, because he's set it up like a storybook at the beginning and so you had time for all the *anagnorises*. And I think that's true of all these kind of Shakespeare plays – the audience have been there so they enjoy all the unravelling. They all have a say and that's like courtroom drama on the television. There's something very satisfying about the end of a who-dunnit when the detective goes through 'it couldn't be x but it could be y'. It's an old enjoyable device. And it's then infused with an enormous emotional and spiritual feeling. Shakespeare *is* a very spiritual writer like that, it's true.

The moral seriousness of the approach owed something to Gill's having been brought up a Catholic as a child:

> I think having had the kind of education that I had which was absolute pre-Vatican II hard down-the-line 'Catholic boys don't go to heaven as easily as Protestant boys, because they know better' then it's bound to affect your approach to things. And once you've had to study free will, on a simple level, just wars, personal responsibility, occasions of sin, the whole to-do, then I do think there's something that you know about what's going on in the world that you can grasp, whether the author's saying it or not. But Catholicism is pretty straight down the line if you take the whole thing. It's not a religion for sissies as far

> as I can see. So I think the redemptive quality is very important in Shakespeare, that there is a possibility for change for the better, that all will come right as long as we hold on. It's the whole notion in Shakespeare – hang in there and it will come right; the fall of man and the redemptive side of it.

Looking back on the production now, Gill feels that he ought to have done more to bring out its kinship with the late Romances:

> I think I got *Measure for Measure* wrong, frankly, on the interpretive side now. I think it is definitely about Puritan England: Isabella and Angelo are really cut from the same piece of stone, aren't they?, and that's part of the peculiar moral insight of the play: that they are *both* being tested. And then you're in the conundrum of the fact that somehow Isabella is seen as being wanting, yet no one could want her to go in for this stage rape in order to save her brother. As usual with me, I tried to address the structural, internal problems of the piece, but I think now having seen a production the other day which had ended with the Duke pointing to a big double bed and the horror starting again of the symbolic rape, I don't think that's what's inside the play. I think it's much more like a romance. A constant theme in Shakespeare is that life is better than death and that people like Claudio are worth more in a way because they are human and alive than these abstractions, these abstracted people like Angelo. But I think it's about how it's all interrelated parts of the same thing. And he shows that it could sort of come right without making a *Twelfth Night/As You Like It* ending. So the play looks forward, it seems to me, to *Cymbeline* and *The Winter's Tale*. I think you have to assume that the Duke and Isabella get on. Otherwise, it becomes horrific in a way that isn't Shakespeare, I don't think. I probably wouldn't be so elaborately in period now because I wanted it to have that slightly the look of when it was written and London and all the rest of it. I think it would be more . . . Simpler. What I did was take the city comedy side of it seriously. We set it in period and perhaps it's that I didn't go enough down the route.

Riverside Studios, home to Gill's productions of *Measure of Measure* (1979) and *Julius Caesar* (1980), as well as of Middleton and Rowley's *The Changeling* (1978), was an arts centre in the London borough of Hammersmith. Gill himself was the Artistic Director, one of the few occasions when he has been in a position to be producer of his own work. Riverside programming was a mixture of high art and social experiment. The Shakespeare productions were part of a whole spectrum of activities which included an international dimension (Tadeusz Kantor, Dario Fo, Shuji Terayama, Joan Miró); fine art (Bruce MacLean, Jon Groom, Renzo Piano and Richard Rogers); literature (Basil Bunting, Douglas Dunn); dance (Merce Cunningham, Rosemary Butcher, Siobhan Davies, Trisha Brown, Lucinda Childs); and new plays (Nicholas Wright, Tunde Ikoli, Hanif Kureshi). This could be seen as the last gasp of 1960s culture before the reaction of the 1980s set in in earnest.

The Riverside *Julius Caesar* had an inventiveness about its staging that looked back to *The Duchess of Malfi* nearly ten years before, and the production had something of a modern-dance feel about it. It had a fine sinewy energy and forward movement and, like a lot of Gill's work, there was nothing you wanted to add (or indeed subtract either):

> We were faced with the problem that there was this big cast and I had a limited number of actors financially available. I had about eighteen, which is quite a lot, but the doubling was very difficult. So, I worked out that you could quite quickly turn everybody into everything – and that I could have a bigger crowd than I'd first thought. Alison (Chitty, the designer) made a folded-in stage – a wooden floor that would be hoisted open and then a series of wood and metal benches that could quickly be made into tables or a kind of chair to carry Caesar on, so we could make very dissolved and quick imagery. And then we put the actors in a very similar sort of practice clothes, I suppose, which was a very good solution because they didn't have to have costume changes and they all had a sort of basic look – it was a palette of varying very soft greys, so everybody could be individual within a general tone. And then we had simple Roman breastplates and broadswords. There were no togas – except that Caesar had a sort of long gown. So we were able to have a lot of quite feisty theatricality of the two men, Brutus and Anthony, being lifted on the shoulders of most of the boys so they created a close-up of a crowd and the base of a tribune. And we worked out the battles which I slightly formalised so there were elements of modern dance in it, and we had occasionally very lavish lighting; and then when it came to the death of Caesar on a simple technical basis of the laundry, which is I didn't see how at Riverside we would get it all done between a matinee and evening with our resources, when they stabbed him they could reveal sleeves underneath which made them look as if they were stained in blood – slightly Japanese but not, a little bit richer – and then we put a great deal of white cloud like a sort of huge lung of white smoke, which was then dyed red, so it started

> white and then we let the red into it so as they were stabbing it became red. So it had a lot of expressionist devices, lots of music, the boys shouting things, and the set was just this wooden stage and the back wall of Riverside. But Alison made gauzes – there was an image thing that in the first half said Senatus Populusque Romanus and then in the second it was taken off and said Gaius Julius Caesar. So it was simple, emblematic but had a kind of slightly expressionist dynamic, I suppose, or expressionist-cum-New-York-dance look to it.

Alongside Gill's full-dress productions, there was other more fragmentary work, mostly behind closed doors or for invited audiences only. In the summer of 1977, for example, there was a workshop, *Shakespeare's Women*, at Riverside Studios. This took five Shakespeare heroines – Cressida, Helena, Viola, Isabella and Rosalind – and looked at two scenes in which they each appeared; five early scenes were followed by five scenes from later in the respective plays. The spectators sat on a large square tarpaulin in the middle of the empty space and swivelled round to follow the action which took place on all four sides. The collage form brought out in a very pure way that sense of unity in diversity, of all these separate diverse creatures being seen steadily by a central consciousness that is typical of Gill's Shakespeare.

There was also a series of workshops, *Shakespeare in Dialect*, investigating the effect of doing Shakespeare in different accents and what they brought to the text in terms of rhythm, speed, pacing, and also different realities. It was an attempt to harness the energy and sense of lived experience lodged in certain corners of contemporary speech and channel this into Shakespeare's language. When Tony Sher performed Hamlet's speech 'Nay but to live / In the rank sweat of an enseamed bed' in an Afrikaner accent, the Puritanism and sexual disgust were vividly present in the room. Other experiments included scenes from *Troilus and Cressida* in Lancashire ('How have I *blabbed*'); from *Measure for Measure* in Scots; and an East London *King Lear*, where the sense of patriarchy and family connection was overwhelming:

> Certain things culturally make the imagery come to life. All the idiosyncratic humour is suddenly unlaboured. And it stops you going down the awful European, post-Meyerhold route that is very un-Shakespearian – that sort of heavy-duty 'meaningful' productions. And individual imagery really seems to jump forward. Certain of the metaphors seem to. But certain of the accents don't have enough variety – the Midlands doesn't have enough variety of cadence. My thing with Shakespeare is that I didn't think it was written in this vapid South of England way and I wanted to find out how it was written. I

> don't know what I think now, because I never did a full production – except the one we did of *Macbeth* – in an accent. We did the Angelo and Isabella scenes in Scottish. What is remarkable was it released the Puritanical side of both characters, so you saw *vividly* what Shakespeare was getting at in his questioning of Angelo *and* Isabella, which is clearly part of the play. The play isn't about the rape of Isabella as far as I can see. It's a very hard look at two over-verbal, fanciful-speaking Puritans, and when we did it with these two actors it came springing to life. And the East London *King Lear* had a marvellous virility. Family had a real meaning. You could have done a *King Lear* like that. I think that play would have obtained it funnily enough. I don't know if it got us anywhere except to help me want Shakespeare to be more like Shakespeare.

Most of this exploration took place at the National Theatre Studio, where Gill was the Director between 1984 and 1990, culminating in a complete production of *Macbeth* in Jamaican dialect in 1987.

Gill's work has not been immune to changes in the wider culture. The figures tell their own story. In the nine years between 1971 and 1980, there were eight productions of plays by Shakespeare and his contemporaries: in the following twenty-five years, 1981 to 2006, there were only four (one of which was *Macbeth*, performed in the Cottesloe for one night only). The Conservative government's pursuit of commercial imperatives closed down Riverside Studios and put the National Theatre itself under siege, shrinking and shrinking and coarsening the repertoire. The ambitiousness of the Royal Court/Riverside endeavour and its sense of civic generosity came to seem quaint and outside the intellectual current. All this was part of a more general waste. Gill's energies went in other directions, most notably into his own writing. Other Shakespeare productions were mooted – *The Winter's Tale, Hamlet, Othello, Anthony and Cleopatra* and *King Lear* – but none came to fruition. It is to be hoped that they still may: certainly our theatre is poorer without them.

Chronology

Shakespeare productions

1939 Peter Gill born September 7
1964 Peter Gill Assistant Director Royal Court Theatre
1969 *Much Ado about Nothing*, Stratford, Connecticut
1970 Peter Gill Associate Director Royal Court Theatre

1971 *Macbeth*, Stratford, Ontario
1972 *A Midsummer Night's Dream*, Zurich Schauspielhaus
1974 *Twelfth Night*, Stratford on Avon
1975 *As You Like It*, Nottingham Playhouse, Edinburgh Festival
1976 Peter Gill Founding Director of Riverside Studios
1976 *As You Like It*, Riverside Studios
1979 *Measure for Measure*, Riverside Studios
1980 *Julius Caesar*, Riverside Studios
1980–97 Peter Gill Associate Director of the National Theatre
1981 *Much Ado about Nothing*, National Theatre
1984–90 Founding Director of the National Theatre Studio
1987 *Macbeth* (co-directed), National Theatre (Studio Night)
2004 *Romeo and Juliet*, Stratford on Avon

Related productions

1967 *A Soldier's Fortune* (Thomas Otway), Royal Court Theatre
1971 *The Duchess of Malfi* (John Webster), Royal Court Theatre
1978 *The Changeling* (Thomas Middleton and William Rowley), Riverside Studios
1984 *Venice Preserv'd* (Thomas Otway), National Theatre

Bibliography

Doty, Gresdna A. and Billy J. Harbin (eds) (1990) *Inside the Royal Court Theatre, 1956–1981: Artists Talk*, Louisiana State University Press.

Findlater, Richard (ed.) (1981) *At the Royal Court: 25 Years of the English Stage Company*, Amber Lane Press.

Gaskill, William (1971) 'Finding a Style for Farquhar', *Theatre Quarterly*, Vol. I. No 1 1971.

Gaskill, William (1988) *A Sense of Direction*, Faber.

Haill, Lyn (ed) (2007) *Actors Speaking*. Introduction by Peter Gill, Oberon Books.

Wardle, Irving (1978) *The Theatres of George Devine*, Cape.

Other sources

All quotations by Peter Gill are taken from a series of conversations with the author which took place in April/May 2006. Tapes are in the author's possession. Further material about Peter Gill, including photographs and reviews of productions, is available at his website: <http://dspace.dial-pipex.co./town/parade/abj76/PG/ index.shtml>.

Recollections of Harley Granville Barker, Dame Sybil Thorndike and Sir

Lewis Casson interviewed by Douglas Cleverdon, was broadcast by the BBC Third Programme on 27 March 1967. Tape No: TLO42/TD32.

About the author

John Burgess is a freelance director and lives in London. He was Associate Director at Riverside Studios, 1978/9, and worked for fourteen years at the National Theatre where he directed works from the classical, romantic and modern repertoires as well as many new plays. He helped found the National Theatre Studio with Peter Gill and was the National Theatre's Head of New Writing 1989–94. He has directed abroad in Switzerland, Scandinavia, North America and Turkey, and is the author of *The Faber Pocket Guide to Greek and Roman Drama* (2005). He has three times been Visiting Professor at the University of California, Davis.

7
HARLEY GRANVILLE BARKER

Christopher McCullough

The phenomenon of the director/*auteur* as a central interpretative figure in the twentieth-century performance of Shakespeare's plays may be traced back to Harley Granville Barker. However, his stage realisation of Shakespeare was limited to only three productions (four if we count his engagement with Lewis Casson's production of *King Lear* in 1940), leaving the mediation of his practice to be disseminated more widely through his writing on the performance of Shakespeare, which grew directly out of his creative sensibility and experience of the material business of making theatre.

There is, often, a perceived tension between the worlds of professional theatre and the scholar/artists who work in universities. While the tension is less so as the boundaries become more indistinct, Granville Barker stands out as a 'scholar/artist' whose breaking with the nineteenth-century traditions of staging Shakespeare, coupled with his commitment to close textual reading, links him down the decades to the rich vein of productive tensions in Cambridge University that emanated from the textual analysis of F.R. Leavis and the directing of George Rylands, which, in their turn, informed the re-established Royal Shakespeare Company under Peter Hall in 1959/60.

Granville Barker's skills were wide ranging, and equal claims may be made for him as a playwright, as an advocate of new writing in the theatre and as a director who swept away the traditions of the actor-manager and pictorial scenography that had characterised the nineteenth-century stage. However, there is a danger that much of the critical commentary on Granville Barker, in claiming him as the radical innovator of modern directing, perceives him solely as an iconoclast who transcended the cultural context of the early years of the twentieth century. What is more interesting is to understand the world of which he was a part and the degree to which he was one of the 'authors' of that culture.

Granville Barker's rejection of the nineteenth-century barnstorming styles of performing, as well as his rejection of elaborate pictorial scenography and the haphazard cutting of the received texts, mark him out as a 'modern' man of the twentieth century. It is this sense of Granville Barker as a man of that moment in history (as far as his productions of Shakespeare are concerned, the time was the first two decades of the twentieth century) that distinguishes him from William Poel, whose aim it was to recreate the performance conditions of Shakespeare's historical period. Whether or not Granville Barker is usefully described as a 'modernist' is a matter for dispute, but his work does contain elements that would not be out of place in any definition of the twentieth century's modernist movement. Perhaps a better term for Barker, appropriated from Raymond Williams (Williams 1958: 9), would be 'palaeo-modernist', a man who sought to recapture the dynamism of sixteenth-century performance within the framework of twentieth-century cultural concerns. Where Poel tried to impose the past on the present, Granville Barker aspired to bring the past up to the moment.

There are many factors that help us to locate Granville Barker's work as more complex – and more interesting – than the simple expression of an iconoclast. The cultural landscape of the period in which Granville Barker's Shakespeare productions made their mark was formed out of the nineteenth-century *fin de siècle*. This ending of a century has often been seen as a 'working out of unfinished lines; a tentative redirection' (Williams 1958: 165). However, more recently, arguments have tended to focus on the *fin de siècle* as a site in which the genesis of the now-familiar fragmentation and cultural crisis of twentieth-century modernism was formed. It would be a mistake to associate Granville Barker too closely with the fading echoes of nineteenth-century high imperialism. The simple point to note is that while Granville Barker was rejecting the more conservative aspects of late nineteenth-century theatre, there is some evidence that he was influenced by aspects of what we recognise as the new art (*art nouveau*) of the *fin de siècle*. This, as will be argued, was particularly so in respect of the decorative style of scenography with which he and his designer chose to replace pictorial literalism in the visual language of stage setting. In our attempt to understand the making of the artist, we need to recognise the polyvocality of the material, social and ideological factors that form Granville Barker's aesthetic.

Granville Barker's rejection of nineteenth-century pictorial staging did not result in an imagined sixteenth-century bare platform for performance. While Granville Barker did work with a thrust stage, seeking the consequent immediacy of performance with the audience, the stage décor he employed for the three Savoy Shakespeare productions owed much to the *art nouveau* movement. This 'new art', while developed in the 1880s, was still a significant influence in the visual imagery of the first two decades of the twentieth century. The essence of the art form is linear, a line extended in a sinuous curve, which could be expressed either in a simple form, or in more complex patterns derived from nature. The patterns of the drapes and the textiles covering stage furniture, as well as the costumes used in the productions, all echo the visual preoccupations of *art nouveau* design. Norman Wilkinson's design for set and costumes for *Twelfth Night*, in particular for the drinking scene, exemplifies this point. The costumes, while inscribed with imagery that is clearly drawn from late sixteenth-century fashion, have evolved into the vogue often found in English Shakespeare productions of the second half of the twentieth century and on into the twenty-first: that is to say, costumes that belong to no specific time and no specific place. Wilkinson's costumes, in fact, owed more to Victorian pantomime than to historical research.

The massive *art nouveau* drapes of all three Shakespeare productions, combined with stylised pillars, furniture and, in *Twelfth Night*, the cone-like trees in Olivia's garden, replace the pictorial landscape backcloths of the previous tradition but also seem part of a new tradition of decorative scenography. Susan Carlson has suggested that the colours pink and green, which were dominant in the production of *Twelfth Night* and were also the colours of the Actresses' Franchise League, signal Granville Barker's support for the suffragist cause (Carlson 2006: 134). The thought is a pleasing one, and not beyond Granville Barker's idiosyncratic range, but the choice of colours is at least equally likely to reflect Wilkinson's artistic taste. The photographic records of these productions cannot be dissociated from other contemporary developments in the visual arts. For example, a cross-reference to the emergent cubism of Picasso and Braque (the pink and the green) combined with the developments in surrealism, constructivism and fauvism all demonstrate the focus of attention away from any concern with pictorial literalism, although the visual codes in the work of Granville Barker and Wilkinson relate more closely to the decorative than to the fine arts (notwithstanding the objections of the *Times* critic to the 'post-impressionism' of the sets for *The Winter's Tale*). And, as a note in passing, if we look forward to Komisarjevski's 1932 production of *The Merchant of Venice*, we can see that his concept of a cultured synthetic theatre is not that far visually removed from the visual codes employed by Granville Barker.

Granville Barker's relationship with the playwright George Bernard Shaw (more of a nineteenth-century man than Granville Barker by some twenty years) is important and, despite the difference in their ages, should be understood as a mutual relationship of very different temperaments, noting that it involved dissonance as well as symbiosis. G.B. Shaw, it should be understood, was one of the major playwrights of the late nineteenth and early twentieth centuries, and while they shared support for aspects of socialism and the emergent suffragist movement, as well the mutual benefit they achieved during their Royal Court years, particularly the seasons 1904–7, they differed in other professional matters. Many external similarities in directing style were offset by Shaw's autocratic assertion of the playwright's right to dictate the actors' movements and the outcome of rehearsals as absolutely as a musical maestro faced with a wayward orchestra. Against this, we see Granville Barker's desire to create an ensemble of actors, with the director taking the role of the ideal audience throughout the rehearsal process (although we will note in the final section on *King Lear* a change in Granville Barker's approach). Granville Barker's rare experience of an apprenticeship in acting while learning how to write plays allowed him a sense of the level of interdependence that necessarily exists between actors and playwrights.

The clear linear patterning of the visual environment of Granville Barker's Savoy Shakespeare productions may be seen to be a rejection of the literalism, or pictorialism, of nineteenth-century theatre scenography, but this should not be taken to mean that he was not concerned with a carefully constructed and pointed realism in his productions of Shakespeare's plays. Among the many new approaches to the stage during the last decades of the nineteenth and the early decades of the twentieth century we cannot afford to ignore the new naturalism in the theatre emanating from Russia, with Konstantin Stanislavsky's developing systems of training for actors, Anton Chekhov's plays (although it is possible that Granville Barker would not have known much of the work in Russia before his visit to Moscow in 1914), and from Henrik Ibsen in Norway. Similarly, the novel's concern with 'real' people in 'real' situations (Émile Zola in particular) is intrinsic to the shift in focus from the broader sweep of history to the interior lives of the Western European middle classes. What is germane to Granville Barker's Shakespeare work is an emphasis on a modern concept of interior character (more so than the social dimensions of character), wherein the representations forming in the arts operate in parallel to developments in science, as may be instanced in the development of psychology. While we cannot – nor do we need to – rely on direct contact between the various players across Europe in our scenario, the important factor to note is the broader ideological development in consciousness. The new languages in the arts and sciences produced new ways of thinking that focused on the inner life (however we define that concept) of the individual rather than relying on a broad representation of characteristics prevalent in the rhetorical spectacle of much nineteenth-century theatre.

While the developments in what we now refer to as 'naturalism' in the theatre may be seen to be central to Granville Barker's playwriting, we do need to wonder how this new aesthetic related to his work with Shakespeare's plays, which are embodied in a poetic form both dramatically and theatrically. Did Granville Barker reconcile character as manifest in the sixteenth- or seventeenth-century dramas with the formulation of character in the late nineteenth and early twentieth centuries?

In his *Preface to Othello*, Granville Barker addresses the difference between the way in which an actor may give substance to the inner life of a character and what he refers to as mere impersonation. Impersonation, in this sense, occurs when the actor remains manifestly her/himself whilst adopting the mere external signs of the character being played. It is as if, by patronising the character, the actor is working to the detriment of the playwright's construction of that character:

> The actor's is, above all, the faculty of sympathy: found physically in the sensitive ear, the receptive eye, the dancer's body that of itself responds, emotionally in the tears or laughter ready at some call, and intellectually in a capacity not only seemingly to absorb some product of another's thought, but to reproduce the effects of understanding it without necessarily having understood it.
>
> (Granville Barker 1937: 106–7)

The end of this quotation may strike a discordant note with many actors today but, necessarily, needs placing in context. Granville Barker is calling for the actor to place her/his personality in service to the character created by the dramatist; to develop the 'faculty of sympathy' and by so doing to absorb 'another's thoughts' as embedded in the language given to the character, rather than allowing her/his personality to override the dramatic character (the rhetorical style of previous generations). 'Much more than interpretation is asked of the actor. He has to *embody* the character' (Granville Barker 1937: 106–7). Presumably this means that a form of symbiosis, between the dramatic character as embodied in language and the actor's personality, has to be achieved. This is a call for a quality of verisimilitude in the actor's deployment of the dramatic language, a notion with which few people would find good reason to disagree. However, many actors of later generations, from a variety of ideological persuasions, would find it difficult to agree with the notion that 'another's thoughts' could be embodied without necessarily understanding them.

The poetic language of Shakespeare's theatre creates another layer of difficulty. The language of Shakespeare's plays is not immediately accessible, whether in the late sixteenth century or the early twentieth century. Certainly, some lines have embedded themselves in the cultural consciousness of the English-speaking world – 'To be, or not to be', 'All the world's a stage' and so on – but the imagery, for the most part, is dense, and there is a world of distance between a popularised seeking after a psychological motive in acting and being able to communicate a character's thoughts to an audience when the language is often couched in complex metaphors. Peter Thomson provides us with an access to Granville Barker's aim for the actor to embody the playwright's character:

> [P]ersonation, if we mean to propose by it that one whole human being (Burbage, say) can substitute for another whole human being (Hamlet), was at best embryonic on the early modern stage. Personation did not abolish the performer's self from the playing space. He had access to the audience, and so could slip easily from dialogue to aside to dialogue to direct address or soliloquy.
>
> (Thomson 2000: 9)

The nature of Shakespeare's dramaturgy requires the versatility of shape-shifting suggested by Thomson; in one moment, the actor is 'in' the character, at another, the dramatic structure and the style of performance require the actor to step aside and 'narrate' the character in a direct address to the audience. In one sense, Granville Barker is taking the notion of personation (perhaps first realised in Hamlet) a number of steps further. He recognises that we can only go so far in adapting our consciousness to the techniques of the sixteenth and seventeenth centuries, as we need to retain a spontaneity that can only come from a contemporary apprehension of the plays, an apprehension that is created by all the voices of the time forming our consciousness. We may assume that Granville Barker's actor 'embodies' the character through an empathetic form of acting that requires a sensitivity to the demands of the theatrical moment – the soliloquy, in sonnet form, startlingly shared by Romeo and Juliet, or the 'narrating' of a character's thoughts to the audience. Intuition, the actor's 'faculty of sympathy' may here take precedence over a critical understanding.

It is vital to our understanding of Granville Barker's work in the theatre that we recognise that, however far *ahead* of his time he may have been, he belonged to it. His sensibility and his aesthetic were conditioned by contemporary axioms. In broad terms, he accepted Poel's thesis that Shakespeare's plays should be performed as Shakespeare wrote them. Putting aside the uncertainty regarding the textual provenance of Shakespeare's plays, or any claim to know precisely what was performed on the stage of the Globe or any of the other London theatres in the sixteenth and early seventeenth centuries, Granville Barker's aim was to clear away what he rightly regarded as the clutter of the generations that had accumulated around the plays, with the aim of restoring their clarity without transpositions, alterations or cuts. But the question raised in his Introduction to *The Players' Shakespeare*, 'whether any omissions whatever from the text can be justified' (Barker 1974: 44) was a thorny one. One of the problems here was the cultural distance between Shakespeare's time and the early decades of a Georgian England still experiencing the constraints of Victorian morality. Granville Barker's concern focuses on obscenity, on Shakespeare's ease with jokes of a sexual or scatological nature. 'The manner of his time permitted this to a dramatist. The manners of ours do not' (Granville Barker 1974: 44). Granville Barker's view is that a joke is measured by its effect on an audience: 'And if, where it was meant to provide a mere moment of amusement, it makes a thousand people feel uncomfortable and for the next five minutes rather self-conscious, its effect is falsified and spoiled [. . .] What is to be the fate of topical allusions whose meaning is lost?' (Granville Barker 1974: 44).

While my main focus now will be on the three productions of Shakespeare at the Savoy Theatre, regard must also be given to Granville Barker's *Prefaces to Shakespeare*, as they, too, form a major part of his work on Shakespeare. Each of the productions, *The Winter's Tale* (1912), *Twelfth Night* (1912) and *A Midsummer Night's Dream* (1914), will be discussed with reference to the preface that was, in the case of these three productions, produced concurrently, and further reference will be made to the much later *Preface to King Lear* and Granville Barker's role in Lewis Casson's production of the play in 1940.

The *Prefaces* are not, in any conventional sense, critical analyses, but rather a director's preliminary notes to the actors at the start of rehearsals, and there is a clear development in style through the three early *Prefaces*. What they all reveal, though, is Granville Barker's understanding of Shakespeare's dramaturgy and stagecraft and the need for a fluency of staging and speech, unbroken by the lengthy intervals required by the complex set-changes that encumbered much of the nineteenth-century theatre.

The Winter's Tale was the production that first gave Granville Barker the opportunity to put into practice his new ideas on the staging of Shakespeare. While recognising his debt to Poel, Granville Barker did not seek to recreate a *faux* Elizabethanism, but to draw on his understanding of the clarity and dynamism of that theatre, while creating performances that would also speak to audiences in 1912.

The production was not universally well received by the press, which was, by and large, out of sympathy with Granville Barker's aims, regardless of whether or not he had achieved them. The main focus of criticism was on the departure from a literal pictorial staging with its reassuring sense of historical definition, on the 'new', and highly decorative, scenic style, which was considered eccentric, and on the colourful but historically imprecise costumes, which were condemned as exotic. The text was hardly cut at all but still only ran between two and three quarter and three hours (with one interval of fifteen minutes) due to the rapidity of the actors' delivery of the words. This would have been a fairly novel experience for both audience and reviewers, who were more used to the complications of pictorial scenography and a stately rhetorical delivery of lines. The speaking of Shakespeare's language was too rushed for hostile spectators, but there were others who welcomed the opportunity to experience the play in a fuller and less encumbered form. Moreover, the performance of the language was not subjected to a process that attempts to turn blank verse into prose – as sometimes has happened in later twentieth-century theatre – but brought character and the rhythm of language together in Granville Barker's concept of embodiment.

The fluidity of staging rendered Perdita's performance too physical and seemingly commonplace, causing consternation to some observers. From this, it would appear that Granville Barker was successful in his aim to allow actors the freedom to develop their moves (and stage relationships) without too many of the constraints of strict prerehearsal blocking, of the kind which directed actors to delivering this or that line from predesignated precise points on the stage. Perhaps the most important element in this production, certainly in terms of future developments in the staging of Shakespeare's plays, was the use of the apron stage and the opportunities it afforded to the actors in developing a direct relationship with the audience, particularly during asides and soliloquies. The picture frame created by the proscenium arch had been a major contributor to the tradition of determining actors' moves so that the 'picture' would read clearly to the audience. More pragmatically, Granville Barker's use of the apron stage also meant that scenes could be performed on the apron stage while other scene changes took place behind it, thus ensuring the continuous flow of action. Of greater theatrical significance, however, was the freedom it allowed for the actors to move forward (downstage) to address the audience directly.

Granville Barker's *Preface* raises three main points regarding the play and his production: the concept of Time as a chorus; the scenic structure of the play and, in particular, the function of bridging scenes; and the way in which Granville Barker understands the function of character in Shakespeare. He recognises that *The Winter's Tale* seems to veer between tragedy and comedy. This is only a problem if we accept that there are strict boundaries between these forms in Shakespeare's art. Attempts to measure his plays by the received notions of Aristotle, or for that matter Seneca, will only lead to dramatic contortions. As Granville Barker points out, this is a play that contains recognisable elements of both tragedy and comedy, and any attempt to align it with one or the other will falsify it. On either side of the gap of sixteen years lie tragedy and comedy, and the demands of both genres must be respected.

Barker was well aware that the lapse of time in the middle of the play serves as a point of transition from one genre to another, with 'Time acting as a Chorus':

> The very artifice of the device, moreover, attunes us to the artifice of the story; saves us, at this dangerous juncture, when Hermione is apparently dead, Antigonus quite certainly eaten by the bear, from the true tragic mood. Moreover, 'Time as Chorus' is the simple way to bridge dramatically the sixteen years, and therefore the right one.
>
> (Barker 1974: 19/20)

Granville Barker states in the *Preface* that he has no contribution to make to the further issue of the division of Shakespeare's plays into acts or scenes. However, the scenic structure of Shakespeare's plays is more essential to his dramatic form than an overarching division into acts (which was more a printer's than a playwright's device). A near-seamless passage from scene to scene allows for the plays to be performed as swiftly and smoothly as possible. As this was Granville Barker's intention, we may suppose he supported, if only by implication, the division by 'scene' as less disruptive of the dramatic flow than a breaking up into acts. However, the audience does need an emotional 'breathing space'. Bridging scenes are useful in that they allow minor plot developments to occur without fracturing or disrupting the progress of the major narrative.

Granville Barker denies Leontes the status of tragic figure. Contrasting Leontes with Othello he conjectures that, while Shakespeare may have seen jealously as the 'centre-point' of the *Othello* tragedy, in making Leontes' jealousy 'perverse, ignoble, pitiable', he seeks to avoid the 'magnificent error' of Othello. (I will not dwell on Granville Barker's unfortunate designation of Othello as 'a primitive and noble creature, building its happiness on a civilised ideal', but it is an interesting comment on prevalent ethnic views of the time, in particular on notions of 'orientalism', as will be observed in aspects of his production of *A Midsummer Night's Dream*.)

The Winter's Tale ran for six weeks, and Granville Barker followed it almost immediately with a production of *Twelfth Night*. This production, again in the Savoy, retained many of the same cast as *The Winter's Tale*, and the leading actor Henry Ainley made the, perhaps appropriate, transition from Leontes to Malvolio. Ainley was an important actor in these early and radical interpretations of Shakespeare in that he brought to the stage an element of the tragic comedian that heightened the tension between the, hitherto, superficial demeanour of what had been expected of the character and exposed the underlying vulgarity of both Leontes and Malvolio. The critical response, unlike that for *The Winter's Tale*, was almost unanimously enthusiastic. Christine Dymkowski notes that:

> the *Illustrated News* found it 'more conciliatory' than *The Winter's Tale*. The *Times* wrote that, in this play, Barker 'sets out chiefly to please rather than [. . .] chiefly to make us "sit up". There is no deliberate challenge now, to the scoffer, no flaunting eccentricity, no obvious search for quaintness for its own sake. Novelty, of course, there is, and an independent touch in everything.' John Palmer, on the other hand, pointed out that this revival was actually no different from the first; it seems that audiences and critics found themselves unconsciously won over to Barker's methods once their initial shock had passed.
>
> (Dymkowski 1986: 46)

While Granville Barker's *Preface to Twelfth Night* is a curious mixture of personal preference and critical analysis, its significant value is that it was written while he was in rehearsal. One of the notable breaks with nineteenth-century practices is the importance Granville Barker gave to the rehearsal process as a journey of discovery for both director and actors. The last paragraph of the *Preface* is particularly revealing, in that it allows us to gain a direct insight into the balance between his ensemble working methods – 'Daily, as we rehearse together, I learn what it is and should be; the working together of the theatre is a fine thing' – and his personal commitment to his developing principles of theatre-making: 'But as a man is asked to name his stroke at billiards, I will now commit myself to this: its [*Twelfth Night*] serious mood is passionate, its verse is lyrical, the speaking of it needs swiftness and fine tone; not rush, but rhythm, constant and compelling' (Granville Barker 1912: 32).

Granville Barker's reading of the role of women playing the roles originally assigned to boy players argues that, to view the play 'rightly', we must 'view it with Elizabethan eyes'. He makes the interesting point that the Elizabethan audience's 'strain of make-believe in the matter ended just where for us it begins, at Viola's entrance as a page. Shakespeare's audience saw Cesario without effort as Orsino sees him' (Granville Barker 1912: 29). At one level, Granville Barker is taking to task those female actors of his time who do not play the man in playing Cesario, particularly in those scenes with Olivia, but instead choose to flaunt the fact that they are really women to the audience, and they do this with the sole aim of entering into a self-regarding conspiracy with the audience to the detriment of Olivia's stature in the play. Granville Barker's point is exemplified in,

> One sees how dramatically right is the delicate still grace of the dialogue between Orsino and Cesario, and how possible it makes the more outspoken passion of the scenes with Olivia. Give to Olivia, as we must do now, all the value of her sex, and to the supposed Cesario none of the value of his.
>
> (Barker 1912: 29)

The assumption is that the Elizabethan boy actor had to suppress his gender as Viola but allow it to come forward as Cesario; whereas the female actor in Granville Barker's Savoy company had to accomplish the reverse. We cannot be certain of how the Elizabethan boy players presented – played with – their own gender and that of the female characters, but we may take the point that Granville Barker's search for integrity with the female character meant that any metatheatrical interplay between the gender of the actor and the character, for whatever reason, good or ill, had to be expunged.

Susan Carlson links Lillah McCarthy's performance as Viola/Cesario with the need to abandon 'feminine charm' in the pursuit of female suffrage, a life-and-death issue in 1912: 'The reconceptualization of Viola/Cesario's breeches part is also enhanced in a suffrage context' (Carlson 2006: 135). This may or may not be so, but the interesting point is her use of the term 'breeches part', which did not come into use in the theatre until the late seventeenth century (Restoration theatre), when women were allowed to act on the English stage. The term 'breeches part' carries with it the negative association of the 'male gaze', the hitherto forbidden licence given to men to look at women's legs in public. We may conclude that Granville Barker's interrogation of gender display may have had less directly to do with the public theatres' practices or the suffragist movement than it had to do with his reaction against eighteenth- and nineteenth-century theatrical practices. By way of an addendum, contemporary reports state that Viola was played in a 'masculine' and 'rational' manner and, as Dymkowski observes, this was a Viola who gained the upper hand in the sword fight with Andrew Aguecheek (Dymkowski 1986: 55).

Less convincing is Granville Barker's defence of Orsino as 'a finely interesting figure' (Barker 1974: 28), who in many critical readings then and now, is a shallow character in love with the idea of being in love. Of course, the same degree of shallowness may be attached to other major characters such as Sir Toby Belch and Andrew Aguecheek, but they belong more legitimately to the 'humours' realm of comedy. There is a strong sense from the *Preface* that Granville Barker's aim to recover the play misses the challenge of the essential breaking of rules by Shakespeare, who is deliberately playing with levels of gender ambivalence, shallowness of character and foolish aspirations to wit in what might otherwise be dismissed as a piece of froth devised to pass the time during the annual Twelfth Night festivities. Of course, as ever with Shakespeare, there is more to it than that, as we may see in the play's darker narrative, driven by the tensions between Feste and Malvolio. It seems that Granville Barker, despite his refreshing reinvention of Shakespeare's theatre and his clear textual interrogation, is still looking for a consistency of form that simply is not there (and all the more exciting for that).

With his productions of *Twelfth Night* and *A Midsummer Night's Dream*, there is a clear sense that Granville Barker is growing in confidence, as is evidenced in the reports on the success of both these productions and in his *Prefaces* to these two plays.

As we may observe, Peter Brook, in his famous production of *A Midsummer Night's Dream* (1971), was one of the beneficiaries of Granville Barker's earlier radical revisions. Both these directors, like others through the twentieth and twenty-first centuries, have started rehearsals by asking the question, how do we represent fairies and magic in a world that no longer believes in such entities? Granville Barker's problem was twofold: to find a way to break away from the sentimentalised image of gauze wings, owing more to children's picture books than to British folklore, and then to find a visual metaphor that would read theatrically as 'other', something related to humankind but not of it. His solution was to employ an overt theatricality combined with the image of an exotic 'otherness'.

Both Granville Barker, and Peter Brook much later in 1971, looked to exploit theatricality in order to articulate the fairy world and to subvert a notion of dainty pictorialism. In Brook's case, the metaphor took the form of a combination of circus and conjuring skills, feats of performance that are, without specialised training, something that we (the audience) cannot emulate. For Granville Barker, the solution was somewhat different and very much connected with the fascinations of his own time and culture. Any director of the modern era has to decide how to distinguish between the fictionalised world of Athens (the world of men – the gender-specific reference is deliberate) and the world of the wood, which is the domain of the fairies and where the accepted social relationships of humans are largely irrelevant. The scenery for Granville Barker's production of *A Midsummer Night's Dream* was once again designed by Norman Wilkinson, and it followed the non-realistic decorative theme established in the two previous productions. In the simplest terms, Athens was formal, symmetric (as was the staging) and consisting of pillars and levels; the world of the wood was signified by a series of richly elaborated decorative drapes supplemented by floral wreaths, offering a sense, for this observer of surviving images at least, of nature encased in the sensual lines of *art nouveau* patterns. The presentation of the fairies was likewise removed from the illusion of any known world and raises another issue that may well be derived from images of an alternative nineteenth century; an avant-garde culture still echoing through into the early twentieth. Granville Barker's reading of the fairies seems to take its cue from the little changeling boy whose mother, 'in the spicèd Indian air by night', communed with Titania (Act II, Scene 1). There is a distinctly oriental 'otherness' to the demeanour of the fairies, surely derived from images popularly supposed to represent aspects of the 'exotic East' (some reports suggest that the inspiration came from Cambodian idols). The fairies were painted mostly in gold and dressed in a range of costumes that carried visual echoes of a range of cultures from 'Arabia' to Hindu gods. One may suppose that this is, like that of images derived from *art nouveau* for the scenography, another example of a popular bohemianism striving to break free from the hegemony of Victorian constraints. Sir Richard Burton (1821–90), adventurer and proselytiser of all matters subversive to respectable bourgeois manners, fascinated the London cognoscenti with rumours of the 'orient', which became a term by which Western cultures described all that was 'East' and exotic. Edward Said has established the concept of *orientalism* as being ideologically rooted and a means by which Western cultures declared (and continue to do so) as 'other' and thus marginalise, or conversely appropriate, cultures colonised by the Western powers (Said 1978). I do not intend to digress too far from the matter in hand, simply to highlight how Granville Barker drew from the cultural fashions of his own time for images of 'other-worldliness'. The exception to the decision to create a sense of otherness in the fairies (the actors on stage were equally removed from 'natural' behaviour by having them move in a staccato fashion) may be seen in Granville Barker's decision to have the Puck (Robin Goodfellow) firmly rooted in an image of English folklore as a hobgoblin in a quasi-Elizabethan costume.

Granville Barker wrote two *Prefaces* to *A Midsummer Night's Dream*, the first concurrent with the production, the other much later (1924) and more detailed in its close critical reading of the text. However, it is the *Preface* (1914) written while he was in rehearsal that seems most germane to this an understanding of his theatrical practice. Reading through the three concurrently written *Prefaces*, one gains a sense of increasing confidence in Granville Barker's writing. Certainly, it is in the *Preface to A Midsummer Night's Dream* that he appears most assured. His starting point is Samuel Pepys' dismissal of the play in performance, about which Granville Barker is surprisingly generous, on the grounds that 'He [Pepys] has done less to keep Shakespeare from his own. If you go to theatre to scoff you may remain to enjoy yourself; if you go to pray (once in a while) you likelier leave to patronise' (Barker 1974: 33). Granville Barker's objection is to the tendency on the part of spectators to become over-pious about the poetry and to see the enactment by mere players as a hindrance to the true soul of the poet. For Granville Barker, Shakespeare may well have been more poet than anything else, but he was inexorably tied to the stage, not least through having to make a living there: 'if it was he [Shakespeare] [who] made the English theatre, did not the theatre make him what he is – what he might be to us?' (Barker 1974: 34).

While so much of Granville Barker's radical reassessment of – and one might assume his progressive thinking about – Shakespeare took place in and through performance, there is one line of thinking in the *Preface* that might appear to be out of kilter with twenty-first-century attitudes to the speaking of poetry on the English stage. And this, in his words, 'opens up the question of the loss and gain to pure poetry on the stage by the coming of women players' (Barker 1974: 36). His discourse seems to stumble into uncertainty over the speaking of verse 'classically', a term whose meaning is made no clearer by the implication that this is beyond the ability of women. The problem perceived by Granville Barker seems to be the inability of his contemporary players (we may assume, male or female) to do justice to 'the merit of Elizabethan verse with its consonantal swiftness, its gradations sudden or slow into vowelled liquidity, its comic rushes and stops, with, above all, the peculiar beauty of its rhymes' (Granville Barker 36). All in all, the problem he grappled with, as directors still do in *A Midsummer Night's Dream*, was how to present the 'dream' in a way that speaks for its generation of actors as well as audiences.

Any, albeit brief, account of Granville Barker's contribution to the mediation of Shakespeare on the stage should not ignore his involvement in Lewis Casson's 1940 production of *King Lear*, well after Granville Barker had formally retired from directing in the theatre. The *Preface to King Lear* was written in 1927 and revised in 1935, and so pre-dated the production by some years. Unlike the *Prefaces* to the earlier three productions, which were written concurrently with the rehearsals and stand as a good example of how Granville Barker's thinking and theatrical practice interacted, the *Preface to King Lear* effectively acted as a template for that production. The 1940 production of *King Lear* is extensively documented and, in addition to the *Preface*, Hallam Fordham took extensive notes during rehearsals and John Gielgud (who played Lear) was centrally concerned with the production in his book *Stage Directions* (1963).

The three productions from 1912 to 1914, ground-breaking though they were, possess all the excitement of discovery, rather than fulfilment. The 1940 production of *King Lear* sees the promise of that early work taken to a conclusion in a way that clearly has influenced subsequent English productions of the play. In his *Preface*, Granville Barker starts in combative mood, challenging the critical tradition (Charles Lamb, William Hazlitt and A.C. Bradley) that argues the case that *King Lear* is beyond staging in its immensity of scale and complexity of human emotions: 'Scholars, in the past, have been apt to forbid this play the theatre; it is my business now to justify its place there' (Barker 1927: 133). Having challenged that view, he then engages in a close critical reading that effectively matches stagecraft with poetry and symbolic setting with action.

Granville Barker's actual involvement in the production is not entirely clear, but from the evidence, it would seem that the fact that his name was not on the playbill as director (or 'producer' as that was the word more commonly employed at that time) should not be seen as an indication that his role was merely that of occasional adviser. Gielgud records that Granville Barker came to London from Paris (where he was living at the time) and 'spent a weekend making preliminary arrangements with Roger Furse, the designer, and with Lewis Casson who agreed to undertake the preparatory work of the production' (Gielgud 1963: 51). Gielgud records that he (Granville Barker), 'came back to London again after rehearsals had already begun and worked with the actors for ten days, but he left after the first dress rehearsal, and never saw a performance with an audience' (1963: 51–2).

Even taking into account the fact that he was writing over twenty years after the event, the immediacy of Gielgud's writing suggests that his memory is clear on the impact Granville Barker's presence made on the actor; for Gielgud, those ten days, 'were the fullest in experience that I have ever had in all my years upon the stage' (1963: 52). While Granville Barker's physical presence in rehearsals was only for that short time, his contact with the production, particularly with Gielgud, continued after the production had opened through a number of short letters Granville Barker wrote to Gielgud advising him on particular moments in the play, which are reproduced in *Stage Directions*. Sadly, Granville Barker's letters to Casson (before and during rehearsal), from which much might have been learned, were destroyed in the London blitz. However, Gielgud did keep detailed notes on his rehearsal copy, recording Granville Barker's directions on the tone, motive and technical delivery of Gielgud's lines, which are published as Appendix I to *Stage Directions*. As an indication of the close work on the text undertaken by Granville Barker, it is worth quoting a selection from Act I, Scene 1 of Gielgud's rehearsal copy of *King Lear*. In the ten-day rehearsal period, Barker was working from his *Preface to King Lear*, which, in its final form, was far more detailed in its textual commentary than the earlier *Prefaces*. Here we gain a remarkable insight to the precision demanded by Granville Barker on an almost line-by-line basis with Gielgud's notes after each line.

Line 102	*Nothing will come of nothing*. First note of danger.
Line 106	*How now, Cordelia, mend your speech a little*. Grind. Intimidation.
Line 124	*By the sacred radiance of the sun*. Big without ponging. [actor's slang for overacting]
Line 131–2	*The barbarous Scythian*. Oath over, sulk over this. Descending passage
Line 139	*I loved her most*. Justify himself.
Line 152	*With reservation of an hundred knights*. He thinks this disposes of the whole thing, lean back, happy as opening.
Line 178	*Kent, on thy life no more*. Dead quiet. Turn. Stare at him.

(Gielgud 1963: 122)

What is clear from these notes is the degree to which Granville Barker had moved in dictating precise actions to moments in speeches. Equally, the letters to Gielgud written from Paris after the run of performances had commenced suggest a deep concern with treating the text as if it were analogous to a musical score. The following quotation contains Granville Barker's own words, whereas the notes in the above quotation are Gielgud's responses to Granville Barker in rehearsal.

> *Edg: Father . . . poor Tom* make much of this; don't hurry; give it a 'Banshee' effect, lilt and rhythm.
>
> At the sound Lear lifts his head. Face seen through his outspread fingers (suggestion of a madman looking through bars).
>
> The Fool screams and runs on: business as at present. This gets Lear to his feet. He turns towards the hovel watching intently for what will emerge.
>
> (Gielgud 1963: 133)

While we may be certain that Granville Barker's presence in the ten-day rehearsal period was absolute and his concern carried on in his letters from Paris, there is, though, a curious appropriateness about the long silence that has surrounded this final venture into the professional theatre. It was Granville Barker's capture of the power of stage silences (e.g., see line 178 above) in *King Lear* that most profoundly impressed Lewis Casson: 'He was a master of silence' (Devlin 1982: 203). Despite its savagery, this is a play full of strangely dramatic silences.

In view of Granville Barker's frustrated hopes for a national theatre, it is an irony that this production of *King Lear* was staged in the Old Vic, which was to become the temporary home of the nascent National Theatre in the 1960s.

The production, in Granville Barker's own view, was not perfect; but what production ever is? What is evident is that it encapsulated his legacy to the generations that were to follow in the (Royal) National Theatre and the Royal Shakespeare Company.

Chronology

1877	Harley Granville Barker born in London on 25 November
1892–1900	Acted in, and latterly, directed many plays
1900	Acted the part of Osric in Johnstone Forbes-Robertson's production of *Hamlet* at the Lyric Theatre, London
1900	Acted the eponymous character in William Poel's production of Christopher Marlowe's play, *Edward II*
1912	Directed *The Winter's Tale* at the Savoy Theatre
1912	Directed *Twelfth Night* at the Savoy Theatre
1914	Directed *A Midsummer Night's Dream* at the Savoy Theatre; also visited Konstantin Stanislavsky in Moscow.
1917	Appointed the first Chair of the British Drama League
1923	First volume of *The Players' Shakespeare* published
1927	The first volume of the *Prefaces to Shakespeare* published
1928	President of the Royal Society of Literature
1931	Went to live in Paris
1940	Undertook a significant role in the London production of *King Lear* with Lewis Casson and John Gielgud (Lear)
1946	Died in Paris on 31 August.

Bibliography

Barker, Harley Granville (1927) *Prefaces to 1st Senes*, London: Sidgwick & Jackson.

—— (1931) *On Dramatic Method being the Clarke lectures for 1930*, London: Sidgwick & Jackson.

—— (1937) *Prefaces to Shakespeare*, London: Batsford.

—— (1974) The Player's *Shakespeare*, London: Batsford.

Carlson, Susan (2006) 'Politicizing Harley Granville Barker: Suffragists and Shakespeare', *New Theatre Quarterly* 22 (2): 130–41.

Devlin, Diana (1982) *A Speaking Part: Lewis Casson and the Theatre of his Time*. London: Hodder & Stoughton.

Gielgud, John (1963) *Stage Directions*, London: Heinemann.

Dymkowski, Christine (1986) *Harley Granville Barker: A Preface to Modern Shakespeare*, Washington, DC: The Folger Shakespeare Library.

Morgan, Margery (1961) *A Drama of Political Man: A Study in the Plays of Harley Granville Barker*, London: Sidgwick & Jackson.

Said, Edward (1978) *Orientalism*, London: Vintage.

Salmon, Eric (1983) *Granville Barker: A Secret Life*, London: Heinemann.

Thomson, Peter (2000) *On Actors and Acting*, Exeter: University of Exeter Press.
Williams, Raymond (1958) *Culture and Society*, London: Ghetto and Windus.

About the author

Christopher McCullough is Professor of Theatre and Head of the Department of Drama at the University of Exeter. He came to university teaching through a circuitous route involving, initially, training in fine art, thence to theatre practice and, later, English literature. He has worked frequently as a visiting professor and director in Italy, the USA and Brazil. His books include *Theatre and Europe* (1996), *Theatre Praxis* (1998), a study of *The Merchant of Venice* (2005). His current research focuses on a perceived influence of Gothic literature on productions of Shakespeare, in particular the work of Edmund Kean. His consistent focus is on the material and cultural conditions within which theatrical performance is constructed and from which stance this essay on Harley Granville Barker takes its starting point.

8
TYRONE GUTHRIE

Robert Shaughnessy

'They won't understand it anyway, so pace! – rhythm – pace!' So began Tyrone Guthie's professional association with Shakespeare in the theatre, in the shape of this repeated command, issued, according to his biographer, during the 'fast and furious' rehearsals for his production of *Love's Labour's Lost* that opened at the newly converted Westminster Theatre on 6 July 1932 (Forsyth 1976: 116). Issued in a spirit of mischievous iconoclasm, Guthrie's ruthless edict to his cast of fourteen indicates an attitude to Shakespeare, to the text, and to the imperatives of performance, for which he would become both renowned and notorious: on the one hand privileging action over introspection, and speed and movement over poetry; on the other caring less about verbal meaning and nuance than the play's liability to test the audience's or, more importantly, his own, patience, and subordinating the sacred writ of the Shakespearian text to directorial caprice. *Love's Labour's Lost* was not, at this time or subsequently, a play that Guthrie especially cared for: here it was introduced as a last-minute substitute for a scrapped production of a second-rate biographical drama about Disraeli because it 'fitted the cast to the extent that there was an actor for each part and a part for each actor' (Guthrie 1959: 75). Nonetheless, Guthrie's insouciant irreverence seemed cannily well judged with regard to the play itself, at the time an unloved, rarely performed, verbally convoluted and obscure early comedy. Staged as 'a masque, with Navarre's court in red and the Princess and her ladies in green' (Styan 1977: 183), it was remembered by the actor who took to the role of the King, the then-absurdly youthful Anthony Quayle, as 'an enchanting production'; it was also the first exposure of the Guthrie approach method of verse-speaking. Quayle explained:

> He was keenly aware of rhythms – the overall rhythm of a scene rather than the clear carving of syllables. So there were often passages where he didn't care if the audience heard exactly what was said. He aimed

> for a general impression; the clarity of dialogue was comparatively unimportant . . . So there'd be a great impression of brouhaha, confusion, noise, embattled opinion, out of which one vital line would emerge – bang! – like that, and hit you with a wallop. He'd throw away twenty lines to achieve one which would slam you in the face.
>
> (Rossi 1977: 19)

From the start, Guthrie's ostensibly casual, even careless attitude to Shakespearian verse was, in actuality, the product of a profoundly musical sensibility, whereby, as Quayle put it, 'he regarded a play as a musical score: its changes of pace, its modifications, its climaxes, crescendos and decrescendos' (Rossi 1977: 19). And, as far as *Love's Labour's Lost* was concerned, it was a method that earned the praise of no less an authority than the editor of the *New Cambridge Shakespeare*, John Dover Wilson, who came to see Guthrie's revival of the second production at the Old Vic four years later and wrote that 'I went, I saw, I was completely conquered . . . Mr Guthrie not only gave me a new play, the existence of which I had never suspected . . . but he set me at a fresh standpoint of understanding and appreciation from which the whole of Shakespearian comedy might be reviewed in a new light' (Wilson 1962: 64). In a seeming vindication of Guthrie's fast and loose treatment of the verbal text, Wilson found that the production 'revealed it as a first-rate comedy of the pattern kind – so full of fun, of *permanent* wit, of brilliant and entrancing situation, that you hardly noticed the faded jesting and allusion, as you sat spell-bound and drank it all in' (1962: 64). Between them, Quayle and Wilson find in this early production the essence of Guthrie's method: rooted in a fundamentally musical, operatic sensibility, it was throughout his directorial career defined by his readiness to subordinate characterisation and verbal detail to the demands of narrative and to the imperatives of the play's larger design, or, as Wilson puts it, its pattern. Although none of these, least of all Guthrie, would have been likely to describe it as such, this understanding of the Shakespearian text as a spatial and temporal entity was thoroughly modernist. As we shall see, it was an understanding that would eventually inform not only a production style but also the architectural poetics of the post-war Shakespearian stage.

At the time he made his London Shakespearian debut, Guthrie had been working both in the theatre, largely on its artistic and commercial fringes, and in the broadcasting industry, for just over half a decade, as a radio producer and scriptwriter for BBC Belfast and for the Canadian National Railways, as a producer with the Scottish National Players, and as Artistic Director of the Festival Theatre, Cambridge. *Love's Labour's Lost* was not Guthrie's first Shakespearian production; he had produced *Measure for Measure* at

Cambridge during the 1929–30 season, but mindful of the Festival Theatre's reputation for avant-garde excess that had been cultivated by his predecessor, the maverick genius Terence Gray (whose travesties of Shakespeare and others had scandalised and delighted 1920s Cambridge), this was a show inflected by the 'slightly classical and conservative bias' (Guthrie 1959: 55) of the theatre under his direction. *Love's Labour's Lost* was sufficiently impressive to recommend him to the matriarch of the Old Vic, Lillian Baylis, at whose invitation he joined the company for the 1933 season. At the beginning of the 1930s, after a decade of frenetic modernist-influenced experimentation, and equally determined resistance thereto, the British Shakespearian stage was reeling, on the one hand, from the excesses, eccentricities and provocations perpetrated by Gray in Cambridge and Sir Barry Jackson and H.J. Ayliff (contrivers of modern-dress productions of *Hamlet, The Taming of the Shrew, Macbeth* and *Cymbeline*) in London and Birmingham, and, on the other, from the soporific solemnities of annual festival and rotating repertory productions in London and Stratford. Guthrie entered the scene as a young producer on good terms with the contemporary avant-garde, the West End and the new broadcast media, who appeared to possess the boldness of vision, the commercial acumen and the respect for the Vic's classical and philanthropic traditions, that might propel the ailing organisation, limping along with its recycled stock sets, costumes and stage business, into a new era. Guthrie had, in 1932, also already published his own diagnosis of the English theatre's current malaise, *Theatre Prospect*, which sketched his ambitious manifesto for its future. Sensing the threat posed by the encroachment of the radio and the cinema, Guthrie argued that the theatre needed to rediscover its own distinctiveness as an artform and to redefine its place within contemporary society. Attacking the dominance of 'bourgeois' naturalism, and embracing 'a reaction from rationalism, a reaction from [the] bourgeoisie', he claimed that what was now needed was a 'break with naturalism' whose implications were both theatrically and culturally revolutionary: 'invading every department of our civilisation with incalculable results, turning all our existing notions and existing institutions topsy-turvy, ending for ever the theatre as we know it, or giving to it another renascence, with another Shakespeare' (Guthrie 1932: 62, 48, 50).

This seemed to be in tune with then-current thinking at the Old Vic: as the organisation's 1929 Annual Report had stated, it was time for the theatre to become 'pre-eminently the place for artistic experiment, even if some eggshells of prejudice have to be smashed in the process' (Rowell 1993: 98). The first phase in Guthrie's Shakespearian work, as represented by his productions at the Old Vic during the 1930s, was characterised by the ingenuity and energy with which he sought to accommodate the spirit of experiment within the solidly Victorian framework of the Old Vic. In a piece for the *Old Vic and Sadler's Wells Magazine* of September–October 1933, Guthrie announced his arrival with news of the scenic reforms that he was about to initiate. Aligning himself, and the Vic, with the moderated and qualified Elizabethanism that Harley Granville Barker had adapted from the more doctrinaire practice of the pioneering revivalist William Poel, Guthrie wrote that the season's permanent setting 'is an attempt to utilize the convention of the Elizabethan stage in a form that can be fitted into the Rococco [sic] framework of the Vic, and that also reflects contemporary taste in its austere simplicity of line and surface' (Guthrie 1933: 3). Designed by leading modernist architect Wells Coates, who was an enthusiastic subscriber to the Le Courbusier *machine à habiter* aesthetic, this was a purposefully functional rather than decorative, non-representational set, intended to facilitate speed and flexibility, to free the plays from period specificity and to liberate the imagination. In the event, however, though the set was 'distinctly handsome' it was also 'wildly obtrusive . . . a powerful, stridently irrelevant competitor for the audiences' attention': 'Painted pinky-grey for *Twelfth Night*, our opening production, it completely dominated the evening and suggested not Illyria but a fancy-dress ball on a pink battleship' (Guthrie 1959: 109). Still, it was relatively inexpensive, enabling Guthrie to allocate the funds that would usually have been spent on scenery to the costumes; more controversially, it allowed him to engage as the season's main attraction the Hollywood actor Charles Laughton, currently starring in the hit Alexander Korda-directed biopic *The Private Life of Henry VIII*. This was a move that inevitably aroused the suspicions of the legendarily parsimonious Baylis, not only on the grounds that Laughton was an American film star who had never previously played Shakespeare, but also because it appeared to contradict the long-standing company ethos of the 'People's Theatre'. The Shakespeare productions of the 1933–4 season were *Twelfth Night, Henry VIII, Measure for Measure*, *The Tempest* and *Macbeth*, all directed by Guthrie; Laughton was something of an embarrassment as both Macbeth and Prospero, although his Angelo was later praised by J.C. Trewin as 'like a great sinister cat' (Rossi 1977: 31). Perhaps unsurprisingly, the only real success was *Henry VIII*, in which Laughton reprised his film performance of the King, and Guthrie craftily recycled the sets and costumes that Charles Ricketts had designed for Lewis Casson's production for the Empire Theatre nine years previously.

Guthrie's rather inept handling of the inevitably bitter and very public spat between Baylis and Laughton that brought the 1933–4 season to a close was one of the factors that led to his not being re-engaged for the following year; as he also observed, the 'old guard of Old Vic supporters' had not been impressed by the limited reforms that he had attempted to introduce: 'This may be clever but it's not our Shakespeare' (Guthrie 1959: 115). Nonetheless, after a brief spell in the commercial theatre in which he honed his talent for choreography, light comedy and for tough handling of star performers, Guthrie returned to the Old Vic at the beginning for the 1936–7 season, to direct *Love's Labour's Lost, Twelfth Night, Henry V* and *Hamlet*. Once again risking the wrath of the stalwart supporters of the People's Theatre, he declared in the *Old Vic and Sadler's Wells Magazine* of September–October 1937 that 'this season we are hitching our wagon to two stars': namely, Edith Evans and Laurence Olivier, to play Hamlet and Henry V. The Guthrie–Olivier *Hamlet* marked a turning point for both actor and director. In some ways, this was a conventional enough production along the lines that Guthrie had already defined for his Shakespeare work: it was fast-paced, staged on a schematic structure of rostra, ramps, levels and stairs, and noted for its fluent handling of public set-pieces; Guthrie's mastery of large group scenes, exercised in particular through his invention of individualised and idiosyncratic business for supernumeraries, was well established. More unexpected, given that the definitive image of Hamlet of its time was the that of exquisitely lyrical and reflective John Gielgud, was Olivier's prince: a man of action, an athletic, restlessly mobile, rampantly masculine figure whose command of the stage was absolute. According to Guthrie and Olivier, however, the production, and Olivier's portrayal, were underpinned by a theoretical perspective that, insofar as it indicated a willingness to engage with advanced thinking that typified the modernist avant-garde, revealed both to be in advance of their time. Taking advice from the leading British disciple of Freud (and author of the 1923 essay 'Hamlet and Oedipus'), Dr Ernest Jones, they accordingly attempted to put into action a fully-fledged Oedipal portrayal of Hamlet; as Olivier subsequently recalled, this was depicted through 'an impressive array of symptoms: spectacular mood swings, cruel treatment of his love, and above all a hopeless inability to pursue the course required of him', as well as in a 'weakness for dramatics' which 'would be reasonable if the dramatics spurred him to action, but unfortunately they help him to delay it' (Olivier 1982: 79). The Oedipal angle was not generally noticed by the reviewers at the time, and it would be for posterity to expose the interconnections between Guthrie's desire for the disclosures afford by the non-illusionist, non-pictorial stage and his growing preoccupation with the potential of psychoanalysis both to excavate the archaeology of human sexuality and belief and to map the deep structure of classic dramaturgy (Shaughnessy 2002: 79–146). In the first instance, psychoanalysis encouraged Guthrie to probe what he later called 'hidden motives' in Shakespeare (1965: 72–109). In the 1937–8 season, Guthrie's and Olivier's shared interests led to a Jones-influenced *Othello* in which the latter's Iago was envisaged as 'subconsciously in love with Othello' and thus compelled 'to destroy him'; unfortunately, there was 'not the slightest chance' of Ralph Richardson as Othello 'entertaining this idea' (Olivier 1982: 82), and the overall result was, as Guthrie put it, 'a ghastly, boring hash' (1959: 173). Nearly thirty years later, in 1964, Guthrie's *Coriolanus* at the Nottingham Playhouse introduced a semi-Oedipal homoerotic reading of the relationship between Caius Martius and Tullus Aufidius, as, 'in a relationship somewhere between a son and a lover' the former 'throws himself on the mercy' of the latter (Guthrie 1965: 92). Yet, Guthrie was also profoundly, even brutally, intolerant of character-centred psychologising, and of the indulgent emoting and over-internalised playing that he associated with actorly egotism, as is evident from a reported incident from rehearsals for the 1956 *The Merchant of Venice*: 'Down on the stage the young actress playing Jessica was lying back enjoying her work . . . Guthrie rose from the auditorium, marched down to the stage and, reaching the actress, he gave her a near karate chop on the bare leg and spoke in fury: "You're feeling it, you silly little bitch! Your business is to make *them* feel it! . . . Do it again!" ' (Forsyth 1976: 255). In his productions of the 1930s, Guthrie demonstrated his mastery of the theatrical idioms which he could not take entirely seriously, resulting, for example, in a *Henry V* in 1937 whose straightforwardly rousing patriotism overrode the pacifist scruples with which Guthrie and Olivier had approached it, and (opening on Boxing Day 1938) a pantomime *A Midsummer Night's Dream* that took the Victorian staging tradition beyond parody, introducing a *corps de ballet* of gauze and gossamer-clad flying fairies directed by Ninette de Valois, luscious painted scenery, and the full Mendelssohn score. In 1938, amidst a cultural climate dominated by a sense of the growing inevitability of war, Guthrie returned to *Hamlet* with Alec Guinness in the title role, in a production which was notable not only for its quietly understated prince but also for its pointed, politically conscious, use of Ruritanian almost-modern dress, in which the chilling martial spectacle of the Ghost in Kaiser Wilhelm battledress was counterpointed by the poignancy of the everyday ordinariness of mourners gathered under umbrellas at Ophelia's funeral.

Of all of Guthrie productions of the 1930s, however, it was the 1937 *Hamlet* that would provide the most significant, not only for its initiation of an Oedipal performance tradition, which was iconically commemorated in Olivier's self-directed 1948 film of the play, but also as a result of what happened when the production was performed at Kronberg Castle, Helsingor, in Denmark some six months after its London run. At the invitation of the Danish tourist board, the Old Vic company took the production, as the first of a series of annual open-air productions in the courtyard of the sixteenth-century castle reimagined by Shakespeare as Hamlet's Elsinore, to be performed before an audience of 2,500 that included members of the Danish royal family. The set of the London production was replicated and a supporting cast of Danish officer cadets recruited; floodlighting and sound amplification was installed, and what had in the confines of the Old Vic been experienced as a dynamically, if shabbily, intimate experience was reconceived as a spectacle, and an exercise in cultural ambassadorship, on a massive scale. On its first night, however, the production fell foul of the one element that could not be controlled (but which could have been readily predicted): the notoriously volatile Danish weather. Hours before the show was due to open, 'rain was coming down in bellropes'; going ahead was impossible, but so too was cancellation. Momentously, according to Guthrie's own account, the decision was taken to relocate the performance in the ballroom of the nearby Marienlyst hotel: 'There was no stage; but we would play in the middle of the hall with the audience seated all around as in a circus. The phrase hadn't yet been invented, but this would be theatre in the round' (1959: 170). Hastily reblocked under Oliver's direction, the performance was an adrenalin-fuelled minor miracle of creative improvisation, and, as a 'plucky gesture' (*Daily Mail*, 3 June 1937), it was gratefully and appreciatively received. But in terms of Guthrie's own personal mythology, and for the proponents of the open-stage movement that he followed in his wake, it was a pivotal moment. The contrast between this ramshackle, improvised, yet thrillingly intense encounter and the event that took place the following night in the castle courtyard, where a *Hamlet* awash with arc-light, boomed through tannoys and fleshed out with massed crowd scenes, must have seemed as much cultural rally as theatrical performance, could not have been more marked; forty years after the event, the critic J.C. Trewin said that it was 'the most exciting performance of *Hamlet* that I've ever seen' (Rossi 1977: 34), while Olivier, similarly, recalled how witnesses of the ballroom *Hamlet* would often claim that 'it was the best thing they'd ever seen' (1986: 55). Of all of the factors contributing to the excitement, the key ones, for Guthrie, were spatial and architectural; the experience confirmed his dissatisfaction with the proscenium stage, in that 'at its best moments' the scratch performance in the ballroom connected the audience, the actors and the play in a 'more logical, satisfactory and effective way than ever can be achieved in a theatre of what is still regarded as orthodox design' (1959: 172).

It would be a decade before Guthrie would next find the opportunity to investigate this relationship in more detail, although the war years did present him with the challenge of developing a peripatetic, and more genuinely populist, form of non-traditional Shakespeare in the shape of the productions toured by a small expeditionary force from the Old Vic around the working men's clubs and cinemas of the mining villages of South Wales between 1941 and 1943. Invited to direct a show for the second Edinburgh International Festival of Music and Art in 1948, Guthrie chose an obscure dialect Scots sixteenth-century Morality play by Sir David Lindsay, *Ane Satire of the Thrie Estaites*, and, as a venue, the Assembly Hall of the Kirk of Scotland. For Guthrie, the seven-hour drama (edited down to a two hours for the production) provided the perfect pretext kind to test his emerging theory of theatre, in that 'scene after scene seemed absolutely unplayable on a proscenium stage, almost meaningless in terms of "dramatic illusion" '; the performance space, consisting of a wooden platform with audience seated on three sides was 'a tryout . . . a first sketch for the sort of Elizabethan stage' that he 'had long hoped, somehow and somewhere, to establish' (Guthrie 1959: 275, 277). Perhaps the ecclesiastical setting also resonated with Guthrie's growing interest in the 'ritual' aspect of performance: believing that 'the aim of theatre should be to transport its audience, but not by illusion', he found that the audiences of *An Satire* 'focused upon the actors in the brightly lit acting area' against a background of 'dimly lit rows of people similarly focused on the actors'; in such a state, 'you are rapt, transported; in that condition you lose almost all sense of identity, of time and place' (Guthrie 1959: 279–80). Amiably described by director Alan Schneider as 'a marvellously counterpointed blend of *Henry V* and the Marx Brothers' (Rossi 1970: vii–viii), *An Satire* was the hit of the Festival: given the almost occult force that its polemicists have sometimes attributed to the open stage, it is worth remembering that its success – as in all of Guthrie's best work – was a product not only of the liberating potentialities of non-proscenium space but also of Guthrie's distinctive ability to animate and energise it.

Finally, in 1952, came the chance of a lifetime. In the provincial Canadian town of Stratford, Ontario, the businessman Tom Patterson decided to capitalise upon the borrowed glory of his home town's second-hand affiliations with Shakespeare's birthplace, by conceiving the idea of an annual Shakespeare festival to be staged in a new, purpose-built theatre. Out of the blue, he telephoned Guthrie inviting him to act as adviser on the project, an invitation that quickly led to Guthrie agreeing to direct the festival. Guthrie managed to persuade the festival planners that the theatre ought to be modelled on the Elizabethan playhouse: as he rather disingenuously put it,

> we were discussing the building from a strictly practical point of view, and I was merely suggesting that the best practical results would be got from a stage which closely conformed to what is known of the stage for which Shakespeare wrote, and by relating the audience to the stage in a manner which approximated to the Elizabethan manner.
>
> (Guthrie 1959: 284)

Importantly, Guthrie was seeking not to replicate the physical structure of the early modern stage (as had his predecessors William Poel and Nugent Monck, and as would his successor Sam Wanamaker in Shakespeare's Globe on London's Bankside) but to fashion a space in which the fabrication of illusion was irrelevant, one that would bring actors and audience into close proximity. Co-designed by Guthrie with Tanya Moiseiwitsch, who had established a partnership with the director at the Old Vic a decade earlier, and the Toronto-based architect Robert Fairfield, the resulting festival stage was a hybrid of Greek arena and Elizabethan playhouse, a modernist machine which, director and designer agreed, determined to 'eschew *Ye Olde*': 'while conforming to the conventions of the Elizabethan in practicalities, it should not present a pseudo-Elizabethan appearance' (Guthrie 1959: 286). In the same way as Guthrie's direction artfully skimmed over the local detail of the text in order to reveal not only its larger patterning, phrasing and orchestration but also its archetypal overtones, his and Moiseiwitsch's stage design aimed to suggest the deep structure of non-illusionist dramaturgy, not to replicate the physical form of the early modern playhouse. At its centre is a tiered polygonal platform, surrounded by an arc of audience seating in which no spectator is more than fifteen rows away from the stage, and from which radiate vomitoria designed for entrances and exits through the auditorium; upstage, a structure of pillars, stairs and balcony provides the equivalent of Greek *skene* and Elizabethan tiring house. For the first two seasons, performances took place under canvas; in 1957 the stage acquired a roof and was enclosed within a permanent structure; subject to a few minor adjustments to the placement of the pillars, this arrangement has remained in place to the present.

For the theatre's opening, Guthrie directed a sharply contrasting pair of plays, between them calculated to serve as vehicles for the English stars (Alec Guinness and Irene Worth), to provide opportunities for large-scale ensemble work and to show off the capabilities of the new stage: *Richard III* and *All's Well that Ends Well*. The first of these, favoured by Guthrie for its 'strong thread of melodrama' (1959: 286), exemplified its director's ritual vision: ceremonial, and hypnotically incantatory, this was a show which made use of an extravagant palette of crimson, black and gold, huge looming crucifixes and glittering halberds, fluttering banners and tolling bells, ghosts rising from trapdoors, a torchlit funeral procession, armies sweeping through the auditorium and across the stage. As sheer visual spectacle, it was breathtaking, and it was anchored by Guinness's diabolic Richard, who gave his first speech in the manner of a fascist demagogue from the balcony and met his end rolling off the stage platform and virtually into the laps of the front row. *All's Well that Ends Well* was a riskier venture: rarely seen on the British stage and never previously staged on the North American continent, this was a play whose sexual frankness and ambiguous, even bitter, comic tone seemed an unlikely choice for a festive opening. Nonetheless, it not only afforded Guthrie's other lead, Irene Worth, a plum role in the part of Helena but also the opportunity to complement the baroque medievalism of *Richard III* with a staging revelling in a modernity that challenged the presumption that the Stratford Festival was an exercise in antiquarian revivalism. Costumed, predominantly, in the high fashions of the European *fin-de-siècle*, with brightly coloured ballgowns, black tails and tunics, where Guinness's sickening King of France languished in an antique bathchair (which had to be specially imported by England, as nothing so iconically Old Worldly could be sourced on the American continent) until brought to his feet by Helena's healing art, *All's Well that Ends Well* inhabited a Ruritanian world whose rigid hierarchies and codes of manners, like the rhymed formalities of the text, 'lent themselves to the devices of dance' (Styan 1977: 197). For its reviewers and audiences, this was exciting, new and liberating, but it had its potential disadvantages too. Guthrie's productions were well known for their relentless, sweepingly choreographed mobility; on the Stratford Festival stage, the presence of the surrounding audience made perpetual motion virtually mandatory, in order to prevent performers from masking each other. As Dennis Kennedy notes, the restlessness that this engendered may have been 'acceptable and even desirable in many comic or ceremonial scenes' but was 'occasionally distracting in the quiet or intense moments' (1993: 161). Guthrie returned to Stratford for the next two seasons: in 1954 to direct a nakedly populist *The Taming of the Shrew*, staged as a Wild West show in which Petruchio made his entrance to his wedding on a pantomime horse, and, in 1955, a sombre *The Merchant of Venice* which powerfully confronted anti-Semitism, notably in its masterly handling of Shylock's final exit, where, as actor William Hutt recalled, 'everybody booed and roared and spit and baited this Jew, there was a sudden hush, and *one* person on stage started to cry . . . That was Shylock's exit, that man crying' (Rossi 1977: 184–5).

Although he accepted the invitation to direct *Twelfth Night* in 1957, Guthrie's association with the Stratford Festival was now pretty well over; his next major theatre project was to launch a bid to establish a repertory theatre in the USA. The Stratford venture had been touted by its founder not only as an innovation in theatre architecture but also as a step towards a new Canadian theatre industry (although Guthrie would have been well aware of the limitations inherent in a seasonal operation whose economic and artistic priorities were necessarily shaped by the rhythms of tourism and cultural pilgrimage); the campaign for an American repertory theatre was driven by the wish to create an alternative to the Broadway commercial system, in which serious and classical drama could be fostered in the context of a permanent company organisation. In an advertisement in the *New York Times* (30 September 1959), Guthrie called for expressions of interest; seven cities responded (including Chicago, Detroit and San Francisco), and Guthrie eventually settled on Minneapolis/Saint Paul, which had the advantage of a large university community, as the home of the new theatre. As at Stratford, Guthrie used the opportunity to build a performance space on the open-stage principles which, thanks in part to his own tireless advocacy, were becoming increasingly adopted in the construction of new theatres across Europe and America, as, for example, in the Chichester Festival Theatre and the Delacorte Theater in New York, both of which opened in 1962, the Mark Taper Forum, Los Angeles (1965), the Sheffield Crucible (1971) and the National Theatre's Olivier auditorium (1976), as well as the myriad smaller-scale provincial arts centres and performance venues that commenced operations in the 1960s and 1970s. Similar in many respects to the festival stage, the Tyrone Guthrie Theater in Minneapolis consisted of an asymmetrical polygonal platform with audience seating for 1,441 on three sides; there was, however, no balcony feature but a removable back wall through which items of scenery could be trucked on and off. The opening production this time was *Hamlet*, and it was performed by a company that included both veterans of the American Shakespearian stage, such as Jessica Tandy as Gertrude, and a complete newcomer to Shakespeare, the young George Grizzard, as Hamlet. Spotted by Guthrie in the original Broadway production on Edward Albee's *Who's Afraid of Virginia Woolf?* the previous year, Grizzard was the production's major discovery: a charismatically youthful and contemporary, all-American figure at the centre of a staging which, though generally accounted modern dress, was eclectically twentieth-century in its range of reference; as the Toronto *Globe and Mail* (9 May 1963) reported, 'the uniforms are splendidly Teutonic, the ladies' travelling clothes quite Edwardian, but Claudius and Gertrude are impeccable in evening dress, Laertes rebellious in a trench coat'. Although hailed by the critic of the *Boston Globe* (9 May 1963) as 'the most remarkable production of "Hamlet" the contemporary theatre is likely to see', there was, in truth, little that was new or particularly innovative in this production: the case for the open stage had, as far as the civic repertory theatres of the anglophone world were concerned, been conclusively made, while Guthrie's staging, though as fluent, inventive and idiosyncratic as ever, showed signs that, in his Shakespearian work at least, the director was content to replay and recycle past achievements, and to quote, or repeat, himself, and (as with the 'tennis rackets and umbrellas' spotted by the critic of the *Minneapolis Tribune* [8 May 1963], which seemed to have been lifted straight from the 1938 Old Vic production). Guthrie may have looked forward in 1953 to a 'ritual' theatre in which we might 'purge our minds of triviality, and

. . . live for an instant at our highest imaginative peak' (Guthrie et al. 1953: 120), but, once they had become accepted as routine, it became evident that the longer-term benefits of eradicating the picture frame and distributing the spectators around the stage, especially in the hands of directors less gifted than Guthrie, were rather more prosaic, and perhaps more disappointing. As one reviewer of *Hamlet* at Minneapolis rather flatly summarised, 'the three-quarter arena theatre is handsome and has good sightlines' (*Variety*, 8 May 1963); its greatest strength lay not its capacity to accommodate ritual but to expose the kind of nuances that would subsequently become associated with the studio-scale Shakespeare of the 1970s: as the *Minneapolis Tribune* reported, 'Gertrude . . . enters in the wedding finery in Act One. She looks at Hamlet; Hamlet looks back; his eyes drop; her eyes drop. The situation is revealed as it could not be on the picture frame stage'. Ironically, the 1963 *Hamlet*, as one of the less consequential of Guthrie's Shakespeare productions, is one of his better documented, being the subject of Alfred Rossi's *Minneapolis Rehearsals* (1970), a volume that includes a detailed log of the rehearsal process (the author played Rosencrantz), a facsimile of the production promptbook, copious photographs and a selection of the reviews, from which the preceding comments are excerpted (Guthrie's direction of the 1953 Stratford Festival was itself the subject of a National Film Board of Canada documentary feature, *The Stratford Adventure* [1954], which contains illuminating footage of the director at work and *Richard III* and *All's Well that Ends Well* in performance, was reissued on video in the 1990s and is now available on DVD; the only one of Guthrie's stage productions to have been filmed in its entirety was his 1955 Stratford *Oedipus Rex*).

Guthrie continued to direct Shakespeare at Minneapolis and elsewhere during the 1960s: *Henry V* and *Richard III* at the Tyrone Guthrie Theater in 1964 and 1965 respectively, *Coriolanus* at the Nottingham Playhouse (1963; the cast included a young Ian McKellen as Tullus Aufidius), *Measure for Measure* at the Bristol Old Vic (1966) and *All's Well that Ends Well* in Melbourne (1970). But these were largely reworkings of productions of plays that (*Coriolanus* excepted) he had directed before; indeed, it is widely acknowledged that the most revelatory, and most heartfelt, work of his last decade was in his productions of Chekhov and of Greek tragedy at Minneapolis: *Three Sisters* (1963), *The Cherry Orchard* (1965) and *Uncle Vanya* (1969), and the epic adaptation of Aeschylus, *The House of Atreus* (1967). Michael Langham, Guthrie's protégé and successor at both the Stratford Festival (from 1956 to 1967) and the Tyrone Guthrie Theater (1971 to 1977), was frank in his assessment: 'It wasn't as if a great man had come to Minneapolis and made something fantastic happen, which is what I'd felt at Stratford. I had been replacing God at Stratford. There was none of that in

Minneapolis . . . I didn't think much of any of the Shakespeare productions he did during the Guthrie Theater years' (Rossi 1977: 284). Rather than seeing this, as some have done, as evidence of Guthrie's personal decline, it is possible to draw a different moral, and one which is perhaps at odds with some of the received wisdom about the post-war open-stage movement which Guthrie is credited with pioneering. Far from providing the expected solution to the problem of staging Shakespeare in the modern age, according to the principle that 'a play can be best presented by getting as near as possible to the manner in which the author envisaged it' (Guthrie 1959: 301), the open stages at Stratford and Minneapolis, founded as they were on sites of cultural contradiction between new world and residually old-world Shakespeares, had the unintended consequence of depositing the drama into an indeterminate, vaguely mid-Atlantic void, in which, as Denis Salter describes it, 'a low-key, methodical and psychologically nuanced kind of modernity was grafted onto a gesturally and vocally heightened, externalizing quasi-Elizabethan kind of theatricality' (1996: 122).

For Langham, and for many other commentators, Guthrie's best Shakespearian productions were not the ones that took place in the theatre of his realised dreams but those mounted on the picture-frame stages which he ostensibly despised: *Henry VIII* (Shakespeare Memorial Theatre (SMT), Stratford-upon-Avon, 1949), *Troilus and Cressida* (Old Vic, 1956), and *All's Well that Ends Well* (SMT, 1959). Guthrie's objections to the proscenium stage were avowedly social and political as well as practical and artistic (somewhat imprecisely, he characterised its division of stage and auditorium as indicative of a 'social chasm', epitomised by the 'iron [safety] curtain, now a world-famous political symbol of separation or *apartheid* [1959: 93]), and his championing of the arena stage was informed by a strong spirit of egalitarianism, as well as hopes for democratic participation and ritual engagement, that harked idealistically back to an imagined Greek example. Yet, the Guthrie who wrote that the 'insuperable problems posed by the architecture' at Stratford-upon-Avon and London compelled directors to resort to 'elaboration of spectacle', so that, 'to give the public something for its money, a Pageant is mounted to the accompaniment of a Shakespearian text' (1959: 192) was himself not only the supreme maestro of such spectacle and pageantry, but also a director whose work seems to have been profoundly energised by the limitations that the picture frame imposed. Almost in spite of himself, and itself, Guthrie's Shakespeare work in the 1940s and 1950s (and his productions of other early modern dramatists) was at its most creatively and politically acute when it inhabited conditions with which it was at odds. *Henry VIII*, in 1949, was remembered by the actor Robert Hardy (who played Griffith) as 'a thoroughly political piece' by a director who 'had an extraordinary comprehension of power politics': 'He made all the political scenes . . . absolutely electric' (Rossi 1977: 138). There was still more than enough pageantry and horseplay to send the Stratford audiences home happy, and Guthrie revived the production at the Old Vic in 1953 to mark the June coronation of Queen Elizabeth II; any suspicion that this might have aroused that the pacifist, anti-authoritarian Guthrie had turned into monarchist, militarist and patriot were dispelled three years later by production at the same theatre of the rarely seen *Troilus and Cressida*. Opening against the ominous background of the military build-up to the Suez Crisis, which at the end of 1956 would culminate in national humiliation, this was a darkly satirical, starkly anti-war reading, which habited the Greeks and Trojans in 'the fashions of 1913, Edwardian England and the Kaiser's Germany', signifying 'the last time when nations could treat war as a game' (Styan 1977: 203). For Kenneth Tynan, who would soon after proclaim the dawn of a new theatrical era with the premiere of a similarly disillusioned response to the condition of post-imperial Britain, John Osborne's *Look Back in Anger* at the Royal Court, Guthrie's production perfectly captured the insolent decadence and casual brutality of the English aristocracy in decline: 'His Trojans are glass-smashing cavalry officers who might pass for British were it not for the freedom with which they mention Helen's name in the mess' (*Observer*, 8 April 1956). The 1950s was also the decade of his stunning, epic *Tamburlaine*: first, with Donald Wolfit at the Old Vic in 1951–2, and subsequently, rather less successfully, with Anthony Quayle in New York in 1956.

The culmination of this, the final genuinely creative decade in Guthrie's Shakespeare work was his extraordinary *All's Well that Ends Well* at the Shakespeare Memorial Theatre in 1959. In some respects a revamping of the 1953 Stratford, Ontario production, this was initially set in the same Ruritanian, middle-European milieu of evening dress and formal dance; but whereas the costumed and choreographed bodies of the performers had provided the primary source of visual satisfaction upon the scenery-free platform at Stratford, here Guthrie's cast of thirty-six (which incidentally included both Vanessa Redgrave and Diana Rigg in walk-on parts) weaved through a landscape of leaf-strewn arbours, vast, echoing ballrooms and cramped prostitutes' boudoirs, a world, sumptuously designed by Moiseiwitsch, that evoked Shaw (and *My Fair Lady*), Wilde, Chekhov, P.G. Wodehouse, Ivor Novello, the cartoon world of Giles and *The Merry Widow*. More controversially, Guthrie elaborated upon the contemporary references that he had introduced in the earlier production, going for anachronistic broke in the scenes set in the French camp by costuming his troops in the berets, khaki and baggy comedy shorts of the British Eighth Army division known as the Desert Rats, circa 1941; and by expanding the Florentine Duke's review of the troops in Act III,

Scene 1, which in the text consists of a mere twenty lines, into an extended sequence of sight gags and pratfalls played amidst the ruins of an abandoned viaduct, involving an erratic PA system, treacherous microphone leads, wayward flags and, for the Duke himself, a lethally funny impersonation of a white Afrikaaner (identified by some reviewers with the former South African Prime Minster General Smuts, notoriously the antagonist of Mahatma Gandhi, but perhaps equally readable as an emblematic incarnation of the apartheid state). For many critics, this was Shakespeare couched in terms of the Crazy Gang at the London Palladium and hit television comedy of conscript life *The Army Game*: most agreed that this was an inspired rehabilitation rather than an outrageous imposition. Perhaps, too, given the violence and the bungling that accompanied the 1950s British history of decolonisation in Cyprus, Western Africa and elsewhere, there was a more bitter edge to the military comedy than the reviewers cared to recognise or admit. Described by Harold Hobson in the *Sunday Times* (26 April 1959) as 'one of the best productions that Stratford has ever done', *All's Well that Ends Well* was part of the last Stratford season to operate under the artistic directorship of Glen Byam Shaw, a season that also saw Tony Richardson direct Paul Robeson at Othello, Peter Hall's productions of *A Midsummer Night's Dream* with Charles Laughton as Bottom, and of *Coriolanus* starring Laurence Olivier, and Shaw's *King Lear*, with Laughton in the title role. Looking to the future of Shakespearian production at Stratford-upon-Avon, *All's Well that Ends Well* offered a life-affirming combination of solemnity and mischief, operatic sweep and exquisite detail, formality and vaudeville vulgarity, that the work of the decade that followed would struggle to emulate.

Guthrie has been celebrated for his achievement as the globe-trotting founding father of the open-stage movement, and in his influence in this respect continues to be felt worldwide: as recently as 2006, the Royal Shakespeare Company finally, albeit temporarily, fulfilled his dream of transforming the theatre-going experience at Stratford (Antony Quayle reported that Guthrie dismissed the Memorial Theatre as 'a dreadfully old-fashioned theatre' fit only for 'old-fashioned work', and urged him to 'Push it into the Avon!' [Rossi 1977: 26])) with the opening of the Courtyard, a 1,048-seater thrust-stage auditorium, in which over 80 per cent of the audience are no more than 10 metres from the stage, designed to house the company's main-stage work during the period of the Royal Shakespeare Theatre's refurbishment. But, as this essay has sought to emphasise, his work within the decaying apparatus of the bourgeous theatre which he affected to disdain in many ways rivals and perhaps even surpasses the work that was staged in settings that carried the hopes of those wished, in vain, to supersede it. Guthrie's presence was also registered more indirectly in the work of the directors he influenced, notably

Peter Hall, whose debt to the man he dubbed the 'sad, mad Don Quixote of the English theatre' (1987) was lasting and profound, and Laurence Olivier, whose Shakespeare films in different ways bear the imprint of their director's mentor, as manifested in the Oedipal introspection and rampant athleticism of his *Hamlet*, as well as in the dazzling stylistic and tonal shifts, the combination of heroic rhetoric and low clowning, that characterised his *Henry V*. 'Thought it was vulgar', was Guthrie's verdict on the latter film; as Olivier observed, this was pretty funny, given that he had 'copied outrageously' from Guthrie's production (Rossi 1977: 96–7). But then, as Olivier also said (Rossi 1977: 102) if anyone was entitled to pronounce such a judgment, it was Tyrone Guthrie, 'inimitable when he was on form' – 'He was a bloody genius'.

Chronology

1932 *Love's Labour's Lost*, Westminster Theatre, London
1933 *Richard II*, Shakespeare Memorial Theatre, Stratford-upon-Avon
1933 *Measure for Measure*, Old Vic, London
1937 *Hamlet*, Old Vic
1937 *Henry V*, Old Vic
1937 *A Midsummer Night's Dream*, Old Vic
1938 *Hamlet*, Old Vic
1941 *King John*, Old Vic
1949 *Henry VIII*, Shakespeare Memorial Theatre
1952 *Timon of Athens*, Old Vic
1953 *Richard III*, Festival Theatre, Stratford, Ontario
1953 *All's Well that Ends Well*, Festival Theatre
1954 *The Taming of the Shrew*, Festival Theatre
1955 *The Merchant of Venice*, Festival Theatre
1956 *Troilus and Cressida*, Old Vic
1959 *The Merchant of Venice*, Habimah Theatre, Tel Aviv
1959 *All's Well that Ends Well*, Shakespeare Memorial Theatre
1963 *Hamlet*, Tyrone Guthrie Theater, Minneapolis
1963 *Coriolanus*, Nottingham Playhouse
1964 *Henry V*, Tyrone Guthrie Theater

Bibliography

Davies, Robertson, Tyrone Guthrie, Boyd Neel and Tanya Moisewitsch (1955) *Thrice the Brinded Cat Hath Mew'd: A Record of the Stratford Shakespearean Festival in Canada, 1955*, Toronto: Clarke, Irwin.

Forsyth, James (1976) *Tyrone Guthrie: A Biography*, London: Hamish Hamilton.

Guthrie, Tyrone (1932) *Theatre Prospect*, London: Wishart.

—— (1933) 'To Introduce Myself', *Old Vic and Sadler's Wells Magazine*, September–October.
—— (1959) *A Life in the Theatre*, London: Hamish Hamilton.
—— (1964) *A New Theatre*, New York: McGraw-Hill.
—— (1965) *In Various Directions: A View of Theatre*, London: Michael Joseph.
—— (1971) *Tyrone Guthrie On Acting*, London: Studio Vista.
Guthrie, Tyrone, Robertson Davies and Grant MacDonald (1953) *Renown at Stratford: A Record of the Shakespeare Festival in Canada, 1953*, Toronto: Clarke, Irwin.
—— (1954) *Twice Have the Trumpets Sounded: A Record of the Stratford Shakespearean Festival, 1954*, Toronto: Clarke, Irwin.
Hall, Peter (1987) Foreword to Tyrone Guthrie, *A Life in the Theatre*, London: Columbus.
Howard, Tony (2000) 'Blood on the Bright Young Things: Shakespeare in the 1930s', in Clive Barker and Maggie B. Gale (eds) *British Theatre between the Wars, 1918–1939*, Cambridge: Cambridge University Press, pp. 135–61.
Kennedy, Dennis (1993) *Looking at Shakespeare: A Visual History of Twentieth-Century Performance*, Cambridge: Cambridge University Press.
Olivier, Laurence (1982) *Confessions of an Actor*, London: Weidenfeld & Nicholson.
—— (1986) *On Acting*, London: Weidenfeld & Nicholson.
Rossi, Alfred (1970) *Minneapolis Rehearsals: Tyrone Guthrie Directs Hamlet*, Berkeley, Calif.: University of California Press.
—— (1977) *Astonish Us in the Morning: Tyrone Guthrie Remembered*, London: Hutchinson.
Rowell, George (1993) *The Old Vic Theatre: A History*, Cambridge: Cambridge University Press.
Salter, Denis (1996) 'Acting Shakespeare in Postcolonial Space', in James C. Bulman (ed.) *Shakespeare, Theory and Performance*, London: Routledge, pp. 111–32.
Shaughnessy, Robert (2002) *The Shakespeare Effect: A History of Twentieth Century Performance*, Basingstoke: Palgrave Macmillan.
Styan, J.L. (1977) *The Shakespeare Revolution: Criticism and Performance in the Twentieth Century*, Cambridge: Cambridge University Press.
Wilson, John Dover (1962) *Shakespeare's Happy Comedies*, London: Faber & Faber.

About the author

Robert Shaughnessy is Professor of Theatre at the University of Kent. His publications include *Representing Shakespeare: England, History and the RSC* (1994) and *The Shakespeare Effect: A History of Twentieth Century Performance* (2002), as well as numerous articles and essays on twentieth century and contemporary dramatists and theatre practitioners; he has edited *Shakespeare in Performance: Contemporary Critical Essays* (2000) and *The Cambridge Companion to Shakespeare and Popular Culture* (2007). He is currently writing on Tyrone Guthrie for the Lives of the Great Shakespeareans series.

9
PETER HALL
Peter Holland

In *Next*, a short animated film made by Barry Purves in 1989 for the Aardman company, a theatre director is sat in the stalls when William Shakespeare himself comes on to audition. In a mimed routine of increasing virtuosity and frenetic activity, using a life-size doll and a variety of props, Shakespeare alludes briefly, at times clearly and at others opaquely, towards his entire corpus of plays, ending as Jupiter in *Cymbeline* in an apotheosis of his glory. The theatre director, initially bored, too engrossed in reading a copy of *Peter Hall's Diaries* even to look at the stage, becomes transfigured, not only attentive but also suddenly haloed, finally seen with angel's wings, and given, as he guffaws with laughter, the film's only words other than its opening call of 'Next!': 'Lord, what fools these mortals be!' (*A Midsummer Night's Dream*, Act III, Scene 2, line 115). The theatre director is not only reading a book by Peter Hall; unmistakably he looks like Peter Hall, probably the only theatre director whose face might be recognised by the audience for an animated short. By the end, Hall becomes both St Peter to the divine Shakespeare and Puck to Shakespeare's Oberon. Peter Hall, the film suggests, has been given a special position in the world of Shakespeare production, a figure uniquely allowed access to Shakespeare himself, the favoured disciple of the master, the rock on whom the church of Shakespeare has been founded.

Comic films, of course, enjoy their own hyperbole. But Peter Hall's work on Shakespeare and for Shakespeare over more than fifty years might reasonably be seen as reducing the extent of this exaggeration, if not exactly verifying it as straightforwardly true. It is not simply the long list of acclaimed productions in each decade since his career began: say, *Coriolanus* with Laurence Olivier in Stratford in 1959, *Hamlet* with David Warner at Stratford in 1965, *The Tempest* with John Gielgud in 1973, the group of late plays as his farewell to the National Theatre in 1988, *Hamlet* for the Peter Hall Company in the West End in 1994, or *As You Like It* in Bath in 2003. Nor can it be defined solely in terms of the creation of the Royal Shakespeare Company, a step that defined an institutional structure within which Shakespeare production in England would most powerfully be articulated, for no single company has had such a broad international effect on the understanding of Shakespeare in performance as the RSC. Nor is it his undeviating belief in the importance of an ensemble company as the only basis for Shakespeare production. Nor is it contained within his writings about his process of Shakespeare production, the definition both of his own practice and of a systematic approach to Shakespeare's language that he profoundly believes in as the only way to work on the plays, so that his writing about Shakespeare and his productions of Shakespeare dovetail as a single coherent project across his career. Nor can it be understood solely in terms of his consistent denial of the widespread assumption among theatre directors of a necessary, self-preserving gulf between their Shakespeare productions and Shakespeare academics, as if scholars were some kind of inherent danger to theatre productions. Nor, finally, can it be seen through the pervasive extent of his influence on theatre directors, on designers and, above all, on actors, those who have worked with or for him and those who have never been close to his rehearsal room. In the complex combination of all these factors and the equally complex way in which Hall has become the cultural marker of a dominant mode of creating and defending principles of theatrical production, of aesthetic values in performance and of social beliefs in the cultural benefits of classical theatre (and therefore supremely of Shakespeare as the English icon of classical theatre), Peter Hall has fully earned the priestly and saintly accolade Purves jokingly but also sympathetically conferred on him in *Next*.

For Hall, the investigation of the Shakespeare text – and his work has been characterised by a consistent sense of the obligation to mine the text rather than impose on it, appropriate it or dislocate it – is a sustained process in the rehearsal room that begins with word and then moves outwards through line, speech, scene and act to uncover for the actor and then make available for the audience the complete play. The Shakespeare play is, for Hall, an early modern text that negotiates with the present in ways that are not to be limited by an arbitrary definition of narrowly manifested ways in which that negotiation is to be understood, as in, for example, a production that displaces the early modern quality of the text in favour of some chosen rehistoricisation. As he commented in an interview in 1989, 'Unless what's on the stage looks like the language, I simply don't believe it. Ruritanian or modern or eclectic costumes are all very well – I can see why people do that – but if you're speaking Elizabethan English, to me there's always a war between the two' (Berry 1989: 209).

Hall's Shakespeare productions have, from the very beginning, been deeply interconnected with his work on contemporary drama. His English-language premiere in 1955 of Beckett's *Waiting for Godot* (a play he revisited fifty years later) and the long series of the first productions of plays by Harold Pinter resonate with his Shakespeare work. But the sense in which Hall's Beckett and Pinter are aligned with Hall's Shakespeare, in ways that, say, his productions of Peter Shaffer were not, may reside less in their modernity than in their unfailingly intense explorations of language, scene and play as rhythmic forms. Their prose is as metrically exact as Shakespeare's verse, and the revealing of that rhythm (and then the revelling in what has been revealed) in *The Homecoming* in productions in 1965 and 1990 is as exacting a demand on the actors as in *Hamlet*. For Hall, meaning can never be solely a product of the semantic fields of the playwright's vocabulary or the structure of his or her syntax, for it is permanently and undeviatingly intertwined with the metrics of spoken language. To ignore the rhythm of a line is to fail to find the meaning of its words; hence, the extension of implication from line to the discovery of character, plot and scenic form would be appallingly fractured by forgetting the supremacy of line as rhythmic form in Shakespeare's verse or ignoring the ways in which Shakespeare's prose is always non-naturalistic. As Hall teaches in his manual for Shakespeare actors, *Shakespeare's Advice to the Players*, 'On the surface, Shakespeare's prose is easier to speak than his verse. But the actor will mislead himself if he thinks of the prose as a more "natural" representation of ordinary speech. The opposite is true. There is always a formality about Shakespeare's prose' (2003: 43). Finding that formality or that rhythm is the actors' and directors' first task.

The rhythm of Shakespeare's language is for Hall a form of music. In 1969, Hall agreed that, when Georg Solti stepped down in 1971 as Director of the Royal Opera House and Colin Davis took over, Hall would join Davis in a partnership, as artistic director to Davis's music director, spending half the year working on opera productions. For the first time, Covent Garden would have recognised in its institutional form the equal importance of drama and music. In the event, just before the appointment was due to begin, Hall resigned, unable to work with the Board of Covent Garden and the production practices for staging opera there. Over subsequent years, he directed opera frequently and with great delight and success in the very different context of the Glyndebourne Festival Company.

Alone among British theatre directors of the century, Hall has been equally adept and triumphant in the opera house and in classical theatre. There has been a two-way influence in his work with his opera productions, especially of Mozart, explored as complex Shakespearian dramas, and with his Shakespeare productions, for example of three of the late plays in 1988, affected in their visual styles by his experiences directing baroque opera. In large part, though, the exchange is a consequence of his attitude to drama, especially

Shakespeare's plays, as score, a piece of writing containing its voicing and staging in precise rhythms through precise codes, so that plays are viewed as being as complete containers of directions for their performance as an opera's musical score contains all the notes the singers and orchestra will need to perform. As Hall complains, 'Most Shakespearian productions are a symphony of mis-scansions and mis-emphases and seem unaware of the fact. There are even misquotes – plain inaccuracies. We wouldn't accept wrong notes in Mozart' (Hall 2000a: 42).

Once the system of the writing is grasped by the actor, then the task is to apply it to the specifics of the text that make up the score for the actor's character in its vast variations of rhythmic detail and the delicate instructions that they reveal, letting the actors know, if they are prepared to listen, exactly how to voice, move, respond and simply be on stage. In a way that long ago stopped being fashionable for most theatre work, especially in contemporary and naturalistic drama, Hall is committed to table-work, the careful exploration of the play by the actors and director sitting round a table, going through the text line by line, discovering what might be possible in terms of meaning and what is, for Hall, unquestionable and necessary in the tightly defined nuances of each line's metrics.

This process is not one that is easy to document in Hall's practice. When in 1984 he directed *Coriolanus* at the National Theatre with Ian McKellen in the title role, Kristina Bedford observed the rehearsals, noting day by day what was happening, what was tried and kept, what was experimented with and discarded, how the production grew. But her book of the experience, *'Coriolanus' at the National: 'Th'Interpretation of the Time'*, begins the 150 pages of her 'Diary of the Rehearsal Process' on 24 October: 'Three weeks into rehearsal – stage of beginning to block the show' (Bedford 1992: 193). Elsewhere she comments, 'After two weeks of preliminary work on language and verse speaking, Hall began to put the show on its feet and establish a skeletal blocking which would be fleshed out later in the rehearsal period' (Bedford 1992: 27). She has no details of and perhaps had no access to those two or three weeks of 'preliminary work'.

But, for Hall, such work is never a kind of incidental starting point, an unimportant preparation for the 'real' work of blocking and moving. Instead, the blocking is a direct consequence of what has been found during the table-work. As a young and over-confident director, Hall used to block all movement in advance of beginning rehearsal. A week into rehearsals for *Cymbeline* at Stratford in 1957, Peggy Ashcroft, playing Imogen, resisted a prescribed move and Hall, realising how wrong he was, gave way completely.

She was right. It was arbitrary. It was a pattern. When I now say

> I never block a play, I have to know what the physical life of a scene will be; I have to know that the exits and entrances are right, and the furniture, but I never give moves any more. I suggest, or say what I like and what I don't. But the actors must always feel that they've invented it. She taught me to have the confidence to use their responses.
>
> (Fay 1995: 119)

Hall is here being slightly disingenuous; as he admits elsewhere, 'I have tried never to "block" a play since. I always have a plan of moves worked out in case there is no creativity in the rehearsal room' (2003: 203). But the assumption, central to his approach to the Shakespeare text, is that, while movement is a process found by the actor freely in the creative space of the rehearsal room, the details of the language as semantics, syntax and rhythm is an exact form that must be learned, understood and accepted before any such creativity is possible.

At the end of *Shakespeare's Advice to the Players*, Hall tries to bring this argument out as a closing article of faith:

> Much of what Shakespeare asks of theatre people is common sense; and much, once the actor gets the rhythm of the verse pulsing in his head, comes instinctively. But it needs learning, and it needs passing on. The need to renew is an absolute necessity of living theatre. Change is life. But you cannot escape Shakespeare's form and you cannot alter the form. You can (and must) find new means of expressing the form . . . Acting Shakespeare is a physical, rhythmical and often musical discipline.
>
> (Hall 2003: 207)

Hence, for Hall, the notion of a production which 'is alive and which lets the text take care of itself . . . is a contradiction':

> If the text is disregarded, the words become a secondary means of communication. The production can only then be creative if something else takes their place – such as music, mime or images. Certainly, such a production would not be Shakespeare, but only something based on Shakespeare. Shakespeare's beginning is the word; and his end is also the word. He tells you what he means, and therefore what he means you to feel. And – if you are an actor – he tells you how to *shape* the words.
>
> (Hall 2003: 207–9)

The freedom to discover movement is a consequence of absorbing the precision and the formal demands of the language. Discovering what the verse-line demands is to find a space that is not, for Hall, a constriction but a liberation, a working through the tightness of precise rhythm to a freedom that comes with ownership, a sharing of the authority of the language between writer and performer.

In 1988, casting three of Shakespeare's late plays (*Cymbeline, The Winter's Tale* and *The Tempest*) for his farewell productions as he ended his time as Artistic Director of the National Theatre, Hall chose Sarah Miles as Innogen in *Cymbeline* (as the role was now named), impressed by 'the daring honesty of her film performances' and unconcerned that she had had no experience of playing Shakespeare.

> Within days I knew I'd made a terrible mistake. Sarah learnt the meaning of Innogen's verse with aptitude, and she worked hard to breathe in the right places and to develop her voice. But she had great difficulty in delivering the words as spontaneous descriptions of her feelings. Too often she sounded false, not to say calculating . . . I realized that her strength as an actress was in conveying emotions below and beyond the words . . . But Shakespeare expresses everything by what he *says*. His characters have the ability to describe and illustrate what they they are feeling *as* they are feeling it. So his actors have to give the impression of creating the text while they experience the emotion.
>
> (Hall 2000a: 350)

On the one hand is the exhausting rehearsal process of finding what has been so carefully calculated in the language as effect; on the other lies the turning of those calculated forms into the illusion of something spontaneous, so that feelings are not implicit in the language or adjacent to it but fully embodied within the language itself. It is a procedure that requires training and experience that develops towards a learned skill, not simply a willingness to try.

From the start of the creation of the ensemble company at Stratford, in the early days of the Royal Shakespeare Company, Hall and John Barton, lured from an academic position at Cambridge to work with the new company, demanded that actors studied verse. Where a company like Brecht's Berliner Ensemble, probably the world's best-known theatre company when the RSC was being formed, was defined by a political position that controlled both repertory and design aesthetic, Hall saw the RSC as

> the product of a group of actors all speaking the text in the same way and a group of directors who agreed that they all knew what to look

> for in the verse . . . [T]he verse-speaking made the Company style. It quickly became famous for the clarity of its communication and the certainty of its speech.
>
> (Hall 2003: 203–5)

It was not, therefore, the case that Hall's young RSC saw its task as some form of archaeology. If there is in the search for what the verse reveals a commitment to Shakespeare, a keeping faith with Shakespeare (and, as with the appropriation of the opening of St John's Gospel in the comment that 'Shakespeare's beginning is the word', the divinity of Shakespeare is often assumed in Hall's language about him), this is not a search for a narrow authenticity such as, for instance, characterises some of the work at Shakespeare's Globe, the current reconstruction of the Globe Theatre, with its attempts at performances in Elizabethan pronunciation or the proud foregrounding in its first productions of the ways in which wearing Elizabethan underwear helped actors create character. While preparing to direct a Shakespeare play, Hall 'still mutter[s] the text to myself in Elizabethan' and is recurrently fascinated by that rougher sound in which, in his favourite example (*Julius Caesar*, Act I, Scene 1, line 75), 'Doth not Brutus bootless kneel' sounds like 'Doath nut Brewters bewtless kerneel' (Hall 2000a: 88).

Hall's RSC, even as its actors were attending verse classes and studying Shakespeare's sonnets, was never locked into a past but, instead, was engaged in the interaction between Shakespeare and an urgency of the present. The two most famous and successful productions of its first phase, Hall's production with John Barton of the first tetralogy of Shakespeare's histories as a trilogy renamed *The Wars of the Roses* (1963) and *Hamlet* starring David Warner (1965), were both marked by their immediacy of a political modernity. Behind John Bury's designs for *The Wars of the Roses*, with their leather and steel, their costumes which had become clothes long lived in and their sets with conference tables at which the characters had plainly spent many long hours, lay a design aesthetic plainly influenced by Brecht's company (which had visited London in 1956). A sequence of plays which had rarely been admired now startled audiences and critics with their insights into *realpolitik*, less a dull succession of battles than a thrilling sequence of unpredictable plotting in rooms and corridors, a revelation of the political processes by which power is sought and gained. As such, *The Wars of the Roses* was, for Hall, 'bred of its time [. . .] We wanted to reveal the political ironies which are at the heart of any power struggle at any time. Hypocrisy and cant were as common on the lips of politicians in Tudor England as they are on television during modern British elections' (Hall 2000a: 184).

Later, Hall came to think that the extent of rewriting and cutting which the co-directors used to adapt the four plays into three was wrong-headed, showing a distrust of the text: 'whatever is done to the great masterpieces only makes the adaptors look silly' (2000a: 184). But few in 1963 would have thought of the *Henry VI* plays as 'great masterpieces' and would instead have thought of *Richard III* as an isolated drama, a leap in Shakespeare's craft from his earlier apprentice labours. That *The Wars of the Roses* showed all four plays to be masterpieces was a significant part of its achievement.

For *Hamlet* in 1965, the play's modernity lay in its being 'the product of a time of doubt', a characteristic Hall saw as shared between Shakespeare's early modern world and Hall's. But it was also a Shakespeare production that connected Hamlet himself more firmly with a young audience than had been the case for centuries: as Hall said in his speech on the first day of rehearsals, 'something inside [Hamlet], this disease of disillusionment, stops the final, committed action. It is an emotion which you can encounter in the young today' (Hall 1967a: 160, 162). David Warner was, for Hall, 'a young actor who [. . .] represented the young intellectual of today' and that group of 'the young of the West' had 'lost the ordinary, predictable radical impulses which the young in all generations have had', leaving them with a 'negative response' which Hall found 'deep and appalling' (Hall 1967b: 155 and 1967a: 162–3).

In the production, Warner was marked as the contemporary student by the long scarf he wore, the badge of 'the modern late-teenager, pathetic in his lack of grip, strangely poignant in his angular helplessness'. But it was not simply Warner's contemporaneity that defined the production; rather, it lay in the interaction between Warner's Hamlet's 'dark despondency' and the harsh 'political world of Elsinore' which lacked any sign of 'a logic, a creative dynamic, a meaning, that is more than based on expediency'. Strikingly, these sympathetic descriptions of the production's immediacy came from a critic, Gareth Lloyd Evans, usually unsympathetic towards the project of Hall's RSC as a company where Shakespeare 'must speak to the twentieth century' (Lloyd Evans 1967: 136, 134). But the quality of speaking verse often displeased Hall's critics. Lloyd Evans found failure in precisely the areas where Hall's later theory and practice for verse-speaking would be strongest:

> Rhythm and music are at a discount, the voice often seems roughly *sotto voce*, the pausing *ad hoc* . . . One can nowadays, perhaps with impunity, democratize the prince, but the archetypal Hamlet exists outside the confines of any fashionable or individual interpretation (although it can contain them) mainly through the poetry he speaks. To denude him and the play of the associative power of poetic utterance is to take away the timeless dimension.
>
> (Lloyd Evans 1967: 136)

Lacking audio tapes of the production, I have no means of knowing whether Lloyd Evans's detailed complaints are justified, whether Warner paused arbitrarily, choosing an effect not built into the structure of the verse. But on the one hand, he himself sounds like the later Hall defining the failure of an interpretation that seeks relevance above historicity while, on the other, the production's modernity seems from others' accounts, the visual record and my own memories not to have been apparent in the simplistic ways that would become the norm against which Hall writing forty years later would be resisting. If *Hamlet* in 1965 became potently modern, it was not a matter of dressing Elsinore's court in business suits or having Fortinbras's troops abseil onto the stage in modern combat dress; rather, it was a finding of connection through meaning that was both early modern and contemporary, not a denial of the former in favour of a glib link to the latter. Lloyd Evans, in other words, perceived a denial of archetypicality and generality in a production that would not now be seen as denying those qualities. Even if we would now deny the desire for some generality as being only the imposition of a narrow model of what constitutes an anglophone model of universality, Lloyd Evans saw in the young RSC only an unjustified and limiting reaching for immediacy.

When, nearly twenty years later, in his National Theatre production of *Coriolanus* (1984), Hall, so exceptionally in his practice, chose to dress the production in modern suits, there was little that made the play more relevant, more contemporary as a result. Driven by the need to form a large-enough on stage crowd (and unable, as any late twentieth-century production was bound to be, to afford to pay a large group of professional actors), Hall sold on stage tickets to people willing, as needed, to be shepherded around the stage by a few actors, becoming a Roman crowd in the process. Clutching their shopping and often looking distinctly embarrassed, this mob proved only the gap between Coriolanus's Rome and the moment of the performance. Never a starving, angry, politicised, vulnerable group of citizens, they shared with Shakespeare's crowd only their confusion. What power the production had in its exploration of the meaning of the politicians' interaction with the community they purport to represent was never a result here of what the amateur conscripted crowd did but, as one might expect, the consequence of the superb exploration of Shakespeare's language by McKellen and the rest of the professional cast.

In the 1960s, Hall knew that fashions shift, in verse-speaking as in everything else: 'The new, cool, intellectual, rather formed, rather witty [. . .] style of speaking Shakespeare which we adopt, which concentrates more on meaning than it does on emotion, will seem in ten years' time the most horrible cliché and affectation' (Hall 1967b: 153). But what came to some to seem affected in Hall's required style of speaking Shakespeare would be the absolute rigidity of the system Hall taught his actors and demanded of them. Where Hall claimed to feel flattered by the joking label of being an 'iambic fundamentalist' that he earned, somebody undeviatingly obsessed with the constituent elements of Shakespeare's blank verse, some of his casts found it impossible to work effectively and creatively in a context where Hall would use a pencil to tap the stresses of each line on his table during rehearsal, head down in the text alertly listening more often than head up looking at what they were doing, and where Hall's notes to actors during a run would more often point accusingly to a missed caesura than to anything that the actors felt would help them maintain the quality of their performance – though for Hall it would be precisely by preserving the caesura that the quality of performance would have been maintained.

In effect, commitment to Hall's principles was the necessary precondition of working in the tight ensemble company that Hall sought to create both in the RSC of the 1960s and the recent forms of the Peter Hall Company forty years later. Creating the RSC was for Hall, to a significant extent – significant enough for him unequivocally to foreground the point – the means of resolving the problems 'of all the differing styles of speaking' Shakespeare's language which he found in 1960s actors (Hall 2003: 203). At the same time, Hall saw, in the very act of defining the RSC as an ensemble company that would play both Shakespeare and contemporary drama (something the ad-hoc companies that had been created for the annual Stratford season had never tried to combine), a possibility both of better verse-speaking and of developing 'the kind of protean actors, alive to the issues of the day, that Shakespeare deserved and that would give his plays contemporary life' (Hall 2000a: 156).

Hall's RSC, playing part of the year in Stratford and part in London, combined the best traditions of Stratford Shakespeare with the new immediacy of the London theatre context but, by creating the Stratford season as a repertory rather than a succession of discrete productions, it allowed the Shakespeare performances to interconnect, the actor moving from role to role within the week of performances as much as across the season. In the company's new and longer perspective, consequent on the actors' being on long contracts, new plays, premiered in London, played alongside the London transfer of Stratford productions, feeding the actors and other creators of the RSC's work with a range of new styles that transferred back into the Shakespeare performances the following season in Stratford. The intermixing of modes was fundamental to the company's meaning and was, in many respects, even more than in the creation of an ensemble company, the crucial innovation that Hall brought to Shakespeare production at this point.

The quest to develop protean actors might seem strangely aligned with the increasing rigidity of Hall's principles for uncovering Shakespeare's meaning in the codes of the verse, but they were part of a commitment to classical forms and the integration, even more marked in Hall's tenure as Artistic Director of the National Theatre from 1973 to 1988, of Shakespeare into a world repertory of drama. Alongside Hall's work on Beckett and Pinter and on opera as signs of the nature of his Shakespeare productions lie his explorations of Greek drama, most especially in the production of Aeschylus' *Oresteia* at the National Theatre in 1981, in Tony Harrison's energised verse translation in a style insistently aware of its own metrics and with the driving rhythms of Harrison Birtwistle's music underpinning the stage action. Hence, Hall was willing to accept 'classicism' as a definition of his theatre style:

> in the sense that one of the things [. . .] that is essential to the concept of classicism is the idea of form. Form is not naturalism [. . .] In a sense, the Greek stage itself is a mask, and behind the mask happens the blinding of Oedipus and the killing of Agamemnon. That in itself is a form, physically. Blank verse is a form, just as singing is a form. These are all artificial means of shaping naturalistic behaviour and speech, giving them a form which enables us to deal with emotions and attitudes and responses which might be too painful or even ridiculous for us if done naturalistically [. . .] So form enables you to deal with tears either by wearing a mask, or by singing an aria, or by speaking blank verse.
>
> (Berry 1989: 208–9)

It is no accident that Hall goes on to praise three contemporary artists for their 'remarkable sense of form': Beckett, Pinter and Michael Tippett (whose operas he directed).

If the verse line is the fundamental building block of Shakespearian drama as form, it does not exclude the ways in which the form can also be apparent in design and movement. In 1975, Hall directed *Hamlet* again, at the National Theatre with Albert Finney in the lead. The rehearsal process was deeply satisfying for Hall. After a four-hour session he noted in his diary: 'it was a wonderful experience. It's really why I do this job. Not for performances – not for plays – not for money – but for the satisfaction of having a really good rehearsal where the excitement of discovery spreads from actor to actor'.

Just before opening night, he recorded his delight in what had been accomplished, bringing together the insights with which his diary had been filled for weeks:

> This is the closest I have reached to the heart of a Shakespeare play in my own estimation; it is the production which [. . .] has the least gap between my hopes and the facts on the stage. It is also pure and clear [. . .] And the production is the closest I have ever got to a unified style of verse speaking which is right [. . .] It has been a very satisfying experience.
>
> (Hall 2000b: 196, 205)

In the event, the production was largely disliked by the critics who focused on the problems in Finney's performance and the arduous audience experience of a four-hour, uncut text. The gap between a director's delight and critics' response is a common fact of theatre. Here it might signal the gap between Hall's concerns and the kinds of effects to which critics more readily react. But it was not only in the verse-speaking for the production that Hall found the coherence of an awareness of form. John Bury's set, a wall with massive double-doors in it and a 30-foot circle on the stage floor crossed by a grid of lines drawing towards a perspective point, could, without any change whatsoever, have been used for a production of Greek tragedy, an abstracted space that did not ever seek to create rooms and halls, battlements and closets, but that instead sought to underline the spatial relationships between characters. Both Greek and Elizabethan in its influences, the set was a formal space for exploring form.

Someone standing at the centre of the circle or prowling its circumference was defining his or her emotional and intellectual response to the network of social relationships as the movement of the play's actions continually sought to identify and reidentify them. Characters' ability to choose where they were, the ease with which they could take up a position or the imposition of a placing by others, also worked as a means for the audience to understand event. Ophelia at the circle's centre for the nunnery scene and Gertrude at the same position in the closet scene were in part positioned there by male figures of authority (Claudius and Polonius) while Finney's Hamlet, ranging warily around the edges of the circle, was both threatening and displaced. Where the 1965 *Hamlet* had seen the play as a young man's response to the strategies of a cerebral and heartless political world, now, with an older Hamlet in a formalised space, the play's action became visible as a geometry of relationships, a structure of form within which emotion itself was dangerous. Not surprisingly, Hall was pleased with the way in which he had learned how to treat the verse so that it is 'based on feeling and passion', where 'in Stratford days what I did was intellectual' (2000b: 205).

I have recurrently been emphasising Hall's demand that actors learn the techniques of understanding Shakespeare's language as the crucial training for understanding and communicating his form. Hall argued for this in 1964, requiring that 'techniques have, therefore, to be learnt and developed until Shakespeare's form is a discipline which supports rather than denies self-expression', while seeing actors' resistance to this discipline at a time when 'rhetoric is now suspect' (Goodwin 1964: 42). But it was not until he published *Shakespeare's Advice to the Players* in 2003 that Hall made the process as publicly clear to a general readership as he had privately to countless casts in the rehearsal room and workshop.

Hall dedicated the book to three people. Dadie Rylands, the first, was the central figure in theatre in Cambridge for much of the twentieth century and a vital influence on Shakespeare production well outside the university through, for instance, his directing John Gielgud. As an example of an academic and theatre practitioner, Rylands embodies the meeting between the two worlds that Hall so admired. John Barton, the second, was Hall's friend and collaborator from his undergraduate days in Cambridge through the creation of the RSC and well beyond. It is the third dedicatee who might seem most surprising: F.R. Leavis. If, at Cambridge, Hall enjoyed Leavis's lectures with their sneering style, he had already learned from Douglas Brown, who coached Hall at the Perse School for university entrance, the value of Leavis's commitment to close textual analysis as the only means through which to value the work of art. Scrutiny, the name of Leavis's academic journal, was a watchword for Hall's directing technique. In *The Wars of the Roses*, 'what we did came out of the most rigorous scrutiny (the Leavis word) of each scene. What was it for? What did it mean? And how could it be expressed to a modern audience?' (Hall 2000a: 187). When Leavis died in 1978, Hall recorded in his diary, 'All the textual seriousness at the basis of Trevor [Nunn's] work and of mine comes from Leavis [. . .] Comical to think that Leavis hated the theatre and never went to it. He has had more influence on the contemporary theatre than any other critic' (2000a: 344).

Leavis's work signified a moral purpose and authority in art to which Hall fully assented and of which he himself became a vocal advocate in berating successive governments of right and left for their underfunding of the arts and berating the Arts Council for the banality of the ways in which it distributed the Government's funding, for Hall saw the arts as the core of the process by which a society came to understand its moral being. But Leavis also offered Hall and others the mirage of a scholarly, scientific analysis of language as the means of discovering that moral purpose. At the same time, and even more completely than Rylands, Leavis stood for what academic study could offer the theatre, and Hall's subsequent fascination with Shakespeare scholarship, his close collaborations with academics such as John Russell Brown and Roger Warren and his engagement with textual scholarship (albeit often imperfectly understood) are indirect consequences of what he took from Leavis.

At the core of Hall's scrutiny of Shakespeare's verse comes the line. He teaches emphatically:

- Try to make every line scan.
- Learn the end of the line.
- Keep the line whole and play lines rather than words.

(Hall 2003: 29)

Preserving 'the sanctity of the line' (again, that religious language for Shakespearian form) is vital and enables the proper attitude towards, for instance, a mid-line caesura in which 'the two halves of the line must make one in tempo, dynamic and volume, even though the emotions are usually different' (Hall 2003: 34). Over and over again, *Shakespeare's Advice* enunciates a rigid set of rules. Noting that a quarter of Shakespeare's lines are made up of monosyllables, Hall rules that 'monosyllables always indicate a slowing up, or a spreading of the speech' so that 'it scans, easily'. Then the actor's task is 'to find out *why* the line is slow, and what emotions he must engender in himself to produce these measured accents. But slow it always is and always must be [. . .] But the line must still hold its iambic purity' (Hall 2003: 35). There is simply no possibility for Hall of a line of monosyllables being spoken in any other way.

Easily and unsurprisingly, he can adduce examples of such lines being delivered badly: when, for instance, an Othello bellowed 'Keep up your bright swords for the dew will rust them' (Act I, Scene 2, line 59), 'the line was too fast to be comprehensible. It was so frantic that it gave no impression of the strong naïvity of this character, so certain of his authority' (Hall 2003: 36). But the poor performance of one actor or many does not prove the rule. More disturbingly, Hall gives an interpretation of the line in a way that is not in the slightest consequent on its monosyllabic nature, for it is equally easy to create an Othello who delivers the line quickly but whose certainty in his authority is at this stage in the play entirely justified and not the product of a posited 'strong naïvity' (2003: 36). Of course, any actor must for any line, not only monosyllabic ones, 'find an emotion that justifies the tempo', (2003: 36) but Hall asserts, from his long experience but without any evidence, a single slow tempo for such lines that he cannot possibly justify.

Throughout the book's examples, there are similar extrapolations from one kind of assumption to another. The final half-line of Claudius' preparation for prayer, 'All may be well' (Act III, Scene 3, line 72), is 'an unconvincing half-line, monosyllabic, colloquial and simple [. . .] He doesn't believe it, and neither does the audience' (Hall 2003: 133). Of course, an actor may well play it that way, and an audience may react as similarly unconvinced, but it is equally practicable for a Claudius to believe it while his audience does not. Again, nothing in the line precludes alternative readings, ones which in no way deny the line's rhythm but depend on a different interpretation of what that rhythm might signify.

The belief in the sanctity of the line also for Hall prescribes stage action. Hamlet, seeing Claudius apparently praying, at some point draws his sword (always assuming that he does not enter with the sword already drawn), for later, at 'Up, sword, and know thou a more horrid hent', he appears to sheathe it again. But Hall's examination of the opening lines of Hamlet's speech,

> Now might I do it pat, now he is praying.
> And now I'll do it; and so he goes to heaven,
> And so am I revenged.
>
> (Act III, Scene 3, line 73–5)

leads him to state unequivocally that it is after 'goes to heaven' that 'Hamlet draws his sword [. . .] There is no justification for the stage practice of breaking the line to draw the sword; it is written quite clearly so that after the line ends, with sword drawn, Hamlet reflects "And so am I revenged" ' (Hall 2003: 135).

Recent stage practice here has, I suspect, been the product of a slavish following of edited texts, for the mid-line drawing of the sword was first marked by Capell in his edition of 1768 and by most editions subsequently. But Hamlet could draw his sword a line earlier than Hall demands, after 'praying' and as a prompt for 'And now I'll do it', just as easily as the mid-line moment Hall detests. Equally, drawing the sword during part of the line (e.g., while saying 'And now I'll do it') would not interfere at all with the smooth rhythm and preserved sanctity of the line that Hall requires. Separation of speech from action is something most Shakespeare actors and directors dislike, preferring movement or 'business' on the line, not after it. Hall seems here to assume a separation that his own stage practice avoids. The point, of course, is not my local disagreement with the constrictions of Hall's analysis of the individual cases but rather the tendency in Hall's writing – and hence in his rehearsal room – for one kind of assumption about the nature of Shakespeare's verse to condition another so that, while the actor may indeed find that 'form comes first and [. . .] helps to provoke the feeling' and may be 'empowered then to make the audience listen and understand' (Hall 2003: 13), the parameters within which that understanding operates are far narrower than Hall represents.

While Hall sees himself as searching for a direct connection to early modern forms of delivery (without adherence to early modern speech sounds), he is also consciously identifying his technique in a long theatre tradition. A further influence on Hall, beyond the dedicatees, was Edith Evans from whom Hall learned 'the rules of Shakespeare's verse and prose that [William] Poel had drummed into her'. The rules matched those he had learned from Rylands but then Rylands' early performances had been with Cambridge's Marlowe Society which 'had been founded [. . .] on Poel's precepts' (Hall 2003: 207). One might, as a result, see Hall as the last great Edwardian director, the last inheritor of a long tradition, rather than as an innovator. There are, for instance, many similarities between the Peter Hall Company as a project and those companies run by actor-managers in earlier eras.

Yet, what consistently marks Hall's work since leaving the National Theatre in 1988, in the various permutations which the Peter Hall Company has undergone, has been the determined attempt at the creation and maintaining of an ensemble company where techniques would be fully absorbed and Shakespeare productions as a result would offer that coherence that Hall prizes. It is a concern that has also, again in a collaboration between scholarship and theatre, driven his commitment to the Rose of Kingston project, a theatre currently being constructed based on the evidence of the archaeology of the early modern Rose Theatre, to be used for teaching graduate courses in theatre (Hall is Chancellor of the University of Kingston) as well as for work by his professional company. The Rose of Kingston stage, a broad traverse within a circular auditorium, is a resistance to the strong thrust of the Globe, its modern recreation and such modern versions of the forms of later Jacobean theatres as the Swan and Courtyard theatres built for the RSC at Stratford. Hall, vocal in his opposition to the placing of the stage pillars in the Globe reconstruction, has now set out to create a theatre that accords both with the archaeological record and with his sense as a theatre director of how early modern stages must have related to their audiences. The Rose of Kingston asks the audience to watch a broad sweep of drama in front of them, rather than integrating them into an action that they surround. It is, for Hall, the right space in which to work on Shakespeare, the proper resistance to the immediacy of connection which the RSC's Swan Theatre so eloquently provides and which he finds unhelpful. When he directed *All's Well that Ends Well* in the Swan Theatre in 1992 (his first RSC production for twenty years), the production was noticeably reluctant to use the kinds of audience engagement that the stage's form so strongly promotes.

In an interview in 1989, Hall envisaged his future Shakespeare productions:

> There are some I haven't done that I very much want to do. I have no ambition to complete the canon.[. . .] I've never done *As You Like It* and *Measure for Measure*. I've never done *King Lear*. I've done all the histories but I've never done *Much Ado*.
>
> (Berry 1989: 214)

Over the next fifteen years, Hall would work through that list: *King Lear* in 1997 with Alan Howard at the Old Vic Theatre, *Measure for Measure* in Los Angeles in 1999 (performed in repertory with *A Midsummer Night's Dream* by a company of twenty-five American actors who, 'within two and a half weeks [were] all speaking Shakespeare the same way, observing the form and relishing the rhythm' [Hall 2000a: 426]), *As You Like It* in Bath in 2003 with his daughter Rebecca as Rosalind.

But for all the excellence of some of these productions and others he directed for the Peter Hall Company, Hall has never been able to achieve with it the sustained ensemble company that he created in Stratford in 1961. The Peter Hall Company produces a number of plays every year, across a broad range of classical repertory regularly including Shakespeare, but it is not a permanent company. Casting for each season is done afresh and, while some actors often return, most do not. Hall has also been unable to find either sufficient funding or attractive enough projects to enable him to cast star actors. In many ways, the ideal that his RSC made possible only marks the distance from that ideal at which he is now forced to work.

Hall's ambition in 1989 was 'a small theatre with a vast sum of money so that I could teach and explore Shakespeare by performing him' (Berry 1989: 214). Though the Rose of Kingston may prove to be that small theatre for teaching, it is unlikely to be backed with enough funding such that he could recreate the conditions for his 1988 *Antony and Cleopatra* at the National Theatre where, as he has recurrently mentioned since, he had the unusual luxury of two star actors (Anthony Hopkins and Judi Dench), an ensemble company for them to work with, and a twelve-week rehearsal period, long enough to allow for four weeks of table-work and for the possibility of the designer, Alison Chitty, having time to develop and refine the set and costumes as ideas emerged during rehearsals. That the production attracted the kinds of glowing reviews and cheering audiences that all directors might yearn for was a triumphant vindication of Hall's ideals. But it has proved an example almost impossible to reproduce in the economic conditions of British theatre, whether at the National Theatre, the RSC or the Peter Hall Company.

In some respects, Hall's recent work has been the victim of the very brilliance of the concept of the RSC and the extent to which he transformed irrevocably the way in which modern British Shakespeare production might best be achieved and within which he was able to define a company's mode of unremitting attention to Shakespeare's text that continues to be his article of faith. Too often since, Hall must have spent many hours in the stalls auditioning, like his animated version in *Next* but without the likelihood of its semi-divine Shakespeare appearing to him.

Chronology

1930	Born in Bury St Edmunds, Suffolk
1950–3	Undergraduate at St Catharine's College, Cambridge
1955	Directs British premiere of Beckett's *Waiting for Godot* (Arts Theatre, London)
1956	First production at Stratford-upon-Avon: *Love's Labour's Lost*
1959	*Coriolanus* (Stratford-upon Avon) starring Laurence Olivier
1960	Creates the Royal Shakespeare Company
1963	*The Wars of the Roses* (RSC), directed with John Barton
1965	*Hamlet* (RSC)
1965	Pinter's *The Homecoming* (RSC)
1967	*Macbeth* (RSC)
1968	Resigns as Artistic Director of the RSC
1973–88	Artistic Director, the National Theatre
1975	*Hamlet* (National Theatre)
1976	The National Theatre moves from the Old Vic to its purpose-built South Bank home
1977	Knighted
1979	Shaffer's *Amadeus* (National Theatre)
1981	Aeschylus's *The Oresteia* (National Theatre)
1983	Wagner's *Ring* (Bayreuth)
1984	*Coriolanus* (National Theatre), starring Ian McKellen
1984–90	Artistic Director, Glyndebourne Festival Opera
1987	*Antony and Cleopatra* (National Theatre), starring Anthony Hopkins and Judi Dench
1988	*Cymbeline, The Winter's Tale, The Tempest* (National Theatre)
1988	Founds the Peter Hall Company
1989	*The Merchant of Venice* (Peter Hall Company), starring Dustin Hoffman
1992	*All's Well That Ends Wells* (RSC)
1994	*Hamlet* (Peter Hall Company)
1997	*King Lear* (Peter Hall Company)
2003	*As You Like It* (Peter Hall Company)
2007	The Rose of Kingston scheduled to open

Bibliography

Addenbrooke, David (1974) *The Royal Shakespeare Company*, London: William Kimber.
Barton, John and Peter Hall (1970) *The Wars of the Roses*, London: BBC.
Beauman, Sally (1982) *The Royal Shakespeare Company*, Oxford: Oxford University Press.
Bedford, Kristina (1992) *'Coriolanus' at the National: 'Th'Interpretation of the Time'*, Selinsgrove, Pa.: Susquehanna University Press.
Berry, Ralph (1989) *On Directing Shakespeare*, London: Hamish Hamilton.
Brown, John Russell (ed.) (1982) *Focus on 'Macbeth'*, London: Routledge & Kegan Paul.
Chambers, Colin (2004) *Inside the Royal Shakespeare Company*, London: Routledge.
Crowl, Samuel (1992) *Shakespeare Observed*, Athens, Ohio: Ohio University Press.
Dawson, Anthony B. (1995) *Hamlet*, Manchester: Manchester University Press.
Fay, Stephen (1995) *Power Play: The Life and Times of Peter Hall*, London: Hodder & Stoughton.
Goodwin, John (ed.) (1964) *Royal Shakespeare Theatre Company 1960–1963*, New York: Theatre Arts Books.
Goodwin, Tim (1988) *Britain's Royal National Theatre*, London: Nick Hern.
Hall, Peter (1999) *The Necessary Theatre*, New York: Theatre Communications Group.
—— (1967a) 'Hamlet', in Charles Marowitz and Simon Trussler (eds), *Theatre at Work*, London: Methuen, pp. 160–3.
—— (1967b) 'The Director and the Permanent Company', in Charles Marowitz and Simon Trussler (eds), *Theatre at Work*, London: Methuen, pp.148–59.
—— (2000a) *Making an Exhibition of Myself: The Autobiography of Peter Hall*, London: Oberon Books.
—— (2000b) *Peter Hall's Diaries*, ed. John Goodwin, London: Oberon Books.
—— (2000c) *Exposed by the Mask*, New York: Theatre Communications Group.
—— (2003) *Shakespeare's Advice to the Players*, New York: Theatre Communications Group.
Lloyd Evans, Gareth (1967) 'Shakespeare, the Twentieth Century, and "Behaviourism" ', *Shakespeare Survey 20*: 133–42.
Lowen, Tirzah (1990) *Peter Hall Directs 'Antony and Cleopatra'*, London: Methuen Drama.
McCullough, Christopher J. (1988) 'The Cambridge Connection: Towards a Materialist Theatre Practice', in Graham Holderness (ed.), *The Shakespeare Myth*, Manchester: Manchester University Press, pp. 112–22.
Pearson, Richard (1990) *A Band of Arrogant and United Heroes*, London: Adelphi Press.
Rosenberg, Marvin (1997) *The Adventures of a Shakespeare Scholar*, Newark, Del.: University of Delaware Press.
Styan, J.L. (1977) *The Shakespeare Revolution*, Cambridge: Cambridge University Press.
Warren, Roger (1990) *Staging Shakespeare's Late Plays*, Oxford: Clarendon Press.
Wells, Stanley (1997) *Royal Shakespeare*, Manchester: Manchester University Press.

About the author

Peter Holland has, since 2002, been McMeel Family Professor in Shakespeare Studies and Chair of the Department of Film, Television and Theatre at the University of Notre Dame. Educated at Cambridge, he was Judith E. Wilson Reader in Drama in the Faculty of English there. From 1997 to 2002 he was Director of the Shakespeare Institute, Stratford-upon-Avon, and Professor of Shakespeare Studies at the University of Birmingham. He is editor of *Shakespeare Survey* and co-editor of *Great Shakespeareans* and *Oxford Shakespeare*

Topics. He is the author and editor of many books, including *English Shakespeares* (1997). He has been a governor of the Royal Shakespeare Company (RSC) and a regular broadcaster for the BBC. The first production by Peter Hall that he saw was *A Midsummer Night's Dream* in 1959 and he has followed Hall's career with deep pleasure ever since.

10
TERRY HANDS
Phillip Breen

Only an unfortunate accident prevented Terry Hands' largely uncut 2004 production of *Romeo and Juliet* running straight through at two hours eight minutes. Christina Cole, making her professional debut as Juliet and in a flurry of first-night excitement ran in to the stage left wing and fractured a toe. With no understudies, Cole played through the six week run in various stages of recovery. Sadly for the Clwyd audiences they were not swept along with the 'the two hours traffic of our stage', but were rather left to puzzle on why 'so light a foot would ne'er wear out the everlasting flint'.

As Assistant Director, I was left to oversee the final run in the rehearsal room on a grey Saturday morning in winter, while Terry began lighting Timothy O'Brien's set, and I was witness to work of clarity, power and emotional complexity. In this production, the heat was palpable and the 'mad blood' was stirring. There was not an ounce of Byronic whimsy about Daniel Hawksford's impulsive, macho Romeo, and the group of Montague Boys lead by former Llanelli prop forward Bradley Freegard seldom discussed homoeroticism. They understood it far more profoundly than that; their scenes came straight out of the team bath. By watching and allowing their natural dynamic to evolve in rehearsal and by handing Freegard an earring to wear at the dress rehearsal Hands had given the Clwyd audience a Verona that his company and his audience understood. Despite its injury, the production was a hit, even though it did play at an epic two hours and twenty-five minutes, sadly including an interval.

With the interval we lost one of the most interesting discoveries of the rehearsal process, the impetus given to the tragic arc of the play and the rich irony of the 'Gallop apace you fiery footed steeds' speech if it follows directly and swiftly on from the death of Mercutio; if she is wading in the blood of her cousin as the story is passed from Romeo to Juliet. But nearly all of the rough-hewn spirit survived. Swift articulation of scenes, swift playing style on a minimally furnished stage has become Hands' style, his way of serving the play above all and the primacy of the actor and the line. He explains that his

> his constant quest is to find ways of releasing the thought and the emotion together and finding ways to support the line. By that I mean the words that are spoken by the actor. You can often say to a young actor 'new line, new thought, new movement'. It may just be a change of weight, a shuffle, it may, depending upon the energy within the line, be a full movement. That movement is part of the energy of the play. A skier doing slalom, doesn't come to the flag, stop and ski off down the other side. It's a drop of the shoulder and on to the next part. The same is true of a Shakespeare soliloquy.

Hands is sceptical of the 'director as *auteur*', preferring to think of himself as 'co-ordinating the specialised talents of others', an invisible hand serving the play. This is expressed in his commitment to the ideals of 'the company', a group of actors that work together over a period of years who have an instinctive feel for how their fellow performers play. While much is spoken about abstract notions of *ensemble*, for Hands whether at the Everyman, Clwyd Theatr Cymru, or most notably at the Royal Shakespeare Company, it has always been a concrete reality, indivisible from his conception of the role of a director and is the beating heart of his work. For him 'a company is worth six months of rehearsals'. Hands, it seems, has always been part Jean Vilar, part Bill Shankly.

After graduating from Birmingham University and the Royal Academy of Dramatic Art (RADA) in 1964, Hands was part of the group that founded the Liverpool Everyman Theatre. The Everyman was founded on a shoestring budget of £3,000 from Liverpool City Council, their first season of productions was a 44-week programme commencing on 28 September 1964 and a company that contained Susan Fleetwood and Bruce Myers – two actors who subsequently worked with Hands at the RSC. The theatre was thrust into the civic consciousness of Liverpool part by accident and part by design. Their first venue in Hope Hall was used as a cinema on Saturday mornings, so they had to find other ways to draw an audience. Hands hit upon an idea to produce plays on the syllabus of schools within a thirty-mile radius of the theatre and avoid the perception that they were solely for schools by putting on evening performances and a beat group in the cellar on Thursday, Friday and Saturday nights, for their adult audience. They were perforce one of the first Theatre-In-Education (TIE) companies.

The demands of 'TIE' projects in Toxteth were far from the make-up classes at the Royal Academy that were still teaching their students how to apply 5 and 9 on Monday, Tuesday and Wednesday and mask a wig-join. The Everyman auditorium itself resembled in shape and dynamic an Elizabethan playhouse with the audience below the stage level, a raised platform at the back of the stage and no fly-tower. This Everyman seated 750 on two levels. The thrust configuration necessarily imposed fluid movement – unlike the Swan at Stratford there were no gangways downstage left and right for an actor to rest during a scene – and the close proximity of the often raucous Liverpool kids compelled actors to play scenes directly and quickly. This was in contrast to the often rhetorical and fairly immobile productions of Shakespeare that were the norm at that time. Consideration of the unfettered responses of this audience was paramount for the Everyman company in their early productions. Then, as now, Hands had the image of a 14-year-old child in his mind when preparing for rehearsals:

> Why fourteen? Because they are hitting puberty and there's a sudden interest in the world around them. We found when we were going out to schools that the kids were tough. They could smell out pretension a mile away. You don't waste time with Liverpool kids, we drove it through very fast. In a sense it must have been like doing the plays for the groundlings in Shakespeare's own time. When I first came into the theatre in the early 60s, there was a lot of disguise, artifice, wigs and whatnot. It didn't fool the 14-year-olds. We asked them why they didn't go to the theatre and they would say because there's a better class of actor on the football field.

Hands' achievements in Liverpool were recognised in 1966 when Peter Hall invited him to Stratford to join the Royal Shakespeare Company. Hall's nascent RSC brought together a generation of directors, graduates in English literature and language who understood the context in which the plays were written, who made detailed studies of the texts, could offer it up to their actors and according to Michael Billington 'shot British theatre forward 200 years almost overnight'. This group contained Hall himself, John Barton, Peter Brook and Trevor Nunn. According to Hands, one of Hall's great achievements was that 'he made it a respectable job for a University graduate to become a theatre director. He allowed the art of the director to emerge and evolve'. He also recalls that this group drew inspiration from the *Berliner Ensemble*'s visits to England in the 50s and 60s: 'no more four walls, no more painted cloths, real bits of wood and metal, people talking straight out, breaking the "fourth wall" all the time'.

As well as the profound influence on the directorate, the *Berliner Ensemble*'s aesthetic was being introduced to the RSC by designers. John Bury in particular. Bury had been working with Joan Littlewood's company in Stratford East, asking their audience to use their imagination; moving from the representational to the expressionistic and the abstract.

Thrust into artistically and intellectually vibrant company, Hands was initially given the brief to run 'Theatre-Go-Round', the RSC's TIE wing:

> Peter gave me a budget, an administrator and he told us we could rehearse in the tin shed (later The Other Place). He told us two things: 'Do what you like' and 'break even'. I said I'd have to go and pinch actors from all over the company and he said 'if Peter Brook complains then we'll talk again'. And within about three months we had about sixteen shows and demonstrations that we could take out on the road to schools and colleges. We even took out Peter Brook's company to do *US* on the road.

After a successful production of pro-Castro Cuban drama *The Criminals* by Jose Triana, in 1967 (the first production Hands had directed in an end-on proscenium arch theatre), Peter Hall invited Terry to direct his first main stage Shakespeare production and was given the choice between *Richard II* and *The Merry Wives of Windsor*. He recalls that he

> 'read them both and didn't want to do either. At that stage I was 27, and I couldn't stand Richard's page after page of self-pity. So I said, with my heart in my mouth, I'll do *The Merry Wives*'.

Work began on the production in 1968 and Hands was given a remarkable cast which included Elizabeth Spriggs and Brenda Bruce as the Wives, Brewster Mason as Falstaff, Roger Rees as Fenton and Ian Richardson as Ford. A daunting task for a junior director and one that prompted fastidious study in preparation for the rehearsal room:

> The more I read the play in the folio, the less sense it made. Then I had a stroke of luck. Oxford University Press at that time were publishing the bad quartos of Shakespeare. I looked at the bad quarto of *Merry Wives*, and there, gaps were being filled in and plotting 'mistakes' corrected. There were missing links and clarifications. There's no clarity in the folio. There is in the 'bad' quarto. So I steadily built up my

own script, one that made total sense. I was excited by the detective work.

The sleuthing continued:

> It does seem to me that a director has two jobs when working on a play. To discover the 'conscious' play and the 'unconscious' play. In the same way that we have an conscious mind and a unconscious mind, so with any playwright, young or old, alive or dead, if they're any good there are at least two plays in there. There's the conscious play, the one they set out to write and there's the unconscious play one that has written itself subliminally. The job of the director it seemed to me was to climb inside the writer's head and to pick out both. With *Merry Wives* I analysed every word in every scene, I still have enormous notebooks to show for it. So whatever was said in the text, 'good morning', 'it's cold today', for example, would go in one list, entitled 'greetings'; that would record how they addressed one another, 'master/sir' or whether first names or surnames were being used. 'Domestic' would go in one list and 'hunting' would go in another list. All in all I had twelve categories, there were categories for emotion, hate, love; just the words that Shakespeare used and nothing else. I would write them down in lists and add them up at the bottom and see what choices of words were predominating in each scene. Then I could decide as a director whether to accentuate that or play against it. All very primitive really, but useful. When I was reading *Merry Wives*, my instinct was that the predominant imagery of the play was 'hunting'. But in the overall summing up, 'hunting' came third behind 'domestic', the talk of laundry baskets, homes, carpets and what not. To a 27-year-old 'domestic' had absolutely no interest, so I didn't see it. It taught me a valuable lesson.

From that came the realisation that what Shakespeare had written was a companion piece to *Henry V*, at around about the same time (c.1599–1600). In *Henry V*, he writes about the unification of a nation, in a sense it's his tribute to Elizabeth I. In the play you have four captains – an Englishman, an Irishman, a Welshman and a Scotsman – and by the end you have a band of brothers, they are a united nation. The comic version of this story of national unity takes place at a crossroads called Windsor. Here, you have a Frenchman, a Welshman, you have the court coming down, you have got the heart of England, the peasantry, and you have the Masters. To be a Master you had to be pretty wealthy, and the soldiers who survived Agincourt were all made Masters. These were the 'new' English, the businessmen, the *arrivistes*, the people who were building the first British Empire and who would soon chop off the head of Charles I. And into this highly organised society is thrown the court and Falstaff, who get their comeuppance for trying to make a few quid by seducing a wife or two. The play is a celebration of the new nation, of the new renaissance nation.

Timothy O'Brien's set reflected Hands' vision of Windsor; that of a new town, newly wealthy, hewn into the forest by its landowning, professional inhabitants. The uprights of the trees were disciplined into a township. There were no walls, the audience were invited to imagine the boundary between the 'domestic' and the forest. This gave each 'domestic' scene a broader social context, lightly pointing up the *nouveau* side of the characters, and by hanging a few dolls from the branches of forest, the darker suggestion that the characters were not very far removed from their pagan past. This gave the Horn's Oak scene overtones of Hallowe'en. Like the *Berliner Ensemble*, social context and social relations were not incidental in this production but became central to the drama.

> Before we get on to the 'design', the question of the space you are working in has to be addressed. If you can get that right, then you don't need a set. Then you can move to the naked actor and what you need minimally to cover him or her to focus the play. That is for me the very first part. I always want air to pass through a set and I want room to move the actors. I prefer to work with very little. Also, it seems to me, that everything that happens on stage whether it is movement or a response has to support the line. And, if you work without furniture, which I for the most part do, all the energy can be directed in to the play and its communication.

Hands' preparation enabled him to be a walking encyclopaedia in the rehearsal room, talking to the actors about who these characters are and continually offering fresh contexts for each scene, rarely interrupting, never pushing, never doctrinaire. As he puts it:

> I was not going to teach Ian [Richardson] or Liz [Spriggs] anything. All you can do is throw them a different colour ball each time and watch what they do with it. The more coloured balls you throw them, the more they'll play and the more wonderful they'll be.

While Hands' resistance to 'blocking', as illustrated by this example from the early part of his career, is rooted in respect for the actor's craft, it also springs from the desire to serve the variety of Shakespeare's text by preserving the variety of the actor performing it. Indeed, it might be said that this is the main focus of his work, the thing that all aspects of his productions are geared towards. When talking about rehearsals for *The Merry Wives of Windsor*, he remarked:

> I wouldn't do blocking. I never do. I don't to this day. You really can't 'block'. Because the way in which Miss A or Mr B speaks and moves is going to be different each time. With 'blocking' you can erase masses of detail, and that detail has to come from the actor. And if you allow them to act freely, it does.

This can also be said of his native suspicion of any 'technique' that interferes with the actor's freedom of movement, anything that gets between the impulse of the actor and his text. For Hands, in the main, excavating and exploring what the playwright has written is difficult enough without muddying the water with extra-textual conjecture. As I witnessed during rehearsals for his 2003 production of *The Crucible*, when an actor asserted meekly, 'My character wouldn't do that', Hands curtly replied, 'There's no such thing. Your character is you, plus what you say, start again'. However, during the 1968 *Merry Wives of Windsor*, his assistant director, the late Buzz Goodbody said:

> 'proper directors do improvisations.' I replied that I think they are a waste of time and she said 'let me do some'. So she took everybody off one day to The Other Place, and the whole 'village' went to church for the day. With a service conducted by Hugh Evans and they sat in pews and they had to decide who would sit next to each other. It was actually hugely valuable. It aided and clarified their behaviour to each other on stage.

This is a useful vignette demonstrating his willingness to explore something counter-intuitive in the rehearsal room. But to any actor, assistant director, designer or stage manager who suggests something off the beaten track, his response will be 'If it works we'll keep it, if it doesn't we won't'. Little time is wasted on discussion, and filibustering is not tolerated.

During his 1971 *Richard III* for the RSC, Hands experimented further with the notion of 'non-blocking', pushing the freedom of his actors to the limit, allowing them almost total freedom to rebuild the stage action every night. His brilliant company (including Helen Mirren as Lady Anne, Norman Rodway as Richard and Ian Richardson as Buckingham) had only sporadic success with this method, finding it difficult to maintain in a busy repertory system. Hands regarded this experiment as a failure. In 1972, he was offered the opportunity to direct a new production of *Richard III* at the Comédie-Française:

> I was about the 15th director to be invited as all the others had turned it down. I agreed to do it mainly because I'd had a flop with the play and I considered it unfinished business. The Comédie-Française *Richard III* was a success. Robert Hirsch was an astonishing Richard, Jacques Charon played Buckingham, all the greats of the French theatre were in it. Abdel [Abd'Elkader Farrah, known professionally as 'Farrah', 1926–2005] designed. It was at this time I began to learn the way that the French language worked. The French actors, of course, having a so-called 'non-tonic language' played the phrase, where we in England at that time were playing the 'word'. What you would hear in the corridors and the rehearsal rooms at the RSC at that time was 'colouring the word'. The result was that we often played very slowly. We had problems in Stratford because our shows had to be down by 10.30 because the bus services back to Birmingham left at 10.50. As a result, the texts of our productions were heavily cut. What I discovered with the French, because they played not the 'word', but the 'phrase', right the way through to the full stop, their work was that much faster and more meaningful. Instead of stressing every other word they were accentuating 'the meaning'.

For the French classical actors, playing through to the end of the sentence came from the tradition of the *tirade*. Actors could use the pattern of the verse line and the thematic repetition to build emotional intensity. Hands started to apply these ideas to English Shakespeare on his 1975 production of *Henry V*:

> After France, I suggested to Alan Howard that we could play like that, through to the full stop, ideally on one breath. It became a company joke at first because sometimes the full stop didn't come for 15 lines, but even if they couldn't do the line on one breath, they could have that point in mind as they started the sentence. Soon we found that we were playing far more of the text than we normally did and we were coming down well within our 10.30 limit. I played *Julius Caesar* without an interval and it was through in two hours fifteen. It became more and

> more popular because it released the actor's instinct. Instead of the heavy preparation of a line, which was basically nineteenth-century, now they were flowing through the play. Most importantly, far more lines were being played so you got more richness from the experience itself, rather than the last minute ad hoc cutting that used to go on in order to get it over with by the required time.

Aesthetically also, Hands and Farrah were able to build on the lessons learned at the Comédie-Française and bring them to their most vivid realisation here. For Hands, this was the play about the theatre building, 'the wooden "o" '. Director and designer had decided to open up the Royal Shakespeare Theatre (RST) and place this epic theatre space at the centre of the production. The back wall of the theatre was revealed, as was the wing space; the stage was thrust as far out in to the auditorium as possible, this was the largest playing area ever used by the company. Farrah likened the set to an 'aircraft carrier landing deck', upon which the play would take place, and then concentrated on the detail of costuming, richness of decoration and a careful selection of props. He also demanded that the lighting should carry an equivalent impact. Hands had been lighting his own work since the all-hands-on-deck days of the Everyman, a skill he had acquired on the primitive Strand Junior 8 lighting board, at the same time as learning to run prompt corner and fumigate the seats. The introduction of computers in 1972 made it logistically possible for him to light work of this scale, and he credited himself as Lighting Designer for the first time on this *Henry V*.

With only an ugly bundle of grey rags centre stage to dress their epic, empty 'wooden "o" ', Hands and Farrah were inviting their audience to 'think, when we talk of horses, that you see them' on a massive scale. They decided that this complicity between actor and audience should start with the actors on a bare stage in rehearsal clothes preparing themselves for the performance:

> In a way, the beginning of the play is spent rehearsing for the play that is to come. The play doesn't really begin until you get to Southampton. So we literally started with the actors on stage at 7 p.m. doing their exersises in their ordinary rehearsal clothes and the first costume we saw was that of the French Ambassador. We felt that this play, as it often is in Shakespeare is about an out-of-date, over-the-hill declining power confronting a new vibrant one. So if you play for twenty minutes in your rehearsal clothes and a spot-on replica of a medieval French Ambassador enters, he will look even more out of place and even more out of date because everybody else looks so relaxed.

The Queen was due to visit Stratford, in this the centenary year of the theatre, certain sections of the audience were very keen that Her Majesty should not see the RSC play *Henry V* in their jeans. Within the company there was unrest too, as the actors attempted to persuade Hands that this lack of costume made the audience see 'them and not their character', he countered that this first section of the play 'became about the words and not about the costume'.

The production hinged on the *coup de théâtre* at the top of Act II that accompanied Emrys James' thrilling delivery of the 'Now all the youth in England are on fire' speech. The true scale of Alan Howard's voice emerged through the indignance of the 'tennis balls speech' in Act I Scene II, as he faced the costumed French ambassador; and over James' speech the ugly bundle of rags exploded to form a great canopy over the stage as a large cart packed with actors came hurtling on, carrying an enormous cannon:

> Often we played the first fifteen minutes to a 1500-seat theatre in icy disbelief. But when the explosion came, the level of warmth that flooded the stage sustained the production from then right through to the end of the evening.

Farrah's costumes and Hands' lighting design combined to create many memorable visual moments, punctuating the rapid tempo of the production:

> I remember saying to Abdel that we could only afford three actors to play the multitudinous French Army that was going to crush Henry. He asked me to keep the light in one tight area, his French knights came out in golden armour. When the light hit it was like a sunrise.

Hands later said of Farrah, 'for me he was more than a friend and collaborator. He was mentor, guide and the strongest artistic influence of my life'. In Alan Howard too he found a strong and lasting collaborator. His vast vocal range and lupine, dextrous, butch physicality gave Hands, in some ways, his ideal leading man. An actor of charisma, technical prowess and variety, able to play with speed but lose none of the articulation and definition in the text.

In this centenary year Hands directed all four productions in the RSC's Stratford season, including a revival of his *Merry Wives* and an acclaimed staging of both parts of *King Henry IV*. He was made Joint Artistic Director of the RSC in 1978 and Sole Artistic Director and Chief Executive in 1986 until his departure from the company he had helped to build in 1991 after 25-years.

After a successful career as a freelance director, winning accolades for productions in Paris, New York, London and Tokyo, Hands took on the task of saving Theatr Clwyd, a repertory theatre in Mold, north Wales. The theatre has two performance spaces: the 550-seat Anthony Hopkins Theatre and the 200-seat Emlyn Williams Studio space. What began as a consultancy contract to reopen the theatre, became an enduring relationship and a new challenge. At the time of writing in early spring 2007, he is still Artistic Director and Chief Executive of the thriving company, with a large audience in Wales and beyond. In 1998, Theatr Clwyd's name was changed to Clwyd Theatr Cymru to reflect its commitment to its Welsh identity and to its Welsh audiences. It has been a galvanising force for Welsh actors, writers and directors. As part of its repertoire the company has mounted ambitious productions of repertory staples such as *Romeo and Juliet*, and *Macbeth* (played by Owen Teale), and it has received critical acclaim for productions of *King Lear* (played by Nicol Williamson) and *Troilus and Cressida*, plays that are rarely mounted in regional repertory houses, due to a combination of cast size, perceived box office draw and the monumental challenge for actors.

Clwyd Theatr Cymru continues to be a political lightning rod in Welsh arts discourse, because of its status as a de facto national theatre in the English language and the role that it might play in building a confident, bi-lingual Welsh identity in a devolved Wales in the twenty-first century. Shakespeare has had a central role in the discourse relating to the establishment of a Welsh national theatre. A Welsh Assembly Nationalist once labelled Shakespeare a 'London writer', writer of the English oppressor and, as such, should not play a role in the development of a Welsh theatre culture. Unsurprisingly Hands passionately disagrees:

> If you want to create a true national theatre in any country, you do need to focus it on a particular writer or writers. In Norway they do the work of Ibsen, Sweden, Strindberg, and so on. England has predominantly Shakespeare but there are many others. It is noticeable in countries that have a 'national' writer, their second writer is almost invariably Shakespeare. Shakespeare in his richness of humanity, breadth of imagination, becomes '*notre Shakspeare*' or '*unser Shakespeare*'. Belonging as much to them as he does to us.

With no dominant national author for the stage, Hands feels that Shakespeare could be:

> crucial to the Welsh experience. If you start with the premise that you do not require special conditions to play it and that Shakespeare

> speaks immediately to the rich and the poor, to the educated and the non-educated. While of course it would be better if there were a Welsh O'Casey or a Welsh Molière, there isn't. Shakespeare should, I think, form the core of a national theatre repertoire.

What then for the future of the production of Shakespeare's plays, not only in Wales but in the broader UK, particularly given the increased commercial pressures on actor availability and on production budgets? Placing this question in a broader historical context, Hands sees a trend not towards too little Shakespeare, but too much:

> [At the RSC] every production we did had to be a major event. We tried to do each production so well that no one would go near the play for five years. Sometimes we succeeded. We never sent a play out on tour until it had been showered with praise in both Stratford and London. Now I feel the attitude is 'Don't worry if you miss this bus, there'll be another one along in a minute'. Shakespeare is championed partly by critics who are bored of Shakespeare Adaptation, partly by bored practitioners. But the fourteen-year-old coming to the theatre for the first time is not bored. Should a great play by Shakespeare (comedy or tragedy) be a great event? Or should it be part of a theme park? At present I feel it's more theme park and I would like to see more event.

But:

> We can't all be Peter Brook. Of course we can't. I was sitting there on the first night of *A Midsummer Night's Dream* and by the interval we all knew we were at a moment of history. I don't mind trying the whole of my life to achieve one interval like that.

Chronology

1964 Founded the Liverpool Everyman Theatre with Peter James and Martin Jenkins

1966 Joined RSC at Stratford-upon-Avon, in charge of Theatre-Go-Round

1975 Directed all four productions in the centenary season at Stratford 1975, *Henry V, Henry IV Parts 1 and 2. Henry V* also on international tour

1977 Directed the three parts of Henry VI, the first time produced in their entirety since Shakespeare's day

1972 Directed *Richard III* at the Comédie-Française, later at the World Theatre Season, London in 1973

1978 Appointed Joint Artistic Director of the RSC and, from 1986 to 1991, Chief Executive: productions included *The Winter's Tale* (with Jeremy Irons), *Coriolanus* (with Charles Dance) and *Love's Labour's Lost* (with Ralph Fiennes)

1996 Joined Theatr Clwyd as Artistic Consultant, preventing its closure after local government reorganisation

1997 Appointed Director and Chief Executive of the renamed Clwyd Theatr Cymru which in 1999 became a Welsh national performing arts company: productions included *Twelfth Night, Macbeth, King Lear* (with Nicol Williamson as Lear), *Romeo and Juliet* and *Troilus and Cressida.*

Bibliography

Interviews with Terry Hands were conducted at various times throughout 2006–7 and are in the possession of Phillip Breen.

Addenbrooke, David (1974) *The Royal Shakespeare Company: The Peter Hall Years*, London: Kimber.

Chambers, Colin (2004) *Inside the Royal Shakespeare Company: Creativity and the Institution*, London and New York: Routledge.

Daniell, David (1980) *'Coriolanus' in Europe*, London: Athlone Press.

About the author

Phillip Breen is Director of New Writing at Clwyd Theatr Cymru. Credits as Director include *Suddenly Last Summer* (Clwyd Theatr Cymru), *The Shadow of a Gunman* (Glasgow Citizen's), *The Birthday Party* (Clwyd Theatr Cymru), *The Zam Zam Room: An Evening with his Royal Hipness Lord Buckley* (Soho Theatre, Ronnie Scott's and Off-Broadway – *Time Out New York* 'Pick of 2005'), *The Resistible Rise of Arturo Ui* (Glasgow Citizen's) *The Promise* (Union Theatre, London) *Far Too Happy* (Edinburgh Fringe, West End and national tour, 2001 Perrier Award nomination), *A Few Idiots Who Spoil It for Everyone Else* by Tim Key and Mark Watson (Canal Café Theatre, London), *Memoirs of A Dead Man* (Edinburgh Fringe), *Destiny* (BAC, Runner Up for 2003 James Menzies Kitchen Award). Phillip was Director of EDGE04, the Chichester Festival Theatre's Fringe Event, where he directed his own adaptation of Bulgakov's *Black Snow* and the BBC rehearsed reading of John Hegley's radio play *The Cat in the Kennel*. Phillip was the curator of the RSC's Laugh-In event which contained original material from Armando Iannucci, Ken Dodd, Alan Plater, Richard Herring, Oliver and Zaltzman, Alex Horne, Mark Watson, and The Cowards. His first play *Past Imperfect* was shortlisted for *Write2002*, the Manchester Royal Exchange's New Writing Award.

11
HENRY IRVING

Russell Jackson

During his lifetime, Sir Henry Irving (1838–1905), born in a cottage, made the first theatrical knight (in 1895) and buried in Westminster Abbey, became an icon of the new-found respectability of his profession. This did not come about without conscious effort: his most recent biographer rightly emphasises Irving's 'promotion of theatrical commemoration and [. . .] publicity management' as contributions to the acceptance of the commercial theatre – and himself – as significant in cultural life (Richards 2005: 73).

As a Victorian actor-manager who supervised meticulously every aspect of his productions, Irving exercised many of the functions subsequently associated with the independent director. This was a theatre of grand pictorial effects and vivid individual performances, with texts tailored to suit the demands of elaborate scenery and the talents of the principal actors. The actor-manager had the last say in matters of lighting, scenic effects, music, costume and casting, rehearsed the members of his acting company, so as to achieve a sense of ensemble, and articulated through the coordination of these elements a consistent interpretation of the scripts he had chosen. In many respects, he resembled the Hollywood executives of the mid-twentieth century, such as Irving Thalberg or David O. Selznick, who exercised effective control over all aspects of their productions. Crucially, though, Irving was *not* independent: the marshalling of these forces – which in the heyday of his tenure at the Lyceum Theatre were formidable – was effected in support of his own performances as an actor. Any discussion of his practice and influence has to take account of the assertion by George Bernard Shaw, the most trenchant of his critics, that 'a prodigious deal of nonsense ha[d] been written about Sir Henry Irving's conception of this, that, and the other Shakespearian character.' The truth was 'that he [had] never in his life conceived or interpreted the characters of any author except himself' (Wilson 1969: 75). Given that Irving's Shakespearean productions were organised around these interpretations of the characters he played, the actor's 'conception' of the plays has to be treated with some caution. Nevertheless, these theatrical spectacles possessed remarkable unity of effect, amounting to a Shakespearian realisation of Richard Wagner's *Gesamtkunstwerk* – the artwork that would bring together all its contributing elements in a unified whole.

Speaking at Harvard in 1885, Irving insisted on the need for an ensemble, but in his case it was to be derived from attention to pictorial effect rather than the actors' work together on the script: 'It is most important that an actor should learn he is a figure in a picture, and that the least exaggeration destroys the harmony of a composition'. The aim of a company should be to 'work towards a common end, with the nicest subordination of their individuality to the general purpose' (Richards 1994: 44). His example inspired not only like-minded fellow actor-managers to comparable feats of scenic elaboration (in many respects, Herbert Beerbohm-Tree was his true heir) but also influenced more radical artists. Edward Gordon Craig acknowledged that his experience of the Lyceum and its ambience was crucial in his own development as a theorist and practitioner.

Craig subsequently celebrated Irving's untiring rehearsal of actors in every detail of their enunciation (like Irving, Craig spent little time on psychological subtleties and motivations), the boldness and scale of his stage pictures and his ability to disregard accuracy in period settings in favour of what would *seem* right and achieve the desired artistic effect. Irving, he insisted, was not a producer – the word commonly used in the early 1900s for the person now called a director – but an actor, and Craig admired and respected his single-mindedness in organising plays around his own performances (Craig 1930: 84). Descriptions of Irving at work in rehearsal have more than a hint of the approach that in Craig's writings led to the concept of the actor-as-puppet, the *Übermarionette*. When he took over management of the Lyceum in 1878 he was able to achieve results that as mere leading actor had been beyond his remit:

> He rehearsed over and over again the first scene [of *Hamlet*], striving to impart into each character the individuality, urgency and power which he deemed necessary to 'start the play a living thing.' With infinite care he worked up the procession which preceded his own entrance – the royal yet subdued pageant advancing and dispersing to reveal the sabled, solitary figure of Hamlet, whose spirituality was accented by a subtle dimming of the lights.
>
> (Irving 1951: 311)

Not only the 'infinite care' but also the final effect and the means of achieving it would become characteristic of Irving's management.

However, unlike Craig, Konstantin Stanislavsky and Max Reinhardt, Irving was not an actor who forsook his original craft to mutate into a director. He did not initiate any new method of theatrical production, still less develop or propound any innovative theories of his art. His published lectures and speeches, although extensively prepared for him (and on occasion probably written) by assistants, reflected his ambitions for the theatre as a respected and socially established artform. His comments on the technique of acting are confined to reflections on the means of achieving effects rather than the mental work needed to 'build' a character in the later, Stanislavskian sense. Irving, after all, had learned his craft in a theatre that left actors, so long they were competent, to look after their own performance. For all his due acknowledgement of and attention to new developments in the visual arts, Irving was effectively elaborating the production style evolved by his actor-managerial predecessors, notably Charles Kean and Samuel Phelps. Irving refined practices derived from the former's mid-century antiquarianism and the latter's forceful acting and sense of company work.

It has been suggested that Irving's work – in particular, his direction of crowd scenes – was influenced by the London visit of the Meiningen Court Theatre company in 1881, but the Duke of Saxe-Meiningen had himself been influenced by Charles Kean's productions and at least one of the visitors, the actor Ludwig Barnay, claimed that the Lyceum performances were 'a complete revelation' (Booth 1981: 56; Jackson 2004: 156). Like the Duke and his stage director, Ludwig Chronegk, Irving aimed for realistic, individualised crowd effects rather than generalised routine behaviour from the 'supers', but there is evidence that the Lyceum effects were more harmonious and less fussy. In this respect, Irving's practice anticipated the more stylised effects achieved in the early twentieth century by Craig and Reinhardt. The numbers involved were very considerable: the wardrobe for the 1888 *Macbeth* had to provide for 165 soldiers, eighty 'flying witches', forty lords and ladies, sixteen waiting-women and at least a dozen other non-speaking roles, as well as the principals (Hughes 1978: 16; Spielman 1889: 99). By the standards of the late twentieth and early twenty-first centuries, not to mention the playwright's own time, Lyceum Shakespeare would seem vastly overpopulated.

Irving's ascendancy as an actor had begun in 1871 with the success of his performance at the Lyceum in Leopold Lewis's melodrama *The Bells*. In 1874, when he first appeared there as Hamlet, he effectively staked his claim to be regarded as a major Shakespearian talent, although there were dissenters, among them William Archer, coauthor in 1877 of a pamphlet, *The Fashionable Tragedian*, that lampooned Irving's vocal and physical mannerisms mercilessly and whose title indicated a sceptical view of his growing status as a celebrity. His first appearance at the Lyceum as Shylock, in 1879, consolidated his reputation in a role where he was less vulnerable to the reservations of his detractors. The span of Irving's career coincided with the heyday (and eventual decline) of the 'Aesthetic Movement' in art and decoration, with its pursuit of subtlety in colouring, evocation of delicately defined moods and atmospheric effects. He was painted by Whistler and celebrated by Wilde, and employed eminent painters – Edward Burne-Jones, Ford Madox Brown and Laurence Alma-Tadema – as designers and advisers.

In a later, more appreciative (but still sharply analytical) work, Archer observed that in the first five years of his management Irving had achieved 'a whole gallery of scenic pictures, each as worthy of minute study as any canvas of the most learned archaeological painter'. The 'minute artistic realism' was qualified, though, by distinctively modern taste: the 'intellect of South Kensington' (that is, the Victoria & Albert Museum) might have been 'taxed' and its resources 'ransacked', but '[n]o previous manager could have produced such effects, for the time was not yet come. The Lyceum drama came into existence with – I had almost said for the sake of – the new art hues and fabrics' (Archer 1883: 97). On assuming management of the Lyceum, one of Irving's first actions, to the dismay and anger of the former managers, Colonel and Mrs H.L. Bateman, had been to replace their daughter Isabel with the infinitely more charismatic actress Ellen Terry as Ophelia. Terry had been married – briefly and unsuccessfully – to the painter G.F. Watts and had lived with the architect and artist Edward William Godwin. (Godwin was the father of her children, including Edward Gordon Craig, who appeared at the Lyceum as an actor.) She brought a direct connection with the new movement in art. As Archer put it:

> Whatever her absolute merits in a part, she always harmonizes as perhaps she alone could with the whole tone of the picture. She gives their crowning glory to the fabrics of South Kensington. She has all the outward and visible signs of the inward and spiritual grace which covers a multitude of histrionic sins – I mean, of course, Intensity.
>
> (Archer 1883: 101)

This key concept of aestheticism, mocked memorably in Gilbert and Sullivan's *Patience* (1882), gives a valuable clue to the effectiveness and popularity of Irving's productions. As an actor, he was 'intense' in conveying by finely tuned external detail the conflicted states of mind of his characters, and he created stage effects to enhance these performances.

Irving's Lyceum favoured revivals of mid-century melodramas, historical subjects and adapted literary texts. The choice of living dramatists was far from adventurous, and Irving's proudest endeavour in that direction (and the play he was acting in the night he died) was Alfred Lord Tennyson's *Becket*. In Archer's words, the Lyceum was dominated by 'a dead drama skilfully galvanised' (Archer 1883: 95). Shakespeare was a major element of the Lyceum's repertoire and provided many of Irving's 'signature' roles. However, his acting, and the atmospherics of his productions, did not suit every Shakespearian play he attempted and excluded many from his repertoire. In effect, Irving's methods turned Shakespearian tragedies into superior melodrama and lent melodrama the aura of high art. In some respects, though, Irving's attention to undemonstrative, natural-seeming detail in his Shakespearian roles (Hamlet, for example) and their freedom from stale convention corresponded with the means by which he achieved a refinement of melodramatic technique in such performances as that of the remorse-stricken burgomaster Mathias in *The Bells*.

Irving's Hamlet was remarkable for its avoidance of 'points', the vivid but too often over-emphasised bits of business or vocal effects by which actors put their signature on crises or high points in a role. 'From the first moment he enters upon the stage,' wrote one admirer of his 1878 performance, 'lounging with a sour discontented air, in the rear of his mother's retinue, we feel that no heroic creature will stride to the front to compel our admiration and carry our sympathies by storm; it is a very human being, with faults and frailties like our own' (Hardy 1879: 19). However, convention was not discarded when Irving saw a use for it. Like many previous Hamlets, he crawled across the stage towards the King during the play scene, having taken Ophelia's fan to hide his face (Hughes 1978: 59–60). The first innovation was the fact that the fan was made of peacock feathers, considered unlucky on stage, and a further surprise came when Hamlet threw himself into the King's throne singing the rhyme 'For thou dost know, O Damon dear' – and then threw the fan aside on the final line, 'A very – very – pajock.' It was a moment that even those who had seen him in the part many times continued to find electrifying (Sprague 1944: 159–60). Irving's Hamlet was a performance skilfully adapted to his capacity for nervous energy underlying melancholy, the kind of divided personality which, as Peter Thomson has argued, gave Irving his direct connection with contemporary preoccupations in psychology. Even his villains had to be conscience-stricken, and 'he was not at ease with sheer evil' (Thomson 2000: 157).

There were also occasions – notably his 1888 *Macbeth* – when a play that ought to suit his penchant for anguished psychology, shadows and vivid contrasts of lighting failed to achieve the anticipated result. In some cases, a handsome production could not compensate for the miscasting of the central male role with an actor (Irving) who lacked the lightness of touch or physical grace it was conventionally held to require, and Irving's Romeo (1882) and

Malvolio (1884) were generally considered inadequate. In at least one case, the absence of a major role suited to his talents prevented him from producing a play that would have been ideal for Ellen Terry: Irving never staged *As You Like It*, and she never got to play Rosalind. It is an overstatement of the case to treat Terry (as Nina Auerbach does in her fine biography of the actress) as a *victim* of Irving's regime – after all, it provided her with her greatest triumphs, and she was a resourceful, brilliant woman with a mind of her own. However, no other London management in the last decades of the century was able to stage productions with the liberality and prestige achieved at the Lyceum, and her presence there was a major element in its attractions. Whether or not she and Irving were lovers in the strictest sense will never be known, but this was a loving artistic partnership. Terry's affection and respect for the man and his artistry are evident in everything she wrote about him, even when – in private – she ruefully admitted that there were limitations to the scope afforded her.

Between 1878 and 1901 Irving staged productions of twelve plays by Shakespeare, including new versions of three in which he already been acclaimed as an actor, *Hamlet, Richard III* and *Macbeth*. There were two histories (*Henry VIII* in 1892 and *Richard III* in 1896); three comedies (*The Merchant of Venice* in 1879, *Much Ado about Nothing* in 1882 and *Twelfth Night* in 1884); and the tragedies *Hamlet* (1878), *Othello* (1879 and 1881), *Romeo and Juliet* (1882), *Macbeth* (1888) and *King Lear* (1892). *Cymbeline* was produced in 1896, and *Coriolanus*, in 1901, was the last new Shakespearian production staged under his management.

Any account of Irving as a director has to take into account the impact of his own acting, just as study of his acting cannot be separated from his staging of the plays with regard to his place in the stage picture. His contemporaries often spoke of Irving's acting in terms of the 'realisation' of a familiar image (in historical roles) or the creation of a vivid and original portrait, describing his demeanour, costume and make-up as though the result were a painting exhibited in an art gallery. Thus, in *The Merchant of Venice*, the impact of his dignified, quasi-tragic Shylock was powerfully reinforced by the additional (and much-imitated) episode he added to the conclusion of Shakespeare's Act II, Scene 6, when Shylock returned to his house to discover that Jessica had eloped. The scene was a fully set stage, with a canal, spanned by a narrow bridge, upstage, and Shylock's house on the quayside closest to the footlights. Lorenzo arrived with a crowd of masqueraders in his (practicable) gondola, and he and his bride-to-be left the stage in a flurry of movement, music and colour. The act drop fell quickly and rose again immediately to reveal the empty street and canalside 'with no light but the pale moon, and all sounds of life at a great distance'. Shylock entered wearily over the bridge and was about to enter the house as the drop fell again (Hughes 1978: 232). Even more memorable (as befitted his final scene) was Irving's exit at the end of the trial scene. It combined elements of 'stage-management' as it was then understood – skilful timing and the deployment of the crowd of 'supers' – with the effect of the individual performance.

> The quiet shrug, the glance of ineffable, unfathomable contempt at the exultant booby, Gratiano [. . .] the expression of defeat in every limb and feature, the deep, gasping sigh, as he passes slowly out, and the crowd rush from the Court to hoot and howl at him outside, make up an effect which must be seen to be comprehended.
>
> (Sprague 1953: 116)

As a director, Irving knew how to shape the audience's perception of the character by well-orchestrated emotional effects at strategic points in the flow of the play.

As was customary at the time, Irving cut lines, passages, scenes and sometimes whole characters from his acting scripts of the plays: even with long intervals between the acts, cuts were needed to allow for the setting and striking of elaborate scenery. However, for the most part, Irving refrained from adding episodes or extended stage business not directly warranted in a play. His 1877 production of *Richard III* broke with theatrical custom by beginning with the play's first lines rather than the preliminary scenes – including the murder of Henry VI – provided by Colley Cibber's 1700 adaptation. Irving was not the first to revert to Shakespeare's text, but his production established it as the norm, at least in London. After 1877, as Arthur Colby Sprague notes in his account of the play's stage history, 'use of the alteration was to be exceptional and a little furtive' (Sprague 1966: 131).

In *Much Ado about Nothing*, though, Irving insisted (to Terry's chagrin) on following tradition with a familiar 'gag' (as actors' additions were called) at the end of the 'Church Scene' (Act IV, Scene 1):

> BENEDICK: I will kiss your hand, and so leave you. By this hand, Claudio shall render me a dear account.
> BEATRICE: My dear friend, kiss my hand again.
> BENEDICK: As you hear of me, so think of me. Go, comfort your cousin; I must say, she is dead.
> BEATRICE: Benedick, kill him, kill him if you can.
> BENEDICK: As sure as he's alive, I will.

Cuts elsewhere in the play amounted to some 569 lines, but this additional exchange earned its keep by providing a 'strong curtain' that set up the challenge before the interval that followed (Hughes 1978: 174). It also shifted the emphasis decisively and in true actor-managerial fashion onto Benedick's masculine resolve and new-found seriousness and away from the couple's emotional situation.

Much Ado about Nothing, by no means a favourite with Victorian audiences, became one of the management's enduring successes, with 212 performances in its initial run, two subsequent revivals at the Lyceum and continuing popularity on tour. A great deal of the attraction lay in Terry's charm and vivacity, complemented by Irving's subordination of his habitually quirky, sardonic humour to a degree of panache and elegance. Common anxieties that Beatrice would seem too 'shrewish' and Benedick too coarse were allayed.

The manager's visual taste was represented most impressively in the set for Act IV, Scene 1, the sanctuary and part of the aisle of a cathedral whose vastness was skilfully suggested by a blending of 'built-out' (three-dimensional) scenery and painted backcloths. The scene was staged with as much of the panoply of religious ceremony as could be achieved without causing offence to those who might object to its accurate reproduction on stage. Clement Scott, an ardent admirer of the actor, was at pains to point out how he had managed to treat this solemn scene 'realistically and still with reverence'. Having taken advice from the clergy on the correct forms and ceremonies, Irving carefully removed specific liturgical symbolism from the staging and the vestments. Both Scott and Irving's business manager and biographer Bram Stoker describe the process (Stoker 1907: 105), and Scott's apologetic description suggests not only the solemnity achieved but also the attitude to 'art' that the Lyceum embodied for many of its patrons:

> There can be no harm in the incense that fills the air as the bridal processions file to the appointed spot; in the plaintive wail of the organ, with its soft and persuasive reed stop, contrasted with the secular music attendant on the bride; there can be no danger in the admirable and effective contrast of the major and minor keys throughout this extraordinary scenic composition; a contrast of priests and courtiers, of ecclesiastical ritual and courtly solemnity; of organ and stringed band; of religion and the world. And the consequence is that there is left impressed on the memory all that is beautiful and nothing that is distasteful. That is surely the highest mission of art.
>
> (Scott 1897: 251)

In modulating the scene's staging so as to avoid direct presentation of religious ceremony, Irving was, of course, complying with the rules the Lord Chamberlain's office would have insisted on as part of the censorship regime that remained in place until the late 1960s, but he was also courting the sensibility of his own devotees.

The revival of *Macbeth* in the 1888–9 season was, in many respects, characteristic of the best in Irving's production style. As Lady Macbeth in the ascendant during the first acts, Ellen Terry wore a brilliant and exotic costume of soft green and blue fabric made to shimmer by being sewn over with real beetle wings and offset by vivid red wig with long plaits: this stood out strikingly against the sombre background of the sets and the tenebrous lighting, as did Macbeth's second costume 'of heavy bullion-coloured silk, with sleeves of light blue silk' and the golden armour he wore in the final scenes (Spielman 1889: 99). Oscar Wilde was prompted to observe that 'Judging from the banquet, Lady Macbeth evidently patronises local industries for her husband's clothes and the servants' liveries, but she takes care to do all her own shopping in Byzantium' (Robertson 1931: 151).

Irving worked up fine torchlight effects for the aftermath of the murder and the banquet, although some reviewers noted the intrusion of shafts of limelight (the equivalent of modern follow-spots) to pick out the principals. Duncan arrived at Macbeth's castle (the play's Act I, Scene 6) at night – allowing for a striking torchlit picture but making impossible any observation of the 'temple haunting martlet' and hardly affording evidence for the King's declaration that the castle had 'a pleasant seat'. Recalling the scene many years later, the dramatist Henry Arthur Jones, generally an admirer of the actor, thought that in this case his preference for atmospheric lighting had got the better of him: 'Shakespeare's words went for nothing, meant nothing, were scarcely heard' (Jones 1931: 60).

Macbeth's return to the witches (Act IV, Scene 1) was staged as a spectacle in which scenic landscape painting was combined with supernatural effects. In the words of the theatrical trade paper the *Era*:

> The figure of Macbeth on a rocky eminence stands out bold and picturesque against the lurid sky, and while the hell broth steams, and the spectres rise there is heard the tuneful chorus the witches chant, 'Black spirits and white' [inserted, as was customary, from Middleton's *The Witch*], while later, the scene changing to a Scotch lake, beneath a stormy sky, the stage is filled with Hecate's host, who waving their arms, break forth with the beautifully melodic chorus 'Come away.'
>
> (5 January 1889)

The reviewer compared this, not surprisingly, to the Brocken scene in Irving's *Faust* (1885), one of the theatre's most successful and profitable productions (Booth 1981: 115–24).

In the overall scheme of the production, Irving's six-act version moved from darkness to greater darkness, with an elaborate cavern setting for the apparitions summoned by the witches, gloomy interiors relieved by torches and an autumnal setting for the final scenes – after a supposed interval of six years during which Macbeth's hair and beard had turned grey. 'The dominant impression left upon the mind', wrote the reviewer from *The Times*, was that of 'a wild, haggard, anguish-stricken man [. . .] visibly an old man when he dies, his grey hair dishevelled, floating wildly in the wind' (31 December 1888). Complemented by Arthur Sullivan's mysterious and compelling score (whose overture has remained in the concert and recording repertoire), the play became an elegiac story of unredeemed guilt.

Unfortunately, it was generally held that Irving and Terry had misconceived their roles. He was doomed from the very beginning: in the words of the *Saturday Review*, 'his lined and haggard features, his restless movements, his wild and wandering eye, [gave] him altogether the air of a prey of the Furies at his first entrance upon the scene' (5 January 1889). Some thought Macbeth cowardly, too easily daunted, while the general verdict on Ellen Terry was that she was too mild and conventionally 'womanly'. On her first appearance, she was revealed seated by a great stone hearth, reading her husband's letter by the glowing embers of the fire and occasionally glancing at his portrait. *The Times* (31 December 1888) noted that she read with little sense of surprise and settled in an armchair to ponder the situation, her reaction being one of joyful satisfaction rather than exhilaration, 'a gentle, affectionate wife, wrapped up in her husband.' Even 'unsex me here' was spoken falteringly, as though she were making 'a manifest effort to repress her feminine instincts'. In a strictly private letter to the critic Clement Scott, Terry defended her interpretation eloquently and in striking personal terms, but in the public world it was counted not unreasonably as an indication that in this role she could not overcome the temperament that made her so effective in comedy or as a virtuously pathetic heroine (Auerbach 1987: 257–8). For all its limitations, the production was successful, playing for 150 nights to capacity audiences until the season ended on 2 June 1889 (Irving 1951: 506).

Irving's later Shakespearian productions included at least one personal triumph, his Cardinal Wolsey in *Henry VIII* (1892), although it was admitted that he modelled the interpretation more on Richelieu than on the historical original, making him a subtle, refined prince of the church rather than an ambitious, overtly combative political animal. The historical pageant dominated what was considered a disjointed and unsatisfactory play. *King Lear* (also 1892), for all its painterly attractions – including a magnificent rendering of the cliffs near Dover for the final scene – was marred by the uncertainty of Irving's performance as the King on the first night.

Nevertheless, Lear's first entrance made a profound impression, framing his character in a striking moment by mobilising the forces of the ensemble in support of an essentially 'picturesque' piece of acting. The Shakespearian enthusiast Gordon Crosse could still recall it in detail forty-seven years later:

> Kent and the others have spoken their opening dialogue ending with 'the king is coming.' And here he comes down the steps, a striking figure with masses of white hair. He is leaning on a huge scabbarded sword which he raises with a wild cry in answer to the shouted greetings of his guards. His gait, his looks, his gestures, all reveal the noble, imperious mind already degenerating into senile irritability and ready to fall into utter ruin under the coming shocks of grief and rage.
>
> (Crosse 1941: 8)

It is likely that, as often happened, Irving's performance was more assured (and less fatigued) after the opening, but by then most of the press reactions would have been registered with the public and, to a degree, posterity.

Among the productions of the 1890s, *Cymbeline* (1896) was outstanding for the appropriate casting of Irving and Terry as Iachimo and Imogen and for its bold choice of a respected but hardly popular play. It was clear from the beginning that despite the presence of the eminently classical Alma-Tadema as an adviser, Irving had insisted on the creation of a fanciful and unusually picturesque version of 'ancient Britain'. The costumes were vivid and rich; there was an elegant palace garden for Iachimo's first attempt on Imogen's loyalty to her husband, and little to imply that the native culture of the island kingdom was more primitive than that of Rome. There, however, the costumes were even more elegant, maintaining a sense of urbane continental sophistication. Even the boys hidden in Wales were well groomed, with immaculate 'fleshings' (the tights always worn to denote bare legs) under tasteful if not altogether accurately chosen animal skins – Irving was willing to set aside Alma-Tadema's objection that there were no leopards in Wales, just as he had politely noted but ignored the information that Messina did not have cedar trees in the period represented in *Much Ado about Nothing*. The scene in Imogen's bedroom afforded Irving an opportunity for one of his favourite dark scenes as he emerged from the trunk to make hypnotic passes over her sleeping form, but in many other scenes, the production was unusually brightly lit. Shaw complained that the 'inappropriate prettiness and sunniness' of the mountain landscape made it impossible for Terry to get the fullest value from Imogen's discovery of the headless corpse she mistakes for that of Posthumous. For the 'gloom amid the wolf and robber-haunted mountain gorges which formed the Welsh mountains of Shakespeare's imagination', Irving had substituted 'a nice Bank-holiday afternoon in a charming spot near the valley of the Wye' (Wilson 1969: 77, 78). Readers of his long notice in the *Saturday Review* were not to know that Shaw had effectively directed the actress in an exchange of letters (not published until 1929) with advice that was noted in her study-books for the performance, leading her through the role in overall conception and textual detail – a kind of support that he knew Irving would not give her (Hughes 1978: 210).

During his management of the Lyceum – his sole ownership ended in 1899 with the establishment of a syndicate to take over the running and leasing of the theatre – Irving effected important technical refinements, particularly in scene design and lighting. In 1911, Bram Stoker published an article giving valuable details of the latter. Electric lighting was introduced gradually, and Irving experimented with combinations of gas- and limelight as well as modifying the colour and intensity of the cooler, but at first harsher, light offered by the new medium (Jackson 1989: 190). By his use of tableau curtains ('tabs') that descended to close in the scene from the sides of the proscenium, and by making many scene changes on the darkened stage without lowering either curtains or a drop, Irving was able to achieve a smooth progression from scene to scene within the plays' acts. He made it a regular practice to darken the auditorium throughout the performance, so that the audience's awareness of its own presence was diminished and a fuller focus of attention on the stage was made possible.

As Jeffrey Richards observes, Irving had 'a precise knowledge of Romantic painting and how it could be deployed to realise his own artistic vision' (Richards 2005: 241). The productions in the 1880s and 1890s reflected on a grander scale an aspect of Irving's personal performance style. The connection can be illustrated in the responses of Henry James, an acute critic of the theatre as well as a great novelist – and, unfortunately, an unsuccessful playwright. In 1877, after noting Irving's lack of proficiency in 'utterance' and effective vocal technique, James had defined the particular quality of picturesqueness by which the actor made up for the deficiency 'by small ingenuities of "business" and subtleties of action; by doing as a painter does who "goes in" for colour when he cannot depend upon his drawing' (James 1957: 104). Twenty years later, reviewing the 1897 revival of *Richard III*, James observed that the interpretation was an example of 'what Sir Henry Irving does best.' He 'makes, for the setting, a big brave general picture, and then, for the figure, plays on the chord of the sinister-sardonic, flowered over as vividly as may be with the elegant-grotesque' (James 1957: 287).

Achieving these 'big brave general pictures' called for extraordinary measures. In her autobiography, Ellen Terry gives a vivid account of Irving's customary rehearsal practice (Terry 1908: 168–70). After some three months of private study and preparatory work, on the first day of rehearsal Irving would read the play 'exactly as it was to be done on the first night' to the assembled company. His own performance was already set, 'and the company did well to notice how he read his own part, for never again until the first night, though he rehearsed with them, would he show his conception so fully and completely'. The readings took place in the theatre's green-room, at the 'Beefsteak-room' – his private dining suite there – or in his house in Grafton Street. Without needing to name the characters, Irving individualised them brilliantly, making notes 'as to the position of the characters and the order of the crowds and processions'. At the end of this, the parts were given out to the actors – though Terry does not make this clear, it appears that they were not given the whole play but rather (as was customary at the time) their own lines and the cues preceding them. She does specify that at the Lyceum the parts were 'written, or printed, not typed', and the actors' next job was to read through the play together 'comparing' their parts to make sure they corresponded to the prompt copy. These meetings were usually held on a Thursday and Friday, with the 'first stand-up rehearsal on the stage' on the following Monday. Each act was gone through twice on a single day, until the play had been worked through, with Irving in sole charge and the stage-manager, H.J. Loveday, and the prompter at his side. Irving 'never spent much time on the women in the company, except in regard to position' – that is, where they should stand – and Terry was often asked 'to suggest things to them, to do for them what he did for the men'.

Irving's demeanour in rehearsals was impressively autocratic but also good-humoured. Edwin Booth, the American actor who shared Iago and Othello with him in 1881, observed that 'from first to last he rules his stage with an iron will, but as an offset to this he displays a patience that is marvellous' (Sprague 1953: 124). Irving's friend Walter Herries Pollock recalled 'that combination of never questioned authority with perfect simplicity which inspired rather than compelled obedience, and with it a real affection in all – actors, supers, and stage-hands alike, who ever worked with or under him' (Pollock n.d.: 8). Ellen Terry recalls the actor-manager patiently labouring with two small-part actors to get the first words of *Hamlet* to 'ring out like a pistol shot.' She urged him to give up, arguing that it would not improve, for all his efforts: ' "Yes, it's a little better," he answered quietly, "and so it's worth doing" ' (Terry 1908: 170). A description of Lyceum rehearsals for *Becket*, published in a magazine in 1893, makes it clear that Irving was able to sketch in bits of business for himself and other principals while supervising the movement of the 'supernumeraries' in the crowd (Jackson 1989: 221–6). The article also shows that he was capable of running through part of a scene in *King Lear* during a pause, and that he expected to have the crowd players at rehearsal from an early stage.

The next round of rehearsals consisted of working through 'half an act once in a whole day', and substitute scenery and properties were provided from the beginning of stage rehearsals. Eventually (Terry does not suggest how long the rehearsal process took overall), Irving progressed to dress-rehearsals and what would now be called technical rehearsals. From Bram Stoker's account (Jackson 1989: 192–3) it is clear that Irving sometimes worked on lighting a new production late at night after rehearsals for the new play in the day and performances of another during the evening: given that he acted in all the principal plays in his theatre's repertoire, the workload of the actor-manager was phenomenal, and there was a danger that (as in the case of *King Lear*), his own first-night performances might suffer as a result. Terry's description suggests not only the limitations of the work but also the fact that in the Victorian theatre Irving's insistence on detail was unusual. Lyceum productions were elaborate in the sense of being fully worked out and composed.

Irving required a full orchestral score, an indispensable complement to stage effect in the period, which was written expressly for the productions and (in the manner of opera, or the great film scores) would support the action with thematic material as well as establishing the general mood. Among the composers commissioned for the Lyceum were Arthur Sullivan, Edward German and Julius Benedict. The resident musical director, Meredith Ball, also provided incidental music and arrangements for entr'actes. The theatre had a full-size band (for some productions numbering thirty or thirty-five musicians) and a proficient chorus and ballet with the requisite chorus-master and choreographer. These forces in themselves, quite apart from the acting company, were effectively those of grand opera. Irving often achieved subtle effects of interpretation that music underlined with more tact than his contemporaries usually achieved. The last scene of *Hamlet* was staged so as to emphasise the isolation of the dying prince and the importance of love, in this case his relationship with Horatio. Hamlet was left alone with his friend in the centre of the stage, as the ladies of the court gathered round Gertrude's corpse and the men surrounded the King's, both groups preoccupied and turned away from the two men. An oboe played the Ghost's music softly as Hamlet spoke, 'If thou didst ever hold me in thy heart' (Hughes 1978: 76). Like other managers of his time, Irving did not include Fortinbras in his *Hamlet* and kept the focus of the finale on the Prince.

This kind of thematic understanding of the text, supported by music and staging, was a hallmark of the Irving style and suggests (as Hughes puts it) 'the seeds of the modern approach' (Hughes 1978: 77). Never one to accept conventional, hackneyed underlining or – worse – bland and generalised musical effects, Irving encouraged his composers to identify recurrent, leading motifs – the Wagnerian *Leitmotiven*. In one notable case he (or his composer) also knew when silence would be the best accompaniment: *The Times*, in a whole column reviewing Sullivan's score for the 1888–9 *Macbeth*, commends the decision to leave the sleepwalking scene without accompaniment rather than provide some conventional 'slow music' at this point. The reviewer also noted with satisfaction that Sullivan had avoided the 'Scotch airs' traditionally associated with the play in the theatre and was concerned with 'giving an emotional emphasis rather than a local habitation to the action, (*The Times*, 31 December 1888). Sullivan received specific instructions from Irving on the musical effects needed in each scene but also discovered that the actor, who had no musical training, seemed able to indicate what was needed by gestures, body movement and vowel sounds (Irving 1951: 502–3; Jacobs 1984: 277–8).

In the 'awakening scene' (Act IV, scene 6) of *King Lear*, on-stage music supported a sequence of powerfully pathetic moments, with the King lying on a couch in his robes of state and Ellen Terry, herself a mistress of tearful effect, attending him tenderly. She shed real tears, and on 'Be your tears wet?', Irving 'touched her with his long, wan fingers and put the salt drops to his lips' (Hughes 1978: 135). This was the culminating scene in a sequence which, because of drastic cuts, brought together three powerfully pathetic scenes: the 'hovel', Lear's meeting with Gloucester (blinded offstage) and the reunion with Cordelia followed one another with little by way of a break (Act III, scene 6, a truncated Act IV, scene 5 and then the 'awakening').

For the achievement of such moments, Irving depended on skilful presentation and the confidence that he could draw on strengths he knew his co-star possessed. Irving could come up with laconic and effective 'notes' for his actors (Craig recalled one illuminating word of advice for his performance as Oswald in *King Lear*: 'Malvolio'), but for the most part he was content to let the principals fend for themselves. Intensive interpretative work on the script with the actors was not part of his method. However minutely and with whatever degree of introspection and use of his own emotional experiences he might study his own roles, for Irving – and for most actors of his generation – this was private work. Its results might be brought to rehearsal, but the exploration would not take place there, and the full effect of the interpretation might even be kept out of view until the opening night. Irving combined and refined many of the activities now associated with direction, but in respect of the actors' detailed work on the script, he remained a product of the mid-nineteenth-century theatre.

Other forces were at work in that theatre that, taken together, hastened the perception that an independent director was necessary. Several successful authors, notably T.W. Robertson, W.S. Gilbert and Arthur Wing Pinero, had secured the right to oversee the rehearsal of their work, and increasing attention to harmonious pictorial effect made the intervention of experts (including chorographers and designers) a necessary adjunct to the actors' work. It was still customary for the scenery of productions to be allotted to a number of artists, but by the end of the nineteenth century it was no longer acceptable in theatres with pretensions to artistic quality to stage productions 'from stock'. Working with actors to achieve personal interpretations that were similarly not taken from stock, and combining these into an ensemble that articulated a view of the play were still a little way off: at the Lyceum, any such development was always subordinated to the demands of actor-managerial regime. Nevertheless, the results could be impressive, effective and, in their own way, comparable with the interpretive efforts of later independent directors. An appropriate concluding image of Irving is his final Shakespearian role in his theatre, Coriolanus, as described by Arthur Symons. It combined pictorial effect, the management of a mass of 'supers' (the 'extras' in Victorian theatre) and a subtle insight into the character:

> A stage crowd at the Lyceum always gives one a sense of exciting movement, and this Roman rabble did all that was needed to show off the almost solitary splendour of Coriolanus. He is the proudest man in Shakespeare, and Sir Henry Irving is at his best when he embodies pride. His conception of the part was masterly; it had imagination, nobility, quietude. With opportunity for ranting in every second speech, he never ranted, but played what might well have been a roaring part with a kind of gentleness. With every opportunity for extravagant gesture, he stood, as the play seemed to foam about him, like a rock against which the sea beats. [. . .] I have never seen Irving so restrained, so much of an artist, so faithfully interpretative of a masterpiece.
>
> (Symons 1909: 58–9)

Chronology

Shakespeare plays directed by Irving at the Lyceum Theatre, London.

1878 *Hamlet*
1879 *The Merchant of Venice*
1879 *Othello* (and in 1881)
1882 *Romeo and Juliet*
1882 *Much Ado about Nothing*
1884 *Twelfth Night*
1888 *Macbeth*

1892 *King Lear*
1892 *Henry VIII*
1896 *Richard III*
1896 *Cymbeline*
1901 *Coriolanus*

Bibliography

Archer, William (1883) *Henry Irving, Actor and Manager: A Critical Study*, London: Field and Tuer; Simpkin Marshall and Co.; Hamilton, Adams and Co.

Auerbach, Nina (1987) *Ellen Terry: Player in her Time*, New York: Norton and Norton.

Booth, Michael R. (1981) *Victorian Spectacular Theatre*, Boston, Mass. and London: Routledge & Kegan Paul.

Craig, Edward Gordon (1930) *Henry Irving*, London: J.M. Dent.

Crosse, Gordon (1941) *Fifty Years of Shakespearean Playgoing*, London: privately published.

Hardy, Lady (1879) 'The Hamlet of the Day', *The Theatre*, n.s. II (February): 17–21.

Hughes, Alan (1978) *Henry Irving, Shakespearean*, Cambridge: Cambridge University Press.

Irving, Laurence (1951) *Henry Irving: The Actor and his World*, London: Faber & Faber.

Jackson, Russell (ed.) (1989) *Victorian Theatre: A New Mermaids Sourcebook*, London: A. and C. Black.

—— (2004) How a Meininger saw us in 1881: the actor Ludwig Barnay on Henry Iriving and others, *Theatre Notebook*, 58/3, 154–8.

Jacobs, Arthur (1984) *Arthur Sullivan: A Victorian Musician*, Oxford: Oxford University Press.

James, Henry (1957) *The Scenic Art: Notes on Acting and the Drama, 1872–1901*, ed. Alan Wade, New York: Hill & Wang.

Jones, Henry Arthur (1931) *The Shadow of Henry Irving*, London: Richards.

Pollock, Walter Herries (n.d.) *Impressions of Henry Irving: Gathered in Public and Private During a Friendship of Many Years*, London: Longmans, Green and Co.

Richards, Jeffrey (2005) *Sir Henry Irving: A Victorian Actor and his World*, London and New York: Hambledon and London.

—— (ed.) (1994) *Sir Henry Irving. Theatre, Culture and Society: Essays, Addresses and Lectures*, Keele: Ryburn Publishing/Keele University Press.

Robertson, W. Graham (1931) *Time Was*, London: Hamish Hamilton.

Scott, Clement (1897) *From 'The Bells' to King Arthur': A Critical Record of First-Night Productions at the Lyceum Theatre from 1871 to 1893*, London: John Macqueen.

Spielman, M.H. (1889) 'Art in the Theatre II: A Shakespearean Revival – *Macbeth*', *The Magazine of Art*, 12: 98–100.

Sprague, Arthur Colby (1944) *Shakespeare and the Actors: The Stage Business in his Plays, 1660–1905*, Cambridge, Mass.: Harvard University Press.

—— (1953) *Shakespearian Players and Performances*, Cambridge, Mass.: Harvard University Press.

—— (1966) *Shakespeare's Histories, Plays for the Stage*, London: Society for Theatre Research.

Stoker, Bram (1907) *Personal Reminiscences of Henry Irving*, 2 vols, London: William Heinemann.

Symons, Arthur (1909) *Plays, Acting and Music: A Book of Theory*, London: Constable and Company.

Terry, Ellen (1908) *The Story of My Life*, London: Hutchinson and Co.

Thomson, Peter (2000) *On Actors and Acting*, Exeter: University of Exeter Press.

Wilson, Edwin (ed.) (1969) *Shaw on Shakespeare*, Harmondsworth: Penguin.

About the author

Russell Jackson is Allardyce Nicoll Professor of Drama in the University of Birmingham. His publications include *Victorian Theatre: A New Mermaid Sourcebook* (1989); a translation of Theodor Fontane's *Shakespeare in London Theatre, 1855–58* (1999) and *Romeo and Juliet* in the series 'Shakespeare at Stratford' (2003). With Jonathan Bate he co-edited *The Oxford Illustrated History of Shakespeare on Stage* (1996; 2nd edn, 2001). He was an editor of *Theatre Notebook* from 1985 to 2004, and has contributed annual reviews of Shakespeare productions to *Shakespeare Quarterly*. His latest publications are *Shakespeare Films in the Making: Vision, Production and Reception* and the second edition of *The Cambridge Companion to Shakespeare on Film* (both 2007).

12
FRITZ KORTNER

Klaus Völker,
translated by Wilhelm Hortmann

During the first two decades of the twentieth century, the most prominent Shakespeare-director of the German-speaking theatre was undoubtedly Max Reinhardt. Of course, there were others, such as Saladin Schmitt who, from 1920 to 1940, produced nearly all of Shakespeare's plays – a most respectable achievement for a middle-sized theatre in an industrial town like Bochum even if the presentations did not go beyond the frame of creditably acted and well-constructed performances of the classics. However, Schmitt's meritorious and continuous efforts to bring all of Shakespeare's works onto the stage could not vie with the highlights elsewhere, notably in Berlin, for example: Leopold Jessner's *Richard III, Othello* and *Macbeth* at the Berlin Staatstheater during the 1920s; Erich Engel's *Coriolanus* and *The Tempest* at the Deutsches Theater during the 1930s, not to mention the legendary production of *Richard III* (1937) directed by Jürgen Fehling at the Staatstheater under Gustaf Gründgens as Intendant, which was understood as an implicit denunciation of the Nazis and their crimes. Fritz Kortner's work as a Shakespeare director falls into the years from 1950 to 1970 when this former protagonist of expressionist acting during the Weimar Republic (1919–32) renewed the German theatre with a number of highly expressive Shakespeare productions in which the light touch of comedy and a reading penetrating to the spiritual core of the plays combined in felicitous union.

Fritz Kortner, born on 12 May 1892 in Vienna as son of a Jewish watchmaker, attended the Imperial Academy for Music and Representational Art. The Board of Examiners of the famous Burgtheater once again proved singularly unlucky in their judgements. Its members had rejected Alexander Moissi (afterwards to become the unaparalleled protagonist of the Reinhardt theatre) 'as totally unqualified for the acting profession', and they characterised the young Kortner after an audition as 'strong in matters of temperament, but due to physique and looks only usable as schemer or villain. Strong inclination to mannered delivery. Lack of personal charm as well as intellectual transparency. Could not promise him an engagement' (Völker 1987: 10). Even without the blessings of the 'Burg' and its hidebound acting instructors, Kortner made his way. After a short interlude at the Mannheim Court and National Theatre, he was granted an audition by Max Reinhardt who instantly engaged him as a member of his illustrious team of actors. Kortner worried less about not being given great parts to play at first than about not working enough under Reinhardt's direction. It was because of Reinhardt's 'sensuous approach to the theatre', as he said later, embodied in actors whom the director had 'inspired with the breath of life' that Kortner had decided to become an actor in the first place. He had seen Reinhardt's *Hamlet* in Vienna as a guest performance – a revelation for the 16-year-old Kortner, because here a director had made *Hamlet* come to life, in decided departure from the usual humdrum production of the classics (Kortner 1991: 80).

But to be playing Laertes in the fifteenth remake of this once-famous production was a sorry letdown, and there was nothing to learn from it. That is why he quit after two seasons in order to look for challenges better suited to, and for directors prepared to make the most of, his abilities, men like Berthold Viertel in Vienna, Alfred Edgar Licho in Dresden and Erich Ziegel in Hamburg. During the First World War, the critic Herbert Ihering gave Kortner lead roles in several plays he directed at the Viennese Volksbühne and recognised that here was an actor who was cut out for a career in directing as well. On account of his looks, he could not be given the parts of Hamlet or Romeo, but Shylock was a different matter. At the age of only 24, he was given the opportunity of acting the part which held a powerful attraction for him on account of its emotional range as well as its complex duplicitous psychology. In the course of the years and fuelled by the growing anti-Semitism in Germany, Shylock was to become his most symbolically charged tragic role. During his first representation of the part (1916 at the Deutsches Volkstheater in Vienna), entering the well-established and accommodatingly unprovocative production as an understudy, he could only give a spirited but diffuse sketch. It was in Berthold Viertel's production of 1923, based on a radical formal concept, that Kortner was allowed to experiment with different extremes and thus to widen the scope of this part while, a year later under the direction of Max Reinhardt in Vienna, he refined, humanised and even subtly spiritualised the part. It was only in 1927 at the Berlin Staatstheater and under Jürgen Fehling, when, finally, he was in congenial agreement with the director's concept that he delivered a provocative, daring but psychologically convincing and mature rendering.

Fehling's concept and Kortner's embodiment of the crazed contradictions in the soul of the hunted revenger were deliberately anti-Reinhardt. According to Kortner, Reinhardt's view of *The Merchant of Venice* was distinctly 'uncritical of society'. With Reinhardt, all the figures in the comedy were captivating, amusing or boisterous, partly charming, partly shrouded in gentle melancholy:

> It is only the intolerance against the Jew which turns Shylock into Shylock. But the splendour of the Venetian *jeunesse dorée* steeps even their affronts in a friendly light. There was much that was amusing and dance-like in this production but at least Reinhardt did not present the dance around the golden calf.
>
> (Kortner 1991: 86)

Reinhardt's idea of Shylock – as shown in Berlin with first Rudolf Schildkraut, later with Werner Krauss, and even in the Viennese version of 1924 in the Theater in der Josefstadt with Kortner – was that of a basically friendly and sympathetic individual, a soft sufferer under slights and injustices until they become unbearable, when, at last, the much-abused victim is driven into terrifying antagonism. Kortner's Shylock of 1927, however, rejected any form of accommodating humour and fought back with the weapons that had been used against him. Leopold Jessner, who had directed Kortner in several other Shakepearean lead roles, did not envy him his success under Jürgen Fehling:

> His recent performance at the Staatstheater was perhaps his greatest victory. For this Shylock showed the protagonist at the peak of his maturity, the terrifying concomitance of all his positive powers as an actor with the material and poetic requirements of the part – in a climax that keeps expectation of what is to come in vibrant tension.
>
> (Ludwigg 1928: 28)

Herbert Ihering criticised the production as excessively theatrical, but he acknowledged Kortner's extraordinary achievement:

> This time he is completely free. An old man, sly and soft, spiteful and broken. A mask that never remains the same. A mask filled time and again by splendid acting, always changing, always heightened. A Jew from the ghetto, without symbolic additions. But, under the influence of the others, through pain and torture becoming the bearer of the sufferings of his race and driven to frenzy and self-destruction, rising through his tragic fall. Kortner will soon have to play Lear.
>
> (Ihering 1959: 297)

Alfred Kerr, another important critic, praised the unusual quality of Fehling's and Kortner's achievement; their merit, he said, consisted in having once for all done away with a comedy which had become unrecognisable through all too many routine productions. 'The only thing to be done with this piece is to play its opposite.' And he thanked Kortner for having acted the 'opposite':

> Kortner is the hero of an unquenchable tragedy. At the beginning, his Shylock feels more cares than hatred. But deep down he smarts under the irrepressible feeling of the crude injustice [. . .] he has suffered at the hands of either triumphant or scheming villains. There is no actor in Germany capable of rendering the speech about bleeding humanity 'If you prick us, do we not bleed?' with such overpowering force and at the same time such urgent and deep simplicity as this fellow. Really unique – beyond Schildkraut, beyond Krauss, beyond Bassermann – I have never seen his equal.
>
> (Kerr 2001: 392)

Kortner was grateful to Fehling for not choosing the easy way out, neutralising the anti-Semitic prejudices of the audience through comic exaggeration of Jewish clichés. Instead, he painted them to frightening effect in crass and daring colours in order to show the abysmal tragedy of the Jew who, driven to terrible hatred, thirsting for revenge, acts like a fiend from hell, is humiliated and has to abjure the faith of his fathers under the scoffing taunts and jeers of the common crowd: 'He does so. But when Shylock then wraps himself in his prayer scarf and stumbles off, an utterly broken man, this is a wordless and most bitter indictment of a type of justice and of judges who lay such ignominy upon a man' (Rühle 1967: 829 f.).

Many critics in 1927 did not like the production because it confronted the prevalent but latent anti-Semitism all too openly. The theatre-going Jewish bourgeoisie especially, found their pro-German and even nationalistic sensibilities offended by a role concept that highlighted the unpleasant and 'evil' traits in Shylock even if their hearts were touched by his tragic fate. They saw themselves as 'integrated' Jews, a quality they hoped would save them from the persecution by the Nazis a few years later. Shakespeare's truth was more contradictory and closer to reality.

In Vienna, Kortner also played Angelo in *Measure for Measure* at the Wiener Volksbühne (1917); in Hamburg, under Erich Ziegel, he played Jacques in *As You Like It*, a part he frequently acted in Berlin. In the early 1920s followed Richard III, Othello, Macbeth (that he had hammered out with director Leopold Jessner), Caliban, Coriolanus and, late in 1926, Hamlet, when long past Hamlet's age. These numerous embodiments of Shakespearian characters formed an important body of experience for his later work as a director. All the leading theatre critics of the Weimar Republic – Kerr, Ihering, Polgar or Jacobsohn – regarded Fritz Kortner as an unsurpassed and suggestive actor who mostly succeeded in measuring out the dimensions of the whole of the drama in the sole focus of the character he portrayed: he struggled to give expression also to the secret elements behind the text. The monstrous rulers he had to embody were never only monsters but also creatures driven by passions and obsessions. Thus, Jacobsohn celebrated Kortner's rendering of Richard III as 'the descent into hell of a steel-clad bloodhound' who, in spite of all his despicable crimes and terror remains a lost and obsessed human being (2005: 380 ff.). Like nobody else, Kerr wrote in his idiosyncratic style, Kortner mastered the final scene:

> When, naked down to the waist, he calls for a horse, it is despair, sheer and raging. A horse – the shout of a madman. A horse – a stammer of forlorn hope. A horse – a last appeal to his former self. A horse – the final knowledge that all is lost. A terrifying experience.
>
> (Kerr 2001: 96)

Kortner was a master at controlling the tempo of delivery, slowing down or speeding up as the situation required. Alwin Kronacher, a director, admired Kortner's delivery as truly creative: 'Since Kainz no one has handled language in such a manner, like an architect running up buildings. He is better than Kainz, builds skyscrapers. Altogether unique in rhythm, clearly structured, no ornaments and frills, no attempts at idyllic emotionalism' (in Ludwigg 1928: 65).

Kortner realised early in his career that he was cut out to be a director. He had experienced time and again that with him in a leading role, productions took a specific direction. From the middle of the 1920s, he attempted to take on directing jobs but received no offers. Only one person, Friedrich Zelnik, himself a director, actor and producer, seemed to realise what was to come: in 1928 he wrote:

> Not every actor is meant to be a director. There are those who need the organising hand of the director to achieve their full stature. Fritz Kortner knows how to guide his own talent. And here lie the roots of Kortner, the future director. He is in full control of his talent, employs it in tempestuous concentration as in flowing dilation. You only have to watch him at work, how he enters into the spirit of each scene, is eager to assist the director, enjoys untying knots and suggesting switches in tempo. He is not the kind of actor who has to be pushed into a specific rhythm he finds and dominates his own. It won't be long

> now before we shall speak of Kortner, the outstanding director, as we are no speaking of him as an outstanding actor.
>
> (Ludwigg 1928: 46)

Zelnik's prediction was correct but was fulfilled only twenty years later when Kortner returned from exile in the USA and began directing in Munich. Of his nearly fifty productions at German-speaking theatres between 1949 and 1970, eleven were devoted to Shakespeare: *Othello* twice, in Munich and Vienna; *Twelfth Night* also twice, in Munich and Berlin; furthermore *Julius Caesar*, *Henry IV*, *Hamlet*, *Timon of Athens*, *Richard III*, *The Tempest* and *Antony and Cleopatra*.

In America, Bertolt Brecht, Berthold Viertel and Fritz Kortner had impatiently been waiting for the day when they would again be able to take up theatre work in Germany and, especially, in Berlin. But when they finally returned from exile they were distressed to see the damage Nazism had wrought in the sphere of art. In the intervening years, most actors had adopted a manner of acting that no longer presented tragic constellations in varied nuances but simply declaimed in plaintive tones about the tragic as such. Kortner wanted an expressive type of theatre, undisguised and devoted to truth, a theatre in which every sentence turns into movement, in which the general drive of the dramatic progress has a realistic underpinning and reveals itself in attitudes. No mere clamour, no hollow words but the careful unfolding of the drama through consciously formed speech. 'And all this very softly, pianissimo, [. . .] a great contrast to the ranting on the German stage of the last fifteen years' (Bruno E. Werner, 1949, in Kortner 1991: 489). Kortner felt the productions he saw in post-Hitler Germany as a noisy theatre of sheer pretence, destroying meaning:

> by clamour, bluff, confusion and speed, hiding its lifelessness in turbulent activity. It numbs the spectator already wearied by the hectic age, spares him intellectual commitment and serves him tasty morsels of pain-, pleasure- and economic miracle-junk in the reconstructed fast-food theatre of his brand-new town. [. . .] The true spirit, up till now drowned in noise, needs to be heard again. Suppressed for too long, it wants to free itself from false melodies. True, in this act of liberation it occasionally sins against poetic tradition by a certain verbal crassness, an excusable fault in those newly liberated. For the future, what formerly was a melodious rendering of verse for its own sake has to give way to a spiritual penetration, melody has to give way to meaning. The delivery of verse must become transparent so that it reveals the condition of the portrayed characters.
>
> (Kortner 1991: 481)

Kortner's *mise-en-scène* and his way of dissecting texts as with a scalpel had something in common with Brecht's efforts to establish a dialectical theatre that would reveal social causalities. Kortner's and Brecht's endeavours challenged the unthinking routine of the municipal theatres which was primarily concerned with the smooth running of a production. Like Brecht, Kortner was horrified to notice how the theatre had deteriorated artistically under Nazism, a state of affairs of which those theatre people who had not emigrated were totally unconscious. They had passed the Nazi years by cultivating a new inwardness and at the same time projecting 'a brilliant technique' to overwhelm their audiences. In a paper Brecht read at the all-German cultural congress in Leipzig in 1951 he said, 'the damage done to the German theatre buildings appears much more visible than the artistic damage is probably due to the fact that the buildings were abruptly destroyed when the Nazi regime collapsed but the theatre arts were continuously compromised in all the years that went before' (Brecht 1993: 150 f.).

Kortner's first Shakespeare production was *Julius Caesar* at the Residenztheater in Munich (1955). He did not share the widespread belief that the play lacked tension and interest because its title hero leaves the stage fairly early on, for Kortner was fascinated above all in the shadow the murder casts on the conspirators who want to end the arbitrary rule of the dictator but only set in motion a new wave of violence, murder and death. Kortner discovered in the Roman tragedy a still topical political whodunit: his production did not so much stress the question of the legitimacy of resistance and tyrannicide but concentrated on the connection between Caesar's fall and the violence it releases. Eliminating Caesar helps the people no whit; if anything, the mountain of corpses grows higher. Because Brutus loves Rome more than anything, he will no longer suffer it to be ruled by one man alone, but he is much too intelligent to fall for the fiction that the will of the people might result in democratic conditions.

> It is the tragic blindness of the ideologue that even though he has a healthy contempt for the populace he does not realise whose servant he becomes when there are no more rulers. In the fourth act he begins to suspect it. This is the point at which the drama begins whose title is neither Julius Caesar nor Mark Antony, but Brutus.
>
> (Jacobsohn 2005: 112)

But Kortner's Brutus was not the victim of his republican zeal. He was full of misgivings; he recognised Caesar's weaknesses, nevertheless regarded him as an able statesman and only reluctantly withdrew his loyalty. The director showed how Brutus's fate was totally linked to a Caesar who was neither hero nor villain but someone driven by ambition, having been lucky so far, and now saw himself surrounded and threatened by envious competitors. Caesar staggered and fell down the steps of the Forum, clinging at last to Brutus, his seeming friend, who embraced him like a lover and killed him.

Kortner did not go for simple actualisation, yet neither should the characters in this tragedy appear as remote figures to whom we can no longer relate:

> These people should be taken out of the abstraction of distance in time and brought to concrete, palpable propinquity to mean something to us here and now. Their language, distinguished by verse which may not be tampered with, must nevertheless contain sufficiently realistic accents to suggest contemporaneity. Similarly, body language and gestures have to interpret the inner action for modern spectators so that, in spite of poetic language, traditional costuming and historical utensils, what is expressed is of our time.
>
> (Kortner 1991: 484 f.)

The director's plan worked: he showed both the sphere of high politics – the race for power in the thoughts and actions of the ruling classes and their demagogy – and the fickleness of the people who remain powerless throughout. The production did not project simple truths in the service of an ideological director's concept. Kortner devoted equal interest to all his figures, and he allowed the tragedy of the futility of every kind of political violence to run its course. Many critics were so surprised that they thought they were seeing the play for the first time. 'There is nothing in Kortner's production that might not be from Shakespeare, but there is very much of Shakespeare in it that has never before been visible' (*Neuer Kurier*, Vienna, 12 April 1955).

Kortner's use of certain 'signs' was indicative. Thus Brutus might try to stress his distance to the other conspirators but, when he finally agreed with them, he covered Caesar's bust with a black cloth for all to see and, later shivering alone in the morning cold, he wrapped himself in this same cloth: a clear sign that black disaster will envelop him too. Brutus, the organiser of the plot against Caesar, was aware that this would not be the liberating deed he hoped for. We hear 'the clock of fate ticking', Alfred Polgar wrote about this dark and oppressive production (*Forum*, Vienna, May 1955). The battle scenes at the end turned into a terrible carnage on a stage floor covered with corpses and cadavers of horses, demonstrating to everyone that Brutus's 'pure' intentions had turned into their bloody opposite. 'Let us be sacrificers, but not butchers', Brutus had demanded, but his 'sacrifice' released a bloodbath.

In Munich during the 1950s, Kortner's deliberately unheroic presentation of heroic figures resulted in an acrimonious controversy. In his autobiography *Aller Tage Abend* he was to explain why the problem of 'heroic' or 'unheroic' acting was so important for him:

> The concept of the hero has to be investigated. If he falls in a bad cause which he thinks is a good one, he is merely stupid. If he realises in his fall that the cause was not worth his commitment, he is a tragic figure. If he falls in a just cause and is convinced that only his death and not his continuing to live will serve it, then he is my man. [. . .] Hero-worshippers don't want to be convinced, they want to be swept off their feet. And heroes who want to sweep audiences of their feet ought to be banned from the modern stage. Being a hero is no profession, but the hero ought to have one. If he has none, he is unemployed, Unemployed heroes constitute a danger. The true nature of a human being with heroic proclivities is better revealed by a kind of distrustful approach than by the usual idealisation. This latter is the attitude of the recruit towards his officer. A heroic character in a play is a military commander neither to the actor nor the director. The substance of the authority wielded by a heroic character has to pass the critical investigation of today's theatre-people. Mindless adulation is silly. A truly luminous character will outshine the dark shadows that may become visible in an objective presentation.
>
> (Kortner 1991: 491 ff.; see also Hortmann 1998: 203–16)

With the exception of *Richard III*, Shakespeare's history plays never commanded as much attention in Germany as his tragedies and comedies. People easily forget that though Shakespeare might take his material from Holinshed's *Chronicles of England, Scotland and Ireland*, he felt free to take considerable liberties where it suited his dramaturgy, fusing several historical personages into one figure, often changing the cast of a particular character and highlighting strokes of fate or attractive episodes that might serve to pinpoint certain lessons for his contemporaries. This 'method' of Shakespeare's strengthened Kortner's resolve to treat classical plays in a similar manner because he too wanted to recover these old works for the contemporary stage. In 1956, he brought out the two parts of *Henry IV* at the Residenztheater in Munich. Kurt Horwitz played Henry IV, Klaus Kinski represented Prince Hal, Gerd Brüdern Percy Hotspur, Friedrich Domin was Sir John Falstaff and Kurt Stieler the Lord Chief Justice. The wealth of characters from all walks of life, high and low, the constant switching between scenes of high import and those of low life, between brutal battles and comic squabbles represented just the constellation to challenge Kortner and tempt him to display a wide panorama of life and to combine the contradictory scenic material into a suggestive and meaningful whole.

This production of *Henry IV* found only gradual approval by audiences and critics because Kortner had strengthened Shakespeare's plurifocal approach to his characters by stressing the contradictions in each, bringing out sharply the mixture of positive as well as negative traits in order to show a convincing dramatic picture of the multi-faceted historical and human reality. The production typified Kortner's complex conception of realism on the stage. He saw in *Henry IV* a marvellous dramatic polyphony 'in which the characters were placed and opposed in complex relationships and actions' (Weiss 1968: 89). It is a comic tragedy in which nothing is what it seems. Kortner took time to bring out the many-sidedness of the characters and showed that slapstick comedy, sharp political criticism, brilliant witticisms and the stupidest of jokes went very well together. The production also contained a political message: an able and good ruler can only mature if he has been through the ups and downs of the school of life. But even so: Falstaff, liar and good-for-nothing, cannot believe that Prince Hal, his companion in debauchery, has truly changed as King and doesn't want to be reminded of their common pranks. Is he altogether wrong when he suspects the King to be merely pretending? As Falstaff says to Shallow, 'this that you heard was but a colour' (*2 Henry IV*, Act V, Scene 5).

Kortner's productions were never quite finished on first nights. He had tried to incorporate too many thoughts and too much material for conclusive perfection. In contrast to other directors, he was not interested in polished surfaces and smoothly rounded products: he did not worry about 'gaps'; his productions were never 'of one piece'; he did not mind 'fissures'. His directing always remained open for alterations or, rather, for further improvement through the actors. In the course of their run, performances improved, their polyphonic effect becoming more patent and was better understood. This was the case in his production of *Hamlet* at the Schiller-Theater in Berlin (1957), where it took quite a few performances for the ultimate coherence to establish itself. 'He wants to say too much in too great detail', the critic Friedrich Luft complained, as it were following the great text 'with a didactic finger'. Luft found the production, as such, impressive but too finely spun in its careful attention to detail and generally not innovative. Furthermore, he disliked 'certain passages the director had unnecessarily heightened and over-accentuated leaving the impression of odd lapses of taste' (Luft 1982: 313–17). But what Luft saw as a strange contradiction was deliberately willed by the director, only the balanced concomitance of the disparate parts had not yet been achieved. The production was neither too long nor too hesitant and carefully detailed. The whole play is but one deferred action after another, that is why *Hamlet* is Shakespeare's 'slowest' tragedy. And yet, it is full of tension. Hamlet's advice to the players: 'Suit the action to the word, the word to the action' (Act III, Scene 2) describes Shakespeare's own handling of language in this play where he adapts the speech to the individual characters and to the changing dramatic situations in a precision unachieved before. Friedrich Luft was relieved to find that Kortner had not used *Hamlet* for an idiosyncratic interpretation of his own:

> Thank God Kortner unfolds what is in this miracle of a drama. He plays the text and not with the text. No extravagant personal interpretation. It is truly as if the director took us line by line through this thought-laden text. A protracted operation, but clear. And it is with a patient impatience (many thanks for this also) that the words of the still unsurpassed Schlegel translation are made flesh on Kortner's stage.
>
> (Luft 1982: 314)

The critic Walther Karsch saw the play again after several weeks and found that the divergent elements now fitted into each other as they had been meant to:

> The surplus freight of interpretation has dropped away, only the 'action' is important, and before we know it we find ourselves in a drama of thoughts. Surprising how the most timeworn phrases achieve new weight. And the Hamlet of the soliloquies and dialogues develops his thoughts solely in reaction to the actual situation, the moment of action.
>
> (Karsch 1962: 66)

Karsch now even no longer objected to the scene that had caused an uproar on the first night (Luft had severely criticised it as superfluous slapstick), the scene in which Hamlet drags Polonius's corpse off the stage:

> The drama contains many things which may appear to us as 'too much'. But as 'not too much' appeared to me the protracted sequence of Hamlet dragging Polonius's corpse across the different sections of the revolving stage. Not too much, because this sequence is the direct translation into grotesque, macabre action of Hamlet's 'This man shall set me packing; / I'll lug the guts into the neighbour room.'
>
> (Karsch 1962: 66 f.)

Kortner made the actors take the text literally. Perhaps sometimes a phrase was taken too literally, especially when an actor had failed in truly embodying it, when it appeared as a disembodied addition, forced instead of powerful.

In the premiere, Joana Maria Gorvin played Ophelia. She was 35 and thought too old for the part by many theatre people and critics. They regarded the young beginner Johanna von Koczian, who alternated in the part, as more appropriate. Once again, Walther Karsch disagreed with general opinion:

> Koczian is certainly nice to look at but she gives no clue that upon the death of her father her world will collapse and her mind will be buried under the debris. What she gives instead is at best touching [. . .] Joana Maria Gorvin by contrast is in conscious control of her art. The decisive difference is this: she makes the stages in the progressive clouding of her mind visible thus revealing the tragedy of this figure. A process which is not merely touching but deeply moving.
>
> (Karsch 1962: 67)

Karsch was of one mind with Kortner: an actor's 'age' is primarily a matter of the actor's power of suggestion and projection, more so than youthful beauty, good looks and mere presence. Similarly Kortner's Hamlet, Erich Schellow, 42, who acted the part with intelligent impetuousness was no longer a 'young' Hamlet. A mature achievement and being one with his role was of more account:

> His Hamlet is tense, cool, sometimes almost hard. He never hides thought behind passion. And in his relation to others, even to his friend Horatio, he always has first to overcome a certain distance because he and the rest are divided by a world of difference. The striking thing about this phenomenon: it was perfectly obvious and at the same time it seemed completely unintentional. Another proof to show that Kortner does not make his actors present a directorial interpretation but follow the meaning of Shakespeare's words.
>
> (Karsch 1962: 67)

Critics were surprised to notice a novel light touch and in parts even an operetta-like manner in Kortner's *Timon of Athens* at the Munich Kammerspiele in 1961. 'Whoever had expected the iambic glamour of "noble Timon" was shocked when Timon popped up again and again as a comic figure out of a cuckoo clock' (Nagel 1989: 23). One critic so shocked was Joachim Kaiser. He conceded that Kortner had 'read Shakespeare's enigmatic text with powerful perspicacity' yet had ultimately only achieved a convincing interpretation, not a successful production. He also complained that Kortner had augmented the 'static' character of the play instead of reducing it and that Romuald Pekny as Timon, far from representing a Shakespearian tragic hero, had from the beginning moved with the wavy gait of someone intoxicated and that the costumes 'such as might have been *à la mode* at the time of the Arabian Nights' had given the whole a fairytale touch but betrayed the tragedy (*Theater heute*, May 1961). For Ivan Nagel, on the other hand, this lightness contained the effective energies 'of a powerful brain': 'Kortner creates extreme tensions, radical results. Where he is great, he is very great; where things go wrong, they go very wrong. But nobody should sit in judgement on the success or failure of his work who will not take into account the tremendous interpretative risks the director takes' (Nagel 1989: 22).

Ivan Nagel, thus, not only defended a much-criticised director, he also described what he had seen:

> Instead of appearing in a beautiful chiton, the scattergood sported bright-red pyjamas, a huge gold lamé scarf slung dandy-like about his shoulders. His gait was not the majestic step of a future tragic hero, he skipped and capered about the stage like someone inebriated on champagne for breakfast and almost floating. His laughter sounded both affable and hollow, he propagated a foolish lightheartedness. The importunate spendthrift seemed to force all on whom he heaped his presents into the concession 'Isn't life wonderful?'. The parasites of his open purse (as well as of his foolish heart) giggled with him, pretended to be enraptured either out of flattery or silliness. It was to 'friends' of this sort that he addressed a toast to friendship: highfalutin phrases, mere embellishments. He bought pictures and poems without really looking at them, enjoying himself in the masquerade of a Maecenas. All in all, the image and manners of a nouveau riche present-day businessman or industrialist, not of a hero from antiquity.
>
> (Nagel 1989: 23)

This was Kortner's view of Shakespeare: tragedy always fringed with comedy and the sublime never far from the ridiculous. *Timon of Athens* was, for him, no Greek tragedy, as his audience knew it from grammar school. How shall Timon's rude awakening, Kortner thought, from his idle pose of a dispenser of wealth convince an audience if we first haven't experienced his self-deceptive intoxication with the abject glitter of hollowness. 'Kortner is never in search of dramatic theories but of the meaning of the particular play in front of him. In *Timon* he found just the figure he presented. His Timon does not know the people whom he showers with presents, and he doesn't want to know them.' He wastes his money in order to be able to feel fortunate, bribing the world so as not to reveal its misery. 'His tragic guilt derives from the infantilism of his comic innocence' (Nagel 1989: 24).

Karl von Appen's set for *Timon of Athens* was highly indicative, visibly representing above and below, appearance and reality, wealth as opposed to poverty, a clear division Appen also marked in the costumes he designed. According to Ivan Nagel:

> Kortner had the space divided into two levels. On the top level (above stairs) (and behind a gauze curtain suggesting fleeting and shadowy unreality) there unrolls a never-ending sequence of festivities while on the grey-coloured level below the philosopher Apemantus (Gerd Brüdern) and the steward Flavius (Peter Paul) prophesy the end. The one, familiar with Timon's soul, and the other, familiar with his master's finances, foresee Timon's inner and outer bankruptcy. In this manner the two acting levels enter into an unspoken dialogue: The turbulent noise of untruth and pretence above is answered by the castigating and mourning double voice of truth below. The two-storeyed set, reminiscent of (and reversing) heaven and hell on the simultaneous stage of the Middle Ages, gives the performance the character of a mystery play.
>
> (Nagel 1989: 24 f.)

Just as in his productions of Shakespeare's tragedies, Kortner gave free reign to all manner of comic diversions, mixing burlesque elements, serene melancholy and even crude jokes with the tragic matter, so – conversely – he revealed the bitter seriousness and poetic pessimism that had long lain unnoticed in comedies like *Twelfth Night*, returning to them their intelligent risibility. His first production of *Twelfth Night* in Munich in 1957 had found only a mixed reception; his second attempt, at the Berlin Schiller-Theater in 1962, was an unquestioned success. Kortner allowed himself no conventional cosiness, neither sweetness nor crudeness, not a whit of thigh-slapping comedy: once again, a precise reading of the text was the prerequisite for the successful scenic realisation, for a whirlwind of comic effects, yet all of them true to life. His cast proved how he had managed to form and guide actors. With equal expertise, they presented exciting alternations between moments of erotic enchantment and melancholy moods, crazy exaltations, brilliant word battles, changeful love scenes, wonderful slapstick numbers and instances of grace and charm. There was an 'aria of laughter' by Maria (played by Carla Hagen) lasting several minutes; there strutting about like a love-sick stork in the park of his mistress was the Malvolio of Curt Bois who had already acted the part in the Munich production and released storms of laughter with his bitterly comic self-deception:

> The Malvolio of Curt Bois is indescribable, a field-mouse giving himself the airs of a gentleman, a megalomaniac, a blown-up dwarf deflated down to his proper size. Bois' clowning is always at high pitch, he uses well-known formulas of the grotesquely comic, then peps and stokes them up with imaginative inventions of his own which take the roof off the Schiller-Theater.
>
> (Luft 1982: 509)

Bois gave the Steward as an evil image of Angelo in *Measure for Measure*, teaching others manners and morals, whose puritanism here, however, is countered with derision and punished even with physical and mental torture applied by the Feste, the clown, in the mask of a puritanical sadist *avant la lettre*. A black comedy at the end that gave a glimpse of a time and conditions without 'entertainments' of which the theatre was one.

A few months before this brilliant explosion of comic talent, Kortner had brought out *Othello* at the Münchner Kammerspiele in a concentrated production exploring all facets of this tragedy. Romuald Pekny, whom Kortner had helped to establish himself as a front rank actor in the part of Timon, played Iago, for Kortner the driving force of the play. The performance lasted four hours but was felt to be shorter: in spite of being divided into three parts by two intervals, tension never slackened. Kortner built his production around the absolute difference between two types of men: Othello (Rolf Boysen), only nature and feeling, full of tender emotions, in fact obsessed by boundless love, which then turns into destructive disappointment. Iago, on the other hand, represented the rational principle: he was ice-cold and insensitive, spoke deceptively low, an unemotional soulless monster ever keen to further his evil plots. He knew the world and would be proved right in the end, even at the price of his own fall.

In *Othello*, Kortner also showed how much life was determined by war. Its agents on Cyprus take a break from fighting and paint the town red, as they go drinking and whoring. But they are none too safe in the port of this island now governed by Othello, and next to him Iago thwarted in his ambition and determined 'to suckle fools and chronicle small beer', i.e., to hoodwink all great and small. The war against the Turks is over but the situation is far from peaceful: Iago's aside, 'O you are well tuned now! / But I'll set down the pegs that make this music, / As honest as I am' (Act II, Scene 1) is meant for the Moor, but it is true for the others as well. It was terrible to watch how Iago's plotting not only raises Othello's jealousy, driving him to madness and murder, but also overshadowed all other scenes likewise, in that every brawl ended in a death, every drinking bout turned the soldiers into a bawling crowd of thugs, and every crass word led to bloody violence. For Kortner, this was not the effect of a fateful mechanism governing a hellish word, it was the work of the individuals themselves who, through war and violence, having lost all inhibitions and been despoiled of their feelings, have forgotten their humanity. This unredeemed condition was not ascribable to a mythic villain or obscure primal forces: both perpetrators and victims were types or characters the contemporary audience could understand. Iago had all the advantages on his side, for Othello is both Moor and Venetian, both lover and commander-in-chief. As a Moor, the lover may not marry a Venetian; as a Venetian he is to command the fleet; but lover and commander cannot be one person. This is the 'knowledge' that makes Othello doubt himself: it prevents his self-confidence from neutralising the poison of jealousy: 'This shaken belief in himself is the soil which makes his jealousy grow' (Szondi 1961: 77 f.). Kortner's *Othello* production, also in the Viennese version of 1966 with Pekny once more acting Iago, was a poignant reminder of the tragic condition that drives human beings into their opposite.

Kortner's last Shakespeare production at the Münchner Kammerspiele was *Richard III* in 1963. Once again, Romuald Pekny was the villain, softly humming, always on the lookout for evil-doing, a coldly calculating, humpbacked, devil-footed and heartless wire-puller. Just as in Pekny's rendering of Iago, there was nothing demonic in his acting of Richard either, and he certainly wasn't a tragic hero. The experiences and memories of the Nazi crimes and the Second World War, which had formed the dark substratum for *Julius Caesar* and *Hamlet* were present here too. Similarly to Brecht whose play *The Unstoppable Rise of Arturo Ui* was only a parable, not a 'realistic' key text about Hitler's rise to power, Kortner did not want to render history as such but aimed at a ghostly history play telling the story of the destruction of humanity, distorting history in visionary images of alienation and showing the deeds of a destroyer whose rise to power was supported by many who felt no qualms about what they unleashed. Richard, for Kortner, was the anti-hero from whose rise many hoped to profit. Not only power-seeking, Richard was 'guilty', and guilty also were the unsuspecting 'good' people who allowed the villain to get away with his crimes. The tragedy Kortner showed might have been entitled *The Stoppable Rise of Richard Gloucester*. There were many incidents to remind spectators of Germany's recent past in the power games of people who seemed to have been infected by the poisonous breath of a fascinating monster. The appearances of the three royal mothers who had been robbed of their children formed an impressive chorus of avengers: Queen Margaret, widow of Henry VI (played by Constanze Menz) supported herself on fearsome outsize crutches; the Duchess of York, mother to Edward IV, Clarence and Richard Gloucester (played by Johanna Hofer) appeared woefully distracted and expressed her hatred almost wordlessly, while Elizabeth, wife of Edward IV (played by Hortense Raky) tongue-lashed the evil schemer with maledictions. Lady Anne, vainly striving with all her reserve and strength to resist the temptation by her husband's murderer, was played by Doris Schade – in *Othello* a few months before she had been a gentle and unsuspecting Desdemona, unable to conquer the 'chaos' in Othello's soul. The final battle scene took place behind a dark gauze curtain which then was raised to reveal a brightly lit battlefield covered with bloody corpses and crowned with the cadaver of a horse. The victors, equally blood-covered, groped their way through this field of death while Richard, half-dead and lying on the ground, shouted for a horse which, had someone brought it, would not have helped him any more: 'Let them not live to taste this land's increase / That would with treason wound this fair land's peace!'

In 1968, the West German theatre scene was thrown into turmoil by the Students' Movement. The young revolutionaries demanded political theatre instead of 'art', no more 'grandpa's theatre'. Kortner countered these alien demands with a production of *The Tempest* (Schiller-Theater in Berlin) excelling in superior humour and steeped in the wisdom of age. Apparently, it was a labour of love, for in spite of several cuts and some reshuffling, he took the greatest care in the unfolding of each scene and sentence:

> The pace, as always, was slow. With every sentence, with every step, gesture and facial expression the actors were expected to prove the authenticity of what they were saying and doing. And when they had finally succeeded in more or less satisfying their severe taskmaster they were to transmit this experience to the spectators with equal force and insistence. Almost like talking to a good child that needs to be continuously admonished before it decides to pay attention. With Kortner, actors were not allowed resounding rhetoric, no pathos, no playing to the gallery [. . .] the shipwrecked lords are treated with the irony their miserable fate deserves. In all their pomp they are stranded on this deserted coast, and they have nothing better to do than to carry on in the style in which they have become rooted: lamenting, scheming, plotting. It is as if they were bound to their world by invisible ties. If proof were needed of Kortner's mastery in forming characters and types during his painstaking rehearsals, this result of the shipwrecked lords as a distinctive social group would be it. And then Kortner drives this group into a gruesome grotesque. He visibly demonstrates the 'theatre of cruelty' which Prospero plays with them. In their panic their eyes pop out of their heads, for a short sequence they wear false eyeballs as in Grand Guignol. And when they remove them they act the

> nonplussed surprise they feel that their madness is really leaving them, that they are healed, healed by 'reason' which, ungraspable to them, was able to forgive.
>
> (Siegfried Melchinger, *Theater heute*, June 1968)

Martin Held embodied Prospero, apparently also as the director's alter ego. Held revelled in the part, acting out whatever imagination or fancy dictated. Sometimes his magic wouldn't function, and then he slapped his forehead before he corrected his error. Held gave Prospero the serene and sharp-tongued irony as if he was a figure invented by Karl Kraus after reading Sigmund Freud. Brilliant intelligence alternated with a crazy logic in this performance. A slow, wonderfully detailed unfolding of an action in which fireworks of slapstick effects enchanted the audience without deflecting it from the main story. Here, as elsewhere, Kortner's chief concern as a director was '*Sprachregie*', conveying the truth of the human action through the authentic tones and accents of suffering and joy. *The Tempest* was Kortner's last impressive and great effort to give Shakespeare's truth a theatrical voice.

Chronology

1892	Born in Vienna
1919–26	Acted Richard III, Othello, Macbeth and Hamlet in Leopold Jessner's expressionist productions
1927	Major success acting Shylock in *The Merchant of Venice*, directed by Jürgen Fehling
1933	Left Germany for London, New York and then Hollywood
1948	Return from exile in the USA
1955	*Julius Caesar*, first Shakespeare production, at Residenztheatre, Munich
1956	Two parts of *Henry IV*, at Residenztheater in Munich
1957	*Hamlet* at Schiller-Theater, Berlin
1959	Publication of autobiography, *Aller Tage Abend*
1961	*Timon of Athens* at Kammerspiele, Munich
1962	*Twelfth Night* at Schiller-Theater, Berlin, and *Othello* at Kammerspiele, Munich
1963	*Richard III* at Kammerspiele, Munich
1966	*Othello* at Būrgtheater, Vienna
1968	*The Tempest* at Schiller-Theater, Berlin
1969	*Antony and Cleopatra* at Schiller-Theater, Berlin

Bibliography

Brecht, Bertolt (1993) *Große Kommentierte Augsabe*, Frankfurt:

Hortmann, Wilhelm (1998) *Shakespeare on the German Stage: The Twentieth Century*, Cambridge:.

Ihering, Herbert (1959) *Von Reinhardt bis Brecht*, Berlin:.

Jacobsohn, Siegfried (2005) *Gesammelte Schriften 1900–1926*, Göttingen:.

Karsch, Walther (1962) *Wort und Spiel: Aus der Chronik eines Theater-Kritikers 1945–1962*, Berlin:.

Kerr, Alfred (2001) 'So Liegt der Fall', *Theaterkritiken 1919–1933 und im Exil*, Frankfurt:.

Kortner, Fritz (1991) *Aller Tage Abend*, Berlin:.

Heinz Ludwigg (ed.) (1928) *Fritz Kortner*, Berlin:.

Luft, Friedrich (1982) *Stimme der Kritik I. Berliner Theater 1945–1965.*

Nagel, Ivan (1989) in *Kortner. Zadek. Stein*, Munich:

Rühle, Günther (1967) *Theater für die Republik 1917–1933*, Frankfurt:.

Szondi, Peter (1961) in *Versuch über das Tragische*, Frankfurt:.

Völker, Klaus (1987) *Fritz Kortner: Schauspieler und Regisseur*, Berlin:.

Weiss Wolfgang (1968) in *Shakespeare Kommentar zu den Dramen, Sonetten, Epen und kleineren Dichtungen*, Munich:.

About the author

Klaus Völker was born 1938 in Frankfurt on Main and studied at the Goethe-University in Frankfurt and at the Free University in Berlin. From 1963 to 1968 he was a freelance writer and theatre critic. From 1969 to 1986, he was a dramaturg in Zürich, Basel, Bremen and Berlin (Schiller-Theater) and collaborated with directors such as Peter Stein, Luc Bondy, Hans Hollmann, Adolf Dresen, Werner Düggelin, Hans Neuenfels and Peter Zadek. From 1982 to 1992, he taught dramaturgy at the Free University in Berlin, and from 1992 to 2005 he was Professor at the Ernst Busch theatre school in Berlin (dramaturgy and history of theatre), in 1993 becoming Head of this institute. He has published extensively on Brecht – *Brecht-Chronicle* (1975), *Brecht: A Biography* (1978) – and books on Frank Wedekind, Irish theatre, Samuel Beckett, Max Herrmann-Neisse, Boris Vian, Johannes Bobrowski, together with others about actors, actresses and directors such as Fritz Kortner, Elisabeth Bergner, Hans Lietzau, Bernhard Minetti, Elisabeth Orth, Kirsten Dene. His translations from French to German include works by Alfred Jarry, Boris Vian, Raymond Roussel, Henri-Pierre Roché, Jean-Paul Sartre, Jean Genet, Copi. He is editor of the collected works of Max Herrmann-Neisse, Alfred Jarry and Boris Vian. He is a member of the Berlin Academy of Arts and of the German Academy of Performing Arts.

13
MICHAEL LANGHAM

Kevin Ewert

Michael Langham's long career encompasses work in Europe, Australia, the USA and Canada. He ran repertory theatres in the UK after the Second World War, was Artistic Director at the Stratford Festival in Ontario from 1956 to 1967 and at the Guthrie Theatre in Minneapolis from 1971 to 1977 and headed the drama division at Juilliard between 1979 and 1992. He has directed in New York and at regional theatres across the USA and Canada. Through all this work, he has developed a distinctive approach to the staging of Shakespeare based around several key factors: exploiting the particular geography of the thrust stage; maintaining a rigorous commitment to making the text come alive; and creating narrative clarity and strikingly theatrical moments through carefully choreographed movement. For Richard Monette, in early years an actor and later Artistic Director at Stratford, Ontario, Langham's work remains the model of how to stage Shakespeare:

> The most important contribution Michael Langham made was discovering how to use the thrust stage, because, they say, even [Tony] Guthrie hadn't solved it. It was Michael who worked on the diagonals and whose work was very choreographic. He was able to bring a dynamism to the stage, invent it in fact, invent how to use that stage. As a director, I have never forgotten those lessons and I adhere to his principals of blocking.
>
> (Interview 2006)

Langham's early training as a director was particularly intense and deeply felt, as it took place not in schools or in theatres but in prisoner-of-war camps. As a young British officer, he was captured in France during the blitzkrieg of 1940 and was moved from camp to camp in Germany until the end of the war. It was in the camps that he grew up and discovered his vocation:

> I had had no experience of life of any significance before I was taken prisoner. I spent the first two years trying to escape and then there came a point when it seemed futile to go on living for nothing else but digging tunnels and forging documents and so on, and I started to turn to something else which was the sort of hobby that I had before [. . .] and I started putting on plays.
>
> (*Behind the Scenes* 1989)

He found that the identification with the experience of the plays went far beyond the aesthetic:

> When one play and then another play that we put on had quite clearly stopped people from committing suicide, at a very impressionable age I began to realize what the theatre could mean, and it had a profound effect on me, and it was then that I knew I really wanted to do nothing else with my life.
>
> (*Behind the Scenes* 1989)

In one of the camps, Langham and a group of prisoners formed a 'Lear Club', and that experience of wrestling with the demons of this play surely lies behind his description of the opening night of *King Lear* at Stratford, Ontario, in 1964: 'It seemed an effortless exercise in human beings going through the challenge of endurance, which is what that play is about' (*Behind the Scenes* 1989). Of course, the exercise was not exactly effortless for the actors on whom Langham could be notoriously tough, or for the director who had had plenty of time to think about the play while enduring imprisonment for five years. His war experiences lie behind his later reputation as cool, intellectual, rigorous, disciplined and controlling, while working to achieve productions often noted for their beauty, humanity and grace.

Langham was born in 1919 in Somerset, England. Before the war, he was enrolled at the University of London as a law student and did a bit of acting on the side, but his experiences in the war camps spurred him to say goodbye to all that. From 1946 to 1948, he directed a regional theatre in Coventry, and from 1948 to 1950, the Birmingham Rep. He first directed at the Memorial Theatre in Stratford-upon-Avon in 1950, where his *Julius Caesar* was noted for its ferocious mob that seemed able to work itself up to its own vivid life independent of the great speeches that are supposed to stir it on. His production of the play five years later in Stratford, Ontario, received similar comments and indicates from the beginning of his Shakespearian career a penchant for striking group choreography over intense individual displays.

Langham directed *Othello* for the Old Vic in 1951, *The Merry Wives of*

Windsor at The Hague in 1952, and *Richard III* in Australia – on a thrust stage – in 1953 while on a British Council lecturing tour. From 1953 to 1954, he was Director of the Citizens' Theatre in Glasgow, and in 1955 he was invited by Tyrone Guthrie to come to Stratford, Ontario. By his own admission, he had a 'very nice thing going' in the UK, but Guthrie was able to convince him that this theatre in Canada was more important and was also the future. Working with Guthrie, working in Canada, and working on the Guthrie–Moiseiwitsch thrust stage all presented difficulties. But Guthrie trusted him and, even though the response to Langham's 1955 *Julius Caesar* was mixed, he was appointed Artistic Director of the Stratford Festival starting with the 1956 season.

Langham was often referred to as a protégé of Guthrie's in the early years, but those who worked with both marked their differences in style. Douglas Rain, a member of the original acting company and a mainstay of the festival for much of its history, offers a vivid distinction:

> Guthrie was a theatrical man. He couldn't put on a production of *Mary Had a Little Lamb* without it being the most dynamically theatrical thing you've ever seen. I would consider Langham to be the master of this particular stage in the way that he could place people so that the audience's eye, instead of wandering back and forth, would always be focused where Langham wished you to be focused. It was like a chessboard with him, and I don't think anybody has quite come up to what he was able to do with diagonals, with people being halfway up a flight of stairs, to create a focal point which would be on the speaker down on the main stage.
>
> (*Butch Blake Video History Project* 1988–97)

Fred Euringer, also an actor in the Festival's early years and later a director and teacher, saw key differences in approach to text, rehearsal techniques and the director–actor relationship:

> Guthrie was capable of cheating the text to achieve something that tickled his great Irish funny bone, at the expense of what Hamlet calls 'some necessary question of the play.' Langham – erring perhaps in the opposite direction – found it difficult to allow the actors to take focus away from the meticulous crystal-clear vision of what he wanted, even though it might lead the actors into mechanical performances at the expense of spontaneity. One felt that Guthrie had no idea where the whole thing was headed, but wouldn't it be fun to find out together. The great joy Guthrie offered actors was to 'play'. The major joy

> Michael gave to actors was to give them a crystal clear idea of what the play was about, and what he wanted from them.
>
> (Interview 2006)

Tony Van Bridge, who also worked with Langham in his early days at Stratford, Ontario, thought the clarity, rigour and control came directly from his war experiences:

> He started working on [plays like *King Lear*] with the prisoners. He had years to do it, so he would work it out carefully in his mind, one piece at a time [and it was] as if he was still in that prison camp to a certain extent. It was what he had spent the war working out.
>
> (Ouzounian 2002: 100–1)

For William Hutt, another festival stalwart, Langham's rigour anchored the company and gave it a more consistent playing style.

> Tony Guthrie's productions featured a lot of improvisation on his part and indeed on ours, and consequently, they seemed slightly to fall apart at the seams in the middle of the season. Not Michael. He was very precise and very good at choreography. He seemed somehow to have the entire production staged in his mind before he went into rehearsals. And each picture wasn't just [. . .] movement for the sake of movement. It illuminated the text.
>
> (Ouzounian 2002: 29)

Some actors enjoyed working this way, others didn't, but the primary beneficiary of Langham's approach was the audience. His productions always told audiences what to look at and how to look at it, as the physical narrative of the piece unfolded.

Guthrie created his Elizabethan-adaptation, anti-illusionist thrust stage in Ontario, and he and his actors played about on it. Langham had to take the next step: to develop and solidify a company, a staging approach and an acting style based around this open, stepped platform, approximately 30 feet wide and 36 feet deep, with a pillared central balcony, central and side onstage entrances and under-the-house front vomitoria entrances. It took a while:

> I found myself fighting it. It's quite a difficult piece of wood to learn to use in a really expressive, creative way, and it was about three or four years before I really felt a marriage with it, that my work could be

> married to it, and that I was really using it in a sympathetic way as opposed to an aggressive way. And yet it did affect my outlook toward Shakespeare especially.
>
> (*Behind the Scenes* 1989)

Langham came to believe that Shakespeare's language, characters and flow of action live best on the thrust – which is what he worked on in Ontario, at the Guthrie and at Juilliard. The greatest strength of the open stage is 'a plasticity of feeling and a more honest physical relationship between people (Behind the Scenes 1989).' The two-dimensional picture-frame stage easily leads to two-dimensional performances, where 'actors pretend to play to each other, when in fact they are playing to the audience; on a thrust stage, if the plays are well staged, you are much more involved in playing to each other, with each other' (*Behind the Scenes* 1989). Langham developed his staging technique directly out of the demands and opportunities of the thrust:

> Shakespeare's theatre was three-dimensional, not only in its physical arrangement but also, presumably, in its acting, its movement and its design. The actors were grouped, I believe, in semi-circular patterns to face one another, not the audience. The effect of this, in my experience, was not to exclude the audience but to involve them more fully in the experience of the play, and, of course, to deepen the relationship between the characters.
>
> (Langham, *Two Programmes* 1962: 23)

Characters facing each other and patterned into constant semicircular movement – this is the hallmark of his choreographic approach, for better or for worse. Most reviews of a Langham production will mention some striking moment composed that way, such as the ring game in his 1989 *Merchant of Venice* at Stratford, Ontario, where '[Bassanio's] balanced clauses [. . .] and Portia's rejoinder were both delivered as the four lovers moved diagonally across stage, weaving their ways among one another, the men in desperate pursuit of the women' (McGee 1989: 114–20). At Juilliard, he worked with fellow faculty member Richard Feldman on an evening of scenes featuring women in Shakespeare. For Feldman, the ever-swirling but perfectly balanced precision engineering of Langham's casket scene from *A Merchant of Venice* typified his style: 'It unfolded across that stage like this miracle of a kaleidoscope of movement. It was my favourite scene of all the things that happened in that evening, but a lot of other people didn't like it. They thought it was cold or something, and I was sure they were insane' (Interview 2006).

In the early years, the ideas he was wrestling with on the stage in Stratford, Ontario, he took to his 1956 *Hamlet* at the Memorial Theatre in Stratford, England. The set was a 6-inch-high octagonal wood platform with a 3-inch step all the way around, surrounded by a sea of black drapes and black felt on the rest of the stage floor. There was a 12-foot-high dark blue drape in the shape of a sail at the back of the platform; a red carpet was laid over the octagon only for the play-within-the-play scene; and a few moveable pieces came in and out swiftly during the action. It was a gesture towards a bare thrust stage dropped into the proscenium space.

Langham acknowledges that this staging was unusual for England at the time, but he also maintains that it was 'revolutionary' for and had 'a huge effect' upon the profession (*Behind the Scenes* 1989, *Butch Blake Video History Project* 1988–97). The production was not well received, and perhaps even less well understood. The Hamlet, Alan Badel, took his knocks for not being whatever version of the prince each critic had in mind, but much sharper barbs were aimed at the director. Many decried the production as far too visually drab, austere and boring for Stratford. An angry letter to the editor of the *Birmingham Post* went even further than the critics, calling the lack of scenery – and furniture, and a front curtain – a travesty and a kind of theatrical nihilism.

There were also complaints about the style of movement and the pacing in the unadorned space. Many critics found that Langham's technique of continuous action on a nearly bare stage – moving between scenes with a lighting shift and by bringing a new group of actors in right on the heels of those that were leaving – quickened the pace but 'confused' the audience about time and place: how could swift movement, reorganised stage groupings and mere dialogue take the place of a thorough set change to indicate where we were? It may have become a commonplace of Shakespearian staging since, but at the time he was pioneering a new approach, physically pictorial rather than scenically pictorial, that would influence a generation of directors. Richard Monette describes Langham's approach as

> very choreographic [. . .] he kept almost constant movement, and as he developed he did an awful lot of overlapping of scenes. I remember him saying, if Shakespeare were alive today he would be writing for the movies because there are so many scenes, so many changes of location, and they are like cuts in a film.
>
> (Interview 2006)

Whether the 1956 *Hamlet* gestured back to Elizabethan practices on a bare stage or forward to techniques associated with the 'new' medium of cinema, many reviewers for the next production at the Memorial Theatre that season made special (and relieved) note of the delicious sets.

Four years after this 'experimental' staging, incoming Artistic Director Peter Hall experimented with the Memorial Theatre itself by adding a jutting apron to try to move the players and the action closer to the audience. He even made special mention in interviews of a forthcoming *Troilus and Cressida* that would be played entirely on the forestage and without settings – in other words, just like Langham's *Hamlet*. Hall's was the first of many attempts to rework the Memorial away from a pictorial stage; the resultant years of mixed architecture and mixed scenic messages end with the transitional Courtyard thrust theatre and the 2007–10 complete rebuild of the Memorial as a thrust space. It is tempting to think that Langham's pioneering work lies behind that decision somewhere. Even in the early 1960s, he was blunt about the value of mere tweaking: 'the great Memorial shrine at Stratford-upon-Avon, in spite of vast expenditure over frequent reconstructions of its stage, remains a most unsuitable, unhelpful building for producing Shakespeare' (Langham, *Two Programmes* 1962: 21).

Hall's opening production for 1960 of *Two Gentlemen of Verona* received mixed reviews, although at least some reviewers positively noted the stage redesign. Up next was Langham's *A Merchant of Venice*, which was greeted as a blazing triumph; perhaps this had more to do with stars Dorothy Tutin and Peter O'Toole, but again the staging stood out. The production was praised for its wit, energy, quick pace, balletic choreography and beautiful stage groupings. Hall made much use of the new revolve in his *Two Gentlemen of Verona* – too much, in some critics' eyes – while Langham didn't use it at all. Instead of the stage, of course, he had his actors in constant motion.

Many critics for the 1956 *Hamlet* described the actors as something like mechanical puppets whirling about the empty space; although decidedly in the minority in 1960, a few were still arguing that the stylistic transplant didn't take. One can tinker with the stage, but without radical adjustment to the house, the Memorial remains a proscenium space: all movement is essentially only displayed on one side and at one angle. Even a lesser production in Ontario such as his 1955 *Julius Caesar* – about which Langham himself later admitted the most interesting bits took place in the aisles – could have the highly choreographed action whirling about the stage and up and down its steps, pouring into its aisles and rushing through the house, and could spur critics to suggest that 'while these Roman mobs are at it, they can tear down the proscenium arch theatre from coast-to-coast' (*New York Herald-Tribune*, 28 June 1955). Langham believes Shakespeare's plays have a physical momentum, a motor, and their energy is released precisely by the geography of the thrust, the rhythm of movement that goes along with it and the direct sharing of the theatrical event without sets and machinery getting in the way. In the late 1950s and early 1960s, his work was at the forefront of a reinvention of the rules of staging Shakespeare – at least when it took place in the right building and on the right stage.

Langham began his directorship of the Stratford Festival in 1956 with *Henry V*. Rising Canadian star Christopher Plummer made his Stratford debut, and leading French Canadian actors came to play the French court – an impressive twin coup for someone who would spend years dealing with nationalist scepticism. 'It's the kind of idea that seems obvious to an outsider', he felt; 'you come to Canada and this is supposed to be a national theatre and you think well, what does Canada mean?' The French actors changed the dynamic of the play from the outset:

> The first day [of rehearsals] the English Canadians had come dressed, as it were, ready for the beach in sweatshirts and straw hats, whereas the French Canadians came in Italian suits. They looked absolutely smashing, with a tremendous sense of presence and panache, and they stood on the stage like no one could stand on the stage better. That sense of cultural identity, cultural difference, really was fused through the whole production, and it couldn't have been avoided, it was a natural ingredient that was very powerful.
>
> (*Butch Blake Video History Project* 1988–97)

The production – described in the programme notes as 'an historical pageant with the theme of Unity through Leadership' – was purposefully optimistic: '*Henry V* is open to all manner of interpretations, but one that seemed reasonable at the time was a hopeful interpretation [. . .] the play end[s] with a peace conference and it was certainly in that spirit we did it, believing it was an expression of the hopes of Canada and Canada's future' (*Butch Blake Video History Project* 1988–97).

With the focus on reconciliation, the peace treaty at the end was elaborately and enthusiastically staged. Burgundy's speech for peace was given almost in its entirety, but the off-colour comments after the wooing scene were cut, as was the sticking point about *heritier* and all bad news contained in the final chorus. The mere presence of French and English actors working together on the Stratford stage, along with Plummer's winning portrayal of Henry, constituted a hit with critics national and international, and the *New York Times* felt the production passed the even more important post-Guthrie staging test: Langham carried on 'the same sweeping tradition' where 'the centrifugal style and the spectacular movement are happily familiar' but also 'added artistic perception of his own' (20 June 1956).

He lost a major battle before the next season began. The festival was born in 1953 in a tent; for the permanent festival theatre being built for the 1957 season, the stage was to remain the same, but there was argument about the size of the house. Since the season was short in those days, the Board wanted as many seats as possible. Langham wanted to keep it intimate. The Board telephoned Guthrie and he recommended, 'get in as many as you can.' The tent held about 1,500 seats, sweeping 240 degrees around the stage; the permanent festival house wrapped 220 degrees around the stage but added a substantial balcony to bring seating to 2,200. Years later, Langham was still arguing that the size and sweep of the house 'impels the actor to push' (*Behind the Scenes* 1989). He saw the bare platform as having great value for acting Shakespeare and the over-extended house as having major disadvantages, especially regarding the conversational rhythm in which he feels the plays should be spoken. When Langham returned to the festival in 1983/4 to head the training programme with the Young Company, he worked in the small thrust space of the Third Stage, later the Tom Patterson Theatre: 'it is much easier to achieve significant results of exploring Shakespeare in spaces that aren't as huge as the Festival Theatre' (*Behind the Scenes* 1989). During his tenure, Richard Monette had the house in the Festival Theatre redesigned; the audience segment was reduced to about 180 degrees, and 400 seats were taken out – much closer to what Langham originally wanted. Ironically, Monette feels that it was finding the solution to the problem of the wider arc in the original house that made Langham's staging so powerful: 'In a way the extended auditorium made the diagonal work better than what I've done because you could reach more people, the person facing upstage would have a greater piece of the pie' (Interview 2006).

For the *Hamlet* that opened the permanent theatre in 1957, Langham wasn't entirely satisfied with Plummer, although Plummer recalls a wonderful trick Langham taught him of thinking of the phrase 'Isn't it extraordinary?' just before speaking passages that might otherwise tend towards complaining or self-pity, to instil a sense of wonderment and discovery instead (Ouzounian 2002: 113). But the real star was always going to be the space itself and, treated with Langham's staging style, it didn't disappoint:

> Michael Langham's production of *Hamlet* showed off [the new theatre] in a unique fashion. From our vantage point [seated in the new balcony], it was possible to draw extra excitement from the swirl of his action. Sometimes the small circling movements of the actors seemed forced, but when there was a large action it held a truly balletic adventure: the players miming on a blazing, flame-colored carpet, the black

> huddle around Ophelia's grave, the madly rushing search for Hamlet after the death of Polonius.
>
> (Whittaker 1985: 73)

Walter Kerr pronounced it 'the only really new stage and the only really new actor-audience experience of the last hundred years on this continent' (*New York Herald-Tribune*, 7 July 1957).

Langham seemed to be hitting his stride with a highly successful *Much Ado about Nothing* with Plummer and Eileen Herlie in 1958. But productions directed by others under his watch were deemed not very impressive, casting a pall on his leadership, and in 1959 he missed a whole season due to severe illness. He came back in 1960 with a successful *Romeo and Juliet* that marked a further advance in his use of the geography of the thrust. For example, the festival to funeral sequences of Act IV, Scene 4 could be played in all their inappropriate, ironic and highly effective simultaneity, since the space allowed Langham to stage Juliet's 'death' on the balcony platform, bring in the bustle of wedding preparations below on the main platform, then discover and lament the loss above while maintaining the revelry beneath. The 1961 season was very nearly lost again to illness, but Langham pushed himself to direct *Love's Labour's Lost* and *Coriolanus*, both with Paul Scofield, and this season became the acknowledged high point of his directorship.

Langham sees in a comedy like *Love's Labour's Lost* a kind of loving chastisement of human follies. He thinks Shakespeare knew the whip had to be cracked but was himself no moraliser: 'He does expose human frailties. And he does correct them. Not openly, though, from the outside. But from within. He refuses to wield the whip himself. He makes his characters do it for him by correcting one another.' The reproof is never bitter or mean-spirited, but gracious and progressive: 'What frailties to correct? Egotism, sentimentality. Pedantry, self-importance. All those follies which [. . .] make men and women unsociable, and unfit for the friendly purposes of life. Those people who, like peevish children, say to life that they won't play, are laughed by Shakespearian comedy back into the game' (Langham, *Two Programmes* 1962).

Still, *Love's Labour's Lost* presents some major problems for a director. The verbal excesses displayed by almost all the characters tend towards the inaccessible, and the jokes towards the unfunny. This can be hidden behind physical slapstick and caricature, but that too can become tiresome and isn't much of an argument on behalf of the text, the characters or the story. Langham's solution lay in creating an accessible, highly detailed play world where the characters don't require mocking but rather where it seems normal that the appetite for talking and listening is huge. The little academe was no retreat but a structure to contain irrepressible enthusiasms, a world where experiences are a series of exciting firsts and where youth might test its ideas and energies in exuberant if often selfish self-expression. In that bigger picture, the tendency to linguistic onanism finally gives way – as it must, when the world intrudes upon this little hothouse – to suddenly serious men and women actually trying to talk to one another.

Langham worked very specifically to create physical actions to bring the language to life rather than hide or cut it. For example, during Boyet's reading of Armado's intercepted letter to the four women in Act IV, Scene 1, a lengthy letter full of obvious questions and answers, Langham 'had Boyet pause on those questions, and the girls interrupt to shout the answers at him. A long, pedantic letter thus became a game between them, without losing one syllable or nuance of its style' (Ganong 1962: 152). All aspects of the production were carefully managed, for audience benefit and for actor immersion; Langham even wrote a paper for the prop department called 'Postal Congestion in Navarre', distinguishing and describing each of the play's many letters in detail.

Langham thought he could make the text work on a technical level if he approached it like a piece of music. He saw the writing structured like musical composition, replete with repetitive artifice and speeches often composed with a statement of theme, then rhythmic variations on that theme and then a summing up. This kind of 'apprentice' Shakespearian writing of repetitive, joyful artifice he believes 'unactable and unenjoyable' without a clear, firm and formal, albeit enthusiastic, style of presentation (Langham, *Two Programmes* 1962: 31).

Frank Euringer played a small role in *Love's Labour's Lost* and recalls Langham's work in rehearsals as marked by 'his rapier-like intelligence and acerbic sensibilities [. . .] he delighted in dissecting the play, filleting it, as it were, and laying it open before the company to digest' (Euringer 2000: 79). The 'filleting' could also be applied to actors. Joan Ganong, who worked in the publicity department at the festival, sat in on a rehearsal where Jack Creley, a well-known comedian and revue star, was going about 'turning every line into a laugh':

> There was quite a tussle about [Holofernes'] whole character, and Michael came up on stage to discuss it.
>
> 'This must be a man of furious enthusiasm about words,' he insisted; 'there has to be a tremendous excitement, tremendous energy – but on a subject for which all that energy is just too much.'
>
> 'Oh, yes. Oh, I see,' said Jack, enlightened. 'Yes, indeed. Energy! Yes,' and back they went to rehearsal.

> The last scene was right square out of this world. Jack did all with his voice what Michael wanted, plus hands, plus head, plus body, plus expression. His hands were going like a windmill. Bill Needles and Butch Blake both nearly broke up. The watching cast were snorting and coughing, and I was weak just from watching this overplus. Michael did not interrupt. Jack's exit from that scene was, at that time, down the ramp. He finished, headed that way with a final flourish. Just as he stepped off stage, through the silence of muted chuckles cut Michael's voice.
>
> 'Jack!'
>
> Jack turned toward him.
>
> 'Michael?'
>
> '*Mental* energy!' That was all. Jack grinned and nodded.

Later, when she talked to Creley about it, he said 'Why, that was the best direction I had [. . .] it took a while, but now I know what Michael wants!' (Ganong 1962: 72–3). The improvised insanity was funny, but those pleasures of the moment were not compatible with Langham's larger conception of the piece. The insane 'overplus' would get laughs for the actor but at the expense of the character, and without explaining him. For the pedants, the comedy was to come not from sending them up but from allowing them, in a more humane and accessible fashion, simply to 'be earnest about their own extravagances' (Ganong 1962: 103).

Love's Labour's Lost became a signature play for Langham. He went on to direct it at the Guthrie and then as a teaching tool at Juilliard and with the Young Company back at Stratford, but those productions were essentially variations on this original staging, reviving much of the design details, business and character conceptions. Langham was not one afraid to repeat himself. The 1961 production had a Caroline setting, mainly because Scofield didn't want both productions of his North American debut to be set so far from the time they were written, and the designs for *Coriolanus* were Napoleonic; later productions shifted to the *belle époque* just before the First World War, and followed the song of winter at the end with the sound of far-distant artillery. But Langham felt that this first production was the one where he figured the play out:

> You do plays more than once in your life and you do them differently, you don't necessarily do them any better. I think there were elements of the magic of that world that will never be recaptured for me as they were for that first time [. . .] a marrying of language and movement [. . .] the last careless summer of youth. It sounds a bit slushy and

> romantic, but I was in touch with something here, a very unforced Shakespeare, effortless Shakespeare.
>
> (*Butch Blake Video History Project* 1988–97)

To maintain that unforced quality, he kept the production in the rehearsal space until the last minute. When he finally moved into the theatre, he encouraged the actors not to force things by trying to fill the space, but instead to get the audience to come to them, as it were. He told them, 'just take deeper breaths and the play will gradually fill the space' (*Butch Blake Video History Project* 1988–97).

With an overall conception of *Love's Labour's Lost* as a summer play with an autumnal end, Langham took pains to prepare for and then manage that final shift. It isn't enough that the shift is emphasised in a kind of dramaturgical split personality; it needs to seem integral to the piece as a whole, the kind of disruption we always knew had to come. Langham planted hints of fragility and melancholy throughout – the entire conception of Armado's character was marked by delicateness rather than bombast, and his chastisement to the boisterous onstage audience for the parade of Worthies to 'beat not the bones of the buried' was especially sobering. With the help of designer Tanya Moiseiwitsch, the final moments were underscored with a deft costume shift. The gowns of the four ladies got progressively lighter and brighter throughout the play, so that by the final scene they were almost white. When Mercade entered at the peak of abandonment dressed completely in black, his contrast was striking in keeping with his message, but more important was the addition of darker cloaks that servants draped over all four women. Berowne's 'the scene begins to cloud' was quite literally realised as the lustre of the stage image was eclipsed even before any lights started to fade. A dissipating brightness accompanied time and the world back into the play. The stage eventually cleared to leave Armado to deliver his final line – 'You that way; we this way' – to the audience as he exited, while autumn leaves slowly tumbled down from the Festival Theatre's very high ceiling to the floor.

Most critics saw this production as confirmation of Langham's status as a master of the thrust stage and a director of Shakespearian comedy without equal. But *Love's Labour's Lost* is an ensemble piece, with no overwhelming star part – the star of the season, Scofield, played Armado. The play could be said to lend itself to a highly technical 'musical' patterning and to be conducted with a firm guiding hand. *Coriolanus* would seem to be a different matter.

Langham directed *Coriolanus* as a tightly choreographed ensemble piece with a star trapped in the middle of it. Euringer, once again in a small role, describes the effect of being in those rehearsals as 'like watching two gladiators circling each other':

> Paul, his nose buried in his tiny book, trying to puzzle out the meaning of the moves he was trying to remember, so that he could figure out what it was that he would eventually have to 'act'; and Langham waiting for Scofield to 'act' something that would support his, Langham's, staging.
>
> Weeks went by: Scofield delivering his lines in a gentle whisper, in much the same softly coveted voice with which he politely ordered tea in the Green Room Cafeteria; and Langham, in his own fashion, trying to solve the play by interminably staging and re-staging the supporting actors around the tormented Scofield, who daily began to look more and more like a baited bear surrounded by a pack of over-reacting pit-bulls.
>
> (Euringer 2000: 171)

Euringer wasn't sure this was helpful: 'Scofield found Michael's way of working very daunting and uncomfortable' (Interview 2006). Ganong, watching those rehearsals from the house, saw something similar, even if she sensed it was ultimately for the best:

> [Paul] had just finished one of his major scenes, and Michael was shoring up some bits and pieces of the blocking which did not suit him. While doing so he began to build the production detail stronger, to make a major production highlight of a scene which should by rights have belonged to Coriolanus. Paul's head turned sharply, he started to speak, but said nothing.
>
> 'All right, Paul?' asked Michael.
>
> 'Yes,' said Paul. 'Yes, of course.' He turned away. But in that turn I caught his expression. It was not temper, Paul never lost his temper; but it was anger, swift, clear anger, the first I had seen him show.
>
> It disappeared from his features instantly. They ran the scene again. The crowds moved around Paul, but it did not matter. The scene belonged by right to Coriolanus, and Coriolanus quietly took it back. [. . .]
>
> The second I saw it, I knew what Michael was up to. [Paul] didn't need [Michael's help]. He needed something else. Something to work against. There wasn't an individual actor in that theatre who could seize a scene from him on his own terms; but Michael had another power – the production. He began to produce Paul Scofield right off the edge of that stage. He did not needle him as he did the others, but he tossed him tough situations, to see what he would do.
>
> (Ganong 1962: 122)

Ganong thought the *production* was dead-on and enormously powerful by opening. Euringer maintains Scofield only found the shape of the piece and the character that *he* wanted to play about a month into the run, and only then by leading the company through one terrifying, awe-inspiring performance where he restructured on the fly almost every aspect of his characterisation (and in places reblocked the action and reshaped the climaxes) through those central scenes leading to the banishment (Euringer 2000: 174–5).

Euringer, who still puzzles over his feelings about Langham as a director, couches his misgivings about Langham's approach in a musical metaphor:

> Directing a tragedy is something like conducting a concerto, as opposed to conducting a symphony which is more like directing a comedy.
>
> If you are conducting a symphony, the orchestra belongs to you, the conductor. The work is held together entirely by the control of the single leader. On the other hand, if you are conducting a violin concerto, at some point you have to give over the control to the soloist [. . .] who finally carries the performance.

Euringer thought the directorial ardour worked for the comedies, which came off 'like brilliant Mozart symphonies: tightly controlled, with a built-in organic metronome-like precision' (Interview 2006). Certainly in the case of *Love's Labour's Lost*, where Langham wanted to project 'a picture of youth in its joyous spring, where physical restrictions on their actions should be nil' (Ganong 1962: 109), its vivid impression of spontaneity came precisely out of the intense physical 'restrictions' of actors being tightly choreographed into constant movement on the thrust. But Euringer, and occasionally others, thought that at times the sheer force of Langham's staging held back or diminished the tragedies, because he couldn't really hand over the production to some necessary solo flights of a Lear or a Hamlet or a Coriolanus.

From the remaining years of his directorship, the production with the most interesting afterlife is his 1963 *Timon of Athens*. A difficult play, with elements that seem unfinished, an overly schematic divide between its first and second half, and an irony that tends towards nihilism, Langham's modern-dress production was exciting and inventive if not whole-heartedly embraced. With much of the staging and its Duke Ellington score still intact, he remounted the production at Stratford in the smaller thrust stage Tom Patterson Theatre in 1991 to unanimous raves, and again in 1993 for the National Actors Theatre in New York where he and his star, Brian Bedford, were both nominated for Tony Awards. Langham changed his mind about the main character, conceiving of him less as a playboy and more as a passionate visionary, whose compulsiveness and vulnerability set up the extremes of both halves of the play. But mostly he attributes the production's rising fortunes to a sense that the play was more appropriate to the 1990s than to 1963. The 1960s had been full of optimism, whereas the 1990s had

> a feeling that the human race is only interested in greed, government is the same, experiments in social reform have all come to grief – the last half of the play now makes such sense, and the first part reminds one of those sort of hopes, the romantic hopes of the 60s.

As perhaps indicated by the lonely, blasted, *Godot*-like tree that provided about the only setting for the second half of the revival, Langham also feels that our increased knowledge and understanding of Beckett 'has made [*Timon*] more available to us' (*Butch Blake Video History Project* 1988–97).

Langham left Stratford in 1967 to direct the Theatre and Arts Foundation at La Jolla, California. He was intimately involved in the design process for the new theatre – with multiple spaces, incorporating things he had learned from Stratford and elsewhere – but the project fell through. Instead, he found himself following after Guthrie once again to become Artistic Director at the Guthrie in Minneapolis, where he inherited an institution with declining attendance, serious financial woes and a lack of clear vision for the repertoire or acting company. There, Langham did much the same as at Stratford: he expanded the season, built a strong ensemble and drew appreciative, and larger, audiences with a repertoire that included a number of plays he had directed with success in Ontario.

Langham accepted the position at Juilliard in 1979 only because it was convenient, since his actress wife Helen Burns had just had a big success in New York. He is typically blunt in his opinion of teaching at that time: 'I didn't believe in it. I had never believed in training schemes. I thought they were usually administered and taught by charlatans and people who had failed in the profession.' But after three years he had to admit, 'I had got hooked by the need for this kind of school in the American culture, a school that was going to be able to encompass training actors to cope with classical plays and fully expressive authors' (*Behind the Scenes* 1989). In a sense Langham had always been training actors. Brian Bedford saw that in all the productions they did together: 'he's [very] technical and [that] can help an actor tremendously. I mean, I've seen him reduce a lot of actors to tears [. . .] but those actors, those crying actors, all said to me eventually, "It was hell, but it was worth it because I learned so much" ' (Ouzounian 2002: 259–60).

A director's approach to acting Shakespeare

> Shakespeare writes about, not incidents of a weekend, but about milestones in people's lives, and when he's played with a sense of immediacy of experience, when he's played with a real raw sense of experience in the actor, as a character traveling through life, he is at his most vivid and exciting.
>
> (*Behind the Scenes* 1989)

The trick is how to play it that way. Langham felt he had to work against a North American tendency to treat Shakespeare's text as an enemy rather than the actor's greatest ally. He didn't exactly try to get students to treat the text like an old chum, as the working relationship and Langham's teaching style were far too intense for that:

> [Michael] knew just about every word of the text by heart, so that if an actor had omitted a 'the' in a particular verse, he would immediately and mercilessly belt the corrected phrase and add 'Shakespeare put that word there for a reason. It doesn't make rhythmic sense without it.' His persistent attention to detail was so relentless that at times his manner came across as downright cruel. Later, one would come to respect these moments for their clarity, integrity and unforgettable impact. [. . .] Eventually this approach gave the actor the form, the structure in which to play.
>
> (Alex Phoenix, *Juilliard Journal*, May 1992)

Langham believes freedom isn't a matter of acting on impulse, but comes from having the support of a solid structure. He doesn't do improvisation work and neither does he believe that there is any subtext in a blank-verse speech; he starts from the rigours of the text of a 'fully expressive author', and encourages his students to release from there. For a visual stylist and choreographic director, his rigorous approach to text is striking:

> I refuse to accept that the day of language is over. [. . .] I think we simply have to work hard and with great skill to reestablish the fact that it's a joyful thing to find words with which to express oneself. Shakespeare's text is built on this assumption: that each character has an overwhelming passion to explain precisely and exactly what he's thinking, and thus what he's feeling. This requires a sort of intellectual glee in the actor, which will give him the power to infect people with the simple joy of utterance.
>
> (Loney 1990: 65)

The actor's technical challenge, which will open up the thought and the feeling and thus be the means of connecting with the text and then to the audience, has to do with mastering a certain speed of thought, especially in soliloquy:

> When you embark as an actor on a phrase of Shakespeare's, you don't know, as you often do with a modern play, what you want to say before you say it. But you have the germ of an idea, and you embark on that idea-journey right up until you find the conclusion of the idea, which obviously comes at the end of the phrase. Each phrase will then have that degree of spontaneous life, white-hot from the mind.
>
> (Loney 1990: 77–8)

'White hot thought' came to represent a central concept for his students at Juilliard, crucial to what creating a Shakespearian character feels like for the actor from the inside: 'With this approach, the freshness of ideas take on new meaning each time they are expressed. They surprise even the speaker and allow him to tap into an emotional center that is vital to any performance' (John Cutler, *Juilliard Journal*, May 1992). The 'white hot thought' process requires enormous intellectual rigour, but getting to the point where you surprise yourself with the ideas that pop up from carefully constructed, memorised and rehearsed text also renders the thought, and the actor, rather vulnerable in the playing. The rush of discovery, the need for the words, is bound to have an emotional or visceral effect for the actor, even if the initial approach is 'intellectual'.

As a teacher/director, Langham was intent on passing on practical skills and the lessons of what works in the theatre; emotional journeys, whatever they are, come from application of craft first, and that can start with something as deceptively simple as the pacing of a line:

> As Berowne lists womankind's accoutrements ["How shall I praise a hand, a foot, a face, an eye, a gait, a state, a brow, a breast"] his mood changes from self-righteous indignation to one of transfixed lovesickness, a comedic transition where timing and pace are everything. After ceaselessly fiddling with this moment throughout the rehearsal process, Michael and I finally settled on a delivery which began rather slowly and accelerated to a feverish pitch, instead of vice-versa. The moment became a real turning point for Berowne and a kind of cause celebre for the audience. Whether Michael directed this moment with all his previous Berownes in exactly the same way,

> perhaps I will never know. But I really feel [. . .] his fierce passion for his craft inspires a collaboration of matching intensity.
>
> (Alex Phoenix, *Juilliard Journal*, May 1992)

It's an outside-in approach but, as even Stanislavsky discovered later in his career, that doesn't negate emotional content, for performer or audience.

Another part of Langham's approach to actor training is a larger cultural project of opposing the diminution of the actor's craft by television and film. Although he believes Shakespeare's words should be spoken with a conversational rhythm – 'It's no good shouting them, or belting them out' (*Behind the Scenes* 1989) – he also wants actors to be ready for the challenge of direct communication with an audience on a larger scale than what a camera might require. This demands a mixture of sensitivity and expansiveness:

> It's good to train in a small place, but life is breath and one could always breathe more deeply. [. . .] Start small with an honest exploration of what the play's about and what the characters are about and what the interplay between people is about, and then having found what you believe to be the essence of the truth of an interpretation [. . .] let that gradually expand by allowing it to become more and more available by deeper breaths, really.
>
> (*Behind the Scenes* 1989)

The expansiveness required does not make the theatre a place for show-offs or loud but empty rhetoric, and neither is it a place for flat naturalism, small truths and the physicality of mere behavior: 'one just craves for the really skilled, sensitive artist actor, and maybe for a little less of the sort of prostitute performer with which the theatre will always be filled, but not exclusively, one hopes' (*Behind the Scenes* 1989).

As a choreographic director intent on making the thrust stage work, Langham was never afraid of just telling people what he wanted them to do. He didn't direct actors in terms of objectives or motives, and he left it to them to figure out how to internalise the moves. But he was often teaching actors about the language of the physical aspects of theatre:

> I remember him talking to a student playing Lear about the power of stillness, so that when you make just a small move that's the equivalent of a close up in a movie. He wasn't talking in terms of intentions, he was talking in terms of understanding the crafts and demands of the theatre, which is also something an actor needs to think about
>
> (Feldman, Interview 2006)

Butch Blake, when asked about his most special memories of performing at Stratford, cites what he learned during Langham's 1964 production of *King Lear*. Blake was afraid of failing when playing Gloucester, especially after the blinding. But Langham worked with him very carefully: 'instead of getting me to scream, Michael said, "Keep it quiet, just whimper, and in any speeches after that, like people in real pain, [that way] you've got the audience in your hands" '. Blake felt a 'sense of great achievement afterwards [. . .] I knew when I was overplaying, and knew that underplaying was better' (*Butch Blake Video History Project* 1988–97). The *technical* lesson – no doubt informed by Langham's war experiences and later battles with life-threatening illnesses but not couched in such personal terms – was *emotionally* effective for the production, and it became a touchstone for Blake's acting career. Some who worked with him caution against over-emphasising his reputation as a bit of a martinet or as uninterested in the actor's and the character's interior life. It's just that emotional responses and vulnerability were not for actors and director to share with one another: these things were always more properly between a production and its audience.

Colleagues refer to Langham as an audience-friendly director but with no hint of condescension. His productions of Shakespeare aren't designed to shock or challenge the viewer or to radically reinvent or make 'relevant' the text; at their best, his productions give audiences the impression that they are seeing, and understanding, and responding to, everything that there is in the play. Richard Monette, the only artistic director whose tenure at Stratford lasted longer than Langham's, feels his predecessor's real innovation was in fulfilling a kind of architectural destiny and passing it on: 'his contribution to Shakespeare and to the use of the thrust stage was incredible. In my view, he was the modern inventor of the staging of Shakespeare on the thrust' (Interview 2006).

Chronology

1948–50 Director of Productions, Birmingham Repertory Theatre, Birmingham
1956–67 Artistic Director, Stratford Festival, Ontario, Canada
1956 *Hamlet*, Shakespeare Memorial Theatre, Stratford-upon-Avon
1956 *Henry V*, Stratford Festival
1957 *Hamlet*, Stratford Festival
1960 *Merchant of Venice*, Shakespeare Memorial Theatre
1961 *Coriolanus*, Stratford Festival
1961 *Love's Labour's Lost*, Stratford Festival
1963 *Timon of Athens*, Stratford Festival

1964	*King Lear*, Stratford Festival
1971–7	Artistic Director, Guthrie Theater, Minneapolis, Minn.
1974	*Love's Labour's Lost*, Guthrie Theater
1979–92	Head of Drama, Juilliard School, New York
1983	*Love's Labour's Lost*, Young Company, Stratford Festival
1988	*Merchant of Venice*, The Shakespeare Theater at the Folger, Washington, DC
1989	*Merchant of Venice*, Stratford Festival
1991	*Timon of Athens*, Stratford Festival
1993	*Timon of Athens*, National Actors Theatre, New York
1995	*The Tempest*, Atlantic Theatre Festival, Wolfville, Nova Scotia

Acknowledgements

Special thanks to the Shakespeare Centre in Stratford-upon-Avon and to the Stratford Festival Archives in Stratford, Ontario, for access to promptbooks, press clippings, production and photo files, and videotapes. Thanks also to the archives at the Juilliard School and to each of my interviewees for their time and generosity.

Bibliography

Cushman, Robert (2002) *Fifty Seasons at Stratford*, Toronto: McClelland and Stewart.

Euringer, Fred (2000) *A Fly on the Curtain*, Ottawa: Oberon Press.

Ganong, Joan (1962) *Backstage at Stratford*, Toronto: Longmans.

Langham, Michael (1962) 'An Approach to Staging Shakespeare's Works', in B. W. Jackson (ed.), *Stratford Papers on Shakespeare 1961* Toronto: W. Gage Limited.

—— (1962) *Two Programmes of Shakespearean Comedy*. A special educational production devised and directed by Langham for tour of Canadian Universities, performed by leading actors of the Festival Company. Script in the Stratford Festival Archives.

Loney, Glenn (ed.) (1990) *Staging Shakespeare: Seminars on Production Problems*, New York: Garland.

McGee, C. E. 'Shakespeare in Canada: the Stratford Season 1989', *Shakespeare Quarterly*, 41: pp. 114–20.

Ouzounian, Richard (ed.) (2002) *Stratford Gold: 50 Years, 50 Stars, 50 Conversations*, Toronto: McArthur & Co.

Pettigrew, John and Jamie Portman (1985) *Stratford: The First Thirty Years*, Toronto: Macmillan of Canada.

Raby, Peter (ed.) (1968) *The Stratford Scene 1958–1968*, Toronto: Clarke, Irwin & Co.

Whittaker, Herbert (1985) *Whittaker's Theatre: A Critic Looks at Stages in Canada and Thereabouts 1944–1975*, Toronto: University of Toronto Press.

Interviews on video, held at the Stratford Festival Archives

Behind the Scenes, interview with Michael Langham, produced by Pat Quigley and Rogers Cable TV, 1989.

The Butch Blake Video History Project, series of interviews with members of the early years of the Festival Company, conducted between 1988 and 1997; interviews used for this piece: Michael Langham, Douglas Rain, Butch Blake.

Interviews conducted by the author

Fred Euringer, 1 October 2006; Richard Feldman, 7 October 2006; Richard Monette, 11 October 2006.

About the author

Kevin Ewert is Associate Professor of Theatre at the University of Pittsburgh at Bradford. He wrote the volume on *Henry V* for the Shakespeare Handbooks series. From 1997 to 2003, he was an Artistic Associate and regular director for the Unseam'd Shakespeare Company in Pittsburgh, where his productions included *Women Beware Women, The Winter's Tale, The Libertine* and *Coriolanus*.

14
ROBERT LEPAGE

Karen Fricker

'If I do Shakespeare, I never really end up doing Shakespeare', the Québécois director Robert Lepage said in 1995. 'It's so basic, with such universal themes, and in French, we rewrite it like we want, so [. . .]: I never have the impression that I'm doing other people's work' (quoted in McAlpine 1996: 151). In its paradoxical blend of insouciant self-centredness and deference to intellectually unfashionable concepts such as 'universality', this is an articulation typical of Lepage and neatly sums up his production history with Shakespeare's plays. Each of his major Shakespeare stagings has involved an intervention or twist of some kind, having to do with language (as with his 1993 Shakespeare Cycle in québécois 'tradaptation'), a bold and unconventional production concept (such as his controversial mud-pit *A Midsummer Night's Dream* at London's National Theatre in 1992), or textual adaptation and interpretation so extreme that it literally reauthors the play (as with *Elsinore*, which toured internationally from 1995 to 1997). These various treatments, as Andy Lavender has argued, have the effect of 'dislocation' (2001: 102): spectators are encouraged to look at familiar texts in new ways and are reminded of their active position in the creation of the production's meanings. This approach can be traced back in some part to the problematically post-colonial status of Lepage's native Québec; his linguistic, interpretative and theatrical playfulness with Shakespeare is legible as a form of 'canonical counter-discourse' (Tiffin 1995: 97) through which former colonial subjects talk back to Empire via an irreverent treatment of sacred literary cows. At the same time, however, Lepage consistently traffics in the language of Shakespeare's essential and timeless meanings but most so in order to frame Shakespeare as a springboard for his own creativity:

> Dealing with Shakespeare, we're dealing with an avalanche of resources, a box of toys to be taken out [. . .] what's so extraordinary about Shakespeare is that this man was so intuitive, he gives us the

> story of mankind. I think he offers a lot of permission to the actor, the translator, the director.
>
> (Lepage and Eyre 1992b: 29)

For Lepage – and this is the crucial twist in his thinking – the perception of the playwright's humanist genius does not trigger protectionist reverence but rather offers enormous scope for contemporary creative intervention. For all this seeming solecism, and for all the productions' interpretative bravado, however, there remains legible in all of Lepage's Shakespeare stagings a strain of conservatism, or perhaps timidity: they still tell their familiar stories and keep characters intact and recognisable. This is far from wholesale deconstruction. Shakespeare is clearly a master to Lepage, or perhaps a parent, to be both deferred to and rebelled against – a theme suggesting the play that haunts his creative imagination, *Hamlet*, which Lepage has described as a channel for his personal filial anxieties.

Born in Québec City in 1957, Robert Lepage became interested in theatre as an escape from a shy and reclusive adolescence. From 1976 to 1979, he studied at the Conservatoire d'Art Dramatique in Québec City, which was staffed by pedagogical descendents of Jacques Lecoq who trained students to approach their work as total theatremakers rather than solely as actors. In the early 1980s, Lepage joined a local company, Théâtre Repère, which used a collaborative, improvisation-based method of theatremaking called the RSVP cycles. Repère became the crucible for Lepage's early work in collaborative creation, and for his first Shakespeare-based production, a version of *Coriolanus* called *Coriolan et le monstre aux mille têtes* (*Coriolanus and the Thousand-Headed Monster*), which played in Québec City in 1983.

In 1985, Lepage's career took a decisive leap forward with the premiere of *The Dragon's Trilogy*, a Repère collaborative creation in which he participated as director/co-creator/performer, and which toured to fourteen countries over six years. A theatrical epic following the story of two québécoise cousins and their families from the 1910s to the then-present day, the *Trilogy* established the visual and transformative *mise-en-scène* and the themes of cultural difference, personal identity and travel that characterise his original work. Along with the solo piece *Vinci* (1986), *The Dragon's Trilogy* made his name internationally and led to coproductions including *Polygraph* (1987–91), an existential thriller inspired by Lepage's experience of having been a suspect in a friend's brutal murder. *Polygraph* was also the first significant theatrical evidence of his fascination with *Hamlet*: within the play's fiction, Lucie, an actress, is cast in the title role of an unconventional production of that play and recites its best-known speech ('To be or not to be'; or as it was spoken in French, 'Être ou n'être pas') while – though this runs against Shakespeare's text – holding a skull, a moment of visual and aural collapse of some of *Hamlet*'s iconic elements presaging a creative strategy that would be fully expressed in *Elsinore*.

While *Polygraph* did not overtly treat themes of Québec cultural difference, the fact that it included Shakespeare spoken in French (even in the play's English-language touring version) inevitably carried a certain political charge. As Leonore Lieblein and Denis Salter have documented, Québec theatremakers have a particularly complicated post-colonial relationship to Shakespeare, given Québec's status as a former colony of both France and England. Shakespeare's plays were seized on as symbolic of the oppression of francophone Canadians by the English majority during the cultural consolidation movement in the 1960s known as the Quiet Revolution. Productions such as Robert Gurik's *Hamlet, Prince du Québec* (1968) and Jean-Pierre Ronfard's *Lear* (1977) appropriated, parodied and carnivalised Shakespeare's texts. Sending up Shakespeare in this way had double political valence: by not choosing a French classic text to parody, these Québec theatremakers were putting two fingers up at their original cultural forefathers, while their treatment of Shakespeare was legible as an expression of resistance to the presence of English-language culture in their society.

The next generation of Québec theatremakers expressed exhaustion with the overt politicising that characterised the Quiet Revolution years. Theatrical production in the 1980s in Québec turned inwards, towards an emphasis on formal experimentation; to the experience of the individual as opposed to family or social themes; and towards the internationalisation of Québec culture – a movement whose paradigmatic figure was Robert Lepage. This young director did not have a strong sense of Shakespeare as a force of cultural oppression but rather saw him as part of popular culture: 'In French-speaking Canada, *Hamlet* is something you've seen on TV at Friday night at 11 pm with Laurence Olivier', he has said (in Lepage and Eyre 1997).

Lepage's first major Shakespeare production was *Le Songe d'un nuit d'été* (*A Midsummer Night's Dream*, translated by Michelle Allen) which broke box-office records at Montréal's Théâtre du Nouveau Monde in 1988. The production was not without its political references – the revolving platform on which the action took place was said to be shaped like England – but was most noted for its focus on the play's dark subtext. With its sleepwalking, partner-swapping lovers and undercurrent of danger and eroticism, this *Midsummer Night's Dream* rehearsed themes that Lepage would more fully explore in his National Theatre production four years later. Lepage's next encounter with Shakespeare was an innovative exploration of Canada's 'two solitudes': a 1989 coproduction between Repère and Saskatoon's Nightcap

Theatre, *Romeo & Juliette* cast the Montagues as anglophones and Capulets as francophones and set the action on the Trans-Canadian Highway.

The following years saw Lepage engaging with Shakespeare's texts with an extraordinary intensity: from 1992 to 1995 he directed twelve Shakespeare or Shakespeare-derived theatre and music productions. This new focus grew out of a concern that the collaborative method of theatremaking may have temporarily run its course:

> The Repère process that I usually use was very successful for two or three productions because I had a lot of things to say. The people I was working with at that time had a lot of things to say. It so happened that our way of working was quite new, and with the method came the successes. But that empties itself. You've said what you have to say, and you have to wait before it comes back.
>
> (Quoted in Johnson 2001: 118–19)

In need of creative refuelling, Lepage threw himself in the world of Shakespearian production with extraordinary energy and conviction; and then just as quickly stopped (see Chronology).

The Shakespeare cycle

The Théâtre Repère coproduction of *Macbeth, La Tempête* and *Coriolan*, featuring a cast of ten québécois actors performing in repertory, premiered in Maubeuge, France in October 1992 and toured for two years in Europe, Canada and Japan. Its starting point was the existence of French-language versions of *Macbeth, The Tempest* and *Coriolanus* by acclaimed Québec playwright Michel Garneau, which Garneau referred to as 'tradaptations.' Garneau's version of *Macbeth*, completed in 1978, is the most politicised and best-known of the three: it places Shakespeare's play into antiquated and ornate language and includes textual interventions to bring out local parallels, using Scotland's oppression under Macbeth to evoke Québec's own fight for cultural and political liberation. The Repère production in 1993 reflected the move in Québec culture away from oppositional politics towards internationalism. *Macbeth* was presented alongside Garneau's tradaptation of *Coriolanus* (1989), which is in an internationalised québécois French, and *The Tempest* (1973), which involves more popularised québécois as well as language shifts between social classes. Promotional materials placed emphasis, however, not on the local politics expressed through the language but on the translator's writerly prowess. Audiences were encouraged to focus on Garneau and Lepage's transformative interventions with Shakespeare, which, it was argued, rendered the productions of a calibre suitable for the international stage (see Lieblein 1996).

All three of Lepage's cycle productions involved strong directorial concepts that drew metatheatrical attention to the acts of staging, acting and spectatorship. These included, as Salter observed, a preoccupation with putting borders and frames in and around the productions, allowing Lepage to place '*everything* – including the fragmented body – into parentheses' (quoted in Salter 2000: 196). Shakespeare in parentheses, or, better, inverted commas: Lepage's comment sums up his irreverent, impatient attitude towards classic texts and the cultural baggage they bring with them. He never just stages Shakespeare; he stages 'Shakespeare', taking account of the mythology and the cultural accretions that surround the plays, and doing so largely via visual means – often, his critics claim, at the expense of text.

In the case of his Shakespeare cycle *Macbeth*, the cultural framing was filmic. Its physical style borrowed openly from Akira Kurosawa's films, particularly *Throne of Blood:* a set of dark wood timbers lashed together created two layered playing areas, the bottom one used both as a corridor and as smaller spaces in which bits of action could be isolated. *La Tempête* was given a metatheatrical frame: the production was conceived as a theatrical exercise, something like a play within a play (which is not, as many critics pointed out, a new idea). The actors were first seen reading the play around a rehearsal table, until their imaginative world took over and they started playing in earnest.

Coriolan, most boldly, was staged in a long rectangular cut-out of a larger blacked-out stage, which focused the action as if spectators were watching a film; the English critic Michael Coveney referred to the production as 'shot' rather than staged. Coveney, who saw the cycle in Montréal, also noted perceptively that *Coriolanus* is 'virtually unknown in North America; the audience reacts as if to a new play, which is how Lepage directs it' (*Observer*, 6 June 1993). While all three plays in the cycle concern power and its abuses, it was in *Coriolan* that Lepage focused most squarely on this theme, playing the text as a ferocious satire of political ambitions and machinations. His innovations also included a radical abridging of the text: the production ran for a little over two hours without interval. It immediately introduced its audacious scenic and interpretative context by skipping the citizens' dialogue in the first scene and opening with Menenius' famous speech likening the body politic to a physical body, delivered in a recording studio as a live radio broadcast. An unseen interviewer's voice spoke the lines usually given to the citizens responding to Menenius' speech.

Act I, Scene 2 was played not as written as a group scene between Aufidius and his senators, but as a bedroom dialogue between Aufidius and a military colleague who was also his lover. After a blackout, Volumnia and Virgilia appeared sitting on the stage, miming some domestic activity; when a servant entered, only his legs were visible, the rest of his body cut off by the top of the portal. In a particularly striking scene, Coriolanus' and Aufidius' first-act battle was played as a nude, homoerotic wrestling match, with the actors lying on the floor and moving together in simulated slow motion, their actions visible via a long, wide mirror tilted towards the audience (a staging trick that would reappear ten years later in the final moments of Lepage's *The Far Side of the Moon*).

Throughout, the frame of the portal was used to create other such unexpected and disorienting effects and shifts of perspective. The battle scenes were played by marionettes, with the puppeteers' legs clearly visible; the 'public place' was a bar in which characters watched political and military news on television. Anne-Marie Cadieux, in an extraordinarily risky performance, played Volumnia on the edge of self-parody, her promotion of her son's interests so blatant and voracious, and her timing so sharp, that she consistently provoked audience laughter and sometimes, rounds of applause. Jules Philip's handsome, young Coriolanus was passionate but indecisive, tortured by pressures on him (gendered and familial as well as political and military); he appeared as one of Lepage's early Hamlet figures.

Thus, a play largely understood as a tragedy of excessive and misplaced ambition and of the conflict between a dispossessed populace and an arrogant, patrician leader was reimagined as a critique of modern media realpolitik. The extraordinary visual surface of the production, so slickly and cleverly imagined, served to reinforce and advance this critique; as did its aural texture – an ingenious soundtrack (by Guy Laramée) of honking car-horns which sounded something like contemporary traffic, something like an old-fashioned trumpet fanfare and, in its slight absurdness, something like snide commentary.

As part of its touring, *Coriolanus* was performed at the Nottingham Playhouse in November 1993, in French with supertitles. The production, as became typical of Lepage's treatments of Shakespeare, divided British critics, some of whom took exception to its treatment of the text, in particular the total excising of the Roman crowd who appear in all but four scenes of the play as written. Without the Roman populace playing its live part in the drama, these critics felt, the meaning of the play had been inappropriately altered. Lepage did have enthusiastic defenders among the British critical corps, who appreciated how the production functioned as a satirical commentary on the play's triumphalism. Such extreme division also marked québécois reaction to the production, with some critics bowled over by the productions' visual élan and accepting its satirical angle on the text, while the powerful Robert

Lévesque in *Le Devoir* – up to this point one of Lepage's strongest advocates – eviscerated it as a 'cheap junk spectacle' (*Le Devoir*, 29 May 1993).

A Midsummer Night's Dream

In July 1992, Lepage became the first North American to direct Shakespeare at the National Theatre (NT) in London with his production of *A Midsummer Night's Dream* on the Olivier stage, it ran for six months in repertory. For Lepage, the core of this play lies in the final word of its title:

> The four lovers, the teenagers, go to sleep in their individual beds on midsummer's night and then enter this common dream. We decided it would be a watery dream, a dark dream, a very muddy, slippery environment. We wanted it to be a dangerous place, like in those dreams where you want to run away but you can't because your feet are stuck. And there is also the idea that you have these white, innocent, pristine teenagers going into their very dirty and sleazy world and coming out of it stained by their own dreams, their own sexuality, their own darkness.
>
> (Quoted in Charles Spencer, 'The Act of Living Dangerously', *The Daily Telegraph*, 6 July 1992)

Calling on a Jungian understanding of the unconscious as a place of dark mystery and danger, Lepage read against the play's comic grain to see it as a frightening rite of passage taking place in the lovers' collective imagination. This understanding of the play was reinforced via rehearsal exercises. He put paper on the walls and asked the NT actors to draw their dreams; what emerged were pictures of 'upside-down forests, mazes, stairs'. Lepage conducted improvisations around these images and became convinced that 'there really is a map of dreams. As if there's a place where people go when they dream [. . .] That is the unknown country that I'm curious to stage or to find' (Quoted in Johnson 2001: 80).

In another interview, he foregrounded the importance of the relationship between the mortal and spirit worlds in the play: 'it's all about this character called Bottom, and there's all these fairies that come from way up above and haunt these poor human beings, and these poor sleepers. Bottom aspires to be the lover of Titania, a goddess. It's a very strong vertical piece' (quoted in McAlpine 1996: 144). For Lepage, what makes theatre a unique and appealing art form is its inherent verticality, as opposed to film, which is a horizontal medium: theatre is the place where humans aspire to be greater than they are, to come 'in contact with the gods' (quoted in McAlpine 1996: 143).

The first moment of Lepage's *Midsummer Night's Dream* signalled his reading of the play as taking place in a space of dreams and darkness. The québécoise contortionist Angela Laurier, playing Puck, scuttled sideways across the stage like a crab, through the shallow layer of mud that was the dominant element of Michael Levine's set, above which hung a single illuminated lightbulb. She reached up and turned off the lightbulb – thus starting the production with the counter-intuitive gesture of a light being extinguished rather than being turned on.

The use of mud became the most-commented-on aspect of the production. It was meant to evoke the murk of the subconscious, with textual support provided, Lepage felt, by the lines in Act II, Scene 1 in which Titania talks about the climate changes that came about after the Indian boy was stolen from her. Research conducted during the rehearsal period found that there was a record amount of rain in England in the year that Shakespeare wrote the play, suggesting that he might have been referencing these weather conditions in Titania's speech.

After Puck's opening gesture, the lights came up on the four lovers, wearing simple white undergarments, asleep on a big iron bed. Hippolyta (the British-Asian actress Lolita Chakrabarti) and a blind Theseus (played by Jeffrey Kissoon, who is black) were seated on either end of the bed, as Philostrate, played by Paul M. Meston, also British-Asian and wearing Indian-style clothing, conducted the bed through the mud with a long pole as if it were a gondola. The production throughout was underscored by live gamelan music. The action followed Shakespeare's script closely – Hippolyta and Theseus discussed their impending marriage, then the lovers awoke to play out the exposition scene about Hermia's unwanted marriage to Demetrius, Lysander's plan for escape, and so forth. The bed was turned on its end to become a threshold through which actors passed to begin their scenes.

Bottom was played by Timothy Spall as a swaggering, buffoonish, 1970s-era macho man with gold chains, platform shoes and (some critics noted) an American accent. Titania's fairies were nearly naked and had their faces painted blue, which the programme said made reference to the Congolese Kota tribe. One of the production's most-commented-on moments was Puck's line, 'I'll put a girdle around the earth in forty minutes', which Laurier spoke while hanging from the cord which held the lightbulb, and then spun violently like a circus acrobat. Some critics read Titania's seduction of Bottom as a rape fantasy, and most noted the uninhibited, brutal nature of their staged copulation. The end of the dark night was represented by the lifting of a black screen behind the action to reveal a beautiful sunrise and the lovers showering away the mud from their bodies in view of the audience. The mechanicals' play-within-a-play used the bed as its stage and saw the actors playing a little gamelan made of kitchen utensils (an intertexual reference to the production itself).

The obvious referent for Lepage's staging approach was Peter Brook's now-iconic 1970s Royal Shakespeare Company production, which took place on an all-white stage and emphasised the idea of playfulness via the performance of circus skills and a lack of recognisably Elizabethan staging elements. Lepage made clear in interview that he saw his production as inspired by Brook's: 'If you look at when Peter Brook did *A Midsummer Night's Dream*, he reappropriated the text but he didn't set it anywhere in particular. He just said, "Play with it, make it yours" ' (quoted in Carson 1993: 36).

Typically, 'reappropriation' is claimed here as a positive action, something that is the director's right and privilege; however, many critics understood Lepage's *Midsummer Night's Dream* as taking too many liberties, radically misunderstanding the play – he was accused of throwing mud at a classic, drawing a moustache on the Mona Lisa. Objections fell into four main categories. Even those who admired the production commented that it was not particularly well spoken, and that more attention was apparently paid to concept and staging than to the verse. In a related criticism, it was felt that the performances varied widely in quality and effectiveness. Another concern was the actors' (and audiences') safety and hygiene; one critic noted that audience members stopped paying attention to the play and started whispering to each other about the actors' tendency to slip and fall on the slick stage. The first three rows of audience members were given plastic macintoshes to protect them from splashing mud, which some saw as evidence of the production's excesses.

Most significant among critical complaint was the argument that the production did not do justice to Shakespeare's text, in that its nightmare-like quality ignored the midsummer setting and lost the sense of the play as a comedy. The single setting of the mudpit did not allow for a clear transition between court and forest, thus making it impossible for the production to effectively communicate the play as a journey from civilisation to wilderness and back. Lepage later said he was aware of this problem. When Richard Eyre told him that he would have 'liked to have seen two worlds – in terms of *mise en scène*', Lepage replied:

> There are many worlds in *Midsummer Night's Dream*, principally the two you were talking about [the court and the forest], but then there's also the world of the dream. We kind of got mixed up in our concepts at one point and were trying to fit in all these places. We had tons of mud on stage, and you don't strike mud. So we were kind of stuck with

> that, which is why we started to have court people walking on chairs on so on.
>
> (Quoted in Lepage and Eyre 1992b: 35)

When Lepage staged the play in Québec City three years later, he addressed this problem by making the central scenic element a pool of water, which appeared as wooden floorboards were pulled back in the transition between Acts I and II, and then disappeared again between Acts IV and V, so that court and forest came through clearly as two different worlds.

As several of the production's more astute commentators noted, for all its seeming radicalism, Lepage's general approach to *A Midsummer Night's Dream* was hardly without precedent but rather followed in the interpretative path laid out by Jan Kott in *Shakespeare Our Contemporary* (which was quoted in the production programme). Highlighting the emotional cruelty of the lovers' partner-swapping, the brutal eroticism of the sexual relationships and representing the action overall as a product of a subconscious fantasy is a standard Kottian reading of the play, one to which, to a certain extent, Brook had also adhered. The relationship of Lepage's production to Brook's was not rupture but continuum. Accounting, therefore, for the very strong critical reaction against Lepage's interpretation, as Barbara Hodgdon has argued, requires an acknowledgement of the 'cultural logic of the post-colonial' circulating around the production and responses to it (1996: 69). Some critics responded to the production as an act of transgression that dragged Shakespeare down from his lofty place as signifier of the purity and excellence of British culture. 'How much of [this production] is really concerned with Shakespeare's original?' asked Steve Grant in *Time Out*, 'how much would someone who hadn't seen or read the play learn about its structure, meaning, and beauty?' (15 July 1993).

At the same time as Lepage's interventions with the play brought the post-imperial anxieties of some of its British observers to the surface, the production also became a canvas for Lepage to play out his own fantasies of otherness. As have several of his original productions, Lepage's *Midsummer Night's Dream* used the theatrical language of Orientalism: its multi-cultural cast, African-inspired costumes and make-up for the fairies, Indian-style costume for the court and Indonesian gamelan playing were all part of Lepage's attempts to, in his words, discover something 'transcultural' in the play, 'something underneath that is universal' (quoted in Carson 1993: 35). Individual elements of non-Western cultures were presented out of context and to give the production a sense of exoticism, thus reinforcing the sense of Asian and African cultures as being 'other' to the Western norm. Lepage defended the staging choices as relating back to his individual artistic quest: 'I'm not trying to take good ideas from other people, I'm just trying to see how that relates profoundly or universally to what I want to say or want to do', he explained, a statement that, as Hodgdon points out, 'mythologises [his] own subjectivity' and uses Shakespeare in an attempt to 'legitimise [his] own intercultural artistry' (1996: 84).

Lepage's *Midsummer Night's Dream* confronted British audiences with colonial subjects of Empire on their national stage, speaking in their various accents and bringing evidence of their varied cultural backgrounds; this clearly destabilised some audience members who see Shakespeare as belonging to a strictly high-culture British tradition. As Lepage himself perceptively noted, 'You can't change the style of acting and break with tradition unless these changes come out of a real need in the *audience* to experience things differently' (quoted in Salter 1996: 118, emphasis mine). Perhaps British audiences (or, at least, British critics) were not prepared for the variety of cultural influences and the very strong visual emphasis brought to this *Midsummer Night's Dream*. The production also made manifest, however, the director's own fantasies of cultural wholeness that are, in their own way, colonising.

Elsinore

Lepage's success and fame accelerated considerably as the 1990s progressed. Having left Théâtre Repère in 1989 and the National Arts Centre in 1993, he formed his own production company, Ex Machina, and opened a multidisciplinary creation centre in Québec City. One of Ex Machina's first productions was *Elsinore*, Lepage's solo meditation on *Hamlet*, which was informed by a personal milestone – the death of his father in 1992: '*Elsinore* deals [. . .] with the emotions of losing your father, and what happens to your relationship with your mother and your Horatios and your Ophelias or whatever' (quoted in Brian D. Johnson, 'The Visionary' *Maclean's*, 11 September 1995).

A basic point about *Elsinore* must be underlined from the start: this was not, and was never intended to be, a production of *Hamlet*. It had a different title: *Elsinore: Variations on Shakespeare's Hamlet* (in French, *Elseneur: Variations sur le thème d'Hamlet de William Shakespeare)* and was variously credited as 'by Robert Lepage' and with 'staging and adaptation by Robert Lepage.' All the words that were spoken on stage, however, were taken from *Hamlet*, and the characters, themes and situations represented were familiar from the play. This tension – was or wasn't this Shakespeare? – was crucial to the production's meaning and its significance and was also in keeping with Lepage's evolving relationship to Shakespeare's texts. He created a new play called *Elsinore* but one that depended on – that was actually *about* – the cultural significance and weight attached to Shakespeare's play and, in particular, to what the character of Hamlet has come to represent in Western society. *Elsinore* was the consummation of Lepage's interpretative approach to Shakespeare. Here, more than ever, was Shakespeare in inverted commas, Shakespeare as cultural tradition, as phenomenon; as a 'game' (Lepage and Eyre 1997) to be played; as a set of ideas, words and clichés to be explored.

As with Lepage's previous Shakespeare adventures, some critics found this kind of playfulness threatening and inappropriate, calling it '*Hamlet* for the short attention span generation' (quoted in Steen and Werry 1998: 138). As Shannon Steen and Margeret Werry have argued, such responses reflect an anxiety that the authority understood to reside in Shakespeare and, particularly, this play and character, was being undermined. Given *Hamlet*'s status as 'one of the founding documents of [the] doctrine of deep subjectivity in the theatre', the fact that this was not an actor's virtuosic playing of Hamlet the character but rather an exteriorised examination of Hamlet's psyche via complex technological staging effects was a threatening prospect for some traditionalists (Steen and Werry 1998: 143).

Lepage had the idea of a one-man *Hamlet* as early as 1990 but shelved the project when he heard that the American auteur Robert Wilson was undertaking a similar project. Come early 1995, however, Lepage could not get the play out of his mind and forged ahead despite concerns he would be seen to be following Wilson's ideas. As Andy Lavender has documented, Lepage and scenic designer Carl Fillion kicked off their work on the production by reading different versions of the text, screening films and talking about their impressions. Lepage brought to the table an image that interested him from Buster Keaton's film *Steamboat Bill, Jr.*: a house falls on a man, but the man is unharmed because he is standing where a doorway falls. Fillion therefore suggested that the actor 'could stand centre stage and have the set come to him' (Lavender 2001: 104). As we have seen, framing and doorways were important in Lepage's other Shakespeare stagings, and here, again, Lepage became focused on the symbolic and staging potential of a hole in the stage: 'That was the only thing I asked for from the set designer', he later recalled. 'Give me that frame' (Lepage and Eyre 1997).

The finished set featured three large panels, one facing the audience and the other two angled on either side. The centre panel could spin vertically and had a circular centre cut-out which could revolve; within this was a rectangular portal. The production featured a score and soundscape by Robert Caux which included recordings of music, sound effects and the live manipulation of the actor's voice; and a complex lighting design including video projections.

The first tour of *Elsinore* travelled within Québec, to the USA and to eleven European countries, with Lepage as performer. In 1997, he reworked the show with a new performer, Peter Darling, who is English; it then toured in

North America and Europe. *Elsinore* evolved considerably over the several years of its existence: when it first opened in Montréal, it was over three hours long, while the version with Darling lasted one hour and forty-five minutes. Lepage continued to tinker with the show (particularly its opening moments) even as Darling toured with it, so that the version performed in Ottawa in September 1997 ended up differing significantly from that seen in New York and Dublin only months later (this account refers primarily to the Ottawa version, which was published in the summer 2002 issue of *Canadian Theatre Review*).

In Lepage's conception, *Elsinore* took place in Hamlet's imagination – when other characters appeared, they did so in relation to Hamlet and as he imagined them. The production's first minutes featured the disembodied voice of Hamlet's father exhorting the Prince to avenge his death. In the 1997 performances, this was visually accompanied by the lone actor sitting on a chair suspended over the stage with his head in his hands, tortured by the sound of his father's voice in his head. The lights dimmed, the set moved, and the actor reappeared in the chair with the projection of a 'King' playing card around him: he became Claudius, dispatching Rosencrantz and Guildenstern to spy on Hamlet; and then, with a switch of posture and a change of projection to a 'Queen' card, became Gertrude. When Hamlet appeared in the open portal greeting Rosencrantz and Guildenstern, video cameras behind the portal caught his image from both sides and projected it on the side panels, allowing the audience to see the action from Rosencrantz and Guildenstern's perspectives.

This staging gesture – placing the audience members in the point of view of the characters themselves – was repeated at several points in the production. When Polonius spied behind the arras during the closet scene, the audience saw the figures of a man and woman (Hamlet and Gertrude) projected on the side panels in silhouette, as if the audience were Polonius himself. The final sword fight between Hamlet and Laertes was played by the actor and his body double Pierre Bernier appearing and then disappearing behind a set piece, with images from tiny video cameras on the end of their fencing foils projected on the side screens. Therefore, the audience saw both the live combat between the actors, and, on the screens, the fight from alternately Hamlet's and Laertes' points of view.

Lepage got his wish of a wall descending over an actor's body in one of the production's most striking pieces of textual intervention and staging. Lepage interwove text from Act II Scene 1, in which Ophelia describes Hamlet coming to her closet, with lines from Act III Scene 1, in which Hamlet orders her to a nunnery, so that the latter scene appears like a stage version of a filmic flashback (even though, in the play as written, the enacted scene happens after Ophelia's monologue). The segue out of the flashback to the end of Ophelia's speech was cued by Hamlet crying, 'Go to, I'll no more of it! It hath made me mad' and throwing his arms in the air. The central wall then lowered with the portal around him. A gauzy fabric had been stretched over the whole top surface of the wall with holes for arms and head, so that, as it descended further, it became a dress, and Hamlet became Ophelia. The other noteworthy moment where Lepage interpolated text from two scenes together was in Gertrude's description of Ophelia's death, which was intercut with Ophelia's mad song from Act IV, Scene 5.

Shakespeare's text, therefore, was manipulated in order to serve the production and effects that Lepage wished to deliver. As Christopher Innes has commented, the text element most frequently retained was Hamlet's soliloquies, thus furthering the impression that its subject matter was Hamlet's psyche. The crux of the production concept was the enactment and delivery of the character's internal life via staging effects, many of them imposingly technical in nature. Many critics commented that someone who did not know Shakespeare's play would have difficulty following the performance, but Lepage's point, clearly, was that it would be hard to find an audience member who *didn't* know the story of *Hamlet*, or have some sort of mythology built up about the character. As Margaret Jane Kidnie has argued, the production's innovation stemmed from 'the way it played with the ability of privileged, even élite, North American and European audiences simultaneously to recognise, and fail to recognise, this most canonical of plays' (1995: 134).

Elsinore looked new and innovative, but, as some commentators have noted, its questions and its methodology had significant precedent in theatrical history. As Innes reminds us, the ideas of an auteur figure with ultimate creative control over all aspects of a production and of theatre as a machine (recall Lepage's company is called Ex Machina) have their roots in theatrical modernism, particularly in the work of Edward Gordon Craig, who conceived of *Hamlet* as a monodrama, including a scene with the stage covered entirely with a gown, and with the set as 'the star of the show' (Innes 2003). Lepage's set of mechanised, moving panels can be understood as the contemporary incarnation of Craig's dream of a theatre whose main scenic effect was moving screens.

The production's treatment of language and of costume reinforced the idea that it was intended as a conversation with *Hamlet*'s theatrical past. When Lepage performed the production in English, he used a Received Pronunciation British accent, because this made him feel closer to the material and its historical meanings than if he were speaking in his own, French-accented English. It therefore follows that he would choose an Englishman when replacing himself as an actor. For performances in French, he chose

François-Victor Hugo's translation, the favoured version in schools and traditional productions, which brought with it a sense of history. With his full-flowing white shirt, black breeches tucked into black leather boots, a long dark wig and closely trimmed goatee, Lepage looked every inch the Romantic Shakespearian hero. It is a measure of how seriously Lepage took the actor's contribution to the production's overall meanings that he did not insist that Darling – who is slight and balding, physically quite unlike Lepage – be costumed exactly like him. Rather, as Lavender recounts, actor and director worked together towards a new physical conception of the role(s) for Darling, who ended up wearing a black shirt, black flared trousers, one boot, and one red high heel, and kept his bare head and clean-shaven face.

One of the most interesting and apposite questions posed by academic commentators about *Elsinore* has to do with the political effects (if any) created by the production. Lepage's textual cutting and interpretation completely excised the play's primary political dimension – the idea of Denmark being under military threat from Norway (removing as well any focus on the idea of Hamlet being mad or suicidal). By foregrounding his personal inspiration for the production and, as we have seen, its modernist, formal qualities; and by authoring it so completely – as text editor, director and, originally, performer – Lepage seems to follow a historic tradition of formalism, which presents the work of art as an end in itself. And, despite extensive cutting, again we find that his textual interventions were not all that radical: the scenes were presented largely in order; the *Hamlet* that was revealed was recognisable from previous interpretations of the play. However, Ric Knowles has argued, Lepage's resistance to completing the show – his constant tinkering – and 'its sheer *excess* (of ambition as well as actorly and technological display)' (1998: 204) certainly give the impression that a resistant, deconstructive politics were at play: Lepage, perhaps, was confronting those forces in theatre and culture that work to close down meaning and protect the eternal greatness of historic texts. However, the production's extreme decontextualisation – the fact that it was not created in, and did not refer to any contemporary social or political setting other than the space of creativity itself – leads to suspicions that the production was complicit with systems of post-industrial capital (Knowles 1998: 206).

Lepage's approach to theatremaking was deeply affected by his brief, intense engagement with Shakespeare's texts. In 1992, he told Richard Eyre that he had come to Shakespeare having 'lost faith in words' because of the barrage of language in contemporary culture (in Lepage and Eyre 1992a: 34). Working with Shakespeare, particularly in England, encouraged him to trust that words remain powerful vessels of communication. This seems to have empowered Lepage to trust himself as a writer: his two subsequent solo productions, *The Far Side of the Moon* and *The Andersen Project*, see him leaning more on language and conventional narrative than in the past. In other works, however, Lepage has striven to move beyond spoken language, as evidenced by his increasing interest in the lyric form (including a Ring Cycle for the Metropolitan Opera scheduled for 2010) and in large-scale spectaculars without spoken dialogue (*Zulu Time, Kà* and his staging of Peter Gabriel's rock-concert tours). After so many Shakespeare productions in such a short period of time, Lepage may have felt he had had enough of language for a while.

Lepage's interactions with Shakespeare have also affected his work formally. He often says that one of the most salutary lessons he learned from Shakespeare is how key decisions are often prompted by practical necessities: soliloquies, for example, were probably written to cover complicated scene and mood changes. This comment informs the formal construction of *The Far Side of the Moon*, which could be described as both one long soliloquy covering one long set change. That production featured a monolithic set of a single wall, which, in an echo of the moving walls of *Elsinore*'s set, glided back and forth to shift fictional locations as the solo actor held the audience's attention by delivering monologues downstage. At the level of content, *Elsinore* may also have helped Lepage exorcise his *Hamlet* demon, in that his preoccupation with father–son relationships has made way for a focus on mothers and children (in *The Far Side of the Moon*) and on the artist's relationship to his artistic milieu and his cultural background (in *The Andersen Project*).

As of early 2007, Lepage's creative attentions seemed wholly focused on original works and opera. The fully staged production of *Hamlet* that he often mentioned during the *Elsinore* process may never materialise. In a short span of time, nonetheless, Lepage made good use of Shakespeare, and his productions and reactions to them paved the way for future directors' innovations and interpretations.

Chronology

1983 *Coriolan et le monstre aux mille têtes*, Théâtre Repère, Québec City
1988 *Le Songe d'un Nuit d'été*, Théâtre du Nouveau Monde, Montréal
1989 *Romeo & Juliette* (co-directed with Gordon McCall), Nightcap Productions, Saskatoon and Théâtre Repère, Québec City
1992 *The Tempest*, National Arts Centre Atelier, Ottawa
1992 *Macbeth*, University of Toronto
1992 *A Midsummer Night's Dream*, National Theatre, London
1993 *Map of Dreams* (excerpts from *A Midsummer Night's Dream*,

Macbeth, and *Richard III*) (in German), Bayerisches Staatschauspiel, Munich

1993 *The Tempest* and *Macbeth* (in Japanese), Tokyo Globe Theatre

1993 The Shakespeare Cycle: *Macbeth, Coriolan*, and *La Tempête*, Théâtre Repère, Maubeuge, France and on tour

1994 *Noises, Sounds, and Sweet Airs* (song cycle with music by Michael Nyman), Tokyo Globe Theatre

1995 *Le Songe d'un Nuit d'été*, Théâtre du Trident, Québec City

1995–7 *Elseneur/Elsinore*, Ex Machina, Montréal and on tour

1998 *La Tempête*, Théâtre du Trident, Québec City

Bibliography

Carson, Christie (1993) 'Collaboration, Translation, Interpretation', New Theatre Quarterly 9(33): 31–6.

Hodgdon, Barbara (1996) 'Looking for Mr. Shakespeare after "The Revolution": Robert Lepage's Intercultural Dream Machine', in James C. Bulman, (ed.) *Shakespeare, Theory, and Performance*, London: Routledge, pp. 68–91.

Innes, Christopher (2005) 'Puppets and Machines of the Mind: Robert Lepage and the Modernist Heritage', *Theatre Research International* 30(2): 124–38.

—— (2003) 'Gordon Craig in the Multi-Media Postmodern World: From the Art of the Theatre to Ex Machina', available online at <http://www.moderndrama.ca/crc/resources/essays/craig_lepage_wales.php>. (Accessed 30 January 2007).

Johnson, Lise Ann (2001) '*Shakespeare Rapid Eye Movement* at Bayerisches Staatsschauspiel', in Mark Bly (ed.), *The Production Notebooks: Theatre in Process*, Volume II, New York: Theatre Communications Group, pp. 74–139.

Kidnie, Margaret Jane (2005) 'Dancing with Art: Robert Lepage's *Elsinore*', in Sonia Massai (ed.), *World-wide Shakespeares: Local Appropriations in Film and Performance*, London: Routledge, pp. 133–40.

Knowles, Richard Paul (1998) 'From Dream to Machine: Peter Brook, Robert Lepage, and the Contemporary Shakespearean Director as (Post) Modernist', *Theatre Journal* 50(2): 189–206.

Lavender, Andy (2001) *Hamlet in Pieces: Shakespeare Reworked by Peter Brook, Robert Lepage, Robert Wilson*, London: Nick Hern Books.

Lepage, Robert and Richard Eyre (1992a) 'Robert Lepage in Conversation with Richard Eyre. 19 November 1992, Lyttleton Theatre', *Platform Papers 3*, London: Royal National Theatre, pp. 33–41.

Lepage, Robert and Richard Eyre (1992b) 'Robert Lepage in Conversation with Richard Eyre. 28 May 1992, Cottesloe Theatre', *Platform Papers 3*, London: Royal National Theatre, pp. 23–32.

Lepage, Robert and Richard Eyre (1997) 'Robert Lepage in Conversation with Richard Eyre', available online at <http://www.nt-online.org/platforms/robertlepage.html>. (Accessed 25 January 2007.)

Lieblein, Leanore (1996) 'Theatre Archives at the Intersection of Production and Reception: The Example of Québécois Shakespeare', in Edward Pechter (ed.) *Textual and Theatrical Shakespeare: Questions of Evidence*, Iowa City, Iowa: University of Iowa Press, pp. 164–80.

McAlpine, Alison (1996) 'Robert Lepage', in Maria M. Delgado and Paul Heritage (eds), *In*

Contact with the Gods? Directors Talk Theatre, Manchester: Manchester University Press, pp. 130–57.

Salter, Denis (2000) 'Between Wor(l)ds: Lepage's Shakespeare Cycle', in Joseph I. Donohoe, Jr. and Jane Koustas (eds), *Theater sans frontières: Essays on the Dramatic Universe of Robert Lepage*, East Lansing, Mich.: Michigan State University Press, pp. 191–204.

Salter, Denis (1996) 'Acting Shakespeare in Postcolonial Space', in James C. Bulman *Shakespeare: Theory and Performance*, London: Routledge, pp. 113–32.

Salter, Denis (1993) 'Borderlines: An Interview with Robert Lepage and Le Théâtre Repère', *Theatre* 24 (3): 71–9.

Steen, Shannon and Margaret Werry (1998) 'Bodies, Technologies, and Subjectivities: The Production of Authority in Robert Lepage's *Elsinore*', *Essays in Theatre/Études théâtrales* 16 (2): 139–51.

Tiffin, Helen (1995) 'Post-colonial Literatures and Canter-discourse', in Bill Ashcroft, Gareth Griffiths and Helen Tiffin (eds.), *The Post-Colonial Studies Reader*, London: Routledge, pp. 95–99.

About the author

Karen Fricker is a lecturer in the Department of Drama and Theatre at Royal Holloway, University of London. She completed a Ph.D. on the original stage works of Robert Lepage at the School of Drama, Trinity College, Dublin in 2005, and from 2005 to 2007 conducted research on globalisation and performance at the Institute for International Integration Studies, also at Trinity. She has published frequently on Lepage in scholarly journals and volumes including *Contemporary Theatre Review*. She reviews and broadcasts about theatre for outlets including the *Guardian, Variety*, RTÉ, the BBC, the *Irish Times*, the *New York Times* and the *Village Voice*. She is the co-founder of *Irish Theatre Magazine*, which she edited from 1998 to 2005. Originally from Los Angeles, she holds a BA and MA in English from Stanford University.

15
JOAN LITTLEWOOD

Lesley Wade Soule

Though she was the first woman to direct his plays in Britain, Joan Littlewood was not primarily a director of Shakespeare. She staged only six of his plays, mainly in the 1950s, along with seven by Shakespeare's contemporaries, some of whom she regarded nearly as highly as she did the Bard. (In fact, she preferred Ben Jonson's comedies to Shakespeare's.) Littlewood treated Shakespeare with a complete lack of deference, having little patience with the notion of 'great dramatists':

> I say to hell with geniuses in the theatre. Let's have the authors by all means, [. . .] but let's get them together with their equals, the actors, with all their wit and stupidity and insight. And this clash, this collaboration, this *anti*-collaboration will create an explosion more important than any bomb.
>
> (Tynan 1967: 316–17)

A central element in her work was the long-term practical study that underpinned everything she and her colleagues did. The ensemble dynamic of her productions came out of serious research and rigorous training. Her stagings of Shakespeare were the fruit of years of sustained ensemble work, unique in the English theatre of her time.

Littlewood's achievement was by no means merely as a director of plays. Kenneth Tynan remarked, 'Others write plays, direct them, or act in them; she alone "makes theatre" ' (Tynan 1967: 317). Littlewood did, literally and almost single-handedly, *make a theatre*, virtually without commercial recompense or subsidy of any kind. As an outsider and as a woman, she faced more obstacles than we can easily comprehend in later, more 'enlightened' times. Partly in consequence, the amount of information about her work now available does not match her contribution to British theatrical culture. The following description, therefore, relies heavily on the recalled and contemporary accounts of those who worked with her, including, notably, her own recollections – no doubt coloured by subsequent experience – in *Joan's Book* (Littlewood 1994). The words of Littlewood and these witnesses can be found in libraries: what follows is a considered piecing together of various accounts and testimonies, with relatively few detailed references, to give not so much an 'objective' picture of her productions of Shakespeare as an impression of the creative process through which these reached the stage.

Her theatrical work and career were prefigured in her personal origins. She was born illegitimate in Stockwell in 1914. 'Common as muck' and full of spirit, she was precocious at school, vividly imaginative and already theatre-mad. At age 11 she directed an impromptu production of *Hamlet*, playing all the parts herself. A few years later, she directed *Macbeth* at the convent school she attended. It was full of blood-curdling, physically inventive touches. The production stunned her audience of nuns and parents, disappointing the young director: they were too timid for her kind of theatre.

At 16, she went to RADA on a scholarship, but she didn't stay the course. She regarded it as a waste of time, however, except for the French classes and those in 'Central European Movement', where she came into contact with Laban's ideas. She left RADA and, after a brief spell in Paris, set off for the north of England, ending up in Manchester. There, in 1934, she met Jimmie Miller (later Ewan MacColl), who was leading an agit-prop group called Red Megaphones, bringing theatre to workers on the streets and at factory gates. Littlewood joined him. Wanting to develop a 'theatre of synthesis', which would combine agit-prop and conventional illusionism, they shortly re-formed into the Theatre of Action, later becoming Theatre Union.

All through the pre-war years, she and MacColl were perpetually engaged in research and practical experimentation, barely taking time for a brief marriage. Their investigations were wide-ranging. The early discovery of Adolphe Appia's ideas on stage lighting had a lasting effect, as did their reading of Leon Moussinac's *The New Movement in the Theatre* (first published in Britain in 1931), especially its striking illustrations of recent work in Russia and America. Meyerhold's constructivism and biomechanics, combined with Stanislavsky's ideas about acting (adapted to both realistic and stylised performance), considerably influenced Littlewood's approach to staging and actor training. Equally important were the ideas of Rudolf Laban, which she used in her work for the rest of her career.

While she and MacColl wrote London off, they continued to be aware of socially committed experimental theatre and kept in touch with what was happening in the USA, the Soviet Union and Germany. Their productions often used techniques influenced by the American Living Newspapers and the political strain of German expressionism. In 1935, she and MacColl were offered scholarships to the Moscow Academy of Theatre and Cinema, but their visas for the Soviet Union never came through. They resumed work in the Theatre Union with productions of Lope's *Fuente Ovejuna* and MacColl's adaptations of Hašek's *The Good Soldier Schweik*. In 1940, they added his adaptation of Aristophanes' anti-war *Lysistrata* and *The Flying Doctor* (from Molière's *Le Médicin malgré lui*). They argued that all the great theatres of the past had been both popular and experimental (see Goorney and MacColl 1986: xlvii). The linkage of classic theatre and political activism was essential to their approach, as their Theatre Union Manifesto of 1936 asserted, 'To those who say that [political issues] are not the concern of the theatre or that the theatre should confine itself to treading the path of "beauty" and "dignity" we would say: "Read Shakespeare, Marlowe, Webster, Sophocles, Aeschylus, Aristophanes, Calderon, Molière, Lope-de-Vega, Schiller and the rest" ' (quoted in Goorney and MacColl 1986: ix).

When wartime military call-ups disrupted casting and petrol rationing made tours impossible, they disbanded the Theatre Union in 1942. But Littlewood and a small group of regulars continued to study and prepare for the future. Early in 1945, with the end of the war in sight, she began contacting old colleagues, and in April a nucleus group met in Manchester. A month later, the Theatre Workshop was formed, and work was begun in donated quarters in Kendal from which they could start touring.

Applications for Arts Council support were consistently rejected, so the years 1945–53 had to be spent mainly touring. They travelled to many of the industrial cities of Britain and to West Germany, Czechoslovakia and Sweden, their repertoire including plays they had done before the war, such as the Molière and Lope adaptations, as well as several of Ewan MacColl's powerfully political expressionist-style plays, including *Uranium 235* (1946) and *The Other Animals* (1948). Despite having to disband temporarily several times, they always reorganised and continued. This was Littlewood's and the company's great learning period, when the theory and research of the earlier years came face to face with both financial necessity and scanty but demanding audiences. Especially between 1949 and 1951 there were frequent schools tours, which not only brought in a little money but also provided free school dinners, a big improvement on their usually meagre diet. They were also able to expand their repertoire, for the first time including Shakespeare.

Most of these early Shakespeare productions, created for school audiences, were free-wheeling treatments of well-known comedies, helping to develop the company's skills in popular, audience-involving performance. In these productions, Littlewood's basic approach to Shakespeare was established. What she and MacColl both liked most about the Elizabethans was their ear for the speech of ordinary people and their ability to turn it into poetry. Littlewood's actors approached the characters in the plays as ordinary people living in a theatricalised world. Not least in her appreciation of Shakespeare's plays was her admiration for the kind of open-to-everyone popular theatre and what she regarded as the rather louche collection of players who performed them. She wanted her actors to have the multiple skills of Elizabethan players, like jazz musicians, she sometimes said, able to switch instruments and styles as the performance progressed. She also felt an affinity for the open and flexible theatrical space of the Elizabethan public theatre. This direct contact with the audience was fundamentally related to her notion of agit-prop: her ideal theatre was always a bare platform, with everything created by the actor in direct communion with the spectators.

Her agit-prop approach to Shakespeare led her to see that most conventional productions of Shakespeare supported present-day class interests and lacked vitality because they reproduced the values of the dominant class. 'It is for us the revolutionary [. . .] to translate Shakespeare and Marlowe and the rest into the living criticism of the bourgeois which they represent' (quoted in Callaghan 1993: 112). This was the message underlying her Shakespeare for schools and later in the company's own East End theatre.

The first of her Shakespeares for school audiences (since *Macbeth* for the nuns and parents years before) was *Twelfth Night*, rehearsed at the end of 1948 and taken on a schools tour of Manchester from January to April 1949, and another in Scotland from September to November 1952. The scenery, given touring conditions and the company's finances, was exceedingly simple. What little money they had went on costumes, which, while not elaborate, were generally flamboyant.

What the company learned about acting by doing Shakespearian comedy was important. A noteworthy example was Harry H. Corbett's experience playing Andrew Aguecheek. The preparation for the role was typical of Littlewood's approach – half Stanislavsky, half political analysis, and always performative: she describes it in her autobiography: 'It was interesting checking up on the politics of the time, finding how the class structure worked. Aguecheek, a poor relation, accepting board from a rich relation, Lady Olivia'.

Her advice to Corbett was straightforward: 'Play him seriously, Harry. Forget that he's played as a funny character.' Littlewood believed that a production only became what it was meant to be in interaction with an audience. Corbett's Aguecheek demonstrated this. The first performance was before a bloodthirsty audience of boisterous schoolboys. Contrary to her usual practice, she spoke to Corbett before his first entrance: 'Stand your ground, Harry . . . Don't let them kill Sir Andrew.' The performance started:

> Sir Andrew's entrance . . . catcalls, wolf whistles. He just stood there, lost – roars of laughter. He didn't react, he held on to the character so painstakingly evolved and at each simple, true reaction the boys yelled with delight . . . He looked vulnerable and the sadder he looked the more those kids roared . . . I waited anxiously for the next performance. Again, it was miraculous. Harry never went back. He couldn't. Once you have experienced the thrill of risk, the elation which often comes with fear, the beaten track is no longer inviting
>
> (Littlewood 1994: 430–1).

In the course of 1949, the company prepared another Shakespearian comedy for a Manchester schools tour, this time *As You Like It*. Little information about the production remains, but it was in the same rambunctious style as *Twelfth Night*.

A Midsummer Night's Dream was produced for schools in 1951, with Littlewood's free editing of Shakespeare's text, cutting some characters and doubling and trebling the rest. The approach was entirely playful, with exaggerated costumes of which the actors made half-hidden changes behind bits of scenery, responding with a wink when the audience hooted at their 'deceptions'. This free admission of the 'fakeness' of dramatic illusion was the kind of actor–audience interplay that Littlewood's style of staging continued to encourage. Critics have often remarked that Theatre Workshop 'was the first theatre to stop pretending that the audience didn't exist' (Coren 1984: 61).

Their next go at Shakespeare was later in 1951, with an adaptation combining the two parts of *Henry IV* (to be developed much further in 1964). Again, little is known of the particulars of the production, but interesting and significant details emerge: about how physically her actors approached characterisation, with respect to costumes, for example. When the company had to borrow costumes from the Old Vic for this production, Littlewood found them in some ways inadequate: 'Our costumes evolved with our characterisations . . . They had to allow for dancing, possibly acrobatics. The pockets must be practical [The Old Vic costumes] may have been effective at a distance, [but they] gave no stimulus to the wearer' (Littlewood 1994: 321).

Schools and other tours (in Britain, as well as to Germany, Czechoslovakia, Sweden and Norway) were their only sources of income. The company's survival was constantly in doubt. The work was heavy: transporting, loading, unloading, de-rigging the set, lighting equipment, curtains, costumes, props, battens, sound equipment and various skips and crates – plus a large switchboard with dimmers on wheels which required four strong men to lift. These pressures were compounded by conflicts and changes within the company, despite their dedication to the cause. An even greater source of frustration was the fact that the perpetual one-night stands of touring made regular and sustained actor training virtually impossible.

Training was essential to develop the kind of theatre Littlewood wanted to achieve. Her ideas had evolved over the preceding years, but Laban continued to inspire her in a dedication to movement as central to all acting. Theatre Workshop were the only company in Britain who made movement training an essential part of their work on a play. She believed that actors' minds should be led by their bodies. They should look for a movement that *conveyed* the feeling of a moment, rather than seek a state of mind in order to *imitate* the feeling. Thus, when they rehearsed a play, after an almost cursory reading of the text the physical became the key to the play's meanings. The actors developed their characterisations 'through an exploration of their movement habits and relationships' (Newlove 1993: 8). After such explorations, concentrated on the characters' physical actions and feelings, they felt able to bring out the script's meaning more fully.

Littlewood scorned what she called the prevailing 'Edwardian' style of English acting at the time as 'acting in the past tense' (Littlewood 1959: 286). In her theatre, acting must always be in the present tense, real and immediate physical life behaviour. Such real life in performance derived not only from what the actors observed but also from their own physical and emotional life, as understood through an intelligent use of Stanislavsky's principles. The actor's living behaviour on the stage became something more than realism; it was often stylised and strengthened by frequent theatricalisation, drawing upon centuries of performance: *commedia dell'arte* was an especially rich source for the company. Acting always employed a variety of traditional skills: dancing, singing, swordplay, and so on. Despite stylisation, however, acting must still be *immediate*, always aware of and responding from moment to moment to actual stage conditions, in particular the other actors. Harry H. Corbett's description was apt: as an actor he must enter the stage properly motivated ('I must go and do such-and-such'), but 'from that point [. . .] play only off his reaction to the other actors' (Hodge 2000: 123). The result was that to many spectators – even experienced theatregoers – Theatre Workshop actors 'didn't look like actors. They looked like people [. . .] They danced, sang, and seemed to do whatever came into their heads next. They lived on the stage' (Milne and Goodwin 1967: 114–15). This was the kind of acting her company brought to Shakespeare and everything else they performed.

But the company's training regime had suffered during the post-war years of homelessness. A fixed place to work and live was desperately needed. Finally, after a number of possibilities had fallen through, Gerry Raffles, the company's General Manager (and the love of Littlewood's life), discovered an old music hall theatre in the East End of London, the Theatre Royal (formerly also the Palace of Varieties) in Stratford-atte-Bow, available to rent for twenty pounds a week. In February 1953, the company moved into what was to be their home for more than twenty years.

They encountered a deluge of practical problems in the damp and draughty old building. The theatre smelled of disinfectant and cat urine; the auditorium was littered with sweet wrappers and orange peel; the stage floor was black and greasy with dirt. More importantly, however, there was enough space for everyone to have a place to sleep, however cramped and windowless. So, the company went to work making the theatre livable and workable – and rehearsing. 'And what rehearsals!' she later wrote. 'I have never known anything like them, before or since. Our release from the slogging routine of one-night stands [. . .] gave us more time and energy for our real work (Littlewood 1994: 448).

They opened the theatre on 2 February 1953 with a performance of a refurbished *Twelfth Night*. Performances recalled their earlier experiences with boisterous school audiences. Spectators shouted at the actors, they threw pennies and toffees on the stage. The performance became a sort of East End block party.

In this first season, they presented eighteen productions, only a few of which were revivals of previous work. They staged O'Casey's *Juno and the Paycock*, Shaw's *Arms and the Man*, Chekhov's *Uncle Vanya* (which they took to the Edinburgh Festival), Gogol's *The Government Inspector* and, in October, Ben Jonson's *The Alchemist*.

The last-mentioned is worth particular attention because it gave more evidence of Littlewood's approach to the plays of both Shakespeare and his contemporaries. Her preference for Jonson's comedies over those of Shakespeare was primarily because of his satirical bite and his language, an artistic version of London street argot. This was the kind of theatricalised realistic language for which she and her company felt a particular affinity. *The Alchemist* gave them a chance to enjoy it to the full. Harry H. Corbett as Face, Howard Goorney as Subtle and Avis Bunnage as Dol Common were sharp, lively and funny, London spivs playing at the height of their con game. The pace was energetic and swift, the total effect 'coruscating' (*Independent*, 23 September 2002).

Their first year in the Theatre Royal reached an appropriate climax on 19 January 1954, when the company opened their overwhelming *Richard II*, which deserves more detailed attention as probably the most brilliant of Littlewood's Shakespearian productions. Howard Goorney describes the company's approach to the play:

> The initial rehearsals [. . .] were devoted to capturing the feeling of the period in quite basic terms. Improvisation exercises aimed at

> developing the enmity between the characters, the sudden outbreaks of violence, the suspicions, the ever present fear of the knife in the back. Joan would say, 'You're in a marketplace and it's full of people. You're getting your shopping and a fight breaks out!' We would fight each other, go berserk, jump on each other. Then she would say, 'Now you're stabbed in the back ... You're on horseback, you're knocked off, you're dragged along, you shout and scream and sweat'.
>
> (Goorney 1981: 167).

The emphasis was always on the physical, as when Richard climaxed his confrontation with Gaunt by striking him with his glove. The characters were developed through the use in rehearsal of specific and very physical images, for example, Littlewood's suggestion to those playing the lords: 'Pretend that stretching out before you is your future, your sons and their sons in a great long line. Behind you is a man with a dagger, about to plunge it into your back' (quoted in Goorney 1981: 171).

John Bury's striking, stark set (available to the actors early in rehearsals) provided a challenging arena for the production's perpetual movement and explosive confrontations: a maze of sloping ramps and a low tunnel the actors had to stoop to go through. They wore heavy coats and helmets that determined and restricted their movements, emphasising their repressed anger and frustration. To add to these challenges, Bury lit the play with stark pools of light surrounded by an enveloping darkness ('excessively grim in scenery and lighting', said the *Evening Standard* [18 January 1954]), and it was performed at almost breakneck speed, one scene moving swiftly into another, with enormous vitality, even crudeness.

The most striking feature of the production was Harry H. Corbett's performance of Richard. Littlewood had worked with Corbett on his rather light voice for a long time, and it became a central element in his characterisation. As one critic described it, 'His high, treacherous, sing-song voice, his glazed eyes, his up-tilted chin, his fancifully managed hands, his swift, light, stooping little runs and leaps are all marks of a man who has only a distorted grasp of reality and is living in an interior world of his own' (*Evening Standard*, 18 January 1954).

To the *Times* critic, Corbett's Richard was

> not merely effeminate, and cruelly capricious, his sudden fluctuations [of mood] are from the outset symptoms of insanity. [. . .] For the deposition scene he shambles on in a coarse and ragged robe and gives away his crown with a crazy cunning. In the dungeon at Pomfret, he

> is tethered by a chain round his ankle like the dangerous lunatic he evidently is.
>
> (*The Times*, 18 January 1954)

Theatre Workshop's *Richard II* can be more fully appreciated through the comparisons made between it and the Old Vic's production, which was playing at the same time. Ewan MacColl described the two productions:

> At the Old Vic you heard deafening flourishes, trumpets, there were banners unfurling, processions [. . .] There was no sustained action but great pauses during which the court assembled according to protocol [. . .] They were making a spectacle. Obviously, they cared a lot about the poetry. They took pains so it would sound beautiful. We hadn't bothered about that. When Mowbray and Bolinbroke met they spat, literally. They spat in each other's faces. There was nothing gentlemanly about it.
>
> (Quoted in Callaghan 1993: 117)

He also compares the different treatments of John of Gaunt's famous set piece ('This royal throne of kings, this scepter'd isle'). At the Old Vic, he came on, says MacColl, 'Now for the big speech . . . and he went off. He could have been going to dinner.' In the Theatre Workshop production, he was dying. The speech was played – convincingly – as that of a dying man, who was carried off at the end, never to be seen again (quoted in Callaghan 1993: 117).

Most critics preferred the Old Vic production as being 'truer' to Shakespeare. The Theatre Workshop staging was simply 'not, all in all, an interpretation of *Richard II* in which we can recognize the play that Shakespeare wrote [. . .] his [. . .] pathetic symphony' (*The Times*, 18 January 1954). The *Evening Standard* felt that Corbett's Richard became at the end an 'ugly and loathsome creature [. . .] for whom we can certainly feel no pity. And without pity, what is there to *Richard II*?' (*Evening Standard*, 18 January 1954). Littlewood's response to such critics was characteristically feisty: 'The critics can't stand it because we're playing in what they call a vulgar fashion – we're playing for action and dynamic rather than for decoration' (quoted in Callaghan 1993: 118).

It was not until three years after *Richard II* that the company undertook another Shakespeare play, though there were productions of five plays by Shakespeare's contemporaries during this period. Marston's *The Dutch Courtesan*, an earthy and exuberant comedy somewhat in the manner of Jonson, lent itself well to the performative comic style the company had developed. The production, according to the Stratford *Express*, was full of 'vigorous clowning' and included 'some exquisite buffoonery' (Stratford *Express*, 23 February 1954).

This was followed in September 1954 by *Arden of Feversham*, which became one of the company's most successful performances. Considerable study of contemporary speech and costumes went into preparing the production, which continued the company's development of an intensely physical and theatrical kind of realism. Barbara Brown's performance of Alice was widely praised: her 'rampant *Bovaryisme* [. . .] could hardly be bettered,' said Kenneth Tynan in the *Observer* (2 October 1954).

In March of 1955, Littlewood returned to her beloved Ben Jonson with a modern-dress production of *Volpone*. There was no altering or cutting of the text, though the action was transposed to modern-day Italy and played as biting, mischievous satire on slick spivs and their hangers-on. Mosca rode a bicycle loaded with pineapples and champagne; Corbaccio wheeled himself around in an invalid chair; Sir Politick Would-Be, the posh Englishman abroad, wore swimming trunks and carried a snorkel. The acting freely adapted the style of *commedia dell'arte*, complete with impudent *lazzi*, especially by George Cooper's Volpone and Max Shaw's Mosca. The production was largely ignored by the British establishment but was nonetheless invited to represent England at the Paris International Festival in 1960.

Learning of the invitation, a West End manager sent a telegram to the festival organisers: 'You have made a terrible mistake. The Workshop are nobodies. They are from Stratford East, not from Stratford-on-Avon' (quoted in Callaghan 1993: 122). With no financial support, they travelled with the stage sets as hand luggage to save money. In Paris, the production was greeted ecstatically. They also presented *Arden of Feversham* at the festival, to equally enthusiastic responses. When the time came to return to London, however, they had no money for their passage; the festival organiser gave them enough to get home.

The following year, the company turned to another Elizabethan classic, this time Marlowe's *Edward II*, which Littlewood had long wanted to direct. The play was staged on John Bury's huge sloped platform stage on which was painted an outline map of England and the northern coast of France. The production was focused less on the downfall of a king than on the puzzlement and desperate struggles of a troubled human being. As Edward, Peter Smallwood, formerly a light comedian, gave a chilling performance of a desperate and neurotic homosexual caught in the cruel traps of court politics. Driven in rehearsals to confront his own latent homosexuality, Smallwood produced a deeply moving portrayal of self-pity, arrogance and suffering. (The stress of rehearsing and playing the role put him into a psychiatric hospital for a period and, eventually, out of the theatre and into the priesthood.) Like *Richard II*, the production was full of intense and threatening physicality, climaxing in the harrowing scene of Edward's buggering: a cloak was held across his body, with only his face showing, and as the red-hot iron was supposed to enter his bowels, the music gave a terrifying shriek. 'There was no false "beauty" about [the production]', wrote one critic, 'and certainly no statuesque sorrowing in the conventional manner of English star performances: rather it was a steadily focused drive to death' (Leach 2006: 113).

Littlewood's attention now focused on her next major Shakespearian production, *Macbeth*, which opened in July 1957 in Zurich. Littlewood was determined to go against the usual approaches to the play, which she felt had too long been distorted by the demands of leading actors and the desire for picturesque pseudo-Scottish pageantry. Approaching it with the same bravado as in her school days, she 'set about stripping the play of the usual trimmings – no Highland mist, no bagpipes, no dry ice for the weird sisters, mine were three old biddies with a penchant for fortune-telling, such as you might meet at any time on a road to the isles' (Littlewood 1994: 480).

In her programme notes for the first performance in Zurich, she refers to the figure from Scottish history which some have thought prompted Shakespeare's play. She insisted Shakespeare's interest was in usurpation, not in a heroic figure he knew nothing about. Macbeth as a historical figure was of no interest to Joan Littlewood, either. Freely rearranging the text, she set her version between the First and Second World Wars and made Macbeth into a military dictator who is finally killed (on stage) by a firing squad. The events of the play are presented as occurring in the mind of the general just before he is shot.

The performances in Zurich were given with incomplete scenery, as was the subsequent performance in Moscow the same summer. The production was not properly completed until the return to Stratford East, where it was performed for five weeks from the beginning of September (and for another week at the Oxford Playhouse in November). John Bury's setting comprised a bare stage, at the back of which rough wooden pillars supported a long balcony of scaffolding, under which were deep recesses receding into darkness. *The Times* review described it as 'an unlovely permanent setting' (*Times*, 4 September 1957), while the *Manchester Guardian* (5 September 1957), better recognising its purposes, called it a 'skillful net of light and dark'. The modern military costumes were designed more to constrict the actors' movement than to enhance their figures.

Rehearsals placed the usual emphasis on the physicality, threats and violence in the play. The actors used games of cowboys and Indians, moving gradually to an improvised battle and finally to the opening scene of the play, using Shakespeare's text. They were also told to work up a scene between

Macbeth and the murderers in a pub. Littlewood's use of specific physical gestures and movements to reveal character and action was also prominent here. The dagger scene, for example, had been rehearsed by Glyn Edwards punching his way through the verse metre with his fists like a shadow-boxer. As he spoke, 'Is this a dagger, which I see before me?', he actually paced it out. 'Come, let me clutch thee' similarly evoked a grasping surge of movement (Milne and Goodwin 1967: 119). Physically underpinned in this way, the performance of the verse made its meaning muscular and clear.

Running through the realistic physicality of the production, there was an expressionist streak (a frequent element in John Bury's sets and lighting). As the whole play became a subjective recollection of events in the mind of Macbeth waiting to be shot, the famous pageant of the Witches' presentation of future kings became Macbeth's nightmare as, tossing and turning in his bed, he imagined the old women in the room with him, seeing the pageant of kings only in his mind's eye. This was the only way the scene made sense to Littlewood; otherwise, it seemed to her little more than a pantomime. Though some of the acting was not up to the level of *Richard II* (many in the cast were new to the company), the performance had all the usual drive of a Theatre Workshop production: the movement was strong and impulsive, the verse delivered with the accents of ordinary modern speech. Despite the worries of some over her rearrangement of the play's action, the performance moved from scene to scene with perfect clarity and dynamic speed.

Macbeth evoked decidedly mixed responses. The first jolt was the generally unfavourable response in Moscow. The critics there felt that her modernisation of the play undermined the audience's belief, a strictly Marxist criticism based on the assumption that the supposed historical 'truth' of a text fixed its meaning. Littlewood defended her approach robustly:

> In presenting Shakespeare in modern dress we are not trying to be clever or experimental [. . .] If Shakespeare has any significance today a production of his work must not be regarded as a historical reproduction, but as an instrument still sharp enough to provoke thought, to extend man's awareness of his problems, and to strengthen his belief in his kind.
>
> (Quoted in Goorney 1981: 154)

Back in England, while, as expected, the *Manchester Guardian* (5 September 1957) found the production 'driving' and 'inventive', most other critics were offended by the supposed lack of 'authenticity'. *The Times* berated 'the insensitive arrogance of the production', adding 'What staff officers would chat to old men in the rain, where private executions were carried out by homberg-hatted hatchet men, where coronation robes and the uniform of a commissar were jumbled together' (*The Times*, 4 September 1957). In general, the critics seemed upset by the production's unmistakable political overtones and by the fact that 'the modern dress lent a touch of satire to the army and (most horrible) to royalty' (Milne 1965: 81). They were, however, undisturbed by a few touches of sentimentality in the production, such as the highland lament sung by an anonymous woman over the bodies of Lady Macduff and her son. In all, it may be said that in this case Littlewood's provocation of the critical and political establishments had been successful.

The last years of the 1950s were filled with enormously popular productions of new plays, most famously Shelagh Delaney's *A Taste of Honey* (May, 1958) and Brendan Behan's *The Hostage* (October, 1958). (His *The Quare Fellow* had been a moderate success in 1956.) It was not until 1960 that Littlewood returned to Elizabethan drama with Jonson's *Every Man in His Humour*, presented with resounding success at the Paris Festival that year.

She left the Workshop in 1961, but returned in 1963 to conceive and direct *Oh! What a Lovely War*, probably the company's most successful production ever. A year later, she directed Shakespeare for the last time. The production was of *Henry IV*, with a text edited by Littlewood to include most of Part I and a few scenes from Part II. It was created for the Edinburgh Festival and performed at the Assembly Hall from 17 August for three weeks. (She had done the play for a schools tour in 1951, but this was a different adaptation and more fully developed staging.)

The use of space was characteristically bold: a large bridge-stage (48 by 15 feet) was constructed across the Assembly Hall from north to south. Thus, the actors (and characters) were displayed openly – one might say publicly exposed – to the audience's potentially critical eyes. The acting was, as was usual for the Workshop, generally free and strong. The exceptions were the 'politician' characters (the king and nobles). Perhaps influenced by Brecht, whom Littlewood had encountered and admired during the 1950s, the high-born characters were deliberately flattened in contrast to the low-lifes of the highway, tavern and rustic scenes. While the power figures wore muted, relatively colourless costumes, the clothes of the lesser characters were more flamboyantly modern, with only hints of the historical in hats and accessories: Victor Spinetti's Poins, for example (an outstanding performance), wore a black velour bowler, single earring, high-heeled blue suede boots and black ski pants. In her intention to show the political impotence of the supposedly powerful characters, Littlewood deliberately introduced notes of uncertainty or bluster into their performances. Slightly recalling Brecht's *Galileo*, the way the actors' way of speaking often deliberately undermined their outward characters. As John Russell Brown has pointed out, Hotspur's (cockney-accented) reading of the letter scene (Act II, Scene 3) used 'added emphasis and quickening tempo' to turn 'assurance into an expression of fear': his 'grandiloquence was *meant* to sound empty' (Brown 1965: 153).

The scenes involving the 'lower' characters were played out more fully, with music and more business for the actors. It is here that the fun of the performance lay, as well as its greater truth. Characters like Poins, Bardolf, Gadshill and Francis became more complex and interesting than in more conventional productions, where they are often reeled off as superficial comic types. George Cooper (who had returned to the company to play the role) made Falstaff 'an unsentimental picture of a public-bar soldier' (Brown 1965: 154), though some thought he lacked some of the energy and colour suggested by the text. John Russell Brown suggested a key to the performance in his description of a striking moment at the end of the first half:

> Hal is backing away on the bridge [stage] Poins remains in the centre [. . .] He bends forward as he listens to Hal's words (addressed to Peto in both quarto and Folio texts): 'We must all to the wars, and thy place shall be honourable [. . .] Be with me in the morning; and so good morrow, Poins.' The delivery of the words is not remarkable and in the centre of the picture is the listener, not the speaker. Poins is smiling; puzzled; embarrassed, perhaps; ingratiating; there is a servility in his jaunty appearance, an insecurity in his knowing manner.
>
> (Brown 1965: 147)

It is in perceptive, interesting moments of this kind (reminiscent of Brecht's approach to history on the stage), where the response of ordinary people to great events is emphasised over the supposed grandness of the events themselves, that the primary strength of the production lay.

Critical reactions were generally negative, some almost rabidly so. Bernard Levin, for example, asserted, 'There is virtually nothing in this production but gabble and shuffle, ill-executed horseplay and unimaginative characterisation' (quoted in Goorney 1981: 130). Even Philip Hope-Wallace, while admiring Littlewood's disrespectful approach to a classic play and liking Prince Hal's Cockney accent and the tactile, Brechtian realness of the props, was disappointed by the roughness of the staging and the actors' lack of clarity of speech. Another critic was disturbed by the production's seeming anarchy, what with the use of music and dance, actors wearing pullovers or string ties purposely visible under cloaks and ermine, and the alternation of presentational and representational acting styles.

And finally, the familiar fallback of so many of Littlewood's conventional critics: the production failed to treat Shakespeare's text with proper respect and the great characters were deprived of dignity. Her response was characteristically assertive. She called a press conference under the chairmanship of Lord Harewood, Artistic Director of the festival and came out with all guns firing:

> We have no respect for Shakespeare. In Scotland, England, the whole world they are bogged down with art and respect for the past. We are not. You can attack the poor Queen Mum but don't attack art. Ever since Queen Victoria, *you lot* [emphasis mine] have been so artistic. I don't know what we're doing here supporting Lord Harewood in his old rubbish. Let's have something of meaning to people.
>
> (Quoted in Goorney 1981: 130–1)

(Earlier, the manager of the Assembly Hall had said that they had sold more unreserved seats for *Henry IV* than he could remember for any first week.)

While she defended herself and her company vigorously, she was fully aware of the gap between what they had attempted and what they had yet achieved. As was usual with the Workshop, they continued working to improve the production throughout most of the run.

Henry IV was the last of her Shakespeare productions. After 1964, Littlewood became less and less involved with the Theatre Workshop, directing only a few productions in the next eight years. More and more, she became involved in a variety of projects in various parts of the world. Her main energies were focused on her dream of a fun palace, based on the eighteenth-century pleasure gardens, like the one at Vauxhall. For Littlewood, the notion of a pleasure garden could provide a more comprehensive kind of participative theatre, embracing all kinds of free activities. Despite numerous attempts to obtain subsidies and several ambitious architectural plans, however, the project was never realised. During the same period, the continued failure of the Theatre Workshop to win sufficient help from public or private sources made its survival more and more uncertain. Littlewood's last production at the Theatre Royal was in 1973: *So You Want to Be in Pictures*, a spoof of the idiocies of film-making. It was well received but did nothing to save the company. After years of struggle, her energies were flagging. The final blow was the death in 1975 of Gerry Raffles. She lived her last years quietly in Paris, as 'Madame Petitbois', writing her vibrant autobiography, *Joan's Book*. She died in September 2002, long after many of her admirers and detractors knew she was still alive.

Inevitably, questions arise about her contributions to the British theatre and to Shakespearian staging in particular. She was an important figure, not only because of her productions but also through her teaching of actors. Many actors and directors who worked with her carried to other companies most of the key elements of Littlewood's way of working: the mixture of contemporary realism and openly theatrical stylisation, often from historical sources; the combination of serious critical politicism and playful popular theatre; the emphasis on movement and gesture as central to the actor's work; language approached as an extension of the actor's body; the crucial importance of acting in 'the present tense'; playing to the audience in a Brechtian way, as coparticipants in the performance; the continued reworking of a production during its run; the elimination of statuesque dignity and poetic recitation as desiderata in classical acting; the constant striving after simplicity and directness in acting.

Despite the acknowledged importance of her work, however, opinions varied about its long-term effect. Michael Billington thought that her influence on other directors was 'fairly minimal' (Coren 1984: 60). Lindsay Anderson felt that the conflict in her work between the politically dissident and the sentimental–popular produced 'a kind of intellectual limitation' (Coren 1984: 40). Peter Hall, on the other hand, was an admirer: 'Joan's theatre was about energy, vitality, blood and sentiment. It could be very common, it could be very vulgar. But it was very very alive' (quoted in Goorney 1981: 166). His high regard for her work was reflected in his invitation of John Bury, for many years Joan Littlewood's lighting and scenic designer, to join him at the Royal Shakespeare Company (RSC) and later the National Theatre, where his work, which had contributed so much to the creation of the Theatre Workshop 'style', enjoyed great success.

The primary elements of Littlewood's kind of theatre were often appropriated, especially by the RSC, but depoliticised. Perhaps fortunately, however, her work on Elizabethan plays does not seem to have suffered quite the same fate. Admiration for her staging of Shakespeare and his contemporaries remains strong, primarily because central to everything she did was the idea that 'theatre must be in the present tense' (Littlewood 1959: 286). 'Theatre Workshop produced Shakespeare or Marlowe as though the play had only just been written', wrote Tom Milne, 'and the playwrights were commenting on life as we know it today' (Milne 1965: 81). Robert Leach has summarised her achievement: 'To make the received repertoire of classic plays into such a coherent critique of contemporary society was an intensely original project, probably unique in British theatre history' (Leach 2006: 114).

Chronology

1934 Meets Ewan MacColl, they form Theatre of Action, later Theatre Union

1945	Theatre Workshop formed
1949	*Twelfth Night* schools tour
1949	*As You Like It* schools tour
1951	*A Midsummer Night's Dream* schools tour
1951	*Henry IV* schools tour
1953	Theatre Workshop moves into Theatre Royal, Stratford East
1953	*Twelfth Night* opens first season at Theatre Royal
1953	*The Alchemist* (Jonson), Theatre Royal
1954	*The Dutch Courtesan* (Marston), Theatre Royal
1954	*Richard II*, Theatre Royal
1954–55	*Arden of Feversham* (anon.), Theatre Royal, and Paris Festival
1956	*Edward II* (Marlowe), Theatre Royal
1957	*Macbeth*, Zurich, Oxford Playhouse, Eastern Europe tour
1958	*A Taste of Honey* (Delaney), Theatre Royal
1958	*The Hostage* (Behan), Theatre Royal
1960	*Every Man in His Humour*, Paris Festival
1961	Leaves Theatre Workshop, Theatre Workshop suspended
1963	Theatre Workshop reconstituted
1963	*Oh! What a Lovely War*, Theatre Royal, later West End, New York
1964	*Henry IV*, Edinburgh Festival
1964	Forms Fun Palace Trust
1978	Theatre Workshop dissolved

Bibliography

Brown, John Russell (1965) 'Three Kinds of Shakespeare: 1964 Productions at London, Stratford-upon-Avon and Edinburgh', *Shakespeare Survey* 18: 147–56.

Callaghan, Dympna (1993) *Shakespeare at the Fun Palace: Joan Littlewood*, Urbana, Ill.: University of Illinois Press.

Coren, Michael (1984) *Theatre Royal: 100 years of Stratford East*, London: Quartet Books.

Goorney, Howard (1981) *The Theatre Workshop Story*, London: Eyre Methuen.

Goorney, Howard and MacColl, Ewan (eds) (1986) *Agit-Prop to TheatreWorkshop: Political Playscripts 1930–50*, Manchester: Manchester University Press.

Hodge, Alison (ed.) (2000) *Twentieth Century Actor Training*, London: Routledge.

Holdsworth, Nadine (2006) *Joan Littlewood*, London and New York: Routledge.

Leach, Robert (2006) *Theatre Workshop: Joan Littlewood and the Making of Modern British Theatre*, Exeter: Exeter University Press.

Littlewood, Joan (1956) 'A Personal Manifesto', *Encore* 7: 283.

—— (1959) 'Plays for the People', *World Theatre* 8(4): 286.

—— (1994) *Joan's Book: The Autobiography of Joan Littlewood*, London: Methuen.

Milne, Tom (1965) 'Art in Angel Lane', in Charles Marowitz, Tom Milne and Owen Hale (eds) *New Theatre Voices of the Fifties and Sixties: Selections from* Encore *Magazine 1956–1963*, London: Eyre Methuen, pp.80–6.

Milne, Tom and Clive Goodwin, (1967) 'Working with Joan', in Charles Marowitz and Simon Trussler (eds), *Theatre at Work: Playwrights and Productions in Modern British Theatre*, London: Methuen, pp. 113–22.

Newlove, Jean (1993) *Laban for Actors and Dancers*, London: Nick Hern.
Tynan, Kenneth (1969) *Theatre Right and Left*, London: Longmans.

About the author

Lesley Wade Soule was educated at the Central School of Speech and Drama, the University of British Columbia and the University of Exeter and is a senior lecturer in the Drama Department at the University of Exeter, where she teaches directing and acting in the MFA Staging Shakespeare programme. Her publications include *Actor as Anti-Character: Dionysus, the Devil and the Boy Rosalind* (2000), *As You Like It* in *The Shakespeare Handbooks* (2005) and *Slovene Theatre and Drama Post Independence* (2007). She is co-editor of the journal *Studies in Theatre and Performance*.

16
NINAGAWA YUKIO

Kawai Shoichiro

Ninagawa Yukio (b. 1935) was born in Saitama Prefecture on the north of Tokyo, the son of a tailor. His mother frequently took him to Kabuki and Bunraku when he was small, and he became well acquainted with traditional Japanese theatre. He first intended to enter a university to study art to be a painter, but finally decided to join the theatre company Seihai in Tokyo in 1955, as a trainee actor, where he got to know Kurahashi Ken, the director and professor at Waseda University, and Abe Kobo, the celebrated playwright. From them, he learned theories of drama such as Brecht's and Diderot's and the Stanislavsky system, which he found useful when he later worked with Western actors. In three years he was promoted from a trainee to an official member of the company as an actor, and acted on television, in films, and on stage. But when Kurahashi left the company, Ninagawa acutely felt the absence of a director in the company and, being dissatisfied with his own acting, decided to turn to directing at the age of 30. In 1967, he gave an atelier production under the title of *Nine Chapters from Wolfgang Borchert's Works* as his first directorial work.

In the late 1960s, Japan was marked by the rise of an 'underground' or anti-establishment little-theatre movement: in 1966, Suzuki Tadashi founded Waseda Little Theatre and gave its first production at the Art Theatre Shinjuku Bunka, the very venue at which another leading avant-garde theatre company, Tenjo-Sajiki, premiered Terayama Shuji's *Marie in Fur* in 1967. In the basement of the same theatre building was another theatre, christened by Mishima Yukio as 'Underground Scorpion'. Ninagawa was determined to produce his favourite young playwright Shimizu Kunio's new play *Sincere Frivolity* in this avant-garde's new Mecca, the Art Theatre Shinjuku Bunka.

He did it in 1969 with a theatre company called the Theatre of Contemporary People which he set up with sixteen friends in 1968 after leaving Seihai. All the plays he directed in those days, including Shimizu's new plays and a modernised version of Kabuki, reflected the contemporary political climate. It was the time when the student protest movement was raging, and terror bomb blasts recurred in Tokyo. Some members of the company regularly participated in anti-war demonstrations, and Ninagawa was not alone in recognising a serious rift between the fictional play-world and the severe reality outside the theatre: the company had to be disbanded in order to start afresh and override this rift.

In 1972, some extreme activists of the United Red Army (Rengo Sekigun) were arrested after a ten-day siege at the mountain lodge Asama Sanso, and it was discovered that fourteen of them had been lynched to death. In commemoration of martyrs to the left-wing movement, Ninagawa formed a new theatre company called Cherry Company in the same year. It was towards the end of 1972 that he came across a young man who thrust a jackknife against his side, threatening to kill him if Ninagawa were not desperately serious in his theatre activities. He later recalled that incident and wrote in his book *A Thousand Knives, A Thousand Eyes*: 'If there are a thousand young men in the auditorium, I should expect a thousand knives. I thought I had to produce performances for those thousand knives' (1993: 55).

When he debuted in the commercial theatre world with his first Shakespearian production of *Romeo and Juliet* in Tokyo in 1974, his aim was not to revere a sophisticated higher foreign culture but to show how relevant Shakespeare could be to our modern life. Much influenced by Mikhail Bakhtin's *Rabelais and His World*, he was determined to make the most of the carnivalesque fecundity and profuse energy of the Renaissance popular culture to depict the salacious and belligerent life force in which the play is immersed just as our contemporary world is. Ninagawa sought to popularise Shakespeare and to reveal how vulgar and subversive as well as lofty and poetic he is.

Although Ninagawa never went overseas to study drama, nor liked to see others' productions, he often visited places to get the image of a play. For his first *Romeo and Juliet*, he flew to Italy, and in a Florentine piazza decided his production should have a piazza-like reservoir of such popular boisterousness as may be observed in Breughel's paintings. This was realised by employing a cast of as many as sixty-five: citizens of Verona swarmed on a tower-like, domineering four-tiered edifice on the stage and, as Elton John's rock music roared, numerous retinues of the two households fought a tremendous battle until Ichikawa Somegoro, the young Kabuki actor, as lovesick Romeo sauntered about in tranquility with a flower in his hand. The dreamy rambling Romeo sprinted at the sight of Juliet: the star-crossed lovers' vehement passions were cogently expressed through the youthful ease and swiftness with which they ran and climbed up and down the high tiers. This fundamental image of running lovers remained the same when Ninagawa staged the play with different cast and design in 1979, 1998 and 2004.

In 1983, urged by his producer Nakane Tadao, he took a production abroad for the first time (Euripides' *Medea*), and not a year has passed since then without an overseas production. In 1985 came his first Shakespearian production abroad, namely *NINAGAWA Macbeth* (premiered in Tokyo in 1980). Thelma Holt the British producer, who was to support Ninagawa's British productions throughout his career, was deeply impressed by *Medea* and *NINAGAWA Macbeth* in Edinburgh and brought them both to the National Theatre in London in 1987, for which Ninagawa was nominated for the Laurence Olivier Best Director Award. Other productions Holt invited for the festival included Ingmar Bergman's production of *Hamlet*.

Alternatively called 'Samurai *Macbeth*', '*Butsudan Macbeth*', or 'Cherry-Blossom *Macbeth*', it was set in the late-sixteenth-century Azuchi-momoyama era of Japan, the age of samurais. A gigantic set, designed by Senoo Kappa, of a *butsudan* or Buddhist household altar, occupied the whole stage to form a kind of proscenium arch. The idea of this set derived from Ninagawa's own desire to speak with the dead, a desire he felt when he prayed for his deceased father and brother as he sat before the *butsudan* at his parental home. It was generally believed in Japan that the living could talk to the dead by opening the shutters of the *butsudan* case and praying for those consecrated there. In the same way, at the opening of the production, a pair of stooped old women opened the massive shutters of the *butsudan*-proscenium and prayed at either side of the stage. They remained there throughout the performance, sitting, eating and watching. Audiences were prompted to join them in watching the story enacted within the *butsudan*. Their presence was for the most part negligible, but when they weep silently at Macbeth's line, 'my way of life / Is fall'n into the sere, the yellow leaf' (or at the 'tomorrow speech' in later productions), audiences were induced to sympathise with the man who was to die bravely. This was Ninagawa's framing device to facilitate audiences to transport themselves into the play-world, a device he almost always employed in different forms in later productions.

At the climax of the play, the Birnam wood, represented by breathtakingly magnificent cherry trees in full bloom, seen through the gauzed trellis of the *butsudan*, swayed to and fro to threaten Macbeth with death. There is a tacit understanding in Japanese literature that beauty is not without some unexpressed sacrifice, and it was imagined especially in Kajii Motojiro's and Sakaguchi Ango's novels that beautiful cherry trees are nurtured by dead bodies buried underneath. Macbeth, who fought under a shower of cherry blossoms, was marked with death.

It was based on this association between cherry blossom and sacrificial death that Ninagawa once formed a theatre company called Cherry Company to commemorate the left-wing martyrs. Accordingly, the cherry blossom in this production was tinged with his sentiment for left-wingers, or for those brave people who, like *Macbeth*, died in fighting. This is why in the early productions of *NINAGAWA Macbeth* we heard the sound of the collision between the police army and the demonstrators, with deafening noises of tear-gas grenades and shouts.

Even for those Japanese who are unfamiliar with the association, cherry blossom does suggest the transience of life, not least because their falling petals are a common metaphor for evanescence. Therefore, the grandeur of the Birnam cherry wood could both delight audiences' eyes and ominously signal Macbeth's death at the same time. The play ended as petals of the cherry blossom fell like snow and choirboys sang Fauré's *Requiem*, replacing Buddhist music heard earlier.

Music, the flower and the crowd were the three things that characterised his productions. As for the crowd in *NINAGAWA Macbeth*, with a cast amounting to thirty-three, he introduced numerous samurais in Japanese armour to fight bloody battles, employing Japanese martial arts. Through such realistic crowd scenes, Ninagawa exhibited the energy of the mass in a spectacular way.

Everything contributed to sumptuous spectacles. The weird sisters were made to look really weird in opulent costumes designed by Tsujimura Jusaburo, and a couple of Kabuki female impersonators performed two of the three gaudy witches to turn the most unrealistic scenes of witchery into something stylised and magical. Malcolm met Macduff at the palace studded with huge, impressive sculptures of warrior-gods, and an enormous chandelier -like circle of ever-burning candles surrounded Macbeth at his 'Tomorrow' speech.

The spectacle was strengthened by its Japanisation. Macbeth had his 'battle fan', unique to feudal Japan, and Banquo's ghost appeared among warriors sitting on the floor in the Japanese style rather than at a table. *NINAGAWA Macbeth* is often compared with Kurosawa Akira's film, *The Throne of Blood* (1957), but it should be emphasised that Ninagawa made it his principle not to change a line of Shakespeare's text. Ninagawa always professed his faithfulness to the text. Throughout his career, his aim was not to reinterpret or to adapt Shakespeare's play but to bring it in close rapport with the modern world and make it easier for his audiences – mainly Japanese – to understand, by means of visualisation and often Japanisation.

Ninagawa was often criticised for his *japonisme*, which critics wrongly believed catered for Western audiences, but it is, as Im Yeeyon argues, 'an easy pitfall to which the so-called intercultural theatre can become prey' (Im 2004: 7). His Japanisation was basically for Japanese audiences, as Ninagawa himself attested:

> I've had very little negative feedback from people involved in the traditional Japanese dramatic arts. On the other hand, a number of scholars of European and English theatre have labelled my work 'Japanesque.' But from my point of view, the only reason I resort to Japanese or Japanesque modes of expression is because I want Japanese audiences to understand my work. It's not that I'm using these symbols for the benefit of foreign audiences [. . .], and I think the best way to enable my core audience to understand my work is through typically Japanese analogies.
>
> (*The Japan Times*, 6 October 2002)

This point is confirmed by *The Tempest*, premiered in Tokyo in 1987. Ninagawa wrote in many places that he had to imagine Prospero to be a Japanese only because a Japanese actor played the role. He hit on the idea that Prospero could be Zeami, the fifteenth-century Noh master, who was once exiled to Sado Island, where many ancient Noh stages still remain. The production was subtitled 'A Rehearsal *on* a Noh *Stage* on Sado Island' (my italics – not 'A Rehearsal *of* a Noh *Play* on the Island of Sado' as it is often taken to be). There was indeed a small Noh stage built on the stage, but 'a Noh stage' mentioned in the subtitle referred to the larger stage on which Prospero rehearsed a play called *The Tempest*. The structure of a Noh-stage-upon-the-Noh-stage strengthened the play's metatheatricality: the stage-managing Prospero produced not only the pageant in Act IV Scene 1 but also the play of *The Tempest* itself, in which shipwreck and wet clothes turned out to be hallucinatory. Ninagawa amplified the significance of this play-within-the-play structure by introducing a framing device that indicated that Prospero and others were being played by Japanese: there was a half-hour pre-show warm-up, in which the cast and staff members, including Ninagawa himself, appeared on stage with the sound of Japanese drums; Ninagawa then left the stage to let Hira Mikijiro assume the role of a director, and eventually Hira began to act as Prospero. When he said, 'Now my charms are all o'erthrown' towards the end of the production, waiting actors, who had been sitting on the stage watching the performance, all came forward, together with the stage crew, to congratulate Hira. This brought the audiences back to the point where he took on the role of Prospero.

Ninagawa's *japonisme* was closely related with his need to eliminate the artificiality or the 'phoniness' of Japanese actors' performance of Shakespeare – 'phony' because the Japanese with their Asian physiognomy have much difficulty in impersonating Caucasian characters in Shakespeare's plays and also because the historical and cultural gap of 400 years makes it difficult for us to reach the great stature of Shakespearian characters. Like Brecht,

Ninagawa felt the need to signal to audiences that they were watching a performance.

At the same time, Ninagawa urged his actors to override the gap. In rehearsals, he often scolded young inept actors by calling them 'convenience-store actors', meaning that they lack the scale of a great character because they are living a basic life on essentials from convenience stores. Ninagawa had a reputation as a fierce martinet, once famous for throwing an ashtray at slack actors, but later in his career, he tried to educate young actors with encouraging words, telling them to reach out for a huge scale as a human being.

That Ninagawa's Japanisation was intended for the Japanese may be confirmed again when we look at the design of *hina-matsuri* or the girls' Doll Festival introduced in his three productions of *Hamlet* (1978, 1988, 1995) all staged only in Japan (although the last production was revived in London in 1998). Any Japanese would instantly recognise it, but Westerners could perhaps only enjoy the gorgeousness of the kimono-clad actors on red-carpeted tiers, who posed like dolls, representing a lord, a lady, their gentlewomen in waiting and their musicians. *Hina-matsuri* is a traditional Japanese festival, celebrated on 3 March, for girls' happiness, and it was a custom to exhibit these dolls on a red-carpeted tiered stand on the day. Ninagawa represented the player-king, the player-queen and their trains as these dolls, not simply for their visual sumptuousness and Japanese quality but also for their suggestiveness in relation to the maimed rite: because *hina-matsuri* was celebrated for a girl's happiness, the overturned dolls adumbrated the loss of Ophelia's bright future.

Kishi Tetsuo, a Shakespearian scholar in Japan, complained that such a visual approach was irrelevant to the play (Kishi 77), and indeed one may prefer non-Japanisation: Ninagawa himself admitted that 'Such surface things' as a pure Japanese style 'cannot evoke the depth and vastness of the world of Shakespeare' (Minami 2001: 214). Nevertheless, we have to admit that even Western directors do adopt some kind of visual approach, like trapezes in Peter Brook's *A Midsummer Night's Dream* or the scrapheap of old cars in Trevor Nunn's *Timon of Athens* (1991), and arguably Ninagawa's spectacular approach is no different from these Western directors in that they both believed that as directors they had to do something to Shakespeare – modernise or Japanise – to make him accessible to the modern audience.

Ninagawa's mastery over a huge set and an immense crowd was noted earlier. In his first production of *King Lear* (1975), with a cast of sixty-five, he actually had Lear's large number of unruly attendants on stage, which seemingly justified Goneril's insistence on reducing their number, and their overflowing existence onstage contrasted with Lear's forlornness in wilderness. In the final scene of *Hamlet* (1978), with a cast of seventy-seven, numerous vassals crawled grovellingly up towards Fortinbras on a huge staircase, a sheer spectacle to indicate the power of the new prince. This *mise-en-scène* recurred in the last scene of his second (1988) and third (1995, revived in 1998 at the Barbican) productions of *Hamlet*.

However, Ninagawa's style gradually changed. The large size of cast in the 1970s was reduced to less than half in the 1980s and 1990s. For instance, his first *Hamlet* (1978) had a cast of seventy-seven, but his second (1988) had thirty-two; his first *King Lear* (1975) had sixty-five, his second *Lear* (1991) twenty-six and his third (1999) twenty-four. Formerly, Ninagawa meticulously prepared his spectacular design, but having established a long-term relation with such collaborators as Nakagoshi Tsukasa, the stage designer, he only had to give them some hints to work on. He abandoned his earlier dictatorial style and began to concentrate more on acting than decorating the stage with a gigantic stage set and atmospheric lighting effects. He began to explore Shakespeare's text more in collaboration with actors and staff.

Having spent ten years in big commercial theatres, he felt a strong need to get back to a small theatre, like the one in which he started his career. Thus, in 1984, he founded a young actors' small theatre company Gekisha Ninagawa Studio (later called Ninagawa Company Dash) in order to experiment in a little theatre called Benisan Pit. There he had freestyle rehearsals, which he compared to jazz sessions. The actors chose scripts by themselves and created several short dramas – not Shakespearian – in groups, and Ninagawa selected, directed and arranged them to make a production. After working for another ten years there, while busying himself with overseas productions, he decided to venture on his first attempt at a Shakespearian comedy. Producers were against this obviously unprofitable project in a small theatre but, because Ninagawa's purpose was not profit, he spent his own money and turned to donations to produce *A Midsummer Night's Dream* in 1994. The result was a breakthrough in his career.

The stage of his *Midsummer Night's Dream* was modelled on the Zen rock garden of the Ryoanji temple in Kyoto, a famous garden that is said to epitomise the universe. The whole stage was covered with white sand, with five threads of sand that spilled from the ceiling down to the stage, as if through invisible hourglasses. The time flowing there was evidently different from ours, and Puck somersaulted through the air and moved about with an astonishing speed: Lin Yung-biau, in the role of Puck, was an acrobat from the Beijing opera. His lines were delivered by Matsuda Yoji, a young Japanese in exactly the same costume as Lin's, wearing a black veil over his face like Kurogo (stagehands on stage) in Kabuki. In this fairyland, Puck seemed double as if seen 'with parted eyes', as Hermia says.

Ninagawa consciously tried to overreach Peter Brook's *A Midsummer Night's Dream* (1970), which he saw performed in Tokyo in 1973, a year before he began to direct Shakespeare. Ninagawa incorporated the best of Asian acrobatic stunts as a response to Brook's dramatic use of such Western acrobatics as trapezes and dish-spinning. Ironically, Ninagawa didn't know that Peter Brook had been also fascinated by the acrobatic feats in Beijing opera: 'My conclusion was that it would be interesting to try to stage *A Midsummer Night's Dream* with a mixed group of Shakespearian actors and Chinese acrobats. This never proved to be a practical possibility' (Brook 1998: 130). What Brook gave up, Ninagawa carried out.

The atmosphere of the rehearsals was convivial and cooperative. Owing to the shortage of budget, Ninagawa made Titania's wig himself by slitting a black plastic bag; Nakane the producer offered free meals during rehearsals; and visitors, including journalists, were asked to make ten paper flowers each, because hundreds of them were needed for falling massively on white dunes and sprouting from the hair of dancing fairies.

The triumph of the production may be partly ascribed to Ninagawa's success in rendering the scene of mechanicals quite contemporary: Daimon Goro as Bottom was a Japanese working-class man in a festive mood, cooking up stir-fry noodles for his friends. Ofuji, the hefty sumo wrestler, as Snug appeared with his corpulent body miraculously balanced on a tiny bicycle only to tumble down in the sand. 'When this man-mountain removes his mask and reassures the ladies that he is Snug the joiner', reported Benedict Nightingale, 'he becomes twice, thrice as menacing' (*The Times*, 6 September 1996). The audiences, smelling Bottom's cooked food, were enticed to experience the real, quotidian world, although they were to be instantly carried away, together with Bottom, to the bizarre, illusionary world of fairies. Shiraishi Kayoko doubling the roles of Titania and Hippolyta, and Sagawa Tetsuro (Harada Daijiro in the original Tokyo production) as Theseus and Oberon transformed themselves from a beaming marrying couple to a gnarling, fighting pair instantly, accentuating the difference between the two worlds.

After the enormous success of this experimental production, Ninagawa failed in his big spectacular production of *Othello* in the same year. He later admitted that the failure was owing to his overemphasis on spectacle (Takahashi 2001: 282). He began to think twice of his use of spectacle, but he had other reasons for his shift in method: he did not want to repeat what he had done before and felt the need to search for something new in order to explore the full meaning of the play. It is precisely for this reason that he ventured on another new approach in the 1998 production of *Romeo and Juliet*: he asked Horio Yukio, a stage designer who had never worked with him, to give *his* plan for Ninagawa to work on. Horio's stage set was a metallic scaffolding enclosing a piazza, which the early Ninagawa would have abhorred for its abstract sternness but, according to what he says in *Ninagawa Yukio: A Theatre Engaged in a Battle* (also mentioned in Takahashi 2001: 300–1), he enjoyed himself struggling to make it look humane by scattering oranges and sprinkling water.

Moreover, Ninagawa shifted from Odashima Yushi's translation to Matsuoka Kazuko's for his third production of *Hamlet* (1995) onwards. Appointed as Artistic Director of Sainokuni Shakespeare Series in 1997 to produce all the Shakespearian works at Sainokuni Saitama Arts Theatre, Ninagawa decided to use Matsuoka's translations. Thus, Matsuoka became the first female translator in Japan to be expected to translate the complete works of Shakespeare.

Ninagawa often referred to the need to electrify the audiences within the first few minutes of a performance so that they are instantly carried into the play-world, not least because he felt the gap between the Shakespearean world and ours was so big that a strong helping hand must be offered for the audience to jump over it. His *Richard III* (1999, 2003), with Ichimura Masachika in the title role, certainly surprised the audiences with many things dropping from the ceiling at the beginning; even a lifelike, full-scale replica of a horse was dropped. More often, Ninagawa gave a half-hour pre-show demonstration onstage, as in *The Tempest*, *Hamlet* and *Titus Andronicus*, to prepare the audiences to join the play-world.

In the 1995 production of *Hamlet*, from thirty minutes before curtain time, actors were seen preparing themselves in each cubicle of a two-tiered dressing-room complex embedded in the back wall of the stage. Here again was a framing device to let the audiences be conscious of the performance's meta-theatricality and, like Snug the joiner, reveal that it was not English actors but Japanese actors who were performing a Shakespearian tragedy. This display of actors' preparation was also resonant with the play's own metatheatricality: Sanada Hiroyuki's acting of Hamlet overlapped with Hamlet's acting of an antic disposition and with the metatheatrical structure of the production. Naturally, as a critic put it, 'It's hard to gauge whether his madness is feigned or genuine' (*Evening Standard*, 1 September 1988). The enigma of the play was deepened.

The enigma was visually expressed by the fluttering curtains of the dressing rooms, blown from behind by electric fans to cause a rippling or billowing undulation, which seemed to suggest the inaccessibility of the interiority: we had no more access to Hamlet's disturbed inner feelings than we did to what lay behind the fluttering curtains, no matter how much they attracted our attention. At times, they indicated a place for furtive surveillance; at other times, one could almost see through the curtains as when they were lit to reveal figures behind, such as Hamlet's mother attending to her make-up or the Gertrude actress attending to her theatrical make-up, or the ghost of Hamlet's father as perceived in Hamlet's mind's eye.

The mirrors in the dressing rooms also had a symbolic effect in this play, for the purpose of playing is to hold 'a mirror up to Nature'. Hamlet's first appearance was staged as he sat pensively in a web of criss-crossing beams reflected off the mirrors, 'reflectively'. The beams looked like white slashes cutting the space where Hamlet was, and it seemed as if he were caught in this web of hurting beams. The same scenic design (by Harada Tamotsu) was employed in introducing the deranged Ophelia to suggest that she, too, almost fell apart as she had herself pierced through by these rays of 'reflection'. At the end of the play, when Fortinbras appeared at the top of the tiers, his soldiers smashed the mirrors in each dressing room, to signify the end of the reflective and torturing play-world, and the sound of traffic noise outside, heard under Fortinbras' final lines, took us back to our everyday world.

Except for the *hina-matsuri* doll tiers, there was no specific Japanisation in the production. Ninagawa began to drop his Japanisation because he felt that the younger generation, to which most of his current audiences and actors belonged, have no national inferiority complex and needed no cultural filtering. Almost everything seemed an eclectic amalgamation of Japanese and Western styles. Komine Lily's costume design for male characters, with a dark-coloured long skirt of no particular national identity, became a basic costume design in Ninagawa's later Shakespearian productions.

It is noteworthy that this was his third *Hamlet* and the first one to be shown abroad. Ninagawa candidly admitted that his previous productions of *Hamlet* were failures, because he had given them crude ornamental forms, putting too much emphasis on some aspects of the play. He realised that his decorative visual approach wouldn't do with *Hamlet* and that he should be more concerned with the interiority of characters and with the delicate balance of the play. He said, '*Hamlet* like Mozart's music stands on a delicate balance. If you put too much emphasis on, say, Hamlet's affection either towards his father or towards his mother, then the whole piece is distorted' (Ninagawa and Hasebe 2002: 283).

In the 1998 production at the Barbican, Sanada Hiroyuki as Hamlet impressed Sir Nigel Hawthorne, who chose him for his Fool when he starred in Ninagawa's Royal Shakespeare Company (RSC) production of *King Lear* (1999–2000). In the rehearsal, Ninagawa was intrigued by Western actors' propensity to pose incessant questions – for example, whether Lear wants to take off his shoes in conversing with Gloucester. Because Japanese actors usually try acting their ideas before discussing them, Ninagawa asked them to try them out. He said in an interview that the opening scene was tried in at least twenty different versions based on actors' ideas until it reached the final version, which turned out to be similar to his original plan (*Ninagawa and Hasebe* 2002: 310). He was ready to sacrifice all he had prepared in order to try new ideas. Uzaki Ryudo, the musician who started collaborating with him in 1984, had spent half a year to compose thirty pieces of music for the RSC *King Lear*, but a week before the RSC actors came to Japan, Ninagawa suddenly decided that he needed stronger Japanese elements in the music, and Uzaki had to compose them all afresh. This was only possible because Ninagawa had established an extraordinarily firm relationship with his collaborators.

He brought *Pericles* to the National Theatre, Olivier, in London, having been invited by its Artistic Director Trevor Nunn, just before his directorship expired in March 2003. This unrealistic and fantastical play is not easy to stage, but Nunn believed that this play, 'with its unusual picaresque structure, following the ceaseless journey of its hero from youth to age, with a storyteller to guide [. . .] has even stronger affinities with Japanese drama' (programme note). In a casual conversation with the present writer during the rehearsal period he said that the play was 'outrageous' (meaning that it is far-fetched and incoherent), but he succeeded in turning the far-fetchedness into an illusory, dream-like atmosphere that governed the whole production.

It was presented as a dream dreamt by modern people in the period of distress immediately after a war. The opening scene looked like a wrecked place after a war. The stage was spotted with taps running water, and bedraggled refugees gathered limping and shuffling to the sound of machine guns and helicopters in order to enact their fabulous story. He doubled the significance of Gower the storyteller, transforming him into an old Japanese couple playing Japanese musical instruments, performed by Shiraishi Kayoko and Ichimura Masachika. Because they emerged from the crowd of refugees, it became clear that 'Gower' was a representative of those people who aspired to dream in order to survive the hardship of the time.

Thus, the fable-like *Pericles* was presented as a dream play, and the audience was constantly reminded that it was being performed by 'Gower' and other people. For this purpose, Ninagawa emphasised the sense of role-playing. Except Uchino Masaaki in the title role, each actor played more than one role: Tanaka Yuko doubled as Thaisa and Marina, and Ichikawa played Gower, Cleon, Simonides and Lysimachus. The sense of a dream was also strengthened by Harada Tamotsu's pin-spot criss-crossing lighting, as well as by Komine Lily's costumes, so gorgeous and colourful that they 'out-Mikado the Mikado' (*The Times*, 31 March 2003). Although to the Western eye, they might look classically Japanese, the costumes in general belonged to nowhere (with sole exception of the traditional Shinto costume worn by maidens at

Diana's temple), just as the world presented had no geographical identity. They belonged to a dream.

The triumph of the production was brought about by Ninagawa's usual emphasis on metatheatricality, which he started in his early career because he wanted to shy away from the 'phoniness' of Japanese actors' impersonation of Caucasian characters, but *Pericles*, conceived as childlike fable, is itself phony enough for his metatheatrical method to fit perfectly.

Ninagawa further challenged himself and discarded all his characteristic spectacular designs in his fifth *Hamlet* (2003), in which he used a new translation by the present writer. The audiences sat on either side of a rectangular stage, which was surrounded by huge wired fences on all four sides, so that it looked like either a cage for an animal or a basketball ground in New York City. Twenty-one-year-old Fujiwara Tatsuya as Hamlet banged the fences and threw himself against them as if to try to free his soul. He was a Hamlet with an entrancing tension, stoic but bewildered, manly but fragile.

With enthralling acting from the cast, Ninagawa ventured to focus solely on the acting. After the intermission, the fences were gone, and the actors were left with literally a bare stage. The closet scene, for instance, had no stage setting at all, and the infuriated Fujiwara-as-Hamlet pushed down Takahashi Keiko as Gertrude on the floor, and Fujiwara used the full range of the stage in railing at her. Polonius' arras was supposed to exist offstage, and when Fujiwara dashed off with his sword drawn, shouting 'A rat!', Taka Takao as Polonius tumbled forward onto the stage covered with the arras. Thus, Ninagawa succeeded in materialising Peter Brook's 'empty space', and proved that his theatre did not consist merely of ornaments and spectacles. He even prohibited himself from resorting to lighting effects. After Claudius learned about the murder of Polonius and alarmedly left the stage, urging Gertrude to come with him, Ninagawa did not use blackout for the scene change but allowed the audiences to appreciate the wordless last minutes of the scene: the worn-out and distressed Gertrude slowly picked up her scattered high-heeled shoes and forlornly but graciously treaded her way out. This moment showed not only her isolation from the King but also her suffering as mother and as woman, while her queenly grace and feminine sensuality elucidated why the King and Hamlet are so obsessed with her.

In rehearsals in his later career, Ninagawa usually let the actors explore their roles freely. For instance, in rehearsing the graveyard scene, Fujiwara as Hamlet jumped into the grave and wanted to deliver his lines – 'What is the reason that you use me thus? I lov'd you ever' – to the dead Ophelia rather than to Leartes. On this point, Ninagawa valued the opinion I advanced during the rehearsal, that although the preceding 'Hear you, Sir' is obviously addressed to Leartes, one cannot deny the possibility of Hamlet's addressing

Ophelia (as suggested in the note in the first series of Arden edition of *Hamlet*). Having heard what his translator said, the director beamingly congratulated Fujiwara on discovering an unconventional way to perform the scene.

Ninagawa also directed the first Japanese-speaking Shakespearian production to be performed in the Royal Shakespeare Theatre when *Titus Andronicus*, starring Yoshida Kotaro, joined the RSC's year-long Shakespeare Complete Works festival in 2006. Just like *The Tempest* and *Hamlet*, his *Titus* had a preshow onstage preparation to give the audiences a metatheatrical framework: some of the costumes were displayed in the lobby for the audiences to see and touch, and actors in the Roman costume were warming themselves up on stage or walking in the aisles; the assistant director occasionally made an announcement of the remaining minutes, exactly as in *Hamlet* (1995, 1998), until Ninagawa's cue for a start was heard in the auditorium, when lighting instantly transformed the stage into a brightly white illusionary play-world.

In this metatheatrical production of *Titus*, Ninagawa avoided such realism as was found in Deborah Warner's 1987 *Titus*, during which, the legend goes, a number of audience members actually fainted. He rendered the horror of the play as stylised and cerebral rather than direct and emotional. As Paul Taylor put it, the play was presented as a myth: 'Everything is symbolic', and 'Red ribbons betoken the gore. Severed limbs and heads are made of translucent plastic' (*The Independent*, 25 May 2006). The stage setting was unmistakably Roman: a colossal symbolic statue of the she-wolf suckling Romulus and Remus dominated the centre of the stage.

At the same time, it was highly stylised; everything on the stage was dazzlingly white, somewhat reminiscent of Peter Brook's white-box staging of *A Midsummer Night's Dream* (25 June 2006); the representation of the blood by red threads dangling from mouth and wounds was a reminder of Brook's 1955 production of *Titus*, in which Lavinia's blood was expressed by streamers at the wrists and mouth. But, added to Brook's stylisation, Ninagawa's *Titus* had power and spectacle and was strong enough to depict the moment when too much anger and sorrow turned into compulsive laughter in Act III Scene 1. Although Brook pre-empted the laughter by cutting some 650 lines, Ninagawa remained faithful to the text, as he always is, and showed the world of Shakespeare, as he understood it, to be both risible and horrible, vulgar and lofty, subversive and conventional.

This brings us back to Ninagawa's starting point, at which he sought to popularise Shakespeare and to reveal how vulgar and subversive as well as lofty and poetic he is. It may be concluded that throughout his career Ninagawa consciously or unconsciously challenged the Western theatre and eventually came to challenge himself by abandoning his early method of *japonisme*, while always attempting to grasp the essence of Shakespeare.

Chronology

1935	Born in Saitama
1955	Joins the theatre company Seihai
1969	His directing debut in Tokyo
1974	*Romeo and Juliet* in Tokyo, his first Shakespearian production
1980	*NINAGAWA Macbeth*, premiered in Tokyo, revived at Edinburgh in 1985
1983	*Medea* at Athens (premiered in Tokyo in 1978, his first production abroad
1984	Founded 'Gekisha Ninagawa Studio' ('Ninagawa Company Dash') for young actors
1987	*The Tempest: A Rehearsal on a Noh Stage on Sado Island*, premiered in Tokyo
1993	Became a professor at Toho Gakuen College of Drama and Music
1994	*A Midsummer Night's Dream*, premiered in Tokyo
1995	*Hamlet*, starring Sanada Hiroyuki, premiered in Tokyo
1997	Appointed the Artistic Director of the Sainokuni Shakespeare Series (SSS) to produce all the plays of Shakespeare
1998	*Romeo and Juliet* in Saitama, the first of the SSS; *Twelfth Night* (SSS 2)
1999	Appointed as Artistic Director of Theatre Cocoon; *Richard III*, starring Ichimura Masachika (SSS 3)
1999–2000	*King Lear* (in English), a joint production with the RSC, starring Sir Nigel Hawthorne, premiered in Saitama (SSS 4)
2000	*A Midsummer Night's Dream* (SSS 5); *The Tempest* (SSS 6)
2001	*Macbeth*, starring Karasawa (SSS 8); the fourth *Hamlet*, starring Ichimura (SSS 11). (SSS 7, 9 and 10 are omitted because they were directed by other directors under Ninagawa's supervision)
2003	*Pericles* (SSS 12); the fifth *Hamlet*, starring Fujiwara Tatsuya, in Tokyo
2004	*Titus Andronicus* (SSS 13); *As You Like It* (SSS 14); the sixth *Hamlet* (in English), premiered at the Barbican, London
2005	*NINAGAWA Twelfth Night* (Kabuki version) in Tokyo
2006	Appointed as Artistic Director of Saitama Arts Foundation; *The Comedy of Errors* (SSS 15); *Titus Andronicus*, revived at the Royal Shakespeare Theatre
2007	*Coriolanus* (SSS 16)

Bibliography

Brokering, Jon Martin (2002) 'The Dramaturgy of Yukio Ninagawa and Tadashi Suzuki: The Fusion of Traditional Japanese Theatrical Conventions with Western Classics', unpublished Ph.D. dissertation, University of London, 2002. (Includes a detailed description of the 1998 *Hamlet*.)

Brook, Peter (1998) *Threads of Time: Recollections*, Washington, DC: Counterpoint; Methuen: London.

Horowitz, Arthur (2004) *Prospero's 'True Preservers': Peter Brook, Yukio Ninagawa, and Girogio Strehler: Twentieth-Century Directors' Approach to Shakespeare's 'The Tempest'*, Delaware: University of Delaware Press.

Im Yeeyon (2004) 'The Pitfalls of Intercultural Discourse: The Case of Yukio Ninagawa', *Shakespeare Bulletin* 22 (4): 7–30.

Kishi Tetsuo, and Graham Bradshaw (2005) *Shakespeare in Japan*, London and New York: Continuum.

Minami Ryuta, Ian Carruthers and John Gilles (eds) (2001) *Performing Shakespeare in Japan*, Cambridge: Cambridge University Press.

Ninagawa Yukio (1999) *Ninagawa Yukio: Tatakau Gekijo* (*Yukio Ninagawa: A Theatre Engaged in a Battle*), Tokyo: NHK Shuppan.

—— (2002) *Note 1969 to 2001*, Tokyo: Kawade Shobo Shinsha.

—— (1993) *Sen no Naifu, Sen no Me* (*A Thousand Knives, A Thousand Eyes*), Tokyo: Kinokuniya Shoten.

Ninagawa Yukio and Hasebe Hiroshi (2002) *Enshutsu-jutsu* (*The Art of Directing*), Tokyo: Kinokuniya Shoten.

Takahashi Yutaka (2001) *Ninagawa Yukio Densetsu* (*The Legend of Yukio Ninagawa*), Tokyo: Kawade Shobo Shinsha.

Yamaguchi Takeshi (ed.) (2001) *Ninagawa no Chosen: Igirisu Koen Kiko* (*Ninagawa's Challenge: The Record of His 'King Lear' in England*), Tokyo: Heibonsha.

Note

This account also draws on its author's personal attendance at rehearsals and conversations with Ninagawa.

About the author

Kawai Shoichiro is Associate Professor of Culture Representations at the University of Tokyo. He has received Ph.D.s from both the University of Cambridge and the University of Tokyo. Since 2002 he has chaired the Sainokuni Shakespeare Committee to support Ninagawa's project to produce all Shakespeare's plays. His translation of *Hamlet* was employed in Ninagawa's production (2003). He has co-written *Hamlet and Japan* (1995), *Japanese Studies in Shakespeare and His Contemporaries* (1998) and *Hot Questrists after the English Renaissance* (2000). He is author of *Kuninusubito*, a Kyogenised *Richard III*, premiered in Tokyo in 2007.

17
TREVOR NUNN

Martin White

Trevor Nunn has been the Artistic Director of the two leading classical theatre companies in the UK – the Royal Shakespeare Company (RSC) and the National Theatre (NT). As a freelance director, he has enjoyed considerable success in the commercial theatre, especially as the director of a series of hit musicals, and he has explored the translation of Shakespeare into the medium of film. However, the following essay focuses only on his approach to the creative practice of directing Shakespeare in the theatre.

Trevor Nunn was born in Suffolk of working-class parents and attended Northgate Grammar School in Ipswich before winning a scholarship to Downing College, Cambridge to read English. While at Cambridge, he acted and directed with the Marlowe Society, directed a *Footlights* revue, took plays and revues to the Edinburgh Festival and mixed with others who would make successful theatre careers, including many – in particular Ian McKellen – with whom he would work throughout his own career. (Nunn's experience of acting, while limited, is of relevance to his directing. He is one of a small number of directors who have also acted, though most not professionally.)

More significant for his development as a director was his contact as an undergraduate with the eminent literary critic, F.R. Leavis. Although Leavis had little interest in drama, concentrating on the novel and poetry, he instilled in students a commitment to the detailed reading and analysis of the language of texts, including an awareness of their social and historical contexts, and the place of the individual in those contexts. Speaking in 2000, Nunn recalled Leavis's influence on his approach to texts:

> Leavis thought of the theatre as a relatively frivolous place. Not that dramatists were frivolous; in his Pantheon some of the greatest works are works of the theatre. But Leavis needed to identify 'moral' purpose in a work. [. . .] the presence of some sort of irreduceable moral centre. And so his take on the great novelists and the great dramatists all

> comes down to their seriousness about society, now and in the future. I confess that I do conduct myself, and my rehearsals, according to humanist principles which lead me to uncover every possible imaginable behavioural detail that makes a writer's humanist observation more truthful and recognisable; and therefore that I also search for some 'moral' core that involves the idea of optimism.
>
> (NT *Platform Papers*)

On finishing university, Nunn, like most aspirant directors, wrote around seeking work but, like most, received the same reply – write again when you have some experience. It is, he has observed, a 'vicious circle; everyone is telling you to go get experience, but you can't unless someone gives you the chance to do it professionally' (*Academy of Achievement* interview). Then he had the stroke of luck that seems so often to kick-start a career, when one of the directors he wrote to (Anthony Richards at the Belgrade Theatre, Coventry) turned out to have formerly been an actor who Nunn, when aged 13, had met when the local theatre company in Ipswich had needed a boy actor for a couple of weeks. Richardson offered Nunn a job as his assistant director. Shortly after, Nunn was awarded a place on the Regional Theatre Young Directors' training scheme, which was run by the Independent Television Fund on behalf of the ITV companies and attached young directors to different theatres in the UK. Nunn was sponsored by ABC TV, which had a base in Birmingham, and was told he could stay on at the Belgrade. Coventry is conveniently close to Stratford-upon-Avon, and his work soon came to the notice of the Royal Shakespeare Company (RSC). Peter Hall saw Nunn's production of *The Caucasian Chalk Circle* and offered Nunn an assistant director post – which with youthful confidence he declined – before he eventually joined the RSC in 1963 as an associate director.

After a very shaky start – Sally Beauman writes that each project he was given 'turned to dust and ashes in his hands' (1982: 289) – Nunn's first success at the RSC came in 1966 with a production of a little-known Jacobean play, *The Revenger's Tragedy*. Neglected since the seventeenth century, the play had been revived, with some success, at the Pitlochry Festival a year earlier. But Nunn's production lifted the play out of obscurity, revealing it as a savage satire of sexual excess and the relentless and reckless pursuit of satisfaction of the senses that caught the mood of the time. Perhaps liberated by the fact that it was his own choice of play, he 'rehearsed it very freely, making use of games and improvisation' (Beauman 1982: 290). When it opened, it was hailed as one of the great productions of the decade, and not just by the critics: Peter Hall, after the dress rehearsal, with a mix of self-regard and generosity, told the company that it 'marked the most exciting directorial debut in the Stratford theatre since his own' (Beauman 1982: 291). Staged of necessity on the same set as Hall's production of *Hamlet, The Revenger's Tragedy* displayed a number of qualities that seem to me to remain constant features of Nunn's work: telling stage images, a vivid theatricality, an emphasis on storytelling, a simple but striking setting and a boldness in seeking contrasting but distinct and defined 'moods' (what Nunn calls 'turning on a sixpence'):

> The actors and the production team identified the problem quite early on, and we said we were going to have to be very, very bold in our attitude from the stage; that we would have to lead the audience. We would have to say 'It's alright – we really are encouraging this response, and now we are being crystal clear that we want you to change your response.'
>
> (Interview with the present writer)

It showed, too, his willingness to take on plays considered 'difficult' or uncongenial and prove them to be quite the opposite, often by treating them, in effect, as 'new', rethinking the accumulated assumptions about a play. A string of successful productions followed, and a year later Hall invited Nunn to succeed him as Artistic Director of the RSC. Nunn was 28.

For his first full season in his new role, in 1969, Nunn chose a programme of three of Shakespeare's Late Plays – *Pericles, The Winter's Tale* (directed by Nunn) and *Henry VIII* – which were complemented by two earlier plays – *Twelfth Night* and *The Merry Wives of Windsor* – and Middleton's *Women Beware Women*. The designer Christopher Morley provided a single setting that could be adapted for each play:

> It was a conscious stripping away of everything extraneous, creating a stage that was like a great empty box [. . .] lit from above by a huge cone of lights [. . .] which could irradiate the stage or be used directorially to pinpoint tiny areas of the stage or individual actors. [In] its exploration of the elements of space, sound and light it marked a seeming decisive break with the naturalistic approach which had dominated the Sixties RSC work.
>
> (Beauman 1982: 301)

Nunn's production of *The Winter's Tale* opened with a striking image (a tactic he has frequently used throughout his career). As he saw each of the late plays as linked by their focus on 'a man – a representative individual [. . .] each of the productions began with an image of the individual' (Ansorge 1970: 17). For *Henry VIII*, it was the famous Holbein portrait of the King; for

Pericles (dir. Terry Hands; des. Timothy O'Brien and Tanzeena Firth), it was a front-cloth with the image of Leonardo da Vinci's 'Vitruvian Man'. The same visual image inspired the opening of *The Winter's Tale*, but here it was a person – Leontes – standing in a tall, mirrored box in the same position as Leonardo's figure, turning slowly in strobe lighting. The figure of Time appeared later in the same box, and it held Hermione's statue at the end. In the play's first scene, set in Mamilius' nursery, a toy version of the same box turned on a clockwork motor (Kennedy 2001: 243–4). The production had a further element that prefigured Nunn's later career in the commercial theatre. In the pastoral scenes:

> Autolycus sang rock songs through a hand-held mike, accompanied by electric guitars, and the dance of the satyrs looked as if it had come from the stage of *Hair*, then playing in London [. . .] though Nunn claimed he did not see the rock musical until two or three months after *Winter's Tale* opened.
>
> (Kennedy 2001: 244)

In an interview with Peter Ansorge in *Plays and Players* the following year, Nunn looked back at the 1969 season and reflected on his own directorial approach to Shakespeare. He began by drawing a distinction between Peter Hall's work and his own. Hall's period at the RSC was characterised, for Nunn, by its politically inflected productions, whereas Nunn confessed that he was less interested in what he described as the Jan Kott-influenced 'images of ladders leading to power' than in 'the human personalities of a king or queen'. To illustrate his point Nunn drew comparisons between his own *Hamlet* – then running in the Royal Shakespeare Theatre (RST) – and Hall's 1965 production, focusing on the last scene:

> In the last scene Peter had built a structure around Fortinbras' returning army: it was a political moment, while Hamlet was dying it was necessary that he made a political decision – he had to make some conclusion to the dynastic struggle, about who was going to take over. [. . .] In my production the stage is very bare, there is hardly anyone watching Hamlet die. [. . .] I'm much more interested in a very private family affair, and in the working out of Hamlet's final confrontation with Claudius and Horatio.
>
> (Ansorge 1970: 16)

He went on to outline that his desire in his first season had been to 'find a way of designing Shakespeare which enables an audience to react to a play at all the basic levels, of storytelling and action, and yet which should be able to crystallise appearances so that what people represent is at least part of what they look like' (Ansorge 1970: 17). The 'chamber' setting, while retaining the symbolic divisions of Heaven, Earth and Hell found in the Elizabethan playhouse could, by 'stripping away more and more scenic effect and working on placing a particular human situation with the right bit of furniture', establish: 'that the most important object on the stage is the actor. [The setting] has to work within the scale of the individual actor – to make his words, thoughts, fantasies and language seem important. [. . .] The middle and far distances are not important' (Ansorge 1970: 17).

With Morley once again as his designer, Nunn clearly hoped to take these aspects of his approach to staging and setting further with *Hamlet*. But this time the results were less successful. Nunn's emblematic use of colours – the setting and costumes were all white, except for Hamlet and, later, Ophelia, who he saw as 'prickly outsiders' in black – led some observers, he confessed, to see an overly schematic simplification in the patterns, 'a kind of chess board imagery' (Ansorge 1970: 17), and the design overall, partly due to the less-than-simple machinery used to open and close shutters at the rear of the stage, did not focus the attention on the actors and their words but proved distracting. The production was coolly received, as indeed were other plays in the season until, finally, Peter Brook ignited audiences with his production of *A Midsummer Night's Dream*. So far as Nunn was concerned, however, a little-publicised event at the end of the 1970 season had an equally significant impact. His *Hamlet* was performed without scenery or costumes at the Downstairs Studio at the Roundhouse in London, where it emerged as a startlingly different production. 'It was', Nunn recalled some years later, 'the experience that gave me the greatest pleasure of the whole year, forgetting about design and presentation altogether. The *Hamlet* was free; it was thrilling' (quoted in Beauman 1982: 308). Nunn's eyes had been opened to a way of staging Shakespeare that would, in time, produce arguably his finest work.

Peter Hall had introduced small-scale work to the RSC through short seasons at the Arts Theatre, Brook's Theatre of Cruelty season at the Donmar and through the touring programme undertaken by Theatregoround (designed to take the company's work to different communities, a policy Nunn continued to support vigorously when he took over). In 1971 (and again in 1973) Nunn ran a studio season at The Place (home of the London Contemporary Dance Company), but he wanted to put 'chamber' productions of Shakespeare at the core of the RSC, and for that he needed an appropriate performance space in Stratford. In 1974, he opened The Other Place (TOP). As well as being a phrase from *Hamlet* – 'If your messenger find him not there, seek him i'th'other place yourself' (Act IV, Scene 3, lines 33–5) – the name was chosen to underline TOP's role as an alternative to the RST. It was created in a former rehearsal room, basically a corrugated iron shed, about 200 metres along the riverbank from the RST. Writing in 1989, Stanley Wells described it:

> Seats are uncomfortable, there is no air conditioning; it's best not to go on Tuesday because that's when the nearby church has its bell-ringing practice, seats are unreserved, and [. . .] many find their view of the playing area obscured by poles and railings, especially in the balcony.
> (Wells 1991: 191)

More importantly, however, as Wells notes, it provided opportunities for 'a rare intimacy of communication and directness of emotional impact' (1991: 191) – exactly the qualities Nunn had been striving for on the main stage. Indeed, it was the 'limitations' of TOP that proved the greatest stimulus to the imaginations of both performers and audiences. Here, there was not only no opportunity but also no need for visually elaborate settings to fill the stage space. Here, actors genuinely had Shakespeare's words as the prime force with which to stimulate the audience, and the smaller space inevitably had an impact on the delivery of those words.

Nunn invited Buzz Goodbody to run TOP with Jean Moore (less heralded than Goodbody but also key to the venue's success) as its administrator. It was an innovative move on Nunn's part. Although not the first woman to direct at the RSC, as is often claimed, Goodbody was the first to become part of the directorial team. In 1975, she opened TOP's season with her own production of *Hamlet*. Staged simply, in modern dress on a white set, and with the actors taking advantage of the space to achieve an intimate, yet intense, vocal delivery, it was critically acclaimed and must have had a particular effect on Nunn after his dissatisfaction with his own production and then his experience at the Roundhouse. Four days after the production opened for previews, Goodbody took her own life. Nunn returned from Los Angeles where the RSC was on tour and took over the rest of the season.

The following year, 1976, Nunn directed his first production in TOP – *Macbeth* – which rapidly acquired the status of a landmark in the recent history of Shakespearian production to set alongside Brook's *A Midsummer Night's Dream*, though, the success of the production came as a surprise, partly because it grew out of comparative failure. Nunn had directed the play only two years earlier in the main house at Stratford, with Nicol Williamson in the title role and Helen Mirren as Lady Macbeth, and it is instructive to compare the earlier and later productions. The setting for the RST, by John Napier, was a black and silver church interior. The opening – an interpolated coronation of King Duncan – illustrated the production's stress on ritual. Suddenly, white curtains were drawn sharply across the stage, becoming a screen on which shadow-like figures were projected, enacting the conflict threatening Duncan's kingdom. Equally suddenly, a horned, devil-like figure opened the curtains to reveal the three witches, suspended from a chandelier. Although there was some praise for Williamson's portrayal of Macbeth's despair (*Observer*) and for Mirren's 'intelligent and irresistible sexuality' (*Sunday Times*), generally the production pleased neither critics nor audiences, nor the director. Nunn transferred it to the Aldwych (the RSC's London home), but despite a number of significant adjustments – he cut the appearance of Banquo's ghost and the apparitions and restored the scene of the death of Lady Macduff (a bewildering omission in the first place) – he remained unhappy.

Now, with a production budget reputedly of only £250 (or £200 in Ian McKellen's recollection), Nunn had the opportunity to explore for himself the virtues of TOP. He cast two main house stars – Ian McKellen and Judi Dench – in the leading roles, and his conceptual take on the play remained virtually unaltered, but, as Dennis Kennedy observes, 'only when completely reworked in the small space did the implications of the interpretation, based on the simplest contrast between good and evil, achieve full strength' (2001: 253). Scenery and lighting were kept to a minimum. A circle of black paint on the wooden-boarded playing area defined the stage, with actors seated on upturned crates outside it, close to the audience, sometimes watching the action. These moments always made a specific point – the witches observed Macbeth damn himself, and Macduff looked on as his family were murdered: 'The sense of peering in at a corrupting spectacle was thus strengthened by a double spectatorship, and became central to the emotional quality of the production' (Kennedy 2001: 254). The circle was carried through into the physical performances: a twirling movement by the actors 'became a feature of the playing and was sometimes continued until the actor's body had passed through 360 degrees in a complete pirouette' (David 1981: 87), while keen-eyed spectators might register that Macbeth moved in an anti-clockwise movement round the circle in contrast to the clockwise direction of the 'virtuous' characters, a pattern suggestive of the traditional association of 'widdershins' with satanic forces. The rear wall of the stage was formed by two upright rectangles of wood, with a narrow gap between them for an entrance. A thunder-sheet hung stage right, and on a table stage left, in full view, were placed the few props used in the play. The proximity of the spectators meant that the performers, in modern dress (though, echoing his *Hamlet*, coloured black and white to signal evil or good), barely needed to project their voices and could speak quickly and 'naturally'. Nunn cut the text down to two and a quarter hours and played it without an interval, though some critics complained (as they often do of his work) that silent, often interpolated, action off the line only served to slow the performance.

Macbeth, like *A Midsummer Night's Dream*, presents a modern director with the fundamental problem of how to create a world in which the supernatural forces and events that drive the action of the play achieve a reality. In this respect, Nunn discovered (as Brook had done six years earlier with *A Midsummer Night's Dream*) that less is definitely more. With no scope for visual spectacle in this austere space, Nunn cut the entrance of Banquo's ghost (which the Folio stage direction, 'Enter the Ghost of Banquo', suggests was staged in the earliest performances) leaving it to Ian McKellen to conjure its reality for the character alone, which he did by staring fixedly on the empty crate. At the play's opening, the witches, two old, one younger, dressed in tatty fur, entered to solemn church organ music, before crouching on stage. Macbeth and Banquo entered and twirled round as they saw them, Macbeth drawing the two daggers that recurred as an image in the play (see below). The witches brought forth no apparitions but, as Macbeth entered, they stripped off his shirt and, with sooty fingers, inscribed 'magic' symbols on his skin, before holding up rag dolls to illustrate their prophecies, which dolls Macbeth then kept clutched in his hand until each was fulfilled.

Battles, too, are frequently problematic on stage. As Shakespeare suggests, too few fighters can reduce the greatest of conflicts to a 'brawl ridiculous' (*Henry V*, Prologue, Act IV, 51), and the reduction in the number of fights in plays written for Jacobean indoor playhouses may reflect contemporary experience of the even greater constraints of a small stage. Nunn solved the problem by letting the audience hear, but not see, the offstage army, while Macbeth desperately piled up the wooden crates as a defensive wall. With the audience within touching distance, Nunn omitted Macbeth's severed head (often, in my experience, a pretty sure-fire source of unwelcome audience laughter). Instead, Macduff, pursued by Macbeth through the narrow gap in the back wall, returned with two bloodied daggers in his hand, an image that – with its echoes of Macbeth confronting the witches, and after the murder of Duncan – forcefully underlined the turn of Fortune's wheel. On the other hand, in the scene of the murder of Lady Macduff and her son, a more traditional realism was sought, with a trick knife being used that enabled the murderer to cut the Lady's throat with the blood appearing to flow from the wound.

McKellen and Dench were widely praised. At the start, Lady Macbeth exerted a powerful sexual hold over Macbeth, using it to drive him to the murder but, rejected by her husband once he had come to power, she is 'Pitched into black desolation, bereft and excoriated. Her mind teeters in knife-edge balance' (*Stratford-upon-Avon Herald*). As he would years later as Iago (see below), McKellen took every advantage of the intimate space vocally and in the detail of his performance. In the *Daily Telegraph*, John Barber traced how the character's decline was physicalised as, at the start of the play, 'in thick darkness', Macbeth:

> prowls with tigerish vitality. After the murder, the daggers rattle in his hands. After the coronation, he exchanges a hideous corkscrew smile with his wife. [. . .] By the end, the evil within has made him a hollow man: empty, weary, flaccid, all hope gone.

That these clear physical expressions of states of mind were the means by which the growing separation between husband and wife were given theatrical form. As Kenneth Rae (1989: 69) has observed, while Nunn's intellectual and interpretative powers are commonly admired, his ability to draw a text and its physical, bodily expression together is less often noted.

For Richard David, however, the strength of the production lay in the overall concept rather than in the performances of the central characters. For him, Judi Dench was too dominant in the opening scenes, making Macbeth 'seem "more pale and green" than is proper, but then 'collapsed' too early, effectively phasing herself out of the play at the end of Act II, and leaving Macbeth to sustain his decline unaided. He found McKellen's Macbeth 'thrilling and unstereotyped', with the actor's apparent reading of the character 'more matter-of-fact' than he expected, giving the character great strength. But, making a comparison with Laurence Olivier in the role, he found too that McKellen 'stifled some of the overtones, the harmonics' of the role (David 1981: 92–4).

In the 1976 season, Nunn also directed *Romeo and Juliet* on the Royal Shakespeare Theatre (RST) main stage which, generally speaking, has not been found by directors or actors to be a congenial space in which to stage or perform Shakespeare. Ronald Eyre's description of it as 'that curious, deformed barn [where] I always have the feeling of a headland on a windy day: bracing, but you've got to shout' (Cook 1974: 47) may be extreme, but its sentiments are not untypical. As Kennedy points out, 'Every artistic director since Bridges-Adams has spent inordinate time and money attempting to lessen the rigidity of the proscenium in what remains – despite architectural and scenic alterations – an adamantly proscenium house' (2001: 250). Nunn himself had made significant alterations to the stage in 1972, when he directed all four of Shakespeare's 'Roman' plays himself (assisted by two junior directors, Buzz Goodbody and Euan Smith, as his senior colleagues declined to be involved). A permanent setting was to be used, but hydraulic machinery was installed to allow the stage to form a variety of shapes and rakes, though Nunn used it less and less with each production, and not at all in the last.

In 1976, as it had been in 1972, the stage in the main house was constructed as a permanent set to be used for all productions that year. Designed by John Napier and Chris Dyer, it was built of timber, with balconies at the rear of the stage in which audiences could sit, and with others cutting across the proscenium line. It looked to all intents and purposes like a replica of an Elizabethan outdoor playhouse set down in the RST, and despite Nunn's protestations that it was not so, many considered it to be 'quite obviously based on Elizabethan models' (Warren 1977: 169). Its purpose, however, was to transport the chamber intimacy, and all its benefits, onto the main stage. The difference between large and smaller spaces can be illustrated by comparison of McKellen's performances that season as Macbeth and Romeo. Whereas in TOP the actor had been able to give an intense and focused performance, physically and vocally, in the RST he seemed excessive in his physical and vocal performance, except in his final speech, which many found moving – partly in its contrast to his earlier performance.

In the late 1970s and early 1980s, Nunn directed two productions – one of a Chekhov play, the other an adaptation of a Dickens novel – which in different ways, and drawing on his experience of small spaces and his skill in handling large ones, made a significant impact on his work on Shakespeare. In 1979, as part of his determined effort to take the RSC's work out to communities, Nunn directed a small-scale touring production of *Three Sisters*. In an interview in 1997, he recalled his approach to the play: 'I thought of it as a *poetic* play, as a play of heightened language and poetic ideas. In a sense I started to think of it in Shakespearian terms [with] an uncluttered environment, the specificity and detail of which could be created through language' (Gottlieb and Allain 2000: 103).

Physical gesture, too, he declared, should be precise and imaginative. Citing the example of how a large number seated at a table for lunch 'could be made by a group of actors using only chairs, forks and napkins', he stressed how it was 'vital that everything be *suggested* and that the demands should be made on the spectators' collective imagination', while the actors 'should be able to crystallise minute behavioural details at this lunch party, so *everything* of their characters' physical lives could be selected to provide a recognisable and convincing clarity' (Gottlieb and Allain 2000: 104). The discipline of removing 'everything of the traditional staging tools' (of a naturalistic play) resulted in 'more poetic and integral answers' to staging issues. The bare white stage provided by designer John Napier (reminiscent of Nunn's 1969–70 work), 'enabled an audience to really see in clear images, [. . .] to see the smallest details of behaviour' and required 'unusual economy from the actors and a strict discipline' (Gottlieb and Allain 2000: 107). Similarly, the settings demanded the selection of precise artefacts: just one chair, for example, to indicate the interior of a house: 'one very large, very male, leather armchair . . . "father's chair" ' (Gottlieb and Allain 2000: 105):

> Because it was the only furniture in the room and because the sisters knew its significance, its presence had nothing to do with answering the usual naturalistic question: 'how is the room furnished?' Rather, it had the identity of another character, a permanent reminder of loss, of change, an anchor that restrained the sisters and which they could not drag in any direction.
>
> (Gottlieb and Allain 2000: 105–6)

At the same time as he was directing *Three Sisters*, and with the RSC facing severe financial cutbacks, Nunn (with his collaborator John Caird) was planning a production of Charles Dickens's novel *Nicholas Nickelby*, the seeds of which idea had been planted in Nunn's mind during a visit to the Soviet Union, where it was common to adapt Dickens for the stage. *The Life and Times of Nicholas Nickelby*, adaptated by David Edgar, opened at the Aldwych Theatre (the RSC's London home) in 1980. The production gave full rein to Nunn's consummate ability to drive a narrative line on stage, but, equally, to identify and pursue the stories of individual characters and present the detail of individual personalities and emotions in the midst of a teeming and swirling humanity. Equally strikingly – as with the lunch party in *Three Sisters* – he created places and objects through his, the actors' and the audience's shared imaginations:

> Trevor had argued early on in the project that it must be done by an imaginative device of some kind, relying on the actors and the materials around them on stage. He was against the use of any additional complex machinery. [The company] began to build up a pile of skips and suitcases on top of tables and other objects capable of supporting heavy weights. Refined by Trevor, it had indeed become a stagecoach. [. . .] Stylistically, the rehearsal was an important achievement as it proved how collective imaginations could achieve startling effects. [. . .] Invention was our greatest ally.
>
> (Rubin 1981: 150–1)

In June 1982, the RSC left the Aldwych Theatre and moved to a new permanent London home in the Barbican Arts Centre. Robert Cushman described the recently opened centre as combining the 'attractions of airport and subway station' (*Observer*), and it became a tiresomely repetitive 'joke' for critics to comment on the difficulties posed by the centre's labyrinthine interior. However, there was virtually unanimous praise for the auditorium itself. Nunn, alert to the tension between the theatre and its location, described it as 'a jewel – set in a concrete sea', though many actors were less complimentary about the backstage facilities, where dressing rooms, for example, had no windows. Nunn inaugurated the RSC's tenure with a production of *Henry IV* (seen in Stratford the previous year), with Parts I and II played together, which in its overall style (and length – it ran to almost seven hours) strongly echoed *Nicholas Nickelby*. A year later (while the stage of the RST was once more remodelled for the season, this time with a thrust stage projecting deep into the stalls), Nunn transferred his acclaimed production of *All's Well that Ends Well* from Stratford. If Dickens was his inspiration for *Henry IV*, here, 'Proust [. . .] was its tutelary novelist' (Shrimpton 1983: 149). The play was set in the early years of the twentieth century, with the Florentine wars becoming a version of the First World War. Harriet Walter, (who played Helena) observes:

> Forget the quibble that there would have been no king of France in those days; in every other aspect the play gained more than it lost. In a conventional doublet-and-hose version, it would be easy to miss the fact that this 'problem' play actually comes down on the side of class mobility, of merit as opposed to heredity, and of female emancipation. By associating the play visually with the worlds of Ibsen and Shaw, these modern themes were brought out.
>
> (Walter 2003: 206)

Praise for the actors' performances was unanimous, especially Walter ('playing the part as if she were one of the *Three Sisters*', *Daily Express*), Stephen Moore as Parolles, arriving in Florence, equipped for the war with his golf clubs ('the Parolles against which all others in our lifetime will have to be measured', *Punch*) and, above all, Peggy Ashcroft's 'extraordinarily lyrical' (*Punch*) Countess, 'her hands flickering with the nervous precision of pointers on a dial [. . .] This, one felt, was a woman who had suffered and remembered the sensation' (Shrimpton 1983: 150). Performances of such physical detail (Helena, for example, reaching out to stroke the absent Bertram's cigarette box on the line, 'my idolatrous fancy must sanctify his relics') and vocal delicacy are clearly more easily achieved in the smaller spaces of which Nunn had become increasingly enamoured. Indeed, Harriet Walter recalls that, when casting, Nunn was especially concerned about the level of detail his chosen setting would require:

> Trevor Nunn, who had seen my Ophelia [at the Royal Court] was sizing me up for the part of Helena in *All's Well that Ends Well*. He had appreciated the detail of my performance but, as he put it, could I preserve that detail *and* reach the back of the auditorium? [. . .] Luckily for me, Trevor took the risk and over the next decade I joined in the effort to combine intimacy with projection, heightened language with naturalistic speech and verbal dexterity with physical strength that has preoccupied the RSC since it first began.
>
> (Walter 2003: 152)

Nunn's query related to Stratford where the production was to open, and Walter analyses how the 'big stage' of the RST required her to devise a way of turning three-quarters so she could share her lines with her fellow actors and audience, while the 'acoustics [. . .] demanded a sort of hiccup of delay around each line to give it time to register with the audience' (Walter 2003: 212). Crucially for Nunn's production, the new Barbican theatre, while still expansive enough to accommodate the epic quality of the RST (seen in *Henry IV*) was, with no seat more than 65 feet from the stage, also able to capture a greater level of intimacy. To underline the class tensions that drive the action, Nunn (further shades of *Nicholas Nickelby* here), in a series of deft directorial touches, enveloped the meticulously plotted journeys of the individual main characters in a fully realised social world: Helena nervously fidgeted with the *chatelaine* at her waist that signified her subservient position in the Countess's house; a cluster of maids busied themselves, tidying the stage between scenes and crowded excitedly onto the stage to greet Helena on her return from Paris; a pair of leather-helmeted aviators bearing despatches to the King 'brought an intoxicating whiff of the great world outside' (Shrimpton 1983: 150) to the gymnasium; Cheryl Campbell's Diana was conceived as an exuberant popular *chanteuse* at the centre of a crowded bistro, while the musicians that accompanied her and provided music elsewhere also had a life of their own as the military band that celebrated the Florentine victory. A key part of Nunn's famed ability to tell a story on stage is his desire to tell as many stories as he can, and nowhere is that exemplified more than in this production.

John Gunter, the designer, created a permanent structure resembling an elegant, steel-framed conservatory, with a silvery limestone-flagged floor that could easily change in mood to represent the play's wide variety of locations: from the home of the Countess of Rossillion, where the play opens, a provincial French chateau – with 'grey shutters and potted orange trees' and an air of being 'contentedly remote' (Shrimpton 1983: 149) – to, in turn, a gymnasium, an officers' mess, a ballroom, a railway station, a field hospital and a crowded soldiers' *estaminet*. The settings were more than picturesque: the sleepy, female-dominated atmosphere of Rossillion, for example, helped make clear Bertram's desire to escape to the testosterone-driven world of the gymnasium, filled with bright young men vaulting and fencing. Indeed, the play's sudden return to the tedium of Rossillion in Act I, Scene 3 made his frustration even plainer.

All's Well that Ends Well conveys an understanding of the 'inaudible and noiseless foot of time' (Act V, Scene 3, line 41), a collision between the old and the new, expressed through a daring blend of comedy (often close to farce) and tragedy. From his early production of *The Revenger's Tragedy*, Nunn had shown his brilliance at sustaining disparate, often colliding moods on stage, and it is unsurprising (especially coming so soon after his *Three Sisters* which he'd treated as Shakespearian) that many who saw *All's Well that Ends Well* shared the view that Nunn had now approached Shakespeare's play 'as if it were a typical Chekhovian exercise in the bittersweet, perplexing dance of life' (Evans 1982: 188). Indeed, dances figure strongly in *All's Well that Ends Well*, and Nunn interpolated yet more and used them as a recurrent motif to cohere the production. The performance opened with the image of a couple, silhouetted in moonlight, waltzing, an image of harmony and unity, ideas that are severely tested in the play. The King's recovery was signified by his dance with Helena (though it was a courtly dance and not the spirited 'coranto' indicated in the text, which presumably gave Nunn his idea), while the moment that follows when Helena is allowed to choose a husband from the young lords was staged as a game of musical chairs, abruptly concluded by Bertram's refusal to accept her. Finally – with Nunn challenging the text's apparent 'happy ending' – Helena and Bertram, in fading light, and in a tableau that echoed the opening, circled each other, fingers barely touching, an ambiguous image of tentative curiosity and resonant of an uncertain future for them both.

Nunn's characteristically forensic exploration of the text (fewer than 100 lines were cut), took 'a play often inconsistent and tedious on the page and magically transform[ed] it into something wholly consistent and compelling in performance' (*Sunday Telegraph*). But he never lost sight of the play's ambivalence – such as its suggestion that noble ends might justify dubious means and its portrayal of characters which are a complex mix of attractive and less likeable qualities. It remains, for me, perhaps Nunn's greatest achievement in main-stage Shakespeare, combining 'sympathetic intelligence and emotional daring' and bringing, fully formed, the qualities of performance he had discovered in small-scale work – in both classic and modern plays – onto the large stage.

In 1986, Nunn realised a long-held dream: to create in Stratford a playhouse that could hold a large enough audience to make staging less well known plays economically feasible, without losing the performance qualities of a small theatre. The result was the Swan Theatre, widely regarded as a near-perfect performance space for early modern plays. Following the launch of the Swan Theatre (inaugurated with Nunn's production of Heywood's *The Fair Maid of the West* – two parts conflated into one and staged in Nunn's post-*Nickelby* style), Nunn left the RSC to pursue a freelance career that included the musicals *Chess* (1986) and, in 1989, *Aspects of Love* and *The Baker's Wife* (one of his few box-office failures). In 1989, he returned to the RSC to close the original The Other Place, prior to refurbishment, with a production of *Othello*, his first Shakespeare production for seven years.

Nunn kept the play's geographical location in Venice and Cyprus but moved the action to the late nineteenth century. Within that loose time frame, observers identified different specific periods. To some, the costumes suggested Austro-Hungary or the Crimea, Strindberg's Sweden to others (though the latter interpretation might have been influenced by the characterisation, especially of Ian McKellen's psychotic Iago). Nunn is often prepared to take risks in casting central roles if in so doing he can open up some new angle on a play. (Later, for example, his decision to cast the 23-year old tyro Ben Whishaw as Hamlet at the Old Vic in 2004 resulted in a youth-oriented modern-dress production that struck a contemporary note that recalled Hall's with David Warner forty years earlier.) As Othello, he cast the black Jamaican-born opera singer, Willard White, who had played Porgy in Nunn's production of Gershwin's *Porgy and Bess* at Glyndebourne in 1986 and now became the first black actor to play Othello at Stratford since Paul Robeson thirty years earlier. White had no experience of playing Shakespeare, a fact that (as a number of reviewers noted) helped emphasise his 'difference' from those around him:

> There was something identifiably careful about [White's] speaking of the verse, a slight sense of awe towards the language that distanced him a little from it, while the rest of the cast, experienced Shakespearean professionals all, part of the RSC club, were taking it in their stride. In a curious, almost disturbing way, this seemed to fit the role rather aptly.
>
> (Smallwood 1990: 113)

It was presumably White's presence that influenced Nunn's decision to make Cyprus also suggestive of the Deep South during the American Civil War of the 1860s, a transposition 'as carefully and as unpretentiously worked' as had been his *All's Well that Ends Well* Crimean setting, and one reinforced with 'plangent music' played on cornet (for the military) and harmonium (for domestic) scenes (Wells 1991: 191). Unlike his TOP production of *Macbeth*, however, in which Nunn cut and reshaped the text, *Othello* was played virtually uncut, resulting in a running time of nearly four hours, prompting Stanley Wells wryly to observe that if the plays were originally performed in complete versions, their audiences must have been 'some of the most intelligent, thoughtful, attentive, imaginative, and intellectually receptive' ever.

The stage design (by Bob Crowley) was simple. The audience was placed on three sides with, at the rear of the small stage space, a central opening and, above it, a slatted wall (resembling Venetian blinds) through which characters could observe the action on stage, such as when Othello spied on Cassio and Desdemona in Act IV, Scene 1. Specific locations were defined by bringing simple but striking items on stage: for the council chamber of the play's second scene, for example, the wood-planked stage was covered with richly patterned Persian carpets, with a baize-topped table around which the Duke's senators conferred over their brandy and cigars, a large telescope on a tripod defined the quayside in Cyprus, and camp beds suggested the soldiers' quarters. The sound and lighting design reinforced location and mood: a crashing storm with strobe lighting took us to Cyprus, where cicadas hummed in the background and bugles punctuated the calm and the wind outside Desdemona's bedroom in the 'willow song' scene.

In all aspects, the production demonstrated the microscopic attention to detail that critics had identified as a hallmark of Nunn's work, on large and small stages, but which particularly suited the intimate nature of TOP. As usual, his close attention to the text revealed new insights – that the play, for example, contains one small tragedy in its opening act, as Brabantio loses his daughter. Detail in gesture enhanced characterisation (such as Iago's obsessive neatness and his tactile behaviour to all except Othello, whom he never touched), while repeated or mirrored actions (such as Othello lifting Desdemona proudly onto a trunk on the Cyprus quayside and later lifting her onto a stool to accuse her of being a whore) enriched the narrative. Although there is no evidence that when Shakespeare wrote the play (probably 1603–4) the King's Men's ambition to regain the use of their indoor playhouse in Blackfriars would be realised, *Othello* has to many critics and audiences seemed essentially a domestic tragedy, its interior settings matching its focus on the mind games of the play. Many who saw Nunn's production in Stratford (and at the Young Vic in London, to where it later transferred), were struck by the impact of the chamber setting, in which the domestic detail in setting and performances felt at ease, while the growing passion and despair of the play's climax was intensified by its constraint within the small performance space.

Two scenes provide good examples of Nunn's mature 'naturalistic' directorial strategies with Shakespeare. The 'drinking scene' (Act II, Scene 3) was set indoors, with two camp beds with grey army blankets, and two portable wash basins (on tripods, such as are used in camping). Iago filled these basins with wine, and in Cassio's brief absence (45–59) he chatted to the audience, added brandy to the mix, tasting it with his finger, like a cook, before putting in more of the spirit. The scene got livelier as the drink flowed, with one of the company having his trousers pulled off. As the others converged on Cassio, clearly intending he should suffer the same indignity, he swayingly asserted his authority (106–16) and, equally shakily, his sobriety. Into the brawl between Cassio and Roderigo, strode Othello – bare-chested, not in uniform – but the men sprang instantly to attention and the evening broke up. Left alone with Iago, Cassio promptly vomited into one of the basins (prompting Iago's 'What, are you hurt, lieutenant', 258), before being helped to a bed and tucked in by Iago, 'with an excess of oily concern' (*Spectator*, 2 September 1989). The text has an exit for Cassio at line 835, but Nunn kept him onstage, asleep, with Iago remaining seated on the bed beside him to speak his soliloquy ('And what's he then, that says I play the villain?'). McKellen, as he did throughout the production, took full advantage of having the audience so close to engage, even implicate, them in his thinking. But Nunn added another telling detail. As Cassio slept, he rolled over and threw out his arm. Iago clearly noted the action, so that later, when Iago describes to Othello Cassio's passionate actions when they shared a bed (Act III, Scene 3, lines 410–23), the audience might recognise that his lie sprang from the distortion of a half-truth, completely in line with Iago's strategies of deception throughout the play.

The 'temptation scene' (Act III, Scene 3) showed Nunn developing the narrative detail of a scene. A table and canvas chairs were set at the rear of the stage with, to the front, a small table and Desdemona and Emilia seated on two outdoor chairs, mixing a jug of lemonade, strained through a small wooden sieve. As Othello entered, Desdemona brought him a glass of lemonade and, while she cajoled him to forgive Cassio, sat on Othello's knee. She had evidently forgotten to sweeten his drink, and Othello grimaced at the sourness but did not complain. Left alone, and to the sound of cicadas in the background, the two men dealt with their papers, and Iago began his subtle insinuations. Entering to tell Othello that the guests had arrived and that dinner was served, Desdemona put a watch on the table, pointedly to remind him of the time and, while offering to mop his brow, dropped her handkerchief. She exited with Othello and almost immediately returned, alone. She was clearly anxious about something she'd forgotten and equally clearly relieved at finding it – the watch – while the handkerchief remained, forgotten, lying on the floor of the stage as the lights came up to signal the interval.

The extensive interpolated business with the lemonade (there's no hint of any of this in the text) seems designed to suggest that Othello, at this point in the play, will accept anything, however bitter, that comes from Desdemona and so was clearly intended to prefigure the section of the scene that immediately follows. But is it more than a superfluous directorial intervention? In the *Independent*, Adam Mars-Jones wondered whether such a physical anticipation of the subsequent action is necessary – he commented that the audience could see the swirling pips as the forgotten sugar was stirred in, and even 'catch the strong whiff of citrus' – while Stanley Wells observed that the production was so rooted in naturalism that a fully written account of it 'would read like a Victorian novel' (*Shakespeare Survey*, 1991: 192). But having decided to give the play a nineteenth-century setting, it was entirely appropriate for the production to be bound together by the naturalistic – and illuminating – detail of its action and acting. Indeed, as Nunn seems to have decided that the play's action turns on apparently trivial moments, which, misunderstood, or distorted in the telling, result in catastrophe – a major task for the director is to ensure that these events are located within a detailed, physical world. And in his creation of such a world lay the production's strength.

In 1997, Nunn was appointed Artistic Director of the National Theatre, a post he held until 2003, during which time the theatre staged seven Shakespeare plays, three directed by Nunn himself. These included a richly detailed and widely acclaimed *The Merchant of Venice*, staged on a traverse in the Cottesloe, a space attractive to Nunn for offering 'a particular intimacy which leads to both a sense of immediacy and danger, and a tangible expectation, to be discovered in performer and audience alike' (Mulryne and Shewring 1999: 47). The choice again showed his characteristic liking for plays often considered problematic (as with *All's Well that Ends Well* or Othello) or even, in the case of *The Merchant of Venice*, distasteful. Indeed, Nunn chose to direct the play in response to the critic David Nathan who had reached the conclusion that in the shadow of the Holocaust, *The Merchant of Venice* should not continue to be produced. Nathan's views resonated to a degree with Nunn's own, but equally (and we might recall the influence of Leavis here) Nunn queried how 'it could be that such a humanist [as Shakespeare] could have written an unsavoury and possibly racist tract' (*Masterpiece Theatre* interview). To test Nathan's proposition, Nunn set his production between the two world wars and a climate of anti-Semitism. Hildegard Bechtler's design placed Belmont at one end of the traverse stage, Shylock's house at the other, a visual emblem of the collision between the hedonism of the Christians and the Hebraic faith, a world of a 'genuine clash of wills, value-systems and revenge-motifs' (*Guardian*). Nunn's production was suffused with a characteristic 'novelistic attention to detail' (*Daily Mail*), that conjured up a picture of social and personal behaviour, with 'imaginative byplay for the lesser characters, fleshing out relationships between them that contribute directly to the portrait of a city, a community, a class' (*The Times*). No aspect of the play was ducked, with Nunn allowing his production (unlike many others) to follow the play's contradictions and complexities, including allowing the serious and comic aspects of the play equal force. Beyond the praise for the performances (especially Henry Goodman's Shylock), one or two brief examples must serve to illustrate the production's quality, the 'dozens of moments that offer [the audience] new perspectives and alignments' (*Independent on Sunday*) on the play: Portia's genuine attraction to the Prince of Morocco; Shylock's fellow Jew, Tubal, leaving the court in dismay as the pound of flesh is demanded; Shylock's painful relationship with his daughter and the 'sudden glimpse of the life of a lonely, desperately over-protective and culturally besieged widower' (*Independent*); the breathtaking moment in the trial, with Portia until the very last moment without any idea of how to save Antonio.

Nunn describes his attitude to a text as one of 'loyalty' (as opposed to fidelity, I assume), but argues that it is at times necessary to remove, telescope, transpose or even add text, taken from other plays or, on occasions, written by himself (Berry 1977: 72–3). The final moments of *The Merchant of Venice* saw him creating a new ending for Shakespeare's play:

> Shakespeare's Folio text ends sort of strangely with some rather crude insensitive jokes from Gratiano. Those lines are often cut. I didn't want to do that, since his insensitivity is an important part of what we're talking about. But there are some earlier lines from Portia where she talks about the strange, unsettled dawn that is arriving. [. . .] I transposed those lines to the very end. Then, as a kind of rumbling, distant thunder becomes apparent, and people slightly shiver with the cold of dawn, Portia says, 'It is almost morning,' which is indeed part of that dawn speech. But that became the last line of the play.
>
> (*Masterpiece Theatre* interview)

For some critics, the final tableau, with Jessica alone, singing once more the melancholy Hebrew song that she had sung earlier with her father, was a sentimental moment, at odds with Nunn's uncompromising reading of the play, while for others it underlined the future isolation of Jessica and, by extensions, others of her faith.

Soon after Trevor Nunn took over as Artistic Director of the RSC, Gareth Lloyd Evans had argued that at the RSC 'experience' was 'being overmounted by "interpretation" '. He characterised Nunn and the directors with whom he had surrounded himself (John Barton, Terry Hands, David Jones) as 'representatives of the "academic" spirit which, both for much good and some ill, has penetrated Shakespearian production': '[The directors] "know" their texts, even if they do not always use all of them. They are meticulous in historical detail – when they decide to be. You can now say [. . .] that Shakespearian production is in the hands of the most knowledgeable directors of all time' (*Shakespeare Survey*, 1970: 132).

Lloyd Evans wrote his essay at the start of Nunn's career, but it rehearses a not uncommon view of the way directors (especially those, the thinking goes, of an 'academic spirit') impose their ideas upon a text. Nunn has acknowledged how 'analysis and having a sense of literature' (*Academy of Achievement* interview) play a key role in his directing. In 2007, nearly forty years after Evans wrote his critique, Trevor Nunn returned to Stratford to direct (interestingly enough) another Shakespeare–Chekhov pairing, *King Lear* and *The Seagull*, this time in the temporary Courtyard Theatre, erected adjacent to TOP to house the company during the major rebuild of the RST. As he prepared his production of *King Lear* – a production that reunited him with Ian McKellen – Nunn gave a number of interviews to BBC Radio 4, reflecting on *Lear*, Shakespeare's plays in general and his own approach to directing. Essentially, Nunn's process as a director, the sequence of his work on a play, has remained the same during most of his career, whether on large stages or small. He comes to a production with his concept for it fully worked out, and although the rehearsal process will develop the detail in the production – and he talks of the 'thrill' of realisation and discovery – 'the exposition I made at the outset has remained our blueprint'. This seems to me partly to explain why he is able to develop the smaller parts and tiny narrative threads that other directors do not: having worked out the overarching concept, he has the time to discover other things. In the rehearsal room, close and unhurried study of the text is his starting point, followed by a period of work on the verse, usually using the sonnets, whose 'highly organised, compressed speech presents every possible language problem, breathing problem, technical problem to an actor'. From there, he moves on to improvisations designed to investigate a character, his or her physical life, interaction between the characters and so on, but always coming back to the text and the textual evidence. However, in addition to these technical, intellectual and interpretative aspects of the director's role, Nunn also brings himself, his own life, to his work:

> The first two productions [of *King Lear*, in 1968 and 1976) were decidedly in the first half of my life expectancy, and then there's been a thirty year gap, and our own personal experiences are stirred and awakened by reading *King Lear* – you realise things about families, things about human behaviour, the regrettable aspects of human

> behaviour, and you perceive them not as academic propositions but as things you have actually encountered in life, or in public events in your life.
>
> (BBC Radio 4)

Peter Hall got it right, I think, when he described Nunn as an 'emotional intellectual', a man whose feelings and thoughts are closely aligned. At his best, it seems to me that Nunn never loses sight of the nuances of character and motive and the human physical expression that reveals them. He is incomparable in his ability to present a complex weave of stories on stage and to reveal the bigger picture while (by?) focusing on the smallest detail. He also wants the plays to speak and to matter to an audience today. In his 2004 Old Vic production of *Richard II*, for example (with the enigmatic film star Kevin Spacey in the lead), he sought to emphasise the play's topicality by employing for the first time in his Shakespearian work many of what have become the signature elements of contemporary performance: television screens, video footage and microphones. The production opened with a lavish coronation scene (echoes of his first *Macbeth*), as Richard, watched by his lords in ermine, was invested with crown – taken from a shimmering mirrored cabinet – orb and sceptre, while the action was filmed and projected, before all removed their robes to reveal their modern suits beneath. Significantly, too, for a director who, earlier in his career, had argued for the personal rather than the political in his approach to Shakespeare, he drew out the play's political dimension, in line with more recent critical and theatrical interpretations. More generally, and for me more successfully, he exposes and explores the resonance and fracture lines between Shakespeare's world-view and our own through transpositions such as he employed in *Othello* or *The Merchant of Venice*. To all his work, however, he brings a vibrant visual imagination, a willingness to take risks in casting and staging, and the capacity to judge with great skill the interaction between stage and audience. For David Nathan, Nunn's *The Merchant of Venice* confirmed him 'as one of the world's truly great theatre directors' (*Jewish Chronicle*). It is a judgement which his work overall merits.

Chronology

1940	Born Ipswich, Suffolk; education: Northgate Grammar School, Ipswich; Downing College, Cambridge
1962	Joined Belgrade Theatre, Coventry
1965	Joined RSC
1968–78	Artistic Director and Chief Executive, RSC

1969	*The Winter's Tale*, RST
1970	*Hamlet*, RST
1972	Directed Romans season, RST
1974	Opened The Other Place (TOP), Stratford-upon-Avon
1976	*Macbeth* (TOP), later for ATV TV
1978	Awarded CBE
1978–87	Joint Artistic Director RSC (with Terry Hands)
1980	*Nicholas Nickelby* (with John Caird), RSC, Aldwych
1981	*All's Well that Ends Well*, RST
1982	Opened RSC theatres at the Barbican Centre, London: *Henry IV*
1986	Opened the Swan Theatre, Stratford-upon-Avon
1986	*The Fair Maid of the West*, RSC, Swan
1987–2003	Advisory Director and Emeritus Director, RSC
1989	*Othello*, RSC, TOP
1995	Directed film version of *Twelfth Night*
1999	*Measure for Measure*, RSC, TOP
1999–2003	Artistic Director, National Theatre (NT)
1999	*The Merchant of Venice*, NT, Cottesloe
2002	Knighted
2004	*Hamlet*, London Old Vic
2005	*Richard II*, London Old Vic
2007	*King Lear* and *The Seagull*, RSC, Courtyard Theatre

Bibliography

Ansorge, Peter (1970) 'Director in Interview: Trevor Nunn talks to Peter Ansorge', *Plays and Players* Vol. 17, no. 12, 16–17, 21.

Beaumann, Sally (1982) *The Royal Shakespeare Company: A History of Ten Decades*, Oxford: Oxford University Press.

Berry, Ralph (1977) *On Directing Shakespeare*, London: Croom Helm.

Chambers, Colin (2004) *Inside the Royal Shakespeare Company: Creativity and the Institution*, London: Routledge.

Cook, Judith (1974) *Directors' Theatre*, London: Harrap.

Crowl, Samuel (1992) *Shakespeare Observed: Studies in Performance on Stage and Screen*, Athens, Ohio: Ohio University Press.

David, Richard (1978, 1981) *Shakespeare in the Theatre*, Cambridge: Cambridge University Press.

Evans, Gareth Lloyd (1970) 'Interpretation or Experience? Shakespeare at Stratford', *Shakespeare Survey*, Cambridge: Cambridge University Press 23: 131–5.

—— (1982) 'Shakespeare in Stratford and London, 1981', *Shakespeare Quarterly*, 33 (1), Washington DC: Folger Shakespeare Library: 184–8.

Kennedy, Dennis (2001) *Looking at Shakespeare*, 2nd edn, Cambridge: Cambridge University Press.

Mulryne, Ronnie, and Margaret Shewring (1989) *This Golden Round: The Royal Shakespeare Company at the Swan*, Stratford-upon-Avon: Mulryne and Shewring.
—— (1999) *The Cottesloe at the National: Infinite Riches in a Little Room*, Stratford-upon-Avon: Mulryne and Shewring.
Nunn, Trevor (2000a) 'Notes from a Director: *Three Sisters*', in Vera Gottlieb and Paul Allain (eds), *The Cambridge Companion to Chekhov*, Cambridge: Cambridge University Press, pp. 101–10.
—— (2000b) 'Trevor Nunn talks about *The Cherry Orchard*', National Theatre *Platform Papers*, 31 October.
Rae, Kenneth (1989) *A Better Direction: A National Enquiry into the Training of Directors for Theatre, Film and Television*, Calouste Gulbenkian Foundation.
Rubin, Leon (1981) *The Nicholas Nickleby Story: The Making of the Historic Royal Shakespeare Company Production*, London: Heinemann.
Shrimpton, Nicholas (1983) 'Shakespeare Performances in Stratford-upon-Avon and London', *Shakespeare Survey*, Cambridge: Cambridge University Press 36: 149–56.
Smallwood, Robert (1990) 'Shakespeare on Stage: Shakespeare at Stratford-upon-Avon', 1989 (Part 1), *Shakespeare Quarterly*, Washington DC: Folger Shakespeare Library, 41: 101–14.
Walter, Harriet (2003) *Other People's Shoes*, London: Nick Hern Books.
Warren, Roger (1977) 'Theory and Practice: Stratford 1976', *Shakespeare Survey*, Cambridge: Cambridge University Press 30: 169–79.
Wells, Stanley (1991) 'Shakespeare Production in England in 1989', *Shakespeare Survey*, Cambridge: Cambridge University Press 43: 183–203.

Reprinted reviews of Nunn's productions in the national press since 1980 can be found in *Theatre Record: the chronicle of the British Stage*.

Internet sources

Academy of Achievement. Sir Trevor Nunn interview, available at <http://www.achievement. org/autodoc/printmember/nun0int-1>. (Accessed 29 January 2007.)
The Merchant of Venice: an interview with Trevor Nunn. Masterpiece Theatre, available at <http://www.pbs.org/wgbh/masterpiece/merchant/ei_nunn.html>. (Accessed 14 November 2006.)
Trowbridge, Simon. *A Dictionary of the RSC*, available at <http://mysite.wanadoo-members.co.uk/stratfordians/stnuntr.htm>. (Accessed 5 February 2007.)

About the author

Martin White is Professor of Theatre at the University of Bristol. His research focuses on early modern commercial English theatre, especially neglected plays from the period. His publications include *Renaissance Drama in Action* (1998), editions of *Arden of Faversham* (1982) and Massinger's *The Roman Actor* (2007), numerous essays and chapters in books and an interactive DVD, *The Chamber of Demonstrations: Reconstructing the Jacobean Indoor Playhouse* (2006). He has directed scores of plays at Bristol, including Jonson's *The Magnetic Lady*, Middleton's *The Witch*, Richards' *Messallina* and Massinger's *Believe as You List*. He works regularly as a consultant to the RSC and advises the Globe reconstruction in London.

18
JOSEPH PAPP
Patricia Lennox

Joseph Papp (1921–91, born Joseph Papirofsky), producer-director and founder of the New York Shakespeare Festival (NYSF), was a director of Shakespeare and a director of other directors' Shakespeare. Charismatic and controversial, he was a Shakespeare entrepreneur, a populist impresario, whose 'principle was escalation or extinction' (Little 1974: 221). When he wanted a theatre for his NYSF productions, he raised the money to build several: a 2,000-seat open-air amphitheatre, a mobile travelling theatre and a complex of small stages housed in a cavernous late-Victorian building. Joseph Papp put his stamp on every production seen in those theatres. From 1960, six years after his New York debut as a director, until his death, he controlled his NYSF with an imperial managerial style that recalled the early Hollywood studio bosses. Later comparisons to mega-theatrical producer David Merrick missed the point that Papp was always the director behind the director. No matter whose name was in the programme, it was Papp who chose the play, approved the production style, the designers and the cast and vetted the director's work in progress.

The following account of Joseph Papp as a Shakespeare director is organised around, but not limited to, four key productions that represent pivotal years in Papp's career: *Antony and Cleopatra* (1963), the NYSF's second summer in its custom-designed Delacorte Theatre in Central Park; *The Naked Hamlet* (1967), the inaugural season of the NYSF's Public Theater, *Much Ado about Nothing* (1972), when Papp was at the height of his success and producing over twenty shows a year, and, finally, *Hamlet* (1982), by which time the NYSF had long seemed another way of saying Joseph Papp. The story of the NYSF is the story of Joe Papp: producer, theatre manager, fundraiser, publicity seeker. It is full of chutzpah, conflict and contradictions. It has a recurring cycle of success–failure–success. The self-repeating patterns include: political and ideological confrontations, financial crisis, dedication to a populist theatre, conflated personal and professional identity . . . and Shakespeare. This was how Joseph Papp created and sustained an American version of Shakespeare, one that spoke to some of the major international changes in Shakespeare performance during the second half of the twentieth century.

Although in many ways he was a very private person, Joe Papp worked hard to create a visible public persona for himself and his role at the NYSF. He always needed the publicity to dramatise and validate the moment. Reviews, articles, editorials, even correspondence from the *New York Times* are quoted extensively in this article because for Papp the press was the 'witness' that marked his cycle of success, failure and expansion. It was an integral part of his work.

Papp loved Shakespeare but disliked traditional productions and distrusted the ideas of most Shakespeare scholars. His goal was to create an American style of acting Shakespeare with multi-racial casts and verse spoken conversationally. He wanted actors to speak in regional or ethnic accents instead of trying to sound like members of the Old Vic. He had great faith in an actor's ability to relate to Shakespeare, and he had equal faith in Shakespeare's words to empower the untrained and inexperienced actor. Among Papp's papers (catalogue series XIII, sub-series 3) in the more than eighty boxes of the New York Shakespeare Festival Archives (NYSFA), are several folders with handwritten and typed notes on Shakespeare. Among these is his comment that the American actor, though challenged by the discipline of Shakespeare, 'finds a way to bring Shakespeare to life [. . .] through the content of Shakespeare's poetic concepts and deep emotive verse'. One of the biggest obstacles to what Papp wanted to achieve was, in his opinion, 'the Shakespeare buff, reared on the operatic style of Shakespearian elocution [who] buries his feelings in the syrup of language'.

Despite the claims that he was creating an American Shakespeare, Papp based many of his ideas on those of Jan Kott, Bertolt Brecht and Eastern European experimental theatre groups. At this time, Papp did not seem to realise – and it probably would not have made any difference – that most of his production goals were similar to those of young British directors like Peter Hall and John Barton. Papp's complaints were really a reaction against the American stage and the previous generation's traditional style based on British 'received pronunciation' and picture-frame staging presented during the 1930s and 1940s by actors such as Katherine Cornell, Alfred Lunt, Lynn Fontaine, Judith Anderson and Maurice Evans. The truth was that director-producer Tyrone Guthrie had long been doing many of the things that Papp wanted, but Guthrie was far away in Minneapolis, Minnesota, and in Stratford, Ontario. Papp, on the other hand, was in New York City where, in 1963, the theatre scene was being revolutionised by the Off and Off-Off Broadway movement. In fact, there was nothing in his productions that wasn't being done in theatres elsewhere. Modern dress/mixed-period costumes, local accents and colour-blind casting were much debated innovations already familiar to more adventurous playgoers – but Papp had a way of making it seem his own invention.

On the whole, the NYSF productions of the 1950s and 1960s were relatively conventional. Papp favoured a traditional text, although sometimes with substantial cuts. The sets, in the first decade usually designed by Ming Cho Lee, were fairly minimal: a series of arches upstage, possibly a catwalk across the back of the stage reached by stairs on either side to provide a second level. Lighting would take care of the remainder – and Central Park under a summer night's sky would do the rest. Theoni V. Aldredge, the designer who would work with Papp for over twenty years, dressed the actors in costumes that were lavish and traditionally appropriate to place or period, although by the end of the 1960s the period was frequently nineteenth century.

Even so, drama critic Robert Brustein felt the NYSF had a special trademark: '[the] quality that makes it so peculiarly American, has always been its volatile, rip snorting, rough-and-ready style' (1965: 228).

What was unique – and much praised – in 'Papp-Style', Shakespeare was the casting, in particular his insistence on setting up a loose-knit and multi-ethnic repertory company that employed many of the same actors season after season. The effect was that of a repertory company, even though nothing of the kind existed in contractual terms. Papp's 'intelligence, imagination, and sheer doggedness' were praised for building an ensemble 'comparable to any in the world, a group so virile that it makes the Old Vic look like a collection of Bennington [College] girls' (Brustein 1965: 225). NYSF productions were not performed in repertory; each play had its own cast and operated as a separate unit. Papp became notorious for his abrupt dismissal of company members and an imperious directing style along the lines of 'You move there because I'm paying you to do it.' Still, he obviously inspired far more than he exasperated. There is a long list of designers, actors, crew members and office staff who stayed with him for decades. Actors include George C. Scott, Colleen Dewhurst, James Earl Jones, Julie Harris and Kathleen Widdoes. Sam Waterston, Kevin Kline and Meryl Streep, among others, are still actively involved with the NYSF.

Everyone worked for minimum salary, often below union pay scale. In his multi-racial casts, he often featured either African-American or Hispanic actors whose experience with Shakespeare was limited. Papp's belief was that 'artists emerge from the mass and are not elite beings who descend from heavens.' James Earl Jones, Earl Hyman, Morgan Freeman, Roscoe Lee Brown and Raul Julia started their careers with the NYSF and continued to return in major roles including Julia's Othello and Jones's Claudius and Lear. In establishing a populist Shakespeare, accessible to everyone, Papp's strongest productions were those that lent themselves to broad comedy, like *The Taming of the Shrew* or to big stage heroics, like the 'muscular, masculine, and leathery' 1960 *Henry V* (Brustein 1965: 225).

During his more than thirty years as producer-director, Papp was accused of being both too reverential towards Shakespeare and, at other times, of taking too many liberties with the plays. In the 1970s and 1980s, more often than not reviews referred to some aspect of gimmickry. Papp's defence was that he wanted to give his audiences Shakespeare productions they could relate to. If vulgar comic bits would help accessibility, or if the audience would come because the cast included movie stars, no matter how limited their skill, Papp had no problem with this and never saw it as a compromise. For him, compromise would be the production carefully designed to meet the comfortable expectations of a middle-class audience.

One of Papp's most consistent ideals – and battles – was for free performances of Shakespeare, supported like a public library through municipal funds. The NYSF was always plagued by lack of money, and Papp's solution was to keep expanding. He spent his life raising money for it, but ironically success increased rather than decreased the financial burden. He claimed his methods for raising funds would have made Richard III blush. The first production in 1954 cost $750; by 1963 the NYSF still had a major deficit after an annual gross of $1 million, and by 1977 the deficit was over $2 million. Although America has no federally maintained theatres, it is possible for companies to raise some money or obtain the use of performance venues through affiliation with educational departments of state and local governments. This type of municipal support, however limited, would remain an important part of Papp's complex financial structure for his theatres and an important part of his ideology. Still, even though his theatres always needed money, he walked away from lucrative contracts and grants if they included censorship or outside control of the production. The free summer productions in the park were partly funded by complicated compilations of local-government grants from the New York Parks Department and the Board of Education. This meant that the NYSF's finances were tied to the city's prosperity – and politics. These included the shift from the entrenched political powers of the 1950s, through a more youthful, new generation of politicians in the 1960s, and a period of urban decay and decline in the 1970s, to a sense of resurgence during the 1980s. Critically needed funding also came through major donations by generous private supporters and, later, with profits from NYSF productions at the Public Theater and on Broadway, especially the millions of dollars from Michael Bennett's *Chorus Line*, originally produced by Papp at the NYSF Public Theater.

Free Shakespeare was idealistic, but also practical. It freed the NYSF from union demands, added romance to private donations and gave Papp much more flexibility in choosing the plays. He did not have to keep an eye on the box office. The 1963 *The Winter's Tale* was typical of Papp's fondness for less frequently seen plays. He would often choose titles that would be new to the majority of his Central Park audience. In contrast, the neighbourhood performances by the NYSF Mobile Theater were plays that were more likely to be taught in school, such as *Romeo and Juliet* and *Macbeth*, or that offered a chance for broad comedy, like *The Taming of the Shrew*. In Central Park, however, in seasons with three or four productions, Papp often included a lesser-known play (at least in America): *Cymbeline* (1955), *Titus Andronicus* (1956, 1967), *Two Gentlemen of Verona* (1957), *Measure for Measure* (1960, 1966), *Richard II* (1962), *Coriolanus* (1965), *Troilus and Cressida* (1965), *Love's Labour's Lost* (1965), *All's Well that Ends Well* (1966) and *King John* (1967).

As champion of the cause of free Shakespeare, Papp fearlessly challenged City Hall and made canny use of the media to promote his causes – and himself. Joe Papp was a seemingly tireless manipulator of his own self-created celebrity status – a status needed for the cycle of fundraising to support the free Shakespeare. He was savvy about publicity and gave countless interviews, lectured widely, received numerous awards, openly embraced controversial causes. He arranged for NYSF-related books to be written and published. He reached hundreds of thousands of viewers with television broadcasts of the NYSF stage productions. All payments went directly back to the Public Theater and NYSF and its most expensive programmes – Shakespeare in the Park, the touring Mobile Theater, and the hundreds of annual performances in the city schools.

A great self-promoter, everything Papp touched had his name on it. This 'Joe Papp Presents' attitude charmed some people and infuriated others. Both his supporters and his detractors (often the same people at different times) were vehement in their praise or condemnation. However, the number of theatres Papp named after their sole benefactors is proof of his ability to inspire both confidence and an impressive degree of monetary enthusiasm: Delacorte, Anspacher, Newman, Newhouse, LuEsther, Martinson and Shiva.

His rise to prominence was fast. In a relatively short time, Joseph Papp became a major figure on the New York City cultural scene where he was celebrated as the award-winning founder, producer and director of the city's most noteworthy Shakespeare company. Only eight years before the opening of the Delacorte Theater, Joseph Papirofsky had renamed himself Joseph Papp and made his New York directing debut with 'An Evening of Shakespeare and Marlowe', performed at the very modest Emmanual Presbyterian Church on the Lower East Side, an area synonymous with the kind of poverty and emigrant background that had marked Papp's own Brooklyn childhood. It was also a district that would later become closely connected with his flourishing success in Off-Broadway theatre, the experimental theatre movement of the 1960s that Papp helped establish. His debut may have been low-key – no budget, a build-it-yourself theatre, actors that kept quitting, hardly any audience – but in two years the Obie, the prestigious Off-Broadway theatre award, was presented to Papp and his Shakespeare Theatre Workshop for: 'the passion, the good humor, the clarity with which it has brought Shakespeare and other Elizabethans back to life in a small East Side playhouse with virtually no budget; and for its simple, whole-hearted love for the English language as it is written and spoken'.

Two years, later in 1958, Papp's work was recognised by the 'big time' Broadway theatre producers. He was given a special citation at the Tony awards for distinguished service to the theatre. In the following decades Papp, the NYSF, and its actors, designers and directors would continue to win many, many Obies and Tonys.

Papp studied acting in Los Angeles at the Actor's Laboratory Workshop, founded by two former members of Stanislavsky's acting company, Maria Ouspenskaya and Richard Boleslavsky. During that time, 1948–50, he also taught courses in acting at the Communist-oriented California Labor School, a connection that would result in his being questioned by the House Un-American Activities Committee in 1958. After a 1950 tour with the national company of Arthur Miller's *Death of a Salesman*, where he was the assistant stage manager and understudy for the salesman's two sons, he returned to New York. In 1954, he was working as a floor manager (similar to a theatre's stage manager) for CBS television when he formed the Shakespeare Theatre Workshop. Papp's early production record was an impressive twenty-two Shakespeare plays between 1955 and 1960, four directed by him (*Cymbeline*, *Twelfth Night*, *Antony and Cleopatra*, *Henry V*), plus Middleton's *The Changeling*. Just as he would do throughout his career, he oversaw every aspect of all the productions. It was his energy and organisational skills that kept the company moving forward. For instance, he made sure their productions were reviewed in the major papers which usually ignored small theatre groups. The first review in the *New York Times* happened only because Papp sat for hours in the drama section's office, refusing to leave until they agreed to send a reviewer to the show. As a producer, Papp also made sure that the ultimate power rested with him. Only NYSF coproducer Bernard Gersten, who handled the financial details, came close to a partnership – until Papp fired him after seventeen years, citing artistic differences.

Papp's first New York performance spaces had been a church, a city-owned outdoor amphitheatre, and another municipal theatre, all of them in Manhattan slums. Papp was dedicated to populist productions of Shakespeare. He wanted the kind of theatre that playwright Clifford Odets described when he said 'real theatre isn't on Broadway – it's got to be played on the back of a wagon and in a union hall' (quoted in Schickel 2005: 65). In the summer of 1957, Papp set up his first travelling theatre on the back of a rickety pick-up truck. The goal was to take Shakespeare to the neighbourhoods in New York's five boroughs. Interestingly, his own first theatre experiences, at least according to Papp, were much more traditional. His high-school English teacher took students to two Broadway productions of *Hamlet* in 1936: one with John Gielgud, the other with Leslie Howard.

This first movable stage would last only a year but would be replaced by a far grander version in 1964. Meanwhile, at the end of the Mobile Theater's first summer, the truck broke down, so Papp arranged for it to be hauled in the middle of the night (by a Sanitation Department truck) into Central Park and deposited in the Belvedere Tower area, near the spot where the Delacorte Theater stands today. Typically, he did this without permits or official permission of any kind and then spent the next five years fighting City Hall in order to return to the park every summer. Also typically, Papp won the fight and ended up with City Hall helping to pay the bills. Papp's battles with city officials for both money and space, all in the name of Shakespeare, were legendary and very public. They already were well established in the public's mind in 1959 when critic John Chapman began his review of *Julius Caesar* (directed by Stuart Vaughn) saying: 'Although we have long been accustomed to it, there was even more fuss about Joseph Papp's free Shakespeare for Central Park – accusations and counter-accusations, loud protests against dictatorship and an assassination from political motives. But this time the drama was staged for entertainment only' (*Daily News*, 4 August 1959).

Free Shakespeare in Manhattan's beloved Central Park was an unbeatable argument, at least as articulated by Joe Papp. Finally, in 1962, the New York Shakespeare Festival moved into its own 2,000-seat, open-air amphitheatre, the Delacorte Theater, designed by Papp and Eldon Elder, built by the City, significantly financed by private supporters, especially George Delacorte whose $150,000 donation rescued the project.

The year 1963 was one of the significant years in Papp's mercurial career. The Delacorte season, which would run between June and the end of August, opened with *Anthony and Cleopatra* directed by Papp, followed by *As You Like It*, directed by Gerald Freedman, and *The Winter's Tale*, directed by Gladys Vaughn. (Both directors would continue with the NYSF for several years.) The previous summer, when NYSF finally moved into its permanent summer home, had been fraught with delays as the powerful City Parks Commissioner Robert Moses tried to block the theatre's opening on the grounds the crowds would destroy the grass. Further, the inaugural production, *The Merchant of Venice*, featuring George C. Scott, was a controversial choice. The New York Board of Rabbis wanted it cancelled, especially the planned broadcast on local CBS television stations. The publicity did the NYSF no harm: Papp would always have a kind of genius for this kind of attention. When *The Merchant of Venice* was broadcast as planned, it was a success and praised for the 'fluid vitality, humor and power of the Joseph Papp production' (Gould 1962).

The following year was the first time that Papp went into a season with no public battles. There were still the usual financial concerns and fear that one of the plays might have to be cut if contributions fell short. Nevertheless, as before, the money arrived, the crowds came, and the critics were pleased. It proved, yet again, Papp's success at following the advice he gave to a young arts activist, 'You can do anything if you have a telephone, chutzpah, and are not afraid of anyone'.

Papp's choice of Shakespeare plays for the summer season was often eclectic. Sometimes, as with the 1963 *Antony and Cleopatra*, the play would be one that had received recent attention elsewhere. Here, the tie-in was with the recently released film *Cleopatra*, the Elizabeth Taylor–Richard Burton extravaganza. In contrast to the massive screen production, Papp presented 'an easy going, friendly performance of the play in which the historical figures seem unremote', and were 'compellingly natural and more credible than many a loftier attempt' (Hewes 1963). The 'loftier attempt' may have been a reference to a production in 1961 by Papp's unacknowledged rival, the prestigious establishment-oriented American Shakespeare Festival in Stratford, Connecticut. The reviews also make it clear that Papp's *Antony and Cleopatra* was perfectly consistent with his goal to achieve a popular, accessible production style for Shakespeare.

The Papp-directed *Antony and Cleopatra* looked traditional. The costumes were standard Hollywood sword-and-sandal epic; the men's lavish armour and capes and the women's diaphanous gowns would have been familiar to any moviegoer. On the simple set by Ming Cho Lee shifts between Egypt and Rome were signalled by a 'lively pageant' of busy flag-changing. These were often carried out by arriving and departing soldiers whose parade-ground manoeuvres were punctuated with non-Shakespeare commands like 'right turn.' The park's Turtle Pond, located just behind the stage, was lit and stood in for the Nile.

But, as with all of Papp's productions, this one neither sounded nor moved traditionally. Cleopatra was played by the Canadian-born Colleen Dewhurst, whose speciality was the very American plays of Eugene O'Neill. The five-foot-six Dewhurst was a rather strapping Egyptian queen, slightly taller than her Antony (Michael Higgins) and compared by one critic to a 'lacrosse-playing and extremely healthy head-girl' (Pryce-Jones 1963). This 'healthy' frankness helped the earthy Dewhurst to get away with emphasising the playful bawdiness in the scenes with Cleopatra's women. In contrast, her gravity and dignity in the final scene gave her death speech an even greater impact. Although judged by *Newsweek* as too American to be regal, Dewhurst's Cleopatra was still a force to reckon with, someone who could turn the hapless messenger's description of Octavia into insults, while 'savoring each bit of bile', and who looked as commanding as a sphinx in a headdress shaped like a mythical bird with long curving metal feathers framing the face.

On the whole, the critics were happy with the production, the cast, the theatre, the romance of watching Shakespeare under a summer sky – for free – and decided that even if the production did not achieve grand tragedy, it was still splendid. At this point, Papp, having reached his goal of a permanent summer stage, began a new quest – the search for a year-round NYSF theatre. This would make the next decade the most successful in Papp's impressive career.

Eighteen years after his first New York Shakespeare production, Papp was at the height of his career, even celebrated in a 1972 *Time* magazine profile 'Joe Papp; Populist and Imperialist'. Five years before, in 1967, Papp had finally opened the NYSF Public Theater (which would eventually house five stages) as the organisation's permanent home. In addition to productions of Shakespeare and new playwrights at the Public Theater and the summer Shakespeare in the Park, in 1972 Papp also negotiated a four-year multimillion-dollar contract with CBS television to broadcast thirteen NYSF dramas, a mix of Shakespeare and new playwrights.

Three Shakespeare productions define this period: *William Shakespeare's 'Naked' Hamlet* (1967), *Two Gentlemen of Verona: The Musical* (1971) and *Much Ado about Nothing* (1972). The rock version *Hamlet*, which reflected a major shift in Papp's production style, offended and outraged its audiences. The other two plays were much loved and became Papp's most financially successful Shakespeare productions – past and future. All three achieved some aspect of his desire for an American Shakespeare.

Papp opened the Public Theater's first stage, the 275-seat Anspacher Theater, with the Galt McDermot innovative rock musical *Hair* – and followed it several weeks later with his own *Hamlet*. The Public Theater on Lafayette Street is located halfway between traditionally bohemian Greenwich Village and the then hippy/punk-grunge East Village, at the epicentre of Off-Off-Broadway. The productions suited the locale. Uptown New York audiences had not seen anything quite like *Hair*, nor had they seen anything like what Papp did to *Hamlet*. It was early days for Off-Broadway, where what were then radical adaptations of Shakespeare would become a staple commodity.

'Naked' Hamlet (as in psychologically rather than physically naked) was a major departure for Papp, who previously had favoured conventional staging, though with a populist twist.

Now his goal was to jolt the paying audience at the Public Theater out of their 'warm glow of past Hamlets' where the lines had taken on the 'same significance to them as doth the Bible'. His notes contain the comment: 'The basic conflict in our production is between the character of Hamlet and the Audience [. . .] the audience is the enemy'. The published script and stage directions, *William Shakespeare's 'Naked'* Hamlet: *A Production Handbook*, complete with Papp's meditations on the staging, contains a sixteen-page preface that discusses the audience members' written responses, ranging from hostile to celebratory. Its main point is that younger audience members were very positive. Papp had wanted to 'bridge the generation gap in appreciation of Hamlet' and wanted the same youthful audience that saw *Hair* to return for *Hamlet*. Advertisements called it 'William Shakespeare's *Hamlet* as a Happening'. Galt MacDermot wrote a rock score for it – and it ran an intermission-less ninety minutes, the standard length of a movie.

Although it may have looked highly improvisational, Papp's own archived notes on the 1967 *Hamlet* fill four folders, a testament to the care and thought that went into the 'rearranged' version. His goal was to present 'an American Hamlet in a contemporary setting' in a way that would force the audiences to 'pluck out the mystery'. 'Denmark is a prism', he wrote. He wanted to set the play in 'a place to crush the spirits', perhaps a hospital room or a police station, because 'Hamlet learned the survival method in a death camp'. The result included a heavily policed Denmark, Ophelia's mad scene as a nightclub performance, and a Hamlet (Martin Sheen) who spends part of the time disguised as a Puerto Rican named Ramon, selling peanuts in the audience and, reverting back to Hamlet, delivers a heavily accented 'To be or not to be' soliloquy (here moved to after Ophelia's mad scene).

The set was part prison, part interrogation cell, described in *Naked Hamlet* as a large, high room with walls and floors of unpainted grey metal with two levels of catwalks running across the stage connected stage right by a circular staircase, while, high up on the back wall, grated windows let in streaks of light. Costumes were modern military uniforms for the men; Hamlet wears a white double-breasted suit with a black mourning band on the sleeve and sometimes puts on a leather bomber jacket; Claudius's uniform was laden with Ruritanian military medals, the Ghost wears a white union suit (never trousers) and sneakers in the first scene and adds a military jacket later; the women wear contemporary dresses, mini-skirted for Ophelia. For her mad scene, Ophelia, now a microphone-wielding chanteuse, wears a top hat and tails with black fishnet stockings as she belts out 'By Gis and by Saint Charity.'

Papp's plans describe a production filled with 'burlesque bits, song and dance routines, familiar vaudeville tricks guaranteed to hold the attention of any red-blooded man, woman or child'. In the production handbook's 'Scene XXVII: Hamlet and His Father Talk Things Over', the Ghost holds Hamlet on his knee and manipulates him like a ventriloquist's dummy as they share the lines of the soliloquy 'How all occasions do [sic] inform against me'. Papp wanted the 'comic act which disarms built-in resistance.' These were tricks 'to reveal the truth and keep the spectator from dropping off'. The play-within-the-play scene looked like a children's birthday party with a cake, balloons and home movies. For Papp, the word 'antic' was the key to Hamlet's behaviour. This Hamlet kept going into the audience, to sell peanuts, to interrogate viewers and brings one of them on stage to shoot Hamlet in the final scene. He also never left Denmark for England, a point that Papp makes much of in his notes. Instead, he lurked about the court in disguises.

When the New York City Board of Education objected and wanted to cancel school tours of the production, Papp wrote to the teachers, admitting that he had taken 'extreme' liberties but explaining that he made a 'radical change in the environment of the play' in order to 'push the meaning forward to an extraordinary degree'.

The production handbook has a description of the opening scenes that captures the production's theatre of the absurd 'push'. Rock music blasts as the audience enters the theatre. The play begins with guards shining flashlights and challenging each other across the auditorium. Gertrude and Claudius are centre stage, asleep in the 'Royal Bed'. Hamlet's bed, set at the foot of theirs, is a coffin fitted up with sheets and blankets. His first action on stage is to remove the blanket from the Royal Bed for his own use. The tug-of-war with Claudius over the blanket is interrupted as two gun-carrying guards enter with Horatio, handcuffed and dressed in prison stripes. An hour and a half later, a blindfolded Horatio (still in prison stripes) has been shot by Laertes; Hamlet dies from an accidental gunshot, and 'as he staggers back on stage, picks up the book [a script of *Hamlet*] and reads the closing lines, "The rest is silence" ' (Papp 1969: 156). Responses were not silent, however, and a debate was carried on in the pages of the *New York Time*'s 'Drama Mailbag'. Years later, critic Michael Feingold fondly recalled the production as 'a real statement of our relationship to the play, rich with Americannesss, with ethnic awareness, with a spirit of fun about poetry and drama, and our awkward attitude toward the classics, half gee-whiz humble and half aw-nuts sarcastic' (14 December 1982).

A bit of *Naked Hamlet*'s controversy spilled over into the summer Shakespeare. Although Papp's more radical productions of Shakespeare were saved for his ticket-buying audience at the Public Theater and, later, at the Lincoln

Center Theaters, the Central Park production in the summer of 1968 sparked debate when Papp directed a *Romeo and Juliet* with a balcony-less balcony scene. In the following years, the park productions would settle back into their more conventional format – far too conventional in the eyes of many of the younger reviewers. Typical of the growing dissatisfaction was Martin Gottfried's complaint that Papp 'invariably sterilizes whatever Shakespeare he directs' (1969). However, as always, Papp would continue to surprise.

Although his Shakespeare productions had been generally well received, occasionally even enthusiastically, as with his *Henry V*, the NYSF had never had a hit show that could be moved to a Broadway theatre for a profitable extended run. Then, in the early 1970s, there were two: *The Two Gentlemen of Verona: The Musical* (music Galt MacDermot, lyrics John Guare, director Mel Shapiro, 1971) and *Much Ado about Nothing* (director A.J. Altoon, 1972). Both shows put a very American face on Shakespeare. This time the critics did not use their habitual Anglocentric benchmark for Shakespeare productions. Instead, they cheered: 'the large American flag on the bandstand places the action right where it belongs and at the same time serves as a kind of private reminder to the audience of all that Joseph Papp [has] done to make good American actors available to us time after time' (Oliver 1972).

For *Two Gentlemen of Verona*, MacDermot and Guare took massive liberties with Shakespeare's plays, but the musical adaptation keeps close to the spirit, if not the words, of the original. Verona is a happy-go-lucky Caribbean island, and Milan is a stand-in for New York City. The 'Love and Peace' musical had a hippy chorus, songs with a heavy emphasis on love and anti-Vietnam War politics. Describing a cast that 'was so racially mixed there were almost no white principals at all' and a score that was 'so *now*', musical comedy expert Ethan Mordden observed in *One More Kiss* that *Two Gentlemen of Verona* 'sounds like Joseph Papp's idea of a musical'. *Time* magazine's Ted Kalem thought it was 'cultural vandalism', but he had also felt the same way about Peter Brook's *A Midsummer Night's Dream* (quoted in Mordden 2003: 11). The nearly sung-through score includes salsa, calypso, jazz, rhythm and blues, rock and roll, what Mordden describes as 'Funky Mandolin with a Latin Pulse' (2003: 10). *New Yorker* critic Brendan Gill reviewed the Broadway opening night at the Saint James Theater, praising the show's 'merry band of marvelous young people onstage, who notable for the variety of their sizes, shapes, and hues, stood singing and dancing and blowing soap bubbles and flaunting yo-yos'. He continued: The 'night marked a sort of apotheosis for Joe Papp the ablest figure known to Off Broadway had stormed and captured Broadway, and I was irresistibly put in mind of a harsh old Yankee saying: "If he ain't happy now, he never will be" ' (1971).

When *Much Ado about Nothing* opened at the Delacorte Theater the following summer, there were more rave reviews for this 'Shakespeare for the contemporary masses' (Gussow 1972). For *Much Ado about Nothing*, Papp had originally wanted Victorian England but became 'charmed' with his young director's plan for an American setting. Today, the changes A.J. Altoon made in *Much Ado about Nothing* would scarcely be noticed, but then the critics were surprised and delighted with the very American version and praised its 'refurbishing of sweetness' and the way 'Altoon is trying to shake out the old sachets in the American attic' (Kroll, 1972). When it moved to Broadway, raves continued to emphasise the American images, where 'the whole stage becomes a Fourth of July fireworks display of Americana' (Barnes 1972).

Altoon, who referred to the show as *Much Ado about Nothing or the Summer of 1905*, placed Messina in Middle America and filled the production with period images. Theoni V. Aldreges' pretty costumes set the tone, as did Ming Cho Lee's transformation of the usual platforms, catwalk and stairs into curlicued Edwardian architecture. The soldiers led by Don Pedro are returning from the Spanish–American war. The local brass band (led by Henry 'Bootsie' Normand) plays Scott Joplin rags at the picnic welcoming them. Beatrice and Hero hide behind their flower-trimmed hats to sneak a cigarette. Benedict, in a striped blazer and white flannel trousers, hides behind an upright canoe in the gulling scene. Dogberry leads a Keystone Kops police force straight from silent films. Except for a few interpolated lines about lemonade and free beer, it was a straight-forward version of the text. The cast included NYSF regulars, the delicately British-influenced Kathleen Widdoes and the very American Sam Waterston as Beatrice and Benedick.

In December 1972, CBS broadcast a staged-for-television version. Seen nationwide, it was a major success, but it became the only one of the thirteen planned NYSF productions to be broadcast. Papp and the network bosses clashed when CBS refused to air the Public Theater's production of David Rabe's anti-Vietnam play *Sticks and Bones*, scheduled to follow *Much Ado about Nothing*. CBS let the lucrative contract lapse, and Papp added the Lincoln Center Theater to the NYSF package in an attempt to recoup some of the financial loss. However, the theatres, located in the cultural complex containing the Metropolitan Opera and New York Symphony Orchestra, were an uncomfortable milieu for Papp, and when they ended up costing the NYSF more than $2 million a year, he ended the affiliation in 1977.

If Joe Papp had a mantra it would have been the comment reported by journalist Stuart Little: 'I do what I have to do when I have to do it' (1974: 253). By the 1980s, Papp's theatres – the Delacorte and the five at the Public were an institution in New York city. Papp had always connected himself with everything done at NYSF, to the point of doing ads, or putting his own picture on the posters and tying his name as close as possible to the productions; by now, he was a star appearing in American Express ads. The Shakespeare in the Park plays, though, were becoming an institution that was increasingly taken for granted. Productions were frequently dismissed as a place for big-name movie stars in mediocre performances. A new generation of critics and audiences was becoming increasingly critical of the Shakespeare productions, finding them old-fashioned, unexciting and poorly acted.

Those charges seemed justified in 1982 when Papp once again directed *Hamlet* at the Public Theater, but in a completely different manner from the 1967 free-wheeling *Naked Hamlet*. The new production used straightforward mid-nineteenth-century costumes, a neo-classical set featuring a white marble floor and walls punctuated with columns, and a text with only minor, but traditional, cuts. In his notes for the 1967 production, Papp said he wanted to 'strip away identifiable characteristics'. This time, the only innovation was casting a woman, Diane Venora, in the lead role. Although the casting was dismissed as another Papp gimmick, his notes show a fascination with the idea as early as the 1960s and include several typed versions of a history of female Hamlets, among them Sarah Siddons, Judith Anderson and Sarah Bernhardt. The critics' major complaint was that Venora's Hamlet was too boyish, but Papp had actually mused much earlier about the possibility of a boy actor aged 12 or 14 instead of Burbage playing the original Hamlet at Shakespeare's Globe Theatre. Something of that boy-actor quality seems to have filtered into Papp's direction of Venora's performance, which had been controlled by this director who allowed his actors very little agency in forming their roles.

Papp ignored his own observation that 'a modern producer must approach it [Hamlet] from a contemporary view and from his personal feelings. There is no way for doing it "straight" without making it a lifeless conglomeration of high-sounding words and affected characters moving around the stage' (notes for his 'Guide to Teachers', 1967). But that was exactly what he did. Critics complained that Venora, a recent theatre-school graduate, lacked the necessary stage experience for Hamlet. They also objected that the lustreless, enervated four-hour production with only a single intermission was far too long and claimed that bored, sleeping audience members only woke up when they heard Fortinbras's trumpeters.

Venora is an intelligent and thoughtful actor, but under Papp's direction her androgynous Hamlet became a nasty adolescent, a 'mean street kid', a 'princeling' instead of a prince. In contrast, Horatio was fortyish, bearded, balding, peered through spectacles and seemed more the professor than a fellow student of this slim, athletic Hamlet. The costumes were vaguely mid-nineteenth century, but Hamlet's black tights, short pants and form-fitting jacket added to Venora's youthfulness and reminded viewers of anything from a bell hop to

Little Lord Fauntleroy. The action was dominated by lulls in which Hamlet was the only character who moved about; everyone else delivered their speeches standing still, muting tones and emotions. Most of the outbursts of action belonged to Hamlet: frenzied dagger thrusts at the unseen Polonius, hurling Ophelia's mementoes in her face, throwing Gertrude to the ground, pummelling her with rabbit punches and half-ravishing her, fighting with Laertes at Ophelia's grave, and histrionically sobbing 'far too many times' (Kerr 1982). The production was nearly universally disliked, and Papp was thoroughly blamed for every failing detail. Undaunted, he would go on to direct well-received productions of *Henry IV Part I, Measure for Measure* and *Richard II* before the end of the decade.

Papp's final major Shakespeare project, planned when he was fighting cancer and when the NYSF was faced with a projected deficit of $4.8 million, was the $33 million, six-year 'Shakespeare Marathon', with six plays a year. Charter members, subscribers to the entire series, received a T-shirt saying 'I've Seen It All' and an invitation to drink champagne with Papp when the curtain came down on 15 September 1993. Papp did not live to see the completion of the marathon. For him, the 'curtain came down' 29 October 1991. Still, Papp *had* 'seen it all' and left behind, for better or worse, more than three decades of an American-style Shakespeare.

Chronology

1955	*Cymbeline*
1958	*Twelfth Night*
1959	*Antony and Cleopatra*
1960	*Henry V*
1961	*Much Ado about Nothing, Romeo and Juliet*
1962	*Julius Caesar, King Lear, The Merchant of Venice; The Merchant of Venice* (CBS)
1963	*Antony and Cleopatra, Twelfth Night; Antony and Cleopatra* (CBS)
1964	*Hamlet; Hamlet* (CBS)
1965	*Henry V, The Taming of the Shrew, Troilus and Cressida*
1966	*All's Well that Ends Well*
1967	*Hamlet, King John*
1968	*Romeo and Juliet*
1969	*Twelfth Night*
1973	*As You Like It*
1976	*Henry V*
1982	*Hamlet*
1982–3	*Rehearsing Hamlet* (ABC-Cable)

1985 *Measure for Measure*
1987 *Henry IV, Part I, Richard II*

Bibliography

Barnes, Clive (1972) 'Ragtime "Much Ado" Comes Indoors', *New York Times*, 13 November.
Brustein, Robert (1965) *Seasons of Discontent: Dramatic Opinions 1959–1965*, New York: Simon & Schuster.
Epstein, Helen (1994) *Joe Papp: An American Life*, New York: Da Capo Press.
Gill, Brendan (1971) 'The Bard, With Affection', *New Yorker*, 11 December.
Gottfried, Martin (1969) '*Twelfth Night*', *Women's Wear Daily*, 14 August.
Gould, Jack (1962) 'TV: "Merchant" Shown', *New York Times*, 22 June.
Gussow, Mel (1972) 'On Stage: "Much Ado" in America', *New York Times*, 18 August.
Hewes, Henry (1963) 'Shakespeare in Central Park', *Saturday Review*, 6 July.
Kerr, Walter (1982) 'This Boyish Princeling is an Unpersuasive *Hamlet*', *New York Times*, 12 December.
Kroll, Jack (1972) 'Duel of Lovers', *Newsweek*, 28 August.
Little, Stuart W. (1974) *Enter Joseph Papp: In Search of a New American Theater*, New York: Coward, McCann & Geoghegan.
Levine, Mindy N. (1981) *New York's Other Theatre: A Guide to Off Off Broadway*, New York: Avon Books.
Mordden, Ethan (2003) *One More Kiss: The Broadway Musical in the 1970s*, New York: Palgrave Macmillan.
New York Shakespeare Festival Archives, the Billy Rose Theater Collection at The New York Public Library for the Performing Arts.
Oliver, Edith (1972) 'Off Broadway', *New Yorker*, 26 August.
Papp, Joseph, assisted by Ted Cornell (1969) *William Shakespeare's 'Naked'* Hamlet: *A Production Handbook*, New York: Macmillan.
Papp, Joseph and Elizabeth Kirkland (1988) *Shakespeare Alive*, New York: Bantam.
Pryce-Jones, Alan (1963) 'Openings', *Theatre Arts*, August/September.
Schickel, Richard (2005) *Elia Kazan: A Biography*, New York: HarperCollins.

About the author

Patricia Lennox teaches at New York University. Her book and theatre reviews appear in the *Shakespeare Bulletin* and the *Shakespeare Newsletter*. Her articles on Shakespeare directors, performers, productions and media versions of the plays are included in *Henry VI: Critical Essays* (2000), *Transforming Shakespeare: Contemporary Women's Re-Visions in Literature and Performance* (1999), *Multicultural Shakespeare: Translation, Appropriation and Performance* (2004), *North American Players of Shakespeare* (2007) and an edition of *As You Like It* for the New Kittredge Shakespeare series (forthcoming).

19
B. IDEN PAYNE

Franklin J. Hildy

During a career that spanned the years 1899–1968, B. Iden Payne directed over 100 productions of Shakespeare's plays, forty of them in Stratford-on-Avon alone. He staged at least thirty-two of the thirty-seven plays that make up the Shakespeare canon, most in multiple productions. It was often claimed for him, though he did not make such a claim himself, that he had directed more productions of Shakespeare's plays than any other director (Gelber 1997: 2) – a claim that was possibly true during his lifetime but is not verifiable. He was, however, the first English director of the Abbey Theatre (home of the Irish national theatre) and the first Artistic Director of what has been called England's model for a modern repertory theatre, the Gaiety Theatre, Manchester. On Broadway, he staged productions for the Shubert brothers, became a staff director for the Charles Frohman Company and was 'loaned out' to David Belasco and Florenz Ziegfeld before directing for the Theatre Guild. Back in England in the late 1930s, he served for eight years as the Artistic Director of the Shakespeare Memorial Theatre in Stratford-upon-Avon. Finally, at an age when most of his contemporaries had retired, he became one of the most sought-after regional theatre directors in the USA. Along the way, he became part of the important 'little theatre movement', managing theatres in both Chicago and Philadelphia. He was a leading figure in the development of Shakespeare festivals in America as his system of 'modified Elizabethan staging' was used by the Globe Theatre company that performed in reconstructed Globe playhouses across the country during the Great Depression was the inspiration for the formation of the Oregon Shakespeare Festival and was used by Old Globe Theatre in San Diego as it began to establish itself as a major regional theatre. As the second Chairman of the first degree-granting Department of Drama in the USA (at the Carnegie Institute of Technology, now Carnegie-Mellon University) and the person who made the Department of Drama at the University of Texas at Austin one of the major programmes in the country, he was a pioneer of theatre in higher education.

One of New York's longest-running musicals, *The Fantastics*, was dedicated to him, and both a theatre at the University of Texas, and the theatre awards given annually in Austin, Texas are named after him. Yet, by the time of his death in 1976, at the age of 94, few beyond those who knew him personally were aware of the extent of his significance or influence.

An attempt at remedying this situation was made with the release of his reminiscences by Yale University Press under the title *A Life in a Wooden O: Memoirs of the Theatre* in 1977. The title was not his but expresses the focus he gave in his later career to the staging of Shakespeare's plays. Payne had actually completed the book under the title, *A Road to William Shakespeare*, a book that chronicled his experience in the theatre of the early twentieth century in order to show how he came to his concept of modified Elizabethan staging. But when this book was posthumously edited by Edward Tripp, he found Payne's descriptions of his life in the theatre more interesting than Payne's explanation of his approach to Shakespeare and therefore cut the latter far more substantially than the former (Gelber 1997: 36–7). As a result, the book provides details only for those parts of Payne's career that influence his approach to Shakespeare, while providing only a rough outline of the modified Elizabethan staging technique he developed in 1925 and used for nearly half a century. As a consequence, his influential approach is still little known and not easy to understand outside the historical context that led him to develop it.

Ben Iden Payne was born in 1881, the same year in which William Poel started the experiments that would lead to the Elizabethan Revival, the movement with which Payne would eventually become most closely associated. He grew up in Manchester, where his earliest exposure to theatre was in seeing touring productions of standard Victorian fare, which he admired greatly. At the age of 17, he was accepted as a 'walking gentleman' by Mr and Mrs F.B. Benson's Shakespeare and Old English Comedy Company, the same company Poel had worked for during the 1884 season. Frank Benson was a legendary figure whose productions of Shakespeare were genuinely admired throughout England, though rarely thought to be the best of their day. Payne spent part of the 1899 season with the Benson company and, after gaining more experience with a lesser touring troupe, returned to the Bensons for the 1900–1 season. In 1902, he toured Ireland with the second Benson company under Mrs Benson, as both an actor and an assistant stage manager. His last tour with the Bensons was to the West Indies in 1904–5. After that, he worked for several touring companies, ultimately graduating to stage manager with Ian Maclaren's Shakespearian repertory company. This was still an age when many of the tasks we now assign to directors were done by the stage manager, and Payne appears to have excelled at it.

In his memoirs, Payne's concern was to tell us about how different the world of Victorian and Edwardian theatre was from that of the post-First World War era. It was a time, he says, when the leading actor or actress in a company, in consultation with those in the major supporting roles, blocked their own scenes, which consisted primarily of setting the exits and entrances. The rest, that is, the scenes the leads were not in, was left to the stage manager to sort out based on traditional practice. Line readings were entirely the business of the performers, although occasionally those new to the trade might ask the stage manager for advice, and Payne found this the most satisfying part of the job. In rehearsal, lines were recited with no attempt at indicating how they would be delivered in performance. In performance, improvisation was a necessary skill for adapting to the many unexpected challenges of staging plays on the road. Payne entered the theatre just as the demands of the new dramas, with their interest in the psychology of characters, were putting demands on actors that their learn-by-experience training could not help them with, thereby making intense rehearsals increasingly important. Payne embraced the new theatre, but he never lost his enthusiasm for the glory days of the old one with its 'quality of glamour, and aura of romance' (Payne 1977: 40), when audiences went to the theatre to see actors, not plays. He always missed the rapport that had existed between the actors and the audience in those early days, and his attraction to the Elizabethan revival seems largely to have been motivated by the belief that it was the best opportunity of recapturing some of that rapport.

While with Benson, Payne acted in at least fifteen of Shakespeare's plays, including *Measure for Measure* (Gelber 1997: 50), a rarely done play that Payne was to come back to throughout his career. Benson was an Oxford graduate with a love for Shakespeare's language and gave Payne a lifelong interest in that language and how it could be understood and spoken. He credits this period with teaching him the value of high-quality costumes in making strong visual statements in staging with minimal scenic means. He also learned how scene changes could alter the flow of a play, and this made him open to approaches that would minimise their necessity. Most significantly, however, he learned pragmatism, which would become the hallmark of his own approach to directing.

W.B. Yeats hired Payne to teach the Irish players how to speak verse drama in 1907. Unfortunately, Payne never got the chance to show what he could do. He arrived for his interview in January, just as *The Playboy of the Western World* opened to considerable criticism from the Irish audience, a number of whom felt libelled by the script. So, those working for the Abbey were quite sensitive about their nationalist credentials and, by the time he took up his post in mid-February, were more resentful than ever of this English outsider. His position at the Abbey was, therefore, untenable, and he resigned in June.

Payne was immediately hired by the Abbey's English patron, Miss A.E.F. Horniman, to become the Artistic Director of her newest project, the 'Manchester Playgoers' Theatre'. This was Horniman's attempt at establishing the first modern repertory theatre in England, and she entrusted Payne with creating it. The project opened in September 1907, and by the following spring had moved into the Gaiety Theatre. Payne ran this company for four seasons, until October 1911, and was largely responsible for its early critical success. He produced a remarkable range of plays, from classical Greek drama, to translations of modern European plays, to the most recent offerings of playwrights like John Galsworthy, George Bernard Shaw and the 'Manchester School' of dramatists, including Harold Brighouse, Stanley Houghton and Allan Monkhouse. But it was his invitation to William Poel to stage, and star in *Measure for Measure* at the Gaiety in April 1908 that had the greatest impact on his future as a director of Shakespeare. This was generally regarded as Poel's most successful demonstration of his approach to Elizabethan staging, and Payne later expressed embarrassment at not having learned more form the experience (Payne 1977: 176). Fortunately, Lewis Casson, who was also in the cast of this production and would later take over the Gaiety when Payne resigned, did remember what Poel had taught them and recounted it for *The Listener* (10 January 1952: 56). Poel, he says, taught the importance of:

1 the full text in its proper order without interpolations or rearrangement;
2 continuity of speech from scene to scene without breaks between 'acts';
3 a permanent architectural set with at least two levels, and an inner stage covered by traverse curtains;
4 a wide platform stage projecting into the audience;
5 Elizabethan dress (with a few period modifications);
6 rapid highly coloured, musical speech, of great range and flexibility.

Payne himself would eventually distil these six points down to what he saw as the two essential points of Poel's teaching:

1 'The fundamental quality of a Shakespearian performance should be the complete fluidity of action' (Payne 1977: 162).
2 'Something approximating to the main features of the Elizabethan theatre (as usually understood) is not only the most suitable but is even essential if the desire of the director is not self-exploitation but an honest determination to make the plays come to life for a modern audience' (Payne 1967: 327.)

Payne came to realise that you could not have complete fluidity of action without 'something approximating' the essentials of the Elizabethan stage, and this formed the basis of what he would ultimately call his modified Elizabethan staging approach, although he would not fully formulate it until he was in his forties.

The seeds of Payne's system can be seen in his later commentary on Poel's *Measure for Measure*. Payne, like many others, noted that in spite of Poel's constant emphasis on performing 'the full text in its proper order without interpolations or rearrangement', he cut the plays to suit his own sense of what was needed to move the action forward for a modern audience. When Payne created his own approach years later, 'fluidity of action' took precedence over purity of text. He always argued that the plays could be cut intertextually as long as the metre was preserved and the 'melodic line' of the action was maintained (Payne 1977: 190).

When considering Poel's ideas of the appropriate speech training for Shakespearian actors, Payne says the entire cast found Poel's training freakish (Payne 1977: 91), largely because of Poel's insistence on the use of an eccentric notion of 'tones'. Poel's production of *Measure for Measure* worked in performance, Payne tells us, largely because the cast ignored what they had learned in rehearsal concerning tones (Payne 1977: 88). But years later, when he wrote about 'Directing the Verse Play' for *Educational Theatre Journal* (1950), Payne stressed the importance of the rapid delivery of verse. Rather than focus on what he viewed as Poel's artificial system of giving emphasis to certain words, however, he focused on vocabulary and the training of actors to speak the lines 'while actually thinking the thoughts'. As a result, his productions were always known for their rapid delivery, careful diction and easy comprehensibility.

What Payne had admired most about Poel's *Measure for Measure*, and indeed just about the only thing he truly did admire at the time, in spite of the positive reviews the show received, were the wonderfully tailored costumes Poel used. The appreciation of high-quality costumes was something Payne had learned from Benson and Poel's approach and reinforced his belief that Elizabethan dress was the most effective way to costume one of Shakespeare's plays, a belief he put into practice in nearly all of his productions of Shakespeare's plays.

Under the influence of Poel's enthusiasm for Elizabethan theatre, Payne directed *The Knight of the Burning Pestle* as the Christmas play for 1908, *Every Man in his Humour* as the Christmas play for 1909, and *Much Ado about Nothing* in 1910. Although he says he made no use of what he should have learned from Poel in these productions, by the time he staged *Much Ado about Nothing*, he had come to appreciate 'the rhythmic flow in the unfolding of the plot – the melodic line of scene development, [. . .] which would be destroyed by the customary omission or transposition of scene to avoid many scene changes' (Payne 1977: 103). This was a clear indication that he had learned more from Poel than he realised. For *Much Ado about Nothing*, Payne came up with a system of staging short scenes in front of a neutral curtain, through which actors could enter on the ends or through the middle, while sets were changed behind in order to facilitate a rapid continuity of action without abandoning the use of scenery. This was only a slight modification of the system Poel had been using since the 1890s, but to understand that, it is necessary to take a quick look at the stage Poel brought with him to Manchester, the 'Fortune fit-up'.

The 'Fortune fit-up' had been built in 1893 for Poel's first full staging of *Measure for Measure*, at the Royalty Theatre in London. Fit-ups were common touring stages during the Victorian era, designed to be erected in halls across the country, but occasionally used even in theatres. Poel called his the 'Fortune fit-up' to give it the authority of the Fortune contract, the most highly regarded document relating to Elizabethan theatre buildings at the time. This fit-up was actually based, however, on a drawing of the interior of the Swan playhouse which had only recently been discovered. The Fortune fit-up stage was just 30 feet wide by 24 feet deep – small when compared to the 43 foot width by 27 foot 6 inch depth that the Fortune contract seems to imply (although this has become a debatable point), but it is actually not significantly smaller than the stage that was discovered in the excavations of the Rose playhouse in 1989. Stage columns, 18 feet tall, standing about 14 feet apart, supported a fake penthouse roof and divided the stage depth in half on Poel's stage. At the back of the stage was a balcony flanked, at stage level, by two doors, as shown in the Swan drawing, and also an 'inner stage' which is not shown in the Swan drawing but was proposed by A.H. Paget in 1891 and adopted by nearly all Elizabethan theatre reconstructors thereafter. When Payne first saw the fit-up, he found it dingy and thought it represented only 'a passing curiosity' (1977: 99), but he gradually came to realise its importance to the staging of English Renaissance drama.

When Karl Gaedertz published the Swan drawing in 1888, he had proposed that the most likely purpose for the stage columns which were such a prominent feature of the drawing was to provide a mid-stage location for stage curtains. This would allow the area behind the columns to be closed off from time to time to facilitate the changing of furniture or other stage decorations on the rear stage while a scene could be played on the stage area in front of the columns. Poel adopted this practice, using costumed stagehands to open and close the curtains. He continued using it long after the objection was raised that in Shakespeare's day a large part of the audience in those polygonal playhouses would have been looking at the stage from the sides. The column curtains worked for Poel's fit-up because the only time he used audiences on the sides, they were actors in the show. (He did not use real audiences on the sides until long after the fit-up was gone.) Payne knew this system was of dubious authenticity, but he recognised the value of these curtains for maintaining a flow in the action while still being able to have scene changes. So, he experimented with what he thought would be an equivalent system of using a set of neutral curtain just upstage of the proscenium arch for *Much Ado about Nothing* at the Gaiety, and he repeated this experiment for a number of years (Payne 1977: 103–4). This was, however, simply the extension of a tradition of using tab curtains to cover scene changes that had long been used in the Victorian era. But the experiment was indicative of the difference between Payne's approach and that of Poel and his other followers. While they railed against the proscenium-arch theatre and argued for a return to the open stage, Payne accepted the proscenium arch and strove to make Poel's approach work within it. Unfortunately, this particular adaptation did not succeed. Payne came to realise that 'the drawing of curtains across the stage near the proscenium is fatal to the flow of action because that movement is subconsciously associated with a feeling of finality – the feeling that something has been finished and something new is about to begin' (Payne 1967: 327). When these curtains were made part of a set representing an Elizabethan-style stage, as Poel's curtains were, they closed off only a small section of the centre stage and so were not seen in this way.

Payne later observed that

> throughout my sojourn in Manchester, it was not the realistic plays dealing with contemporary life that interested me most intensely. The plays that stirred my imagination and gave me the most satisfaction as a director were, on the one hand, poetic plays and on the other, plays of fantastic comedy.
>
> (Payne 1977: 109)

He also says that it was during this time that he began to study Shakespeare intently, beginning to read the research upon which Poel's theories were based.

Payne had formed his own company with his wife, Mona Limerick, before leaving the Gaiety and had another company on the road as soon as his resignation at the Gaiety was accepted. But when Ms Horniman told him of an opportunity to open another repertory company, this time in the USA, at Chicago, he jumped at the chance. The Chicago Theatre Society project did not work out. He did stage *Measure for Measure* there for the first of many times in his career but insists that he used little of what he had learned from Poel beyond his own modification of the curtains he had already used for *Much Ado about Nothing*. Far more significant was his introduction to Thomas Wood Stevens.

In 1913, Stevens was in the process of creating the first degree-granting programme in theatre at the Carnegie Institute of Technology in Pittsburg, Pennsylvania. The programme was the inspiration of the institute's President, Arthur Hammershlag, but Stevens designed the curriculum and ran it for its first decade. By the time he left, Stevens had succeeded in getting the professional theatre to accept that theatre could be taught in a college setting. One of the ways in which he did this was by hiring professionals to teach in the programme, and Payne was his first recruit. It was while working there that Payne would finally develop his modified Elizabethan staging, a system that fit Poel's approach to Shakespeare comfortably within the proscenium-arch stage.

But before that could happen, Payne took a job to create a repertory theatre in Philadelphia in 1914. Like the project in Chicago, however, it did not develop as he had hoped. His last production for this group was a revival of Sheridan's *The Critic*, which he had originally staged in Manchester. This production was picked up by the Shubert organisation for a short run in New York City, becoming the first of a long list of shows he staged there including *Justice* by John Galsworthy (1916), which gave John Barrymore his first leading role; *Dear Brutus* by J.M. Barrie (1918) with William Gillette and Helen Hayes; and *Embezzled Heaven* (1944) with Ethel Barrymore. Only his last Broadway production was of a Shakespeare play, *The Winter's Tale*, which he did for the Theatre Guild in 1946. Payne's work in New York was generally well received, but he found it stultifying. It was during this time, he says, that he realised he was no longer a theatrical pioneer (Payne 1977: 149).

More and more he was drawn to his work at Carnegie Tech, where he had started staging plays in 1914 and an annual Shakespeare play in 1917. Poel had been invited to stage a play there in 1916, and, although Payne was unable to see it, the response it got from the students and audience made him think that Poel was right when he told the *Daily Chroncle* in 1913, 'Some people have called me an archaeologist, but I am not. I am really a modernist. My original aim was just to find out some means of acting Shakespeare naturally and appealingly form the full text as in a modern drama' (Speaight 1954: 90). Here was a pioneering approach to which Payne felt he could make a contribution. Unfortunately, when he proposed to do *Richard II*, staged 'in the Elizabethan manner' in 1917, he was prevented from starting his experiments by Stevens, who designing an attractive but conventional proscenium-arch set for the show. It was not until Stevens stepped down as chair in 1924 and

Payne accepted the post for the 1925–8 term that he was finally able to experiment with the concepts he had been formulating over a period of more than fifteen years. He first applied his ideas, he says, to a student production of *Hamlet* in 1926.

What Payne had come to realise was that Poel's version of the Elizabethan stage, and just about every other version of his day, created distinct areas which he call 'zones of interest'. Poel had talked of three areas – the thrust stage, the inner below and the inner above – but Payne saw six. Perhaps the best way to understand this is to first put it into art terms, thinking of the stage as having a background, middle ground and foreground. The background consisted of the tiring-house façade with an 'inner above' or balcony, flanked, at stage level, by two doors which provided access to the stage, and the 'inner below' or discovery space between these doors. The inner below may lack historical justification, but it seems necessary for some plays and is certainly convenient. For Payne, the inner below and the inner above created two zones of interest in the background and, in most reconstructions of Payne's day, generally had their own curtains and scenery. The middle ground, which was the most important to Payne's scheme, consisted primarily of the rectangular area at centre defined by the inner below and inner above at the rear and the stage posts at the front. Payne called this area the middle stage, or sometimes the penthouse. This was not a very large area, as the posts were generally only 12 to 16 feet apart and about 12 feet from the façade. Payne was well aware of the lack of any historical evidence for Poel's usage of curtains between the posts to close off this space, but, like the questionable inner below, Payne found it useful to his scheme. To each side of the middle stage were small side stages. On stages like the Fortune fit-up, these side stages were in front of the tiring-house doors, the primary entrances and exits. In the proscenium-arch stages Payne normally worked on, these areas were in front of the primary entrances and exits coming in from the wings. Payne adhered to the notion that 'for some obscure psychological reason, entrances made on the left side of the stage (the audience's right) make a more dynamic impact' and used these side stages accordingly (Payne 1977: 164). These side stages were not closed off when the middle-stage curtains were shut, so significant entrances and exits could continue to occur. The foreground was everything in front of the post. He called this the 'forestage'. In many productions, however, the forestage was broken up into three subdivisions, and sometimes even six. Payne became convinced that Shakespeare's 'practical dramaturgy' could be seen 'in the allocation of the different portions of the stage to the scenes as they unfold – the zones of interest as I call them' (Payne 1967: 329). This could be discovered on a stage like that of the Fortune fit-up or it could be discovered on a stage like that of Copeau's

Théâtre du Vieux-Columbier in Paris. All that was important were the six zones in their proper locations.

Payne often talked of what he learned from using these zones of interest. The forestage, he says, was most appropriate for scenes that needed no identifiable location, leaving each audience member free to imagine their own setting. This included scenes that indicated a passage of time (sometimes required to allow for costume changes) and scenes in which the audience was addressed as with soliloquies and expository scenes (Payne 1977: 169). The middle stage was used for localised scenes and the 'inner below' at the back of this area was important in helping to establish the location. For this reason, he was happy to use painted backdrops within the inner below and even at other locations on the stage when the rear façade did not cover the entire space. Once the location was established for a scene, the action could spread out onto the side stages and the forestage. The inner above could be used as its own location or in conjunction with the middle stage, and Payne did not hesitate to use stairs that connected the two areas. It could have its own scenic background that did not need to relate to any background shown in the inner below. Payne later observed that 'the Inner Above should be used only where necessary or in situations where it obviously assists the action' (Payne n.d.: 256), thus indicating that the placement of a scene within a zone was largely a matter of personal aesthetics. The side stages were where most of the exits and entrances occurred. He found that stage entrances did not have to be at stage level and could incorporate stairs. The stage posts were also an important feature, although they were not assigned a zone designation. They were especially important for scenes of overhearing as a person on the middle-stage side of a post was readily accepted as being unable to see someone on the side-stage side.

Payne's method was to divide a play into rehearsal units, usually consisting of two scenes together but sometimes up to four scenes made up a unit, while at other times only a single scene did. Act divisions were ignored. These were rehearsed in the same order they would be performed in the production which was generally, but not always, the order in which they appeared in the text. The zone of interest for each scene was then plotted.

While Payne did numerous productions of many of Shakespeare's plays, only a few were well documented, and it may be most instructive to look at his *Measure for Measure* in 1927, as that would lend itself most readily to a comparison with Poel's staging. Payne first cut nearly 900 lines from the text, focusing it on three dramatic movements involving three sets of characters; the undercover spying by the Duke, the corruption of Angelo and the moral decay of the city (Rucker 1982: 270). The first four scenes of the play (Act I) were then plotted as follows:

- Scene 1: 'the Dukes Palace,' middle stage;
- Scene 2: 'a street,' forestage;
- Scene 3: 'a monastery,' inner below;
- Scene 4: 'a nunnery,' inner above.

The next four scenes (Act II) alternated between the forestage and middle stage with the last scene incorporating both. But in order to make this possible, the actual Act II, Scene 3, set in 'the prison', was cut, and in its place Act III Scene 2, set on 'a street', was substituted. Although Payne, like Poel, argued forcefully against the wholesale removal of scenes and reorganisation of the text in this way, both violated their own teachings when they felt it improved the flow of the action in the drama. The first scenes of Act III, 'the prison', took the production into intermission, making use of the middle stage in conjunction first with the inner above and then with the inner below. The first three scenes of Act IV, which followed the intermission, continued to use the middle stage in conjunction with the inner below and the inner above (Rucker 1982: 268–95). The last three scenes made use of the forestage, including Scene 4, which is localised as 'a room in Angelo's House' and therefore should have been on the middle stage. But Payne considered this an expository scene and therefore appropriate to the forestage location. The play closes with Act V, Scene 1 'the City Gates' which made use of the full stage for the first time. In theory, then, a scene was assigned to a zone based on the kind of scene it was thought to be. But, in practice, Payne often experimented as he changed his mind about what kind of scene he was really dealing with. Ultimately, zone placement seems to have been determined by Payne's intuitive sense of what felt right for the production, causing Shattuck to comment that 'his breakdown of the dramatic and psychological significance of the various portions of the platform – Middle stage, Fore stage, and right and left Side stages – which he calls "zones of interest," seems quite too private a set of distinctions to be worth spelling out' (1978: 307). But the system did work, and was generally found quite effective.

Once the zones were set, the details could be worked out. Furniture and properties were selected to localise scenes staged in the middle, inner-below and inner-above zones. More importantly, the opening and closing of the curtains on the inner above, inner below and between the posts had to be choreographed. Young men, or young women dressed as boys, were blocked into the performances to open, close or partially close the curtains in whatever combination was needed in as unobtrusive a manner as possible. Eventually, Payne found the use of the curtains behind the stage posts predictable and not nearly as necessary as he had originally thought. Although he never fully abandoned them, he used them less and less. This was made possible, however, by Payne's most significant break with Elizabethan staging practices, the use of electric stage lighting. Like Poel's most accomplished follower in England, W. Nugent Monck, Payne embraced stage lighting and used it not only for its intrinsic beauty but also to reinforce the focus on a given zone or a given character.

Payne's primary interest, however, was always on the verse. Though he did not follow Poel's systems of tones, he did read the play to the cast at the beginning of each rehearsal period, giving them an indication of proper pronunciation, inflection and the emphasis that would make the meaning of each speech clear. Much of the early rehearsal period was spent going over character relationships and word meaning. Scene rehearsals saw Payne reading each speech before the actor was asked to deliver it (Bowmer 1974: 29). Again, Payne seems to have grasped Poel's goal but modified the approach to achieving it.

Between 1917 and 1949, Payne did twenty-seven productions of Shakespeare's plays at Carnegie Tech, all the while refining his staging technique. After he left the chairmanship in 1928, he joined Stevens for three years at the Goodman Theatre in Chicago where he both acted (he was an accomplished actor) and directed, then returned to his freelance work. He served as an artist in residence at Washington State University in 1930, where his work was seen by Angus Bowmer, who later created a Shakespeare festival in Ashland, Oregon (Bowmer 1979: 10–11). This festival was founded on Payne's modified Elizabethan-stage system, which they used for decades. But before that festival was created, Payne was invited by Stevens to join him in a project to stage cut-down versions of Shakespeare's plays in a reconstructed Globe playhouse for the second year (1934) of the 'Century of Progress' World's Fair in Chicago. Payne did a thirty-six-minute version of *Comedy of Errors* for them, and a thirty-seven-minute version of *As You Like It.* He was unable to stay with the company as it set up similar Globes at the California Pacific International Exhibition at San Diego (1935) and both the Texas Centennial Exposition in Dallas and the Great Lakes Exposition in Cleveland, Ohio (1936), but the productions done on those stages used the zone system that Payne had developed, and actors from those productions took their own versions of modified Elizabethan staging into colleges and universities for many years thereafter. One of those actors, from the Cleveland company, was Sam Wanamaker, who thirty-five years later would start the project that eventually lead to the creation of Shakespeare's Globe in London.

What took Payne away from the Globe company was being hired as the Artistic Director of the Shakespeare Memorial Theatre in Stratford-upon-Avon where he worked from 1935 to 1942. Payne did over forty productions using his system there, including *Measure for Measure* and a *Hamlet* (1940) that was considered the fastest production of that play ever staged. He also discovered Donald Wolfit, who he taught to speak verse and who became his son-in-law. Payne says almost nothing of his years at Stratford in his memoirs. When Ruth Ellis wrote the history of the Memorial Theatre in 1948, she referred to Payne as a scholar-director whose productions were seen by the critics as 'sound but not inspired' (1948: 82). Yet, at the same time, she notes that the festivals, attendance figures were breaking records under Payne's leadership. Shattuck seems to have put his finger on the problem when he noted that by the 1920s 'interpretations' of Shakespeare had come into vogue. At the same time that Payne was doing his modified Elizabeth staging for many (but not all) of his productions at Stratford, Tyrone Guthrie was running the old Vic with unusual stage business and 'astonishing displays of costume and scenery' to wow the critics. 'The discerning few who took their Shakespeare neat, as they would take Michelangelo or Mozart, appreciated his [Payne's] intelligence, integrity, and faithfulness to the texts' (Shattuck 1978: 306). But Payne's approach, no matter how successful it was with the public, lacked the innovation that critics fixated on in the early twentieth century.

After leaving Stratford, Payne returned to his freelance directing career in the USA, doing several shows on Broadway. He was the first big-name hire for the Department of Drama at the University of Texas in 1946, at the age of 65, and a regular director for the Shakespeare theatres in San Diego, California and Ashland, Oregon after 1949. For over twenty years, he worked at universities and regional theatres around the country and inspired a whole generation of theatre departments and Shakespeare festival directors to emulate his approach. During this period, he repeated *Measure for Measure*, both for the old Globe in San Diego (1955) and for the University of Texas (1965). He directed his last play, *The Tempest*, at the University of Texas in 1968, sixty-nine years after he first joined Frank Benson's company.

The system Payne taught was based on the pragmatism he learned in his early years in the Edwardian theatre. This was both its great strength and its major weakness. As a strength, Payne's system was flexible enough to ensure that no hard and fast dogma got in the way of staging Shakespeare's plays effectively. Zone theory, especially, was an art, not a science, and it relied on the intuition of the director to make it work. As a weakness, his 'modified Elizabethan staging' system seemed to depend too much on compromises to be dynamic. It did not have the idealistic purity of Poel's dictates, even if it was in some ways truer to Poel's ideals than Poel himself was. It did not have the radical modernism of the 'concept' approach to Shakespeare, even though it was more appealing to the average audience. But modified Elizabethan staging was a consistently effective and highly influential system that brought breathtaking speed and clarity to the performance of Shakespeare's plays in a manner that was both aesthetically attractive and economically cost-effective.

Chronology

1881	5 September, born at Newcastle-upon-Tyne, England, son of Alfred and Sarah Payne; Moved to Manchester the following year
1898–1902	spent 4 weeks with Benson Company (1898), toured with Mile Gratienne's company (1898–99), returned to Benson Company for provincial and Irish tour (1899–1900), and joined Carlyn and Charlton 'fit-up' company (1900–2)
1902–6	did another Irish tour with Benson's second company (1902–3) as assistant stage manager and actor, toured as stage manager and actor with *A Pair of Specticals*, and *The Importance of Being Earnest* for Arthur Hare Company (1903–4), did West Indies tour with Benson company (1904–5), followed by various tours during which he first worked on Rostand's *Les Romanesques*, translated as *The Fantastics*
1907–11	hired as producer for the Abbey Theatre (Feb–June 1907) and for the Manchester Playgoers' Theatre (Sept 1907–Oct 1911); started Payne company with wife Mona Limerick (Dec 1910)
1911–15	ran Payne company with his wife and a second company with his friend, H. Theodore, which continued until August 1914. Does 12-week inaugural season for Chicago Fine Arts Theatre (1913), before returning to England for tour that includes 4 weeks at Gaiety Theatre, Manchester, started a repertory company in Philadelphia, directed first summer show at Carnegie Institute for Technology and started working for the Shuberts with *The Critic* (1914), directed *Hobson's Choice* and *Desire Under the Elms* for Shuberts (1915)
1916–34	director and then staff director for Frohman organization (1916–22), his programme credit reads 'staged by' until 1920 when he is first listed as director, a term not common until 1940s; continued directing summer show at Carnegie Tech, where he became visiting professor of Drama (1919–34) and acting chair of the Department of Drama (1925–28); developed 'modified Elizabethan staging' (1925). Did freelance directing on Broadway including season with the Theatre Guild (1928–9) and both acted and directed at Goodman Theatre in Chicago (1928–30); directs *Love's Labors Lost* at University of

Washington (1930), and creates 40-minute stagings of *Comedy of Errors* and *As You Like It* for Old Globe playhouse at Century of Progress World's Fair in Chicago (1934); similar Globes at San Diego, California (1935), Dallas, Texas, and Cleveland, Ohio (1936), used versions of Payne's zone staging

1934–43 served as artistic director, Shakespeare Memorial Theatre, Stratford-upon-Avon

1943–6 lectured for British Ministry of Information in USA and returned as freelance director to Broadway and as visiting professor to Carnegie Tech (1944–9; also was guest director at University of Washington and University of Iowa (1943)

1946–68 joined faculty at University of Texas at Austin; worked for San Diego National Shakespeare Festival (1949–52, 1955 and 1964) and for Oregon Shakespeare Festival (1956, 1958 and 1961) and was a guest director at the Universities of Missouri (1947–8), Colorado (1953), Michigan (1954) and Alberta 1958–60 and 1962) and at the Baniff School of Fine Arts, Alberta, Canada (1957–64)

1976 Died 6 April.

Bibliography

Allard, Stephen (1916) 'William Poel in America', *Theatre Arts* (November): 24–6.

Bowmer, Angus L. (1974) *As I Remember Adam*, Ashland, Oreg.: Oregon Shakespearian Festival Association.

—— (1978) *The Ashland Elizabethan Stage*, Chapbook #1, Ashland, Oreg.: Oregon Shakespearian Festival Association.

—— (1979) *Acting and Directing on the Ashland Elizabethan Stage*, Chapbook # 2, Ashland, Oreg.: Oregon Shakespearian Festival Association.

Ellis, Ruth (1948) *The Shakespeare Memorial Theatre*, London: Winchester Publications.

Feldman, Donna Rose (1953) 'An Historical Study of Thomas Wood Stevens Globe Theatre Company, 1934–1937', Ph.D dissertation, University of Iowa.

Gaedertz, Karl Theodor (1888) *Zur Kenntis der altenglischen Bühne, nebst andern Beiträzur Shakespeare-Litteratur*, Bremen: C.E. Müller.

Gelber, William Francis (1997) 'Ben Iden Payne: His Road to Shakespeare', Ph.D. dissertation, University of Texas.

Harris, Arthur John (1988) 'William Poel's *Measure for Measure* at Stratford-upon-Avon, 1908', *Speech and Drama* 37 (1): 13–21, 51–4.

Hildy, Franklin J. (1986) *Shakespeare at the Maddermarket: W. Nugent Monck and the Norwich Players*, Ann Arbor, Mich.: University of Michigan Press.

Paget, Alfred Henry (1891) 'The Elizabethan Play-House', *Transactions of the Leicester Literary and Philosophical Society*, (January): 237–50.

Payne, Ben Iden (1950) 'Directing the Verse Play', *Educational Theatre Journal* 2 (3): 193–8.

—— (1967) 'Shakespeare at Work in His Theatre', *Educational Theatre Journal* 19 (3): 327–32.

—— (1977) *A Life in a Wooden O: Memoirs of the Theatre*, New Haven, Conn.: Yale University Press.

—— (n.d.) 'A Road to Shakespeare', manuscript, Hoblitzelle Fine Art Library, University of Texas at Austin.

Rucker, Patrick Casseday (1982) 'Ben Iden Payne and the Development of the Modified Elizabethan Stage', Ph.D. dissertation, Texas Technical University.

Shattuck, Charles H. (1978) 'Memoirs of B. Iden Payne: Review of *A Life In a Wooden O: Memoirs of the Theatre*. By Ben Iden Payne', *Shakespeare Quarterly* 29 (2): 304–8.

Speaight, Robert (1954) *William Poel and the Elizabethan Revival*, Cambridge, Mass.: Harvard University Press.

About the author

Franklin J. Hildy is Professor and Director of Graduate Studies in the Department of Theatre at University of Maryland. He is author of *Shakespeare at the Maddermarket: Nugent Monck and the Norwich Players* (1986), editor of *New Issues in the Reconstruction of Shakespeare's Theatre* (1990), co-author, with Oscar G. Brockett of four editions of *History of the Theatre* and over fifty articles on a wide range of topics, including the history of efforts to reconstruct the theatres of Shakespeare's day. He as severed as an adviser to Shakespeare's Globe, London since 1984 and has been a consultant on numerous reconstruction attempts in the USA.

20
ROGER PLANCHON

Gerry McCarthy

There is a photograph in the archives of *Le Parisien Libéré* depicting a provincial event: a 14-year-old Roger Planchon receiving the Croix de Guerre. He stands in his Boy Scout uniform before the Collège au Lazaristes and is invested by the provincial military commander. In July 1944, Planchon had been entrusted by a wounded *résistant* with the task of bringing news to his fellows. Arrested by the Germans, he was beaten and imprisoned but hid the written message. He subsequently escaped to complete his mission.

This encounter was never lost on Planchon and, later, when he staged Brecht's *Schweyk dans la deuxième guerre mondiale*, he described his fear at the sight of a stage property – a German soldier's helmet. He has more generally expressed a delight in the immediacy of dramatic performance and its distillation of 'real' experience in time and space, which he sometimes describes as 'poetic'. This 'reality' of the stage performance reappears in Planchon's statements on theatre and on his own performances as an actor and director. The term will serve here when considering the place of Shakespeare in the first phase of work after childhood years spent in a country at war and under occupation. For Planchon, work in the theatre was grounded in experience, as much as were the issues of politics and history of the second half of the twentieth century.

The nation that emerged from the war was ready for change and celebrated the spirit of resistance, hardly universally expressed during the conflict. A need was felt for a new representation of the nation and its heritage. The dominance of Paris and its political cadres was challenged, and cultural policies were adopted to address all France and all its classes. This was to involve support for a decentralised theatre – a policy of change but also of conservation and extension of a heritage.

Roger Planchon, born in 1931, came to theatre at a moment when it was being recreated for a public and in regions where it had been too little known. His formal education had ended early. He came from a poor family in the rural Ardèche and was born in St Chamond in the Lyonnais, where his parents kept a café near to the steelworks, and thus his first occupations were herding his grandfather's four cows and waiting at table. (He was to say that Shakespeare wrote for his mother who could not read.) He owes much to the friendship of a Brother Paul at his Lyon college who introduced him to poetry and painting. He discovered difficult and 'marvellous' works of modern writers, and in the cinema he was stunned by Orson Welles and the masterpiece he saw seven or eight times, *Citizen Kane*. He began to think of becoming an actor and, guided by his readings, undertook his own physical training. At the time of Orson Welles's death in 1985, he offered *Le Monde* an appreciation of the film and of Welles the actor. Planchon describes him as a 'poet'.

> A tidal wave carried me away. Even more than the skill of the scenario, than the invention of the narrative scheme, than the cunning of the linking of images and sequences, which are studied in schools and in books on cinema, there are his eyes that laugh, his inner gaze. A clear, precise and dreamlike manner of looking at the real. A singular gaze, immensely generous and noble, of such great goodness that one stands dumbfounded. Because he was authentically a poet, the gaze of Orson Welles is nothing but goodness.

He goes on to identify the sense of reality as conveyed by Welles's art, returning to his own life experience of the war:

> No words of an adult on the death of one of my fellows, on the cruelty of war and its misery, both of which, however, I have known in full measure [. . .] have made me sense, as did this film, the very heart of reality, its size, its weight, its violence, its hidden inconsistency.

A number of factors intersect here that will become characteristic of Planchon: the preoccupation with the real and its kinship with imagination and dream, and the moral power of the actor. The bridge between stage and spectator is the actor in whom the audience shares a way of seeing and experiencing human action. 'Reality' is a question of knowledge, embedded in physical experience, and it is felt in the shared rhythms of actor and spectator.

Roger Planchon is, in his own words, a provincial, rooted in the Ardèche. Creating with a handful of friends in 1952 their first theatre, the Théâtre de la Comédie in the centre of Lyon, was an onerous business, which involved the negotiation of subsidies and the mollifying of the city council. When a space could be found for performance, their repertoire was criticised, resulting, on one occasion, in eviction from a parochial hall for an irreligious programme of Marlowe's *Edward II* and *Faustus* (inspired by Artaud and his affinity with seventeenth-century texts). While homeless, the newly professional company played Shakespearian comedy, conceived for outdoor performances. Both *Twelfth Night* and *The Merry Wives of Windsor* reflected another enthusiasm, for comedy and the Italian tradition, and a concern to create an audience for the auditorium that by day they were constructing in the city.

In these early productions one may see the embryonic style of Planchon and his unified troupe (immediately identified by the press as *Les Planchon*), and it stresses materiality. Everything was the work of the acting company: lighting, stage costume design, construction and musical composition and execution. *Les Planchon* worked as labourers building their theatre and the fit-up stages for Shakespeare in Lyon parks. Costumes aimed at a period effect but were cut with a necessary improvisation; and spaces and ramps served the merely efficient movement of actors. Evening performances relied on simple lighting: ghostly footlights bathed the feet of the actors and spilt onto the makeshift facings of rostra and steps. Planchon's productions reveal the sheer effort needed to create both theatres and shows with the most scanty of means. The corresponding effort in performance, however, produced work that, uninhibited by material restrictions, attained an accuracy and expression unexpected in a young company.

The freshness and sensibility of playing was frequently noticed. A programme note invited the audience outdoors to share the physical quality of acting, of the human voice and presence in space, rather than any poetical notion of a 'garden theatre'.

> If the theatre goes to take breath in the open air, this is not for reasons of aestheticism but of hygiene. The actor needs to feel the words of his role melt in the wellsprings of the night; the spectator needs to encounter the calm mass of shadows.
>
> We invite you to this communion which we know to be necessary, through the shattering of auditorium and stage, by the fusion of fiction and reality, by what that reality brings to the dream. If there is magic in the theatre, it rediscovers its sense in the open air. There, thanks to a bare stage, the drama can find its true measure, farce its true element and enchantment its springboard.

Their confidence is striking. Shakespeare in the open air led Planchon to a deeper understanding of drama in time and space, beyond the confines of the tiny theatres where the company had begun its professional activity. 'Reality' and 'dream' are coupled to express the actors' living realisation of a *virtual* world, *actually* felt by the spectator. All this is 'thanks to the bare stage'. The feeling of words as a physical phenomenon resonated in space and registered in the nervous experience of the actor was to be a crucial element in Planchon's philosophy and practice of drama.

When he next turns to Shakespeare, Planchon will have a different concern for scenography and a more assertive stage presentation, customarily expected of a great theatre director, but in these early productions (*Twelfth Night* remains in the repertoire for five years), the company was at home in the hands of a dramatist who became Planchon's master. Looking back on these early years (and on his staging of the sometime surrealist poet, René Char), Planchon explains his concerns for text and for 'reality' in performance:

> in the theatre, it is not the density of language which creates its poetry but its exactness with respect to the sharpness of the dramatic situation which is presented [. . .] Beyond the words, often between the lines, the landscape of the unsayable is present. It is always necessary to make the characters speak in an everyday fashion, to make them speak, moving between ideas and emotions, but also while placing them on the edge of the abyss of reality, there where precisely the poets dwell and keep watch.
>
> (Bataillon 2001: I, 96)

We shall return later to these remarks, which express the (surprisingly) surrealist nature of Planchon's aesthetic. For a director whose first statements, above, include a rejection of aestheticism in favour of 'hygiene' in performance, Planchon's search for poetry at the edge of the 'abyss' of reality sounds surprisingly theoretical. Nonetheless, and particularly in his relationship with Shakespeare, he thinks in terms of a medium that is material and yet that transforms mental experience in its audience. Shakespeare's alchemy transmuted material life into the dreamlike experience of art. And this resembled his way of contemplating the rigour of peasant life and experiences. When speaking of his forebears, he describes feeling as a boy, in clogs and short trousers, herding cattle on the mountainside under the Ardèche skies, that his people was 'the stuff (*matière*) of their own dreams'. Three terms later, he found expression for his feeling in Shakespeare's 'striking words': *une phrase fulgurante*.

When, in 1957, Planchon was given control of the municipal theatre in Villeurbanne, a working-class borough in the Lyons conurbation, he surveyed his audience: the two writers Villeurbanne wanted were Dumas and, the second more clearly a dramatist, William Shakespeare. The tradition of the house in playing light musical comedies was dear to the town council and was a 'popular' genre they wished to continue. It was also required by the terms of

Planchon's contract. In his inaugural season, Planchon duly played an adaptation of *Les Trois Mousquetaires*, but first of all he programmed the two parts of *Henry IV*: he did not include any operetta, and his decision was defiant. He staked his personal vision of a popular theatre, and all hinged on the success of a monumental undertaking: the staging of the two parts of *Henry IV* subtitled *Le Prince* and *Falstaff*: five and a half hours of theatre with one long interval. The minutes of the town council show the incomprehension of his paymasters:

> Monsieur Brinon reproaches Monsieur Planchon for having signed a contract that he has in no way respected. He regrets that no operettas are performed in order to make way for *The Life of Henry IV* which interests no-one, and in particular the Villeurbannais. The theatre must be for the worker a relaxation, a rest and not a Chinese puzzle [. . .] Monsieur le Maire sums up what has been said and declares: *If the theatre could be closed, I should be the happiest of men.*
>
> (Bataillon 2001: II, 48)

But Planchon could claim that his popular audience liked this allegedly alien and complicated entertainment. In the discussions that regularly followed performances, it was clear that uneducated spectators enjoyed the history of an English king, and they were shrewd judges of the play. Above all, and to the satisfaction of the director, they understood the play as a struggle for political power and for class domination. Planchon was fond of quoting the worker who stood up to explain the action: the son of the factory boss, who disappoints his father, hanging about in the bistrot with common workers, subsequently goes to the wars (in Indo-China). When he comes back, restored in his father's estimation, he takes over the factory and is a more brutal boss than his father before him.

A wide popular audience implied no lessening of artistic quality in the show, nor any lowering of intellectual demands, but it required a campaign of information and dialogue aimed at the workers of the city, who were unfamiliar with the customs and practices of the stage. This was a campaign that Planchon led, loudspeaker in hand, at the gates of the Berliet truck factory, debating the accessibility of theatre to his chosen audience. Planchon firmly believed that his audience possessed awareness and judgement and cited its sophisticated response to cinema and the montage of images, which went unremarked by hostile critics but bore a clear relationship to the speed and complexity of the images of Shakespeare's open stage.

Planchon already understood how the power of drama can be felt by the common man who sees in the fiction of the stage a structure of action corresponding to life around him. This is an embedded understanding (Michael

Polanyi calls it *tacit knowledge*) of fellow human beings in action, which leads to apprehension in general of patterns of events. That knowledge leads to the recognition of the events that Planchon called the *fable* of the play. When, in the wake of the success of *Henry IV*, Planchon was seen as a Brechtian, he was identified with a theory, and this consecrated his work among intellectuals. Planchon was more attentive to the practice of Brecht, whom he had met in 1955, having studied *Theaterarbeit* and a year after a somewhat tentative production of *The Good Person of Setchuan*. Brecht confirmed his instinctive belief that the *fable* was the armature of the dramatic performance: one should not enquire, he would later say, 'Who is Tartuffe?' (as did much academic criticism), but 'What does Tartuffe do?' Planchon, involved with his working-class audience, naturally responded to the concept and spirit of Brechtian Epic theatre, and when still engaged with *Henry IV* was arguing that practical models should be studied to learn how to make the form more effective.

More important than theory were Brecht's use of scenic space and his stage language. Planchon's way of understanding the Brechtian lesson was to stress the need for scenic elements to discharge a 'responsibility' to the play, meaning, one may infer, that these elements are 'answerable' to the evolution of the action, the *fable* played out on the stage. In the same way, the text was responsible. It is not helpful to assert, as has been done, that this means simply that the scenic language is as important as the text but rather that they are both similarly a function of what is *really* or, better, *actually*, done in performance.

For *Henry IV*, René Allio joined Planchon as designer, and their working relationship was to be close and fruitful. Allio was able to realise Planchon's notion of the 'responsibility' of the set and in ways that showed the absorption of Brecht's scenographic techniques. The design that he produced for *Henry IV* was an open stage with screens, showing maps, contemporary with the historical period of the play and a minimal setting of furniture and props for different locations. The set supports the action by the use of captions specifying the progress of events and resuming their content. Planchon here draws on Brecht's practice and his own observation of the popular cinema audience and the effectiveness of a montage of episodes.

The playing of the scene is contextualised by the detailed use of objects. But in Planchon's work the object does more than localise the performance, it grounds the performance in the material world. More than a scenic indication, the stage property, or the stuff of a costume, becomes part of the sensory world of the performer. In the progressive restagings of the play (four further seasons between 1958 and 1965), one sees the search for a material quality of properties and costumes. Some of this is preserved in the production photographs, in, say, the scene between Prince Harry and the King (*King Henry IV*, Act IV, Scene 3), where the attention of the two actors to the crown conveys the disciplined physical power of the performance. Similarly, in the tavern scenes, the personal space of the actor contains textures and materials that create the sensual immediacy that is a vital aspect of Planchon's 'reality'. The performance of Jean Bouise was, this early in his career, received as the greatest French Falstaff, so intense was the living presence of the actor. Planchon later discussed this feeling for life in a 1972 interview for *Theatre Quarterly*: 'I have a passion for what is concrete. Everything that is really palpable, concrete, pleases me. I like life in its most elementary state, without heightening [. . .] It's the whole feeling of life passing, something very fragile which doesn't last, which is miraculous in the truest sense of the word'.

Thus he spoke of his set and staging in *Henry IV* as following Shakespeare in assembling different elements of the dramaturgy:

> we needed to show, to get across, changes, apparent contradictions. Our costumes are then as little decorated as possible: their function is above all to classify. [. . .] Similarly for the set. But here we have tried something new: a set in three elements whose functions are distinguishable. The first, this is the equivalent of stage blacks; we call this, with Allio, the closed space, the container. The second is the commentary. But, for *Henry IV*, the commentary and the container are the same: these are the contemporary maps which both frame and indicate the place of the action, at the same time placing it in historical time. Finally the third is the different locations.

Planchon and Allio were conscious of the scenic language they adapted from Brecht but also knew from Jean Vilar's work at the Théâtre National Populaire in Paris, and at the Avignon Festival: '. . . we have taken from Vilar his principle of the spotlight, of the cone of light which circumscribes a place, and which enlarges or diminishes it at will. All of that, deliberately not real. But what is real is everything that touches the human body: here, we have real objects'.

Asked if he betrayed Shakespeare in any way with this narrowing of focus on the material reality of life, Planchon replied confidently, opposing philosophical materialism and 'spiritualism': 'Our Shakespeare appeared quite natural, and it is [. . .] We played Shakespeare in the most literal, the most material manner possible. And then, our public does not know Shakespeare, it has not meditated on *Hamlet*, it has no spiritualistic prejudices' (Bataillon 2001: II, 31).

Planchon's set fixed the play within a framework of history, while the environment was immediately sensed by the actor's body. The acting was deliberately reserved, close to a 'degree zero' Planchon later described. It was 'prosaic', not high-flown. If ever the actors pursued an effect, an inflated generalisation, the production 'let them down, they could go no further, or if they tried, they fell flat on their faces' (*se casser la gueule*). Respect for the text meant understanding of its dramatic quality, creating the texture of life and living that the actor *actually* encounters in Shakespeare's *fable*. It was a text where imagination and actual sensation were interdependent and interactive: poetry and reality were reciprocally alive.

Undoubtedly, the 'prosaic' realisation of the stage event might be the consequence of the French director's lack of the original text. However, with *Henry IV* and in later productions, Planchon took pains with language. In a preface to the play, he later explained the material life of text:

> Theatrical dialogue is a *matière* in the sense in which the term is used in modern painting. Squeezed out of the tube, it does not serve to define the problem, but hardens to fix the nature and contours of human beings caught up in a particular action. Conflict of ideas abstracts the character; the course of the action and the *matière* of the dialogue give him a solid base. Shakespeare makes use of all the verbal ironmongery of the tournaments, or courtly love and knightly jousting. He turns it into honey by distilling the poetry from it [. . .] In order to enjoy the story you must like paddling in this verbal compost, where part of our childhood comes back to us.
>
> (Planchon: 1972: 8)

This reminds us that Planchon was and is an actor. And he is a dramatist. The familiar academic analyses of plays express only one *abstract* level of drama ('the conflict of ideas' every French schoolchild would know as the phrase which would express the pressure of love and duty in the Cornelian tragedy), whereas the deeper understandings of drama are momentary and evolving in the play of bodies and human minds in the space blatantly before us:

> The average speech in the theatre develops an argument, but these long speeches of Shakespeare's are arguments whose words radiate outwards and explode. I find myself appreciating the substantial difference between unreeling and radiation, between the linear and the circular expression of ideas.
>
> The fact that my English is rudimentary will explain this naïve approach, but I believe in it.
>
> (Planchon 1972: 9)

The materiality of the actor explains Planchon's idiosyncratic linking of reality and poetry. One can believe, if not his 'rudimentary English', that this play, his 'first great pleasure in the theatre', was to change the course of his life. One can also see how the English play could be effective in a working-class French town, in another language. Planchon's politics and his poetry flourished in a culture of work and struggle, which echoed the sonorities of Shakespeare.

He needed his audience and his workers' theatre in order to create his style. And the assurance of that style was seen in the next classic play performed at Villeurbanne: Molière's *George Dandin*. Here, the short three-act play, originally the basis for a *comédie-ballet*, was staged with an enlarged cast creating vignettes in place of the dancing: short scenes of life in the farmyard of a prosperous peasant in a comic misalliance to a young gentlewoman. This provided a background upon which the lighter action of the cuckolded husband and social antagonism could be felt and understood. Allio's work for both *George Dandin* (1962) and then *Tartuffe* (1964) subtly embraced the plays by a design that 'commented' upon the action, and did it in a remarkably beautiful materialist fashion.

Planchon's new designer, André Acquart, developed this house style for Planchon's next Shakespeare production, *Troilus and Cressida* (1964). The set would brutally change and vary space according to the demands of groups of actors and the different styles of action in different scenes. One critic describes the effect as being like the shuffling of a pack of cards, while another evokes the hectic rhythm possible on this set, described by Planchon as a 'tool for acting'. Planchon departs from the *netteté*, the clarity of Vilar's unencumbered style which he admired, to experiment with his other model, Brecht. Views divided on the effect, and even those who admired the conception convey something of the heaviness of the method:

> André Acquart has conceived a changeable set of monstrous proportions. At the beginning of the action, a double wall separates the Greek camp from that of the Trojans. This wall, within which the gates of Troy open, pivots stage left and right, unfolding with its movement very realistic settings for a *salle d'armes*, a royal tent, a palace, for a garden or for the lists. While the action is unfolding in an opened set, another is being prepared. Stagehands, mingling with the cast, move the wall, and the new setting appears, completed with a few props brought on naturally by the actors. In the last act, that of the battle, the wall comes apart into movable flats, which change position with the rhythm of the fight, creating a feeling of uncontrolled movement. This set takes on a fundamental importance, for it is thanks to it that the play can proceed helter-skelter. Without a dead instant.
>
> (*La Vie Lyonnaise*, 22 January 1964)

The staging was not universally liked, nor was the acting, Planchon's greatest strength. Where one critic defends the production, he adds that doubtless Planchon will, as he always does over a period, find improvements. And yet the play, although little known, was judged startlingly modern. For an audience that remembered the Occupation, only twenty years past, and had scarcely recovered from the trauma of the war in Algeria, the effect was staggering. A reviewer conveys something of the impact of the playing and the context that was generated: 'I greatly admired the Thersites of Gerard Guillaumat. His sniggering clown has a tragic breadth, and an overpowering humanity. A cold comic performance of utter despair' (*Le Progrès*, 25 January 1964).

Planchon had nevertheless given himself and his actors a new challenge in preparing the script. Jacques Rosner and Yves Kerboul, his assistant directors, initially constructed a draft translation from all the available French versions and had the aid of a panel of distinguished academics when necessary to clarify the structure of the language, its levels of style and range of reference. Thus they were able to supply Planchon with a first text which, if somewhat literal, preserved the complexity of the original, and on this basis he wrote the performing version, reinforced by his study of French baroque writers of the late sixteenth century.

When *Troilus and Cressida* was subsequently performed in a Paris season at Barrault's Théâtre de l'Odéon, the text was criticised and questions raised even as to its understanding by the actors. On the other hand, the dramatist, Michel Vinaver, acknowledging a problem, found that at the second hearing he could appreciate the quality of the production. When Planchon had prepared *Henry IV*, he had adapted the text to promote the swift progress of a lengthy action and to aid an audience and actors unused to Shakespeare's style. The attempt in *Troilus and Cressida* to render the density of the *matière*, the 'circular' rhetorical text, was only a qualified success. Planchon's efforts to engage his actors can be judged from later remarks on the actor Michel Bouquet. He requires a reserve in the actor, who must not overpower the text but be available (*disponible*) and attentive to it. Planchon gives an example of the physical preparation of text and the address to muscle memory: 'I explain to the actors that one must apply a *pressure* (*une pulsion*), a feeling, upon a phrase, and a different pressure upon another, while trying to pass from one to another through a zero point'. The failure to achieve this alternation of effort and recovery is accurately described: 'in general the beginning of the second phrase retains the tone of the previous one'. Stated thus, Planchon describes a familiar phenomenon: generalisation. This produces the progressive inflation of an unspecific emotion instead of the incisive *feeling of what happens* (to borrow from Antonio Damasio's discussion of human consciousness).

Planchon requires the actor 'not to play, to hold back, and to have first of all a memory'. Before one dismisses the comments as too banal – a memory is obviously required! – Planchon conveys the physical quality of the player's memory: 'Bouquet is a machine that records everything. The text, of course, and movements, that is the minimum memory. But also the impulses stored away [. . .] In a great actor you have five thousand pieces of information concerning the scene' (*Paris Hebdo*, 17 March 1977).

There is more than a hint of the practice and thinking of Louis Jouvet, recorded in his Conservatoire classes of 1940, where similarly the lesson for the actor of the classical dramatist (in his case, Molière) is a restraint and a physical disposition to accept the rhythms of life that are formed in the execution of text. Jouvet describes this as 'respiration', both a matter of control in the execution of a performance and the organic basis of life – breath – felt by the actor and resonated by the operation of sympathetic response in the audience.

Two years later, Planchon returned to Shakespeare in accepting Jean Vilar's invitation to Avignon where the Theatre de la Cité would work alongside Maurice Béjart and the Ballet du XXe siècle. With Michel Auclair already in the company playing Tartuffe and free until August, Planchon chose Shakespeare and *Richard III*: 'I think I have assembled one of the finest Shakespearian casts possible. What is more, I have chosen Richard *III* in accordance with the actors available. Even the smallest roles will be taken by excellent actors' (Bataillon 2001: II, 252).

Given the pressure on Planchon at this time, as working actor, director and the manager of a company touring abroad and working periodically in the capital, the exposure as the virtual successor of Vilar was an enormous burden. Thus his return to Shakespeare was significant. The casting of Michel Auclair, known as a screen actor, was as notable as Vilar's similar collaboration with Gérard Philippe a decade earlier in Corneille's *Le Cid*. Francine Bergé, who had played in Planchon's successful *Bérénice*, would play Lady Anne. At every level, there were huge expectations from a curious public.

Vilar had created a vast stage and a new auditorium – of 3,000 seats – outside the walls of the Petit Palais, but the environment was not the magical setting Planchon evoked in his thoughts on *Twelfth Night* a decade earlier, given the exposure to the blistering sun during nine days of get-in and technical rehearsal and, in performance, the ever-threatening Mistral. Nonetheless, the result was remarkable. Above all, Planchon's ability to discover the springs and motors of the action was noted, as was his detailed understanding of individual roles:

> He makes no difference between the good and the wicked. He simply

> puts in place the mechanisms and the men and invites us to observe as under a lens these human brothers who devour one another. Richard III is not a black hero of traditional interpretations but the emanation of an age without pity. [. . .]
>
> In this Shakesearean *Richard III*, scrutinised with penetrating intelligence by Roger Planchon, it is solely a question of the lines of force between characters of guts and power.
>
> (*Le Progrès*, 29 July 1966)

Not only was Planchon's understanding of the action judged masterly but also his method was well adapted to this vast popular amphitheatre and was applied with a sure hand. Planchon later explained to *L'Humanité* the appeal of the play for the modern audience:

> It is, in 1967, an interesting play, for it takes politics seriously. It is a description of political behaviour which is capable of bringing the citizen to his senses. Shakespeare is the only one who has known what happens in a council of ministers in a period of crisis. As to the play, it is a game of political negations. As to the problem posed, this concerns the assumption of power. It is a miraculously successful play, where history and psychology and individual pathology intersect exactly.

The design executed by Claude Lemaire answered Planchon's need for concrete images and solid masses on the stage. Costumes served to *reduce* the classification of groups (unlike *Henry IV*) their similar egg-shell colourings integrating them with the sandy stone wall against which they performed. When it came to battle scenes, the large company (fifty-nine actors on the vast stage) could indifferently represent soldiers of any party. The material feeling of the stage was further increased by the contrast of different instruments, or machines, for the making of war, or for torture or punishment; and, as if part of this fearsome array others simply for seating or for eating. This quality goes so far as the rough-hewn wood of the coffin (rather than any cloth bier), which Lady Anne follows.

The word that best described Planchon's qualities as director of this massive show is 'intelligence'. The outdoor space was vast, but Planchon sought and preserved a clarity that seized and compelled the imagination. The critic of *Le Soir* was totally disarmed:

> I remain still dazzled by this miracle of a show which, for four hours, made me forget the discomfort of the seat, the chill of the wind which got up, tiredness, sleep. Better still, had the herald announced two

> hours of extra playing time I would have gladly stayed, until dawn, fascinated by this new form of theatre, by these fantastic actors, by the mystery taking shape before my eyes.

Planchon had reached a point of impasse. His materialist and grounded production allowed the play to speak for itself, with no repeat of the textual difficulties criticised in *Troilus and Cressida*, and the actuality of the acting style he encouraged served the text and did not compel meanings or interpretations. On the other hand, the resources needed – large casts and, increasingly, talented actors, supplementing the Villeurbanne company – were expensive and managerially onerous.

His earlier *Tartuffe* had indicated a direction in which he perhaps needed to move. He regarded Molière's play as 'Shakespearian' and his production refined qualities seen in his *Henry IV*. Writing to René Allio about their ideas for the set, which would include elements, paintings, that 'commented' on the action and that would then be flown out over the five acts, he said:

> What strikes me in your proposals for designs is that I see there a Shakespearianising of the play. That is true, for *Dom Juan* and *Tartuffe* are the most Shakespearian plays of Molière [. . .] that is to say in its [*sic*] way of paring down the whole by succeeding *coups de théâtre* right down to its core. And that reduction, you have translated by a series of unveilings in space.
>
> (Bataillon 2001: II, 196)

Planchon's work with Allio opened a vista on a scenography where the level of 'commentary' could develop with ever-greater boldness and imagination. Working with other designers, again on Molière, Planchon took the reflection of politics and history into almost surreal realms with a ravishing and sensual restaging of *Tartuffe* with Hubert Montloup, and then, with Ezio Frigerio, of *Dom Juan* and Racine's *Athalie* in a unified set; and then again *L'Avare*. Such was the beauty of these designs that some critics felt the need to defend Planchon against the charge of aestheticism, and others were positively reminded of the Shakespearian beginnings of the impoverished company under the actual stars and trees and backdrop of the night.

In a 1977 discussion (at the time he was working with Bouquet on his own play *Gilles de Rais*), Planchon placed himself in the context of contemporary theatre directors: 'The great [directors] today conduct above all research into scenic writing. At certain moments the theatre is scenic writing alone, and at other moments is only dramatic writing. I am one of those rare persons who try to hold both threads'.

Despite his declared admiration for those other *great* directors (chief among whom he would name Bob Wilson), Planchon became ever-more confident that scenography could not constitute the ultimate work in the theatre, which must respond to human life, evolving over time, and be apprehended in the being and performance of the actor. He recalled that as early as 1955 (before *Henry IV*) he was aware of the direction that theatre might take towards a purely *scenic* expression, independent of text. Given his love of painting, he was excited by the 'adventure' of it passing from the frame into a different plastic medium in the theatre, but he was quick to perceive the consequence as being the passage of the spectator from 'mental time to mental space'.

In a telling phrase, he expresses the impossible achievement of such a scenography: 'Time is hollowed out, there is a presentation of dilated instants'. The instant in drama, however, is both "fragile and miraculous", like life itself, and lives in the physical performance of the actor'. This requires a due proportion between the scale of staging and style of performance and the reality of the expressive human figure, moving through an *undilated* sequence of instants. In his early Shakespeare production, Planchon was already aware of the two threads of dramatic and scenic writing. As he approached a milestone in his career, Planchon returned to Shakespeare in the face of a theatre that had diverted its attention to scenes rather than stages.

In August 1977, announcing his coming season, consecrated to Shakespeare, Planchon planned a repertoire of three plays:

> because, for a long time our public has asked for this, and because it is always necessary to get back to basics. With great pleasure we shall present three plays in repertoire: a tragedy, a comedy and a romance dream-play. The three are marvels: 'masterpieces' as the dictionaries and literary guides tell us. [. . .] The predominant theme is love [. . .] But where did Shakespeare draw the strength to conceive such a vision, so far from effete, which upholds and carries along his whole theatre, and which illuminates with life and nobility all of his characters? In these days of mental pollution, we no longer know what, deep down, love is at all. Who, since André Breton, has been able to recharge love with energy and produce beautiful flashes of lightning?
>
> (Bataillon 2005: I, 208)

This almost valedictory repertoire was to include *Love's Labour's Lost*, abandoned because of cost, and the ultimate diptych of *Antony and Cleopatra* and *Pericles, Prince of Tyre*. With his theme of love in Shakespeare, Planchon returns to the quality that he repeatedly identifies with the inspirational world of the dramatist:

> From the moment I read those so lovely scenes between Olivia and Viola, I understood something that I had never understood in my life. [. . .] In *'Tis Pity She's a Whore* [. . .] there is the very simple idea that that love is possible only against society. It is the surrealist notion, I don't know if it is very profound, but I have always found it very good, very appealing. [. . .] In *Twelfth Night*, without a conflict between love and society, there is the same violence, the same sense of the absolute between two beings.
>
> (Bataillon 2005: I, 246)

Planchon links Breton, the prophet and legislator of surrealism, across the ages to Shakespeare, in the way that his staging of the diptych explores a contemporary sensibility, shaping a space for the playing of the two stories of love, one in historical and one in mythic time. With the cinema image of Burton and Taylor everywhere, Planchon conceived a production where the stage became a dream factory in its own right. First, for *Antony and Cleopatra*, a studio where a film is shot of the Roman campaigns in Egypt, including cinema footage for the sea battle. Then, for *Pericles*, using the same basic set, a different but more fantastic texture of images: Pericles' dream of his wanderings. The set thus moved from the realism of not only the stage image but also the technology of its creation to the dream-world of Shakespearian romance.

The first play was, in ways, familiar, and the set evoked, beyond the costume drama of Hollywood, the fascist dream of a Roman Empire reborn in the legions of a Hitler or a Mussolini. Thus, the setting of the Cinecittà inaugurated by Il Duce in 1937 inspires *Antony and Cleopatra*. The second play was not only unfamiliar but also its world of tests and temptations, shipwreck and a princess born from the waves might not possess the qualities to command the attention of an audience that suffered the 'mental pollution' of its imagination . . . The programme note urged the audience to abandon itself to the progress of a dream. 'Pericles', explained Planchon in an interview, 'dreams the dream of his own tale of chivalry upon the seas'.

The reception of *Antony and Cleopatre* was appreciative, but *Pericles* disappointed. Planchon's thoughts on the show were almost a farewell to the dramatist whose works he could stage only at the cost of monumental personal efforts and the deployment of considerable resources. Ironically, Planchon's own performance (where he doubted he had the physical, or the physiological, resources to play the warrior in Antony) was well received, perhaps because Planchon revealed in himself the toll taken by the efforts of production. Antony, the 'victim of the madness of history', was 'admirable.' The same critic labelled *Pericles* 'a nonsense, a fiasco'.

Although critical reaction to *Pericles* was not uniformly hostile, Planchon's commitment to this play was difficult for many to understand, and, in particular, his insistence on a further shuffling of the images of the play, perhaps because of the new accent in his work, where his material sense of reality incorporated a greater awareness of the power of the theatrical image. In *Le Monde*, Planchon wagered on his audience being capable of listening to a fairy story:

> It is a speech of a child whose heart tells of the enchantment of the world. But Shakespeare never betrays reality. His principle of improbability consists of placing his characters in peril at the heart of the real. It is a matter of convincing them [i.e., the spectators] that, at any moment, the heavens can fall about their heads. And whosoever goes towards the real, unprotected, is convinced that is in fact what happens.
>
> It is a fairy story, but is that anything other than a dream?

This reads like an epilogue, and a possible new beginning. Shakespeare nourishes the most profound theatre, that which escapes our scientific age and yet seems to express its modernity:

> I shall soon have presented ten Shakespeare plays always with the same twin aims: to learn the craft that I follow and to reflect calmly beneath a clear light on the problems that chill us: power, morality and political murder, power relationships between states, between parties [. . .] And the questions which concern us from adolescence to the grave, the passions between fellow beings.
>
> (1 December 1978)

Chronology

Shakespeare productions at Théâtre de la Cité, Villeurbanne

1957	*Henry IV, le prince*
	Henry IV, Falstaff
1958	*Henry IV, le prince*
	Henry IV, Falstaff
1959	*Henry IV, le prince*
	Henry IV, Falstaff

1960	*Henry IV, le prince*
	Henry IV, Falstaff
1961	*Henry IV, le prince*
	Henry IV, Falstaff
1962–3	None
1964	*Troilus et Créssida*
1965	*Henry IV, le prince*
	Henry IV, Falstaff
1966–7	*Richard III*
1968–78	None
1979	*Antoine et Cléopatre*
	Périclès, prince de Tyre

Bibliography

Bataillon, M. (2001) *Un défi en province*: tome 1, *Planchon*, (Paris, Marval), 2 vols.

—— (2005) *Un défi en province*: tome 2, *Planchon, Chereau*, et leurs invités. (Paris, Marval), 3 vols. Volume 1 *Planchon*.

Damasio, A. (2000) *The Feeling of What Happens: Body and Emotion in the Making of Consciousness*, London: Vintage.

Daoust, Y. (1981) *Roger Planchon: Director and Playwright*, Cambridge: Cambridge University Press.

Fayard, N. (2006) *The Performance of Shakespeare in France since the Second World War: Re-imagining Shakespeare*, Lampeter: Edwin Mellen.

Jacquot, J. (1964) *Shakespeare en France: mises en scène d'hier et d'aujourd'hui*, Paris: Le Temps.

Jouvet, L. (1986) *Molière et la comédie classique: extraits des cours de Louis Jouvet au Conservatoire (1939–1940)*, Paris: Gallimard.

Kustow, M. (1972) 'Roger Planchon, actor, director, playwright (interview, assessment and checklist)' in *Theatre Quarterly* 5 (January–March): 42–57.

Planchon, R. (1972) *Introduction* to Shakespeare, W. *King Henry IV part I*, London: Pan Books.

Polanyi, M. (1967) *The Tacit Dimension*, London: Routledge Kegan Paul.

Vilar, Jean (1955) *De la tradition théâtrale*, Paris: Gallimard.

About the author

Gerry McCarthy was until recently Professor of Theatre Studies at the University of Ulster. Before this he was Director of the Department of Drama and Theatre Arts at the University of Birmingham. He has taught and directed in Canada and in France where he was invited by Jacques Fornier at Besançon to work with French actors on the performance of Shakespeare in English. He has particular interests in classical acting and is the author of *The Theatres of Molière* (2001).

21
WILLIAM POEL

Peter Thomson

In the spring of 1875, when he was working for a firm of building contractors, the 22-year-old William Pole (1852–1934) saw and heard (in Italian) Tommaso Salvini as Othello at the Theatre Royal, Drury Lane. As his brief diary entry for 11 April records, he was already kicking against the pricks of his daily routine: 'I seem to get no nearer to the change I long for and this makes me sad. I am still under the bondage of Hell [the City]. I saw Salvini in *Othello* the other day, a great treat' (Speaight 1954: 26).

The juxtaposition of the last two sentences is more telling than the particular sentiment expressed in either. In the years to come, he would monumentalise the 'great treat' as one of the determining events in the transformation of Pole (trainee building contractor) into Poel (man of the theatre). Coincidentally, on one of Salvini's later tours, the wealthy young Konstantin Alekseev, already well on the way to becoming Stanislavsky, saw and heard the same Othello in Moscow. He would devote a chapter to Salvini in his distractingly overwritten autobiography, *My Life in Art* (1924). 'How simple, clear, beautiful, and tremendous was everything that Salvini did and showed!' (Stanislavsky 1962: 272). 'The Othello of Salvini is a monument, a law unto eternity which can never change' (Stanislavsky 1962: 268).

On the face of it, we would not expect to find much common ground between the modernist Stanislavsky and the revivalist Poel, but their shared excitement over Salvini provides a useful insight into the work of two men who took it upon themselves to change the nature of theatrical performance at the end of the nineteenth century and into the twentieth. Poel never approached Stanislavsky's mastery in the training of actors, but he recognised and sought after the *simplicity* of naturalness which both men saw in Salvini. More important, though, is the intensity of their spiritual commitment to the art of the theatre. Actors who undertook to rehearse with Poel, like those who remained with the Moscow Art Theatre, entered the straitened world of the seminary. Stanislavsky's self-portrayal as Tortsov, particularly in *An Actor*

Prepares, is that of a Jesuit disciplinarian – and there was something of that in Poel, too – but there is also a Stanislavsky who expresses his vision of the theatre, 'a law unto eternity', in the language of religious ecstasy; and the fierce combativeness of an 'old-time religion' underpins Poel's assault on the battlements of the Victorian stage. Interviewed for the *Daily Chronicle* of 3 September 1913, he explained his choice of the theatre as a reaction against the ugliness of poverty in London:

> I have striven to change the dramatic world, to alter life on the stage as we know it, to make it what obviously it should be, and what plainly it must one day become, an experience of the spirit of man evolving through beauty and knowledge towards the fullness and perfection of existence.
>
> (Speaight 1954: 59)

In the foreground of any treatment of Poel are issues of material circumstance, but this should not blind us to the urgency of his ambition. He belonged to a colonial age in which the Christian missionary was still a British hero, and the gospel he brought to a disbelieving theatrical world was Shakespeare untrammelled.

Confronting Victorian Shakespeare

William Archer was stating what virtually every interested party took for granted in 1896 when he wrote that 'scenery should as nearly as possible express to the eye the locality which was present to the author's imagination' (Archer 1896: 432). Book illustrations, photographs, picture postcards, posters, the novelty of the moving image all fed off and into the largely uncritical dependence on pictorial information that characterised most earnest Victorians. Poel himself was a lifelong devotee of historical painting – with Jennie Moore, his regular costume designer from 1892 to 1914, he would look to sixteenth-century art for guidance – and the lonely theatregoing of his youth familiarised him with the lavish sets, conditioned by ideas of historical and/or architectural accuracy, that were the stock in trade of metropolitan Shakespeare. To achieve the stature of an iconoclast, he had first to overcome an addiction to Henry Irving – an addiction about which, in later life, he was notably reticent. During the 1870s, when Poel's ideas were beginning to take shape, Irving appeared at the Lyceum as Hamlet, Macbeth, Othello, Richard III and Shylock, on occasions topping off his performances with a recitation of Thomas Hood's doom-laden poem, 'The Dream of Eugene Aram'. When, in 1879, Poel took his first step into management with the foundation of 'The

Elizabethans' and toured unfashionable towns in Britain with costume renderings of scenes from, among other plays, *Hamlet, Macbeth, Othello* and *The Merchant of Venice*, he liked to round off the evening with his own recitation of 'The Dream of Eugene Aram'. There may have been challenge, as well as the flattery of imitation, in the selection of material. Lacking the support of the Lyceum's great scene-painter Hawes Craven, he and his company were testing the power of language on bare, or sparsely furnished, small stages. Anything Irving could do . . . He was by no means the first actor/elocutionist to put himself at risk in unadorned Shakespeare. Following the example of her father Charles, Fanny Kemble (1809–93) presented desk-readings of twenty-four of Shakespeare's plays over more than twenty years from 1848, and the forgotten eccentric Samuel Brandram (1824–92) would recite whole plays by heart to any audience hardy enough to pay and listen. The programme for Poel's 1893 production of *Measure for Measure* promised that 'All money taken, over and above the expenses, will be given to the "SAMUEL BRANDRAM FUND".' What we cannot trace is the precise phasing of the progress of Poel's thinking that led him to the conviction that bare-stage Shakespearian production was not a compromise but an ideal. It was an astonishingly bold conclusion in its time. Well into the next century, the popular view remained Herbert Beerbohm Tree's, that 'Shakespeare regretted the deficiencies of the stage of his day' (Tree 1913: 60). Unsurprisingly, Tree relates his argument, throughout which Poel is the unnamed adversary, to the (apologetic, as he supposed it) Prologue to *Henry V*. No longer do the audience's 'thoughts' need to 'piece out our imperfections'. Modern technology, in combination with superior artistic taste, has done the job for them. In defence of the extensive cutting and rearrangement of Shakespeare's texts, Tree lazily lapses into issues of time: three hours may be tolerable, but it would take five to mount a fully scenic production of any of the favourite plays. And is it not better to group the 'palace' scenes or the 'garden' scenes than to omit a good one altogether? To be sure, that involves transposition, but such transposition is licensed by the demands of pictorial truth and beauty. Already by 1889, in a lecture to the New Shakspere Society, Poel was resonantly complaining that 'with the demand for carpentry comes the inducement for mutilation' (Poel 1913: 150)

Respecting the text

> A critical and genuine appreciation of the poet's work imposes a reverence for the constructive plan as well as for the text. Why should a Shakespeare whose cunning hand divined the dramatic sequence of his story, have it improved by a modern playwright or actor-manager? The answer will be: Because the modern experts are familiar with

> theatrical effects of a kind Shakespeare never lived to see. But if a modern rearrangement of Shakespeare's plays is necessary to suit these theatrical effects, the question may well be discussed as to whether rearrangements with all their modern advantages are of more dramatic value than the perfect work of the master.
>
> (Poel 1913: 119)

This is the introductory paragraph of an essay Poel entitled 'Some Stage Versions' in order to give a semblance of unity to a sequence of discrete lectures delivered to the New Shakspere Society between 1879 and 1881 and an article published in the *New Age* in 1909. Together they amount to a cogent attack on two fronts: first, on the blatant self-interest of actor-managers who deform dramatic structure in the name of theatre and, second, on literary editors whose ignorance of theatre distorts their presentation of play-texts. Poel's eventual plea will be for standardised stage versions that are 'the joint-work of scholars and actors' (Poel 1913: 60), a proposal still capable of ruffling academic feathers and alarming actors in the twenty-first century. Promptbooks of Poel's own productions survive as unruly witnesses to his methods, but none approaches the status of a definitive stage version, and a superficial reading of the published promptbook for *Fratricide Punished* is more likely to inspire derision than enlightenment. The uncomfortable fact is that, faced with the exigencies of performance, Poel's practice was always more half-hearted than his theories; but it was the theories, backed up with the fire of his polemics, that harried the theatre into reappraising its approach to the staging of Shakespeare's plays.

Working, as he did throughout his life, in the protective ambience of his own sealed personality, Poel adopted, as a workable hypothesis, the view that the plays would be best served in theatrical conditions that closely approximated to those of the stages on which they were originally performed. If he knew of the precedent set by the Ben Webster/J.R. Planché production of *The Taming of the Shrew* at the Haymarket in 1844, he never said so, and never needed to. Webster had acceded to Planché's proposal in the pursuit of novelty, and the production advertised its 'pastness'. Poel had his eye on the future. His scholarship was erratic, but capable of providing insights. In an extended argument against the custom of breaking the action between scenes, for example, he finds support in the observation that 'of the plays wholly written by Shakespeare, with the one exception of "The Tempest," all are so constructed that characters who leave the stage at the end of an episode are never the first to reappear, a reappearance which would involve a short pause and an empty stage' (Poel 1913: 41). It was a point he phrased more succinctly in the latest of a series of articles on 'Shakespeare's Prompt-Books' submitted to the *Times Literary Supplement* in 1921 (18 August): 'Shakespeare abhorred the vacuum of an empty stage'. In retrospect, it can be reasonably argued that this was the most influential of all his theatrical *dicta*.

It is all too easy to undermine Poel's authority by reference to his practice. Despite his ideal of unbroken performance, his Shakespearian productions incorporated intervals, and, despite his objections to the mutilation of texts, he cut heavily, not always in accordance with his 'one rule' that lines may be omitted 'but never an entire scene' (Poel 1913: 180). The actor Robert Atkins, who came under Poel's influence in 1919 after formative experience in the school of Beerbohm Tree, was shocked to discover that he was 'a grand slasher of the text', and also 'a re-writer of the verse' (Atkins 1994: 52), but Atkins gives no specific instances. Recorded examples suggest only a nervous impulse to bowdlerise, as in the 1893 *Measure for Measure*, when Claudio's offence ('He has got a wench with child') was tamed to 'He will shortly be a father'. The choice seems to be between blaming Poel for not trying hard enough and admiring him for trying at all. Great directors are not satisfied by imposing their own convictions on actors, and even a more daring Poel could never have been a great director. Any kind of seductiveness, whether of audiences or performers, was missing from his constitution.

Speaking the text

It is a pity that circumstances militated against Poel's putting to the test his conviction that 'with an efficient elocution and no "waits," the Elizabethan actors would have got through one-half of a play before our modern actors could cover a third' (Poel 1913: 17). Working predominantly with amateurs, as much from choice as from necessity, he laboured to rediscover the 'efficient elocution' that had been lost. For most of the actors who have written about working with him, the dominant memory is of his insistence on their following his manner of speaking the lines. Basil Dean remembers Poel, during his 1908 guest direction of *Measure for Measure* at the Gaiety Theatre in Manchester, 'holding the book in his left hand and tapping out the stresses on his knee with the long fingers of his right hand' (Dean 1970: 53–4); Robert Atkins recalls that, in Poel's marked text for the concert performance of Calderon's *Life Is a Dream* (in Edward Fitzgerald's verse translation) at the Ethical Church in Bayswater in 1920, 'many words were underlined. They were the key words, to be hit with a high, low or middle tone. The space between the written lines contained upward and downward slanting lines, denoting the tonal approach to the key words; a squiggly line meant on the level' (Atkins 1994: 107); Margaret Webster summarises Lewis Casson's recollection of Poel's priorities:

> What he was fighting was the Victorian method of speaking the verse, slow, ponderous and accented all over the place; whereas Poel thought it should be rapid, with as few heavy stresses as possible – about one every three lines. The meaning should be clearly represented by melody, which supplied most of the necessary accents. He rebelled also against Irving because he broke the natural rhythm of speech by trying to make it 'modern'.
>
> (Webster 1969: 295–6)

Webster notes that Casson's wife, Sybil Thorndike, added that Poel 'hated accents on auxiliary words'. That there were quirks and eccentricities in his pursuit of the 'tuned tones' of Shakespearian blank verse is well attested. It is even probable that his ear for the music of poetry was less reliable than that of some of the actors under his tutelage. That was certainly the view of his biographer, Robert Speaight, when he acted under Poel's direction (Speaight 1954: 100). In the end, though, the detail of Poel's speculative probing into the speech patterns of Elizabethan actors is less significant than the generality of its impact on later directors. His insistence that the lines are best delivered 'trippingly on the tongue', as Samuel Brandram delivered them, has too often been overlooked by those who focus on his musical vocabulary. The outcome is a distorted sense of Poel's unquestionable peculiarity. 'He encouraged', writes Frances Hughes, 'a rapid, incantatory form of speech with great emphasis on the operative word whether verb or noun' (Hughes 2002: 5); but we should pause on 'incantatory', just as we should on J.L. Styan's claim that he required from each speaker 'a vocal range of two octaves' (Styan 1977: 49). In fact, Poel set out to overturn the current fashion for enunciating Shakespeare in an elevated, 'poetry' voice:

> In the delivery of verse [. . .] on the stage, the audience should never be made to feel that the tones are unusual. They should still follow the laws of speaking, and not those of singing. But our actors, who excel in modern plays by the truth and force of their presentation of life, when they appear in Shakespeare make use of an elocution that no human being was ever known to indulge in.
>
> (Poel 1913: 57–8)

In the desperation of Poel's own remedies, there was much that was strange and enough that was ill judged to have led posterity to underrate him. Too often distracted by detail, and not above the temptation to court controversy by exaggerating his opposition to conservative practices, he could lose sight of his grander purpose, which was to rediscover the naturalness of Elizabethan acting. Such naturalness was as distinct from 'naturalism' as it was from Tree's realistic staging and unrealistic elocution. Poel's own name for it was 'exaggerated naturalness'. Significantly for the future of Shakespearian production in England, Granville Barker understood Poel's aims:

> In the teeth of ridicule he insisted that for an actor to make himself like unto a human megaphone was to miss, for one thing, the whole merit of Elizabethan verse with its consonantal swiftness, its gradations sudden or slow into vowelled liquidity, its comic rushes and stops, with, above all, the peculiar beauty of its rhymes.
>
> (Barker 1974: 36)

Poel was not so naïve as to suppose that his vocal innovations would adapt well to the large proscenium theatres of Victorian England. It was his attempt to recreate the Elizabethan stage that attracted the most (though never as much as he hoped) attention in his own time.

The quest for Shakespeare's stage

Poel's early thinking about the Elizabethan stage pre-dated the discovery, in 1888, of the De Witt/van Buchell drawing of the interior of the Swan playhouse. For his first significant venture, the production of the *Hamlet* First Quarto at St George's Hall in April 1881, he surrounded the stage with red curtains, though with openings where the proscenium doors of the Restoration and eighteenth-century theatres had been and a join upstage centre to allow for the creation of an inner recess. Only the sparse furnishings – a bench, a graveyard mound with a free-standing grave for Ophelia, an easel for the old king's portrait, four chairs and a stool in front of a low platform for the play-within-the-play – reflected Elizabethan practice. At this early point in Poel's career, the bee in his bonnet was the belief that the quartos at large, and this one in particular, were better 'acting editions' than the Folio texts. (It took all his stubbornness to maintain this belief for as long as he did.) The promptbook records that scene changes required the lowering and raising of the front curtain six times during the course of the performance. Poel had not yet felt the force of his later formulation: 'Among all innovations on the stage, perhaps the most far-reaching in its effect on dramatic construction was the act-drop' (Poel 1913: 119). In the title role, though, Poel was already experimenting with rapid delivery and infrequent stresses, to the general displeasure of the handful of reviewers in attendance. Had he been a finer actor, his ideas may have earned him more support. On stage, he was always in better control of his voice than of his body. He knew this and was inhibited by the knowledge: 'A stage manager at the Haymarket Theatre who was teaching me elocution in the seventies', he recollected in 1922, 'said he could get my voice right in two years but that it would take seven years to get my movement right' (quoted in O'Connor 1987: 17). In the modern theatre, as Poel was slow to learn, most spectators hear only what they see.

The achievement of bringing the 'bad' quarto of *Hamlet* to theatrical attention did not much advance Poel's career. He spent the summer of 1881 as director/manager of the Bijou Theatre in Gravesend and the next twenty-six months as the hands-on overseer of Emma Cons's Royal Victoria Hall and Coffee Tavern, before its evolution into the Old Vic. A six-month period, in 1884, as stage manager for Frank Benson's fledgling company of touring Shakespearians must have affected his developing consciousness, but Benson was six years his junior and Poel had always a tendency to think he knew better. It was his 'conducting' (unpaid, I believe) of rehearsed readings for the Shakespeare Reading Society that gave him the control he craved during what would otherwise have been fallow years. It was through his link with the society that Poel launched his second significant foray into Shakespearian production. His *Measure for Measure* (Poel as Angelo) was originally recited in 1891 at Ladbroke Hall in Notting Hill Gate, but there was sufficient belief among the amateur members of the society that they were involved in something remarkable to encourage the financing of a run at the small Royalty Theatre in November 1893. Now, for the first time, Poel was to present a play by Shakespeare on a specially built model of an Elizabethan stage, based on the builder's contract (8 January 1600) for the Fortune Theatre. We know, in detail, the dimensions of Poel's significantly scaled-down model. It was 30 feet wide, 24 feet deep and 21 feet high. The oak-framed fit-up stage (with bolts and nuts) included a tiring-house façade and was augmented by 'a practical rostrum and balcony and canvas painted cloths, representing galleries, boxes and amphitheatre' (O'Connor 1987: 28). There were two entrances under the balcony and a wide central entrance which could be closed off by two 'painted oak doors'. A roof or 'heavens' was suspended from the tiring-house to two 18-foot-high pillars at mid-stage, each supporting a practical curtain which could be drawn to block off the upstage area. In the Royalty, this stage projected beyond the proscenium into the auditorium, without affording room for members of the audience to sit at the sides. Instead – surely his daftest inspiration – Poel imported male members of the Shakespeare Reading Society to sit, in Elizabethan costume, on either side of the stage and often in front of the actors (and a handful of female members, in period attire, to sit in the balcony behind the actors). He was using people as 'period' scenery.

The Fortune fit-up continued to feature in Poel's productions for more than a decade and might have been used for longer had it not been for the new safety regulations enforced by the London County Council in 1907. He had seen how fit-ups could create theatres in almost any sizeable social space during his early years as a jobbing actor, when touring Yorkshire towns with James Scott's ramshackle company, and, since he was quite as likely to be staging productions in social spaces that were not theatres, the model made sense. For the full realisation of the revivalist experiment, though, it was seriously flawed. In the first place, it was too small. Poel had no conception of the broad sweeps of action on the Elizabethan platform. Even in his conjectural reconstruction of the Globe – admirable in many aspects – he restricted the stage to something like fit-up dimensions (see White 1999). We should think of him, perhaps, as a miniaturist. Certainly he admired stillness in actors and preferred curtains to choreography. The dependence on curtains is the second flaw. On the Fortune fit-up, they could be used to create an inner stage – a proscenium arch in miniature to preserve pictorialism in defiance of the open platform – and, stretched between the mid-stage pillars, they could be drawn to imply change of location or simply to conceal scene changes. From early on, Poel found it convenient to close this mid-stage traverse for exterior scenes, thus confining them to an often contradictorily small downstage area and confronting the onlookers with 'a mass of imitation tapestry' (Mazer 1981: 61). There were curtains to conceal the balcony, curtains to conceal the inner stage, curtains to conceal curtains. It was not long before the draped stage of the revivalists (Poel had his imitators) became as unsurprising as a cliché. Even Granville Barker fell back on a version of the act-drop in order to isolate the apron for some of the scenes in his Savoy *Winter's Tale*. Edward Gordon Craig's *Hamlet* screens may plausibly be seen as a brilliantly imagined alternative. The third flaw is implicit in the whole idea of an Elizabethan fit-up. This is not a recreation of Shakespeare's stage so much as the sculpture of a recreation of Shakespeare's stage, within which actors may move like gallery visitors in an installation. The extent of Poel's initial dependence on this artefact is demonstrated by his staging of *Twelfth Night* in 1897. This was a revival of the first production by the Elizabethan Stage Society, which Poel had founded in 1894 with the aim of extending his readings into fully staged performances; but the venue this time was the Hall of the Middle Temple, where Shakespeare's own company had presented the play in 1602. The Hall's oak screen has two large doors and a balcony above, and the obvious playing space is, in this respect, comparable with the stage of De Witt's Swan drawing. To perform in front of the screen would have challenged, perhaps released, Poel's revivalist vision. To install the Fortune fit-up there, as he did, was to place a pretence in front of a reality. I have irresistibly in mind the memory of Jonathan Pryce's drunken progress through the Stratford auditorium, before the opening of Michael Bogdanov's 1978 *The Taming of the*

Shrew, to tear down the tatty scenery of the fit-up company that had come to Shakespeare's birthplace to present a play. But it is unfair to expect too much of Poel at this pioneering period of his career. He needed his curtains as much as Tree needed his proscenium arch and could not yet envisage a truly continuous production without them. Together with doors, a balcony, a recess (inner stage) and what he called a 'forward stage' they represented the essentials of his defiantly minimalist concept of the ideal setting for Shakespeare's plays.

Spatial language

It was Poel's intuition that the flow of Shakespeare's dramatic language through a play could be sustained only if transitions from scene to scene and location to location were effected without any interruption to the rhythm of speech and action. The further possibility that the placing on the platform of particular episodes or characters might illustrate the deeper meaning of the spoken text may have come home to him during his work on *Doctor Faustus*, either for its first production in 1896 at St George's Hall or for its revival in 1904 at the Court Theatre and on tour. Here, the upstage area of the Fortune fit-up was the territory of Lucifer, Mephistopheles and the minor devils, who appeared on the balcony, entered from under it and were there at the end to receive the damned Faustus into the hell mouth of the inner stage. With this moral low ground behind it – looming over it – Faustus's study was placed in a middle area, separable from the 'forward stage' by the traverse curtains slung between the pillars. The textually fraught 'comic' scenes (with the exception of the papal banquet and the imperial court, which called for a modicum of scenic decoration) were isolated on whatever apron was left available in the chosen venue by the closing of these curtains. The aura of amateurishness in Poel's productions is nowhere clearer than in surviving photographs of actors clustered in uncomfortably flat lines along the shallow jetty that was all that remained of the raised stage area once the fit-up was in place. Reviewers were understandably reminded of family shows in Victorian parlours, with the audible whispers of concealed cousins advertising the preparation of the next scene during the progress of the present one. What needs to be emphasised about this tripartite division of the stage is that it attempted, without the vivid aid of painted scenery, to localise each successive episode. Poel did not question the legitimacy of the audience's curiosity about where exactly any particular scene was taking place, and he did his best to satisfy that curiosity. It was not he, but Granville Barker, who queried the Elizabethan audience's reliance on localisation: 'if they stopped to ask themselves where such and such a character, under their eyes at the minute, was supposed to be,

"On the stage" might well have served for an immediate answer' (quoted in Mazer 1981: 129–30). Taking into account Poel's urge to localise alongside his preparedness to cut heavily and even, on occasions, to break his own rule by transposing scenes, as in his ninety-minute *Coriolanus* at the Chelsea Palace Theatre in 1931, William Archer's jibe that he was nothing more than Beerbohm Tree without the scenery has its own satirical force (cited in Speaight 1954: 262). As almost always with Poel, we are pushed into regretting the limits in his courage of his own convictions.

The creation of acting zones within the Fortune fit-up was a further scaling down of the scaled-down Elizabethan platform. Poel's actors were almost always in close proximity to each other, and their range of movement bore no comparison with that of their Shakespearian forebears. He accepted spatial constraints with evident equanimity. It is doubtful whether anyone but Poel would have agreed to squeeze *The Alchemist* (1899) into the small Apothecaries' Hall, where his reduced fit-up stage confined the actors within a space 24 feet wide by 12 feet deep. At its simplest, his staging alternated scenes set upstage of the pillars (generally 'indoors') and outdoor scenes set downstage of them in front of closed curtains. Cary Mazer deploys the terms 'alternation theory' and 'zone theory' to describe these two approaches to the staged text. The use of the balcony and the area underneath it as a separate third zone was intermittent, and sight lines dictated that the inner stage should serve only for exits, entrances and tableaux. Even so – and this is what made Poel so influential – his determined pursuit of forgotten styles of performance necessitated a reassessment of the nature and function of performance space. Ironically, it was not in any of Shakespeare's plays that he had his first (some say, only) undoubted success, but in the fifteenth-century morality *Everyman*, first staged alfresco in the Master's Courtyard of the Charterhouse in 1901. Here, the three zones of *Doctor Faustus* were physically separated. Raised high (just how high is not recorded) was the heaven from which, at the opening of the play, God (Poel, in characteristic defiance of ridicule) called Everyman to account. Beneath it was a raised acting area, housing, inside flats, Everyman's domestic life. Not much room for movement so far. But when Everyman began his inevitable pilgrimage towards death, he and his companions descended into the courtyard and crossed the 40 feet to a third stage in the corner. This early example of promenade performance was not without precedent during a period when open-air performance was in vogue. But new questions arose for Poel when he came to transfer the production indoors. He had now in mind, willy-nilly, a new concept of multiple staging. It was a concept that he initially compressed into conformity with the Fortune fit-up, but it lingered. In so far as his natural stubbornness allowed, the *Everyman* experience changed his life. First, it rescued his reputation as a director;

second, it established him as a discoverer of forgotten gems (rather than, as after the fiasco of *The Coxcomb* in 1898, a man who could not distinguish between a good old play and a dud one); and third, it pointed the way to new ideas about exploiting the uncluttered stage.

The three stages of *Everyman* owed something to Poel's limited research into medieval pageant wagons. Only in the final scene, when the Angel spoke from on high to proclaim Everyman's ascent to heaven, was there any sharing of focus between the separate areas. But Poel, who had earned a reputation as a man who stuck to his guns, was more adaptable than has been generally recognised. The late production (in 1927) of Samuel Rowley's *When You See Me, You Know Me* – and, indeed, most of his work with the Elizabethan Stage Circle over the next five years – is, in this respect, exemplary. Much had changed in the years since the *Everyman* premiere, owing not least to the well-publicised disputes between Poel and Ben Greet over the ownership of the production (see O'Connor 1987: 74–6). Although himself still a marginal figure, Poel had, by 1927, ample evidence of the impact on the profession of his revivalist style. Now in his late seventies, and without the Fortune fit-up at his disposal, he made a slight, but significant, adjustment. The production of Rowley's oddball chronicle history was implicitly a claim that, given the appropriate setting, neglected plays of the late sixteenth and early seventeenth centuries could be effectively staged in the twentieth. (Poel would follow up with Jonson's *Sejanus*, Fletcher's *Bonduca*, Chapman's *The Conspiracy and Tragedy of Charles, Duke of Biron* and Peele's *David and Bethsabe*.) But a bigger claim was being made on 10 July 1927. Over the day, and in preparation for the performance of *When You See Me, You Know Me* in the evening, Poel supervised the transformation of the Holborn Empire into an approximation of an Elizabethan playhouse (see Somerset 1966). This involved the surrounding with curtains of the area upstage of the proscenium arch, the provision of a balcony with a curtained inner stage below it and the building out 27 feet over the stalls of a platform 45 feet wide. If this could be done at the Holborn Empire, Poel was implying, it could be done in any other theatre, converting the picture-frame configuration into something more like an end stage. But this was something more than an end stage. Even a scattering of spectators in the side boxes provided a rare chance to test the value of a three-sided audience; Ivor Brown, writing for the *Saturday Review*, shrewdly observed that 'soliloquies and asides, on a full platform stage, are spoken quite naturally to the surrounding audience' and concluded that, in this production, 'one could understand the plasticity and variety of the Elizabethan stage method' (Brown 1927: 90).

In his programme note for *When You See Me, You Know Me*, Poel alluded to the hotly debated revisions to the Prayer Book, under consideration in

1927: 'Will Summers, who represents the opinions of the audience on the subject, tells the King, on whom the Pope has conferred the title of Defender of the Faith, that the people can defend their own Faith and do not wish anyone else to do it for them'.

The note has a *post hoc ergo propter hoc* flavour, as if Poel were trying to convince himself, as well as the audience, of this old piece's contemporary relevance. His own religious (and political) radicalism was certainly of the individualistic kind, and his treatment of the play (more than a third of the lines were cut, and Poel supplied fifty of his own) was designed to enforce an argument that Rowley had handled more tentatively. But it was the staging opportunities that attracted Poel in the first place, and the government of belief by the state was never more than a secondary issue. Conscious that, for a change, he had a large empty space to fill, he had assembled a cast of forty-one, backing up the speaking roles with extras garnered from the Elizabethan Stage Circle and Elsie Fogerty's Central School of Speech and Drama. There is no evidence, in the generally tepid reviews, that he deployed his crowds particularly effectively, but the occasion was significant in two ways. First, it witnessed the extension of the timid apron into something that might legitimately be called a thrust stage, and second, it showed Poel experimenting with simultaneous, as well as multiple, staging. It is that second departure that merits particular attention.

Poel's division of his fit-up stage into three zones of action necessarily cramped performance in an already restricted space. The platform constructed in the Holborn Empire, though, provided a new depth, ripe for exploitation. Two or three times during the production, when the dialogue referred to historical figures, Poel placed them in dumb-show on the balcony *behind* the actors who were speaking about them; a trick more obviously cinematic than theatrical. But his major innovation was to fuse together scenes that Rowley had set out in sequence. Thus, Henry VIII on the forestage was intercut with Prince Edward behind the proscenium arch, and they remained in place for the arrest of Katherine Parr: three separate scenes in simultanous action. Predictably, though, Poel sought to localise his characters by building two pavilions, one on either side of the proscenium. The King had possession of one while Cardinal Wolsey and the bishops had the other, which became the site of Katherine Parr's arrest. Simultaneous use of these pavilions was established from the outset, with Wolsey hosting the French ambassadors at the same time as Henry was addressing his court. The actors could see each other across the stage, but the characters could not – a staging convention which Poel had never previously employed to such good effect.

Poel's legacy

As a director, Poel was less remarkable for what he did than for what he led others to do after him. Safe in the knowledge that they did not need to employ him, his successors were generous in their acknowledgement of his pioneering impetus. George Bernard Shaw, too, was a powerful advocate; and all this despite the fact that Poel's productions of Shakespeare were decidedly dowdy. He was determined to prove, to educate, to disabuse rather than to entertain. Great directors release great performances from their actors. Poel, even on the rare occasions when he had access to actors of quality, tended to constrain them. They were part of his programme, not independent artists. Probably the most accomplished cast he ever worked with was provided for him at the Gaiety Theatre in Manchester for *Measure for Measure* in 1908. More characteristically, he surrounded himself with amateurs, 'those rare birds Poel gathered about him, who loved to be associated with the resuscitation of unknown or half-forgotten things' (Bridges-Adams 1971: 81). The critic of the *Saturday Review*, having endured, rather than admired, the ground-breaking production of the First Quarto *Hamlet* in 1881, noted that these rare birds 'displayed the airy confidence of ineptitude' (quoted in Speaight 1954: 51), and similar complaints were still being made after the 1927 *When You See Me, You Know Me*. Against such cavillers, though, it can fairly be said that Poel had an eye for undiscovered quality. He launched the careers of Maud Holt (later Mrs, then Lady, Beerbohm Tree), Lillah McCarthy (and her first husband, Granville Barker) and Edith Evans, and he was respected, and to a degree emulated, by Martin Harvey, Robert Atkins and Lewis Casson. The impact on the young Casson of Poel's ideas is particularly vividly described by Casson's granddaughter, Diana Devlin (see Devlin 1982: 21–5). Of more enduring significance, perhaps, is the incorporation of his views on the speaking of Shakespearian verse into the training programme of the Central School of Speech and Drama under its founder and first director, Elsie Fogerty, who had played Viola in Poel's 1897 *Twelfth Night*.

Although critical of the Victorian actor-managers, Poel was one of them, and the fact that his influence lay behind the development of specialist, non-acting directors through the twentieth century reflects both his own deficiencies as an actor and the greater power of his polemic. It would be an overstatement to say that, without Poel, the largesse of the Elizabethan open stage would have been forgotten for ever, but without him, the exploration of its potential would have been delayed. He had neither the flair nor the temperament to popularise his own approach to Shakespeare's plays. The approach itself was too rigid anyway, as even so gifted a showman as Tyrone Guthrie discovered during his 1933–4 season as director of the Old Vic:

> We would follow Poel and Barker and Shaw, make no cuts merely to suit the exigencies of stage carpenters, have no scenery except a 'structure', which would offer the facilities usually supposed to have been available in the Elizabethan theatres; stairs, leading to a balcony; underneath, a cubbyhole in which intimate scenes can occur and where, concealed behind a curtain, thrones, beds and so on maybe stored.
>
> (Guthrie 1959: 108)

Guthrie had been preceded as director at the Old Vic by Robert Atkins (1921–5), who had been more respectful of his manager's penny-pinching policies. The unadorned staging of Shakespeare at Lilian Baylis's Old Vic from 1914 until her death in 1937 did more to popularise Poel's notions than anything he himself achieved (see Schafer 2006: 129–60), but only Atkins among her chosen directors was consciously an apostle. Guthrie was too much a devotee of the startling to surrender even to Baylis, whose presence was peremptory: Poel, over eighty when Guthrie launched his first Old Vic season, was never his mentor and certainly no longer a threat. But what Guthrie learned, and Poel was reluctant to acknowledge, was that a permanent 'Elizabethan' structure – certainly one as architecturally intriguing as that designed by Wells Coates (or one as makeshift as Poel's) – on a picture-frame stage is likely to draw attention to itself to the point where it lessens the audience's concentration on the play. It may be argued, though, that Poel was more aware of this risk than his detractors admit and that his awareness fuelled his campaign for the building of a Shakespearian playhouse in London. Even so, given the freedom of the New Globe, he would probably have grouped his actors in localised 'zones', with the eliding of scenes an occasional 'simultaneous' variation.

The various ways in which Poel's cause was sustained – by Nugent Monck at the Maddermarket in Norwich, Ronald Watkins at Harrow School or Sam Wanamaker on the South Bank of the Thames – is not the business of this essay. As Cary Mazer has argued, Poel's revivalism was absorbed into, and transformed by, the 'new stagecraft' of the early twentieth century. It was after seeing Reinhardt's *Oedipus* at Covent Garden in 1912 that Poel wrote:

> although, as an Englishman, I may claim that Shakespeare's country was the first to agitate for a return to the open platform, I do not overlook the fact that it was Professor Reinhardt's genius which gave practical shape on a larger scale to the principles of Elizabethan staging, and that he showed himself capable of understanding and adapting those principles to modern conditions while at the same time

> he proved himself to be a genuine artist by his ability to subordinate the setting to the requirements of the drama.
>
> (Poel 1929: 84)

Granville Barker, an English exponent of the 'new stagecraft', neither forgot nor underrated Poel's influence on him since, as a novice actor, he had rehearsed and played Richard II (1899) in a University of London Lecture Theatre and then (1903) Marlowe's Edward II. 'Mr William Poel', he later wrote, 'with a fine fanaticism, set himself to show us the Elizabethan stage as it was'. But the distance Granville Barker had travelled from Poel by the time he staged his Savoy Shakespeares is neatly expressed in the reflective hiatus between the two sentences of another observation he made: 'What can this scenic equipment do for drama whose virtue it was to be independent of it? One need not perhaps jump to the conclusion that it can do nothing at all' (Barker 1974: 161 and 48). The question is Poel's, but the qualification is all Granville Barker's.

Chronology

1877–8	On tour in Yorkshire with James Scott's fit-up company
1879 (June)	Founded and toured with 'The Elizabethans': 'professional ladies and gentlemen whose efforts are specially directed towards creating a more general taste for the study of Shakespeare'
1881 (16 April)	Production of the First Quarto *Hamlet* at St George's Hall
1881–3	Manager of the Royal Victoria Coffee Hall
1884	Stage manager of F.R. Benson's Shakespearian company
1887–97	Instructor to the Shakespeare Reading Society (he was variously associated with the Society from 1878 to 1919)
1891 (18 November)	Directed costume recital of *Measure for Measure* (himself as Angelo) in Ladbroke Hall, Notting Hill with the Shakespeare Reading Society
1893 (November)	Three-night run of *Measure for Measure* at the Royalty Theatre, with the Shakespeare Reading Society (first use of the Fortune fit-up)
1894–7	Founded the Elizabethan Stage Society
1895 (June)	Directed *Twelfth Night* at Burlington Hall and St George's Hall (first production of Elizabethan Stage Society)

1896 (July)	Directed *Doctor Faustus* at St George's Hall with Elizabethan Stage Society
1897 (November)	Directed *The Tempest* at various London venues with Elizabethan Stage Society
1899 (February)	Directed *The Alchemist* at the Apothecaries' Hall with the Elizabethan Stage Society
1900 (February)	New production of the First Quarto *Hamlet* at Carpenters' Hall, with Elizabethan Stage Society
1901 (July)	First of many performances of *Everyman*, initially in the Master's Court of the Charterhouse, with the Elizabethan Stage Society
1902 (July)	Short run of *Everyman* in the Imperial Theatre
1904 (October)	Guest production (invited by Granville Barker) of *Doctor Faustus* at the Court Theatre
1905 (May)	Directed *Romeo and Juliet* at the Royalty Theatre (last production of the Elizabethan Stage Society)
1905 (July)	Sale of properties, etc. (including the Fortune fit-up) of the Elizabethan Stage Society
1908 (April)	Directed *Measure for Measure* at the Gaiety Theatre, Manchester
1920 (March)	Directed a vocal recital of Calderon's *Such Stuff as Dreams Are Made Of* at the Ethical Church, Bayswater
1924 (August)	Directed *Fratricide Punished* at the Oxford Playhouse
1925 (December)	Directed *Arden of Faversham* as an early experiment in multiple staging at the Scala Theatre
1927 (March)	Founded the Elizabethan Stage Circle
1927 (July)	Directed *When You See Me, You Know Me* on a specially constructed thrust stage at the Holborn Empire, with the Elizabethan Stage Circle
1931 (May)	Directed a ninety-minute *Coriolanus* at the Chelsea Palace Theatre, with the Elizabethan Stage Circle

Bibliography

Archer, William (1896) 'Art in the Theatre: The Limitations of Scenery', *Magazine of Art* 19.

Atkins, Robert (1994) *An Unfinished Autobiography*, London: Society for Theatre Research.

Bridges-Adams, W. (1971) *A Bridges-Adams Letter Book*, London: Society for Theatre Research.

Brown, Ivor (1927) Review of *When You See Me, You Know Me*, in *Saturday Review*, 16 July.

Dean, Basil (1970) *Seven Ages*, London: Hutchinson.

Devlin, Diana (1982) *A Speaking Part: Lewis Casson and the Theatre of His Time*, London: Hodder and Stoughton.

Granville Barker, Harley (1974) *Prefaces to Shakespeare*, Vol. VI, London: B. T. Batsford.

Guthrie, Tyrone (1959) *A Life in the Theatre*, London: Hamish Hamilton.
Hughes, Frances (2002) *A Brief History of the Shakespeare Reading Society*, London: Society for Theatre Research.
Isaacs, J. (ed.) (1956) *William Poel's Prompt-Book of* Fratricide Punished, London: Society for Theatre Research.
Mazer, Cary M. (1981) *Shakespeare Refashioned: Elizabethan Plays on Edwardian Stages*, Ann Arbor, Mich.: University of Michigan Research Press.
O'Connor, Marion (1987) *William Poel and the Elizabethan Stage Society*, Cambridge: Chadwyck-Healey.
Poel, William (1913) *Shakespeare in the Theatre*, London: Sidgwick & Jackson.
—— (1929) *Monthly Letters*, ed. A.M. Trethwey, London: T. Werner Laurie.
Schafer, Elizabeth (2006) *Lilian Baylis: A Biography*, Hatfield: University of Hertfordshire Press.
Somerset, J.A.B. (1966) 'William Poel's First Full Platform Stage', *Theatre Notebook* 20(3): 118–21.
Speaight, Robert (1954) *William Poel and the Elizabethan Revival*, London: Heinemann.
Stanislavsky, Konstantin (1962) *My Life in Art*, trans. Elizabeth Reynolds Hapgood, London: Geoffrey Bles.
Styan, J.L. (1977) *The Shakespeare Revolution*, Cambridge: Cambridge University Press.
Tree, H. Beerbohm (1913) *Thoughts and After-Thoughts*, London: Cassell.
Webster, Margaret (1969) *The Same Only Different*, London: Victor Gollancz.
White, Martin (1999) 'William Poel's Globe', *Theatre Notebook* 53(3): 146–62.

About the author

Peter Thomson is Emeritus Professor of Drama at the University of Exeter, where he worked from 1974 until his retirement. For five years in the 1970s he reviewed the productions of the RSC for *Shakespeare Survey*. His books include *Shakespeare's Theatre* (1983 and 1992), *Shakespeare's Professional Career* (1992), *On Actors and Acting* (2000), three on Bertolt Brecht and, most recently, *The Cambridge Introduction to English Theatre, 1660–1900* (2006). He is the General Editor of the three-volume *Cambridge History of British Theatre*, editor of the journal *Studies in Theatre and Performance* and a research associate of the *New Dictionary of National Biography*.

22
MAX REINHARDT

Peter W. Marx

Born to a Jewish family in Baden, a small town near Vienna, Max Reinhardt (1873–1943) was deeply influenced by the rich and vital culture of the nearby metropolis, quipping ironically that his cradle had been on the fourth gallery of Vienna's famous Burgtheater. Fascinated by its remarkable protagonists, Reinhardt himself became an actor, starting his career in a minor theatre in Salzburg (Austria). He was soon discovered by Otto Brahm (1856–1912) who hired him for his legendary Deutsches Theater in Berlin, where Brahm had brought naturalism to the German stage.

This engagement at the Deutsches Theater brought Reinhardt from the Austrian provinces to the heart of Europe's most vibrant German-speaking metropolis and the 'Theatre Capital' of Germany. In spite of his youth, Reinhardt primarily played old or elderly men, like Engstrand in Ibsen's *Ghosts*. After a few years in the ensemble, Reinhardt became dissatisfied with the consistent naturalism that Brahm tried to apply even to classical plays. In 1901, Max Reinhardt proclaimed his own vision of theatre:

> I have in mind a theatre that returns joy to the people. It should lead them out of their grey everyday life to the bright and pure air/sphere of beauty. I can sense how people are tired of recognizing their own misery on stage again and again. They long for brighter colours and a heightened vision of life.
>
> (Reinhardt 1989: 73)

With this in mind, he founded a cabaret ensemble named Schall und Rauch (Noise and Smoke) with a small group of colleagues. In the guise of parody, these young actors did not simply mock prevailing theatrical styles but rather experimented with the diversity of theatrical languages outside the rigid, programmatic constraints of the conventional stage.

Eventually, the undertaking turned into a small theatre, and Reinhardt, leaving Brahm's company after a resounding éclat, became head of Schall und Rauch. Numerous contemporaries saw this step as symbolic patricide, a young man firmly rejecting naturalism and realism on the stage. Reinhardt developed an increasing interest in 'classical' plays and his love of Shakespeare became a driving force in his comet-like career.

Overwhelming success for Reinhardt's 1905 production at the Neues Theater of *A Midsummer Night's Dream* brought the offer to become Head of the Deutsches Theater, succeeding Brahm at Germany's most prestigious theatre. In 1913, Reinhardt announced a cycle of Shakespeare productions, including *A Midsummer Night's Dream, Much Ado about Nothing, Hamlet* and *The Merchant of Venice*. By this time, he had already widened his area of activity to include all of Europe as well as the USA. In London, *Reinhardtism* had become a keyword in theatrical discourse.

Unlike many British contemporaries, such as Henry Irving or Herbert Beerbohm Tree, Reinhardt was not an actor-manager; he soon gave up acting in order to focus on directing. He was also a dynamic and restless entrepreneur, aided by his brother and business manager Edmund. In his heyday, he simultaneously managed several theatres in Vienna and Berlin, organised national and international tours of his productions, and, in 1920, founded the Salzburg Festival. As early as the first decade of the 1900s, Reinhardt had negotiated the opening of a Reinhardt Theatre on Broadway, which would have meant dividing his activities between Europe and New York. While the grandiose plan never worked out, his tours and productions in the 1920s were huge box-office successes, and his name became widely known.

In 1933, Reinhardt's career in Germany came to an abrupt end; though the Nazi Government offered him the status of an 'Honorary Aryan', Reinhardt refused, leaving Germany and going into exile in Austria, England and the USA where he arrived in 1934. But he was unable to live up to his former achievements: his actors' studio in Hollywood and several productions in New York were economic failures. He twice returned to *A Midsummer Night's Dream*, the play that had laid the foundation of his career, in Hollywood and Chicago. Once again, the old magic worked, as it did in the wonderful film he made for Warner Brothers but, given the wartime situation and the hand-to-mouth existence of theatres in California, he found it increasingly difficult to find an audience. In 1943, Reinhardt, considered the inventor of directorship in the modern German theatre and someone who had celebrated brilliant successes for more than thirty years on almost every stage of the Western world, died in reduced circumstances in New York.

In contrast to many of his contemporaries, such as Edward Gordon Craig and Konstantin Stanislavsky, Reinhardt did not tie himself to a single style: his productions neither belonged to a specific school nor followed a particular programme. Among the surge of 'isms' at the beginning of the twentieth century, Reinhardt, unlike many in the avant-garde, pursued no exclusive aesthetic vision, trying instead to create a unique atmosphere for each individual production. This eclecticism puts him outside the clear classifications of traditional theatre history. None of his contemporaries possessed his gift for using (and developing) the rich diversity of theatrical languages and forms.

This versatile pragmatism combined several streams of the contemporary theatre. Despite his scepticism about Brahm's insistence on naturalism, Reinhardt was nonetheless influenced by the latter's urge to overcome the traditional declamatory style. He also stood in a line of succession from George II, Duke of Meiningen, who had both revolutionised stage design and insisted on ensemble acting. Reinhardt also travelled abroad for inspiration and became familiar with Beerbohm Tree's work and the London theatre, as well as with the work of Craig and Stanislavsky.

In order to govern his theatre empire and keep it running, Reinhardt and his staff developed a complex organisational structure. Along with an elaborate and effective system of advertising and public relations, the aesthetic process itself was tightly controlled and structured. In close cooperation with his set designer and composer, Reinhardt prepared each production meticulously, beginning work well before the start of rehearsals. The complete structure of the production would be laid down in a *Regiebuch* (prompt book) which was updated until opening night and beyond. The annotations gave detailed descriptions of the main actions on stage, the lightning and other technical installations, resulting in an extensive documentation that allowed productions to be kept in the repertoire for years: even in Reinhardt's absence, the cast could be changed and the production revived, with rehearsals conducted by one of his numerous assistants, using the *Regiebuch* as a guide. All this touring was exhausting and time-consuming, but Reinhardt's stunning ubiquity was based on his efficient, industrial-like organisation.

Such a complex theatre operation also called for a sizeable company. Apart from members from his own school of acting, Reinhardt would hire talented young actors wherever he found them. For opening nights and first performances, he employed his star actors and later replaced them with lesser-known ones; in this way a single production could run for several hundred performances, the most successful for more than a decade. Artistic standards were undoubtedly compromised when whole casts or individual actors were replaced, but this was the only way to run such a theatre empire with hundreds of performances a year in several theatres with no public subsidy.

From the beginning of his career, Max Reinhardt was concerned about training young people for the acting profession. As early as 1905, he founded the school of acting at the Deutsches Theater, even though he himself never elaborated a 'system' of training. His prompt book for *Macbeth*, however, shows clearly what was expected: basically to follow Hamlet's advice to the actors in Act III, Scene 2: 'Be not too tame neither, but let your own discretion be your tutor; suit the action to the word, the word to the action'. Reinhardt left nothing to chance: in the soliloquies, for example, he prescribed not only the pauses and stresses in verbal delivery but also orchestrated accompanying gestures and facial expressions. Fortunately, however, his best actors were not limited by his dictates.

In his ensemble, Reinhardt assembled outstanding artists, but many of them did not fit the prevailing categories of type-casting. Actors such as Gertrud Eysoldt, Fritz Kortner, Alexander Moissi and Rudolf Schildkraut might not suit the common taste, but Reinhardt integrated their specific appearances, physiognomies and timbres into his productions, making inventive casting a hallmark of his aesthetics. Though the productions were conceived in advance, in rehearsals Reinhardt guided his actors towards a concept that was based on his intuition and joy in experimentation.

Reinhardt's Shakespeare productions, which spanned his entire career, may be exemplified in *A Midsummer Night's Dream*, *The Merchant of Venice* and *Hamlet*.

A Midsummer Night's Dream

On 31 January 1905, at Neues Theater in Berlin, audience and critics were stunned by the lavish and opulent performance. Friedrich Düsel declared: 'This production of *A Midsummer Night's Dream* ranks among the most beautiful ever seen on a German stage' (*Deutsche Zeitung*, 2 February 1905).

The enchantment was due neither to the plot nor to any particular actor but to the stage setting. Gustav Knina had designed scenery which was dominated by the Athenian wood. In contrast to then-current convention, Reinhardt and Knina had decided not to use painted backdrops but to construct a genuine three-dimensional wood: actual trees reached up to the roof, surrounded by little bushes, and a small pond gleamed in the silver moonlight. And, as if this were not enough, the whole wood was installed on a revolving stage. The legendary Munich stage engineer Karl Lautenschläger had invented the revolving stage about ten years earlier; it was widely used to speed up scene changes but had never before been seen in Berlin. Moreover, Reinhardt used it for dramaturgical effect: during the performance, the wood started to turn, so that the audience's perception was as bemused as those of Shakespeare's dreamers.

This device not only affected the décor but had a significant impact on the actors as well. With the wood conceived as a practical space, the actors could use the entire stage, in all its dimensions. Restrictions posed by painted backdrops were no longer an issue. The entire stage became a playground for the elves who, dancing and frolicking all over, animated the sylvan landscape. They were not played by children, as was traditional, but by young girls in light green costumes with veils that resembled wafts of mist and gave a subliminal eroticism. This innovation was further emphasised by Reinhardt's decision to abandon conventional ballet movements so that the elves appeared to be truly revelling. And, as Nina Zabludowski put it, 'The sliding, the hopping and jumping appeared unconventional, elementary and thus much more expressive' (Zabludowski 1930: 49).

Oberon's entourage was in contrast, as the *Regiebuch* indicates, rather a rough crowd: 'His followers are trolls, dwarfs, gnomes and pixies, and they skip along behind and jump in front of him from the grass and the hill, down left, and tumble in his path' (quoted by Styan 1982: 58). Their costumes were furs and enormous headdresses made of leaves and branches. They practically melted into the woods when the Athenians stumbled over the roots that, moments later, turned into wood sprites, cowering on the floor. These forest-dwellers suggested late-nineteenth-century depictions of mythical creatures and were considered not mere fairytale characters, but allegories of the elemental, uncivilised core of human beings.

To present the wood as a sphere of its own, Reinhardt imported several technical devices from Herbert Beerbohm Tree's legendary 1900 production. The floor, for example, was covered with a carpet of moss and grass, in order to avoid any resemblance to the bare stage. In a manner similar to Beerbohm Tree's real-life rabbits, which have come to epitomise the over-reaching Victorian stage pictorialism, Reinhardt installed small lights suspended from the ceiling to represent fireflies. Reinhardt did not merely copy Beerbohm Tree – as claimed by some of his critics – but developed new devices that were subsequently patented. Among these was the *Rundhorizont* (cyclorama) that clothed the stage's background. Huntly Carter gives a detailed account:

> [T]here is a vast horizon or heaven which passes round the back and side of the stage. It has a slight dome, [. . .]. This huge segment of a circle is a light iron structure covered with plaster. [. . .] This heaven is lighted by an enormous 'Oberlicht' (overlight) [*sic.*] [overhead light], placed above the centre of the stage and so constructed as to throw its rays of light horizontally and not *vertically*.
>
> (Carter 1914: 175–6)

The *Rundhorizont* soon became a hallmark of Reinhardt's aesthetics and epitomised his use of the stage as a three-dimensional space. Taking full advantage of its depth, he freed it from two-dimensionality and graphic illusionism, turning it into a true *Lebensraum* for his figures. The *Rundhorizont* accomplished this by evoking a sense of infinity within the artificial space.

The apogee of Reinhardt's art was his masterful lightning: having developed the techniques for using light dramaturgically, he painted his wood with broad strokes of light. Even Paul Goldmann's mockery suggests the effect: 'One saw a wood or many real trees. One saw the floor covered with real moss. One saw a moon that shone so magnificently that the real moon would not bear the comparison, if the Lord assigned the celestial illumination to Max Reinhardt' (Goldmann 1908: 232).

Athens and her dwellers stood out in contrast against this fairy world and the vibrant chaos of the wood, an effect furthered by the costuming. While those of the elves and goblins matched the dark tones of the wood, the Athenians wore the conventional costumes of stage Greeks in bright colours.

Because he wished to make the woods the central focus of his production, Reinhardt reduced the first scenes in Theseus' palace to a brief episode, for which only a small part of the stage was used. The last act, on the other hand, mobilised all theatrical means to stage the splendour of Theseus' festivity: when the curtain was drawn, the audience saw a deep blue sky and a brightly shimmering marmoreal amphitheatre, as a torchlight procession approached. The brightness of marble and torchlights provided a picturesque contrast to the gloomy colours of the wood. Reinhardt used all possible theatrical means to establish Athens and the fairy world as antipodes, not only the text, dramatis personae and plot.

Although Reinhardt used August Wilhelm von Schlegel's (1767–1845) classic translation without major changes, he was much more creative in his appropriation of the music of Felix Mendelssohn-Bartholdy (1809–47). Mendelssohn's composition for *A Midsummer Night's Dream* (Opus 61) was not presented as a whole but divided into several parts adjusted to the requirements of the scene and used as dramaturgical devices;

> Some themes are repeated if it stands the stage in good stead. Some motifs function as sounds of the wood as well. The rhythm of movement and language on one hand and the music in the background on the other, merge in an integrated expression that matches the meticulously chosen, warmly illuminated colours.
>
> (Zabludowski 1930: 48f.)

Nina Zabludowski's description recalls Richard Wagner's concept of *Gesamtkunstwerk* postulating that all elements of the stage should melt into a singular work of art. Many representatives of the avant-garde, such as Adolphe

Appia and Edward Gordon Craig, had taken up this idea to articulate their vision of a genuine theatrical work of art. These approaches favoured stage design, lightning and costumes at the cost of the formerly dominant drama. Even though Reinhardt himself never took an explicit stand on this topic, his audience recognised that his style of directing was related to the idea of the *Gesamtkunstwerk*. His *A Midsummer Night's Dream* was consistently praised as a 'polyphonic composition' and a coordinated mobilisation of all theatrical elements.

Reading the literature surrounding Reinhardt's 1905 production, it is striking that the cast is so rarely mentioned, even though highly regarded actors were in the production, for example Tilla Durieux (Oberon), Friedrich Kayßler (Theseus) and Eduard von Winterstein (Demetrius). Yet, any astonishment diminishes when remembering that *Gesamtkunstwerk* implies a synesthesia without privileging any single element: the actor should cede his central position to the *mise-en-scène* as a whole and to the director as its creator.

Among the cast, only Gertrud Eysoldt's (1870–1955) Puck was widely mentioned in the press and raised a controversy among the critics. Along with Reinhardt's renunciation of conventional patterns for *A Midsummer Night's Dream*, Eysoldt divested Puck of all traditional elements. Until then, Puck had been played by a girl, as a ballerina-like figure with little wings on her back. Eysoldt, in contrast, was clad with furs, leaves and branches. Usually, Puck had been a whimsical, cute, little being but Eysoldt was an ugly, untamed sprite, a Robin Goodfellow in all his ambiguity.

This interpretation echoed Eysoldt's earlier stage appearances as 'wild' female characters, such as Frank Wedekind's *Erdgeist* or Oscar Wilde's *Salome*, who claim the right of their erotic desire. These self-confident women, standing in sharp contrast to dominant role models, haunted her stage persona, as Marvin Carlson would put it, and these overtones irritated some critics deeply: 'Oddly enough Mrs. Eysoldt, an expert for perverse female characters, played Puck. She turned the elf into a gross goblin lacking any poetry. But his clowneries entertained the audience' (*Neue Freie Presse*, 2 February 1905).

Conversely, more open-minded critics regarded Eysoldt's Puck as the key to a new reading of the play:

> We understood laughingly the eternal, unchallengeable philosophy of eroticism. We laughingly accepted Puck among the world's sages because he whiningly forces the stallion to choose between oats and mare. This animal parable taught us what we were about to observe soon after in the realm of higher desire: in a world of wild drives, it is foolish to insist on the superiority of the human consciousness.
>
> (Harden 1905: 195)

According to this proto-Freudian reading, Reinhardt's production was not restricted to mere aesthetic or technical changes but was based on an innovative reading of the dream with the primal wood as its sphere: the *mise-en-scène* did not conjure up a fairyland but staged an allegory of the *conditio humana*. The lavish production celebrated infatuation, eroticism and desire, beyond all social or moral considerations.

Reinhardt's *A Midsummer Night's Dream* offered a counter-image to the Wedekind and Wilde plays he had previously staged. Whereas their protagonists are inescapably mired in the antagonism of their emotions to social expectations, Reinhardt read Shakespeare's play as a miraculous and utopian solution of these conflicts. This harmony guaranteed the acceptance and success of the production. Besides earning Reinhardt a place among the foremost artists of his time, his 1905 *A Midsummer Night's Dream* was also a major box-office success, its 500 performances marking an outstanding record for a classical play in those days.

Throughout his entire life, Reinhardt repeatedly returned to this play, which suited his flair for colours, music, atmosphere and fantasy. Succeeding productions basically followed the model developed in 1905, but some stand out among the recycling. In 1910, he staged the play for a single performance in a private garden in Nikolassee, close to Berlin. This kind of site-specific performance obviously intrigued him very much, since he came back to it several times, staging *A Midsummer Night's Dream* in the 1930s in both Oxford and Florence. Such open-air performances might be taken as proof of a hidden craving for realism, but he did not favour a real wood over the one on the revolving stage: rather, he took pleasure in theatre's many different genres.

While an opulently equipped stage was a key to Reinhardt's success, it was not an indispensable precondition. In 1909, Reinhardt was invited to bring his productions to the Munich Künstlertheater (Art Theatre), a theatre built to embody the ideas of Georg Fuchs (1868–1949) who had proclaimed that a radically new theatre should be centred on the actor. The audience was seated in an amphitheatre facing a stage with no orchestra pit, the so-called *Reliefbühne*; the actors performed on a shallow stage in front of stylised backdrops, so that they appeared as in bas-relief. This denial of space did not harmonise well with Reinhardt's style, and his contemporaries considered he and Fuchs to be opposites rather than allies. Those critics who had castigated Reinhardt's lavishness expected a spectacular failure, but he proved able to adapt his production to the Munich conditions. While in Berlin, his production depended on the free and imaginative use of the depth of the stage, now he stripped away all decorative luxury and opted for a minimal staging. A couple of trees sufficed to conjure the summery wood near Athens. The elaborate wedding procession was replaced by Mendelssohn's famous march. Reinhardt's success in Munich proved that he exploited, but did not depend on, technical devices.

In his American exile, Reinhardt again turned to *A Midsummer Night's Dream*, staging it, in 1934, in the Hollywood Bowl and touring it to Berkeley, Chicago and Milwaukee. These performances were conceived as the beginning of an annual festival, but the plan was never realised.

The Merchant of Venice

The Merchant of Venice was well established and Shylock a fixture in the repertory of the great virtuoso actors of those days. To gain a new perspective, however, Reinhardt started not with this central figure but with stage and costume design. He assigned these tasks to the painters Emil Orlik (1870–1932) and Ernst Stern (1876–1954), the latter becoming Reinhardt's main stage designer in following years.

As with *A Midsummer Night's Dream*, Reinhardt used a revolving stage to create a three-dimensional space. The circle was divided into several parts, each presenting a different locale and with a canal, complete with bridges, open stairs and Venetian gondolas, occupying the central axis. This arrangement provided quick scene changes and allowed figures to move through the city as the stage turned slowly; with a film-like effect, the scene transitions were visual surprises in their own right.

This emphasis on the scenery changed the focus of the entire play, as Reinhardt's dramaturge Arthur Kahane has pointed out: 'Venice is the heart, centre, and essence of this production. Not Shylock but Venice: the perpetually singing, perpetually humming Venice. This city vibrates with love of life, pleasure, joy, and exuberance. It considers itself the capital and centre of the world' (1914: 116). This setting provided not only splendid decoration but also a frame for the director's interpretation: the grandeur of Venice eclipsed Shylock's fate. Whereas the stage genealogy of the nineteenth century focused on Shylock as the tragic protagonist of the play, Reinhardt insisted on comedy. According to Kahane, the Venetian *jeunesse dorée* was nothing but 'a charming, frivolous community of careless aristocrats ready and gifted for all kinds of adventures and pranks'. In order to maintain a happy ending, Shylock should be nothing but a 'sinister stranger vanishing in a sea of music' (Kahane 1914: 116–17).

This elegant stage contrasted with the Shylock of Rudolf Schildkraut (1862–1930), a senior actor already a legend in his lifetime. According to rumour, he had been born in Constantinople and raised in Romania and had started his career in minor Yiddish theatre troupes in Eastern Europe before he was discovered for Hamburg. This personal legend added to his stage appearance, because he embodied Oriental stereotypes, both fascinating and mysterious to his audience. Moreover, Schildkraut's physical appearance was not at all attractive, being rather bulky, with protruding eyes, but critics praised his daunting presence on stage.

Schildkraut's costume stressed these physical features: he had an oriental coat of precious fabrics with rich ornaments, tailored in a way that gave him an angular contour. He wore a turban and big rings on his fingers. His face looked grotesque, with a smile baring several tooth gaps, and it was framed by a fringe of beard, and long hair with traditional sidelocks (*Payot*). The contrast to the elegant and fashionable environment of Reinhardt's staged Venice clearly marked him as an outsider.

The effect of Schildkraut's Shylock can be exemplified by the pantomime scene of Jessica's abduction which Reinhardt added to the play's action. The air is filled with music and laughter while athletic figures kidnap Jessica from her father's house; then, as the music dies away, Shylock appears on stage, quietly humming an old Shabbat song. He knocks on his door, but when no one answers, he grows nervous and calls for Jessica. All of a sudden, he panics: he runs up the stairs, looking for his daughter and his money, crying out for both. The clumsy body has turned into an agile figure, speeding all over the stage. Without another thought, Shylock runs to the Rialto.

This scene – paradigmatic for Reinhardt's directing – drew much attention from audience and critics for its beauty and insight into Shylock's motivation: he loves both his daughter and his money – and is robbed of both. Contrasted music further distinguished the two worlds: the Venetians accompanied by ubiquitous music and laughter, Shylock's quiet humming uniquely his own. Schildkraut's physical performance added strongly to the scene, with rapid changes of body language and movement reflecting his inner disturbance and despair. His initially grotesque appearance elicited compassion in this moment of defeat and betrayal: he is no longer the 'annoying stranger' who 'invades like a cloud the bright Venetian sky' (Kahane 1914: 117); his cruelty was a response to lifelong discrimination and exclusion. The impression of the wordless scene was too imposing to allow a return to comedy, and the tensions eventually culminated in the trial when Shylock – calm on the outside but trembling with inner feeling – stumbles off the stage while the Venetians burst into jubilation. So, the production finally redirected the focus to Shylock and Venice's splendour, Reinhardt's original focus, is rendered culpable as it becomes obvious that the carefree life of the young Venetians was at the cost of others.

This reading against the grain of tradition relied on Schildkraut's acting and appearance. Without trying to turn Shylock into a tragic hero, the actor embodied the character's despair, and his own persona strengthened this effect:

he radiated an aura of authenticity and veracity that became entangled with Shakespeare's character and made visible the political dimension of the play. Arnold Zweig has described this effect in terms of the Jewish Dietary Laws: 'Schildkraut's Shylock smells of onions and garlic. This is at least as delicious and odorous as butchered pigs and a goatling boiled in its mother's milk. [. . .] This very Rudolf Schildkraut, stubby and fidgety, was a major mesmerizing and shocking appearance on the German stage' (Zweig 1928: 177f.).

The character's implicit appeal for tolerance was not verbal but lay in the physical and sensuous reality of Schildkraut's Shylock.

Reinhardt restaged the play in the Grosses Schauspielhaus, a former circus transformed into a vast theatre for about 3,200 spectators. The enormous space, with a regular stage within its arena, was a challenge for actors, and not all Reinhardt's stars managed to master the gigantic theatre vocally or physically. Reinhardt had experimented with mass spectacles since 1910, but it was not until 1919 that he could acquire the former Zirkus Schumann as a permanent theatre. While it was suited to the performance of Greek tragedies, including mass choirs, the development of a repertoire for such a huge room was yet unsolved. Transferring *The Merchant of Venice* to this new format was highly ambitious, especially since most of the audience and critics had vivid memories of Schildkraut's Shylock and the enchanting stage by Ernst Stern. Owing to the extended dimensions, the new production lost much of the former's glamour. The revolving stage had shown a Venice in miniature, but the enlarged proportions could not conjure up the same enchantment. Critics mocked the set as a 'sports field'.

These conditions also required a different style of acting. Werner Krauss (1884–1959) as the new Shylock handled the dimensions of the Grosses Schauspielhaus well and even took advantage of its magnitude. He relied on a method of 'optical acting', as Herbert Ihering has put it (1997: 55). Contemporaries criticised Krauss's approach as superficial in that he did not aim at a psychological reading but rather worked with gesture and voice. However, his demonstrative style suited the huge stage that could not create an intimate atmosphere but required large gestures. His Shylock of 1921 appeared in a dark caftan with a *kippah*, the traditional Jewish head covering. But more remarkable was his use of a red wig that had been an attribute of Jewish theatrical figures until Edmund Kean (1787–1833), in 1814, performed Shylock for the first time without it. Some historians have traced back the wig to Medieval Passion plays that caricatured Jews as antagonists of Christ. Kean led Shylock away from this stereotypic representation, but Krauss's choice of the wig deliberately echoed the earlier tradition. His costume suited his highly agile and aggressively physical style of acting. Critics also noted the increase of physical violence against Shylock that might be due in part to the enlarged stage but, together with the *genius loci* of the former circus, the violence recalled the brutality of slapstick jokes:

> Krauss ripped stumblingly through the arena. He was an angry, dangerous clown, a ghostly, weird Ahasver. He stumbled; he fell, and rolled on the floor. He kicked and he was kicked. He nagged and trumpeted. Medieval hell had spewed up this red, ugly, joking devil. He was a spookily deformed nightmare. An eerie vision.
>
> (Ihering 1997: 60)

Krauss's energetic clowning did not allow any deeper emotions, neither suggesting heroic resistance nor intended to elicit compassion. He openly exploited anti-Semitic stereotypes. The comic happy ending excluded the Jew but also bore an awkward message. Emil Faktor noticed these ambivalences in the audience reactions: 'If a certain party cheers with ostentation at the first appearances of Shylock, one wonders whether this play is really a good choice in our days of racism' (Faktor 1921).

Keeping historical development in mind, Krauss's Shylock of 1921 can be read as a double key scene of German (theatre) history: in the course of Krauss's further career, his superficial, mask-like style of acting led him to the Nazi movie *Jud Süß* (1940) where he played all the Jewish side characters. His abnegation of any psychological or emotional approach culminated in a caricature-like appropriation of these characters. Though the 1921 Shylock does not directly foreshadow this later production, Krauss's ambivalent aesthetics were already fully developed by then.

The production is also revealing about Reinhardt. While he was personally very aware of increasing anti-Semitism in German society after the First World War, he did not consider his artistic profession in any way political. He was too fascinated with the possibilities of a new interpretation, as offered by Krauss, to question its political implications. While such a naïveté was still possible in 1921, this Shylock already mirrored the tensions in Germany that led to the catastrophe of 1933.

Hamlet

The Tragedy of Hamlet remained a major challenge. The play was considered part of the German literary canon and, strangely, a symbol of German identity; the widely repeated saying 'Germany is Hamlet' underscored the expectations of the audience. Reinhardt's first *Hamlet* premiered in 1909 during his guest performances in the Munich Künstlertheater. Its shallow stage called for a novel solution. Reinhardt could not unfold lavish decoration but had to work with reduction and abstraction. The set he used only gave a view of sections of rooms that were never closed and in every case had a gallery or stairs leading up or down. An audience was given the impression of a fragmented space in which the actors could vary entrances and exits: it appeared to be a labyrinthine and sinister palace with an atmosphere of ambiguity and gloom.

Alexander Moissi (1879–1935), an actor of Albanian-Italian descent, played the title role. One of the most dazzling stars of the German stage at that time, he was slender, with big dark eyes, wavy black hair and a high, singing voice; furthermore, he never abandoned his accent. His voice and pronunciation were not suitable for traditional declamation but had a very special appeal. While he soon became famous for his impersonation of broken and troubled characters so fashionable in contemporary plays, such as Osvald in Ibsen's *Ghosts*, his classic roles were controversial.

In view of the German claim to *Hamlet*, the part did not offer much variety of interpretation. In contrast to the anglophone countries where a Hamlet born to set an 'out of joint' time to right and a 'sweet Hamlet' were two possible models, the German tradition demanded the heroic Hamlet. Josef Kainz (1858–1910) was widely held to be the ultimate Hamlet. Whereas he appeared strong and superior, Moissi's rather boyish prince was considered wilful and effeminate. According to Siegfried Jacobsohn: 'The hallmark of Moissi's Hamlet was not melancholia but defiance' (1910: 153).

When Reinhardt transferred *Hamlet* to Berlin the same year, he tried to adapt the Munich setting to the Deutsches Theater, but the effects that had created a dense atmosphere in Munich were lost on the larger Berlin stage. More crucially, in January 1909, Kainz had given a guest performance as Hamlet in Berlin at the Neues Schauspielhaus under the direction of Alfred Halm. While the production was considered humdrum and unexciting, Kainz's Hamlet was highly praised and, according to several critics, Moissi's lost in comparison.

In 1913, Reinhardt returned to *Hamlet*. This time, employing more money, time and effort, he found an inventive solution for his Berlin stage and astonished his audience with a totally new approach. He abstained from all technical and decorative endeavours and implemented a radical abstraction and reduction of scenery. He extended the stage by covering the orchestra pit and the first rows of the stalls, gaining an enormous forestage that reached deeply into the audience. The space was more or less empty, only three steps led to a small podium; the back was bounded by a cyclorama. Thanks to these alterations, the stage had a new depth that could be extensively used.

In this empty space, curtains were flown in, their different colours marking both mood and setting: violet for Laertes' farewell from his father, dark green for the praying king, red for Gertrude's closet. Almost no architectural pieces were used, only a wall at the back during the first scenes and a statue to mark the graveyard. The stage did not evoke the illusion of Elsinore but became, as Arthur Kahane had it, 'Hamlet's soul' (1914: 115). This new solution demanded the audience's active participation: it 'appeals to our imagination. The space is wonderfully neutralized' (Jacobsohn 1910: 159).

This time, Moissi alternated in the role with Albert Bassermann (1867–1952), whose interpretation was widely appreciated: trained in naturalistic theatre, he did not use the language musically as Moissi spoke so that he revealed his character's inner thoughts and feelings. His Hamlet was judged to be in a major key, 'not, as usual, in [a] minor' (Jacobsohn 1910: 162).

In his long-lasting preoccupation with Shakespeare, Reinhardt showed sensitivity towards the tone, rhythm and scenographic potential of each text. In theatre history, he occupies a middle ground: stressing the stage as a genuine art, he tried to engender a dialogue between literature and theatre in order to recreate a play's characters on stage. In contrast to the proponents of the *Shakespeare-Stage*, Karl Lautenschläger and Jocza Savits, Reinhardt did not try to exhume an 'authentic' Shakespeare. While he repeatedly expressed his admiration for the Elizabethan theatre, he also insisted that its aesthetic means were too meagre for an audience of the twentieth century. When Reinhardt repeatedly praised Shakespeare as an actor-playwright, he implicitly laid out his ideal of directing as a process of mutual enrichment, not of dominating the text.

Chronology

1873	Max Reinhardt is born in Baden (Austria)
1905	*A Midsummer Night's Dream*
	Reinhardt becomes Head of the Deutsches Theater Berlin
	The Merchant of Venice
1909	Guest Performances in the Munich Künstlertheater including *Hamlet*
1910	Guest performances in London
	Oedipus Rex – Reinhardt's first mass production in a circus arena
1913–14	Shakespeare cycle in Berlin
1919	Opening of the Grosses Schauspielhaus (the former Circus Schumann)
1920	Founding of the Salzburg Festival
1923–24	Guest productions in the USA, including *The Miracle*, running 298 performances on Broadway
1933	Reinhardt leaves Germany after the Nazis seize power
1934	*A Midsummer Night's Dream* in the Hollywood Bowl

1935	*A Midsummer Night's Dream* – movie for Warner Bros.
1937	Reinhardt directs *The Eternal Road* in New York – his last major production
1943	Reinhardt dies in New York

Bibliography

Carter, Huntly (1914) *The Theatre of Max Reinhardt*, London: Frank & Cecil Palmer.
Faktor, Emil (1921) 'Der Kaufmann von Venedig', *Berliner Börsen-Courier*, 13 (3).
Goldmann, Paul (1908) *Vom Rückgang der deutschen Bühne. Polemische Aufsätze über Berliner Theater-Aufführungen*, Frankfurt/ Main: Rütten & Loening.
Harden, Maximilian (1905) 'Theater', *Die Zukunft* 52: 186–96.
Hortmann, Wilhelm (1998) *Shakespeare on the German Stage: The Twentieth Century*, Cambridge: Cambridge University Press.
Ihering, Herbert (1997) *Werner Krauß: ein Schauspieler und das neunzehnte Jahrhundert*, Berlin: Vorwerk. First published 1944.
Jacobsohn, Siegfried (1910) *Max Reinhardt*, Berlin: Erich Reiß.
Kahane, Arthur (1914) 'Max Reinhardt's Shakespeare-Zyklus im Deutschen Theater zu Berlin', *Jahrbuch der Deutschen Shakespeare-Gesellschaft* 50: 107–20.
Marx, Peter W. (2006) *Max Reinhardt. Vom bürgerlichen Theater zur metropolitanen Kultur*, Tübingen: Francke.
Reinhardt, Max (1989) *Leben für das Theater: Schriften und Selbstzeugnisse. Hrsgg. von Hugo Fetting* (ed.), Berlin: Argon Verlag.
Styan, J.L. (1982) *Max Reinhardt*. Directors in Perspective, Cambridge: Cambridge University Press.
Tollini, Frederick (2004) *The Shakespeare Productions of Max Reinhardt*, Studies in Theatre Arts, 31, Lewiston, Queenston and Lampeter: Edwin Mellen.
Williams, Simon (1990) *Shakespeare on the German Stage*, Vol. I: *1586–1914*, Cambridge: Cambridge University Press.
Zabludowski, Nina (1930) 'Ein Max-Reinhardt-Jubiläum: Reinhardts "Sommernachtstraum" vom 31. Januar 1905 und die Neuinszenierungen von 1907, 1909, 1913, 1921 und 1925', *Die Scene* 20 (2): 47–53.
Zweig, Arnold (1928) *Juden auf der deutschen Bühne*, Berlin: Welt-Verlag.

About the author

Peter W. Marx is Junior Professor of Theatre Studies at the Johannes Gutenberg-University of Mainz (Germany). His main fields of research are theatre history, cultural studies and interculturality. He has recently published a monograph on Max Reinhardt *Vom bürgerlichen Theater zur metropolitanen Kultur* (*From Bourgeois Theatre to Metropolitan Culture*) (2006), tracing Max Reinhardt's career with an emphasis on its social and cultural contexts. Reading theatre and its aesthetics as a forum for cultural negotiations, Marx analyses Max Reinhardt's work as essential for the emergence of the modern concept of directorship as well as central in mediating between high art and forms of popular culture such as the circus or the revue.

23
BARRIE RUTTER

Christian M. Billing

Biography is important in a study of Barrie Rutter's work, for to understand where the man is from and the route he took to a career running one of Britain's most significant alternative classical theatre companies is to understand much about his approach to the direction of Shakespeare, his stripped-down production aesthetic and his oftentimes audacious performance style. Rutter was born in Hull, East Yorkshire in December 1946. The town, still based at that time very largely around its maritime economy, had only recently had the guts bombed out of it during the Second World War and was struggling to rebuild itself. His family lived in a fish-dock house: a two-up, two-down Victorian terrace in the deprived Hessle Road area of the city; both generations of immediate relatives worked in the fishing industry, an insular working-class community that limped its way unsteadily from wartime damage to eventual destruction in the next conflict to hit: the Cod War with Iceland in the 1970s. Although not particularly gifted in an academic sense, Rutter benefited from one of the brief blips of egalitarianism to light on the British education system and went to one of the bog-standard grammar schools that the socialist educationalists of post-war England allowed working-class children to attend. He there found refuge from a home life that was in his own estimation deeply unpleasant and, despite setbacks like a grandfather who burned his grandson's schoolbooks, achieved moderate success.

At first, any activity that extended his hours away from home appealed; as he grew older, however, it was performance that attracted most. During the 1964 academic session, he was cast as Macbeth in a school production and discovered his acumen for acting. He subsequently joined the National Youth Theatre, for whom he played Nipple in *Little Malcolm and His Struggle against the Eunuchs* at the Royal Court and Shakespeare's Falstaff. Despite a difficult training period at Glasgow's Royal Scottish Academy of Music and Drama, Rutter's talent was such that in 1968 he had written for him the part of Douglas Bagley in Peter Tierson's television drama *The Apprentices*. A career in professional performance thus began on a high, and he worked successfully during the early 1970s as a jobbing actor in theatre, one-off television dramas and a number of well-known situation comedies before joining the Royal Shakespeare Company (RSC) in 1975. At the RSC, largely as a result of the class- and region-based prejudices of the Cambridge-educated élite that ran the institution at that time, he performed in a variety of only minor roles until he left in 1980 – when a mixture of frustration at being habitually overlooked for major Shakespearian parts and an opportunity to engage in more genuinely experimental theatre practice led him to join the National Theatre (NT) in London. It was here that he met the man who was to become the greatest influence over his subsequent career and artistic philosophy: Leeds-born poet and intellectual Tony Harrison. Harrison gave Rutter significant roles in all three of his NT productions: *The Oresteia* (dir. Hall, 1981), *The Mysteries* (dir. Bryden, 1985) and *The Trackers of Oxyrhynchus* (dir. Harrison, 1990), shows written expressly to celebrate the poetic rhythm and expressive beauty of the northern voice. It was in the last such production that Rutter experienced the events that led him to found his own company and to become a director of Shakespeare. Like many tales in the history of theatre, the story is one of coincidence and accident.

Trackers premiered in Delphi in 1988 before transferring to the NT two years later. The play took the 400 surviving lines of Sophocles' *Ichneutai* (discovered in an Ancient Egyptian rubbish dump by Oxford scholars Bernard Grenfell and Arthur Hunt in 1907) and created from them a play for the historical and cultural landscape of late-1980s Britain. As an oppositional, working-class and deliberately northern poet, Harrison reworked one of the very few surviving Athenian satyr plays as a commentary upon the ways in which he saw theatre's original unity of purpose as having been lost (or at least artificially divided into 'high' and 'low' by the Nietzsche-following, upper-class, southern-English guardians of post-nineteenth-century culture, education and theatrical practice). Seeing partition as an unnecessary perpetuation of divided audiences and divided societies, Harrison used Grenfell, Hunt and a clog-dancing chorus of Satyrs to demonstrate Athenian acknowledgement of humanity's need to combine Apollonian and Dionysiac elements of the psyche:

> With the loss of [satyr] plays we are lacking important clues to the wholeness of the Greek imagination, and its ability to absorb and yet not be defeated by the tragic. In the satyr play, that spirit of celebration, held in the dark solution of tragedy, is precipitated into release, and a release into the worship of the Dionysus who presided over the whole dramatic festival.
>
> (Harrison 1991: xi)

Whilst Harrison's overarching project was to critique elite educationalists and right-wing politicians who divided art and society into popular (Dionysiac) and refined (Apollonian), his use of the northern vernacular and material reminders of his working-class heritage to do so were powerful aspects of the project. Importantly also, the venue chosen to accommodate *Trackers* between its showings in Delphi and London was a 'homecoming' to Titus Salt's disused textile mill three miles north of Bradford. Such a venue made Harrison's geopolitical intentions clear:

> The play is part of my slow burning revenge against the teacher who denied me an opportunity to read poetry and take part in plays because of my accent. We chose Salts Mill because we needed a venue where the ghost images of the past were strong. Clogs are one of the principal expressions of the rhythm of life and they gear the satyrs into action.
>
> (Harrison, *Daily Telegraph* 23 February 1990)

A world tour was planned but never happened. Rutter was devastated and immediately decided to set up his own company in order to offer the world what the conventional practices of subsidised theatre had denied. His project would be as political as Harrison's; only this time, it would reappropriate for the working-class northern voice the works of the greatest English theatre writer: William Shakespeare. As part of his open declaration of war on the established southern elite, Rutter christened his brainchild: Northern Broadsides.

> The Oxbridge lot have appropriated Shakespeare for long enough [. . .] We are our voices, whether we change them or not [. . .] the biggest injury for a human being is for their voice to be taken away [. . .] I don't care if somebody [. . .] hate[s] it – they'll get both barrels, put it that way. We're not called Broadsides for nowt.
>
> (Rutter, *Yorkshire Post* 22 June 1992)

On Thursday 11 June 1992, in a boatshed on Hull Marina, Barrie Rutter walked onto a concrete-floored stage accompanied by fourteen fellow actors who had committed themselves to a project that would: 'explore the dignity of native speech [. . .] assault the "refinement" of culture [. . .] and explore [classical] texts using the Northern voice' (Publicity flyer). Shod with a well-heeled leather shoe on his good foot and a wooden-soled orthopaedic clog on his disfigured other (together with a white-collar shirt covered by a soldier's plain khaki bomber jacket), Rutter's costume choices, like his consonants, made obvious reference to the divide between high and low, North and South, that the actor, now perforce director, sought to redress. The production had been rehearsed in just four weeks at Salt's Mill and opened against a Spartan setting that the director had acquired, magpie-like, from that industrial rehearsal venue and elsewhere in the northern working man's world. With boats undergoing repair put temporarily back into the water, Rutter constructed inside the boatshed a 700-seat traverse auditorium; his audience accordingly faced each other in two end-on rakes whilst the play took place in the flat open space between them. Actors and spectators were illuminated by a combination of just two open-white lights, one at either end of the stage, as fading daylight turned into a full moon at the production's conclusion. This was the rough theatre of Peter Brook; Grotowski's poor theatre in action. Tickets ranged from just £2.50 to £9.00. In an advert placed in the local press, the general populous were invited to, 'Come to the Marina Boatshed to see *Richard III*' and advised, 'along with your picnic you'd better bring a muffler and hip-flask – it can't half get parky when the wind blows' (*Hull Daily Mail* 5 June 1992).

With actors dressed in eclectic modern dress and using minimal props to tell the story, Rutter placed his emphasis on the muscularity and narrative force of Shakespeare's verse, deliberately drawing attention to its heightened artificiality and the power of language to communicate compelling dramatic narrative: 'you never see a juggler apologising for his skills, and that's what verse does – [it] draws attention to itself all the time' (Rutter, *Financial Times* 10 June 1992). Critics applauded the approach: 'the result is a revelation. Shakespeare's verse emerges as clear, supple, rhythmic, playful and witty' (*Guardian* 12 June 1992); 'Shakespeare sounds terrific in authentic Northern voices. The flattened vowels, dropped aspirates and use of words like owt and ee [. . .] give the language a real immediacy and speed' (*Daily Telegraph* 14 December 1992). Proximity and pace were equally key to the production's success: running at a little over two-and-a-quarter hours, the actor-director made much of his lead character's liminal relationship with fellow players and performed the machiavel at the edges of the stage – a closeness to audiences that enabled him to strike up a strong performative bond in the manner of a medieval vice figure.

Rutter's no-nonsense show played to deliberately heterogeneous audiences and appealed to most; ensemble playing was praised, as were the performances of major characters. The fact that the project had taken place at all was evidence of Rutter's administrative acumen as much as his ability to direct and perform. Much has been made of the show's paltry £2,000 production budget (for set, props and the hire of technical equipment), but two years' graft behind the scenes had led to £110,000 being raised from

Hull City Council and Yorkshire and Humberside Arts. This funding supported wages and a five-week tour of 'non-velvet' spaces throughout the North (planned for when the show closed in Hull). Rutter had also garnered support in kind from each of his venues, from Yorkshire brewers Theakstons and £10,000 in free advertising from Hull-based radio station Viking FM. Bradford Alhambra agreed to provide essential administrative support.

Although his career as a director began from a combination of chippiness and gimmick derived in large part from oppositional intent, Rutter proved to be no flash in the pan. Following a successful tour of the north of England, *Richard III* transferred to the Riverside Studios in London and closed to critical acclaim at the Albertslundhuset, Copenhagen. Since 1992, his company has toured extensively in the UK and worldwide, bringing lively, fresh and invigorating interpretations of ancient Greek and Shakespearian texts to numerous diverse audiences. He has also presented world premieres of new commissions by Yorkshire playwrights Tony Harrison, Blake Morrison and Alan Plater. Each production is presented with minimum theatrical paraphernalia but maximum theatrical force – and is proudly articulated using the rich cadences of northern English.

From 1992 to 2007 Barrie Rutter directed nineteen plays by Shakespeare, drawn from every genre in which the playwright wrote. His rehearsal method and product have developed significantly over the years, yet they have always been rooted in two principal elements: music and geometry. The first comprises all that is spoken, sung or played on instruments (conceived of as a cohesive whole); the second, all physical movement, including blocking, dance and combat (treated equally holistically).

Rehearsals begin with a read-through, about which he confesses: 'I often shut my ears and just get through the play [to] make sure everybody's read it' (Rutter 2005: 269). He finds much of what is taught in English and American Drama Schools ineffectual with regards to classical performance and deplores what he calls adjectival and pronoun acting, as well as the fact that actors frequently pause at punctuation marks inserted by post-seventeenth-century editors and constantly feel the need to construct notions of psychological depth for the dramatic constructs they are required to play:

> I don't believe in the word 'character.' I think everything on the page is the poet's imagination with characteristics. You play the characteristics. I don't believe there is some psychological being somewhere up there on the astral plane, and through the process of rehearsal we can climb up this umbilical chord towards them.
>
> (*Financial Times* 10 June 1992)

Rutter eschews entirely the psychological interpretations of Shakespeare that have characterised most performances since the late nineteenth century and offers in their stead the Shakespearian text as a material document that testifies to various interconnected events and their consequences. He never bothers to attempt to present the interior workings of the human mind because he does not believe that actors can adequately convey them, and he leaves it up to audiences to decide what events on stage might actually mean. His approach has consistently led to the presentation of Shakespeare exactly as it is written, with no attempt to excuse via psychology the oftentimes disturbing attitudes of an early modern playwright with regards to gender, race or class.

For *The Merchant of Venice*, Rutter took himself the role of Shylock but saw the play as a romantic comedy with tragic elements. He directed it accordingly; not so much resisting as not feeling any temptation whatsoever to play the kind of post-Holocaust Shylock-obsessed vision that characterised the majority of late-twentieth-century productions. Unapologetic about the play's anti-Semitism, the production led audiences frequently to laugh, like the play's Venetians, at and not with Shylock – a strategy that led to numerous powerful moments. Yet, these were always constructed theatrically rather than psychologically. One such moment came as the *yarmulke* was ripped from Rutter's head towards the end of the trial scene, at which point there was often an unsettling number of guffaws from audiences. Some critics baulked at this, speaking of a production that lacked psychological depth and presented cruelly only the surface events of Shylock's narrative; yet surely such a visceral visual moment represents the very point of Shakespeare's play – a tale that takes audiences to a point of moral vertigo in which the safe ground of their own (mostly Christian influenced) identities (and concomitant prejudices) suddenly drops away from their feet and a Jew who has hitherto been seen as despicable, whose mind and psychological interiority has hardly been considered, is unexpectedly understood to be frail and human. Lyn Gardner observed in this regard that Rutter's approach turned Shylock into 'a genuinely tragic figure – a flawed, suffering human being, not a racial stereotype' (*Guardian* 25 February 2004). This is true; but the work of arriving at such a conclusion was done by Gardner as an audience member reading the scene's staging, rather than by Rutter acting any notion of interiority. Here and elsewhere in the production the director credited audiences with the ability to decode for themselves the visual and aural signs from which theatre is constituted and was justly proud that his approach repeatedly led to '[hardly] a dry eye in the house' by the end of Act IV, Scene 1 (Rutter 2005: 277). The refusal to apologise for Shakespeare's thorny text, or to render psychological its protagonists' motivations led most critics to applaud the show's honesty and to celebrate a production that brought them face to face with the sheer nastiness of religious prejudice. One particularly astute reviewer began by acknowledging the significance of the Holocaust to modern spectators, before asserting that contemporary theatrical fashion derived in response to these appalling historical events had turned Shakespeare's play on its head. He praised Rutter for restoring the right balance and observed that the show was 'closer to Shakespeare's original intentions than many more fêted productions' (*Daily Telegraph* 25 February 2004).

Avoiding psychology and not demanding the preparation of character by his actors, Rutter starts rehearsals from absolute basics – and those basics are text. He is firmly convinced that if the performance of Shakespearian verse and prose is right, actors are freed up to explore more fully their roles and that this leads to elevated levels of performance. Accordingly, he strives for meticulous understanding by his cast of the rhythms, imagery and meanings of Shakespeare's language. This knowledge, once owned by and embodied in performers, acts like the modal structures within which great jazz players improvise: when all actors are in tune, are keyed to the same interlocking rhythms and have well-developed understandings of the philosophical substance of what they are saying, things begin to happen. In early rehearsals, Rutter's eyes are always on book rather than on actors, and he directs much of his first phase of preparation with his ears. As a result of years of attention to detail in this regard, his understanding of the complexities of Shakespeare's many and varied verse and prose rhythms, forms and styles far exceeds the nonsensical platitudes spouted by most directors concerning iambic pentameters.

Added to linguistic precision is Rutter's unalterable commitment to the articulation of classical verse in the northern voice. He is not afraid to correct vowels or consonants that have drifted too far south for his liking. The issue is both political and aesthetic: he believes passionately in the right of working-class northerners to hear the nation's greatest theatre poet spoken with the rhythms and inflections of their own vernaculars; he is equally convinced that the flat vowels and granite consonants of the English north better suit the linguistic forms and intended speed of articulation of Shakespearian drama. Accordingly, he nearly always casts actors born, raised and preferably trained in the north of England. From the very start of his directing career he has suppressed not only southern English speech patterns but also references to the south in Shakespearian texts. His *Merry Wives* (*of Windsor*) was a version of Shakespeare that dropped all southern references not only from the play's title but dialogue; his pared-down edit of Shakespeare's first tetralogy removed much of Shakespeare's dealings with France and proudly advertised itself as the first Rose-based (i.e., York and Lancastrian) *Wars of the Roses* to appear on the English stage.

This approach has not only led to the garnering of a hugely faithful regional audience but also to wider questioning of the cultural hegemony of Received Pronunciation as the accepted manner of classical acting. The matter is not simple parochial recalcitrance from a regional director, as some denigrators have insisted. The way in which Rutter and his actors spoke Shakespearian text on early international tours led foreign journalists to remark:

> Many of us will remember a teacher at school reading one of Hamlet's dark and evocative soliloquies with an accent that better befits Tamil or Punjabi; and some of us were, perhaps, even asked to read out Mark Antony's impassioned funeral speech with a pronunciation that one can only call one's own. In this respect, 'our Sak-es-pare' has always been different to that of the English [. . .] a dramatic world populated by spiffy southern England voices [. . .] epitomised by the likes of Sir Laurence Olivier [. . .] If Shakespeare ever needed a bit of demystification [Rutter's approach] couldn't have served the purpose better.
>
> (*Indian Express*, Madras, 15 December 1993)

The debate concerning the appropriateness of different localised voices in the global performance of Shakespeare has continued since; but one point cannot be overstated: it is largely as a result of pioneers like Rutter that audiences in the UK and abroad have been politically engaged by versions of Shakespeare that offer an attack on the language-based cultural imperialism of the traditional British élite. Much of the territory gained by advocates of national and regional identity since the early 1990s has been secured as a result of successful cultural projects such as his.

As one might expect from a director who places so much emphasis on the interplay between the human voice, politics and identity, Rutter achieves his most profound directorial inflections through uncomplicated use of language. Northern Broadsides actors regularly tease laughter from lines that other companies struggle with, or find down-to-earth pathos in those that elsewhere seem laboured. In *King Lear*, the unremitting starkness with which his performers uttered Shakespeare's flinty poetry 'crashed over [audiences] as relentlessly, as unpityingly as breakers slamming upon Dover beach, leaving [them] unsheltered, without respite to regroup emotion, simulating [. . .] in the theatre the experience the King and his daughters suffer in the narrative' (Rutter 2003: 249). Equally trademark is Rutter's insistence on pace, which makes his show timings much closer to those of original performances than those of other directors and leads to performances as 'refreshingly different from the norm as early music played on original instruments' (*Yorkshire Post* 23 February 2000). *Romeo and Juliet* brought in Shakespeare's supposedly impossible two hours' traffic at two hours and ten minutes, of which critics spoke of the thrill of being taken along by Shakespeare's verse at full tilt. Rutter is firmly convinced that if Shakespeare is produced with minimum histrionic trickery and technical paraphernalia, if it is given back to actors to perform, then the playwright's language emerges most powerfully – and it is in speed and clarity of vocal expression that Rutter believes Shakespeare's full dialectical force to lie. He habitually reminds actors in rehearsal of the three cardinal virtues: 'faith, hope and clarity', stressing that 'the greatest of these is clarity'. His work has accordingly been praised for its accessibility and lucidity. Of *Antony and Cleopatra* one accomplished critic confessed that until he had seen Rutter's version he had regularly 'sat through [the play] dutifully, but never experienced the full blast of its poetic majesty and brilliance'; seeing Northern Broadsides he was converted to 'Shakespeare's insistently glorious and beguiling text' (*Observer* 8 October 1995).

The desire to present Shakespeare through his language and on his own terms is not, however, to say that Rutter shies away from interpretative decisions. Productions regularly speak about contemporary issues, particularly those relating to social class. *A Midsummer Night's Dream* placed Shakespeare's mechanicals at the play's centre and created actors whose intense affinity with their dramatic creations led them to observe: 'they represent us. They are [. . .] working people who are craftspeople, as are we, and we're going to give them their proper dignity' (*Times Educational Supplement* 9 September 1994). *Twelfth Night* saw characters of high or aspirationally elevated social status revealed as buffoons in a production that brought to the fore the artificiality of social distinction. Rutter also picked up on other aspects of the play's deep-rooted class-consciousness, in particular for Feste's comings and goings, which were presented as evidence of financial insecurity. In *King Lear*, a working-class music-hall comic, Duggie Brown, was cast as the Fool to make forcibly the point concerning the way the lower orders simply drop out of Shakespeare's narrative: Brown departed in a 'glorious backward exit to oblivion and infinity in the great depth of the [Salt's Mill theatre] lobby' (*Daily Mail* 10 September 1999). *Antony and Cleopatra* likewise brought attention to its lead characters' politically significant alter egos as flawed and failing despots who were dignifying as world governance what was really just exploitation. Equally politically, Octavius Caesar was played as a besuited managerial type who delighted before the show proper in watching a semi-pornographic, transvestite parody of Antony and Cleopatra's love antics paraded before him on a trolley – a framing device that not only affirmed Cleopatra's suspicions and pointed to her suicide as an act of victory but also commented on the rise of a particularly unctuous managerial class in 1990s Britain.

Rutter directs predominantly from the floor. If required in a scene, he uses his own lines to cue other actors neatly and lets a dramatic unit run until performers encounter a problem or he sees something that could be done better, at which point he stops and directs in more interventional fashion. His many explications include demonstrations of Shakespeare's verse patterns; sermons on the power of the caesura; homilies on monosyllables; discourses on the authority of accretion and the effectiveness of lists; word definitions and historical or mythological clarifications. Like many auto-didacts, he is a passionate accumulator of fact (and theatrical precedent) and often directs by reference to well-known performances, good or bad. He habitually uses actor's shorthand to explain requirements rapidly: proper nouns become imperatives: 'Norman Hunter it' (move backwards quickly and keep open in the manner of 1960s and 1970s Leeds United and England winger Norman Hunter); 'this is *Ab Fab*, this' . . . 'we're in danger of getting a bit *Brigadoon* here' . . . 'this is pure Greek, we see his dead body in your face' . . . 'have you seen *Papillon*? Run on like that'. The result is an uncluttered economy of direction that reaps rewards in both rehearsal and performance.

Rutter's processes create strong ensemble mood. Northern Broadsides actors have fun, both inside and outside the rehearsal room, but their pleasure in no way impinges upon the serious work of each day. For their most ambitious production, *The Wars of the Roses*, most members of a twenty-one-strong company were called to rehearse music, practise dance and play various character parts during several sessions of a working day that lasted up to twelve hours, often six days a week; yet actors are nearly always empowered by this approach – not merely in terms of individual performances but also with regards to the ensemble interpretation of whole scenes and plays. The power of Shakespearian set pieces such as battles and festive revels comes in no small measure from two significant factors: (i) the director is always onstage with his actors, never asking them to do anything that he is not prepared himself to undertake and (ii) there is common ownership of ideas built up organically by the company. This is not, of course, to say that Rutter directs by committee or accepts each and every suggestion made by an actor. He always listens, thanks colleagues genuinely for input, but frequently drops ideas after running with them only very briefly, or ignores them immediately by moving rehearsal in another direction.

Put-downs can be withering. After watching actors' first attempts at a scene he might offer: 'Thanks for that. It's a bit Cheltenham Ladies College, but I see what you're doing . . . we'll go for something a bit less Am Dram'. The ironic denigration is well intentioned, however, and it works both ways. In one rehearsal in which Rutter played Richard III for an indisposed Conrad Nelson (a role he has played in four productions over hundreds of performances), an uninvolved actor went to the props cupboard, brought out a plastic leg of ham and waved it above the director's unsuspecting head as he performed the hunchback King and the rest of the company slowly corpsed one-by-one around him. Playful affection and admiration such as this come in equal measure because Rutter understands as an actor-director the physical needs of his actors: to one looking askance at a metal trolley after he has been told he must mount it whilst playing a madman he immediately offers: 'don't worry, you can wear knee pads and we'll pad it up'; to another looking for a powerful exit trajectory: 'use the vom; it'll give them your face all the way out'. Actors appreciate such practical thoughtfulness and perform better as a result of it. In performance too, he is just as likely to let another actor take the crowning moment of a scene as he is to let his own overwhelming passion for acting lead him to steal the limelight. Like a talented centre forward who makes it his unselfish business to cross to team-mates better positioned in the six-yard box, he (nearly) always does what is best for his fellow performers.

Alongside the emphatic treatment of language, Rutter's greatest tools in rehearsal are music and dance; both of which form just as important a part of process as they do Northern Broadsides' unique performance style. A day's rehearsal typically begins with a music call, during which members of the company either divide into choral sections to practise vocal parts before coming together as a single choir, or practise instrumentals individually or in sections. He weaves the musicality of Shakespeare's verse seamlessly into his shows' musical scores and has, since setting up his company, collaborated extensively with composer, musical director, actor and subsequently associate director Conrad Nelson. Music is central to Rutter's vision and is always arrived at by consideration of the rhythmic and dramaturgical demands of the text in question. Accordingly, Nelson's scores differ hugely and have included: folk-inspired guitar, fiddle and bodhrán; fairies playing Dixieland jazz on kazoos; *a capella* settings of Shakespearian lyrics (including Bottom singing 'The ousel cock' to the tune of *Ilkla Moor Baht' At*); Southern Gospel; part song; bursts on the mouth organ; barber-shop quartet; jive; swing; slap-bass solos and medieval liturgical harmony. For *Macbeth*, a cast of seventeen actors was driven by double bass, percussion- and brass-infused music throughout much of their 105-minute, interval-free performance. If a production involves warfare, it is represented symbolically, often using complex percussive figures for which extensive and detailed drum practice takes place. Many members of the company consequently learn to play competently the snare, side and kettle drums during rehearsal. The focus achieved by beginning a day's process with drum practice is outstanding: by the end of music rehearsal, actors are habitually so aligned as an ensemble that changes of mood and tempo are achieved through simple eye contact with each other or the musical director. This militaristic focus and its energy are then taken over by Rutter as he directs. The fact that each actor is required to perform musically in practically every one of his shows adds significantly to company cohesion. More than this, however, the strategy contributes to overarching forms of rehearsal and actor training that better position performers to tackle Shakespeare as physical machines, rather than the sort of 'head-up' players produced by most British and American drama schools.

Biomechanical training is equally evident in the company's use of clogging. Rutter has used this northern English dance-form to great effect in nearly all of his productions: *Richard III* used it to represent the battle of Bosworth field; *A Midsummer Night's Dream* offered a fairy *pas de deux* between Oberon and Titania that took clog-dancing to the boundary of flamenco; the ball to celebrate the affiancing of Juliet to Paris in *Romeo and Juliet* was a stave-dancing barn dance in which the clatter of wooden soles underlined the sexual tension of the lovers' first meeting. Clogs have also been used more subtly to underscore significant passages of verse, such as Mercutio's rhythmic evocation of horses' hooves during the Queen Mab speech, or eerie underscorings of Richard III's soliloquies. In *Macbeth*, the witches rolled back a carpet to clog out satanic incantations, led by a demonic Rutter as Hecate (one of the rare appearances of this character in modern performances and an echo of the male sorceress in Orson Welles' Federal Theatre Project production). While on one level it is important for actors to tackle in rehearsal the dances that emerge in final performance, Rutter's use of the artform goes far beyond simple preparation and constitutes one of the most significant aspects of the company's physical rehearsal style.

On most days of rehearsal, all members of the company clog. Sessions can last for up to an hour and a half of intensely physical work. A typical session involves: gentle lower-body workouts, heel and toe tapping, ankle rotations, foot shake-outs and lower leg rotations; followed by the teaching of step combinations (often led by different members of the company and based on traditional dances from the northern English regions). As clogging continues, its complexity increases and session leaders (Conrad Nelson or previously laktismographers Lawrence Evans and T.C. Howard) begin to take over the session. Work is continuous and actors are typically asked to add to whatever metre they are performing previously learnt step patterns in a variety of alternate metres (3/4, 5/4, 7/8 and so on). Actors are tenaciously focused upon their work and might be directed to 'march' across the room in facing lines using different metre patterns (a technique similar to that employed in Tadashi Suzuki's marching soldiers exercises). Session leaders begin rapidly to call out numbers denoting metre changes, or indicate these by raps on a snare drum. As work becomes more detailed, drummers come out of the group to overlay snare and long drum patterns. Actors never look at their feet but stand upright, with relaxed upper bodies, eyes focused on each other. Frequently, the company is split into groups whilst clogging so that each group can be given a different metre. The numbers of actors in each group and the metre used may then be varied. As metres and group sizes change over time, different percussive patterns emerge. The effect is very much like listening to the phase compositions of minimalist composers such as Steve Reich. With numbers, patterns and volumes constantly changing, progressive combinations of steps are added. Eventually, the noise of multiple pairs of clogged feet rapping on a rehearsal room floor, together with complex cross beats and militaristic paradiddles on snare and long drums becomes intense. In this environment, the company might be instructed to perform together patterns of steps in units of threes, fours, fives then fives, fours and threes: creating a percussive chiasmus that emulates the spoken patterns of Shakespeare's lines. Slowly, clogging will wind down as actors are instructed to tap out only the first beat of each unit until eventually representative actors are selected as the rest of the group stop, watch and listen to the chosen actors bring the session to an end.

The physical effort required to produce such complex rhythms and musical dynamics is remarkable; yet, it is the effect that it has on actors that is most impressive: after clogging, the company often move straight into performance and run entire scenes, or suites of scenes. What this does to the articulation of verse is astounding and testifies to the utility of incorporating sustained, methodological approaches to physical actor training within rehearsal processes. It is not for nothing that Renaissance theatre incorporated numerous dances and ended its performances with jigs – or that ancient Athenian tragedy was based around the stylised dancing of a well-trained chorus of ephebes. Choreographed physical movement of this type has frequently gone hand in hand with poetic drama. Divorcing them is not a form of folly from which Rutter suffers.

The director's attitude towards set, costume and staging is straightforward. This is in small part dictated by the financial and logistical constraints of touring; but overwhelmingly it is driven by the director's opinion that classical texts need simply an empty space and actors' bodies to communicate most effectively their meaning. If any proposed prop or scenic item gets in the way of an actor's performance it is deemed unnecessary and never makes its way on stage. Most frequently, shows are set in modern dress, or uncluttered modern spins on historical costume. *Merry Wives* used brightly coloured 1970s garb, with a collection of garish ties for Falstaff; *A Midsummer Night's Dream* had ribbon-bedecked, Morris-dancing sprites, mechanicals in overalls tapping out rhythmic accompaniments to the play's opening verses as they worked their various trades and lovers dressed in calico shirts and cotton jumpers that spoke of the industrial spaces that produced them. Colour is frequently used symbolically: the battle of Actium in *Antony and Cleopatra* was presented by opposing groups of actors drumming each other out of existence: Caesar's army in blue; Antony and Cleopatra's in the complementary orange. As each group beat out its battle plan in a series of percussive rhythms (using reclaimed metal oil drums and plastic chemical containers so to do), an orange-suited actor crossed the floor indicating that an Egyptian had changed sides. Audiences immediately knew that Antony's cause was lost. Following the defection, the rhythms of Egypt's army became infected by those of Caesar's and began slowly to disintegrate. In *Romeo and Juliet*, Rutter likewise divided warring families and their acolytes into visually spectacular complementary colours: the Capulets in oceanic greens and blues, the Montagues in vivid oranges and reds. The production was equally immediate: warring youths fought with sickles and bale-grabbers (industrial implements appropriate to the majority of venues they played); the set comprised a single scaffold that stood for balcony, bedchamber and mausoleum. *Macbeth* was performed on a rectangle of russet-coloured sheepskin surrounded by a low-level metal walkway; colour was used to great effect both to hide and to bring actors to the fore: witches, clad in burnt sienna and orange costumes trimmed with fur, dropped to the ground to become camouflaged in a rug that represented both the blasted heath and the flames of hell; Macbeth wore a red tie once he had killed Duncan; Lady Macbeth had red sleeve lining added to her black dress at the same point. *The Merchant of Venice* again employed Rutter's favourite 'football team' aesthetic: Venetians wore dark blues, Belmont ladies reds, Jews black and white – all of which were set against a simple white set that Rutter linked to that used in Brook's *Dream* (Rutter 2005: 277–8). The colours undoubtedly helped tell the story, but were also, perhaps not-so-coincidentally, the primal hues of European fascism – and the Union Jack.

In uncluttered environments such as these, Rutter's shows abound with pace and energy; more importantly, the slightest directorial touch may easily be seen. *A Comedy of Errors* took place in a minimal blue octagon with banners denoting sky and a miniature house and nunnery. In this virtually empty space, actors dressed in late-1950s costumes combined fast-paced vocal delivery with exquisitely choreographed comic *lazzi*. The result was an apparent farce based almost entirely around actorly skills. Shakespeare's early comedy was thus presented as intellectually underpinned slapstick – with just the right amount of distance to communicate its subtle point about the potentially disorientating and tragic consequences of routine circumstances. Playful but disturbing, the show had a bright hallucinatory feel and caught the sombre underside of a drama that is for the characters involved 'a Kafkaesque nightmare rather than a jolly romp' (*Financial Times* 4 May 2005). Simplicity such as this is, of course, always deceptive. While audiences may quickly be sucked in by the verbal banter and physical clowning of productions that have planning, precision and no small measure of actorly skill, they are at the same time exposed to a director who treats the Shakespearian text with sophistication and uses deliberately Spartan scenographic environments to their full potential. Focused relentlessly on performance rather than paraphernalia, *A Comedy of Errors* caused critics to laugh so much that it hurt but also offered a subtext with more chilling elements – such as the arrival of a line of psychiatric doctors who wished to take control of the crazed Antipholus, all flexing their rubber-gloved fingers. With theatrical economy of this sort, Rutter produced a disturbing world in which Shakespeare's 'nimble jugglers [. . .] Dark working sorcerers [. . .] Soul-killing witches [and] Disguisèd cheaters' (Act I, Scene 2, lines 98–101) had a very visceral air about them. With so little to distract audiences from actors' performances, physical and verbal comedy was so successful that reviewers resorted to the finest comedians of the twentieth century in their appraisals: Tommy Cooper, Eric Morecombe, Vic Reeves and Phil Silvers all served as comparators. Fine praise indeed.

Venue is equally important to Rutter's work. Northern Broadsides was created with a remit to play as often as possible what the director calls 'non-velvet' spaces. The policy came from a dislike of traditional theatres, particularly those designed in the late nineteenth and early twentieth centuries, which he considers separate too artificially actors from audiences. For this reason, Northern Broadsides has taken Shakespeare to venues as diverse as riding schools, cattle markets and the Tower of London. Perhaps the director's favourite venues, particularly at the beginning and in the middle sections of his career, were converted industrial locations – especially disused textile mills. In the new millennium, however, lack of availability of such venues (most have been turned into expensive apartments as a result of the 'northern [economic] renaissance'), cost of hiring those left and difficulty in complying with increasingly draconian health and safety legislation have made the playing of such spaces more problematic. Nevertheless, the company still tours to several, largely because spaces of this sort not only speak powerfully of northern England's industrial heritage but also because they add a special quality to Northern Broadsides performance style: *A Midsummer Night's Dream*, which opened at Manor Mill, Oldham, achieved much of its class-based focus amidst the paint-peeling columns of a manufacturing venue that once housed the very types of workers Rutter presented as mechanicals. In spaces of this sort, the various designers with whom Rutter has ongoing collaborative relationships produce evocative scenographic environments that bring to the fore the ubiquitous utility of products previously prepared in England's now-neglected mills. Actors become the working northerners who fashioned them. Space accordingly dictates theatrical effect: *King Lear* was rehearsed with Salt's Mill in mind, particularly for one image that Rutter had held in his mind for six years (since first rehearsing *Merry Wives* in the space): Lear walking the entire length of the longest loom room in Europe crying 'Howl, howl, howl!' (Act V, Scene 3, lines 256ff). His lament was ostensibly for a dead daughter; but it echoed inside a hollow vault that was testament to Yorkshire's industrial demise. The production took Rutter's austere scenographic aesthetic to its limits and demonstrated in concrete terms Shakespeare's repeated insistence that salvation, beauty, love and great art all spring from the nothingness of unaccommodated performance. In his home theatre, the Viaduct (formed from the underground level of another ex-mill: Dean Clough in Halifax), Rutter frequently exploits the architectural potential of found space. Here, Banquo entered the eerie subterranean playing space holding a flambeau as his death scene's only light. Quickly snuffed out, audiences were left to experience the sound of murder in a dank and murky cellar – sending 'primal panic sweeping through [them]' (*Daily Telegraph* 20 March 2002).

The rigour of his creative processes and the range and vitality of his theatrical output have made Barrie Rutter in the fifteen years from 1992 to 2007 not only one of the UK's most powerfully dramatic but also most prolifically active directors of Shakespeare. He has made lively, fresh and invigorating theatre in non-traditional spaces throughout the north of England, as well as in the major receiving houses of England Wales, Scotland and Ireland. He has also toured to significant regional theatres specialising in Shakespeare and Renaissance drama such as the Swan in Stratford-upon-Avon and the Globe in London. He has undertaken site-specific performance in venues as diverse as an indoor riding school in Nottinghamshire and the Tower of London. Additionally, he has toured abroad to the USA, Greece, Germany, Denmark, Brazil, Poland, Austria, China, the Czech Republic and India. When in 2006 his *Wars of the Roses* approached its conclusion, critics felt that his company had come full circle from its humble beginnings in 1992: as clogged battle and porters' trolleys carrying rival kings emerged in homage to the director's first show, they observed: 'it's a measure of how far Northern Broadsides has come that they can now return to [this] work as part of a seven-hour cycle' (*Guardian* 3 April 2006). The company's repertoire has become expansive, including new writing, the inventories of classical Greek drama and every genre in which Shakespeare composed. Barrie Rutter's stripped-down approach to Shakespeare in the northern voice allows playwrights' language to speak for itself, yet he consistently finds new theatrical environments in which it can do so. The result has been critical acclaim, hosts of awards and the establishment of a loyal audience who come repeatedly to listen to the tragic, funny, complex, dialectical, philosophical plays of the world's greatest theatre writers presented with level-headed clarity in the uncluttered performance style for which they were originally conceived.

Chronology

1992	*Richard III*
1993–4	*Merry Wives*
1994–6	*A Midsummer Night's Dream*
1995–7	*Antony and Cleopatra*
1996–7	*Romeo and Juliet*
1999	*Twelfth Night*
1999	*King Lear*
2000	*Much Ado about Nothing*
2001	*Merry Wives, King John*
2002	*Macbeth*
2003	*Henry V*
2004	*The Merchant of Venice*
2005	*The Comedy of Errors*
2006	*Henry VI, Edward IV* and *Richard III: The Wars of the Roses* composed from Shakespeare's first tetralogy of history plays
2007	*The Tempest*

Bibliography

Interviews with Barrie Rutter conducted at the West Yorkshire Playhouse, Leeds, 21 April 2006, Dean Clough, Halifax 26 October 2006 and with Conrad Nelson at the West Yorkshire Playhouse, Leeds 21 April 2006.

Harrison, Tony (1991) *The Trackers of Oxyrhynchus*, London: Faber and Faber.

Rutter, Barrie (2005) 'A Production Diary: The Merchant of Venice', *The Shakespeare International Yearbook*, Vol. V, Aldershot and Brookfield: Ashgate Press.

Rutter, Carol Chillington (2003) 'Northern Broadsides at Work at Play,' *Shakespeare Survey* 56.

About the author

Christian M. Billing studied drama, theatre studies and Greek civilisation at the universities of Kent, London, Leeds and Warwick. He joined the permanent academic staff of the Department of Drama and Music at the University of Hull in 2001 after eleven years working professionally in film and theatre and teaching dramatic literature and theatrical practice at various universities in the United Kingdom and the USA. He has directed numerous productions of contemporary and early modern playtexts at venues as diverse as the Institute of Contemporary Arts in London and a disused basement in Leeds. Technical work as a lighting designer and scenographer has seen him at work in an equally disparate variety of professional contexts. His research and publication interests lie primarily in the performance of historically distanced texts and in the theoretical and practical investigation of early modern English and ancient Athenian drama and society. Within this field, a particular interest is transnational and intercultural exchange in theatrical literature and practice.

24
MARK RYLANCE
Bridget Escolme

In 1995, Mark Rylance was appointed as Artistic Director of Shakespeare's Globe, the London reconstruction of the Shakespeare's public playhouse. He differs from many of the directors in this volume in that he performed in, rather than directed, much of the work there; he has been called, by himself and others, an actor-manager. He has spoken out against awards for individuals in the theatre and has repeatedly drawn attention to the achievements of the ensemble at the Globe. During his tenure, his starting points for producing Shakespeare were not only the plays but also a range of external influences and pressures, both material and spiritual: the demands that the architecture of the reconstructed theatre make of text and performance, his sense of the English Renaissance's spiritual relationship with the classical world, the meanings potentially created in the live encounter between performer and audience. He was the director of a building and a set of experimental artistic practices rather than, very often, the director of plays. However, his work at the Globe makes an important intervention in a volume about 'Directors' Shakespeare', as it challenges the very notion of a Shakespeare waiting to be released by one man or woman's creative vision.

Rylance wanted the reconstructed theatre building, and the audiences that came to it, to play a primary role in 'directing' the meanings that were produced there. The Shakespeare productions that he led and performed at Shakespeare's Globe ranged from the *Henry V* in the theatre's opening season, produced according to founder Sam Wanamaker's desire for one production per season to follow historically researched early modern theatre practices, to Rylance's last appearance there, a three-man *Tempest* haunted by three female 'fates' in contemporary dress. The original practices remit was criticised by some for producing too broad and populist a 'heritage' Shakespeare. Rylance's approach to the reconstruction of Shakespeare's theatre has seemed to some pragmatic and materialist, to others archaic and esoteric. However, his vision for the theatre was primarily that it should be an experiment in historically researched theatre practice, and I am going to argue that the Globe under Rylance staked out new ground for British Shakespeare production in terms of the audience's role in the production of meaning.

Mark Rylance was born in Ashford, Kent in 1960; his family moved to Connecticut when he was two, then to Milwaukee, Wisconsin, when he was nine. In 1978, he returned to England to take up a place at the Royal Academy of Dramatic Arts (RADA). Though he first played Shakespeare at his American high school, his early professional experiences tread a very British line between theatrical tradition and experimentation. His pre-Globe professional acting credits offer an impressive narrative of artistic growth through all that was respected in the British subsidised theatre during the late twentieth century. He worked with Mike Alfreds of Shared Experience, whose early presentational narrative techniques and metatheatrical aesthetic must have proved something of a perfect training for eventual work in a theatre so dependent on the performer–audience relationship. Alfreds was eventually brought to the Globe by Rylance in 2001, to direct *Cymbeline*. Rylance played Romeo in the inaugural production at the Swan in Stratford, whose stage thrusts its actors into the presence of the audience. His work with Max Stafford-Clark at the Royal Court, with his task-based approach to Stanislavskian objectives, chimes well with Rylance's sense of the Globe as a meeting place for presentation and interiority, for inner and outer worlds: 'The Globe stage thrusts in to the centre of the theatre, no part of it is without the circle as in the proscenium theatres [. . .] And Shakespeare plays on our inner selves with his outer show' (Rylance 1996). Rylance embraces opposition and contradiction with enthusiasm. He has an acute sense of the materiality of the meanings produced when the architecture and texts of history come into contact with the actors and audiences of the present, but his descriptions of the Globe project also demonstrate a spiritual investment in the project. He has described it as a space to play, between 'heaven and earth', 'imagination and matter', 'spirit and body': 'and when we play with these, we are sustaining our souls, for the soul thrives when it acknowledges a divine factor in human endeavour. Or for that matter, a human factor in divine endeavours' (RSA lecture 1996).

Once appointed Artistic Director, Rylance wanted to realise Sam Wanamaker's vision for the reconstruction: a theatre as near as possible to the original site, one that recreated the architecture of the first Globe and the active, participatory, face-to-face relationship between performer and audience that might have existed in Shakespeare's theatre. Critics leapt to point out that this was an inherently problematic project. Late-twentieth-century audiences were not late-sixteenth-century ones: their understanding of what it was to visit a theatre, their journey to that theatre, their behaviour, their smell, their *Shakespeare*, were all radically different from the cultural references and material conditions of Shakespeare's first audiences. Undoubtedly there was a sense, from the project's outset, in which Shakespeare was to be *discovered* or *revealed* in this space; the theatre was built on a faith in the historical research into the original's architecture and a belief that certain historical performance energies might be recreated within it. Rylance's commitment to the exploration of 'original practices' was always part of what he regarded as an essentially experimental brief, however. The work with all-male companies, the use of early modern music and instruments, research into the accurate reconstruction of Elizabethan and Jacobean costume using 'original' materials, research into early design elements, a direct relationship between performer and audience, the finale 'jig', were as much indicative of an openness to the materiality of meaning and its production, as of a museum-piece reverence for 'authenticity'. Indeed, Rylance never claims to have found an authentic Shakespeare, and Wanamaker's 'authentic brief' was soon replaced in Globe parlance by 'original practices' to describe the productions based on historical research. What Rylance set up here was a series of historically researched *restrictions* on artistic practice. What might Shakespeare mean if electric light did not focus audience attention, if the audience stood, or sat on benches, sometimes in potentially uncomfortable proximity to one another, if changing from one costume to another was cumbersome or impossible, if men played women? His determination to put historical research into theatrical practice has often cut through the bardolatry that suggests Shakespeare is always our contemporary. His passionate support, for example, as a continuing member of the Architectural Advisory Group at the Globe, for the decoration of the auditorium in similar painted style to the pillars and *frons*, flew determinedly in the face of modern conceptions of the 'historic' as tastefully plain and rough-hewn. Rylance often spoke of Globe productions as site-specific; he worked with the restrictions and impositions, as well as the obvious opportunities, offered by the architectural reconstruction, to produce Shakespeare at the Globe.

The commitment to original practices that Rylance shared with the Globe's Musical Director, Clare Van Kampen and its costume designer Jenny Tirimani, was a logical extension of the Globe's experiment with historic theatre architecture. This commitment also gave rise to quite different kinds of experimentation, inspired by the original practices remit. The all-male shows, and others during Rylance's tenure, used costume produced as far as was possible according to period design and methods of construction. The opening production, *Henry V*, used historically accurate underwear and dyes. *Julius Caesar*, on the other hand, used period costume for most of the characters but had plebeians emerge from the audience in contemporary street clothing.

Original-practices clothing at the Globe was sometimes startling. It did not conform to the taste for the subtle and the muted, characteristic of much late-twentieth-century theatre design – the post-Brechtian beiges we might expect with our historical realism. These clothes refused to signify the pre-consumerist functionality or faded grandeur offered by many heritage sites. They were newly made clothes, produced according to historical research into dying and construction. The clothing of aristocratic characters displayed the riches of early capitalism in an overtly presentational way, as their originals might have on the backs of the Chamberlain's Men's aristocratic sponsors. When the clothing gave rise to objections by actors for its impracticability (ties and loops caused problems during quick changes that Velcro has since been invented to solve), and by audiences for its bright cleanness, Rylance's commitment to the experiment was undiminished. 'The clothing that made up the costumes was so expensive', argued Rylance; 'you wouldn't have broken it down. So some people felt that wasn't very realistic, but the realism is being carried by the words, not by the matter' (Rylance, Globe Exhibition interviews). What was carried by the 'matter' was a double gesture of display – the social display of hierarchical colour systems, of doffing hats and of wearing weapons (all supported by the historical research of the Tudor Group, whom Rylance invited to work with a number of Globe companies) and the theatrical display of huge, bright figures against an intricately painted *frons*.

I will not re-rehearse here the debate as to whether men, as opposed to pubescent boys, might have played women at the first Globe. What was significant about the all-male – and indeed about the all-female – productions at the Globe under Rylance were the ways in which gender was intermittently denaturalised and placed in quotation marks on this stage. Intermittently, because, as some scholars have speculated might have been the case at the first Globe, it was often possible to forget that men were playing women on the reconstructed stage (see Dawson and Yachnin 2001: 31–7 for a summary of arguments regarding the visibility of the boy player's gender on the early modern stage). In John Dove's touring production of *Measure for Measure*, for example, Edmund Hogg wheeled around the stage in his vast black and white farthingale, held his Isabella straight, stiff and contained, and spoke with an uncanny, soft precision – the epitome of virtuous modesty, onto which Angelo could project his fantasies. Angelo then destroyed the woman of his imagination in a disturbing short-circuiting of stage convention: he gave his 'sensual race the rein', and grappled the gendered epitome of virtuous modesty to him. Hogg's audiences reacted in shocked silence or with nervous laughter. The wreck of theatrical illusion mapped uncomfortably but productively onto the wrecked and trembling Isabella. In Giles Block's *Antony and Cleopatra*, the Egyptian queen's acts of anger and vulnerability, and Rylance's constructions of them, were both part of the entertainment and produced a figure both highly theatrical and highly empathetic. The effect was of an actor standing up for as well as standing in for his character, very different from that produced by the naturalistic actor in a space intensely focused by stage lighting. This effect was successfully capitalised on in Phyllida Lloyd's all-female *Taming of the Shrew*, in which Janet McTeer's strutting *gestus* of maleness is finally out-performed by Katherine Hunter's Kate, who enacts her final submission with such wild enthusiasm as to embarrass the men into awkward silence.

The most powerful legacy of Rylance's actor-management of the Globe, however, is an 'original practice' that every production there is forced to experiment with: a direct relationship between performer and audience. An awareness of the production of meaning in the moment of contact between actor and spectator underpins many of Rylance's statements about the theatre, his talks to actors as rehearsals begin and his own performances. It is this, above all, that makes him a significant figure amongst the directors of Shakespeare analysed in this volume: he directed the modern British actor's preoccupation with the invented inner lives of characters outward, to the audience.

Mark Rylance's production of *Julius Caesar*, the one production for which he took the role of 'master of play' during his tenure as Artistic Director, attracted a remarkable range of contradictory notices. The 'masters' system had been developed during the play's first season: the titles of Masters of Play, Verse, Voice, Music, Costume, Movement were coined to suggest an assemblage of experts, bringing their crafts and abilities together to make theatre. Two years after the theatre's opening and preview seasons, the Globe had established itself amongst its large audiences as a space for open, presentational, participatory performances. Alongside the theatre's own productions of Shakespeare and his contemporaries, created by a range of 'Masters', the preview season had included *A Midsummer Night's Dream* performed by Northern Broadside, a company who focus on popular Shakespeare spoken by Northern English actors, and the use of direct performer–audience contact. The Johannesburg Civic Theatre's *Umabatha: The Zulu Macbeth* played the opening season and further demonstrated the appropriateness of the space for powerful traditions of storytelling. As Paul Prescott's analysis suggests, a number of critics felt uncomfortable about the notion of a popular, participatory Shakespeare (see Prescott 2005), and when reading newspaper reviews, it is sometimes difficult to separate critiques of the artistic quality of the productions from snobbish assumptions regarding the proper make-up and behaviour of audiences. At any rate, those who disliked *Julius Caesar* found it broad, unsubtle and lacking in the naturalistic character development they expected of modern Shakespeare. More favourable reviews suggested that there was something here to replace the fully, psychologically drawn characters supposedly to be found in the best of the early modern drama. Comment in the *Independent* points to the novelty, in 1999, of Rylance's attention to the performer–audience relationship at the Globe: 'The artifice is blatant and unapologetic: the main event has to take place within an imaginative world that – if this doesn't sound too pretentious – relies as much on the participation of the audience as it does on the actors' (Robert Butler, *Independent on Sunday*, 30 May 1999). At the time of Rylance's resignation in 2005, it would have seemed odd for a critic to express the need to apologise for pretentiousness when commenting on that relationship.

During rehearsal for *Caesar*, Rylance was very conscious of the dimensions and intimacies of the spaces used for rehearsal and how they differed from the theatre itself. Alongside the familiar, post-Stanislavsian exercises – building 'character' through discussion of the play's imagined past, asking actors to speak out everything their character says about another – Rylance incorporated site-specific process into rehearsal. He invited audiences to watch work in progress, so that the performer–audience relationship could be discovered and continually remade; once rehearsal transferred to the Globe, he had groups touring the theatres stand in for the groundlings in the crowd scenes, so that the plebeians' rousing of the theatre audience could be tried (see also Bessell 1999). The admixture of character-development techniques and metatheatrical approaches did not work for every actor, and the transfer onto a stage surrounded by greater numbers of visible witnesses appears to have been a difficult one for some. Toby Cockerell, particularly, who doubled as Portia and Octavius, resorted to a forced shouting in the latter role, which suggested he felt more comfortable with the female presence he had established in the space than the young, patrician, male one. Despite some awkwardness, however, and a problem with some performances 'flattening out' in the transfer from indoor rehearsal to outdoor performance, *Julius Caesar* is a key production in terms of the discoveries Rylance made about performer, architecture and Shakespeare at the Globe.

Rylance and Tirimani's scenography for the production was typically simple. A curtain depicting the Roman goddess Fortuna was drawn across the opening to the tiring house; Roman statues were set in the gallery; a little avenue of orange trees in pots created Brutus and Portia's domestic space. Ancient Rome was evoked through explicit visual reference to the feast of Lupercal (Antony wears a wolf mask and skin in Act I, Scene 1) and through the kinds of costuming detail that the Peacham drawing suggests would have been worn by Shakespeare's actors – there were togas over doublet and hose for the assassination of Caesar. The plebeians emerged from the audience in

T-shirts and baseball caps, signifying that, just as Shakespeare's Rome resonated for Shakespeare's England, so Shakespeare's England could be used to reference ours. Through these figures in street clothes, the audience was asked to witness and, to some degree, take part in decisions, power-broking and acts of violence that unfolded in the theatrical present.

Rylance wanted the Globe companies to achieve *eloquence* during the 1999 season – eloquence according to the *Oxford English Dictionary* definition: 'to speak with force, fluency and appropriateness'. Maintaining a theatrical 'appropriateness' in the presence of an audience who are 'there with a chance to voice their own thoughts' (Rylance, in Bessell 1999) requires a degree of flexibility, however. A stage manager's account of drunken groundlings taking a dislike to Cassius from his entrance, and pre-empting lines from their own copies of the play, demonstrates that the work of pulling the visible, contemporary audience into a narrative burdened with cultural baggage can be challenging, and a number of significant changes were made during previews that shifted the performer–audience relationship radically.

One area of speculation at the Globe was the use of the yard for acting. Towards the end of Rylance's tenure, little action took place there, and Rylance had decided it was unlikely that Shakespeare's company had used it. Indeed, there is no evidence for an early use of the yard by actors, and conclusions about whether *Julius Caesar*'s experiment with plebeians performing there 'proved' anything must remain speculative. However, the presence of Rylance's t-shirted, baseball-capped plebeians, shouting from the crowd and climbing onto the stage, foregrounded the political control of crowds in the play and drew attention to the class tensions explicit in the first scene. The first performance was introduced by a London 'town crier', who announced the opening of the 'four hundredth season at the Globe' and concluded with a shout of 'God bless you all! God bless Sam Wanamaker and God bless the Queen!'. A cheery shout of monarchist acquiescence arose from the playgoers, which died awkwardly when one of their number, or so it seemed, disrupted the celebratory proceedings by calling out 'Hurry up, we're getting wet!'. There were nervous titters; the wit in the baseball cap was carrying a can of beer, and those around him were clearly unsure as to whether he was going to prove a disruption throughout; this was a crowd that was going to need controlling. Caesar, it seemed, knew exactly how to do so, swiftly casting the audience as enthusiastic Caesar-worshippers in a raucous and populist Lupercal procession, headed by Antony in a wolf-skin and little else; there were clamorous cheers and catcalls from audiences throughout the run. The entrance of the train, directed in the early previews so as to maintain a fluidity of action from scene to scene, had to be delayed so that the last lines of Act I, Scene 1 could actually be heard above the mob of Caesar-worshippers.

The casting of audience as pro-Caesar mob had implications for Cassius, who, in Act I, Scene 2, had to break down the Globe's cheery holiday mood and reconstruct the audience as thinking, freedom-loving classical patricians. The audience's own foregrounded presence in this theatre drew attention to the contempt with which Cassius speaks of the crowd to Casca: we must hush up and listen, or we stand exposed as the hooting 'rabblement', the 'rag-tag people' who would have accepted Caesar had he 'stabbed their mothers' (Act I, Scene 2, lines 244, 258, 274). The audience, conscious of having been a rabblement, listened to rabblements denigrated. This made for a wryly self-conscious crowd of playgoers, aware of the parts they were being asked to play in the fiction.

By the end of the run of *Julius Caesar*, though, this construction of a cynical, knowing audience had been complicated, via decisions made about the use of the yard, and by Mark Lewis-Jones, who began the run as something of an ironic Mark Antony (see also Koch-Schulte 1999). He caused gales of laughter, and one shout of 'Liar!', when he assured the audience, before the Caesar's coffin, that he 'only speak[s] right on' (Act III, Scene 2, line 218). Each of Mark Antony's actions – including his clambering down from the stage into the yard to show us Caesar's bloody robe – was clearly a rhetorical device, and the audience were in on the game. By the end of the run, Lewis-Jones was working to persuade on a much more emotionally engaging level, and though the audience were just as willing gleefully to demand 'The will!' as in early performances, 'Friends, Romans, countrymen' was far more of a sincere tribute to a dead friend. By the end of the run, Antony was moving from gallery to stage to show the crowd Caesar's robe, rather than climbing into the yard, and the calls of the plebeians came from the audience instead of from on stage. The small group of plebeians had made something of a feeble crowd early in the run, and though Brutus and Antony speaking to the audience across the empty stage space had its own awkwardness, the later staging was the more effective, as Antony filled the empty space not with mere rhetoric but with the material body of Ceasar. In early performances, Antony's line 'now let it work' (Act III, Scene 2, line 253), as the plebeians ran off to wreak havoc, was all part of the manipulative plan; later in the run, the line rather served to complicate and interrogate a performance of sincerity. *Julius Caesar* at the Globe was an experiment in the political meanings produced by the occupation of theatrical space.

An intuitive understanding of where Globe audiences might productively laugh, or raucously participate, developed throughout the production's run, particularly in the case of Benedict Wong's Calphurnia. Wong was beset with nervous giggles from the audience when first called centre stage by Caesar early in the run. In later performances, s/he was accosted by a raunchy Antony in his Lupercal costume, so that laughter at a man in a dress was released in a comic moment more in keeping with the world of the play. By 2002, when Rylance played Olivia in the Globe's *Twelfth Night*, much had been learned at the Globe about permitting the audience their incredulity and finding valves whereby laughter could be productively released.

Performer, audience, women and men

Rylance's intuitive understanding of how to move, speak and make his presence felt in the Globe reconstruction offered some of the most powerful direction to actors working with him, the invaluable contributions of a rich range of Masters of Play notwithstanding. Rylance's presence has sometimes dominated the Globe stage, because he understands that the stage demands a kind of honourable showing off, a theatricality centred not only on the generous giving of focus but also on the shameless taking of it. This has been clearest in his performances of female roles. The shameless taking of focus is perhaps familiar in the case of Cleopatra, whose theatricality is clearly central to the fiction. It is more unusual to witness a production of *Twelfth Night* in which Olivia is such a dominant figure.

The Globe's 2002 *Twelfth Night*, produced for a short season of performances at the Middle Temple Hall, was redirected by the production's Master of Play Tim Carrol for the outdoor playhouse, with a partly different cast. It was powerfully centred on Rylance's Olivia: on her shifts from close retirement to social participation, from control to vulnerability, from death to life. Though Rylance is a RADA-trained actor with as much concern about Stanislavskian superobjectives and psychological intentions as the next, his interest as Artistic Director of the Globe in the performer–audience relationship lead him to foreground the *theatrical* powers and vulnerabilities of the fictional figure in Shakespeare's theatre, and a particular kind of theatrical femaleness was produced as a result.

When Michael Brown's Viola emerged through the trap door in the middle of the Globe stage into Illyria, the audience were strange creatures to her; she looked about the galleries in wonder and appeared instantly vulnerable, both on the shores of this new country and to the gaze of the paying audience. Rylance's Olivia, on the other hand, made little direct contact with the audience at first. She entered in ceremonious procession with her household, as if to restore order after two scenes in which the central characters have appeared somewhat out of control, stranded or in love. Dressed in black and wheeling effortlessly around her domain, she began Act I, Scene 3 at the head of a long table, signing papers to signify the competent ordering of her household. Her mourning dress and absorption in her papers, her reluctance to engage with Feste's foolery, then her good-humoured refusal to be unnerved by his mockery, all signalled a determination to create an impenetrable space of ordered calm. This mourner appeared determined to let nobody – neither Orsino nor the spectator – into the privacy of her mourning. Once Olivia had met Cesario, all semblance of self-control dissolved, and Olivia ricocheted about the space, fanning herself and stumbling over words much to the audience's delight. Her self-revelation from behind the mourning veil – 'But we will draw the curtain and show you the picture' (Act I, Scene 5, line 223) – catapulted her into self-revelation, and her soliloquy after Cesario's departure had her cringing with embarrassment at her own imperious questioning of Cesario's 'parentage' (Act I, Scene 5, line 279).

As a portrayal of someone plunged into emotional confusion and vulnerability, this Olivia was both a comic and a sympathetic one. Interestingly, the presentational nature of the Globe had a very different effect on Sir Toby's relationship with the audience. Bill Stewart's Toby Belch was a cynical, knowing old lush. When he cried for Aguecheek to caper 'Higher! Higher!' (Act I, Scene 3, line 137) it was clear that he is happy to humiliate the foolish knight for our enjoyment, and his final rejection of Sir Andrew came as no surprise. In fact, Stewart might have productively made *more* contact with the audience; after all, as a lively production of *Richard III* will demonstrate, the most iniquitous vice figures on the Shakespearian stage can draw us into complicity. However, the tendency of the actor trained in the principles of psychological character study may be to regard anything but the most fleeting moments of direct address, outside of soliloquy, as unforgivable mugging. Liam Brennan (Orsino) uses a telling phrase where he explains that he 'spoke very directly to the audience in my first scene, but I felt thereafter the object of Orsino's attention is Viola [. . .] The same was true last year with Macduff [. . .] he was so driven and focused that *it wouldn't be right to be "courting" the audience*' (Brennan in Ryan 2002, my italics). What Rylance's tenure at the Globe demonstrated was that the variety of potential modes of direct address in this theatre are huge: 'courting' the audience is only one of them. Rylance's Olivia moved from complete indifference to the opinions of audience and other characters alike, to a highly sympathetic self-consciousness in their presence. He glanced nervously or joyously out at his audience according to the progress Olivia was making with Cesario, indicating a figure highly self-conscious about the suddenness of her love and her lack of control over the behaviour it seems to be inducing. As Brennan himself showed in his Angelo soliloquies in the Globe's *Measure for Measure*, direct address is not merely what Hamlet accuses the clown of doing. The actor/character on the Globe stage can confront the audience, appeal to them, conspire with them, acknowledge his vulnerability in their presence. Having questioned Brennan's dismissal of direct address as 'courting', I should say that his Orsino, particularly at Act II, Scene 4's moment of awkward intimacy with Viola, demonstrated a supreme sensitivity to the extent to which Globe audiences can be drawn in to the fictions presented to them, and the production gave the lie to the figuring of Globe crowds as tourist dilettantes. The actor's work at the theatre is a testimony to his own flexibility and to the success of Rylance's policy of inviting actors back to the Globe for future seasons.

Rylance's commitment to all-male production at the Globe allowed him to develop techniques for playing female that illuminate an aspect of a number of Shakespeare's women that rarely emerges in modern production. Rylance's permits the female figures he plays to be ludicrous as well as vulnerable, comical figures as well as funny women. In playing, rather than being, a woman, Rylance has explored the comic vulnerability of the female figures he has played, where actresses have perhaps been more inclined to discover their strengths. This is not the soft vulnerability of sexist stereotype; indeed, it is not necessarily a gendered vulnerability at all as is most clearly demonstrated by Rylance's hapless Duke Vincentio in *Measure for Measure*. It is, rather, the vulnerability of the modern clown, who is always conscious of the judging gaze of the audience, whether he bends before it, courts it or defies it. Rylance was clearly able to make comic sense of Olivia having played Cleopatra three years previously.

As I have suggested elsewhere (Escolme 2006: 128–34), the key to the critical success of the Globe's 1999 *Antony and Cleopatra* was the way in which Rylance's theatrical persona and Cleopatra's theatrical manipulations within the fiction map onto one another in Rylance's performance. This was a key season for the Globe's original-practices remit. After the run of this production, Rylance became convinced that Shakespeare's company would have cut the plays rather than spoken with a rapidity that the acoustic of the theatre would have made impossible; he determined that the inside of the theatre needed a unified, painted design rather than a stage area anachronistically separated from the auditorium by a décor the auditorium did not share; he found that an extended balcony was a practically and theatrically successful solution to the design of the *frons scenae* (see Bessell 1999). In the (ultimately unsuccessful) attempt to cut playing time down to two hours with few cuts in the text, speed became of the essence for the season's Red Company and the best use to date was made of the potential fluidity of the bare platform stage. The rapid shifts from the tragic to the comic became particularly evident through rehearsals and performances of this play, and Rylance's Cleopatra was memorably funny:

> I learned more about the dynamics of the plays this year. The audience

> teaches me each year to be more confident, to let the play swing into comedy, in order for a bigger swing *back* into tragedy to occur [. . .] [T]he audiences here [. . .] seem to respond strongly to that antithetical relationship between comedy and tragedy in both plays [The audience have taught me that] it's all right to laugh at Cleopatra's line 'How heavy weighs my lord!' (IV. xv. 32), because the relief in laughing opens them up and catches them unaware; fifteen seconds later they see her howling in despair as Antony dies suddenly in her arms.
>
> (Rylance in Bessel 1999)

Cleopatra's relationship with the audience in this production swung from defiant obliviousness, to blatantly manipulative performance, to raw vulnerability in Antony's death scene. She skipped exuberantly about the stage, followed by the tolerant but weary Charmian and Iras, who dropped cushions wherever she deigned to sit down. Paul Shelley's Antony endeavoured to rediscover the authority of the centre-stage space but had his theatrical status repeatedly undermined by her lively possession of the space and her court. The production repeatedly demonstrated the ways in which actor and space produce meaning in this theatre. Centre stage can be an 'authority space' (see Kiernan 1999: 63–4) but is also a risky, exposing place, where one's authority can be undermined. Moving back and forth or standing for too long at the front of the stage reads as weakness: Paul Shelley told us that he 'must from this enchanting queen break off' in this position (Act I, Scene 2, line 121) – and his declaration seemed like a desperate bid for the audience's help and support in achieving the impossible. Charmian's parody of Cleopatra's constant, flitting movement as she teases the Queen over 'brave Caesar' (Act I, Scene 5, line 67) is amusing – but Charmian gives her parodic performance across the front of the stage and demonstrates nothing like her mistress's mastery of the space. It is Cleopatra who understands the power of acting on this stage and in this Egypt.

Rylance's expansive gestures, often a feature of Globe performances, read as spontaneous exuberance in one moment, highly performed in the next. A speech that often reveals whether a Cleopatra is of the more manipulative or the more sincerely in-love variety, was significantly hard to read here: 'all the gods go with you. Upon your sword / Sit laurel victory, and smooth success / Be strew'd before your feet!' (Act I, Scene 3, line 100–2) says Rylance, with the deepest of historically researched curtsies, and because bowing, curtseying, shaking hands and doffing hats are all so carefully socially encoded, we cannot know how sincerely Cleopatra means this performance of loving lady bidding adieu to her lord.

Rylance's Cleopatra took her costume for Acts IV and V from Plutarch, who, after Antony's death, had 'rent her garments' and 'scratch[ed] her face and stomach' (Plutarch 1964: 310); he wore a filthy shift and had removed Cleopatra's wig of auburn curls to reveal a shaved head with tufts of torn hair. Cleopatra's performances of royalty and femininity were stripped away. However, this vision of broken humanity did not indicate a privileging of sincerity over performance, a revelation of the 'real' Cleopatra behind her 'becomings'. Her pathetic, self-abused figure re-dressed itself for her last performance in death, and she constructed her own monument to time from her own body and costume. Immediately before taking the asp, she knelt and kissed the feet of the ultimate performer, the clown, who had cheekily got up onto the throne in which she would take the snake's bite. What Rylance revealed here were the ways in which 'woman' and 'queen' and 'human' might be constructed theatrically, and in opposition to Roman masculinity and war machine.

'That within which passeth show': *Hamlet*

Given the attention this account has paid thus far to the metatheatricality of Rylance's work at the Globe, the theatre's 2000 *Hamlet* is of particular and paradoxical significance because of its interest in interiority – both in terms of psychology and imagined architecture. This production offered an alternative to the presentation/personation binary that underpins much speculation about early modern acting style. Rylance's Hamlet presented 'interiority' to the audience, and the emotional impact of his performance was produced in moments when Rylance's work at playing Hamlet was foregrounded most clearly.

As records of design meetings suggest, the creation of interior spaces on the Globe stage was an early focus for *Hamlet*. Tiramani and Rylance's idea of suspending a false ceiling under the heavens was finally abandoned, but a low rail was built around the edges of the stage for *Hamlet* which 'contained the world of the play' and 'was an attempt to define the "interior" feel of the play' (see Bessel 2000). Four benches were used throughout and created further enclosed spaces for action. The yard was not used by actors at any point in the production: 'The world of the Danish court needed to feel [. . .] enclosed and claustrophobic' (Bessel 2005: 5). Though Giles Block was appointed 'masters' of both 'play' and 'verse', Richard Olivier, who had directed Rylance in the Globe's opening production of *Henry V*, worked with the company on a period of rehearsal at Otley Hall, an Elizabethan mansion in Suffolk. Here, the company played through the text in 'real' time, with the Ghost appearing on their first night and the graveyard scene occurring on the second (Bessel

2005: 10). The play's scenes of spying and surveillance took place in rooms in the house, and all this was intended to give the company a sense of how the action might 'really' have felt in the dark, in a gallery, in a mother's 'closet'. An experience was being created here that actors could recall in the moment of performance – a technique that rather recalls Stanislavskian techniques of emotion memory than site-specific metatheatre. Attention to another, more spiritual sense of interiority was, moreover, taken to something of an extreme when, on Olivier's suggestion, Rylance underwent a meditative burial ritual in a hole dug for him by the production's gravediggers, 'in order to get in touch with the earth' (Bessel 2005: 11). These narrative, psychological and spiritual exercises manifested themselves on stage in a performance of emotional intensity on display. Rehearsing *Hamlet* as if it were a naturalistic drama of families in domestic (albeit royal) settings, combined with attention to the demands of audience and architecture at the Globe, produced a compelling emotional theatricality that renewed old questions of Hamlet's madness, his relationship with Ophelia, his procrastinations.

As I have discussed elsewhere (Escolme 2005: 63–4), Rylance's Hamlet was intensely emotional. He wept where other recent Hamlets had sneered and ranted, begging Ophelia to leave for the nunnery as if he genuinely felt this was the only safe retreat for her from the ghastliness of the court and the world; he was horrified at his accidental killing of Polonius and wept once more as he lugged the guts into the neighbour room. From the moment in his first soliloquy when he turned to the yard and galleries (he begun, as he did at the RSC in 1989, with his back to the majority of the audience), he was a painfully vulnerable figure, aghast, it seemed, at having to reveal everything he was keeping from the court to over 1,000 paying spectators. From these spectators, however, he took courage, energy and a need to communicate all this horror. The performance reinvigorated voice-training truisms about Shakespeare and the 'need for words'. Hamlet compulsively talked to us, performed the clown for us, rehearsed the revenge hero for us and offered us both his inadequacy and his contempt for that hackneyed role. This Hamlet knew he had no fixed role to play at court or within the conventions of stock revenge tragedy, and the 'character' of this emotionally intense Hamlet was produced by his relationship with the audience. Where Polonius was assured that the audience would find his comments on Hamlet's madness sublimely sensible, Hamlet never seemed sure of what our judgements would be. He was a small, dark blot on the bright red velvet world of the court – or a small, dark blot outside of it, as he would not move up towards the happy tableau of family and good government Claudius was endeavouring to create at the beginning of the play. Even when others were on stage, Hamlet often appeared to be alone with the audience.

Then, at the point where many a school pupil is taught that Hamlet learns to act, Hamlet told us that the readiness is all and withdrew his presence from us, slipping into another plot, a stock revenge one written by Claudius, in which a show is set up to disguise a murder, and avenger, innocent bystander and villain alike end up strewn dead across the stage. It is as if this complex, questioning being, whose presence before the audience produces his 'character', is finally too complex for a revenge drama and has to withdraw from us so that the play can end. One reading, then, of this production is that the metatheatrical self-consciousness of its performance throws Hamlet, who continually and painfully interrogates theatrical and cultural convention, into dark relief against the simple ethic of revenge tragedy and finally establishes tragedy as a withdrawal of theatrical presence. For Rylance himself, the physicality of the play's final dual is a theatrical distillation of a new sense of ethical and political responsibility on Hamlet's part, a demonstration of the character's willingness to enter the drama appropriately and actively, if not mercifully. Though Rylance's own reading partakes of the meta-narrative of spiritual journey that underpins many humanist and actorly readings of tragedy, unlike many such readings, it is theatrically informed. 'Sword-fighting is, after all', Rylance remarks, 'one of the most dangerous, immediate and demanding pieces of acting you can do and requires incredible presence and willingness to "be" ' (Rylance, personal correspondence to Escolme). In this description, and in acting Hamlet, Rylance has mapped the actorly notion of the character's inner journey onto the formal theatricality of the virtuoso end-piece of tragedy, so that theatrical acting and fictional action appear simultaneously to dissolve into and stand apart from one another.

Director's Shakespeare

In his assessment of the question 'Who will succeed Rylance at the Globe?' theatre critic Michael Billington argued that 'the choice is crucial, since it will determine whether the Globe continues to be an old-fashioned, actor-driven company or whether it opts for intellectually challenging, director-led reinterpretations of Shakespeare' (Billington 2004). Billington thus suggests that to challenge the intellect, Shakespeare must be 'directed' in ways that the first productions were not. What these analyses of moments from Shakespeare production at the Globe have endeavoured to show is that the singular vision of the director, as constructed by contemporary convention, is not the only way to produce intellectually challenging and emotionally engaging Shakespeare. At the time of writing, the Royal Shakespeare Company has recently completed a reconfiguring of the performer–audience dynamic in their own work through a refurbishment of the Royal Shakespeare Theatre at Stratford; at the company's Swan Theatre, recent productions of *Pericles* and *The Winter's Tale* have been performed to standing audiences in a stalls stripped of seating. Mark Rylance's work at the Globe has done much to foster what Billington called a new 'hyper-theatricality' at Stratford (Billington 2003). Rylance's reappearance, after Hamlet's death, in the signature end-piece 'jig' of his tenure at Shakespeare's Globe (for this production a *dance macarbre* complete with leaping skeleton), was a distillation of the nature of the live theatre event in this space. Rylance ceased to be Hamlet and became a dancing actor, signifying anew that Hamlet was really dead: there was no escape from mortality here via Horatio's legacy or some universal sense of the Shakespearian tragic. In Rylance's/Shakespeare's Globe, meaning has been produced in the gap between actor's work and character's action and in the awkward, exciting, shifting space between performer and audience.

Chronology

1982–3	First season as an actor with the Royal Shakespeare Company
1984	With actor David Moylan, forms the London Theatre of Imagination, an actors' cooperative without a director
1989	Marries Claire Van Kampen, later Musical Director at Shakespeare's Globe
1990	Founds Phoebus' Cart theatre company, with Claire Van Kampen, to perform Shakespeare in sites of ancient spiritual significance and to marry the disciplines of music, dance and acting
1991	Joins Board of Directors of Shakespeare's Globe project under Project Director Sam Wanamaker
1991	First production, *The Tempest*, on the site of the reconstructed Globe
1995–2000	Artistic Director of Shakespeare's Globe
1996	Proteus, *Two Gentlemen of Verona*, dir. Jack Shepherd
1997	Henry V, *Henry V*, dir. Richard Olivier
1998	Bassanio, *The Merchant of Venice*, dir. Richard Olivier
1999	Cleopatra, *Antony and Cleopatra*, dir. Giles Block
1999	Director (Master of Play) *Julius Caesar*
1999	Collaborated with Peter Oswald in the writing of *Augustine's Oak*, the first new play produced at the Globe reconstruction
2000	Hamlet, *Hamlet*, dir. Giles Block
2001	Posthumus and Cloten, *Cymbeline* (Shakespeare's Globe, then Harvey Theatre, Brooklyn Academy of Music, New York, 2002), dir. Mike Alfreds

2002	Olivia, *Twelfth Night* at Middle Temple Hall, then Shakespeare's Globe and US tour, dir. Tim Carroll
2003	Richard II, *Richard II*, dir. Tim Carroll
2004	Duke Vincentio, *Measure for Measure* (mixed cast, Shakespeare's Globe; all-male cast, US tour 2005) dir. John Dove
2005	Prospero, Stephano, Sebastian, Alonso, *The Tempest*, dir. Tim Carroll
2005	Rylance resigns as Artistic Director of Shakespeare's Globe

Bibliography

Bessell, Jaq (1999a) *Antony and Cleopatra*, Globe Research Bulletin, available online at <http://www.shakespeares-globe.org/docs/Antony_and_Cleopatra_1999.pdf>. (Accessed 15 September 2006.)

—— (1999b) *Julius Caesar*, Globe Research Bulletin 1999, available online at <http://www.shakespeares-globe.org/docs/Julius_Caesar_1999.pdf>. (Accessed 15 September 2006.)

—— (2000) *Hamlet*, Globe Research Bulletin, available online at <http://shakespeares-globe.org/docs/Hamlet_2000.pdf>. (Accessed 15 September 2006.)

Billington, Michael (1999) 'They come to bury Caesar', *Guardian*, 29 May.

—— (2003) Review of *Cymbeline*, Royal Shakespeare Company, *Guardian*, 8 August.

—— (2004) 'Brave New World', *Guardian* 20 September.

Butler, Robert (1999) 'All the Globe's a Stage', *Independent*, 30 May

Dawson, Antony B. and Paul Yachnin (2001) *The Culture of Playgoing in Shakespeare's England*, Cambridge: Cambridge University Press.

Escolme, Bridget (2005) *Talking to the Audience: Shakespeare, Performance, Self*, London: Routledge.

—— (2006) *Shakespeare Handbooks*: Antony and Cleopatra, London: Palgrave.

Hopkins, Lisa (1999) 'Review of *Julius Caesar*, Shakespeare's Globe', *Early Modern Literary Studies* 5 (2), available online at <http://purl.oclc.org/emls/05–2/hopkrev.htm>. (Accessed 15 September 2006.)

Kiernan, Pauline (1999) *Staging Shakespeare at the New Globe*, Basingstoke: Macmillan.

Koch-Shulte, Eva (1999) 'Know You How Much the People May Be Moved? Aspects of Audience Communication at Shakespeare's Globe Theatre, London, Exemplified by Moments of the Production of *Julius Caesar*', MA dissertation Friedrich-Alexander Universitaet Erlangen-Nürnberg.

Plutarch (1964) 'Lives of the Noble Grecians and Romans', in Geoffrey Bullough (ed.), *Narrative and Dramatic Sources of Shakespeare*, Vol. V, London: Routledge & Kegan Paul.

Prescott, Paul (2005) 'Inheriting the Globe: The Reception of Shakespearian Space and Audience in Contemporary Reviewing', in Barbara Hodgdon and W. B. Worthen (eds) *A Companion to Shakespeare and Performance*, Oxford: Blackwell, pp. 359–75.

Ryan, Jessica (2002) *Twelfth Night*, Globe Research Bulletin, available at <http://www.shakespeares-globe.org/docs/Twelfth_Night.pdf>. (Accessed 15 September 2006.)

Rylance, Mark (1999) 'Artistic Principles, Goals and Means', held in Mark Rylance archive, Shakespeare's Globe.

—— (1996) Notes for lecture given to RSA, Mark Rylance Archive.

—— (n.d.) Transcripts for interviews made for Globe exhibition, held in Mark Rylance Archive.

About the author

Bridget Escolme is Senior Lecturer in Drama at Queen Mary, University of London, where she teaches theatre and performance studies and researches early modern drama in current and historical practice. Her monograph *Talking to the Audience: Shakespeare, Performance, Self* (2005) and her contribution to the Shakespeare Handbooks series, *Antony and Cleopatra* (2006) are concerned with the ways in which meaning is produced in the moment of live performance and with the relationship between performer and audience. She is currently researching for a book project, *Madness and Theatricality*, exploring recent production of historical plays featuring madness. She is a member of the Architectural Advisory committee for Shakespeare's Globe, and the case studies contained in this essay are based on extensive experience of live performance at that theatre.

25
PETER STEIN

Michael Patterson

Peter Stein began working on Shakespeare relatively late in his career, and his productions can literally be counted on the fingers of one hand. While most young directors cannot wait to take on the challenge of Shakespeare, Stein's first production, *As You Like It*, opened just days before his fortieth birthday. Until then he had made his name with spectacular and intelligent productions of contemporary pieces like Edward Bond's *Saved* (Munich, 1967) and *Early Morning* (Zurich, 1969); German classics like Schiller's *Intrigue and Love* (Bremen, 1967) and Goethe's *Torquato Tasso* (Bremen, 1969); and by causing a furore with his provocative staging of a play about the USA's involvement in Vietnam, Peter Weiss's *Vietnam-Discourse* (Munich, 1968; Berlin, 1969). In 1970 he cofounded a theatre collective in Berlin, based at the Schaubühne am Halleschen Ufer, where, as their leading director, he staged a succession of striking productions, including Brecht's *The Mother* (1970), Ibsen's *Peer Gynt* (1971), Kleist's *Prince of Homburg* (1972) and Gorky's *Summerfolk* (1974).

He first cautiously approached Shakespeare 'as we would a great continent' (Patterson 1981: 132). Six years before he ventured to stage one of his plays, he embarked on a voyage of discovery that would take him and his actors through the world which the playwright inhabited in an attempt to understand the social and cultural forces that shaped his writing. The methods of the Schaubühne ensemble were rooted in the democratic ideal that the actors should be as well informed as the director, allowing them to participate in all decisions regarding a production. Thus, from 1971 to 1973, the ensemble met regularly for seminars on Shakespeare, which Stein joined when the group reconvened early in 1975. The performers learned new skills, e.g., acrobatics, playing the lute, singing madrigals, while studying various topics on which they reported back to their colleagues at weekly meetings.

After so much work, it was felt that the Schaubühne ensemble should present its findings to the public. The result, a kind of living museum of the Elizabethan age, was given the English title of *Shakespeare's Memory* – the English word containing a double meaning, expressed by the German *Erinnerung* (the thing remembered) and *Gedächtnis* (the faculty of memory). It was presented over two evenings in film studios in Spandau, opening on the 22 and 23 December 1976.

The programme of events has been documented in detail in English by Peter Lackner (1977). The first item consisted of various forms of folk entertainment: masked procession, morris dancing, fencing, acrobatics, musical contributions and folk drama. For the second item, banquet tables were rolled out, and the audience were invited to sit for food and drink, while the show continued in the aisle between the tables. Pageant wagons were pulled in, one at first bearing personifications of grammar, rhetoric and dialectics, and then academicians in debate. Another wagon carried a 'cage of fools' who dismounted to perform *The Revesby Play*, a piece of folk drama incorporating a dance with swords. Interspersed with this, speeches were delivered from galleries around the hall – for example, Elizabeth's Tilbury speech before the battle against the *Spanish Armada*.

The final item of the first evening was entitled 'The Museum'. It was here that the ensemble displayed its erudition about astronomy, using models, instruments and a planetarium. This developed into presentations of astrological theory and concluded with a visit to the adjacent 'Garden of Sympathies', where intersecting passages displayed exhibits about the Renaissance conception of humours and correspondences, and to the 'Cabinet of Utopians' containing life-size models of various utopian beings: the hermaphrodite, the androgynous man, the hermit, the embryo and the man of humours.

The second evening opened in 'The Museum', recapitulating elements from the previous evening. In place of the planetarium, a 'perspective cage' had been erected, a construction of cardboard figures and wires demonstrating theories of perspective in Renaissance art. In a 'Cabinet of Emblems', two actors humorously demonstrated rhetorical gestures. Most of this section, however, was devoted to the theme of melancholy.

'The Museum' now turned its attention to the figure of Elizabeth. Christine Oesterlein as the ageing Elizabeth and Sabine Andreas as the young Queen, both in richly authentic costumes, delivered speeches from raised platforms, litters and pageant wagons. These were interspersed with addresses to the Queen and statements about the nature of kingship. At the same time, a scene from *The Revenger's Tragedy* was performed. A huge cross-section of a ship was then wheeled in. This provided the setting for accounts of voyages into the New World and of the effects of colonisation. Nearby, using model ships, the course of the Battle of the Armada was explained.

The whole event ended with a series of set pieces from Shakespeare's plays, performed on an 'island' of tables, wagons and rostra. It was here that one might have expected the preparation to have borne fruit in performance. As it was, the delivery of the speeches was singularly unexciting. There were some inventive elements in the presentation: the figure of Time from *The Winter's Tale* hovered over the island in the reconstruction of an Elizabethan flying harness; Banquo's murderers gathered quietly and slipped away into the audience after completing the deed; Titania addressed her speech to a life-size stuffed donkey. But the quality of acting in these 'highlights from Shakespeare' left much to be desired. As Benjamin Hinrichs observed (*DieZeit*, 31 December 1976):

> there might have been satisfactory ways of performing this revue – academically as careful recitation, or in a popular manner with the joyful panache of travelling players. What made a mockery of the idea was the communal attempt in the last of the seven hours to attempt to play Shakespeare properly – it ended in an exhibition of outmoded theatre styles, in Christmas-card schmaltz, repertory theatre emotionalism, and mannered intensity.

Indeed, throughout the programme the ensemble had difficulty in communicating the enthusiasm they had experienced in gathering their information. As Hinrichs said (1976), a lion hunt may be exciting, but all that remains is a stuffed head: 'The Schaubühne cannot present its explorations to the public but merely its results; not the adventure itself, only a few trophies.' The trophies that were on display did, however, communicate some important ideas to the audience. Because Shakespeare's genius makes his plays so vibrant and still so relevant to our own era, it is easily forgotten how much a man of his own age he was, conditioned by the politics and philosophy of his times. For one thing, his plays were not composed as timeless literary products but as popular art forms, incorporating and exploiting many of the folk elements of his culture. Hence, there was an identifiable value to the ensemble in becoming familiar with folk plays, dances and acrobatic feats.

Despite years of careful preparation, Stein was still apprehensive about his forthcoming production of *As You Like It*. He admitted this play seemed 'totally foreign' to him, 'so full of ideas, so complex and so lacking in consistency that he for one found it hard to come to terms with' (Patterson 1981: 133). By all accounts, the rehearsal period was not a happy one. Overwhelmed by the vastness of Shakespeare's genius, Stein at times seemed to lose his nerve. He did not provide the calm leadership the ensemble had come to expect of him, and the confident clarity which had consistently characterised his work now appeared almost impossible to achieve. Stein seemed intimidated by the complexity of the material, and this crisis of self-confidence created within the cast the kind of tensions common to many theatres but which were mercifully rare at the Schaubühne.

Whatever the roads that led there, Stein's production of *As You Like It*, which opened on 20 September 1977, was to be the most spectacular presentation of Shakespeare in Germany since Reinhardt and arguably the most significant Shakespeare production anywhere since Peter Brook's *A Midsummer Night's Dream*. It took place in the film studios where *Shakespeare's Memory* had been performed nine months previously. On arrival, the audience were herded into a long, high hall, where they remained standing for the first part of the play. The walls and ceiling were of a pale powder blue, illuminated from spots set below grills in raised walks and platforms on three sides of the hall. The pale-blue tone and concealed lighting produced an unreal, cold effect, as though one were standing inside a glacier. On the platforms at the perimeter sat the actors and actresses, so immobile (with the exception of Rosalind who wept silently) that they seemed like waxworks. The costumes, designed by Moidele Bickel, were authentically Elizabethan, elaborate affairs encrusted with pearls and fretted with gold and silver, but, except for Touchstone's motley, muted in colour – blacks, chocolate browns and greys. The scenes near Oliver's house and in Frederick's court, that is, the first act and Act II, Scenes 2 and 3, and Act III, scene 1, were cross-cut in a cinematic style of juxtaposition. One actor or group would speak a few lines and then freeze into a tableau while a passage from another scene was interposed from other players elsewhere in the hall. In place of the leisurely exposition of Shakespeare's play, therefore, one had the exciting rhythms of montage.

The physical use of this area was doubtless a result of the ensemble's researches into Elizabethan theatre, in particular the Great Hall performances. The audience standing at the feet of the actors and free to move towards the focus of attention shared something of the experience of the Elizabethan groundlings. Touchstone was particularly able to exploit this informal relationship between actor and audience, directing many of his asides to spectators a few feet away from him.

The most exciting and authentic moment was on the entry of Charles to the wrestling match. He was preceded by a lord who created a path through the middle of the audience. The wrestling match itself was the showpiece of this first part, and for it Stein had engaged a professional wrestler. As a result, Charles's lines had to be re-allocated, and most of them were spoken by Le Beau, referring to Charles in the third person. Orlando, played by the strikingly beautiful Michael König stripped to a loin-cloth, matched himself against this forbidding heavyweight. After a sequence of carefully rehearsed holds and throws, Orlando found himself almost to his own surprise lifting Charles upside down off the ground to dash him to unconsciousness at the Duke's feet. The whole thing was so polished and the moves so premeditated that it failed to convince as a spontaneous conflict.

The wrestling match characterised the whole level of performance of this first part. The acting was neither strongly stylised nor did it possess the naturalness and spontaneity of good realistic acting. Oliver (Eberhard Feik) was a melodramatic villain; Adam (Gerd David), bent double and falsetto-voiced, presented an actor's stereotype of senility. The performances had in general something of that irritatingly stilted manner that characterises the acting style of inferior German municipal theatres. Only Jutta Lampe as Rosalind displayed cross-currents in her playing. Consumed with grief over her father, she could still giggle with Celia (Tina Engel) and both touch and amuse us with her sudden love for Orlando. After giving her chain to Orlando, she shyly ran away behind a pillar, peered round, then asked, 'Did you call, sir?' And before the love-struck Orlando could reply, she leapt down the steps to him to confess, 'Sir, you have wrestled well, and overthrown / More than your enemies.' Such spontaneity broke through the stiff formality of the court and was a clue that the stilted playing proceeded from a deliberate and brave directorial decision. The slow pacing of the lines, the rhetorical gestures, the pedantic delivery of 'Stage German', the rather unsubtle characterisation, all these were means to make the court scenes of the play uncomfortable and oppressive. The only adequate and sensitive response was to seek to escape from this cold, blue-white world, in which dark-clad actors from above bore down heavily on the audience. Stein risked the dissatisfaction of the audience in order to prepare for the entry into the Forest of Arden. Here, the audience did not merely observe characters moving into the green innocence of Nature; they experienced the release themselves. This was achieved as follows: the first part ended with Frederick issuing orders to Oliver to pursue Orlando into the Forest of Arden. Over loudspeakers, the barking of hounds resounded around the hall, and Oliver and his servants exited by a door in one of the walls. The audience were invited by the actors to follow and left the hall in single file, each like Alice at the door into Wonderland garden.

The audience found themselves in a dimly lit, green labyrinth, artificial creepers hanging from above, water dripping down the walls. As they followed the twists and turns of this passage, they passed curious collages pasted on the walls, small booth-like openings containing, for example, an Elizabethan workshop or, more strikingly, the androgynous man from *Shakespeare's Memory*, a life-size plaster statue with fully formed breasts and a penis bulging from his/her breeches. As the sound of the barking dogs grew distant, the hunting-horns of Arden could be heard. The conception was brilliant: to pass from the formality and brutality of the court through an underground labyrinth to the freedom and innocence of the forest was like being born anew – a metaphorical journey through the uterine canal.

The audience entered into Karl-Ernst Herrmann's magnificent set for the Forest of Arden. A complete woodland environment had been created in the vast film studios. The air was filled with the sound of birdsong and music, golden light fell from above, some of it through the leaves of a fine beech tree, which had been transplanted from woodland on the outskirts of Berlin. Beneath the beech was a shallow pool of water bounded at one side by a field of corn. This sylvan scene formed a backdrop for the main acting area, which measured some 40 feet by 100 feet and which was surrounded by a horseshoe arrangement of about 300 seats. There were more acting areas on catwalks around the walls of the studio, in the aisles between the seats and on raised levels amongst and above the audience: Audrey's home, the farmstead which Rosalind purchases, and so on. The woodland setting was further achieved by suspending tree trunks around the studio and filling empty areas with foliage, greensward and articles of rural life – a loom, a butter churn, a rowing boat – and collections made by the nobles in exile: cases of stuffed birds, insects and fossils. More arbitrary were some remnants from *Shakespeare's Memory*, as, for example, a huge model of the Ptolemaic universe suspended from the ceiling of the studio.

The costumes in this part of the play were totally different from the authentic dress of the court scenes. With a vague suggestion of the late nineteenth century, for example in the elegant beige suit and wide-brimmed hat later worn by Orlando, the costumes lifted the Forest of Arden out of the historical setting of the court into a virtually timeless situation. So, when Rosalind entered with Celia and Touchstone (Act II, Scene 4), it came as no surprise to see her with a fur cap and jerkin and Touchstone pulling a cart laden with seven suitcases.

Some of the folk elements which the ensemble had explored for *Shakespeare's Memory* could now be recalled here. As the exiled lords sat down to a meal (Act II, Scene 7), they protected themselves with a circle of brushwood, a practical device to deter snakes but also a magical encircling. Orlando burst in upon this merry gathering, his sword drawn in a display of youthful bravado, bringing with him the violence of the court. The Duke and his followers unflinchingly calmed his aggression, and Amiens soothed him with music in characteristically Elizabethan fashion. When Jaques prepared to deliver his 'Seven Ages of Man' speech, Stein indicated that this was no spontaneous philosophising by Jaques but the recitation of a familiar piece of folk wisdom. Encouraged by the lords to perform his 'party piece', Jaques moved to a raised piece of greensward and, striking a series of rhetorical poses, delivered the speech in its English original, to the delighted applause of the Duke's entourage. With the Duke's welcome to Orlando, this section of the play ended: Rosalind and Orlando were both established now in the Forest of Arden, and the ground was prepared for their first meeting.

This took the form of a peaceful interlude – a bucolic idyll after the movement, humour and loudness of the second act, as though Nature were quietly gathering its strength to move forward into the summer scenes of Act III. The lighting grew warmer; organ music (composed by Peter Michael Hamel) quietly played; Phebe (Elke Petri) sauntered to the pool and began, Narcissus-like, to admire her own reflection; Corin unpacked bags of stones, sods, herbs and flowers into piles on the central acting area; and Orlando wandered amongst the trees, hanging up sheaves of love-poems to Rosalind. Meanwhile, Touchstone and Corin discussed the 'shepherd's life' on a platform in front of Rosalind's homestead. Rosalind was dressed in a loose-fitting shirt and white cotton trousers which reached to her calves, with a floppy hat on her head and a moustache painted on her upper lip – more an urchin than the pretty boy common to productions of *As You Like It*. The more strongly built Tina Engel, as Celia, wore a 'sailor-suit' dress and carried a butterfly net – all youth and sunshine, reminiscent of Edwardian summers.

When Orlando and Rosalind then met, and he agreed to her plan to personate his sweetheart, Stein did not attempt to force psychological naturalism on this or their other encounters. In January 1975, he had already said of Rosalind: 'it is impossible to approach these events in a psychological manner, because they cannot be played that way.' They would have to find 'something more theatrical, treat it like some kind of a sport (e.g. a boxing-match)' (Patterson 1981: 142.) The reference to boxing suggests one progenitor of this acting style: Brecht. While not specifically 'Brechtian', the acting style Stein devised for the forest scenes certainly possessed Brechtian elements: a beguiling informality, a cheekily irreverent tone and the emphasis on situation rather than on individual psychology.

Thus, the mock-wedding between Orlando and Rosalind/Ganymede was performed like a children's game, with Celia assuming a priest-like voice and striking the couple with her butterfly net to prompt them. The disadvantage in rendering the relationship between Orlando and his substitute beloved so innocent, childlike and flirtatious, was that the dangers of the situation never became apparent. What if Orlando came to love the pretty boy more than his absent sweetheart? How much was his love already a homosexual passion? 'There was no trace of these perilous depths in the relationship of the main characters', commented Benjamin Hinrichs (*Die Zeit*, 30 September 1977).

Once more eschewing psychological subtleties, Stein externalised this androgynous nexus in the most effective and disturbing part of the play. The short scene (Act IV, Scene 2), in which a slain deer is brought in, included the actual skinning of the deer and the draping of the hide over one of the lords. The other lords with horns on their heads danced a primitive hunting dance. The lights dimmed eerily and Rosalind and Celia fell asleep in each other's arms. Orlando could be observed painting his face like a woman and caressing his breasts. The figure draped with the deerskin then confronted Orlando, and they became locked in violent struggle, while Rosalind and Celia rolled across the ground in a tight embrace.

A rational interpretation would not exhaust the implications of this episode, but it is clear that the erotic implications of Shakespeare's play, which Jan Kott discusses in his 'Bitter Arcadia' essay, reprinted in the Schaubühne programme, were here explored. Rosalind, originally played by a boy actor, pretends to be a boy, who pretends to be Rosalind. This blurring of sexual difference is more than an excuse for an intriguing plot: it represents the ancient search for a love that transcends the division between male and female, not the love of man for woman or woman for man but a total union of loving in which, to use Jungian terms, *animus* and *anima* are at one. So, while Rosalind and Celia experienced the sexual embrace of two women, Orlando struggled with a wild, horned beast, emblematic of his violent masculine nature. Exhausted but victorious, he was now able to be truly worthy of Rosalind's love.

Finally, the plot complications could be resolved: Rosalind promising a solution to the yearnings of Orlando, Silvius and Phebe, expressed in their formal declarations of love (Act V, Scene 2, lines 91–109). Reflecting the liturgical character of this hymn to love with its antiphonal responses, Stein placed the four actors in exact symmetry in a circle so that the expressions of love passed from one to another with Rosalind's 'And I for no woman' delivered to the world at large.

At this point, there was a crashing and tearing, and some dozen knights in armour burst through the tall door at the opposite end from the pond. Again, Stein had taken a reported incident, Duke Frederick's intended invasion of Arden, and acted it out. As the warriors hacked their way through the undergrowth, they began to grow weary, as though overpowered by some magic power of the forest. They cast off their armour piece by piece and collapsed on to the ground or into the pond. Yet again, the utopian spirit of Arden had repelled this violent onslaught launched from the court.

Now the wedding wagon rolled in, with Hymen (Gerd David) standing aloft, a gilt figure in an ornate tunic and skirt surrounded by gilt branches. This apparition of Elizabethan kitsch was a warning of the return to artificiality that was to befall the Duke, his followers and the newly wed couples. Already Celia and Rosalind stood resplendent in their court clothes, and they were joined by Orlando and Oliver, once more wearing the dress of Elizabethan noblemen. Dressed less stylishly, but with a sense of occasion, were Touchstone and Audrey, and Silvius and Phebe. The last, miserable to discover Ganymede's true identity, howled throughout the ensuing courtly minuet. Civilisation had come to Arden, and Jaques moved amongst the dancers, giving his final blessings before going to join the usurping Duke in his 'religious life'. The wagon began to roll off, and all on it called for Jaques to come with them: 'Stay, Jaques, stay', but he bowed his way out, determined to enjoy his melancholy solitariness. As Jan Kott astutely observes: 'At the end of the play everyone will leave the Forest of Arden; except Jaques. He is the only one who has no reason to leave the forest because he has never believed in it, has never entered Arcadia' (Kott 1965: 231)

The Forest of Arden was a temporary respite from the violence of political life, a glimpse of a world where ideal love might be attained, but it could only be an illusion.

> Shakespeare has no illusions, not even the illusion that one can live without illusions. He takes us into the Forest of Arden in order to show that one must try to escape, although there is no escape; that the Forest of Arden does not exist, but those who do not run away will be murdered.
>
> (Kott 1965: 226–7)

The by-now slowly and silently dancing couples approached the far end of the forest area, about to enter the same cold, white hall from which they had originally made their escape. Just as the wagon reached the doorway, there was a jolt, and the courtiers hurtled off towards their icy world once more. Meanwhile, in Arden, Corin began the laborious task of clearing up the mess left by civilisation, the abandoned weapons, armour and clothing.

In this piece, Stein summarised his view of Arden: the freedom of nature is an illusion. So, while it is valuable and important to glimpse Utopia and to experience it for an evening, the way forward is through restructuring what we have, not through escaping to what we may never have. How this restructuring is to occur, it was not Stein's intention to discuss in this play. He presented us with a vision not a political programme. That this vision did not possess Stein's accustomed clarity was a source of dismay to many critics, who felt – as Stein seems at times to have done too – that Shakespeare had gobbled him up. On the contrary, it would be fairer to say that Stein had had the courage to work with images he perhaps could not fathom totally himself.

Unnerved as he may have been by the experience, it was an essential stage in his maturing as a director and an indication that *As You Like it*, while standing at the end of a period in Stein's development, also represented the beginning of a new creativity. This new creativity asserted itself in producing new plays by Botho Strauss (1978), in spectacular versions of Aeschylus' *Oresteia* (1980) and O'Neill's *The Hairy Ape* (1987), and thoughtful productions of Chekhov's *Three Sisters* (1984) and *The Cherry Orchard* (1989), but it would not be for another twelve years that Stein returned to Shakespeare with his first foreign-language drama production, *Titus Andronicus* in Italian at the Teatro Ateneo in Rome in November 1989.

Stein was attracted to *Titus Andronicus* by its fragmentary nature and insisted, as was his wont, that he had no prior conception for the play. In the event, the star Italian actors (for example, Raf Vallone as Marcus) with whom he worked at great expense, performed in a histrionic style ill suited to the subtleties of Stein's direction. The set by Moidele Bickel was a large space contained by arched white walls blindingly lit through overhead glass panels, creating an antiseptic world in which the horrific acts of the play appeared cruel and efficient rather than viscerally shocking. Her costumes (suits with togas thrown around the shoulder), like the Mussolini-style helmets, created modern references that invited a contemplation of the parallels between Renaissance violence and the savagery of our own times, so that the piece worked as a political parable, an invitation to intellectual reflection in contrast to the shockingly violent stagings by Peter Brook in 1955 and Adrian Noble in 1978.

As codirector of the Salzburg Festival, Stein decided to produce *Julius Caesar* in the summer of 1992, a year later transferring it to the Edinburgh Festival, where he took over the Royal Highland Exhibition Hall and caused something of a stir by pleading that the flight paths of incoming aircraft should be changed so as not to interfere with his performances. The premiere took place in the Felsenreitschule in Salzburg, where the large arena (almost 200 feet wide) had been covered with a marble playing area and steps backed by tiers of arches. The audience, seated at anything up to 200 feet from the action, were therefore treated to a spectacle involving 240 performers, reminiscent of the massive stagings by Reinhardt in a circus arena. This functioned well in the public scenes, for example, the assassination of Caesar or Mark Antony's speech to the Roman populace. As Michael Billington wrote (*Guardian*, 3 September 1993):

> In the Forum scene both Brutus and Mark Antony are confronted not by the usual apologetic handful but by a milling, angry, boiler-suited crowd that has to be forced to listen by guile and rhetoric. One of the production's most thrilling sights is seeing this throng of individuals turned into a collective force who weave and sway around the orators and then tear their temporary trestle stage to pieces.

The vast amphitheatre worked less well in the more intimate scenes. As Peter von Becker observed, the danger was that the performers, many of them leading German and Austrian actors, might 'easily be turned into declaiming dwarfs' (1992: 20). Indeed, Stein reinforced arguments and confrontations with carefully thought-out moves, in which the steps played a significant role: 'Each human emotion and its accompanying movement became a piece of choreography' (Becker 1992: 20). Inevitably, though, some of the subtleties of the confrontations like that between Brutus and Cassius in Act IV, Scene 3, were swallowed up in the vast arena. Thus, despite the gesture towards modern relevance in the costumes (yet again contemporary suits with a toga thrown over the shoulder), the political insights of the play, which Stein in the past would have revealed with astonishing clarity, were here submerged. Once more, it may have been that Stein was so impressed by the vastness of Shakespeare's vision that he felt that only by performing *Julius Caesar* on a grand scale could he do justice to the original. Although Stein's production offered an unforgettable four-hour spectacle, it is perhaps worth remembering that, despite their capacity, the theatres for which Shakespeare himself wrote offered much greater proximity between actor and audience and so created a greater sense of intimacy. After this spectacular event at the Edinburgh Festival, Stein was eventually invited back to direct there again, and his next Shakespeare production – apart from his four-hour *Antony and Cleopatra* staged at the Felsenreitschule in Salzburg in 1994 – would be his first attempt at working with British actors on Shakespeare.

To anyone who has been excited and enthralled by Peter Stein's past productions of European classics, his 2006 staging of *Troilus and Cressida*, first at the Edinburgh Festival then at the Royal Shakespeare Company in Stratford, will have come as a disappointment. One looked in vain in this 'flamboyantly mediocre production' (Nicholas de Jongh, *Evening Standard*, 16 August 2006) for the daring interventions that have characterised Stein's past work, offering perspectives on classics like Kleist's *Prince of Homburg* or Ibsen's *Peer Gynt* that has made it now difficult to stage these plays again without reference to Stein's insights. In vain one searched for the spectacular stage effects like the Forest of Arden created for *As You Like It*, the vast scale of the *Julius Caesar* production, or the bough of the cherry-tree that came crashing through the roof at the end of his 1989 production of *The Cherry Orchard*. One was not even treated to the piercingly fresh intelligence that has usually informed Stein's work in the theatre.

Admittedly, *Troilus and Cressida* is a problematic piece. Its combination of lyrical young love with lecherous commentary, of genuine heroism with male posturing, of passion with cynicism, means that its intention is never clear. It has tragic elements, but no resolution; the title suggests that the focus is on the ill-fated love of Troilus and Cressida, but the events of the war are far more than a backdrop and dwarf their personal problems. Stein admits that it was this very complexity of the plot and themes of *Troilus and Cressida* that attracted him to the piece:

> This is just why I do theatre. I say, 'Let's do this play, which is so problematic and puzzling, and then I might understand it.' [. . .] In all his other plays, after disasters or comic resolutions, there is the feeling that things can start up again, can go on. But here – no . . . It's an ending like no other, completely nihilistic.
>
> (Interview in *The Scotsman*, 9 August 2006)

In fact, it was only with the ending that Stein made a major intervention in the text (apart from a few cuts and mercifully omitting the tediously unfunny scene between Pandarus and a Servant at the start of Act III). In the original, Troilus curses Pandarus and exits to leave the older man alone on stage to deliver his vicious epilogue. In Stein's version, Cressida reappeared to beg forgiveness of Troilus, was violently rejected by him, and Troilus in an act of suicidal desperation ran at Achilles' Myrmidons and was impaled on their lances. Only then did Pandarus launch into his monologue. Despite the muttering of some critics about Stein's mistaken attempt to resolve a deliberately inconclusive ending, his conclusion certainly made for a more coherent narrative.

Indeed, it might be argued that Stein should have taken more liberties with the original. Once again, he seemed almost intimidated by Shakespeare, modestly asserting that his role was to learn, hoping that the actors 'can make me understand this play, in a language that is not even my own' (Interview in *The Scotsman*, 9 August 2006). Stein concentrated on the spoken word, placing nearly all the scenes on a bare stage before a huge metallic wall, presumably representing the walls of Troy. This massive wall, designed by Ferdinand Wörgerbauer, was intended to slide forward and tilt to provide the battlefield in Act V. The mechanism failed at the Edinburgh premiere, leading to the performance being abandoned halfway – the kind of decision it is hard to imagine a British or American director taking, given our tradition that 'the show must go on'. By the time the set was brought to Stratford, the recalcitrant wall remained firmly in place.

The costumes, designed by Anna Maria Heinreich, were a strange mixture of authentic Trojan and Greek armour with shabbily contemporary overcoats worn by the Greek generals, suggesting the decayed command of the remnants of some Balkan army. The set-piece battles were also inconsistent: most were choreographed as a dance with warriors spinning gracefully before their opponent – a patently fatal move in close combat; and yet the main encounter between Achilles and Hector was played out with exciting realism. For most of the play, soldiers returned from battle completely unscathed, their shields intact, their small golden loincloths still neatly in place. Yet, at the end, the Trojan army stood around drenched in stage blood.

The characterisation was curiously inconsistent too, ranging from the modern figure of the thoughtful politician Ulysses (David Yelland) to the cartoon figure of Ajax, played like a mindless thug by Julian Lewis Jones. While there was much talk of lechery, the production was virtually devoid of sexuality. There was a good deal of nakedness but little eroticism. It is not unreasonable that Troilus (Henry Pettigrew) and Cressida (Annabel Scholey) should have a coyly restrained consummation of their love. However, Helen (Rachel Pickup) and Paris (Adam Levy), a pleasant-looking couple flown in together on a spectacular red bed, were playful but never passionate.

Most contrary to the spirit of *Troilus and Cressida*, however, was the tepid relationship between Achilles (Vincent Regan) and his catamite Patroclus (Oliver Kieran-Jones). Theirs was a cosy companionship which entirely lacked the erotic charge that was so powerful in John Barton's 1968 production, which, according to the programme note, inspired Stein to direct *Troilus and Cressida*. Even the powerful figure of Cassandra (Kate Miles) created hardly a flicker of interest: she was brought on to screech her lines without having significant impact on either the Trojans or the audience. It may well be that Stein failed to recognise that while German actors impress with their intelligence and discipline, British actors score through their energy and charm. His failure to harness these qualities made his *Troilus and Cressida* simply dull.

When asked why his approach to Shakespeare has been somewhat tentative, Stein admitted that he found Shakespeare very difficult and modestly asserted: 'I'm not a very good Shakespearian director' (Interview on BBC Radio 4, 5 August 2006). He also vigorously rejects what he regards as the slapdash treatment of Shakespeare particularly prevalent among British and American directors who want to stamp their own vision on to the text, and famously described the improvisational approach of his fellow countryman, Peter Zadek, as 'Shakespeare in underpants' (Patterson 1981: 131–2). Stein does not see himself as a visionary director:

> I always have certain difficulties in understanding myself as a director. A director – that would be more in the sense of someone arrogant, fascinating, radiating genius, his head full of images and visions, which are then transmitted in a mysterious way so that the actors burst into flower under this visionary spell.
>
> (*Die Zeit*, 2 January 1976)

It is never his intention to 'rescue' a play with some brilliant directorial vision. His preferred method is 'beginning from zero' (Patterson 1981: 4), quietly appraising the text and then constructing his production on the basis of the discoveries yielded by the words: 'the simple act of going back to the text is the most radical thing that you could do now' (Interview in the *Guardian*, 9 August 2006).

In Shakespeare's text, he has been regularly confronted by richness, complexity and ambiguity, a confusing mixture of tragedy with humour, intimacy with spectacle, psychological insight with exciting stage effects. While repeatedly attracted to this 'box of rare delights', to use Goethe's phrase, Stein sometimes appears to lose his way when it comes to staging the plays. Significantly, when questioned about the striking scene of Orlando's fight with the deer in *As You Like It*, Stein refused to 'explain' this episode: 'Orlando's fight was not one of the most thought-out aspects of my As *You Like It* production. It formed a part of a dreamlike mime sequence which possessed musical and visual meaning rather than any narrow interpretable significance' (Personal communication, 18 October 1980).

Stein's great strength lies in the clarity of his vision: 'if nothing occurs to you, the least you can be is precise', as he said in an interview with Jack Zipes (1977: 53). However, beginning with *As You Like It*, when Stein even expressed his doubts about being a director, he has found it difficult to be precise when confronted by the richness and complexity of Shakespeare. If he could have surrendered himself more in the way that he did with the imprecise but theatrically stunning fight of Orlando, he might have achieved more as a Shakespearian director. Instead, he seems to have been all too easily tempted towards spectacle (as in *Julius Caesar* and *Troilus and Cressida*). This worked well with pieces like *Peer Gynt* and *The Hairy Ape*, where the text is less subtle. However, in Shakespeare this tendency towards using large casts and expensive settings, the cost of which has repeatedly priced Stein out of the market, tends to submerge the psychological tensions of the original. As a consequence, Peter Stein, who is unquestionably one of Europe's leading directors, justifiably famed for his clever and inventive stagings of a wide range of works, from Aeschylus to Nigel Williams, from Verdi to Chekhov, can claim only in his first Shakespeare production to have done justice to his reputation. *Richard II*, planned for 2007, a project Stein had been considering for thirty-five years, focuses more closely on individuals rather than on grand spectacle, so it may well be that this text is better suited to his intelligence and clarity.

Chronology

1967 Bond: *Saved*
Schiller: *Intrigue and Love*
1968 Brecht: *In the Jungle of Cities*
1969 Goethe: *Torquato Tasso*
Bond: *Early Morning*
1970 Middleton and Rowley: *The Changeling*
Becomes director of the Schaubühne am Halleschen Ufer, (from 1980 Schaubühne am Kurfürstendamm), Berlin
Brecht: *The Mother*
1971 Ibsen: *Peer Gynt*
1972 Kleist: *Prince of Homburg*
1974 Gorky: *Summerfolk*
1976 *Shakespeare's Memory*, CCC Film Studios, Berlin
1977 Shakespeare: *As You Like It*, CCC Film Studios, Berlin
1980 Aeschylus: *The Oresteia*
Leaves Schaubühne to work freelance
1984 Chekhov: *The Three Sisters*
1989 Chekhov: *The Cherry Orchard*
Shakespeare: *Titus Andronicus*, Teatro Ateneo, Rome
1992 Shakespeare: *Julius Caesar*, Felsenreitschule, Salzburg
1994 Shakespeare: *Antony and Cleopatra*, Felsenreitschule, Salzburg
2000 Goethe: *Faust*
2003 Chekhov: *The Seagull*
2006 Shakespeare: *Troilus and Cressida*, King's Theatre, Edinburgh

Bibliography

Becker, Peter von (1992) 'Ein Kinderspiel – was sonst? Peter Stein inszeniert Shakespeare's "Julius Caesar" in der Felsenreitschule', [A child's game – what else? Peter Stein stages Shakespeare's *Julius Caesar* in the Felsenreitschule] *Theater heute*, September 20–2.

Brook, Peter (1968) *The Empty Space*, London: Penguin.

Kott, Jan (1965) 'Bitter Acadie' (essay) *Shakespeare our Contemporary*, London: Methuen.

Lackner, Peter (1977) 'Peter Stein', *Drama Review*, T74: 79–102.

Patterson, Michael (1976) *German Theatre Today: Post-War Theatre in West and East Germany, Austria and Northern Switzerland*, London: Pitman.

Patterson, Michael (1981) *Peter Stein: Germany's Leading Theatre Director*, Cambridge: Cambridge University Press.

Sebald, W.G. (1988) *A Radical Stage: Theatre in Germany in the 1970s and 1980s*, Oxford: Berg.

Zipes, Jack (1977) 'Utopia as the Past Conserved' (interview with Dieter Sturm and Peter Stein)', *Theater*, Vol. 9 (1): 50–7.

About the author

Michael Patterson read modern languages at Oxford and then studied theatre at the Freie Universität in Berlin, where he became familiar with the contemporary German theatre scene. This resulted eventually in his survey, *German Theatre Today* (1976). After spending some time researching at the Schaubühne am Halleschen Ufer in Berlin he then wrote the first monograph on Peter Stein (1981). In 1977 he attended Stein's spectacular production of *As You Like It* in film studios in Berlin. Subsequently he has seen and been impressed by many further Stein productions, although he feels that Stein never achieved the same quality in his later productions of Shakespeare. Patterson has published a definitive bibliography of German theatre and studies of German expressionist theatre and of German theatre in the late eighteenth, early nineteenth centuries. More recently, he has widened his perspective to write on British political theatre and to single-handedly author *The Oxford Dictionary of Plays*. He is now Emeritus Professor of Theatre at De Montfort University, Leicester.

26
GIORGIO STREHLER

Donald McManus

Giorgio Strehler (1921–97) was the single most important figure in post-war Italian theatre. He was more than just a director. He was actor, scholar, dramaturg and scenographer. The renowned American theatre scholar Ruby Cohn interviewed Strehler for the *Tulane Drama Review* in 1964 when his status as an international theatre figure was in its ascendancy. His accomplishment as a director, according to Cohn, was the 'distillation of a culture and a historical situation, of a moral attitude and a psychology' (Cohn 1964: 34). If this statement were true of his work in 1964, it became ever more true as his career continued. His productions became increasingly self-referential, even autobiographical, as he matured. Although he directed definitive productions of Brecht, Goldoni, Pirandello and many others, his productions of Shakespeare's plays mark key points in his development and have had a lasting effect on approaches to Shakespeare in performance.

Strehler was born into an upper-middle-class family of intellectuals and artists in a small, seaside town outside of Trieste. His father died when he was about two years old. Giorgio's mother raised him with the help of his maternal grandmother. Both of these women were accomplished musicians. They instilled an appreciation and deep understanding of music in the boy that helped him when he found his own artistic *métier*. He grew up fluent in German and French as well as Italian. His mother wanted him to study law, but he became obsessed with the theatre at an early age and entered the Accademia Filodramatici in Milan to study acting.

The young artist's rise to prominence in Italian and European theatre was stalled by Italy's entry into the Second World War. His fluency in German served him well during the war. He managed to escape to Switzerland and pose as a German Swiss under the assumed name Georges Firby, thereby avoiding military service in the Italian army. Although this period was one of great stress and privation, he managed to stay connected to the theatre during his exile and even produced plays by Pirandello and Eliot while living in a refugee camp.

After the war, he readily found work as a freelance director but longed to establish a permanent company. He had known the scholar and critic Paolo Grassi (1919–81) in Milan before circumstances forced him to flee to Switzerland. The two men shared both aesthetic tastes and political ideals. In 1947, Strehler and Grassi occupied an abandoned cinema, which had reputedly been used by the Nazis to interrogate prisoners, and established the Piccolo Teatro di Milano as an art theatre for all. Their goal was to create a people's theatre devoted to the highest artistic quality, where egalitarian, socialist political values would coexist with a cultural product on a par with those of France, Germany and Britain. The Piccolo was the first state-subsidised resident company in post-war Italy. The Piccolo represented a change in the structure of Italian theatre away from touring companies headed by a star actor and towards a resident company where the director's vision was paramount.

The new theatre's mission was published as a manifesto, *La Lettera programmatica*, in which the founding directors announced that the Piccolo's focus would not be words or gestures, authors or actors, but the spectators. Their first priority was creating theatre that was in dialogue with its audience and, by extension, Italian post-war culture. What would comprise this new civilisation? How would the Italian theatrical community overcome the legacy of the Fascist era? *La Lettera programmatica* said nothing specific about the performances or texts that would create the desired bond between company and audience. No one who read the Piccolo's 1947 mission statement would have guessed that Shakespeare productions would form such a large part of the Piccolo's repertoire.

In the first two years of the new company, Strehler directed *Romeo and Juliet*, *Richard II* and *The Tempest*. By 1952, he had staged eight of Shakespeare's plays ranging through all the genres, including *Macbeth*, *Richard III*, *Henry IV*, *Twelfth Night* and *The Taming of the Shrew*, establishing the primacy of Shakespeare in the Piccolo's first few seasons. Although the number and frequency of Shakespeare plays lessened after the intense pace of the early years at the Piccolo, his last two encounters, *King Lear* and *The Tempest* respectively, were defining moments in his career.

The Tempest was the only one of Shakespeare's texts that he staged more than once. His initial production was in the summer of 1948 a little over a year after the opening of the Piccolo's first season. His second, radically rethought version, was a full thirty years later in 1978 and was the last Shakespeare play that he mounted. Both *Tempests* were well received by audiences and critics, and serve as convenient bookends for Strehler's career as a Shakespeare interpreter.

The Tempest, 1948

Although produced under the auspices of the Piccolo Teatro di Milano, the 1948 *Tempest* was staged out of doors in Florence's Boboli Gardens. French director Jacques Copeau (1879–1945) had presented *As You Like It* in the gardens ten years earlier, and Austrian/German director Max Reinhardt (1878–1943) had staged *A Midsummer Night's Dream* there in 1933. Salvatore Quasimodo's (1901–68) Romantic-tinged translation was selected as the Italian text for the Boboli *Tempest*, and the design was by Gianni Ratto, with whom Strehler had collaborated for *Richard II* in Milan only a few months earlier.

Together they devised an elaborate spectacle that took advantage of the park's existing architectural features, statuary and waterways. The literal presence of water separated the audience from the performers. A multi-levelled playing space was constructed on a circular butt of land that could be accessed from additional bridges. The stepped hill that formed the stage resembled diagrams of the levels of Hell stretching through Purgatory and Earth to Heaven in Renaissance bookplates accompanying editions of Dante's *Divine Comedy*. Each level was symbolically connected to an appropriate action with the apex of the hill reserved for the masque scene and the lowest level for Caliban's hut and the antics of the clowns.

The Dantesque imagery of the island created a universe in miniature and also conveniently reminded the audience of Italian cultural history while watching this English play. The masque scene incorporated anachronistic Italian opera arias, while the clowns, Stephano and Trinculo were derived from Italian *commedia dell'arte* characters who performed extraneous bits of comic business. This device of mixing and matching cultural references in the same production would be repeated and refined as Strehler matured.

In addition to the expanse of water between the spectators and spectacle, fountain pipes sprayed water into the air surrounding the peninsula. The cascading water formed a curtain that could obscure the island from sight when desirable. The water was used to bounce light onto the set, and when disturbed by the spray from the fountain, this reflected light created a rippling effect on the playing space. The curtain of water was contrasted in the finale by having the island explode with fireworks. The entire event was a celebration of theatrical devices on a grand scale.

The concept of rooting the *mise-en-scène* in contradictory images such as fire and water would become another marker of Strehler's style. The literal realisation of fire and water in 1948 was replaced with lyrical evocations in the subsequent 1978 production. The two stagings, thirty years apart, both stressed the joy of theatrical artifice and spectacle, but where the 1948 production brought elements to the audience in a tactile way, the later, more universally celebrated version, used more subtle stage devices with their mechanisms clearly visible.

Despite the splendour and success of the Boboli Gardens *Tempest*, many of the Piccolo's early attempts to stage Shakespeare's plays were hastily produced and largely derivative in concept. The director himself was dismissive of his accomplishment in the 1948 *Tempest* saying that while it was a principal moment in his formative work, there was little rehearsal, little reflection, and 'Caliban didn't exist' (Horowitz 2004: 42). He was struggling to strike a balance between his penchant for theatrical display and showmanship, executed in the extreme for *The Tempest*, and his interest in using Shakespeare's plays to reflect and comment upon Italy and Europe's post-war, political reality. The inspiration for how to strike this balance came from an unlikely source: German director and playwright Bertolt Brecht (1898–1956).

Although he had wanted to direct a Brecht play for years, he wasn't sure how to balance the theatricality and the political argument inherent in the text. He felt that his experience directing Shakespeare helped give him the confidence to tackle epic theatre and visited Berlin to ask the playwright for advice while planning a production of *The Threepenny Opera* in 1955 (Hirst 1993: 90). He questioned Brecht about the theoretical fine points of epic theatre and how they worked in practice. He was worried because almost none of his company of actors at the Piccolo had experience with the 'alienation effect', 'gestus', and other specific concepts of the epic approach. Brecht was sufficiently impressed with the interview to visit rehearsals and the opening night for *Threepenny* the following year in Milan. If Shakespeare helped the director to prepare for Brecht's theatre, personal contact with the playwright and mastering the epic style also had an effect on Strehler's approach to Shakespearian texts.

In Strehler, Brecht found one of the only directors who appreciated that his theatre was meant to be theatrically effective as well as didactic. Brecht's theoretical writings had been widely interpreted as anti-naturalistic or anti-Stanislavskian, but Strehler believed that truly epic theatre must be a synthesis of presentational and representational techniques. Brecht endorsed this philosophy by pronouncing Strehler his heir apparent. When he died later that year, his widow, the actress Helene Weigel, offered Strehler the directorship of the Berliner Ensemble. Although he turned down the position, his work was broadly interpreted as 'Brechtian' until the end of his life. During the short time that the two men knew each other, the German playwright had been struggling with his own adaptations of Shakespeare's plays.

One year after Brecht's death, and the season following his first mounting of *The Threepenny Opera*, Strehler directed *Coriolanus*. This production directly reflected his mentor–protégé relationship with Brecht, who had been obsessed with this particularly difficult play in his final years. *Coriolanus* was a stylistic turning point because he found a way to physically underscore the political argument of the play by stressing dialectical oppositions of class, historical forces and gender. He described the unity between the plebeians and the tribunes as 'thesis and antithesis in movement' (Strehler 1974: 315). His approach throughout rehearsals and the design phase was to emphasise the many interpretive problems of the play rather than attempt to solve them. The set by Luciano Damiani was extremely simple. Each scene had a different configuration of columned porticoes, varying in size and number, but never varying in their orientation to the audience. The columns and arches were always parallel to the edge of the stage, presenting a flat row. The persistently flat composition suited the dialectical conception as each scene could be read as another set of oppositions. Ultimately, Strehler wanted Coriolanus' personal tragedy to be clearly contextualised within the broader play of social forces and for this dialectic to be visually coherent to the audience.

Shakespeare output slowed markedly after the successes with *The Threepenny Opera* and *Coriolanus*. Strehler directed four other Brecht plays and a composite evening of his German mentor's poetry and songs before returning to Shakespeare in 1965. When he did return, it was with an epic production that combined various scenes from the *Henry VI* cycle entitled *Il Gioco dei Potenti* (*Power Games*). The set, codesigned by Carlo Tommasi and Strehler himself, was even more minimalist than *Coriolanus* had been. The primary scenic element was the stage floor, which was wooden, slightly raked and hexagonal in shape. Strehler wanted as little interference as possible with the entrance of bodies into the space. The physical collision of armies on a huge game board defined the rhythm of *Il Gioco*.

The success in applying a Brechtian approach to *Coriolanus* and *Il Gioco* was a considerable accomplishment, but these productions retained a derivative quality. Strehler was gaining a reputation as a Brecht interpreter who applied epic theatre to classic plays. As such, he was his master's pupil rather than a unique creator. *Coriolanus* was a play that the Berliner Ensemble had produced, and *Power Games* was a Brecht-styled adaptation of a group of plays. Where these productions were conceptually tied to the Brecht–Berliner theory, and the aesthetic programme that went with it, over the coming decades his approach was to be more clearly driven by formal and aesthetic considerations. In the 1970s, his *King Lear* and *The Tempest* were as concerned with the relationship of human bodies to space, light and form, as much as they were with human beings caught in the class struggle or the march of history.

As his directing style became more identifiable, he increasingly quoted other works of art, including his own productions from the past. This tendency towards self-reference, which he liked to call meta-theatre, became less and less of a Brechtian alienation device with a didactic political motive and more and more of an aesthetic principle. As with other areas of the modernist art movement, which flourished in Europe during the 1960s, political motivation was not abandoned but treated as one part in an increasingly complex discourse with formal, as well as historical and critical points of departure. All of his productions had a meta-theatrical frame and, in most cases, referred clearly to a theatrical and cultural past. The 1948 *Tempest* was an early example of this tendency with its combination of *commedia dell'arte*, Dante, grand opera and spectacle.

Strehler's greatest contribution to Shakespeare in performance would probably never have been produced if he hadn't had a political and personal crisis and had been forced to leave the very theatre that he had cofounded on political principles. The instability of political labels and artistic programmes was brought home to him in 1966 only a year after his Brecht-inspired production of *Il Gioco dei Potenti*. It was the period of student unrest in Italy and most of western Europe. The 'contestazione', as it was called in Italy, was a student-driven movement that protested against everything from college entrance exams and the war in Vietnam to cultural exclusivity. He suddenly found himself accused of being the bourgeois manager he sought to differentiate himself from when founding the Piccolo Teatro in the first place: 'The contestazione taught me a terrible lesson: one wakes up one morning and discovers that one is right wing, considered conservative by everyone, while the night before you felt that you were left wing and one of the avant-garde' (Strehler 1974: 51). Much to his surprise, he was targeted as one of the establishment figures against whom the students voiced their discontent. The Piccolo Teatro was picketed and the resignation of its artistic director demanded. He shocked the city, and probably the protesters more than anyone, by promptly quitting. He was to take a six-year hiatus from the Piccolo. During his absence from the theatre he had cocreated, he worked as a free agent in France, Germany and Italy directing mostly opera but also sporadic productions of plays by Brecht, Weiss and Gorky. He directed no Shakespeare plays during his self-imposed exile from the Piccolo. His defining style came after the shock he had at discovering he was part of the establishment after all. When he finally returned it was to mount *King Lear*. With this triumphant resurrection, it seemed that his artistic palette was more variegated than ever.

King Lear, 1972

The Piccolo *King Lear* was based on circus, and it was the director's darkest vision of the theatrical metaphor. The periphery of the acting area in *King Lear*, when it was visible, was clearly defined as a circus tent with ropes anchoring a canvas awning. This awning defined the perimeter of the playing space. Even when the stage was well lit, the circus motif reminded the audience that their vision was being defined, hemmed in and constrained. Inside the tented playing space there was a circus ring with a wooden edge and a sandy interior. Strehler described his concept for the setting of the production: 'A place that is empty and tiring: desolate. A tragic surface, muddy, primordial, in which we walk and tire. Where one's feet sink in and where one is made filthy when one falls' (Strehler 1973: 264). Most of the characters were caught in the mud and advanced only slowly through an apparently tiring and tragic substance. They seemed to be struggling to advance and sometimes delivered key dialogue in semi-darkness. The one character who was free from the mire and shadow was the Fool, who could appear and disappear like a circus star doing a clown entrée, popping in and out as if by magic, frequently tripping lightly along the edge of the ring while balancing with a tiny umbrella so as not to fall into the mud that made others filthy.

The tent and the ring seemed to represent two variations on a bleak, foggy world of illusion and obfuscation. Truth, or the enlightenment that Lear sought as the play progressed, seemed to lie outside the tent, possibly outside the world of the theatre and the play. The Fool was patterned after the Swiss circus clown Grock, yet played by a young actress, Ottavia Piccolo, who also played Cordelia. Strehler was very taken with the notion that Shakespeare's lyrical clown, Robert Armin, had played both parts in the original Globe production. He wanted to draw attention to the Fool as a doppelgänger of Cordelia, but he also conceived of her as a supra-gendered entity capable of transcending the gap between narrative and audience:

> To me there can be no question as to whether the Fool is young or old or whatever, or happy or sad, or half mad or not. She is an oral-physical-mimetic entity who performs a specific function. Here it is to contradict (which is a characteristic of a clown relationship to their 'masters'), to comment, to demystify, etc. Above all she must be anonymous, physically malleable, be able to sing, dance and move mimetically with agility and assurance. The Fool is continually inside and outside of the tragedy; she has a gestural legitimacy in the scene and

> out of the scene – as an intermediary figure between the stage-actors and the stalls-audience.
>
> (Strehler 1973: 31)

The Fool would appear and disappear by means of a follow spot, making it seem as if she was the only source of light in a ponderous world of confusion. The follow spot had the additional effect of reinforcing the presentational nature of the circus motif and reminding the audience of the anachronistic representation of ancient Britain in this version. Although the Fool/Cordelia character was unambiguously positive in Strehler's *King Lear*, the theatrical metaphor as a whole seemed to indicate corruption. As the tragedy progressed, Lear's character took on more and more of the aspect of a circus clown as well. His face got paler, and his ruffled collar and running eye make-up all made him appear as if he had become a white-faced clown who was being teased into understanding by the Grockesque Fool.

Many aspects of the production were reminiscent of Federico Fellini's (1920–93) film *8½* (1963). *8½* had a similar circus motif and critiqued the decadent tendencies of the art-making process and increasing materialism of both daily life and culture in 1960s Italy. Strehler was also influenced by the theatre of Irish playwright Samuel Beckett (1906–89). The idea of there being a connection between *Lear* and Beckett's *Endgame* had already been established by Jan Kott (1914–2001) and was tested by Peter Brook in his 1962 production. The Piccolo *Lear* additionally seemed to repudiate popular culture by making the circus world one of horror and violence. Lear's whitened face was equated with both circus and madness, implying a morally corrupt sub-text to theatrical artifice. The real world beyond the walls of the theatre, or at least offstage seemed, by contrast, more positive than the depicted universe.

It is tempting to read this production of *Lear* as a taciturn reflection on Strehler's career to that point (just as *8½* was a reflection on Fellini's career after having made eight films). Included in this self-evaluation is a pervasive negativity with regard to the illusion making that goes hand in hand with theatre directing. The protestors' criticism of him, which he felt so painfully during the *contestazione*, was tangible everywhere in *King Lear*. He withdrew and had an extended period of depression during his self-imposed exile from Milan, and the *mise-en-scène* for *Lear* reflected this bleak state of mind. Even death was presented as a more positive, natural alternative to the corrupt circus world. Whatever the personal motives behind his directorial choices, he wanted Lear's final act to be an active choice rather than a pathetic exit.

There were several unusual decisions concerning the final scene in order to arrive at the effect of Lear's death as a conscious and positive choice.

Rehearsal diaries indicate that he developed his concept for the denouement over several months of trial and error in which he reversed major decisions as late as two weeks from the first public presentations. Finally, he decided to have a seamless sequence with the final battle between Edgar and Edmund and the death of Goneril and Regan all enacted in a central coral into which Lear would carry the dead Cordelia for a macabre family reunion. The dual casting was most important to Strehler in the death scene where he felt that the Fool's lessons should be present both physically and intellectually:

> The fact is that the Fool is only of service to the negative character Lear, so as to comment on that negativity. He can no longer be of service once Lear's personality emerges out of the darkness and is reborn, becomes the opposite of what he was. [. . .] But then it isn't possible, or at least it doesn't seem possible here that the Fool must disappear. He is no longer needed as he was, but rather, in a new form and with a new substance. And so we have Cordelia.
>
> (Strehler 1973: 44–5)

Radical as the dual-cast Cordelia and Fool seemed at the time, perhaps the most interesting decision was to leave Lear alone with the dead for his final stage moment rather than surround him with Kent, Edgar et al. as the text indicates. When Lear said 'thank you sir' after asking someone to undo his button in the death scene, there was no one to whom he could direct the line. He said it to himself and followed it with direct address to the audience in the final lines: 'Look there, look there!'

The Tempest, 1978

In many ways, the definitive staging of *The Tempest* in 1978 was a conceptual complement to the *King Lear* of six years earlier. The two productions cannot be completely understood separately because in many ways they were mirrors of each other. Both were products of Strehler's post-*contestazione* crisis and exile. Both used space and light in a dramatically different way from the earlier forays into Shakespeare. Each relied heavily on theatrical metaphor, or meta-theatre, but where *King Lear* seemed to represent the stage as false and even morally inferior to reality, *The Tempest* represented a kind of rapprochement with the maestro's art-making *métier*. Prospero's island was a stark patch of boarded stage with a trapdoor out of which a pseudo-native Caliban appeared, while Ariel's entrances defied gravity and defined the gulf between floor and rafters as theatrical playing space.

Where the 1948 *Tempest* presented images as literally as possible, such as a

Dantesque hill for a stage, an island surrounded by real water and exploding fireworks, the 1978 version evoked waves with silk sheets. The stagehands were always completely visible to the audience whether they were manipulating huge blue silks to create the illusion of water or pulling ropes to make Ariel fly. The design strategy managed to quote elegant, Italian Renaissance stage devices, such as the wave machines of Niccolà Sabbatini, and make these devices seem modern by their frank, Brechtian execution. Resident dramaturg Agostino Lombardo created a new translation especially for the production to replace the Quasimodo version and give the text a fresh, brisk sound.

The meta-theatrical devices in *The Tempest* were extraordinarily complex and grounded in meticulous historical research and precise application of theatrical quotation. Where his *King Lear* evoked the circus with an androgynous Grock-like character in the Fool and a harried, white-faced clown for the King, the characters in *The Tempest* derived from contrasting styles and epochs of theatrical tradition. He drew on three distinct clown traditions as part of his *mise-en-scène*. Alonso, the displaced monarch losing his mind, was presented as a white-faced clown and was an obvious, self-referential allusion to *King Lear*. The audience was reminded of the previous production, monarch and use of clown imagery for a tragic situation, but ultimately the meta-theatrical imagery created the opposite effect.

Trinculo and Stephano were patterned after *commedia dell'arte* characters and included bits of traditional *commedia* business as they had in the 1948 production. Stephano was a conniving Brighella and Trinculo was a simple-minded Arlecchino. However, there was a class-consciousness about the revisiting of the *commedia* clowns that was less overt in the 1948 version. Stephano and Trinculo were presented as the proletariat, one with petit-bourgeois aspirations, the other decidedly lumpen. Ariel, played by the actress Giulia Lazzarini, recalled a French Pierrot in billowing white silk tethered to a harness that allowed her to fly to the top of the theatre but also represented her physical bond to Prospero. Lazzarini's Ariel always kept her dignity, moving one moment like a dancer, the next like a trapped servant or slave.

Because Prospero manipulated her action, she seemed like a marionette and he the puppeteer at times. Where the female Fool in *King Lear* was the dominant character in most interactions with the King, Ariel was almost always submissive to Prospero. Her subservience was both psychological and tactile. When she asked for freedom, she pulled on her always-visible rigging. Even as the tether kept her a servant to Prospero, it also allowed her to fly, opening the space vertically while the other characters remained earth-bound.

Calilban was a median character between the contrasting clowns of Ariel, Trinculo and Stephano. He had no costume other than a vaguely native make-up. His initial appearance was crab or perhaps spider-like, and at other times he distorted his body in various animalistic contortions, but he was an unadorned, simple, man-creature who walked erect, as a normal human, when alone on stage with no one watching him.

The Ariel/Pierrot contrasted the proletarian Arlecchino and Brighella and delivered a subtle social and historical message at the same time. All of the clowns maintained their comic spirit. The themes of freedom and dignity inherent in Shakespeare's text were expressed with a consistency of motif and comic tone. The audience was encouraged to empathise with the proletarian clowns even while they laughed at their stupidity. Ariel's free flight, combined with her own desire for genuine freedom, was elegantly joined to the other clowns and Caliban, even as the narrative pitted these characters against each other in the battle for domination of the island. Although they were at odds, they shared a common heritage as antique, stage characters.

Ariel was, in many ways, a re-vision of the Cordelia/Fool idea. She appeared to be both puppet and second daughter. In the final scene of *King Lear*, Strehler had Cordelia's arm swing lifelessly while Lear held her in his arms. He was trying to evoke the image of a broken puppet and had the light focus on her face to make it as bright as the white face of Lear at that moment. The purpose of this final tableau was to remind the audience of the relationship between Cordelia and the Fool, who were played by the same actress. The imagery was similar in *The Tempest* but the effect was the opposite. Rather than Ariel being broken when her strings were cut, she was liberated. The audience was elated when Prospero ultimately freed Ariel, but her flight to freedom was an earth-bound run, although a joyous one, through the stalls.

The power of authority was a thematic focus of *The Tempest*, just as it had been in *King Lear*, but escape from that authority was equated with maintaining the illusory world of the island, a place that the audience cherished. As was the case with so many elements of these two productions, the final sequences mirrored each other. Prospero was left alone on stage just as Lear had been. Both protagonists had come to the end of their voyage of enlightenment. Where the bleak stage environment of *King Lear* created a longing for the world outside of the circus ring, the *mise-en-scène* of *The Tempest* suggested that the world outside of the theatrically constructed island was far less inviting than the stage space, however flawed, that Strehler and his surrogate, Prospero, had constructed.

Moments prior to the final soliloquy, Prospero breaks his staff to represent his resolve to leave the island for good. When the staff broke, the entire set fell apart as well, pitching the stage, which had been lit with increasing brightness throughout the play, into semi-darkness. The final scene was the darkest in the production with the possible exception of the storm scene at the beginning. The darkness that was so pervasive in *King Lear* was always present in *The Tempest*, but it was always somewhere in the distance just at the edge of the expansive horizon that led away from the island. Conversely, light was always present in *King Lear* but only on the other side of the circus tent, blocked off from the characters and the audience. So, too, the reversal of light and dark in these two productions seem to correspond metaphorically. Where actual light seemed to represent spiritual enlightenment always just beyond Lear's living space, so the light of Prospero's island seemed to represent a superior quality to the real world of both Shakespeare's and 1970s Milan.

During the final soliloquy, Tino Carraro, the actor playing Prospero, walked out into the audience with his cloak removed and his entire demeanour suggesting the honest plea of the actor after a long performance asking to go home. Once 'Carraro' had asked the audience to let him return to his dukedom, however, his 'Prospero' voice returned, and Strehler answered Prospero's request on the audience's behalf by making Prospero return to the stage and having the island return to its former state. Tino Carraro was ostensibly returning to the stage in order to take his curtain call, but the image was also that of Prospero choosing the imaginary world of the island over the world of his dukedom in Milan. Since the Piccolo is itself located in Milan, Prospero's final recanting of his decision represented a rejection of the corruption of Milan.

Strehler's legacy

Strehler's productions of Shakespeare's plays challenged his creativity to such an extent that they stretched the potential of the old Piccolo to the limit. The construction of a new theatre and the Piccolo Teatro Studio in particular, became an inevitable coda to his long career. The Studio theatre is an extraordinary space, built to address the scenic limitations of the old Piccolo. The Piccolo Studio, designed under Strehler's supervision and completed in 1989, evokes the idealised 'wooden O' of Shakespeare's Globe but is such an all-encompassing circle that it feels like an appropriate space for Greek tragedy as well. Much more than a thrust stage, it is almost equivalent to an arena space. Added to this is a deep and wide proscenium space, allowing traditional, baroque renderings and hearkening back to the Italian Renaissance experiments in illusionist theatre. Five galleries stacked one on top of the other evoke the great opera houses of Italy and Germany. It is a space designed to represent all things to all theatregoers, yet has a remarkably warm and cohesive quality unlike generic, multi-purpose houses that feel utilitarian rather than exceptional.

Strehler kept a close rein on all aspects of his projects. He served as lighting designer for the majority of his productions and was an aggressive partner in all aspects the design process. Josef Svoboda (1920–2002), who collaborated with Strehler on a mammoth production of *Faust* in the 1990s, spoke of the quality of their working relationship:

> He is professional through and through. The level of his philosophical thinking is remarkable. He has great artistic, literary and musical feeling. In addition, he is a wonderful actor; after all, he played Faust in the production, which involved exacting performances from a directing and stage-designing point of view. With a partner like that it is possible to communicate with few words. We understood each other perfectly. I discovered a lot of things from him.
>
> (Svoboda 1992: 55)

Svoboda's phrase 'literary and musical feeling' was paraphrased by many of Strehler's collaborators.

His rehearsal process was unlike that of any other director. In many ways, his rhetoric and actual behaviour were contradictory. While the ethos of the Piccolo Teatro was ostensibly egalitarian, Strehler ran his rehearsals like a symphonic maestro conducting his actors like musicians in an orchestra and manipulating them physically in the manner of a choreographer. Indeed, he was used to directing opera, having worked frequently at La Scala and many of the other premier opera houses of Europe.

Visitors to his rehearsal hall were sometimes shocked to see specific line readings and physical instructions given to actors of the highest calibre and reputation. The leading actors of the company were loyal to him, however, and continued to work with him until his death. Giulia Lazzarini, who played Ariel in the second version of *The Tempest*, returned to play the character of the same name in Strehler's version of Goethe's *Faust* in the early 1990s. Although fifteen years had passed since she had put the flying harness on, she flew around the stage again when Strehler wanted to quote his own *mise-en-scène* for *The Tempest* in *Faust*. Similarly, Tino Carraro, who had played Lear and Prospero as well as major roles in Strindberg and Chekhov at the Piccolo, also made an appearance in *Faust* in a costume calculated to remind audiences of his past glories in Shakespearian productions. Giulia Lazzarini said working with Giorgio allowed her to be completely free in performance. She acknowledged that he was extremely precise in directing vocal and physical nuance but said that this specificity, paradoxically, allowed her to relax.

The maestro-like attention to physical gesture and vocal inflection was tempered by a willingness to experiment in rehearsal. During rehearsals for *King Lear*, for instance, he had the Fool shadow Lear, literally imitating his gestures throughout the denouement, after her final exit from the actual text. He encouraged actors to explore personal connections with characters and situations in the Stanislavsky–naturalism tradition, yet always built in a formal exit for the actor: a kind of escape from the role where they could distance themselves and allow the audience to critique what had happened. This formula of juxtaposing formal gesture, in Brecht's terms *gestus*, with naturalistic, empathetic characters, allowed actors to exhibit excesses in the emotive scenes that would have seemed self-indulgent in strictly realistic staging. It was this combination of techniques along with attention to the visual-design elements that led some critics to coin the term 'lyrical realism' to describe the Strehler style.

Work habits at the Piccolo were rigorous by Italian standards. Actors were rehearsed up to twice as many weeks as most other theatres and usually for nine hours a day. Rather than feeling constrained, or manipulated, most actors felt liberated by working under these conditions. They were allowed great freedom in many aspects of the rehearsal process even if Strehler became almost absurdly specific with final presentation. He said that the 'actor's effort is often subordinated to the activity of the director, but it shouldn't be' (Strehler 1989: 62). Ideally, the creative process of textual interpretation was a collective act to him, even if his powerful personality needed to assert itself eventually.

As Strehler's career wound down, the laurels piled up. He was elected to the European Parliament in 1982 and was appointed Senator to the Italian Republic in 1987. In 1989, he gave the convocation address at the University of Toronto in Ontario, Canada. During his lecture he posed the theoretical question, 'Who is the author of the staged performance? Who is the author of tonight's performance of *The Tempest*?' (Strehler 1989: 58). He spoke of translation and language in general as 'ideology'. 'When a work outlives its geographical and historical boundaries, the original author–audience relationship is severed immediately' (Strehler 1989: 60). He believed that it is the act of reassembling that lost relationship that constitutes authorship and that this activity is always a collective and ideological enterprise. Translators are, therefore, authors of the texts they publish, and directors and actors are coauthors of the texts they perform.

His own performance as Faust near the end of his career was marked with none of the precision he expected from actors under his command, but he had not been on the stage for decades. His shortcomings as a performer were irrelevant in the case of his Faust. The production was a series of fragments from Goethe's massive play translated by the director himself into Italian. *Faust* was more about Strehler than Goethe, and, as such, it quoted his greatest productions of Shakespeare. Perhaps knowing that he would die soon, he produced a play that could sum up his career and place his 'authoring' of Shakespeare at the summit.

Chronology

1947 Cofounder and Artistic Director of the Piccolo Teatro di Milano *Arlecchino servitore di due padroni*
1948 *Richard II*, *The Tempest*, *Romeo and Juliet*
1949 *The Taming of the Shrew*
1950 *Richard III*
1951 *Henry IV*, *Twelfth Night*
1952 *Macbeth*
1953 *Julius Caesar*
1956 *The Threepenny Opera*, *Coriolanus*
1965 *Il Gioco dei Potenti* (*Power Games*) based on *Henry VI* cycle
1972 *King Lear*
1973 *Il Gioco dei Potenti* (remounted in Salzburg)
1975 *Il Gioco dei Potenti* (remounted in Vienna)
1978 *The Tempest*
1982 Appointed Director of the Théâtre de L'Europe
1982 Elected to European Parliament
1987 Appointed Senator of the Italian Republic

Bibliography

Cohn, Ruby (1964) 'Sixteen Years of the Piccolo Teatro', *Tulane Drama Review*, 8(3): 27–49.

Colli, Gian Giacomo (2004) 'Shakespeare in a Fountain: The First Italian Production of *The Tempest* Directed by Giorgio Strehler in 1948', *Theatre Research International*, 29(2): 174–85.

Hirst, David (1993) *Giorgio Strehler*, Cambridge: Cambridge University Press.

Horowitz, Arthur (2004) *Prospero's 'True Preservers': Peter Brook, Yukio Ninagawa, and Giorgio Strehler. Twentieth-Century Directors' Approach to Shakespeare's The Tempest*, Newark, Del.: University of Delaware Press.

McManus, Donald C. (2003) 'Clown in Giorgio Strehler's Theater', in *No Kidding! Clown as Protagonist in Twentieth-Century Theater*, Newark, Del.: University of Delaware Press, pp. 90–108.

Strehler, Giorgio (1973) 'Appunti per la Regia', *Il Re Lear di Shakespeare*, Verona: Bertani, pp. 214–67.

—— (1974) *Per un teatro umano*, Milano: Feltrinelli.

—— (1989) *Incontro*, Toronto: Istituto Italiano di Cultura.

—— (2002) 'Notes on *The Tempest*', trans. Thomas Simpson, *PAJ 72 A Journal of Performance Art* 24(3): 1–17.

Svoboda, Josef (1992) 'Even a Disciplined Stage Designer Has His Dreams: An Interview', *Theatre Czech & Slovak*, 4: 54–80.

Trousdell, Richard (1986) 'Giorgio Strehler in Rehearsal', *The Drama Review* 30(4): 65–83.

About the author

Donald McManus is Assistant Professor of Theatre Studies at Emory University and Resident Artist at Theater Emory in Atlanta, Georgia. He was born and raised in Montreal, Quebec and has worked professionally as an actor, director, musician and clown in Canada, the USA, Asia and Europe. He studied theatre and Italian at the University of Toronto and received a doctorate in theatre studies from the University of Michigan, Ann Arbor. He attended staged readings by Giorgio Strehler of works by Dante and Shakespeare at the University of Toronto in 1989 and visited rehearsals and performances at the Piccolo Teatro di Milano in 1990 and 1991, where he interviewed members of the company about their experiences working under Strehler's direction. Dr McManus is also a translator and published the only English-language version of Eduardo De Filippo's first full-length play *Uomo e galantuomo* (*Man and Gentleman*) in *Forum Italicum* in 2001. His book *No Kidding! Clown as Protagonist in Twentieth-Century Theater* (2003) examines the pervasive use of clown in the works of major twentieth-century theatre artists and includes chapters on Giorgio Strehler and Bertolt Brecht.

27
JULIE TAYMOR

Douglas Lanier

Though the recipient of numerous theatre awards, a Guggenheim and a MacArthur 'genius' grant, Julie Taymor was not well known with general audiences until her extraordinary success as director of the musical theatre adaptation of *The Lion King* (1997), a production that introduced the American public to a number of avant-garde stage techniques and for which Taymor won two 1998 Tony awards: for best costume design and best direction. Welcome as popular recognition was for Taymor, it was rather belated, given that her distinguished career in American theatre extends back to the mid-1970s. Her productions include stage adaptations of novels and short stories (*The Transposed Heads*, from the novel by Thomas Mann, 1984; *Juan Darién*, from a story by Horacio Quiroga, 1988; *Fool's Fire*, from the story 'Hop Frog' by Edgar Allan Poe, 1992; the opera *Grendel*, from the novel by John Gardner, 2005), operas (Stravinsky's *Oedipus Rex*, 1992; Mozart's *The Magic Flute*, 1993, Wagner's *The Flying Dutchman*, 1995), original works (*Way of Snow*, 1974; *Liberty's Taken*, 1985), plays by Carlo Gozzi (*The King Stag*, 1984; *The Green Bird*, 1996), films (*Frida*, 2002; *Across the Universe*, 2007) and three well-regarded stage productions of Shakespeare, one of which has been reworked for film. Taymor's extensive œuvre was honoured by an exhibit at the National Museum of Women in the Arts in Washington, DC, in 2000. The catalogue for that exhibition, *Playing with Fire*, offers the most comprehensive overview of Taymor's work to date and is particularly valuable for Taymor's own reflections and reminiscences about her many stage and film productions. Because Taymor's career has been so varied, understanding her approaches to Shakespeare on stage and screen requires us to situate those productions in the context of a developing artistic sensibility marked by stylistic restlessness, daring eclecticism and an attraction to mythic storytelling.

A profoundly visual stage director, Taymor emphasises simple, bold stage images that show a general affinity with magic realism. Her costumes and set designs are often exaggerated and stylised, use striking contrasts in scale and evince a flair for totemic figures, surrealistic or fantastical juxtapositions and dark humour. Especially distinctive is her imaginative adaptation of mask and puppetry techniques drawn from a variety of world theatres, particularly non-Western ones. In the manner of postmodern pastiche, her work often mixes time frames, performance traditions and visual allusions taken from widely different sources. The use of cross-cultural allusions, freely adapted non-Western performance techniques and recurrent elemental symbols (fire, clay, water and food prime among them) give her stage productions the quality of mythic storytelling, a quality she has actively embraced and cultivated. With many other stage directors of the late twentieth century, she shares a self-conscious celebration of theatricality. For that reason, her works often foreground their ability to get maximal effect from a minimum of theatrical means and feature moments that bare their theatrical devices or encourage the audience's delight in unusual technique. Related to this quality is Taymor's interest in juxtaposing performer and prosthetic. She often allows, for example, the face or body of the actor to be seen beneath the mask or puppet, thereby enabling a simultaneously double performance, or she includes moments that involve transformation of a character represented by a mask or puppet into the flesh-and-blood actor. Thematically, Taymor is strongly attracted to material that explores the relationship between civilisation and the darker impulses – especially monstrosity and violence – that underlie or threaten it, issues that surface with particular force in her productions of *The Tempest* and *Titus Andronicus*. Taymor characteristically handles these themes with a degree of aesthetic stylisation, even grotesque beauty, an approach that has generated some controversy in reception of her Shakespearian productions.

Above all, Taymor's work is marked by her eclectic appropriation of design techniques and performance styles from an extraordinary range of sources – children's theatre, avant-garde theatre, director-theorists like Jerzy Grotowski, Jacques Lecoq and Herbert Blau, politically oriented designers like Peter Schumann of Bread and Puppet Theater, various Asian and Latin American theatrical traditions, European art film and opera among them – a list which reads like a compendium of influences upon contemporary Shakespeare production more generally. To understand the distinctive eclecticism of Taymor's Shakespeare productions, it is necessary to trace her early artistic education. Born in 1952 and, by all accounts, a precocious child, Taymor came of age in the political turbulence and artistic experimentalism of the 1960s, an era to which she pays extended homage in her film musical *Across the Universe*. Though Taymor is now renowned for her facility with non-Western performance techniques, her earliest experiences with the theatre as a child in a suburb of Boston, Massachusetts involved Shakespeare. The first live performance she recalls attending was of *A Midsummer Night's Dream* when she was six or seven, and by the age of nine she had played the part of Hermia in a production by the Children's Theatre Company of Boston. In her teen years, she became the youngest member of the Theater Workshop, an experimental company based in Boston influenced by Grotowski's ideas of 'poor theatre'. Taymor credits her experience in the Theater Workshop with giving her 'a very early understanding of how to be a creative theatermaker – a theater-maker, as opposed to a playwright or an actor' (Gold 1998: 21). Taymor's interest in world cultures developed alongside her early professional experience in the theatre. As a high-school student, Taymor participated in a summer exchange programme in Sri Lanka through the Experiment in International Living. The connection between theatre and an internationalist, particularly non-Western, sensibility would be a prominent theme in Taymor's subsequent work.

Graduating from high school early, Taymor left the USA in 1969 to study mime with Jacques Lecoq in Paris for a year. Lecoq's emphasis upon the body rather than the face as the primary instrument for visualising emotions and abstract qualities was particularly influential upon Taymor's developing aesthetic. At Lecoq's École de Mime, Taymor was also first awakened to the expressive possibilities of masks and puppetry and was introduced to performance techniques that owed much to the then-current vogue in Asian, particularly Japanese, stage traditions. Her work with Madame Renée Citron on puppets initiated Taymor into the dialectic between puppet or mask and actor that has since become one of her thematic hallmarks. As Taymor puts it, 'Madame Citron animated objects, so it was really about mime, about understanding shape, form, and substance [. . .] you can really put life into inanimate objects. That's the magic of puppetry. You *know* it's dead and therefore you're giving it a soul, a life' (Schechner 1999: 37). It was also in Paris that Taymor first encountered the films of Fellini, a important touchstone for her film *Titus*. In 1970, Taymor returned to the USA to attend Oberlin College. Her self-designed major in folklore and mythology reveals her continuing interest in the intersection between non-Western cultures and theatrical practice: 'I was always kind of moving toward being an anthropologist. I loved to study the culture of other people, and that included religion and theatre, and the origins of theatre in shamanism. That provided a very good basis for the kind of work I've done since' (Gold 1998: 22). Oberlin enabled Taymor to pursue some of her studies off-campus as an apprentice with Peter Schumann's Bread and Puppet Theatre in New York, a company whose work she had first seen in Boston as a youngster. Under Schumann's mentorship, she deepened her interest in puppetry and honed her skills in sculpting and design, and Schumann's experiments with large-scale puppets seem also to have sensitised Taymor to the theatrical possibilities of spectacular contrasts in scale. Perhaps most important, Schumann encouraged her to develop her own eclectic approach, independent of commitment to an ideological programme.

Upon her return to Oberlin, Taymor joined Kraken, the theatre company Herbert Blau founded at the college in 1972. Blau's performance techniques and philosophy provided Taymor, so she has repeatedly claimed, with one of the central foundational principles of her own practice, the 'ideograph'. The ideograph is an immediately apprehensible emblematic stage image, a simple movement or gesture that epitomises the central concept or emotion of a work. Taymor describes it as 'an essence, an abstraction [. . .] boiling [an idea] right down to the most essential two, three brush strokes [. . .], one beautiful, little, sculptural, kinetic move' (Schechner 1999: 38–9). Her brush painting metaphor underlines the fundamentally visual nature of the ideograph and its close kinship with Asian artistic traditions. Taymor's drive to capture the gist of a character's manner, a narrative moment or a theme in a single, simple, concentrated stage image is central to her methods for developing a visual style for a production and lending it a mythic, iconic quality. Of her creative process for developing her 1982 production of Christopher Hampton's *Savages*, she notes that 'in ideographing the gestures for each of the figures and eliminating extraneous movement, I looked for what was the most minimal action to express the essence of the moment in time' (Taymor and Blumenthal 1999: 82). In practice, the ideograph serves as a means through which Taymor and her actors can identify in bodily form the thematic and characterological fundamentals of a production. Ideographs, Taymor has stressed in interviews, need not appear in the final productions, but where they do, they often function like musical motifs, as does the circle of life motif in *The Lion King*, an ideograph that signifies at once the life cycle, the cycle of revenge and the ritual space within which ancient theatre occurs.

From the mid- to late 1970s, Taymor's immersion in Asian theatrical traditions would be considerably expanded. As part of her preparation for writing her senior thesis on Indonesian *wayang kulit* (shadow puppetry) and masked dance, Taymor attended a summer programme in Seattle under the sponsorship of the American Society for Eastern Arts, her first direct contact with Asian performance techniques. After her graduation, a Watson Fellowship enabled her to study 'visually oriented theatre as well as experimental and traditional puppetry' in Indonesia, Japan and eastern Europe for a year (Taymor and Blumenthal 1999: 13). Upon arriving in Indonesia, however, she became so enamoured of the culture that she spent almost all of the next four years in Java and Bali, eventually forming her own multicultural theatre company – Teatr Loh – and creating her first original plays, *Way of Snow*

(1974) and *Tirai* (1978). Taymor's four-year Indonesian experience introduced her to native performance techniques and iconographies, including *wayang kulit*, which she has used in several subsequent works. A brief sojourn to Japan during this period allowed Taymor to study Noh theatre and *bunraku* puppetry, the latter of which she showcased in her production of *The Tempest*. But her work in Indonesia may have 'shaped her working process and artistic philosophy more profoundly than it did her visual style' (Struve-Dencher (n.d.) 10). In chronicling her experiences with Teatr Loh, Taymor speaks not only of the exhilarating vitality of the Indonesian arts and the central place of ritual and theatre in community life but also of her own difficulties in navigating barriers of language, gender, race, nationality, collaborative styles and artistic philosophy in a multicultural troupe and culturally diverse audiences (see Taymor 1979). Of her *Tirai*, for example, Taymor reports that 'the Javanese thought the play to be about Bali, the Balinese thought the play to be Javanese, the Sumatrans thought the play to be about somewhere else, and the Westerners thought the play to be about Indonesia as a universal model for other cultures' (Taymor 1979: 73). The perils of specific cultural references may have reinforced Taymor's penchant for blending allusions to performance styles from disparate cultures rather than remaining rigorously faithful to her sources. Such an approach stresses the inclusively communal ideals of her theatre, her desire to create stage spectacles with transcultural and mythic resonance. Such ideals have been the hallmark of her many contributions to American theatre since returning to the USA in 1979. Not least among Taymor's influences has been noted film score and orchestral composer Elliot Goldenthal, whom she met in 1980. Besides becoming life partners, the two have collaborated on a number of projects, including his 2006 opera *Grendel*; Goldenthal has supplied the music for all of her Shakespeare-related projects. Goldenthal's score for the film *Titus* provides a good example of his musical idiom, which is characterised by dense textures, minimalist patterning, expressive use of dissonance and Stravinsky-like rhythms and allusions to disparate musical genres whose clash mirrors the postmodern collision of styles in Taymor's visual design.

Taymor's interests in arresting ideographic visuals, masks and puppetry, free adaptation of world performance traditions and mythic storytelling inform her approach to staging Shakespeare. Although Taymor worked as a designer for Amy Saltz's 1984 production of *A Midsummer Night's Dream* at New York's Public Theatre, her stature as a Shakespearian director rests upon three productions for the stage – *The Tempest* (1986), *The Taming of the Shrew* (1988) and *Titus Andronicus* (1994) – as well as her film *Titus* (1999), based upon her stage production. All of Taymor's Shakespearian stage productions have been for the New York-based Theatre for a New Audience, a company founded by Jeffrey Horowitz and committed to bringing classical theatre to ethnically and economically diverse New York audiences not typically reached by professional stage performances. The production's visual design for *The Tempest* pared down scenery to bare essences. (G.W. Mercier, a collaborator with Taymor on several projects, is credited with the set and costume design and Taymor with puppetry and masks, though Taymor's comments in interviews suggest she is a hands-on designer of all aspects of her productions.) To indicate Prospero's island, the steeply raked stage was covered with black sand; above the horizon line was a white fabric panel lit with bold primary colours to indicate changes of scenes or moods, a technique that allowed for silhouetting of characters at key moments. Forms of magic in the production were realised through various techniques freely adapted from Asian theatre. For the play's visual prologue, Prospero drew a magic circle in the sand to conjure the storm; at the same time, on the horizon above him to the left, Miranda sat before a small sand castle. Two figures clad entirely in black appeared and poured water from watering cans in front of Prospero and Miranda, spotlights emphasising the shimmering water. In Prospero's case, the water served to cleanse him in preparation for his magic ritual; in Miranda's, it led to the destruction of her castle. Throughout this sequence, a puppet of a ship mounted on a pole slowly travelled across the horizon towards Miranda. When Prospero conjured the storm with his magic staff, a shadow of the ship puppet was projected onto a billowing sail, while the ship's passengers acted out their travails in front of it. At the end of the scene, the sail dropped away and the ship puppet burst into flame, signifying its wreck. This prologue established a subtle and somewhat ambivalent analogy between Prospero, whom she characterises as 'the master puppeteer, the stage director' (Taymor and Blumenthal 1999: 115), and Taymor herself, the woman director, an analogy that surfaced at several moments in the production. This prologue also aptly exemplified Taymor's interest in contrasts in scale – we see versions of the same events in two scales at once. Taymor characterised this opening sequence as an ideograph of the production's key theme, 'the conflict between nature and nurture' (Taymor and Blumenthal 1999: 118). Puppetry figured throughout the production. For the masque of Ceres and Juno, white puppets on poles, one a huge stylised figure with articulated arms in a Prospero-like robe, the other a smaller version with a streamer body, were seen from behind a black scrim lit from the front with dots of light, so that both figures seemed to be made of stars in a night sky. When Prospero punished Caliban, Trinculo and Stephano for pilfering, the three were chased by canine spirits represented by huge red dog heads and long silk streamers, rendered in vaguely Asian style and mounted on poles.

Taymor's most innovative use of puppetry came with her handling of Ariel.

Ariel was represented by a stylised white oval face mask and white silk streamers; the mask, held in the hand and not worn on the face, was manipulated *bunraku*-style by an actor clad entirely in black except for a white hand-glove which gave the disembodied spirit an additional means of expression. Taymor intended for the face to be 'androgynous and non-characterological, in the manner of Eskimo and African masks' (Taymor and Blumenthal 1999: 123). Its expression – one eye open, one closed – suggested Ariel's mythic duality, poised between the waking and dream worlds. The mask allowed for simple but powerful effects. When Prospero quarrelled with Ariel in Act I, Scene 2 over his demand for freedom, the magician took the face-mask from the puppeteer and held it out of reach, momentarily rendering the puppeteer helpless and immobile and leaving her resembling a blasted tree stump. Taymor's approach to the island's other native inhabitant, Caliban, and his compatriots Stephano and Trinculo, also involved masks. Caliban entered the play by emerging from the sand, an indication of his association with the element of earth but also a reminder of his birth as Sycorax's demonic spawn emerging from the underworld. Clad only in a loin cloth, his body was covered with white clay, and, most strikingly, his head was entirely encased in a crude stone mask reminiscent of the face-masks of Japanese *haniwa* effigies or New Guinea 'mudmen', a rough-hewn block with nothing more than expressionless holes for eyes, mouth and ears. The idea for Caliban's mask, Taymor explained, sprang from his complaint to Prospero, 'here you sty me / In this hard rock' (Act I, Scene 2, lines 342–3), but the mask also served to literalise Caliban's primitive nature as 'a freckled whelp, hagborn – not honoured / With a human shape' (Act I, Scene 2, line 283–4), and for the play's first half it made Caliban resemble a living, life-size, dehumanised puppet. Stephano and Trinculo were also fitted with partial face-masks that matched their exaggerated *commedia dell'arte* costuming, and both roles were played by actors associated with clowning.

Though the production nodded in the direction of colonialist readings of *The Tempest* by casting the troupe's only black actor as Caliban and giving him a Caribbean accent, the imperialist and racial politics of the play remained largely unexplored. So too Prospero's relationships with Miranda and Ferdinand (whom the reviewers uniformly saw as overly conventional lovers) and with the marooned Neapolitans (a reviewer for *The Village Voice* dubbed them 'playing-card royalty'). Rather, Taymor focused the production on Prospero's spectacular feats of magic and on his island's native inhabitants, both of whom serve as the magician's puppets. Dressed in a muslin robe and with a head of long, wild grey hair, Robert Stettel's Prospero had the bearing of an ancient magus, resembling Charlton Heston's Moses *sans* beard. Because Prospero was portrayed as all-powerful, with minimal qualms about his powers, the freeing of Caliban and Ariel from the bonds of puppetry took on particular significance. Caliban's release came in Act II, Scene 2, when Trinculo and Stephano convinced him they will overthrow Prospero. At this, he bashed the stone mask open with one of the logs Prospero forced him to carry, fastened the fragments to his loin cloth as totems of enslavement and then sang his freedom song. At play's end, chastened by Prospero, Caliban, kneeling at his feet, offered to place a piece of the mask back onto his face, resuming his status as puppet; Prospero's forgiveness came in the form of gently rejecting that gesture (Taymor and Blumenthal 1999: 122). His release of Ariel was even more metatheatrically resonant, for Prospero freed his servant by laying the Ariel mask on the sand and removing the black veil from the kneeling actor before him who had played Ariel's part throughout. Her face now revealed for the first time, the actor beamed with joy, acknowledged the presence of the spectators and theatre, then strode wordlessly through the audience and out of the performance space, breaking the dramatic illusion and thereby slipping free of Prospero's power. Prospero then repeated this gesture for himself. When he broke his staff moments later, the house lights immediately came up, shattering the theatrical spell. Dominating the largely positive reviews of the production was praise for its 'lovely effects' (*Village Voice*, 18 March 1986: 90) and 'visual delights' (*Shakespeare Bulletin*, July/August 1986: 18) and emphasis upon 'the play's kind, healing spirit' (*New York Times*, 27 March 1986: C15). In 1987, the production was remounted at the American Shakespeare Festival in Stratford, Connecticut.

Taymor's next Shakespeare project, *The Taming of the Shrew* (1988), was a conscious departure, for it is one of her few productions in which none of the characters used stage prosthetics. Taymor left much of the design to others and, indeed, the only puppet was Petruchio's horse, a giant wicker hobby-horse on wheels. Her directorial approach was decidedly language-oriented rather than visually oriented. Taymor has said that her impetus for the project was to direct 'an "actor's play" ', to take an approach that was 'very physical, that wouldn't utilize masks or puppets – at least not literally' (*Boston Phoenix*, 29 April 1988: 3, 7); perhaps also influential was the fact that she had performed in a production of *The Taming of the Shrew* while a college student. Inspiration for costuming came from Breughel and Bosch, in part, Taymor stressed, to situate the action firmly in early modernity where patriarchal assumptions held firm. The primary set was a haystack which converted into an oversized gazebo, which allowing for easy transition between the induction and the main action. Uncharacteristically for a Taymor production, the points of cultural reference for the design were fairly self-consistent and decidedly western European. Emphasis fell rather upon character relationships, particularly that of Petruchio and Katherine.

Taymor eschewed both the misogyny of the whip-cracking shrew-taming and the farce of the mating-of-madcaps approaches to the play. Instead, she conceived of Petruchio as an unconventional gentleman – one reviewer calls him a 'shrewd, swashbuckling shrink' (*Boston Phoenix*, 29 April 1988: 7) – who undertook only to mirror Kate's antisocial behaviour back to her and insisted quite sincerely that he does all for her comfort. Kate's shrewishness sprang from her needy desire for love, and her relationship with Petruchio liberated her into an partnership with a man of equal intellectual fire. In the couple's first encounter in Act II, Scene 2, Taymor stressed not the physical violence or bawdiness but the erotic excitement of the two's intellectual thrust and parry as Kate and Petruchio discover an equal partner: it was 'as much a chess game and mating dance as it is a male-female bethrottlement' (*Boston Phoenix*, 29 April 1988: 8). Observes one reviewer, from Petruchio Kate learns 'how to arrange a mask to shield her most private needs from public scrutiny, at the same time that she learns to appreciate her husband's qualities' (*Shakespeare Bulletin*, May/June 1988: 9). The production's turning point comes when Kate begins to collude with Petruchio in lampooning Vincentio in Act IV, Scene 5. Their relationship thereafter comes to turn on a conspiratorial alliance based upon their shared wittiness, delight in game-playing and anti-conventionality. As for the other characters, Taymor singled out their stultifying propriety: 'Half of the characters in *Shrew* are dominated by the bourgeois, petty society, concerned with flirtations and traditional male-female roles [. . .] I asked the actors to create a "mask" for these characters without actually wearing one. Juxtaposed against this stylized world are Kate and Petruchio.' (Taymor and Blumenthal 1999: 127).

As Taymor's description suggests, notions of the social mask and of Kate and Petruchio's shared theatricality dominated her conception of the play, and so, despite its lack of visual fireworks, the production does in fact accord with her abiding thematic interests. Nowhere was this more so than with the handling of Kate's final speech. She delivered it from atop a banquet table, magnifying its quality as a stage performance, and though she offered her pronouncement about female submissiveness earnestly, it was filled with private sneers at those gathered, particularly her sister Bianca. When Kate turned to Petruchio to place her hand beneath his foot, she gave him a long, knowing, joyful look that signified their private understanding of the moment – it was not so much a public taming (as the banqueters clearly understood it) as a clever, multilayered performance offered to him alone. 'She was willing to play the woman', Taymor claims, 'much as it might hurt her pride, because she loved him. The gesture was grand, and it moved him' (Taymor and Blumenthal 1999: 128). The speech thereby exemplified Taymor's penchant for 'double performance', where the audience was invited both to experience the stage event and to appreciate the exposure of its theatricality.

Heightening that quality of double performance was Taymor's choice to retain the play's induction. Instead of stressing the farcical or violent continuities between the induction and main action, Taymor stressed their contrast. Unlike Petruchio, Christopher Sly was a drunken, raucous lout who, transformed into a lord, awakened in a bathtub filled with suds, a preposterously literal version of ritual cleansing. The acting style of the induction was comically broad, even cartoonish, punctuated with slapstick sequences and goofy cross-dressing gags. When, for example, Sly chased the broad-shouldered page who pretended to be his lady around the room, she defended herself by throwing at him the apples that filled out his/her costume's bodice. Periodically, Sly and his companions would reappear in the audience to remind spectators of the theatrical frame, and at play's end Sly walked back onstage as the characters froze in place, as if to underline that he could never enter their world. By stressing the comical stylisation of the induction, Taymor highlighted the earnest psychological naturalism of her approach to Kate and Petruchio's developing romance. Perhaps for that reason, reviewers saw the production as 'uncompromising, unsullied, and unsouped-up' (*Boston Phoenix*, 22 April 1988: 8), 'direct, sound, unfussy, and well acted' (*New York Post*, 14 March 1988: 28), and 'workmanlike [with] no strong political viewpoint' (*New York Times*, 16 February 1988: 25). One reviewer perceptively argued that Taymor's approach allowed the production 'to have the play every which way' – as 'love match', 'taming', 'male chauvinist tract', and 'feminist tract' – 'without any sacrifice of fun, without the pain some of us experience when fun is had at someone's expense' (*Shakespeare Bulletin*, May/June 1988: 9). The production also had a brief run in Beverly, Massachusetts at the North Shore Music Theatre.

Taymor's most ambitious and provocative Shakespearian production has been *Titus Andronicus*, first produced in 1994 for the Theatre for a New Audience in New York and reworked for the screen in 1999. Taymor reshaped Shakespeare's notoriously bloody Senecan tragedy into a disturbing commentary on cycles of violence and on the act of viewing violence as entertainment. Her focus fell particularly on Titus and Aaron who, she argues, changed positions in the course of the play: whereas Aaron, fuelled by his racial victimisation, moves from frighteningly gleeful malevolence to fatherly tenderness for his son, Titus moves from paternalistic devotion to Rome and his children to appallingly cruel revenge against Tamora and her sons (Johnson-Haddad 2000: 36). To underscore the historical pervasiveness of her central concerns, the production design intermixed iconographies from several imperial civilisations – ancient Rome, Fascist Italy, 1950s America. Costuming was dictated by developing personalities within the narrative rather than chronological consistency. In the course of the stage production, Titus was garbed as a series of archetypes: a Roman centurion, a dapper general in an Eisenhower jacket, a kindly grandfather in grey cardigan and plaid shirt, a madman in a bathrobe and a pastry chef. Tamora dressed like a 1930s blueblood (out of Visconti's *The Damned*, notes Taymor), whereas Lavinia appeared early on in 1950s *haute couture* and later in bloodied chiffon. The stage set was dominated by grainy blown-up reproductions of ancient Roman columns which operated as movable flats and a deliberately battered, ink-smeared back screen on which photos of Roman settings were projected. These roughed-up photographic elements were calculated to remind the audience of 'the weight of history' (Taymor and Blumenthal 1999: 192), as well as of reproduction itself, associating it with its own kind of distorting violence. Central to the set was a 1950s-style formica-and-chrome kitchen table which signified itself in the opening sequence but later on functioned as a sacrificial altar and banquet table. A bathtub was equally multifunctional, serving as a place of cleansing for the soldiers, the pit into which Bassanius is cast and Titus' personal bath. The palette was pared down to black, white, red and blue, 'the colors of the veins beneath our skin' (Taymor and Blumenthal 1999: 192).

Given Taymor's desire to use *Titus Andronicus* to interrogate the West's long-lived culture of violence, the question of how to stage the play's many murders and mutilations posed a special challenge. Instead of choosing between theatrical stylisation and graphic realism, Taymor used different styles at different moments, juxtaposing each against the other to complicate the audience's response. In the play's opening scenes, the violence was ritualised. Titus' army entered the play, for example, in a slow synchronised march, as if a squadron of automatons; they were dressed in black battle regalia, with one hand of each soldier encased in a bayonet, in grimly ironic anticipation of Titus' severed hand to come. The mechanical, inhuman quality of these soldiers visually established the rigid mercilessness of Roman militarism that Titus then pursued in his killing of Alarbus and Mutius. Later scenes were increasingly graphic. The mutilation of Lavinia was both horrifying and abstract at once: when Marcus discovers her, she stands in agony in a blood-spattered petticoat atop a pedestal, mortified and quivering, unable to move, a spectacle presented to his and the audience's gaze. She wore black gloves, the fingers of which were mere twigs, a grotesque reminder of her lost limbs and an oblique allusion to the Ovidian tale of Philomele, Shakespeare's mythic source for Lavinia's story. In Act II, Scene 3, Aaron cut off Titus' hand with a jackknife, with all the gruesome bloodiness and pain in full audience view, and the head of Titus's sons were returned to him, like grotesque lab specimens, in large glass jars, one of which Titus carried under his arm as he delivered his vow of revenge. Particularly unnerving was the murder of Chiron and Demetrius, for the two were strapped upside down on operating tables, fully exposed to the audience as Titus summarily slit their throats. Even the final banquet scene offered a juxtaposition of modes. After Titus suddenly snapped Lavinia's neck and again after Lucius dispatched Saturninus with a gunshot, several dinner guests at the table mechanically raised their glasses in a bizarre synchronised toast, an echo of the automatonic entrance of Titus' army which both distanced the spectator from the horrors and reflected sardonically upon that distance.

Taymor made two large additions to the play, both addressed to the dual issues of violence and spectatorship. First and most controversial were what Taymor called 'penny arcade nightmares' (PANs), five brief surrealistic spectacles interpolated into the action at key moments. These sequences used Taymor's trademark puppetry to literalise Shakespeare's poetic imagery in the play, but they also often portrayed acts or aftermaths of violence that Shakespeare did not depict onstage. For example, in the second PAN, inserted between Act II, Scenes 2 and 3, Lavinia, apparelled in a doe headdress and ripped petticoat and standing on a pedestal, was ritualistically assaulted by Chiron and Demetrius manipulating lifesize tiger puppets. Though this sequence presented a stylised vision of Lavinia's rape, it also drew attention to the sequence as theatrical spectacle, for it, like each of the PANs, was presented within a gold frame – a miniature proscenium – with crimson curtains that parted to reveal the vignette. Elliot Goldenthal's dissonant carnival music lent this moment the unsettling quality of a freak show, and a distressed, bespattered plastic scrim between audience and actors reminiscent of a television screen reminded spectators once again of the distorting violence of representation. As the play progressed, the PANs became more integrated into the main action, so that the fifth PAN – the appearance of Tamora and her sons as Revenge, Rape and Murder – was treated not as a narrative digression but as Titus' nightmarish fantasy of revenge which he hallucinates as he bathes in his tub, a visual allusion to David's *Death of Marat*. The play's horrifying final banquet became, in effect, the culminating PAN, for the entire scene was set within a giant gold frame emphasised by footlights. As Taymor suggests, 'suddenly the entire play was a Penny Arcade Nightmare' under Titus' direction (Taymor and Blumenthal 1999: 190). This framing at once stylised the pile-up of revenge killings that end the play and reminded the audience of their uncomfortable roles as consumers of violent spectacle.

Taymor's second addition was of a framing character, a modern boy who watched the events at hand and played the role of young Lucius. He figured strongly in the play's visual prologue and final scene. As the production opened, the boy, dressed in a homemade paper-bag mask, played with toy soldiers at the kitchen table. A collage of cartoon sounds identified the cultural catalyst for the boy's increasingly frenetic abandon: contemporary media violence. As his play reached fever pitch, Titus' army marched onto the stage, their faces in black masks dimly reminiscent of the boy's. In effect, his toy soldiers have become real, and the boy was thereafter swept into the drama's action as the character Lucius. In the course of the play, the boy moved from an initial delight in violence to observation of its escalating consequences and barbarism. The fruits of that observation were made clear at play's end. After Aaron received his death sentence from Marcus, the boy focused his gaze upon a small black coffin, representing Aaron's doomed son. As the lights faded, he placed his hand on the coffin in a gesture of compassion for the innocent child victims of this cycle of revenge, a gesture that reached across boundaries of race and nation and measured the distance the boy had travelled since the opening scene. Mingled sounds of shrieking birds and crying babies reminded the boy (and the audience for which he was surrogate) of the persistence of violence and of the pain its innocent victims continue to suffer.

Critics have often remarked upon the cinematic qualities of Taymor's production style, and so it is understandable that she would want to transfer the production to the screen with *Titus* (1999), her first feature film. (In interviews, Taymor has repeatedly articulated her desire to preserve her most ambitious or successful stage productions on celluloid.) *Titus* followed the design of her stage production remarkably closely, using the resources of the film medium to extend her iconography and interpolations in several ways. The iconography of her PANs remains generally the same, though the style shifts to surreal, computer-graphic montages. Myriad images of a she-wolf, ironic reminders of Rome's legend of Romulus and Remus, appear throughout, most notably above Saturninus' throne. Shooting on location allowed Taymor to include monumental architecture of the recent and ancient past, retaining her mix of time periods. A Roman-style coliseum frames the film, emphasising Taymor's central theme of violence as entertainment – it is there that Titus' army first enters and there that young Lucius witnesses Aaron being condemned. Saturninus' and Bassianus' vying for power in Act I, Scene 1 takes place before the Esposizione Universale Roma, Mussolini's governmental headquarters, with characters dressed in a jarring jumble of antique and modern dress. Ruins of ancient Rome and fragments of statuary appear in many scenes, most notably when Titus begs for the lives of Quintus and Martius as they are taken to execution; this scene is set on a bleak deserted crossroads dotted with ruins, an ideograph for Titus' isolation and desolate state. Taymor situates the revelation of Lavinia's mutilation, one of the most surrealistic and disturbing scenes in the film, in a swamp littered with broken branches. Lavinia stands not on a pedestal but on a tree stump, and in an effects shot at once horrifying in its realism and yet eerily artistic, her hands appear to have been replaced by black twigs.

Nevertheless, Taymor does make several changes for her film version. In part as a concession to the practical needs of cinematic realism, after her mutilation Lavinia is fitted with carved hands which young Lucius, out of compassion for her, procures in a woodworker's shop. The change lends her the quality of a broken doll. Stylistic allusions to Italian cinema abound, especially to Fellini's *Satyricon* in scenes of Saturninus's decadent court. Her casting of Anthony Hopkins in the title role (Robert Stettel played Titus in the stage version) brings into play memories of his portrayal of Hannibal Lecter in *The Silence of the Lambs*, which figure strongly in the film's last third. Indeed, many of the most significant changes are concentrated on the final banquet scene and epilogue. Taymor particularly accentuates the scene's black humour. The banquet is visually prefaced by a shot of pies cooling in an idyllic kitchen, and Hopkins plays Titus as a goofy gourmet chef who relishes the black wit of his cruel surprise. In this version, Lavinia kills herself with a knife, and the succession of murders ends with a 'bullet-time' effect reminiscent of *The Matrix*, connecting the sequence to contemporary spectacles of media violence. When the camera pulls back from the banquet table, we discover that it is in the middle of the coliseum where the narrative began, though this time the coliseum is filled with ghostly spectators who witness Aaron's condemnation and, it is implied, the entire cycle of revenge we've just seen. In this version, young Lucius retrieves Aaron's son from a tiny cage and carries him out of the coliseum towards a just-breaking sunrise, the film slowing into a still before he can fully exit.

Titus brought wider attention to Taymor's Shakespearian productions among critics and, with it, considerable debate. Her interpolated ending has proved one of the film's more controversial elements. Some have praised this gesture of hope, particularly in the context of the coliseum's actual location in strife-ridden Croatia; others have seen it as a betrayal of the production's critique of media violence, little more than a tacked-on Hollywood happy ending. The other major critical controversy surrounding the film has concerned its stylised approach to portraying violence. The largely positive reviews of the stage production consistently dubbed it 'grand Guignol', a phrase which testifies to the tension between horror at the bloody effects and fascination with their theatrical aestheticisation. More mixed responses to the film suggest that this tension was heightened by the cinematic medium and by Taymor's changes. Some writers have argued that Taymor's critique of spectatorship was blunted by the very different horizon of reception associated with film (McCandless 2002), that her evocation of fascist iconography 'depoliticizes violence and universalizes the Holocaust' (Burt 2001: 100), or that her focus on Titus and Aaron minimises Lavinia's too-stylised suffering (Aebischer 2002). Others have offered spirited defences of Taymor's strategies, detailing in depth her problematising of the psychology of horror film spectatorship (Starks 2002), analysing Lucius' function as interpolated spectator (Cartelli 2005), stressing the Brechtian effect of Taymor's ritualisation of violence (Hopkins 2003), or noting her sensitivity to the plight of the 'other' (Vaughan 2003). By contrast, journalistic reviews, while generally respectful of the film's ambitions, suggest that it is Taymor's postmodern violations of cinematic realism rather than her treatment of violence that pose the greatest challenge for popular audiences. Despite these debates, reviewers agree that *Titus* is a major achievement and has done much to raise the stature of Shakespeare's much denigrated early tragedy.

Taymor's accomplishment as a Shakespearian director is considerable. Her skill in crafting powerful, visually beautiful or grotesque ideographs is a distinctive feature of her approach. So too is her eclectic appropriation of theatrical styles from a variety of world traditions and her fascination with ritual and stylisation, elements she shares with another noteworthy Shakespearian director and pupil of Jacques Lecoq, Ariane Mnouchkine. Taymor's interest in masks and puppetry, both as stage techniques and as themes, are typical of her work. By regularly including elements of self-reflexivity and 'double performance' in her productions, Taymor encourages a sophisticated engagement with issues of spectatorship and theatricality, yet she tends to shy away from Brechtian critical distantiation in favour of making more positive thematic statements, particularly in the endings of her Shakespeare productions. Perhaps most important, her central concern with the power of performance and ritual gives her work a mythic sensibility unusual for postmodern directors.

Chronology

1984 *A Midsummer Night's Dream*, Theatre for a New Audience, New York City
1986 *The Tempest*, Theatre for a New Audience, New York City
1988 *The Taming of the Shrew*, Theatre for a New Audience, Beverly, Mass. and New York City
1994 *Titus Andronicus*, Theatre for a New Audience, New York City
1999 *Titus*, Fox Searchlight Productions

Bibliography

Aebischer, Pascale (2002) 'Women Filming Rape in Shakespeare's *Titus Andronicus*: Jane Howell and Julie Taymor', *Études Anglaises* 55(2): 136–47.

Burt, Richard (2001) 'Shakespeare and the Holocaust: Julie Taymor's *Titus* is Beautiful, or Shakesploi Meets (the) Camp', *Colby Quarterly* 37(1): 78–106.

Cartelli, Thomas (2005) 'Taymor's *Titus* in Time and Space: Surrogation and Interpolation', *Renaissance Drama* n.s. (34): 163–84.

DeLuca, Maria and Mary Lindroth (2000) 'Mayhem, Madness, Method: An Interview with Julie Taymor', *Cineaste* 25(3): 28–31.

Ellis, Hazel 'Shakespeare's Sister: Julie Taymor Talks about *Titus*', Reel.com, available online at <http://www.reel.com/reel.asp?node=features/interviews/taymor> (Accessed 21 September 2007).

Gold, Sylviane (1998) 'The Possession of Julie Taymor', *American Theatre* 15(7): 20–5.

Hopkins, Lisa (2003) ' "A Tiger's Heart Wrapped in a Player's Hide": Julie Taymor's War Dances', *Shakespeare Bulletin* 21(3): 61–9.

Johnson-Haddad, Miranda (2000) 'A Time for *Titus*: An Interview with Julie Taymor', *Shakespeare Bulletin* 18(6): 34–6.

Academy of Achievement (2006) 'Julie Taymor Interview' *Academy of Achievement* website, available online at <http://www.achievement.org/autodoc/page/tay0int-1> (Accessed 21 September 2007.).

McCandless, David (2002) 'A Tale of Two *Tituses*: Julie Taymor's Vision on Stage and Screen', *Shakespeare Quarterly* 53(4): 487–511.

Pizzello, Stephen (2000) 'From Stage to Screen: Interview with Julie Taymor', *American Cinematographer* 81(2): 64–73.

Schechner, Richard (1999) 'Julie Taymor: From Jacques Lecoq to "The Lion King": An Interview', *The Drama Review* 43(3): 36–55.

Starks, Lisa S. (2002) 'Cinema of Cruelty: Powers of Horror in Julie Taymor's *Titus*', in Lisa S. Starks and Courtney Lehmann (eds) *The Reel Shakespeare: Alternative Cinema and Theory*, Madison, NJ: Fairleigh Dickinson University Press, pp. 121–42.

Struve-Dencher, Goesta (n.d.) ' "Theater is my Skin": Tracing Julie Taymor's Creative Ethos', available online at <http://goestas.com/files/ideas/misc/taymor.pdf> (Accessed 21 September 2007.).

Taymor, Julie (1979) 'Teatr Loh, Indonesia, 1977–8', *The Drama Review* 23(2): 63–76.

Taymor, Julie (2000) *Titus: An Illustrated Screenplay*, New York: Newmarket Press.

Taymor, Julie and Eileen Blumenthal (1999) *Julie Taymor: Playing with Fire*, New York: Harry N. Abrams.

Vaughan, Virginia Mason (2003) 'Looking at the "Other" in Julie Taymor's *Titus*', *Shakespeare Bulletin* 21(3): 71–80.

Wrathall, John (2001) '*Titus*: Bloody Arcades. John Wrathall Talks with Julie Taymor', in Ginette Vincendeau (ed.) *Film / Literature / Heritage: A Sight and Sound Reader* London: BFI, pp. 125–9.

About the author

Douglas Lanier is Professor of English at the University of New Hampshire. His publications include *Shakespeare and Modern Popular Culture* (2002), as well as many articles on contemporary audio, stage and film productions of Shakespeare. He is also a contributor to the SourceBooks editions of Shakespeare's works on the subject of Shakespeare and popular culture.

His most recent publications include 'Shakespeare on the Record' in *The Blackwell Companion to Shakespeare and Performance* (2005); 'Shakespeare and Cultural Studies: An Overview' in the journal *Shakespeare*; and an annotated bibliography of over 900 film adaptations of Shakespeare for *Shakespeares after Shakespeare* (2007).

28
DEBORAH WARNER
Carol Chillington Rutter

London. December 1997. Wilton's Music Hall. A ghostly scene of Victorian dereliction. Barley-sugar cast-iron pillars hold up a sagging horse-shoe sweep of balcony in a gloomy, barrel-vaulted auditorium. The place, the actor will say later, is 'a cross between a dreamscape and a synagogue' (*Guardian*, 10 December 1997). It's unheated. The wooden seats, hard. On the dark stage the shape of a figure in black, bare-armed, looms out of the shadows. A hand reaches up, switches on a single bulb hanging from a bare flex. In the sudden, mean glare, an image of angular physical austerity comes into focus, and hard words: 'April is the cruellest month.'

First beginners

Unmistakably, the line was T.S. Eliot's. The voice, the body were Fiona Shaw's. And, just as unmistakably, the theatre-making intelligence directing the production was Deborah Warner's. No one could misread the signature. Deborah Warner is, for actors like Brian Cox, Simon Russell Beale and Fiona Shaw, quite simply the most meticulous, continuously challenging and surprising Shakespeare director of her generation, a reputation all the more impressive because it rests on only five professional Shakespeare productions in the UK in a career launched in 1987 with *Titus Andronicus* for the Royal Shakespeare Company (RSC) followed by *King John* (RSC, 1988), *King Lear* (National Theatre [NT], 1992), *Richard II* (NT, 1995), and *Julius Caesar* (Barbican, 2005). That this 'great Shakespearian' should have been directing not Shakespeare but Eliot in Wilton's mouldering East End saloon in 1997, only ten years after her stunning debut in Stratford-upon-Avon, was entirely in character. Warner's clarity of vision and obstinate determination to serve her vision has meant that she has regularly fled from the kind of 'institutional' Shakespeare too often produced by the RSC in 'deadly theatre' mode (certainly throughout the 1990s) into opera, film, installation art; into Euripides, Beckett and Brecht. Wherever she goes, her work as a theatre 'maker' – the term she prefers instead of 'director' – has utter integrity. The opening of *The Waste Land*, then, gives insight into her 'making' of Shakespeare; it reads like a brief anthology of her practical and creative 'genius'. (That's Russell Beale's word: she's 'utterly unique; a genius' [Interview, May 2007]. But 'a genius' is what Shaw and Cox call her, too.)

So what does this opening show? For one thing, her brilliance at negotiating space, whether it's the wasteland stretch of Wilton's music-hall stage; the vast exposed tract of the Barbican; the hemmed-in claustrophobia of The Other Place or The Pit; the improvised 'get-up' installations of productions on tour. Her visual aesthetic is minimalist, austere: Shaw, naked-armed in a black sheath dress and boots, alone among the 'heap of broken images' of Eliot's poetry, offers a typical stage image. It's a style, Warner says, based on her own 'shyness and reticence'; on her belief that 'the theatre experience is about something laid bare' (*The Times Magazine*, 27 January–2 February 2001). Emptiness appeals to her. She wants, says Hildegard Bechtler, a designer who has worked with Warner regularly, 'a playing space which is free enough for her and the actors to invent in' (*Daily Telegraph*, 2 June 1995). Design isn't prearranged. It evolves in the rehearsal room but into sets that don't work like sets, into 'anti-"set" sets' that strip down, that strip away. (For contrast, says Bechtler, compare the full, elaborately stuffed worlds designed for Shakespeare by, for example, Bob Crowley and Mark Thompson.)

The effect of such visual austerity is to fix the theatrical focus on the actor – Shaw, for example, marooned on Wilton's stage – and to make the actor what a play called *King Lear* or *Richard II* is about, what poetry like Eliot's is 'doing'. 'I don't direct plays', Warner says. 'I direct actors'. There's a difference. 'I don't just find the play, decide what it's about and then push actors [into embodying] what it's about': 'I direct actors' ideas' (*Observer*, 30 April 1989). As a result, Warner's rehearsals proceed at a snail's pace. Her patience with actors is legendary. She 'celebrates the performer', says Fiona Shaw of this director whom she's described as egoless, 'a cipher'; someone who, instead of pushing her own concepts, throws the play open to actors, to work by trial and error, to get lost and, slowly, by stripping away received ideas, to get to the heart of things. She 'fine tunes the actor', wanting 'you to be more yourself than you've ever been before: more grandly poetic, more vulgar, more beautiful, more physically dangerous' (Interview, May 2007). Her method? 'She pours love into you', says Simon Russell Beale:

> *ruthlessly* pours love into you, gives you limitless praise, determined to make you feel confident. YOU WILL FEEL absolutely every time

> you walk on stage that you are THE BEST. Which makes an actor willing to take risks. Her particular genius is in releasing an actor into his personal territory of crisis – unsettling his fixed positions, the performance he knows how to give. She's obstinate, dogged at getting an actor to do something he doesn't want to do.

And then finds out he can.

One other trademark: Warner's genius for giving actors 'things that are real' (*Independent*, 8 May 1987) to ground their performances, ordinary objects, their simplicity charged with unstagey truthfulness, like the light bulb switched on in *The Waste Land* that clearly had practical work to do in Shaw's performance but that figured metaphorically as well. Such objects, literally, illuminate. (And the naked light bulb turns out to be a recurrent motif in Warner's work.) On Warner's visually starved stage, props are few, sensations, reticently withheld. So when they come, their impact is staggering: a dropped pomegranate in *Electra* that opened up like a split head; a handkerchief offered to Titus to dry his eyes that turned out to be useless, already soaked with his brother's tears; the crown that, in *King John*, the infantile king, stepped out of A.A. Milne, kept strapped to his waist with a bicycle chain and that, in *Richard II*, the usurped king delivered to his cousin-turned-usurper, stripping the handover of the legitimating dignity that Bolingbroke so desperately required by sliding the royal headgear down a length of domestic drapery; the silly party hats and whistles of the opening scene of *King Lear* that were somehow remembered in the Fool's 'comic relief' red nose – which, by the end, had found its way into the wrecked king's pocket, Lear trying it on, trying to joke Cordelia back into life, then, when he failed, fixing it to her dead countenance instead, making it an unutterably black joke that 'a dog, a horse, a rat' should 'have life / And thou no breath at all' (Act V, Scene 3, lines 282–3).

A brief life

Born in 1959, Deborah Warner grew up in Oxfordshire in a house full of Elizabethan and Jacobean furniture – her father was an antiques dealer at a time, she says, when the trade was 'a true arts and crafts profession' – in a town within striking distance of Stratford. The Royal Shakespeare Theatre (RST) was her local Shakespeare 'rep'. Educated in a Quaker boarding school, she opted, after A-levels, against university, taking a place instead at Central School of Speech and Drama on the stage-management course and spending most nights in the theatre seeing everything going. (Later, in her first jobs, competing for work with university-educated directors of her generation who, inevitably at that time, were men, she would feel less disadvantaged by her gender than by her lack of a degree. Ten years further on, however, she would see that lack as her salvation, a lucky escape from instinct-deadening training in the habits of over-intellectualising.)

In 1980, Warner founded Kick Theatre Company, spending the next seven years working with unpaid actors, 'practising to be a theatre director at the Edinburgh Festival'. 'We were about the actor and the text, nothing else', she says – which was just as well because they couldn't *afford* anything else: 'we didn't have any money, any sets or any breakfast' (*Independent on Sunday*, 17 July 1994). But Kick did have spectacular success – with productions of *Wozzeck, The Good Person of Sichuan, Coriolanus, Measure for Measure* and, in 1985, *King Lear*, which won a *Time Out* Theatre Award, a *Drama* magazine Special Achievement Award and notices from reviewers hailing Deborah Warner as 'the great new hope for British Theatre' (*Guardian*, 23 November 1988).

The following year, though, when the Arts Council failed to produce a grant for the company, Kick was forced to disband. Soon after, Warner went to the RSC to direct *Titus Andronicus* (1987) and the following year *King John* and *Electra*, Euripides's play marking her first collaboration with the actor, Fiona Shaw, a collaboration that initiated a lasting creative partnership that they themselves describe as 'one of the great gifts' of their professional lives. (In Paris, where their touring appearances are front-page news in *Le Monde*, they've been dubbed 'le tandem anglais'.) In 1988, too, Warner was appointed RSC Resident Director, a success she trumped the following year by winning an Olivier Award, 'Best Director of the Year', for *Titus*. But the ironies of her Edinburgh triumphs were set to replay themselves at the RSC. That January, the company announced new scheduling policies that would doom the kind of labour-intensive rehearsal work Warner insists on as the condition of her employment. She decamped to the NT and beyond, directing Shaw as Shen Te in Brecht's *Good Person of Sichuan* (1989), as Hedda in *Hedda Gabler* (Abbey Theatre, Dublin, 1991); in *Footfalls* (1994) at the Garrick (which caused a furore, first threatened with an injunction then closed down by the Beckett Estate because Warner had presumed to reassign a number of lines from one character to another); in *Medea* (2001) and, that same year back at the NT, in Jeanette Winterson's devised piece, *The Powerbook*. Perhaps most provocatively in these years, Warner directed Shaw as a cross-gendered Richard in *Richard II* at the NT in 1995.

By the mid-1990s too, Warner was directing opera (getting rave reviews for *Wozzeck* at Opera North in 1993 but catcalls 'from a certain kind of comfortable opera audience' for her *Don Giovanni* at Glyndebourne the following year [according to the *Independent on Sunday*, 17 July 1994]). There was a finely judged film of *The Last September* (1999), set on the eve of the

Irish civil wars among the dilapidated great houses and batty remnants of the Anglo-Irish ascendancy playing parlour games in shabby drawing rooms while IRA gun-runners stashed explosives in the outbuildings. And there were first experiments in site-specific performances made without actors that redefined, for Warner, the notion of 'the audience' and 'the performer'. Her 'St. Pancras Project' treated the interior of the 'fantastic' abandoned gothic hotel on the Euston Road as 'a sort of "found poem" on the theme of suspension between two lives'. ('The space', she said, 'was abstract'; 'almost like walking into someone's brain' (*Independent*, 13 April 1996).) It offered spectators, 'a strange solo walk' along 'empty corridors through spaces [. . .] enhanced' with 'little hauntings, little strangenesses': a breakfast tray left outside a door as if a guest had just set it out; a nineteenth-century maid's crinoline on a hook on the back of a door. 'Sometimes you'd hear voices, sometimes you'd hear pianos playing, sometimes you would see figures flitting through' (Radio 3, Warner interviewed by John Tusa).

Warner's admirers had to be happy that she was exploring new forms and media and recharging her batteries devising work like the 2003 'Angel Project' in Midtown Manhattan. But what of Mr Shakespeare? By 2005, Warner had been silent on Shakespeare for a full ten years. Then, the Barbican International Theatre Event announced that she would be directing *Julius Caesar* for BITE:05. What actors experienced in *Julius Caesar* rehearsals, what spectators saw on the Barbican stage, they recognised as the genuine article, true Warner, 'fresh and fearless', her 'egalitarian' methods 'harnessing the total input of the total cast' (which here included a 100-strong crowd of volatile plebs); the 'coolness and authority with which she allowed the play to grow' truly 'awesome' (Jackson and Smallwood 1993: 177). Those comments on her work were Brian Cox's, thinking about 1987. But they were just as relevant to 2005. Warner directing *Julius Caesar* was making Shakespeare as if she'd never been away.

Working

In rehearsals, Deborah Warner sits on a table, her feet shelved on a chair, a position that puts her eye in line with her actors (as against, says Fiona Shaw, directors who direct with their eye on the book). She comes to the first day having put herself through 'meticulous personal study', holed up alone (Shaw again) with 'piles of dictionaries' so that she knows the meaning of every word in Shakespeare's script – and she needs to, because it's a precondition of her contract that she works from an uncut script. (Compare her promptbook for *Titus Andronicus* with Peter Brook's [1955], both held in the RSC archives at the Shakespeare Birthplace Trust: Brook cut 650 lines; Warner, not one.

Examine her *King John* promptbook: again, no cuts). Other directors pay lip-service to 'trusting' the Shakespeare script; Warner means it. Cutting knotty text – the editor's get-out is to call the text 'corrupt', the director's license to dodge it – is, for Warner, cheating, a failure to do the work of rehearsal, to unpick the knots. She doesn't read academic criticism. Mostly, she sees plays refracted through other playwrights: 'Shakespeare is like Sophocles'; 'Euripides is like Edward Albee'. She comes to the first day, also, having cast the play as 'big' as she can possibly manage: it's imperative in Shakespeare, she believes, that supporting roles be played as heavyweight as principals. (Ralph Fiennes was her Dauphin in *King John*; Fiona Shaw, Portia in *Julius Caesar*; Paola Dionisotti, the Duchess of Gloucester in *Richard II*). Two side effects of her casting policy are, first, that actors queue up to work with her and remain immensely loyal, returning to work with Warner as often as they can (Brian Cox, Susan Engel, Derek Hutchinson, Ralph Fiennes and, of course, Shaw); and, second, that young actors who start out with her have a habit of growing into the self-expectations she plants in them (Richard McCabe, Eve Matheson – and, of course, Shaw).

Read-throughs – not just one, but several of them throughout the rehearsal period – go line by line, word by word, actors reading any part except their own. Putting actors on their feet (which may happen before, after or alongside the first read-through), Warner gets them to play games – '*real* play', says Shaw, 'child's play – not fake play with an ulterior purpose'; 'very precise play', says Beale, 'play that produces very specific, geographical and physical pictures'. (His favourite, he remembers from *Julius Caesar*, was a game called 'people you like; people you don't like'. His Cassius finished up stranded in a corner alone; the crowd was at the other end of the room, mobbing Brutus.) He calls Warner a 'very materialist' director: she's interested in the human minutiae of Shakespeare's parts, in the specific visual detail – like the sight of blood smeared on glass, or children's toys bobbing in a paddling pool – and the taste and smell of things. She gets actors 'to remember physically', and by precisely physicalising a situation, to release their role's emotional life. For Russell Beale, it was the sensation 'of the wet shirt, sticking to me' that let loose his Cassius. 'Remembering physically' was for him a revelation: 'Deborah Warner's legacy to me as an actor', he says, 'is to be less interested in what a character is saying than in the precise situation of his speaking: the night, the thunderstorm, the clothes plastered to the body; the way you talk in the middle of the night'.

She casts actors not because she wants them to inhabit her interpretation of the part but because she sees something in the actor that the part might release, or that the actor might release in the part. It's an experiment, a kind of arranged marriage. In rehearsal, she works with the material the actor brings.

It's not an unthreatening process – and not every actor, by any means, thrives under Warner. (Older actors, Graham Crowden, Michael Bryant [to name two] baulk at the improvisations, the painful meandering of rehearsals conducted democratically.) Starting out on *Julius Caesar*, Russell Beale admits he was deeply anxious. 'I'd just done *Macbeth*; my reviews – understatement – were mixed' (the nice ones called him 'portly'; the others, plain 'fat'):

> Deborah had offered me Cassius. *Cassius!* Surely she meant *Brutus*! I was overweight. I was worried about that line – the one about Cassius's 'lean and hungry look'. So when the actor who'd been cast as Brutus had to drop out, I asked Deborah if I could swop roles. I told her I couldn't risk the battering my self-confidence would take. She said she'd think about it.

And she did.

> She *seriously* thought about it, which is unusual for a director. And she came back and said, 'No, I want you to play Cassius. *And I will promise you* that I will support you – that you will not be humiliated.' So humane! But she'd touched my crisis. And she knew it – and that's her genius, to release the actor into the territory of crisis that lets him make huge discoveries. My Cassius used 'Simon's' crisis. My Cassius was *hurting*. My Cassius didn't have a seat at the top table. He was clever, clever, clever, but he needed Brutus: he was the lone grammar school boy amongst a load of Etonians! Socially, he was furious – and then he got seduced by nice cuff-links.

What Warner did for Russell Beale as a director was to strip away his preconceptions, to get rid of 'cool' – what he'd assumed Cassius was about – to find 'needy'; and continuously to 'keep me moving towards the "what ifs" of the role'. Cassius, Russell Beale observes, 'is a man who threatens to commit suicide in every scene. So "what if" those threats aren't hysterical outbursts but deeply felt ideas, the committed ideas of a politician?' It's with the 'what ifs' that Warner's rehearsals are occupied.

Warner, says Shaw, 'allows a kind of chaos in rehearsal, the chaos necessary to free actors, to make discoveries and TO GET LOST.' So, for example, says Shaw:

> she allowed me to rehearse Shen Te *for weeks* in high heels; and she let me pretend to be Mark Rylance for ages in *Richard II* rehearsals: I was supposed to be playing Richard, but I thought Mark was perfect

> casting [. . .] so I wandered around trying to be him. Lost – desperately lost. The point is that she wouldn't force me to make a decision – to throw away the high heels. To ditch Rylance. I had to find my way.

Getting lost, playing games, finding things and discarding them, working line by line on *every* line: the pace of Warner's rehearsals is slow, very, very slow. (The same company rehearsed first Warner's *King Lear* then Richard Eyre's *Richard III* back to back in 1992; eleven weeks went on *King Lear*; five on *Richard*.) While actorly chaos goes creatively, if waywardly, on, what is Warner doing? 'Watching', says Shaw. 'Totally absorbed. Waiting. Patient. Keeping her nerve.' Waiting? 'For something to happen.' Like what? 'Like, in one of those games, something you do that she sees and catches and holds like a butterfly: it's that captured thing she sees that is the real truth of what the actor is doing'. Capturing butterflies is a metaphor for anchoring performances in detail. Nothing the actor does in her rehearsal room that moves into the performance is generalised. She is 'meticulous about the *beat* of every moment' in a play. Such meticulousness is costly. It means she works twelve-hour rehearsal days – and works actors, too, for 'hours and hours and hours', says Russell Beale:

> She's an incredibly hard taskmaster on the floor. She's not satisfied with settling for what actors think is subtle. She won't let you fall back on irony, on wryness. She pushes you up and up and up. With her, there are no half states. She tires you out until there's a sense of desperation in your acting – and *that's* when something creative happens. When you're exhausted, you're released. Into unself-consciousness.

'Savage release at the end of a long period of emotional paralysis' is how Warner describes the revenge ending of Euripides's *Electra*, which is not a bad description of her rehearsal process.

What she achieves by choosing, as she says, 'to create conditions in which there is no world outside the rehearsal room', conditions in which the rehearsal room *is* the world, is remarkable (*Observer Review*, 21 January 2001). 'Deborah', says Russell Beale, 'gets you STARTED where most people begin Act V'. He cites Shaw's astonishing first entrance as Electra, 'pushing open those doors like she was pushing against the weight of the world'. For another director, the actorly presence, the theatrical force delivered in that moment would have been the climax of the actor's performance; for Warner, it was the starting premise.

But for all the 'hours and hours and hours' of work, there's a lot of laughter in Warner's rehearsal room. 'She adores having fun. She loves anarchy, quirkiness, bad behaviour, the *truth* of child's play', says Shaw. And Russell Beale: 'She allowed Portia and Cassius to be terribly naughty, to hang around together at the back of the Roman crowd. We were shameless, really. Portia and Cassius became quite good friends'. In all of Warner's work, 'childness' (as Polixenes in *The Winter's Tale* calls it) is evident: Titus is a kid sticking fingers in his ears when he wants to stop listening; Lear is a kid playing dodgems in his wheelchair; Richard is a kid playing paddy-whack with his cousin Bolingbroke like a million times before, only this time for the crown. She aims, she says, always to 'keep a little toe rooted in the rehearsal room': to keep the molten vividness of rehearsal alive, night after night, when the work of performance takes over and replaces the daily anarchy of discovery with the physical art of mechanical reproduction (*Independent*, 8 May 1987). But she aims too, it seems, to keep a foot planted in the nursery, where the child never gives ground to the adult, never gags the joke. Famously, Peter Brook cut all the lines in his *Titus* that threatened to spoil the play's 'beautiful barbaric ritual' with 'mocking laughter' (Dessen 1989: 15, 22); Warner, by contrast, didn't duck the laughs; in her *Titus*, laughter belonged; it constituted the authentic territory of the tragic grotesque.

The time she devotes to actors in rehearsal, setting up personal dialogues that 'fix' every actor in his part, don't end on press night. For most directors, that's the last time they see their production: their contract ends when it's up. Warner confesses that she finds this abandonment of the 'baby' odd: she's in the theatre night after night, seeing the show, watching, scribbling, continuously giving actors notes – '*deep* notes', Shaw calls them – to bring the production on. The work is never finished. She's 'more of a gardener than a director', says Brian Cox (*Sunday Telegraph Magazine*, 17 December 1988). She 'tends' the show. She watched *Titus Andronicus* more than seventy times in a run of 120 performances – and gave Cox notes the night they closed.

Playing

The 1987 *Titus Andronicus* staged a number of RSC 'firsts'. It was the first Shakespeare on the brand new Swan stage (not counting the part-Shakespeare *Two Noble Kinsmen* that had opened the theatre the previous year, nor indeed Cheek by Jowl's flying visit to the Swan with *Twelfth Night* some months earlier). It was the first Swan production to be directed by a woman – though Warner herself never made much of this 'first'. It's true that she was the first woman director appointed by the RSC after Buzz Goodbody's tragic death, too young, in 1975. But if, in 1987, Warner was the *only* woman on the RSC directorate, the following year there were seven more, and together they were responsible for half that season's work. 'It's a curtain of water', Warner has since said about women breaking into the profession. 'Not a glass ceiling' (*The Times*, 4 May 2000).

Most significantly of all, this was the first *Titus* that offered twentieth-century spectators the whole story, the full text; a *Titus* not subjected to the 'textual fiddling' that Kenneth Tynan, in 1955, supposed was 'required if we are to swallow the crudities' the play serves up. In 1955, Laurence Olivier's Titus had made his first entrance 'not as a beaming hero but as a battered veteran, stubborn and shambling, long past caring about the people's cheers', a 'hundred campaigns' having 'tanned his heart to leather'. When that heart cracked, Tynan wrote, there issued 'a terrible music' – *tragic* music – the 'noise made in its last extremity by the cornered human soul' (*Observer*, 21 August 1955). Warner's *Titus* produced a very different sound: on her stage, the heart cracked, but when it did, the cornered human soul cracked a joke. Brian Cox's Titus was more Archie Rice than Hamlet (Jackson and Smallwood 1993: 178). Laughter – snorting, incredulous, grim, choked, desperate, crazed, triumphalist – rolled off this stage, the bizarre acoustic to a world that, at its sanest, was evidently mad.

The opening scene set up this core observation, giving Titus' triumph as a spectacle of absurdly mismatched pieces. The stage (all scrubbed pine) was by Habitat; the characters (cartoon Romans) by Asterix. Titus entered held shoulder-high, wearing an 'antique Roman' breastplate and an 'authentic' oaken garland of the wars. But his face was caked with mud, weirdly making him appear halfway through an Ovidian metamorphosis, part man, part monument; his boots were an all-in wrestler's; his cloak, a dosser's blanket; and the captives – dressed in modern metal-studded bomber jackets and Cuban-heeled boots – who carried him were 'yoked' to a painter-and-decorator's aluminium ladder carried sideways, he perched aloft, their heads sticking out between the rungs, bizarrely decapitated, like pigs' chops on a butcher's slab. This spectacle gradually came into focus as offering a kind of ludicrous physical caption to what was happening in the scene, the grotesque 'rituals' Rome was performing as 'culture'. There was Titus, father of twenty-five sons, *celebrating*, as he buried the latest, that twenty-one of them had died for Rome. There was Titus, handing over 'the proudest prisoner of the Goths' (Act I, Scene 1, line 96) for 'sacrifice', deaf to the frantic mother's plea which was also a caution – 'Andronicus, stain not thy tomb with blood' – assuring Tamora that this killing was *piety*: 'Religiously [. . .] your son is marked' (lines 116, 124–5). But what kind of religion lops limbs and roasts entrails into smoky 'incense' to 'perfume the sky'? This 'sacrifice' was worse than cultural oxymoron – 'cruel, irreligious piety!' as Tamora calls it (Act I, Scene 1, line 130). By rhetorical revisionism (slaughter = sacrifice) it had made death a species of black joke – and that was insane. 'Civilised' Rome had gone mad, was acting like the gothic 'barbarian'. (But 'handy, dandy', as the Red Queen might ask of Alice, or mad Lear of blind Gloucester, in Titus's Rome, which was the 'civilised', which the 'savage'?)

On Warner's stage, the collision of (modern) ladder with (antique) armour was a materially precise visual proxy for the collision of ideas located at the heart of her production, the way something could be itself and its opposite *at the same time*. (Later on, the simplest of means would yoke primitive atrocity to modernity, to a 'now' that refused spectators permission to locate atrocity in a primitive past that was safely finished: a cheese-wire attached to a metal bucket; a pristine white uniform on the 'chef' who served up boy pie.) Warner's actors, wrote Cox of the experience of performing this play, walked a 'tightrope of absurdity between comedy and tragedy' (Jackson and Smallwood 1993: 175). The daft was never very far from the utterly appalling.

If the sacrifice of Alarbus enacted sick culture, the rape and mutilation of Lavinia (which somehow answered that original violence, spoiling the play's love story as the barbaric sacrifice spoiled Titus's triumph) enacted sick sport. Tamora's 'boys', Chiron (Richard McCabe) and Demetrius (Piers Ibbotson), were adolescent nasties or overgrown Asperger children (a syndrome new to England in the 1980s), sharp-witted but dead to sensation, who, released into Roman culture, overran the space. The production promptbook marks their re-entrance at Act II, Scene 1, line 25, 'dancing/sparring (braving!)' Then adds: 'N.B. quite a free section' – a clue not just to their performance but to Warner's direction. Being 'free' to roam, 'free' to improvise every night as actors – to play – made the 'boys' dangerously unpredictable. And dangerous play was what they committed. The rape was a game. Lavinia (Sonia Ritter), in a simple saffron-coloured shift, a doll-sized creature with a Raphael-angel head of tight curls, was human bait they toyed with, circling, feinting, blind-siding her as she shrank from each 'play' attack, from which they, 'playful', withdrew. Her last appeal to Tamora – who stood impassive, immobile – 'No grace? . . . Confusion fall' triggered Chiron's witty response: 'Nay then, I'll stop your mouth' (Act II, Scene 3, lines 183, 184). The promptbook records the onstage business that elaborated the pun on 'stop', and the sequel: 'C. savagely kisses L – spits out piece of her tongue'; 'D. pulls up her dress – dagger in floor between her legs'; 'lifts L by hand between legs . . . exit with her'.

Their re-entrance in Act II, Scene 4 gave spectators a first bewildering experience of the incomprehension Marcus would, minutes later, encounter ('Who is this – my niece . . .? / . . . If I do dream' [lines 11, 13]). Initially, the action didn't register, didn't make sense. From upstage right, slowly crawling on knees and forearms, their hands drawn up into their sleeves, clutching their cuffs, making stumps as if they were playing some sort of kid's game, came first Chiron then Demetrius. Arriving centre stage, they sprawled together in a collapsed heap of laughter – as, after a long pause covered by their hilarity, behind them entered the crawling, agonised, lurching *and completely silent* figure of Lavinia. Understanding dawned: they, the 'play' version; she, the thing itself. Assaulted. Mutilated. Her hands gone. A wounded animal, a butterfly beating its wings against a closed window, Lavinia struggled centre stage, her crippled 'movement including with arms' (promptbook) mimicked by sadistic cartoon gestures from her guffawing rapists. She willed herself to stand, swayed, then fell. Chiron mounted her. He went 'to kiss her' (promptbook) then, disgusted, 'pull[ed] back', exiting on a final joke about hanging herself – if only she had hands to knit the cord.

This scene epitomises Deborah Warner's work as a director: its austerity and audacity; its focus on actors; its unsentimentality; its attention to every beat of the sequence; its acknowledgement on the nerve endings of pain rendered simultaneously as suffering and joke. Brian Cox sees *Titus* as 'the work' of 'an acute visceral sensibility', the work of 'a very angry young man' (Jackson and Smallwood 1993: 175). Equally, Warner's *Titus* can be seen as the work of another 'visceral sensibility', a young woman's work: fearless, uncompromising. Not angry, but unflinching. (Perhaps not insignificantly, Warner, directing the play, was about the same age as Shakespeare, writing it.) Years hence, directing Medea-the-child-killer, Warner would identify in contemporary society a 'neurotic inability to look at things that horrify' (*Observer Review*, 21 January 2001). In *Titus*, she laid out her theatrical project for the future, 'to look', to observe, see, see more and see differently, but never to avert the gaze from those 'things that horrify'. One of Warner's revelations in *Titus* was to see the rape of Titus's sole daughter as an act of pollution: dirt, not blood, covered Lavinia's body and garments, dirt that connected the extravagant violence perpetrated on her to the extravagant violence perpetrated by her father on Rome's enemies. Caked in dried filth, she looked like him, the returning hero. (Later, the extravagant shedding of blood into a basin held in Lavinia's stumps, when Titus, in a crisp white butcher's apron, cut the throats of each of the boys in turn, worked like a cleansing ritual, like cartharsis. People in the audience regularly cheered.) Another revelation was to understand the theatrical need for Marcus's long speech of reaction to the mutilated Lavinia – all of it. What Brook cut, Warner played: it was there, this production discovered, *for the audience*, to give them time to look, to acknowledge, to recognise, to double up with grief and to regain their footing.

The unflinching gaze, the freakish generic wedding of horror show to clown routine: these were ideas Warner returned to in *King John*, staged in the RSC's bare black-box studio, The Other Place, with a few chairs, some naked light bulbs, and a thicket of scaling ladders, and *King Lear* at the NT's Lyttelton Theatre, played on a Bechtler-designed set that Michael Billington described as 'stunningly ugly', consisting 'largely of a mud-coloured tarpaulin' (*Guardian*, 12 May 1988). In King *John*, the 'wannabe' king (Nicholas Woodeson) was a clown with a mean streak: cosying up to his little cousin, Prince Arthur, he tried to embrace him from behind – 'like a game' (promptbook). But the kid bit him. So he thumped him in the back of the neck, felling him. The Citizen of Angiers (Robert Demeger) was a comic Frenchman in a standard-issue striped shirt and beret who cheerfully chewed a sandwich while he inspected, below, the assault on his town (stunningly conducted as ladder after ladder was slammed clattering against the walls), then doubled as Hubert, ordered to put out the child Arthur's eyes. On the one hand, international politics were conducted as a series of outsized (male) posturings, 'English history', wrote Irving Wardle, 'as seen through the eyes of George Grosz' (*The Times*, 4 May 1989): John in a coat three sizes too big and a coal-scuttle helmet; Austria in a lion skin remaindered from Oz. On the other, the domestic moments – Constance keening for her child, Hubert setting out a bucket for the blinding irons – were breathtaking in their economy. Warner's direction for the blinding, recorded in the promptbook, matter-of-factly conducts 'things that horrify' in real time. Dragging 'A to centre with difficulty', the executioners are instructed to 'lift him upside down over chair so that his head almost touches floor & his legs are over back'. One of them 'Binds his legs with belt. Straddles him. Has hold of his hands finishes binding his legs and turns on him. Takes A's right arm stretches it out. Does same with left. Grabs A's face by chin pushing it down.' (Warner is no sensationalist. But she's curious about human violence. 'I want to know', she says, 'what's in the empty beat after someone's seen her husband killed in front of her' [*Observer*, 16 February 1992].) This sequence ended with Hubert weeping into his hands. And Arthur, exiting, stooping to pick up the handkerchief he'd thrown away.

In *King Lear*, the 'don't wannabe' king (Brian Cox with Howard Hughes hair and a straggling beard sitting bundled up in a wheelchair) reminded Paul Taylor 'of a disgruntled granny in a Giles cartoon' (*Independent*, 28 July 1990). His Fool (David Bradley) was 'Lanky and lugubrious', a 'northern comic in half-mast dress-trousers and aviator cap' (Taylor) who looked 'oddly like a neglected water-spaniel' (Michael Billington, *Guardian*, 28 July 1990) and kept 'making self-dismissive gestures, as though to apologise for his duff material' (Taylor), delivering his lines 'as an extended epitaph, with a shrug and a grimace' (Michael Coveney, *Sunday Observer*, 29 July 1990). If Warner's *Titus Andronicus* three years earlier had served Brian Cox as an extended audition for this *King Lear*, the discoveries he made then – Titus as Archie

Rice; madness as harsh but wisecracking lucidity, repositioning sanity as a tale told by a demented Glaswegian stand-up comic who'd discovered that 'normal' life was bonkers – equipped him now to twin suffering with absurdity in this much bigger play. Characteristically, Warner endowed her production with the simplest of materials to achieve its effects: party hats, a lap rug, a pillow. Early on, Lear and the Fool delivered their patter act duet ('Nuncle, give me an egg', Act I, Scene 4, line 139) 'before a front cloth like a dead-end vaudeville act'; later on, the hovel scene 'amazingly' took on 'Bedlam echoes of the "catch" party in *Twelfth Night*' (Irving Wardle, *Independent on Sunday*, 29 July 1990). Like that earlier 'good idea', the sacrifice of Alarbus, the division of the kingdom – that saw Cox's Lear in party mode 'scissoring pieces off the map like slices of chocolate cake' (Wardle) – was lunatic. But Lear had to travel through the territory of the grotesque to understand it. In the storm – made of deafening percussion and hand-held torches sweeping across the dark – Lear and the Fool used an upraised cymbal for an umbrella; on Dover beach, Lear stomped around in plastic bags stuffed with petals – 'felt' shoes to silence horses – like an overgrown toddler; organising the mock trial, he casually tipped the Fool out of a wheelbarrow where he'd fallen asleep; at the end, he trundled Cordelia on in his wheelchair upside down, red hair streaming, 'like someone pushing a trolley of groceries' (Taylor). In Warner's *King Lear*, the 'side-piercing sight[s]' of Shakespeare's script (Act IV, Scene 5, line 85) penetrated to the heart, conducted there by dark laughter: in this production, to 'see [. . .] feelingly' (Act IV, Scene 5, line 145) meant acknowledging that tragedy's native dress is motley's cap and bells.

Comparing this *Lear* to its sister show, *Richard III* (with which it toured as a double bill), Irving Wardle shrewdly observed that where Richard Eyre's production advanced 'towards a pre-arranged destination', Warner's made 'its discoveries along the way' (*Independent on Sunday*, 29 July 1990). Exactly so. But sometimes with Warner a discovery *anticipates* the way. In 1995, she began her work on *Richard II* by casting Fiona Shaw as the King.

The furore in the media that ensued largely passed Warner by. Just as she directs actors, not plays, so she casts actors, not gender. Shaw, she always maintained, was 'the most exciting and suitable Richard I could think of' (*Guardian*, 31 May 1995). So, she remained unperturbed by the silly season among arts journalists as they threw up their hands in horror at 'Gimmick casting'; 'the sort of thing you might expect to see at the end of term in a boarding school' (*Independent on Sunday*, 21 May 1995), or filled their imaginations 'with panicky images' of cross-gender confusion: 'the Maggie Smith Falstaff, the Nicol Williamson Desdemona, the Raquel Welch Titus Andronicus' (*The Times*, 5 June 1995). Historically, Richard II has regularly been played as a study in effeminacy, as Shakespeare's 'girly king' (Rutter

1997: 316–18). Casting a woman in the part, Warner (paradoxically but entirely characteristically) ignored the obvious, the 'womanish', to explore instead the idea that intrigues King Richard himself, that his body is double, that he is both the 'gorgeous' king (divinely appointed, anointed, hedged in with majesty) and the needy mortal 'subjected' to 'live with bread', 'feel want', 'taste grief', 'need friends' (Act III, Scene 2, lines 171–2). Constituted as duplicitous, Richard sees himself as a 'player' king, initiating a profound meditation on selfhood that Warner set up from the beginning in a dumb-show, staged as spectators took their seats in the theatre. At one end of the traverse playing space, behind a gauze curtain lit uncertainly with candles, actors entered, began warming up, then finally lifted down a heavy coronation robe that stood against the back wall and invested a slight figure who stood there ready to take the weight, a body whose torso was wrapped tight in white bands as if, proleptically, swaddled for death. Robed as king, the figure turned as if to make the big ceremonial entrance. But didn't walk on. Walked *off*. Seconds later, having thoroughly disconcerted the audience with the joke exit, Shaw-as-Richard appeared from another door, but in none of those ostentatious trappings, only now visibly established as two-bodied, and quite evidently a player king. Designed by Hildegard Bechtler, the playing space staged constitutional doubleness in spatial terms: in the intimate Cottesloe Theatre, a narrow traverse stage in bare, honey-coloured wood was flanked by steeply raked seats that rose behind barricades. Spectators were at a tennis match. Or on benches in the House of Commons. Or behind barriers at a joust. Heads had to swivel left, right; to take in this, then that; there was no consensus viewpoint, no way of looking 'from the front', and every scene played to a double audience, spectators seeing across the space the mirror image of themselves (Rutter 1997: 319).

Offering spatial doubles and body doubles, the King's formal body doubling the body beneath, Warner's production found one more uncanny double, discovered in rehearsal, an accident of casting: that the cousins, Bolingbroke (David Threlfall, crop-haired, beaky, angular) and Richard (Fiona Shaw, crop-haired, beaky, angular), were identical twins. Or halves of 'a platonically divided creature seeking to unite' its split self (Irving Wardle, *Independent on Sunday*, 4 June 1995). Wardle saw them 'magnetically circling each other' – the one, flanked by pretty boys in high Renaissance fashion, the other, by heavies in medieval chain mail – and saw, too, that the 'theatrical fascination of the process' was that it operated 'simultaneously as a love journey and a power struggle'. The political story of usurpation (or was it abdication?) that Warner's *Richard II* told emerged as a personal story of these two cousins who were somehow the same – but different. It was a story of failed intimacy, of familiarity disowned: a wrecked love story that remembered childhood, and shared games, and fear, and loss. There was plenty of clowning around: Richard arrived at Uncle Gaunt's in a black armband – only to discover he wasn't yet dead; 'unkinged', he delivered up his crown to his cousin in a wicker shopping basket. But comedy in *Richard II* anchored the cousins' tragedy, the fierce irony that, says Shaw, 'one of them gives his crown away to one who ultimately may not even want it', which 'taps in to our emotional lives, where we give our hearts away to people who don't want them' (Rutter 1997: 318, 323). As in *Titus* and *King Lear*, Warner discovered a terrible joke at the heart of the play, that Richard wins everything by losing, and Bolingbroke loses everything by winning. The last time spectators saw 'the emotionally tongue-tied Bolingbroke', he was 'wracked with tears of remorse for the man who stole his land' (Wardle), the man whose crown he wore, but wearing it, discovered he'd emptied it of meaning.

It's well understood among actors that one of the stories any production tells is the story of its rehearsal. In rehearsal, playing Warner's rehearsal games, one of the stories Shaw and Threlfall found was a story of Richard and Bolingbroke's childhood, growing up together, the runt-prince protected on the playground by his hunky cousin, sharing a secret language, 'one of those languages', says Shaw, 'that exists *underneath* language', that 'discloses secret histories' (Rutter 1997: 320). Ten years later, imagining just such a childhood back story occupied Simon Russell Beale, Anton Lesser and Ralph Fiennes in *Julius Caesar* rehearsals – and similarly supplied depth of field to their tragedy (Rutter 2006: 73). They'd been, they decided, schoolboy contemporaries in the Class of 60 BCE – and sibling rivals: Beale/Cassius, the boffin and butt of every playground joke who'd learned to survive by flattering his doltish comrades that the latest brilliant idea he produced was theirs; Fiennes/Antony, 'a twit' whom the other two couldn't take seriously – until, says Beale, he 'turned into one of the greatest orators of our day and completely f****** us up' (*Time*, 18 April 2005); Lesser/Brutus, the golden boy who'd somehow never quite come good, who moped, peevish, when Antony dethroned him as teacher's pet; a narcissist who *naturally* annexed Cassius' ideas.

Unlike earlier Warner productions where costumes eclectically matched old with new, *Caesar* was set in a definite 'now': Armani suits, designer sportswear, Ministry of Defence-issue flak jackets; 'Rome', a cool, minimalist city designed as if by Norman Foster in steel and glass (a couple of broken columns remembering its ancient past); the war zone, a vast vacant hangar like some depot outside Baghdad, littered with junk and, weirdly, a clapped-out television marooned centre stage, tethered by a long lead stretching across the endless stretch of concrete floor. (Warner's 'modern dress is unlike any modern dress I've ever known', says Russell Beale. 'It has such a rich physicality. When you're inside it, it's like mulch to the performance; a sort of dirt, like manure, or hung meat. Cassius was so pleased with his red tie.') The design of the production (by Tom Pye) stated in visual terms Warner's claim that *Julius Caesar*, in 2005, was 'a play for now': 'a moment to look at issues of power and whether democracies can survive' (*Observer*, 10 April 2005). Spectators saw themselves in this production: they looked at a crowd on stage – 100 milling 'extras' – that looked like the milling crowd thronging the Barbican foyer. They looked at a war that looked like the images of Baghdad, Basra, Beirut that appeared nightly on their television screens. Most significantly of all, they heard in (Rome's) speeches and rhetoric the noise of the (British) nation's daily political jawing. The clarity of Warner's direction (paying meticulous attention, as Shaw says, 'to every beat of a scene', locating the actor in space) meant that spectators were positioned to really listen to the play's arguments – the breathtaking double-think of Brutus' 'It must be by his death' soliloquy, for instance, a speech that felt unnervingly topical in a world post-Saddam Hussein, post-weapons of mass destruction: 'since the quarrel / Will bear no colour for the thing he is, / Fashion it thus' (Act II, Scene 1, lines 10, 28–30). Ultimately, though, *Julius Caesar*, like *Richard II*, was less a history play than a wrecked love story. Cassius, the self-loathing wooer, a man with the mind of Ariel trapped in Caliban's body, picked his way across the 'Tell me, good Brutus, can you see your face?' (Act I, Scene 2, line 53) speech like Quasimodo rescuing some worthless Esmeralda. How apt that this deeply thoughtful political idealist should make himself the mirror, the 'glass', to show Brutus to himself: for, like Richard and Bolingbroke in that other play that calls for a mirror on stage, Cassius and Brutus were also somehow twins. That they died was somehow less tragic than that they killed each other with accusations of false loyalty first.

After words

Warner's typical lighting plot calls for strong, even, unbroken light. (*Titus Andronicus*' opening scene played with the house lights up; *King Lear*'s lighting was 'open, subtle, ascetic – you barely notice it' [*The Independent*, 25 July 1990].) Such lighting shows her hand. She wants spectators to look on objects, people, stories steadily. (In *Caesar*, though, after the full illumination of the great public scenes, she used strong cross lighting, 'brutalising, exposed, angry lighting', as Russell Beale describes it, 'lighting where you can't see the other person': a metaphor for the failed conversations in this play.) Looking steadily herself, she sees the proximity of opposites – the deeply serious, the totally absurd – that meet in the space of the grotesque where she observes much of Shakespeare to be pitched. A final production image: Titus, in a string vest like a navvy, a knotted handkerchief covering his head like some feeble-pated geezer at the seaside, sat hunched over his documents in his gallery under a single dim light bulb, refusing to admit Revenge to his study because opening the door might make his 'sad decrees [. . .] fly away'. But what a joke! He would show his busy-body intruder how he'd outsmarted her. The papers were irrelevant, he chortled, 'for what I mean to do / See here in bloody lines I have set down' (Act V, Scene 2, lines 11, 13–14). Cox's Titus turned out front. He exposed his torso. He'd carved 'STUPRUM' – rape – across his chest, his daughter's violation inscribed on his flesh, his heart. Such moments define the directorly art – and craft – of Deborah Warner. Doing Shakespeare is never about doing 'something with the text'. It's simply about 'making another three-and-a-half-hour attempt to touch the heart' (Warner in *The Observer on Sunday*, 30 April 1989).

Chronology

1980	Kick Theatre Company founded: productions of *The Good Person of Sichuan* (1980); *Wozzeck* (1981); *The Tempest* (1983); *Measure for Measure* (1984); *King Lear* (1985); *Coriolanus* (1986)
1987	*Titus Andronicus*, Royal Shakespeare Company (RSC) (Swan)
1988	*King John*, RSC (The Other Place)
1989	*Electra*, RSC (The Pit)
1989	*The Good Person of Sichuan*, National Theatre (NT) Company (Olivier Theatre)
1991	*Hedda Gabler*, Abbey Theatre (Dublin, then RSC, London)
1992	*King Lear*, NT Company (Lyttelton Theatre)
1993	*Coriolan*, Salzburg Festival; *Wozzeck*, Opera North Festival
1994	*Footfalls*, Garrick Theatre, London; *Don Giovanni* (Glyndebourne)
1995	*Richard II*, NT Company
1995–7	*The Wasteland*, London, New York
1996	'St. Pancras Project', London
1998	*The Turn of the Screw*, Royal Opera House, Covent Garden, London
1999	*The Last September* (Trimark Pictures)
2000	*St. John Passion*, English National Opera (London)
2001	*Medea* (Dublin, London, New York); *Fidelio* (Glyndebourne)
2002	*The Powerbook*, NT
2003	'The Angel Project' (New York)
2005	*Julius Caesar*, BITE:05 (Barbican Theatre, London)
2007	*Death in Venice*, English National Opera (London)

Acknowledgements

I am grateful to Simon Russell Beale and Fiona Shaw for talking to me at length and on several occasions in May 2007 about Warner and her work.

Bibliography

Cousin, Geraldine (1994) *King John: Shakespeare in Performance*, Manchester: Manchester University Press.

Dessen, Alan C. (1989) *Titus Andronicus: Shakespeare in Performance*, Manchester: Manchester University Press.

Jackson, Russell and Robert Smallwood (eds) (1993) *Players of Shakespeare 3*, Cambridge: Cambridge University Press.

Rutter, Carol Chillington (1997) 'Fiona Shaw's *Richard II*: The Girl as Player-King as Comic', *Shakespeare Quarterly* 48 (3): 314–324.

—— (2006) 'Facing History, Facing Now: Deborah Warner's *Julius Caesar* at the Barbican Theatre', *Shakespeare Quarterly* 57 (1): 71–85.

About the author

Carol Chillington Rutter is a Professor of English at the University of Warwick, where she has won a university award for distinguished teaching. She is the author of *Clamorous Voices: Shakespeare's Women Today* (1988) and *Enter the Body: Women and Representation on Shakespeare's Stage* (2001). She is General Editor of the Shakespeare in Performance Series for Manchester University Press, co-author of *Henry VI in Performance* (2006) and has edited *Documents of the Rose Playhouse* (1984) for the Revels Plays Companion Library. Her latest book is *Shakespeare and Child's Play: Performing Lost Boys on Stage and Screen*, published by Routledge in 2007.

29
ORSON WELLES

Matthew Wilson Smith

Who can say when Orson Welles first encountered Shakespeare? As always with Welles, some tales are taller than others. We hear of a teenage Orson reading the *Collected Works* while tramping across North Africa. We hear of a ten-year-old Orson declaiming *King Lear* to his parents. We hear of Orson's mother teaching her son to read by means of the Bard. We learn that his mother's name was Beatrice and wonder whether his Shakespearian wit didn't grow *in utero*.

Whichever myth of origin we choose to believe, one thing is clear: no single figure was so central to Welles' artistry as that of Shakespeare. Throughout Welles' extraordinarily varied career, Shakespeare – in particular, *Macbeth, Othello, Julius Caesar, King Lear, Twelfth Night*, and the 'Falstaff' plays – was the touchstone. Moving between high-, low-, and middle-brow (sometimes within a single scene), Welles produced, adapted, directed and acted in remarkably varied Shakespearian productions on stage, radio, record and film. Of the many Shakespeare productions he directed, three are among the most important: the Harlem *Macbeth* of 1936, the Mercury *Julius Caesar* of 1937 and the *Othello* film of 1952. The first was his first triumph as a professional director, the second was a critical and commercial success that solidified the Mercury Theatre, and the last initiated a new cinematic style for Welles. Taken together, they provide an outline of Welles' career as one of the handful of American directors of Shakespeare whose influence has been truly international.

The stage production for which Welles is best remembered is the Harlem staging of *Macbeth* – the so-called 'Voodoo *Macbeth*' – of 1936. Welles, twenty years old at the time, had significant professional acting experience (chiefly with the Gate Theatre in Dublin and with Catherine Cornell's touring company in America), but little to show for himself as a director. At best a risky proposition to lead this difficult project, he had managed to charm one of the greatest risk-takers of the American stage, John Houseman. The director/producer/impresario, who had already staged Virgil Thompson and

Gertrude Stein's avant-garde opera *Four Saints in Three Acts* in 1934, Houseman had recently been made the de facto Head of the Negro Theatre Unit of the Federal Theatre Project, a project funded by Roosevelt's Works Progress Administration (WPA). Having met Welles some months earlier in New York, Houseman decided to gamble the entire production – and the future of the Negro Theatre Unit – on the young artist.

The sponsorship of the WPA, combined with the charged political atmosphere of the mid-1930s, created ideal conditions for the creation of a production at once popular and avant-garde. Egalitarian policies dictated much of the production. Like many Federal Theatre Project commissions, the Negro Theatre Unit had a mandate to hire a large cast and crew in order to keep people employed and, at the same time, had to keep ticket prices low for the broader public. Including cast, crew, understudies, musicians and so forth, the *Macbeth* troupe ran to 137, all of whom were paid the same weekly sum of $23.86. The all-black cast included over 100 performers, but only four professional actors. Turning such an enormous troupe of what were essentially amateurs into a professional company, even given the relatively generous rehearsal period of four months, would have been a daunting task for the most seasoned of directors. From the outset, however, Welles had no interest in attempting to turn Harlem into Drury Lane; his rehearsal process would emphasise, above all, choreography, dance, music, rhythm. The idea behind his production of *Macbeth*, first conceived by his wife Virginia, would place the tragedy in the Haitian court of Henri Christophe, the revolutionary general who proclaimed himself king in 1811, eventually committing suicide in the face of a coup. Where Shakespeare had looked to Scotland for his primitive Other, Welles would look to the Caribbean.

In hindsight, and even to many at the time, such gestures smacked of racism, with their straightforward lumping together of different groups (Harlemites, Haitians, Sierra Leoneans, Dahomeans) into a single category and their association of 'blacks' with primal rhythms and subconscious horrors. *Heart of Darkness*, the novel that did as much as any to popularise and legitimate such associations for modernist literature, was one of Welles' favourites, and surely an inspiration for the Harlem *Macbeth*. The more direct influence, however, was Eugene O'Neill's *The Emperor Jones* (1920), which was also based on the story of Henri Christophe, and used similar expressionist techniques to explore a racialised subconscious. Unsurprisingly, several reviewers of Welles' production (including Edith Isaacs, John Mason Brown, Arthur Pollock and Burnes Mantle) compared it to the O'Neill play. Unlike *Emperor Jones*, however, the 'Voodoo *Macbeth*' combined racial fantasy with an anthropological exhibition at which New Yorkers (white and black alike) could witness 'real' witchcraft 'right here' in New York. The leader of Welles' drumming troupe,

Asadata Dafora Horton (later to become Minister of Culture of the Republic of Sierra Leone), was overshadowed by a man known simply as Abdul, whom Houseman refers to as 'an authentic witch doctor, [who] seemed to know no language at all except magic' (1972: 190). According to Welles, Abdul was joined onstage by thirteen other 'real sorcerers' from Dahomey. As Houseman tells it, the whole drumming troupe practised 'tribal ritual', sacrificed live black goats at the outset of rehearsal (to use their skins for their drums) and chanted spells during rehearsals and performances. According to Houseman again, many Harlemites feared that the production would be 'a vast burlesque intended to ridicule the Negro in the eyes of the white world' (1972: 191). It did not help that racial politics had worked in favour of the hiring of Welles himself, since the WPA had wanted the works they sponsored to be produced and directed by whites. The highly charged atmosphere finally ignited when Welles was attacked by four blacks, 'determined to prevent this insult to their race', after leaving one rehearsal.

That Welles' production reinforced racist stereotypes is clear, and yet to view it only by this light would be to miss half the picture. Much like *Emperor Jones*, the 'Voodoo *Macbeth*' challenged white ideologies of race even as it reiterated them. It is worth recalling that white audiences, in mid-1930s America, almost invariably witnessed black actors (when they saw them at all) playing stock roles such as slaves, domestics and vaudeville clowns. Black audiences, too, had rarely seen black actors in Shakespearian roles, and, on the whole, reactions among the Harlem community seem to have been far more positive than negative. When a free preview was offered, 3,000 more spectators arrived than the theatre could accommodate. This set the stage for the 14 April premiere, loudly proclaimed by the sixty-five-piece marching band of Elk Monarch Lodge No. 45, a powerful Harlem benevolent society, which marched down Seventh Avenue to a grandstand in front of the Lafayette Theater. Five thousand Harlem residents turned out to greet the production, stopping traffic for more than an hour; according to one report, it was the largest crowd to date for a Harlem premiere. Expectations were not, in the main, disappointed. 'At the conclusion of the performance', wrote the *New York Times* the next morning: 'Orson Welles, who adapted and staged the play, was virtually dragged out of the wings by members of the company and forced to take a bow. There were salvoes of applause as numerous bouquets of flowers were handed over the footlights to the leading players'. Applause continued for a quarter of an hour before the cast was allowed to leave. Though newspaper reviews would ultimately prove mixed, popular opinion was overwhelmingly favourable, and remained so throughout the run. To the end of his life, Welles spoke of the premiere of the Harlem *Macbeth* as the greatest moment of his career.

It was also the fruit of a particularly gruelling process. Rehearsals often ran until the early hours of the morning, making use of any space available ('this theatre, auditoriums, hallways, fire escapes, paper bags, coal scuttles, trash barrels and my apartment', in Welles' account). The peculiar hours were largely forced upon the company due to the demands of Welles' radio schedule, though the testimony of his entire career suggests that Welles preferred to work at a breathless pace, attacking in all directions at once. Houseman estimated that Welles worked twenty out of every twenty-four hours, which, when taken together with the time he is supposed to have spent in Harlem's bars and brothels during this period, would have left the young director with no time to sleep whatsoever.

Both contemporary witnesses and Welles' rehearsal notes indicate that his overriding concern was to transform *Macbeth* into a single adrenaline rush. The transformation began with the playtext itself, already Shakespeare's shortest, but heavily cut and rearranged by Welles to stress a narrative arc of the Witches manipulating and destroying Macbeth. While actually cutting many of the Witches' lines, his script called for them to chant their remaining words incessantly, thus reducing the linguistic complexity of Shakespeare's text but increasing its ritual energy. The Witches (together with Hecate, their 'voodoo master') were also seen in all but two of the production's eight scenes, overshadowing and channelling the course of the tragedy. Act I, for example, culminates in Welles' version with Macbeth proclaimed King of Scotland by 'a grotesque, silent little army', while, from above, the three Witches 'quickly and sharply' chant Shakespeare's line for the First Witch in Act I, Scene 3 ('Weary sev'nights, nine times nine. / Shall we dwindle, peak, and pine'). Welles, who rarely missed an opportunity for a dramatic climax, describes the ending of the act thus:

> The three Witches are seen huddled on the wall. Under their chant has come a rapid throb of drums. This reaches a crescendo under a new voice that is Hecate's, loud and rasping. He is seen suddenly at the very top of the tower, leaning over the throned Macbeth below. The light of an angry dawn flames brighter behind him as he speaks. The courtyard is in shadows. The cripples are strange shapes in the gateway. Hecate and the three sisters are birds of prey.
>
> (Welles 1990: 62)

Hecate pronounces a final curse on the newly crowned king, concluding with the line 'He shall live a man forbid' (also taken from the First Witch of Act I, Scene 3). There is a final thump on the word 'forbid', and the drums come to a dead stop. The curtain comes down, and the single intermission of the evening begins. The emphasis, here as throughout the production, was on the expressionistic energies of primordial ritual and visceral scream.

Welles' focus on integrating music, movement and text meant that he spent little if any rehearsal time on such staples as dramatic elocution and conventional stage gesture. The lack of attention to 'proper' Shakespearian acting was in part motivated by the centrality of music and image in Welles' directorial vision, but it was also inspired by his scorn for conventionality and appreciation of his cast's strengths. 'You see', he told the *New York Times*: 'the negro actors have never had the misfortune of hearing Elizabethan verse spouted by actors strongly flavoring of well-cured Smithfield. They read their lines just as they would any others. On the whole, they're no better and no worse than the average white actor before he discovered the red plush style'.

Welles' popularising scorn for the 'red plush style' (a style he had undoubtedly learned as a member of Katherine Cornell's troupe two years earlier) dovetailed with his desire to draw on the strengths of his largely untrained actors. As he recalled in a 1974 interview, '[D]uring all those rehearsals, I never once suggested an intonation to the actors. The blacks invented the whole diction of Shakespeare. It was very interesting and very beautiful. I didn't suggest anything about Shakespearian tradition or the white way of reciting Shakespeare' (Estrin 2002: 154).

It is with *Macbeth* that Welles' talent for adapting his directorial style to his specific collaborators first emerged. This talent was particularly important when it came to the man on whom the success or failure of the production depended: Jack Carter, cast as Macbeth. Though he had previously performed in some notable roles (including Crown in *Porgy and Bess*), Carter was not a regular actor and was by most accounts a man – much like Welles himself – of furious appetites and mercurial habits. Welles' strategy for working with Carter, and perhaps Carter's strategy for working with Welles, relied heavily on building bonds of trust and affection. 'From the moment at the first reading when Orson threw his arms around Jack, his eyes brimming with tears of gratitude and admiration, a close and passionate friendship had sprung up between these two giants', recalled Houseman (1972: 195). Throughout the remainder of the rehearsal period, Welles and Carter were all but inseparable, with Carter showing up to every rehearsal, after which Welles and Carter would tear through the local clubs. Though not so close, Welles adopted a similarly affectionate style with his Lady Macbeth, the professional actor Edna Thomas. At the other extreme, things went very differently for Abe Feder, the lighting designer whom Welles abused throughout the rehearsal process. Houseman has speculated that Welles may have regularly attacked Feder, who was in any case 'a garrulous masochist', as a means of retaining the loyalty of his cast: the company was 'so delighted to hear someone else (a white man, especially) catching hell, that they persevered with their own stage maneuvers long after their normal span of patience had run out' (1972: 192). Whether or not this was Welles' strategy, he was clearly exploring a number of different techniques, ranging from close friendship to outright cruelty, to bring his directorial vision to life. Adaptability under pressure was always a strong suit of Welles', and it was a suit on which he would draw liberally in the forthcoming years.

Macbeth ran for sixty-four performances in Harlem, another eight weeks at the Adelphi Theatre on Broadway and finally toured through seven WPA theatres across the USA. The tour included a notable stop in Indianapolis where Welles performed the title role in blackface, but otherwise Welles had long since moved on to other projects. Among these were radio versions of Shakespeare plays for Columbia Workshop, including a *Macbeth* (performed live on 2 May 1937) that differed radically from the Harlem production. Though this version was also adapted and directed by Welles, it featured an all-white cast, starred Welles and returned the play to Scotland. Still essentially a man of the theatre, Welles was learning his way around the medium of radio and ended up alienating the composer Bernard Herrmann (who would later compose the score to *Citizen Kane*) by forcing upon him a highland bagpipe that effectively drowned out the studio orchestra. A Welles production of *Twelfth Night* would follow on 30 August of the same year, with Welles as Orsino.

Welles' next triumph as a Shakespearian director, however, was his stage production of *Julius Caesar*. Premiering on 11 November 1937 after a month of rehearsal, this was the first work produced by the Mercury Theatre, a company formed by Houseman and Welles in the afterglow of the Harlem *Macbeth*. The title of the production – *Caesar: The Death of a Dictator* – announced Welles' directorial vision. This would be a staging of Shakespeare's play that identified Julius Caesar with fascist dictatorship, Brutus with doomed liberalism and the crowds of Rome with the mass audiences of modern propaganda. Such analogies were underscored by the costuming of the Roman aristocracy in fascist uniforms and the crowds in twentieth-century street clothes. The stage design was based around simple multi-level platforms and vertical lights, both of which were inspired by Albert Speer's designs for the Nazi Party rallies at Nuremberg (including a lighting cue that directly referenced Speer's 'Cathedral of Light' effect).

The idea of a fascist Caesar, like that of a tragic hero inspired by Henri Christophe, was not original to Welles. The Federal Theatre Project in Wilmington, Delaware had produced a *Julius Caesar* targeting Mussolini some months earlier, and Sidney Howard and Hallie Flanagan had separately recommended the idea to Welles and Houseman. But originality only counts for so much, and the fact remains that Welles was the first to turn an anti-fascist *Julius Caesar* into a critical and commercial success. Moreover, the fascist context of his *Julius Caesar* has since inspired a number of subsequent Shakespeare productions, including Peter Hall's 1959 *Coriolanus* (with Laurence Olivier and Edith Evans) and the 1990 stage and 1995 film versions of *Richard III* starring Ian McKellen.

Welles came prepared to the first rehearsal, showing up with costume sketches, staging notes, light and music cues and a model of the set. As to the text, he had altered it drastically. Welles cut the opening confrontation between the tribunes and the plebeians, opening his play instead with the entrance of Julius Caesar. On the other end of the drama, he eliminated all the battle scenes as well as almost all of the final two acts. As he would throughout his career, Welles pared down scenes and interpolated lines from other Shakespeare plays to better express his overriding directorial vision. The role of Lepidus was cut entirely, while the characters of Octavius and Antony were much reduced, choices that further focused the play upon Caesar as the personification of dictatorship. The result of such alterations was a production of just over ninety minutes. As with *Macbeth*, Welles' predilection was for the breathless aesthetics of the expressionist stage: speed, concision, looming shadows, subconscious horror, death drive. That these were favourite aesthetic techniques of fascism itself is one of the many political ambiguities of Welles' Shakespearian stagings.

The rehearsal process for *Julius Caesar* was just the sort of organised chaos in which Welles thrived. 'When he felt like rehearsing, we rehearsed', recalled stage manager Howard Teichmann. 'When he felt like sleeping, we didn't rehearse. If he felt like rehearsing from 11:00 at night to 6:00 in the morning, damn stage-hands' overtime, full speed ahead' (Callow 1995: 326). One particular difficulty arose in the second week. Welles was determined to block the crowd scenes on the stage set, designed by Samuel Leve based on Welles' plans and being built at a warehouse in Fort Lee, New Jersey. Moving the set to the Mercury Theatre ahead of schedule would have been prohibitively expensive (a point that technical director Jean Rosenthal and producer Houseman were at some pains to explain to Welles). Undaunted, Welles ordered all forty members of the company to make their way out to Fort Lee, travelling from subway to ferry to bus and back again for the next ten days. Arriving already half-spent, his cast rehearsed in the sweltering heat of an airless warehouse, often drowned out by the noise of set construction. Welles insisted that all this inconvenience and lost time was necessitated by the complexities of the set itself, on which the actors needed to rehearse regularly to feel comfortable. As usual, Welles' dramatic instincts proved right, for the set – with its multiple levels, steps, risers and trapdoors, much of which had to be negotiated in utter darkness – proved at once a *coup de théâtre* and a serious threat to the actors' safety. Thanks largely to the Fort Lee rehearsals, the only actor injured on set was Welles himself. Having spent far more time directing the company than rehearsing his own role of Brutus, Welles lacked familiarity with the set from an actor's perspective. Predictably enough, he plummeted down one of the open traps in the first dress rehearsal, sprained his ankle and knocked himself unconscious. The accident was typical for Welles, who frequently sustained stage injuries; typical, too, was the fact that he was performing again the next night.

During the final week of rehearsal, Welles focused most of his attention on the actors' performances, leaving technical elements largely in the hands of Rosenthal and others (including Marc Blitzstein, who was responsible for the music). Having saved himself the time, as well as the expense, of the battle scenes, Welles was now able to devote himself to the crowd scenes and to individual performances. Welles was particularly meticulous in rehearsing the crowd's responses to the orations of Brutus and Antony. Wanting the responses to sound spontaneous and yet be precisely timed and linguistically Elizabethan, Welles developed an innovative strategy. He first recorded the two orations to disk, then played the disks to the actors playing the plebeians, who ad libbed specific lines, in modern English, to say at specific moments. Once these lines and their timing were established through improvisation, Welles replaced the modern words with similar exclamations from other Elizabethan plays.

One scene that was not so easily solved was Act III, Scene 3, the murder of Cinna the Poet by the plebeians who have mistaken him for Cinna the Conspirator. Though a relatively peripheral scene in Shakespeare's drama, it became, by opening night, a dramatisation of the Kafkaesque brutality of a dictatorial state. The scene was described by Joseph Wood Krutch in *The Nation* as an 'unforgettably sinister thing', and was similarly singled out by Grenville Vernon (for the *New Republic*) and Stark Young (for *Commonweal*) as a highlight of the production. In rehearsal, however, it was the last thing to emerge. The first trouble was a disagreement between Welles and Norman Lloyd, who was playing Cinna, as to how to interpret the character. Welles imagined him as a romantic hero, defiantly protesting his innocence to the assembled mob. But Lloyd envisioned Cinna as a shuffling scribbler, less Lord Byron than Mr Zero of Elmer Rice's *The Adding Machine*. At a creative impasse, Welles shelved the scene. Returning to it again three weeks later, he enlisted the aid of Marc Blitzstein, who built the crowd chants into a menacing rhythm that quickened as it continued ('Come. Kill. Ho. Slay . . .'). The underlying troubles continued, however. Compounding them was a larger hitch in the production, which was that the recorded sound score Welles had hoped to use (created by Irving Reis, Welles' sound technician at the Columbia Workshop) proved too much for the Mercury Theatre's amplification system. The trouble might have been anticipated, for Welles and Reis were ahead of their time; theatres in the mid-1930s were simply ill equipped for the kind of sophisticated sound collages that had become the staple of radio theatre.

Given the chaos of the Cinna scene and the inadequacy of the sound system, among other troubles, it's hardly surprising that the first preview of *Julius Caesar* was a disaster. Running with the Cinna scene removed (in part due to Lloyd's refusal to participate) and the speakers overloading, the curtain came down to complete silence. 'My God, we didn't even get a curtain call', shrieked the press officer backstage, according to one account, whereupon Welles spat in his face. Aside from the humiliation of artistic failure, Welles was fully aware that his *Julius Caesar* had to succeed – and succeed enormously – if the Mercury Theatre was to avoid dying in the cradle. Suspending future previews, Welles plunged himself into the business of salvaging his production. He eliminated the sound score entirely and made further cuts to Octavius and Antony's parts. He also returned to the Cinna scene, this time fully embracing Lloyd's reading of the character and using every device he could think of to make the new interpretation work. Now the arc of the scene ran, not from heroic defiance to grand tragedy, but from comic pathos to grotesque horror. Lloyd opened the scene playing Cinna as a Chaplinesque clown, looseleaf sheets spilling from his pockets, imagining himself a great artist amidst admirers. Then, suddenly, the derisive mass chanting began and increased in intensity, the lights turned red, the mob turned vicious. Surrounded now on all sides, Cinna screamed his last words – 'The poet!' – and disappeared down a trap, only his hand visible in the blood-red light. The sudden, starkly political reversal captured the sensibility of the whole production. Finding the key to Cinna's death scene was critical to finding the soul of the production, and the work quickly came together in time for opening night. Premiering to almost universal praise, *Julius Caesar* became the Mercury Theatre's greatest critical and commercial success.

Welles's next major Shakespeare production deserves at least a mention. In terms of sheer ambition, Welles' *Five Kings*, which premiered on 27 February 1939, outshone even his 1936 *Macbeth* and 1937 *Julius Caesar* productions. In terms of critical and commercial success, it fared incomparably worse. Adapted by Welles from *Richard II, Henry IV, Parts I and II*, and *Henry V, Five Kings* was produced by the Mercury Theatre together with the Theatre Guild. The play, which Welles intended to be only the first part of a two-part epic that would play on consecutive evenings, originally ran five hours with two intermissions and featured an enormous cast, including Welles as Falstaff, Burgess Meredith as Hal/Henry V and a host of Mercury Theatre regulars. Many reviewers complained that the play's enormous length and sprawling structure overwhelmed any virtues that might be found in particular scenes or individual performances. Touring through Boston, Washington and Philadelphia, *Five Kings* slimmed down by forty minutes but never made it to New York.

In the hopes of someday reviving the production, Welles kept the sets and costumes in a Bronx warehouse for almost twenty years after the Philadelphia closing. And, in a sense, he did revive it, though not with the same materials. On 20 February 1960, Welles would premiere a new version of the work, built around his performance as Falstaff, entitled *Chimes at Midnight*. The stage version of *Chimes at Midnight* would run for five performances at the Grand Opera House in Belfast before moving to the Gaity Theatre in Dublin, where it ran for another month. Once again, lacklustre audience response kept the ultimate goal – this time London rather than New York – out of reach. Still, Welles persisted. On 8 May 1966, after a year and a half of on-again, off-again production, he would finally finish the film version of *Chimes at Midnight* – once more a commercial failure but regarded by at least some cinéastes (including Steven Bogdanovich and Welles himself) as a masterpiece overshadowing even *Citizen Kane*.

The early 1940s saw Welles making his name, and losing it, in Hollywood. *Citizen Kane* was released in 1941, *The Magnificent Ambersons* in 1942, *The Stranger* in 1946, *The Lady from Shanghai* in 1947, and by 1948 Welles was *persona non grata*, bound for Europe in self-imposed exile. For his final film for the studio system (at least until his brief return in 1958 with *Touch of Evil*), Welles went back to Shakespeare. His *Macbeth* film was a prestige project for a studio usually associated with low-budget Westerns, Republic Pictures, which forced Welles to complete the picture in just three weeks with a tight budget of $700,000. Planning to have the play fully rehearsed before filming, Welles first staged it in May as part of the 1947 Utah Centennial Festival in Salt Lake City, with almost the same cast as would eventually be in the film (including himself as Macbeth and Jeanette Nolan as Lady Macbeth, as well as Dan O'Herlihy, Roddy McDowall and much of the Mercury company). After six performances, Welles moved the company to California to continue rehearsals for the film.

Expanding the rehearsal schedule on the one hand, Welles worked to reduce costs on the other. The Utah Festival had already paid for many of the costumes and props that Welles would reuse in the film; as for the sets, they largely consisted of abstract rock formations constructed out of papier mâché. Filming time would be reduced by setting up three cameras at angles that allowed several scenes to be shot simultaneously. Perhaps most critically, all dialogue was recorded beforehand, with the actors lip-synching along with their recorded voices during their performances, and some re-recorded dialogue added after filming. The decision to prerecord the voices proved a mixed blessing. While it kept costs down by eliminating all on-set sound recording, it also presented technical difficulties of sound synchronisation that, as with his subsequent *Othello* film, were never fully overcome.

In the end, however, *Macbeth* came in on time and on budget, a remarkable achievement for a director often unfairly accused of profligacy. Set in an abstracted Scottish landscape and structured around visual motifs rather than rhythms, it was a sharp departure from the Harlem *Macbeth* of twelve years earlier. Indeed, with tongue perhaps slightly in cheek, Welles remarked that the two productions shared nothing in common. Or *almost* nothing: when asked about any similarities between the two *Macbeths*, his answer was brief: 'When Macbeth goes up to Duncan's bedchamber, for me – I don't know why – he simply has to move stage right to left. That's all'. But Welles was obviously overstating the case, as both play and film exhibited a peculiarly Wellesian indebtedness to expressionism, a love of archetypal figures, dark shadows and chthonic energies bursting forth from a sharply streamlined text.

In September 1948, Welles set to work on his *Othello* film, a project that would consume about four years of shooting. Unlike his *Macbeth*, Welles' *Othello* would be shot entirely on location, in Italy (principally in Venice and Rome) and Morocco (principally in Mogador, Safi and Mazagan). As with the *Five Kings/Chimes at Midnight* project, Welles' struggle to complete *Othello* has since become legendary. 'Orson worried about money': this is the leitmotif of Micheál MacLiammóir's account of the filming of *Othello*, aptly titled *Put Money in Thy Purse*. Welles was able to earn some funds himself through his more remunerative side projects, but he was also forced to spend inordinate amounts of time going cap in hand to a motley crew of investors (including Hollywood mogul Derryl Zanuck, a Russian millionaire named Michel Olian, and numerous others), and it is quite likely that, by the time of the film's completion, Welles had sold more than 100 per cent of it. Money shortages led to other difficulties. Whenever shooting stopped, some of Welles' crew decamped for better-paying jobs (or, in some cases, jobs that paid at all), which meant rehiring at least some crew members after each hiatus. The same was true of actors, some of whom took occasional jobs in order to support their work on *Othello*, and some of whom simply left.

Welles' original Desdemona, the Italian actress Lea Padovani, fell into the last category. After shooting some scenes in the fall of 1948, Padovani left during an interruption in filming to star in a London production of *The Rose*

Tattoo, and never came back (though it remains unclear whether her departure was due to financial considerations, creative frustration, a romantic split with Welles or some combination of all three). Two substitutes (Cécile Aubry and Betsy Blair) failed to work out, and Welles finally settled on a French Canadian actress named Suzanne Cloutier. By the time the film was finished, Desdemona had become a Bride-of-Frankenstein creation: some of Padovani's scenes were reshot with Cloutier, some medium and long shots of Padovani were left in, and, after editing was completed, Cloutier (whose voice Welles increasingly disliked) was entirely dubbed with the voice of a Scottish actress named Gudrun Ure.

This process of multiplication, fragmentation and recomposition exemplifies Welles' broader procedure for the film (and subsequently for *Chimes at Midnight*), a procedure forced upon him by financial constraints but also occasionally embraced by Welles as a way of gaining total control over the final product. The result was that Welles generally filmed in a catch-as-catch-can manner, composing individual scenes from shots that were often taken in different locations, with different actors, over a period of years. The ultimate coherence of the work is a testament both to Welles' brilliance as a film editor and his uncanny ability to maintain a single artistic vision – down to the precise details of specific scenes – over four years filled with distraction. 'There was no way for the jigsaw puzzle to be put together except in my mind', recalled Welles. 'Over a span, sometimes of months, I had to hold each detail in my memory' (Brady 1989: 436).

Welles was always a master of that sort of creative jujitsu that flips adversity into inspiration, and nowhere was this more in evidence than in his work on *Othello*. A representative example was his work on Act V, Scene 1, in which Roderigo is killed (in Welles' version, by Iago rather than Cassio). By the time Welles had assembled actors, crew and equipment in Mogador to begin shooting, only the costume for Iago (played by MacLiammóir) was near completion; costumes for Othello (Welles), Roderigo (Robert Coote) and Cassio (Michael Laurence) were still far from finished. Welles was distraught at the prospect of losing yet more precious time and money and spent a sleepless night oscillating between rage and despair. By the next morning, however, he had reached a conclusion: he would set the scene not on a street, as text and tradition suggested, but in a steambath. While Iago would be fully costumed, Roderigo and Cassio would be dressed only in towels, surrounded by bathers and masseurs. In the resulting scene, the sultriness of the tightly packed bathhouse creates an atmosphere of claustrophobic menace, which builds to the conflict between Roderigo and Cassio, both of whom are rendered more vulnerable (as well as, in an intriguing twist, more comic) by their semi-nakedness. The scene culminates with Roderigo hiding in a low crawlspace; we see him in close-up at the bottom of the frame. He calls out for Iago, who stands in long shot, physically distant from the camera but immediately above Roderigo in the frame. Hearing Roderigo's call, Iago turns and moves towards the camera, spots Roderigo immediately below him, and suddenly strikes downward at him between the loosely spaced floorboards. The scene concludes with a montage of the diagonal lines of the floorboards punctured over and again by the darting line of Iago's sword. Equal parts revenge tragedy and film noir, the steambath scene became one of the most effective in the film.

Unlike *Macbeth*, and to a greater degree than *Chimes at Midnight, Othello* is a film that foregrounds and reflects upon cinematic technique. Welles' greatest contributions to film-making are typically associated with the techniques of *Citizen Kane*, especially his use of deep focus and the long take. Ironically perhaps, these innovations would likely never have occurred had it not been for Welles' relative ignorance of standard studio cinematography and, just as importantly, for his years in the theatre. For both techniques actually bring film closer to the experience of theatre: the use of deep focus recalls the theatre by allowing the audience to choose where to focus its gaze rather than having the camera 'choose' for it, while the use of the long take recalls the theatre by allowing a scene to continue for a lengthy period without cutting. With *Othello*, however, all of that was abandoned, and Welles allowed more essentially cinematic techniques such as montage and camera movement to dominate. With the exception of one long tracking shot of a dialogue between Iago and Othello, the *Othello* film is a highly cinematic montage closer to the work of Eisenstein than that of the earlier Welles. While relationships between the characters are de-emphasized throughout – there is an odd stasis to the characters that sometimes makes the film resemble a particularly hierophantic production of Racine – more peculiarly filmic relationships (such as that between the length of individual shots and the broader flow of dramatic action) and techniques (such as arresting camera angles) are stressed. Thanks in part to the fragmented production schedule forced upon it, and in part to Welles' inspired response to these constraints, *Othello* marks a revolution in Welles' film aesthetic.

Othello won the Palme d'Or at the Cannes Film Festival in 1952, but, like *Macbeth*, enjoyed little commercial success. It would be followed fourteen years later by Welles' equally ambitious, equally troubled, equally brilliant, equally unremunerative Shakespeare film, *Chimes at Midnight*. There would, of course, be other Shakespeare projects as well; with Welles, there were *always* other projects. Immediately after the release of *Othello*, a modern-dress production of *Julius Caesar* was planned but never realised; it was to be shot in news-reel style, funded by King Farouk of Egypt and starring Richard

Burton. The idea would return again in the late 1960s, when Welles reimagined the same production with Christopher Plummer as Marc Antony, Paul Scofield as Brutus and himself as Caesar; again, the project refused to take flight. Acting work was easier to come by, and Welles, despite his detour into auteurism, remained attached to his earlier cultural populism. Welles played Lear in a Peter Brook production for American network television in 1953 and played the role three years later at the City Center in New York. The same year would also find him alternating his Las Vegas magic act with recitations from *Julius Caesar, Merchant of Venice* and *King Lear*.

Card tricks and soliloquies: in a later age, such a high–low mish-mash might have been dubbed 'postmodern'. But Welles never fit such genealogies. Too enamoured of mass culture to be quite a modernist, he was also too rooted in what he understood as tradition to be quite post. Thirty years of Shakespearian productions reveal a wide range of approaches across many media, an overabundance that spilled over established boundaries of high and low, artistic and commercial, enduring and topical. Some patterns emerge, however, from the initial successes of the Harlem *Macbeth* and the Mercury *Julius Caesar* through to his late Shakespeare films. Though Welles never invented language for Shakespeare's characters to speak, he was otherwise unabashed about radically altering the texts, often cutting drastically, rearranging scenes and interpolating lines from other plays of the period. Welles' rehearsal style, meanwhile, could best be described as organised, inspired chaos – a tempest lasting anywhere from a day (on some radio performances) to several years (on some films). Finally, Welles' productions were generally marked by a distinctive interest in quickening rhythms and arresting images, dark shadows and unconscious drives, that make them as much the heirs of expressionism as of Shakespeare.

Chronology

1915	George Orson Welles born 6 May in Kenosha, Wisc.
1936	Directs *Macbeth* for the Negro Theatre Unit of the Federal Theatre Project
1937	Forms the Mercury Theatre with John Houseman. Directs and acts in *Caesar*, the Mercury Theatre's inaugural production. Directs and acts in two Shakespeare plays for Columbia Workshop radio, *Macbeth* and *Twelfth Night*
1938	Directs and acts in a radio production of *Julius Caesar* for Mercury Theatre on the air
1938–40	Records *Julius Caesar*, *Twelfth Night*, *Merchant of Venice* and *Macbeth* for Mercury Text Records; the records are intended to

	accompany his student editions of selected Shakespeare plays, co-edited with Roger Hill
1939	Directs and acts in *Five Kings*, which performs in Boston, Mass., Washington, DC and Philadelphia, Pa.
1941	*Citizen Kane* opens
1942	*The Magnificent Ambersons* opens
1947	Directs *Macbeth* for the Utah Festival
1948	*Macbeth* film opens
1951	Directs and acts in *Othello* at Theatre Royal in Newcastle
1952	*Othello* film opens
1956	Directs and acts in *King Lear* at the New York City Center Theatre
1958	*Touch of Evil* opens
1960	Directs and acts in *Chimes at Midnight* at the Gate Theatre, Dublin
1966	*Chimes at Midnight* film opens
1985	Welles dies in Hollywood

Bibliography

Anderegg, Michael (1999) *Orson Welles, Shakespeare, and Popular Culture*, New York: Columbia University Press.

Brady, Frank (1989) *Citizen Welles*, New York: Macmillan.

Brode, Douglas (2000) *Shakespeare in the Movies*, New York: Oxford University Press.

Callow, Simon (1995) *Orson Welles*, Vol. I: *The Road to Xanadu*, New York: Penguin.

—— (2006) *Orson Welles*, Vol. II: *Hello Americans*, New York: Viking.

Conrad, Peter (2003) *Orson Welles: The Stories of His Life*, London: Faber & Faber.

Davies, Anthony (1988) *Filming Shakespeare's Plays*, Cambridge: Cambridge University Press.

Estrin, Mark W. (2002) *Orson Welles Interviews*, Jackson, Miss.: University Press of Mississippi.

France, Richard (ed.) (1990) *Orson Welles on Shakespeare: The WPA and Mercury Theatre Playscripts*, New York: Greenwood Press.

—— (1977) *The Theatre of Orson Welles*, Lewisburg, Pa.: Bucknell University Press.

Houseman, John (1972) *Run-Through: A Memoir*, New York: Simon & Schuster.

MacLiammóir, Micheál (1952) *Put Money in Thy Purse: The Filming of Orson Welles'* Othello, London: Eyre Methuen.

Mason, Pamela (2000) 'Orson Welles and Filmed Shakespeare', in Russell Jackson (ed.), *The Cambridge Companion to Shakespeare on Film*, Cambridge: Cambridge University Press, pp. 187–202.

Rosenbaum, Jonathan (ed.) (1992) *This Is Orson Welles*, New York: HarperCollins.

Thomson, David (1996) *Rosebud: The Story of Orson Welles*, New York: Vintage.

Welles, Orson (1990) *Macbeth, Adapted and Directed by Orson Welles*, France, pp. 37–101.

About the author

Matthew Wilson Smith is the author of *The Total Work of Art: From Bayreuth to Cyberspace* (2007), a study of the influence of Richard Wagner on modern performance. He has also written widely on modern drama and film. His published essays include studies of Wagner and American cinema, Riefenstahl's *Triumph of the Will* and the American film designs of Joseph Urban. He is an assistant professor of English at Boston University.

30
PETER ZADEK

Michael Raab

Born in 1926 in Berlin as the son of Jewish parents, Zadek's family emigrated to London in 1933. During the Second World War, he was an outsider on two counts: as a Jew and German among the English and as somebody strongly anglicised among the other refugees. He decided not to finish his studies in French and German at Jesus College in Oxford. Instead, he got a place at the Old Vic School where Tyrone Guthrie became his main mentor. Kenneth Tynan called Guthrie's approach an 'infuriating blend of insight and madness' (Tynan 1975: 259). The same could be said about his pupil's later Shakespearian efforts. After having started out in weekly rep at Pontypridd and Swansea, followed by similar jobs in the English regions, Zadek's last British production was the world premiere of Jean Genet's *The Balcony* at the Arts Theatre in London. The enraged author protested against what he perceived as a vulgarisation of his text, threatened to shoot the director and had to be barred from attending the first night.

From early on, Zadek was interested in open forms and plays with strong contrasts. In Shakespeare's work he found a mixture of 'enormous naivety and sophisticated refinement. No theories, no moral lessons, no aesthetic principles, no fashionable updatings' (programme for *Measure for Measure*, Bremen 1967). Already prior to his move back to Germany he had voiced strong objections against any kind of moralising and a directorial method he labelled 'intellectual': 'Theatre is no place to declare intentions. It must not be didactic but entice the audience to ask questions. A play should not contain a message but a vision' (Canaris 1979: 29). Categorically, he stated, 'Shakespeare is characterised by an elementary curiosity, whilst Brecht and Schiller always know everything better from the outset. Probably that is the main difference between the Anglo-Saxon attitude towards theatre and life and the German one' (Lange 1989: 59).

From England he brought a kind of showmanship and revue-like elements unusual in the German theatre at the time, which was still understood as educational in Schiller's sense of 'the stage as a moral institution'. Many of the leading artistic directors liked to call the theatre 'a metaphysical space'. After 1945, there was no significant break in their work, as they stuck to a kind of pathos-drenched declamatory style on abstract sets while professing to let the plays speak for themselves.

All that was anathema to Zadek, and he could not find work in contexts dominated by such outdated aesthetics. After a brief interlude in Cologne he became one of the stalwarts of Kurt Hübner's teams at Ulm and later at Bremen. Hübner was a director of rather modest abilities who never strayed beyond conventional limits. In that respect, he appeared not very different from the old guard his protégés reacted against. But his big quality was being generous enough to gather a group of collaborators with extremely varied styles. In Ulm, Zadek's extrovert theatricality and the rather dour austerity of the former Brecht assistant Peter Palitzsch could not be further apart. Palitzsch in retrospect said about his colleague: 'Everything about him was different from what I had known until then, the way he talked about theatre, his approach to plays, his humour, his cosmopolitan *savoir vivre*' (Iden 2005: 66).

Moving to Bremen, Zadek's main rival was Peter Stein, whose stringent analytical clarity was alien to him. Between them there was not much love lost. 'Shakespeare in underpants' (*Der Spiegel*, 20 December 1976), Stein derided Zadek's method. His opponent, on the other hand, professed himself to be profoundly bored by 'perfectionist packaging' (Canaris 1979: 228) that stifled any remnants of spontaneity in Stein's productions. Both had such a high reputation that they were able to form an excellent ensemble of mostly young actors. Bruno Ganz, then an absolute beginner trying to get out of his native Switzerland, thought only of two theatres he wanted to work at: the Berliner Ensemble and Bremen. Zadek always looked for actors with the potential to surprise him in rehearsal by throwing overboard the usual proprieties of their profession. When he saw that potential, he was perfectly willing to cast people Stein or Palitzsch deemed insufficiently trained.

The strongest link between Zadek and Stein was the designer Wilfried Minks who introduced many of the new trends in the visual arts to the German theatre. For Zadek's *Measure for Measure* in 1967, he reduced the set to a frame of coloured lightbulbs and a couple of chairs. The actors wore jeans and T-shirts or suits, the disguised Duke's cowl being the only costume in the traditional sense. In this brightly lit, uncluttered environment, Zadek was able to radicalise his previous attempts at Shakespearian innovation. His biggest success in that respect had been *Hero Henry* (1964) after *Henry V*, which demythologised war by demonstrating the cynicism of military codes of honour in the manner of Joan Littlewood's *Oh! What a Lovely War*. With *Measure for Measure*, according to a statement in the programme, Zadek at first had 'a more or less realistic production' in mind, but after two weeks of rehearsals, he realised 'that what I saw on the stage strongly differed from what I envisioned myself'. Consequently, he took the text only as the starting point for 'a production of the play's contemporary substance on a free stage'.

The adaptation by the Bavarian dramatist Martin Sperr divides the play into twenty-five scenes, savagely cutting and rewriting the text and including a final massacre, leaving most of the characters dead on the ground. Throughout the evening, Zadek aims for big emotions. To establish their mutual dependence, Angelo (played by Bruno Ganz) and Escalus have a shouting match standing unsteadily on the same chair whilst desperately clinging to each other. They screech the words in a staccato almost unintelligible for the audience. Claudio and his pregnant fiancée are placed head down for their pillory scene whilst the guards converse through the open legs of their prisoners. Isabella jumps at Angelo from behind, screams hysterically into his ear, crawls all over him when she attempts to persuade him. Wanting to prepare Claudio for death, she sits behind him on the floor and slings her legs around his hip. As if to break his inner resistance, she then tries to force her brother's thighs open. Peter Palitzsch was particularly impressed by the passage in which Isabella and Mariana arrange the cheating of Angelo. During their negotiation, they sit next to a beehive, and the whole discussion is also a fight to fend off the bees: 'You had to laugh, and yet it stayed true to the meaning of the scene. Later on Zadek's way to deal with death had nothing esoterically mysterious: that these people who overreach themselves die like cattle is also a tragic joke' (Iden 2005: 66).

Zadek's fellow director refers to the production's most controversial aspect, when at the end the Duke Claudio, Angelo and Mariana are killed off one after the other. The Duke's position in the meanwhile has been taken by Mistress Overdone, here called 'Frau Meier' and impersonated by a male actor, an early instance of Zadek's liking for cross-gender casting. It did not exactly contribute to the understanding of the play when, as a rather feeble in-joke, the actor Georg Martin Bode is named out of character and his execution is called for. Even without going as far as Peter Stein, who called the final murder orgy 'fascist', it appears as a too-easy way to round off a production which, after a powerful series of bravura turns, has become increasingly unhinged. The question whether Isabella might be able to accept the Duke's proposal of marriage gets completely sidestepped. A wish to liken the Duke to a bawd is not enough to justify the rewriting of the ending. The characters are not granted any kind of development, and there is no attempt to investigate the conditions which make it possible for Isabella to utter a plea for Angelo's life.

In none of his previous and none of his subsequent productions did Zadek as ruthlessly put a sledgehammer to a play's form or give a process of self-exploration by a group of actors during rehearsals precedence over his own view of a text. The play was used as material for a string of individually convincing and spectacular visual moments. Despite the mounting inconsistencies towards the end, the flair and the sheer power of the interpretation led critic Georg Hensel to resume, 'All theoretical queries are brushed aside by the way the production works' (Hensel 1983: 13). Peter Palitzsch, however, was right with his warning that 'Zadek opened up dimensions that were later misunderstood by others' (Iden 2005: 66). The director wanted a Shakespearian production without any kind of 'intimidation by the classics' in Brecht's famous phrase. He did not seek improvisation for its own sake. The physical turns were artfully choreographed and demanded the technical skill missing in a lot of feeble attempts to copy it.

Together with Peter Stein's *Torquato Tasso* in 1969, *Measure for Measure* proved one of the two crowning glories of the Hübner years in Bremen and pivotal for the development of the German brand of directors' theatre that dominated the 1970s. For a few years, the Hanseatic town of Bremen was the theatre capital of Germany, a feat only possible due to this country's strong federal tradition of financing the arts, so that regional companies were able to compete successfully with those in the bigger cities. Berlin did not regain the leading position it had enjoyed in the 1920s when it was every actor's aspiration to work there. In Bremen, as in all German municipal theatres, the theatre had a permanent company and a repertory of plays that allowed the scheduling of a different performance every evening. The stylistic richness on offer there was due to Zadek and Stein but also to other outstanding directors like Rainer Werner Fassbinder, Klaus Michael Grüber and Peter Palitzsch.

At the end of the Bremen years, Zadek and Stein parted company. In the 1970s, Stein made the Schaubühne in Berlin the leading German theatre, politically far to the left and very much in accordance with the mood of the time during and after the student rebellion. Zadek, between 1967 and 1972, somewhat vanished from the picture after having accused Stein of having wrecked the artistic work at Bremen with indoctrination, incitement to political hysteria and demands for an amount of democratisation he thought impossible in a theatre. Himself too much of an outsider, Zadek was absolutely unwilling to think about 'training to become a good communist', as Stein and his followers tried at the time. When he took over the artistic directorship of the Schauspielhaus Bochum in 1972, Zadek rejected the cloistered atmosphere at the Schaubühne and instead opted for Joan Littlewood's dream of a fun palace.

Bochum, in the centre of the Ruhr valley with its strong mining industry, has a less bourgeois audience than Bremen but an even stronger theatre tradition, particularly with regard to Shakespeare. The Schauspielhaus claims to have been the first theatre worldwide that produced all thirty-seven of Shakespeare's plays. Under the artistic director Saladin Schmitt there were two famous cycles:

all of the histories in 1927 and the Roman plays ten years later. When Zadek arrived, the funding situation was even better than at Bremen, as Bochum concentrates exclusively on the legitimate theatre, which, therefore, does not have to share the same building with an opera and a dance company. At the time, Bremen had a budget of 12.8 million marks for all three genres and Bochum almost the same amount exclusively for the straight theatre. Zadek provided some much-needed colour for an architecturally and atmospherically rather drab city. He started with a very successful revue version of Hans Fallada's novel *Little Man, What Now?*, organised weekend parties opening up the whole building and cooperated with the local football club, unfortunately rather the 'grey mouse' of the Bundesliga. But brash entertainment was only one side of the coin, and Zadek persistently returned to his basic interest in outsiders.

The artistically most convincing example for that was not premiered at Bochum, but with *Othello* 1976 at the Deutsches Schauspielhaus Hamburg. Bochum, however, had seen a trial run for the underlying conceptual idea with *The Merchant of Venice* four years earlier. Hans Mahnke's Shylock appeared almost like a caricature from the pages of the vicious anti-Semitic Nazi paper *Der Stürmer*. He wore a dirty and torn sackcloth kaftan, and his body language and exaggerated intonation were reminiscent of Veit Harlan's notorious film *Jew Süß*. No non-Jewish director would have got away with a Shylock scraping the dirt from underneath his toenails at the time. Zadek rebelled against then-current philo-Semitic German versions of Shylock as a rather kind old gentleman. His point was, only if you accept this Jew as he is can tolerance be worth its name.

The same could be said of his production of *Othello* where the eponymous part was again portrayed as a grotesque stereotype of the audience's worst imaginations for a black man. Ulrich Wildgruber broke radically with the tradition of Othello as some kind of noble savage and looked more like King Kong on the rampage than a believable commander of the Venetian fleet. The critic Peter Iden wrote:

> Wildgruber in the course of the evening throws over board any kind of control, shows the negro as a seedy, eye-rolling, jerkily gesticulating, most of the time half-naked, always profusely sweating monster, a being outside of any order, excessive with every action. For minutes he fills the stage with explosions of a maniacal frenzy, he rants and raves, tumbles to the floor, roles around spasmodically, kicks, beats himself with his fists, spits, shouts – a riot of emotional excess, so that the feelings are no longer convincingly translated.
>
> (*Frankfurter Rundschau*, 17 May 1986)

Zadek defended his protagonist and thought Wildgruber perfect casting for what 'mind you, is a Shakespeare-negro, not a real one', because he was capable of bringing out 'this invented kind of naiveness and to voice it without in the least trying to embody a negro' (*Theater heute*, 7/1976, 24).

Whilst Othello in Hamburg retained not a shred of the dignified commander, Desdemona was a bored and spoilt young thing trying to compensate for the emptiness of her life by constant changes of dress. The way Eva Mattes played her, it was only too possible to believe Iago's insinuation that she would soon be fed up with the attentions of a husband considerably older than herself. To underline the outwardly scandalous side of their relationship, Zadek used a simple and convincing visual means: whenever Othello touched Desdemona, his black make-up rubbed off on her. The director explained, 'The idea which I and I think every child, every white child, first have is: "If you touch a negro, mummy, does the colour come off?" ' (*Theater heute* 7/1976, 28). Although he heavily stereotyped the other characters – Brabantio as Pantalone, Iago with Mephistopheles's feather in his cap, Roderigo wearing a clown's nose, Emilia as a vapid society lady – Zadek this time sketched the social context he so rigorously denied in *Measure for Measure*. On a set designed by the director himself and Peter Pabst, who was also responsible for the costumes, Cyprus was characterised as a colonial tourist resort by just a few props. Whilst Wilfried Minks provided Zadek with designs formulating a strong aesthetic statement of their own, with other collaborators the director brought as much as possible of the rehearsal room onto the stage, even if the result looked rather scrappy and provisional. For *Othello*, the ladies wore bikinis on the beach where they were waited on by native servants and got photographed by a local official for later publicity purposes. There were street musicians; Bianca was looking out for punters. In this environment, rumours and intrigues flourished, lazy hanging around at a flash turned into violence.

Bianca's unsubtle solicitation by lifting up her skirt or Iago's lascivious storing of the handkerchief in his underpants did not much bother the Hamburg audience. But in the last act, the production turned into one of the biggest scandals in Hanseatic theatre history. Already, earlier on, Wildgruber in his shaggy and matted wig and uniform jacket straight out of operetta provoked a number of angry calls due to his slurred enunciation. In one instance, he calmly stepped off the stage, walked up to the heckler and repeated the passage in question exclusively for him before returning to the play's action. Zadek easily took elocutionary problems in his stride:

> Where I have to choose between a formalism of language alien to the actor's own rhythm and a partial inaudibility or sloppiness, naturally I opt for the sloppiness. I don't always and, I believe, only when the

> quality of the sloppiness is really big. I don't do it [. . .] to provoke anyone.
>
> (*Theater heute*, 7/1976, 24)

A substantial part of the audience understood the treatment of the murder scene as a clear attempt at provocation. After the line 'put out the light', the stage remained dark for a couple of minutes whilst Othello hunted down Desdemona who desperately shouted for help and was brutally mistreated. Zadek staged a sex murder rather than the usual tasteful suffocation with a pillow. Hellmuth Karasek compared the spectators' reaction to the voyeurism of gapers at traffic accidents or punch-ups and commented:

> The audience could see and experience that even in a tragedy dying is a nasty business. They would not mind the same thing happening in the yellow press. But [on the stage] this has to be done as a laying-out, as proper obsequies, in white linen and candlelight, preferably accompanied by music for strings.
>
> (*Der Spiegel*, 17 May 1976)

Zadek, with *Othello*, tried to achieve the biggest possible reversals of feeling, again and again veering between moments of terrifying rage and intense calm. Touching situations were immediately followed by coarse exaggeration. Desdemona movingly sang the willow song cowering naked on the floor, but the director soon broke the elegiac mood when Emilia fondled her mistress's nipples, although the text does not indicate any such sexual intimacy. During the murder scene, next to all the squealing and shouting there were instances of enormous intensity, as described by Benjamin Henrichs:

> [Othello] suddenly turns silent, sits down on the edge of the bed, next to the dead Desdemona, and seeming greatly amazed asks in his most childlike tone: 'Who killed her?' And one realised (if one wanted to) that in a tragedy people get utterly destroyed, not only the theatre, the scenery, and the good taste.
>
> (*Die Zeit*, 14 May 1976)

For some spectators, it was in the worst possible taste that Othello then threw Desdemona's dead and naked body unceremoniously across a washing line.

With this *Othello, The Merchant of Venice* as well as *King Lear* in 1974 and *Hamlet* three years later in Bochum, Zadek achieved what was widely rated as the outstanding quartet of Shakespearian productions in the German theatre of the 1970s. After his Hamlet, Wildgruber described the principle of his cooperation with the director: 'The idea was to do something like jazz. A certain amount of improvisation is possible in the context of a specific theme and the acting among the group' (*Theater heute*, 3/1978, 32). Zadek himself often used the comparison with free jazz or a football match and wanted his work to be different with each performance. At the end of a speech at the Deutsches Schauspielhaus in 1979, he said:

> In the theatre, in contrast to the technical media, the special thing is that nothing can be repeated in exactly the same way. There are few actors who even in a Shakespeare part are capable every evening of giving the impression that suddenly something completely unexpected might happen, be it a cry or an exaggerated gesture, so that in the end they ought to be carried away by the people in white coats.
>
> (*Die Zeit*, 4 May 1979)

During rehearsals, Zadek only used solutions which initially came from the cast: 'What I simply am unable to do is to tell an actor: now do that for this reason in a certain way at this moment and over there you react like that' (Zadek 1990: 150). He insisted that the first impulse had to come from the actor and only then did he help to develop it. If somebody was unwilling to work according to this principle, he ruthlessly replaced him. Over the years, he brought together a group of regulars who knew each other increasingly well and were able to adapt to different surroundings when Zadek took them out of their familiar theatre buildings in his quest for a new audience apart from the usual bourgeois circles. *King Lear* was rehearsed and shown in a cinema, *Hamlet* in a factory hall in Bochum-Hamme, a decidedly unfashionable part of the city. Even though *Othello* had its premiere in the plush opulence of the Deutsches Schauspielhaus, at first it was scheduled outside the theatre's usual subscription system as a late-night show. But the four-hour running time and its big success with the audience after the initial protests had calmed down made a start at 10 p.m. unfeasible. One of the few dissenting voices was Georg Hensel who complained about:

> the reduction of complex, intricately motivated stories to a tabloid headline: Shylock or The justified hate of a betrayed Jew. Lear or The destruction of an old fool. Othello or The black man as an unfortunate outsider. Hamlet or The world as total theatre.
>
> (*Frankfurter Allgemeine Zeitung*, 30 October 1977)

Hensel summarised his criticism: 'Zadek's theatre is satisfied to be nothing else than theatre: it follows the principle of the show. Shakespeare is only necessary to provide the trigger for the various turns' (Hensel 1983: 335). The director himself admitted that in Bremen he and his collaborators had stressed the metatheatrical components too blatantly. But the more he worked on Shakespeare, the less he felt it necessary to set off his work quite so demonstratively from other current interpretations. Even though he regarded translations of the plays as inherently reductive to a massive degree, he no longer took extreme liberties with a text as in *Measure for Measure*, where some of Isabella's utterances were reduced to infantile babbling to turn her into an overexcited teenager. In *Hamlet*, he even used passages from the Romantic Schlegel/Tieck version, allowing the Prince's soliloquies and his scenes with Ophelia a kind of lyricism unparalleled before, and generally retained a rather full text.

In 1977, *Hamlet* marked the end of Zadek's artistic directorship in Bochum. Already in 1975 he had relinquished sole responsibility and had become part of a directorate. Despite initial mistakes due to inexperience in his new function, his period in office was rated a success artistically as well as for the sheer energy his team invested. Against all warnings to the contrary, Zadek's daring gamble paid off when he scrapped the theatre's subscription scheme (whereby spectators had to prebook certain productions) and replaced it with one that allowed them to choose only those they really wanted to see. Tickets were available in two categories at only 5 and 10 marks, subscribers got a reduction of 20 per cent. In the end, even a difficult evening in an alternative space like *King Lear* sold almost the same total amount of seats as more conventional fare like Hecht/MacArthur's *The Front Page* on the main stage.

Bochum under Zadek offered a popular theatre which was unique in Germany at the time. In 1985, it therefore seemed a logical step that he became Artistic Director of the Deutsches Schauspielhaus Hamburg, where he had worked as a guest director a number of times. Hamburg, like Bremen a Hanseatic town and economically more potent than its smaller rival, with the Deutsches Schauspielhaus and its 1,200 seats not only has the biggest German auditorium but also the Thalia, a second equally important and well-funded theatre. The Schauspielhaus then had a budget of 28.6 million marks, 24.7 million of which were state subsidy. The figures for the Thalia were 23.2 million and 17.8 million marks respectively. Unfortunately, Zadek's time in the north of Germany turned out to be a sad contrast to the bright and cheerful, if somewhat anarchic, years in Bochum. In Hamburg, from the outset, he antagonised many critics and spectators by a strident trumpeting of his own virtues which was deemed rather 'un-Hanseatic' in a city whose leading exponents take pride in their unostentatious behaviour in public. Even an old colleague like Ulrich Wildgruber went on record to maintain:

> I did not care much for all this bragging; the PR was dreadful and seriously impaired my sense of proportion. Everything was talked up so much, I thought this simply won't work out, you can't always say: 'I am the greatest, the only one!' Perhaps he hid behind this attitude, I could not reach him any more.
>
> (Lange 1989: 112)

Unfortunately, Zadek's announcements were not matched on the stage. After the success of the Shakespearian work in the 1970s, a tritely infantile version of *As You Like It* was a particular disappointment. The director inserted clumsily staged references to then popular soap operas and, with such extraneous business, gave the impression that he did not trust the text. His later reaction to the negative reviews reeked of pure cynicism, as he gleefully recounted that during the first-night party someone had asked him, 'Mr Zadek, wasn't it immensely difficult to get all those star actors to a point where they appear like dilettantes?' He claimed this man was the only one who had understood his intention with the production (Lange 1989: 73).

Shakespeare's comedies never were Zadek's forte – most disastrous was in 1981 *The Taming of the Shrew* at Kurt Hübner's Berlin Freie Volksbühne, listlessly executed in a setting reminiscent of *Arabian Nights*. Not only was his own work – with the exception of Wedekind's *Lulu* in 1988 – not on a par with the Bochum years, but he also invited mostly second-rate colleagues who were just as luckless. As he had again changed the subscription system to give the audience more choice, hits like *Lulu* sold out, but the flops in the huge auditorium were often not even half-full, and the Schauspielhaus lost ground against its local rival, the Thalia. Whilst in Bochum, Zadek had increased the amount of subscribers already during the first season of his artistic directorship, in Hamburg there was a fall in numbers which proved a liability for his successor Michael Bogdanov. Zadek's artistic directorship was increasingly marked by absentee landlordism; colleagues complained that he spent more time in his flat than in the theatre; and, to add insult to injury, he saved up all his contractually guaranteed time for directing elsewhere in order to go away for more or less the last complete season of his period in Hamburg (see *Theater heute*, 11/1989, 1).

As so often with Zadek, just when he appeared to be critically in the doldrums, he bounced back with a huge success: *The Merchant of Venice* in 1988 – at the Vienna Burgtheater, by far the highest-funded German-speaking theatre, which received twice the amount of subsidy the Deutsches Schauspielhaus or the Thalia Theatre in Hamburg could draw on. For Zadek, it was his fourth production of the play, after an early attempt in England about which he remembers nothing, and then at Ulm and Bochum. Going back to his old interest in outsiders, he had chosen the Shakespeare play he thought closest to his own experience, 'so that basically every 15 years I investigate and describe my own situation' (Lange 1989: 54). It had been one of the very first his parents took him to in England:

> I remember very well John Gielgud as an extremely nasty and repulsive Shylock and Peggy Ashcroft hovering around as a lovely, very young Portia. I went with my parents, I must have been 10 or 11. I still remember that my mother was a bit embarrassed when she had to explain to me why this Jew was so hideous.
>
> (Zadek 1990: 274)

In his own work on the play he always thought it: 'fascinating that as a director you can make Shylock as repugnant, vengeful, loathsome and evil as you like – and yet he remains a sympathetic character. You simply don't get him really vile, I don't know why. With Hans Mahnke I really tried to give my best in this respect' (Zadek 1990: 274)

Being an assimilated Jew himself, in Vienna Zadek wanted a Shylock outwardly undistinguishable from the other characters, and in rehearsal was amused that Gert Voss watched him very closely for details he might use. Voss had expected Zadek to cast him as the merchant and Ignaz Kirchner as Shylock, but the director thought it possible to make Shylock's Jewish thinking clearer by going against type. For Portia in the trial scene, it made absolute sense to ask which is the merchant here, and which the Jew, as both wore the outfits of late 1980s brokers – Shylock, if anything, the flashier and more elegant of the two. The biggest laugh of the evening was due to Antonio's appalled look when Portia asked him 'Is your name Shylock?', and Kirchner's cold cigar dropped from his mouth. Shylock was modelled on Michael Douglas, as Voss had seen Oliver Stone's *Wall Street* while preparing for the part and had given Zadek the video. Whereas the director in the 1970s had disdained stylistic unity for his Shakespearian productions and had used a very eclectic approach to costumes, this time he created a stringent environment for the whole play. The huge and mostly empty stage of the Burgtheater was dominated by an elevator at the back for the entrances and exits, Belmont was only marked by a painted backdrop (set by Wilfried Minks, paintings and costumes by Johannes Grützke). The characters looked dwarfed, exposed and forelorn on these vast expanses, an effect diminished when the production later transferred to the more intimate Berliner Ensemble.

Voss voiced surprise about the way Zadek was able to approach the text as if he had never done it before. But the director has always stressed the importance of the very first impression when encountering a play and despite thorough preparatory reading tries to regain the state of greatest possible innocence when starting to work on it. In an interview, Voss assumed that Zadek was especially interested in the fact that a Jew, however assimilated and demonstrably German, is still not properly integrated and even more in presenting a Jew who is not a passive victim but fights back and shows his pride (see Dermutz 2001: 99). In the Vienna version, he enjoys his job because he is very good at it, whilst Antonio always looks like an advertisement for a stomach remedy. When Shylock demands his rights, he clearly knows that there will be some kind of hidden trap. He basks in his intermediate triumph by sharpening the knife on the sole of his shoe, and even when he is outmanoeuvred by Portia briefly considers whether it might still be worthwhile to have a go at Antonio. When he desists, he does not let his enemies see any disappointment. Still on his knees from pleading for his life as demanded by the Duke, he checks the date on his watch, calmly writes out two cheques with an exquisite golden pen, hands them over, puts on his hat and leaves with the smiling assertion, 'I am content'. The Venetians view this spectacle with rather mixed feelings, because they seem to know that this Shylock will bounce back, and then the situation might no longer be saved by Eva Mattes as a very earnest and even somewhat sad Portia.

Nonchalance was not only the keyword for Voss's acting but a characteristic of the production as a whole. Voss and Kirchner had been particularly worried about Shylock and Antonio's first meeting and were surprised that Zadek asked them just to go through their lines without colouring them. Their surprise turned into disappointment when he told them that this was exactly the way he wanted the scene. During rehearsals, they still tried all kinds of elaborate arrangements. Shylock sat at a table in his office in front of a computer and held hectic telephone conversations with the Stock Exchange. He asked Antonio to take a seat and typed in the newest figures. Only then did he say 'Ay, ay, three thousand ducats'. Zadek indulged them, but in the end he got rid of all the furniture and props and told them just to stand there as if at the Globe. Similarly, they rehearsed for a long time that when Antonio asks Shylock for mercy, the merchant crawls along on all fours whilst Shylock whistles at him as if he were his dog. But after a while, Zadek got bored by his own idea. In his less successful productions, exactly this kind of thing did not get thrown out, and there were lengthy improvisations, as if the director wanted to signal to the audience that he did not care for any kind of dramaturgical consistency. Unusually for Zadek, the Vienna *Merchant of Venice* had a playing time of under three hours and an overarching conceptual idea was followed through without surprise contraventions of the play's structure. The only exception was Jessica's narrowly avoided rape by the drunken carnival revellers.

Gone were the barely controlled explosions described by Peter Iden when reviewing *Othello*. As a protagonist, Gert Voss could not be further from Ulrich Wildgruber. His Shylock never for a moment got loud. He briefly showed how much Jessica's flight hurt him, but only when alone with Tubal. In all the other scenes, he was a model of self-control. Whilst the keyword for Wildgruber's Lear, Othello and Hamlet seemed to have been 'emotional excess', Voss maintained, Zadek 'does not aim for extending oneself to the last but for discretion' (Dermutz 2001: 101). His elegance and lightness were a long way from Wildgruber's extrovert artificiality. Over the years, the director established a kind of travelling circus with a permanent group of actors he brought with him, a system the critics labelled 'Lufthansa theatre'. This was not only costly but also caused a lot of internal problems for the theatres he worked at. If they were lucky, their investment led to an artistic success, however difficult to schedule, when the circus in the meanwhile had moved on to rehearse in a different city. If not lucky, it took some time to write off the costs and recover, as Zadek's results were either absolutely brilliant or, if he lost interest on the way, an outright disaster. But, even in his acclaimed work, whole scenes might be carelessly arranged while the most detailed attention was paid to others.

Increasingly, apart from the Burgtheater and the Berliner Ensemble, hardly any theatre was able to afford Zadek, and even they needed the help of the coproducing Vienna Festwochen. Not only were his personal fees among the highest in Europe, if he directed a Shakespeare, Marlowe or Ibsen, there were translator's royalties for his wife Elisabeth Plessen despite the often rather questionable quality of the text. The fees, travel and accommodation expenses for the production team and the guest actors were way out of the reach of even comparatively affluent theatres. To make matters worse, Zadek usually refused to use the normal rehearsal spaces and insisted on specially rented buildings where he was able to work in splendid isolation. This included his own catering via buffet lunches as he did not want his actors to frequent the ordinary canteen and get distracted through conversations with people not involved in the production. It was mandatory for the whole cast down to bit players to attend every rehearsal over periods of up to five months.

Only once did Zadek not come with his usual stalwarts and agreed to work basically with the resident company. This was in 1997 at the Munich Kammerspiele, where he directed his own adaptation of *Alice in Wonderland* and *Richard III* translated by Elisabeth Plessen. For the latter, however, he insisted on bringing along the protagonist Paulus Manker, in the full knowledge that the renowned ensemble of the Kammerspiele had at least five suitable Richards in its ranks. Zadek obviously wanted to use the psychodynamics created by his central casting decision and exploit group mechanisms as he had done successfully in the past. Manker, indeed, was the expected focus for a lot of pent-up frustration from his colleagues but without himself being able to rise to the challenge of the part. He proved a far cry from the likes of Wildgruber with his elementary power or Voss with his finesse. In continuous bright light on Karl Kneidl's pseudo-Elizabethan plywood set, the production looked deliberately shabby apart from Modesta Maselli's garishly coloured costumes inspired by playing cards. Well-meaning reviewers assumed that Zadek aimed for some kind of naïve, cartoonish storytelling style reminiscent of medieval ballads. But for this rather limited approach to carry four long hours, he would have needed a protagonist with less limited means. Even the star actors among the supporting cast were almost unrecognisable in their indifference either due to a lack of care by the director or missing motivation on their own side. Many scenes looked as if they just had been blocked and then not touched again. The few directorial ideas were of the triteness Zadek himself would gladly have thrown away in a production like *The Merchant of Venice*.

As so often in his career, triumph and disaster alternated quicker than with any other director of his standing, as in 1996 Zadek's highly acclaimed *The Cherry Orchard* had premiered in the Vienna Akademietheater, the Burgtheater's smaller auditorium. Chekhov's text lent itself better to the kind of underplaying increasingly favoured by Zadek than a Shakespearian history like *Richard III*, which would have demanded more directorial intervention than he was then prepared to give. Ranevskaja was played by Angela Winkler, who appeared a surprising choice for Zadek's production of *Hamlet* (his twentieth of a Shakespeare play) for the Vienna Festwochen in 1999. She gave the Prince as a spoilt and vicious child ruining the whole state by a fundamentalist moral stance. Zadek's detractors claimed that in his later years he liked to act the spoilt and vicious child himself with more energy going into backstage shenanigans about money and prestige than into the work proper. Despite his avowed intention not to run a theatre again, being part of a directorate of initially five directors at the Berliner Ensemble proved a brief and troubled interlude from 1992 to 1995. Approaching eighty and after falling out even with the generous Burgtheater, Zadek then turned to setting up his own production company and acting school in a villa in rural Brandenburg. At the time, he would often speak out publicly against the young generation of directors. When he taught workshops he told them, ' "Stop, stop, you are directing a play. That means first you must think about what is this play, what was in the author's mind." But they don't care at all for that. Instead, they add a play of their own with some additional text and the result is their invention' (*Frankfurter Allgemeine Sonntagszeitung*, 18 July 2004).

The former iconoclast started to insist on the priority of the text and was highly distrustful of the kind of single conceptual approach Georg Hensel had attacked him for in the 1970s. In the Bremen programme for *Measure for Measure*, he had voiced a particular dislike for any 'underplaying' and called for 'big passions' on the stage. This kind of extreme energy also characterised his and his protagonist Ulrich Wildgruber's Shakespearian work in the 1970s. The basis for Gert Voss's Shylock, on the contrary, was a move towards bigger discretion and a more coherent conceptual framework. In yet another change of direction, Zadek's Shakespearian productions of the 1990s opted for a greater reliance on the text while practically letting the actors do their own blocking. This led to sometimes shambolic results only partially redeemed by outstanding actors like Angela Winkler as Hamlet. The mildness of old age suited Zadek's productions of Chekhov or Ibsen very well, Shakespeare increasingly in the director's long career would have demanded a bit more of his early passion and energy.

Chronology

1926	Born in Berlin
1933	Emigration to England
1947	First productions at the Old Vic school
1957	World Premiere of Jean Genet's *The Balcony* at the Arts Theatre
1958–60	First German productions in Cologne, Ulm and Hanover
1960	Kurt Hübner makes him resident director at Ulm
1962	Follows Hübner to Bremen
1967	*Measure for Measure*
1967–72	Freelance work in Wuppertal, Stuttgart, Berlin and Munich, work for film and television
1972	Appointed Artistic Director of the Schauspielhaus Bochum; *The Merchant of Venice*
1974	*King Lear*
1976	*Othello* at the Deutsches Schauspielhaus, Hamburg
1978	*Hamlet*
1985–9	Artistic Director of the Deutsches Schauspielhaus, Hamburg
1988	*The Merchant of Venice* at the Burgtheater Vienna
1990	Publishes interviews, programme notes and short articles under the title *Das Wilde Ufer*
1992–5	Member of directorate at the Berliner Ensemble
1997	*Richard III* at the Munich Kammerspiele
1998	First part of his autobiography: *My Way, 1926–1979*
1999	*Hamlet* with Angela Winkler for the Vienna Festwochen

2003 His book *Menschen Löwen Adler Rebhühner* documents two workshops given at the Ernst Busch acting school in Berlin
2005 Founding of myway PRODUCTION-company, later renamed wasihrwollt PRODUCTIONS
2006 Second part of his autobiography: *Die heißen Jahre, 1970–1980*

Bibliography

Canaris, Volker (1979) *Peter Zadek: Der Theatermann und Filmemacher*, Munich and Vienna: Carl Hanser Verlag.

Dermutz, Klaus (2001) *Die Verwandlungen des Gert Voss: Gespräche über Schauspielkunst*, Edition Burgtheater, Vol. II, Salzburg, Frankfurt and Vienna: Residenz Verlag.

Hensel, Georg (1983) *Das Theater der siebziger Jahre. Kommentar, Kritik, Polemik*, Munich: Deutscher Taschenbuch Verlag.

Hortmann, Wilhelm (1998) *Shakespeare on the German Stage: The Twentieth Century*, Cambridge: Cambridge University Press.

Iden, Peter (2005) *Peter Palitzsch: Theater muss die Welt verändern*, Berlin: Henschel Verlag.

Lange, Mechthild (1989) *Peter Zadek: Regie im Theater*, Frankfurt: Fischer Taschenbuch Verlag.

Mauer, Burkhard and Barbara Krauß (eds) (1973) *Spielräume – Arbeitsergebnisse: Theater Bremen 1962–73*, Bremen: Theater Bremen.

Tynan, Kenneth (1975) *A View of the English Stage 1944–63*, London: Davis-Poynter.

Zadek, Peter (1990) *Das Wilde Ufer: Ein Theaterbuch*, ed. Laszlo Kornitzer, Cologne: Kiepenheuer & Witsch.

—— (1998) *My Way: Eine Autobiographie, 1926–1979*, Cologne: Kiepenheuer & Witsch.

—— (2003) *Menschen Löwen Adler Rebhühner*, Cologne: Kiepenheuer & Witsch.

—— (2006) *Die heißen Jahre, 1970–1980*, Cologne: Kiepenheuer & Witsch.

About the author

Michael Raab is a translator, journalist and lecturer and lives in Frankfurt/Main. He studied English, German and French in Marburg, London and Hamburg. For his dissertation ' "The Music Hall Is Dying": The Portrayal of the Entertainment Industry in Contemporary British Drama' he received a Ph.D. at the University of Hamburg. After two years as a producer for German television ZDF he worked as Literary Manager (Dramaturg) at the Staatstheater Stuttgart, the Staatstheater Mainz, the Munich Kammerspiele and the Schauspielhaus Leipzig. He has translated plays by David Hare, Kevin Elyot, J.B. Priestley, David Storey, Michael Frayn, Simon Gray among others. As a writer and lecturer at universities and acting schools, his main fields of research are new British and Irish drama and Shakespeare in production. On those topics he wrote numerous articles and essays as well as a book on English drama in the 1990s. In 1985 he published *Des Widerspenstigen Zähmung: Modern Shakespearean Productions in Germany and England*. From 1985 to 1987, as the Hamburg Theatre Correspondent of the national daily paper

Frankfurter Rundschau, he was able to follow Zadek's work at the Deutsches Schauspielhaus during his artistic directorship there. Whilst working as a dramaturg at the Munich Kammerspiele he observed the production process of *Richard III* at close quarters without being directly involved.

31
FRANCO ZEFFIRELLI

*Tom Matheson**
(with Russell Jackson and Robert Smallwood)

** The sudden death of Tom Matheson, our dear friend and colleague, on 16 October 2006, before he was able to finish this essay, has left us with the privilege of bringing his work to completion. We could not hope, of course, to reproduce the flair that he would have brought to the task, or the instinctive personal enthusiasm for so Anglo-Italian a topic, but we trust that we have fulfilled his main intentions for the piece and we respectfully and affectionately dedicate our endeavours to his memory* (*R.J., R.S.*).

'Franco Zeffirelli's *Romeo and Juliet*', the drama critic of the *Observer* ringingly declared on 9 October 1960, 'is a revelation, even perhaps a revolution'. On the other side of the Channel, its director was embarking on his next project, a production of *Rigoletto* in Brussels, having left London dejected by a chorus of reviews in the daily press 'so damning they beggared belief'. But reading Kenneth Tynan that Sunday, Zeffirelli could take comfort: 'it no longer mattered what the others had said; the master had spoken' (Zeffirelli 1986: 164).

What the others had said, and would continue to say, matters a great deal, or books such as this one would not exist; but unless Tynan was right that the 1960 Old Vic *Romeo and Juliet* was something, at least, of a revolution, Franco Zeffirelli's presence in this pantheon of Shakespeare directors would hardly be justified. For it was his first independent Shakespeare production and, as far as the English theatre is concerned, there would be only two more, an *Othello* for the Royal Shakespeare Company (RSC) the following October and a *Much Ado about Nothing* for the National Theatre (NT) in February 1965. Three Shakespeare productions in five years, and two films shortly afterwards, *The Taming of the Shrew* in 1966 and *Romeo and Juliet* in 1968, with a film of *Hamlet* very much later, in 1990, is a somewhat limited œuvre upon which to base a Shakespearian directorial reputation. What is it about this small body of work that gives it a significant place in the history of twentieth-century Shakespeare production?

Zeffirelli had come to the Old Vic at the invitation of its director, Michael Benthall, with an international reputation as an opera director. He was 37, and his directing career had been almost exclusively in opera for the preceding decade, with a long list of work at La Scala and at other major opera houses in Italy, in Amsterdam, Tel Aviv and Dallas. His first work in London had been in the preceding year, when he directed and designed the Covent Garden début of Joan Sutherland in *Lucia di Lammermoor* and where, later that season, his double-bill of *I Pagliacci* and *Cavalleria Rusticana* had had an enormous success. But at the time of Benthall's invitation, Zeffirelli did not have a Shakespeare production to his name.

Franco Zeffirelli was born in Florence in February 1923 and was a student of architecture at the Liceo Artistico there when his studies were brought to a temporary end by Italy's entry into the Second World War and, shortly afterwards, his own enrolment with the Partisans. His account of these early years, and of his life in theatre down to the time of its publication in 1986, is to be found in the English version of his autobiography, created through a series of recorded conversations with David Sweetman. (In 2006 Zeffirelli himself produced, in Italian, a new *Autobiografia* that offers a fuller account of his personal life but, except for the *Hamlet* film, adds nothing to the earlier book's account of his work on Shakespeare.) His early years were much influenced by time spent receiving English lessons from Mary O'Neill, one of a group of expatriate English women in Florence of whose lives (and of his own, both somewhat fictionalised) he made an affectionate, and engaging, record in his 1999 film *Tea with Mussolini*. With Mary O'Neill, he first became acquainted with Shakespeare, reciting dialogues with her from many of the plays, including *Romeo and Juliet* (Zeffirelli 1986: 19). During the same period, he also worked with various drama groups in Florence and saw a great deal of cinema. Not surprisingly, therefore, one of the first films he went to see after the war was Olivier's *Henry V*, an occasion which he repeatedly presents as a turning point in his life. He left his architecture course and was working as an assistant to the scene painters at the Teatro della Pergola in Florence when he met Luchino Visconti, Milanese nobleman and communist, theatre and film director and producer, and former assistant to Jean Renoir, who, through their partnership over the next decade and more, was to have a profound influence on Zeffirelli's career.

The details of Zeffirelli's work during these years need not concern us here.

It included a certain amount of acting, a good deal of assisting with design and direction and, later, increasing responsibility for set designs. And it was through design that he first encountered Shakespeare professionally, as Design Assistant to Salvador Dali in a Visconti production of *As You Like It* at the Teatro Elisio in Rome in 1948. It was, wrote Mario Praz, in its 'riot of colour and wild imagination [. . .] one of the strangest performances of Shakespeare that the present age has seen', with a backdrop image of Arden as a huge apple in a cube and its court framed by golden elephants on long legs (Praz 1950: 118 and Plate VIIB; Kennedy 1993: 196). Zeffirelli's first work as an independent designer was in Visconti's 1949 production of *A Streetcar Named Desire*, and in that same summer he designed his first Shakespeare, an outdoor production of *Troilus and Cressida* on a grand scale. Visconti 'wanted to create an image of Troy based on Persian miniatures, an exotic city invaded by western barbarians' (Zeffirelli 1986: 94), and the Boboli Gardens in Florence were transformed (at enormous expense) into a walled Troy, all in white, with access for the audience only by drawbridge (Kennedy 1993: 196) and with 'unparalleled magnificence of costume and circus-like pageantry' (Praz 1950: 118). And that was to be Zeffirelli's last Shakespeare until, eleven years and nearly thirty operas (as designer and director) later, he arrived at the Old Vic to direct that revelatory, and possibly revolutionary, production of *Romeo and Juliet*.

Three points are worth observing from this briefest of résumés of Zeffirelli's career before his first Shakespeare production. Most important is the long association with Visconti who, despite that uncharacteristic excursion into the surreal with Dali, may be seen above all, in those immediate post-war years, as the apostle, on film and in the theatre, of neo-realism. Visconti's ambitious film of Giovanni Verga's *La Terra Trema*, set in Verga's own Sicilian fishing village and using local peasants rather than professional actors, was Zeffirelli's first full assignment as Assistant Director. 'Visconti's way', he wrote later, 'was to be faithful to the setting of a play as its author had conceived it and to render it in the most precise detail [. . .] This way of working is my greatest debt to him' (Zeffirelli 1986: 93). Second is the route into theatre, via a long (if interrupted) architecture course, a first job as a scene painter and a lot of time spent as a design assistant. The director who came to the English Shakespearian theatre at just about the time that its direction was being taken over from the theatre-educated by the academically educated (Smallwood 1996: 178) had not, up to that point, directed anything that he had not also designed – and, he told the *Observer* during rehearsals, it was his belief that the director's function must necessarily always include design as well (2 October 1960). Third is the fact that one of the enterprises that immediately preceded the Old Vic assignment was the Covent Garden production of

Cavalleria Rusticana, an opera based, like that first film on which Zeffirelli had assisted Visconti, on a story by Verga; it was for his vivid realisation of the 'verismo' tradition in the presentation of its Sicilian peasant setting that Zeffirelli's production had been so much admired. This was the director who was introduced to his cast by Michael Benthall.

The very phrase 'introduced to his cast' would surprise many modern directors and actors. Estimates of the amount of his or her power over the way the production of a play will work that a director has used up when the casting process has been completed vary according to the actor, or director, to whom one talks, but one rarely hears it put much below half. Yet, after propounding his theories to Benthall about the need for young performers, Zeffirelli records (1986: 163), 'Yes, I could have young new players, but he led me. He suggested that Judi Dench and John Stride, both just starting out, would be ideal for the play. And how right he was'. Judi Dench's account of the casting process is rather simpler: 'When he was brought in to do the play', she writes, 'Benthall cast John Stride and Alec McCowen as Romeo and Mercutio and me as Juliet. He took us to meet Zeffirelli, who just looked at us very searchingly and then said "Yes, very good" to Benthall' (Dench 1996: 201). She goes on to describe Zeffirelli's concern

> to get rid of 'English' passion and get a really 'Italian' feel. I remember the audience gasped when the curtain went up because it was all misty in this very real-looking Italian street and people were throwing out sheets to air: nothing as realistic had been seen in Shakespeare for a very long time.

And that was precisely the gist of Tynan's response:

> The characters were neither larger nor smaller than life and we watched them living, spontaneously and unpredictably. The director had taken the simple and startling course of treating them as if they were real people in a real situation. [. . .] Handled thus realistically, it is sometimes said, Shakespeare's essential quality gets lost. I passionately demur. What gets lost is not Shakespeare but the formal, dehumanized stereotype that we have made of him [. . .] Every director in the audience is biting his nails and wondering why he never thought of this before.

Zeffirelli simplifies the issue when he says that everyone was hostile until Tynan came along. Most of the popular newspapers responded enthusiastically to what the *Daily Express*, in a telling phrase, called 'the new, almost strange, vitality' of the piece (5 October 1960). It was the reviewers in the heavyweight press who wielded the hatchets, and that because they had not heard what they wanted to hear. Darlington put it most bluntly in the *Daily Telegraph*, spicing his remarks with that touch of xenophobic arrogance that is just below the surface in much of the hostile reaction to the production: 'Franco Zeffirelli, the Italian director', he observed, though he had created

> a brilliantly composed picture of a small Italian town full of hot-blooded young men [. . .] who will gaily slit your throat as soon as look at you [. . .] has not avoided the pitfall into which nearly all foreign directors of Shakespeare fall: he has not realized how much the poetry matters to an English audience.
>
> (5 October 1960)

Looking back on the production a few years later, John Trewin saw the issue even more simply: 'Zeffirelli drove the action along with ample vigour [. . .] but had looked at the play like an ardent Italian who could not hear English verse' (Trewin 1964: 244).

Zeffirelli may inadvertently have brought this xenophobic drubbing upon his own head. His *Romeo and Juliet* came three years after Italy had been one of the original six signatories of the Treaty of Rome and thus made the first decisive step towards the creation of the European Union, a full thirteen years before Britain's belated entry. Zeffirelli had spent years directing opera in cities all over Europe; he was the pupil of Visconti, who was the pupil of Renoir; and to London he came, imagining that Shakespeare might be regarded as part of European, rather than merely English, culture – and with a remarkable (and clearly personal and unedited) pan-European message for the Old Vic programme. It described his initial hesitation about directing Shakespeare in England and his change of mind, 'for idealistic reasons beyond the limits of theatre'; and it went on to express the hope that the present production's 'combination of Italian feeling applied to a masterpiece of English theatre [. . .] might prove, if successful, that times have changed in Europe' and that the 'new Europeans' of his cast will show 'that people of different backgrounds may easily work together for creating a new European conscience'.

'Rare words! Brave world!', but the response in England was, and remains, at the 'Hostess, my breakfast' level. Not a single review of the production mentions a syllable of this earnest message, and half a century later, Britain stands disdainfully aloof from the first Europe-wide currency since the Roman Empire and its press moves in an ever-more Europhobic direction – and Franco Zeffirelli remains the only director from continental Europe to have produced a Shakespeare play for the NT or for the RSC. If he is important for nothing else, Zeffirelli is important for so sharply raising the question of why, since the internationalism, the supra-nationalism, of Shakespeare's plays is beyond dispute, the English Shakespearian theatre remains so defiantly insular.

Like Peter Brook's production of *A Midsummer Night's Dream* ten years later, the 1960 *Romeo and Juliet* 'was soon being cited as a point of no return in dealings with the play' (Jackson 2003: 16), the peeling sun-baked walls of its set achieving something of an iconic status that could be alluded to in later productions. Jill Levenson, in an illuminating analysis of the production and of its set – 'as close to neo-realism as theatre could be' – adds the telling anecdote of Zeffirelli himself, just before the curtain went up on opening night, 'flicking a brush with dirty, watery paint about eighteen inches above the floor. "This is where the dogs pee on the walls", he explained. Then he flicked a little higher, saying "and this is where the men pee" ' (Levenson 1987: 100). Such pursuit of naturalistic detail famously included a good deal of eating – 'great munching of apples among the lower orders', as Richard David put it – and eating, or drinking, quickly became a 'token of verisimilitude' that was to prove 'a tic of Shakespeare production in the ensuing decade' (David 1978: 64).

But was Tynan right to see the production as a 'revolution' in Shakespeare production in Britain? Zeffirelli himself (1986: 320) provides one answer to the question: 'The only "revolutionary" claim any director can make is to have seen what no one has bothered to see since the author compiled the work' and he cites his decision to cast young actors in the roles of Romeo and Juliet as 'no more than what Shakespeare would have done'. The constant complaint of the denigrators of the production, even while they were admiring its vitality and the realism of its spectacle, was that it failed to serve what they called 'the poetry' – T.C. Worsley, for example, stating flatly that 'the poetry and the realism simply do not match' (*Financial Times*, 5 October 1960). Tynan believed that 'this argument is only valid if one agrees with those blinkered zealots who think that poetry is an arrangement of sounds, instead of an arrangement of words'.

Debate about the appropriate theatrical treatment of Shakespeare's language had been going on for a long time before Zeffirelli's *Romeo and Juliet* and has continued unabated. But the production undoubtedly intensified it, for, in its emphasis on spectacle and on naturalistic behaviour, it challenged that obsession with the language, and only the language, that has had such a stultifying effect on English theatre, and on Shakespeare in particular. Zeffirelli expressed the belief that 'to listen for beautiful sounds undoubtedly takes you away from intellectual and emotional truth and reality [. . .] Shakespeare was writing to be *believed*, so it is essential to make everything natural in every detail' (*Stage*, 13 October 1960). This is precisely the point that John Russell Brown took up in an important essay in *Shakespeare Survey*. It was the vivid immediacy of behaviour, the lived-in quality of the costumes, the 'unpompous behaviour' of the characters, its 'immediacy, zest and delicacy', that he thought had been the innovations of the production, along with Zeffirelli's making 'the actors' speech as lively and fluent as their physical action'. He felt that too many set changes in pursuit of realism had necessitated excessive cutting in the later scenes but still regarded the production as one of 'unique and consistent achievement' and concluded that 'it is a long time since Shakespeare's text has been so enfranchised' (Brown 1962: 147–9).

Zeffirelli himself (then and later) was entirely unrepentant about cuts: 'No damage is done, it seems to me, when cuts are made in order that the drama may progress in a manner convincing to our own times', he said in an interview in October 1960 and declared – in anticipation, perhaps, of his future Shakespeare films, none of which uses more than a third or so of Shakespeare's text (though that is not, of course, exceptional for filmed Shakespeare) – his belief in the director's absolute right to delete 'things which hold up the flow of the action' (*Stage*, 13 October 1960). Looking back on those films thirty years later, his view was unaltered: 'if [. . .] to make the audience be there with their guts and heart [. . .] it means surgery on the text [. . .] you'd better do it' (Zeffirelli 1990: 262). His confidence in his own role as purveyor of the dramatist's intentions is equally clear: 'theatre [. . .] depends on the people who work in it [. . .] to comprehend and reinterpret for their generation what the original author intended', and once again it is Visconti whom he identifies as having taught him 'how to conceive an idea and [. . .] to make a simple, clear interpretation that can be worked out in theatrical ways' (Zeffirelli 1986: 341, 251). In an interview during rehearsals for the 1960 *Romeo and Juliet*, a similar point is made: 'You don't need many ideas, you need one. On that you work, and the idea carries you if it's right' (*The Times*, 19 September 1960, quoted in Levenson 1987: 87).

Those 'theatrical ways' of working out an idea usually involved months of research into the work's background, in particular the visual and behavioural background, be it pre-revolutionary Russia for *Three Sisters*, Goldoni's Venice for *The Mistress of the Inn*, tuberculosis in the nineteenth century for *La Bohème*, or Renaissance Italy for *Romeo and Juliet*. 'We are unmistakably in Italy' wrote Tynan, 'the director has even taught his actors how to shrug' – and, no doubt by example, for, as Judi Dench recalled, 'you'll be rehearsing and suddenly, out of the corner of your eye, you'll see him standing beside you doing it much better than you. [. . .] He made you *feel* something with an intense, incredible passion', and she recalls the instruction 'don't cry like that, cry like a child', that is, crouching down and with hands to eyes (Dench 1974: 138). When he was in the later stages of filming *Romeo and Juliet*, Zeffirelli offered his own account of such methods: 'I usually demonstrate very much. I am not too good at explaining in words. I don't think it is useful to discuss with actors, who are very simple creators [sic]. They work on simple, basic images. They should be given an image which is clear and not confused'. Excessive discussion of motivation has, he says, been disastrous: 'so much discussion about what an actor should feel, instead of showing him freely and simply what the author expects him to do' (*Guardian*, 2 March 1968). And, in a talk given over two decades later, he makes the same point: 'To my company I never try to articulate, to tell them with words what they have to do. I say, "Well, let's stop this. I'll show you how it happens"; and you show the thing, even if you don't know the words, but the feeling is there. Actors are very visual' (Zeffirelli 1990: 243).

Zeffirelli's desire to achieve, as realistically as possible, his conception of what the author 'intended' was given specific impetus four years after the Old Vic *Romeo and Juliet*, when he was invited to direct (and, of course, design) an outdoor production of the play (in Italian) in Verona itself, with the old buildings beyond the Teatro Romano becoming part of the set and the city's bells part of its soundscape. The idea of youthfulness was now taken further with the casting in the title roles of actors who were making their theatre debuts. Peter D. Hall again designed the costumes and Nino Rota again provided music – as, indeed, they did for all Zeffirelli's Shakespeare productions in the 1960s. The production led more or less directly to Zeffirelli's celebrated film of the play in 1968, with the young and unknown teenagers Leonard Whiting and Olivia Hussey as Romeo and Juliet, and a filmic realisation of all those elements of passion, heat, dust and violence that had been remarked upon in the stage versions but which clearly lent themselves more appropriately to film. 'I had', Zeffirelli remarks revealingly in his autobiography (1986: 262), 'always tried to bring some of the size, scope and glamour of the big screen to the stage', and Levenson (1987: 92) describes the Old Vic production, particularly in some of the juxtapositions produced by the cutting, as an attempt 'to create cinematic theatre'.

The film also featured, in John McEnery's performance, a Mercutio who took even further the manic energy and volatility which had first been seen in Alec McCowen's Mercutio at the Old Vic, where – in, for example, its naturalistic, broken delivery of the Queen Mab speech, the images spontaneously 'coined' – it had astonished critics used to the old debonair–poetic reading of the role and pointed the way to the long line of disturbed, and disturbing, Mercutios that has since become the norm. For Levenson (1987: 98), the 'controversial but electrifying' interpretation of Mercutio was one of the genuine revolutions of the 1960 production. 'You never know on which side you are with Mercutio', Zeffirelli remarked during work on the film:

> certain characters of Shakespeare are 'way out' and this is the way we play Mercutio: extreme in all directions. He is a rebel, fascinating and charming, but very unpredictable, always on the edge of breaking into . . . madness, yes. And a character like that is punished by Shakespeare, to die in a most stupid way, one hot day of summer, for a jest.
>
> (*Guardian*, 2 March 1968)

And the jest, as in the stage version, seemed to Mercutio's friends to be just that, the joke about 'a scratch' strained, as usual with Mercutio, a little too far, so that the shock of the final realisation that he isn't joking, that the scratch will, indeed, 'serve', is all the greater. Mercutio, Zeffirelli remarked many years later, is a character repeated by Shakespeare 'through practically all his plays [. . .] a kind of evil, witty, funny, pessimistic, cynical and existentialist character – which is himself' (Zeffirelli 1990: 246).

In its passionate immediacy, in its spectacle and colour and energy, in its locative verisimilitude, in the precision and exuberance of visual detail of its sets and costumes, much of it based on Renaissance painting, and, of course, in its freedom with the text, Zeffirelli's film of *Romeo and Juliet* distils for posterity something of what he was doing in his theatre work. Levenson describes it as 'a version of the famous legend more uniform in tone, beautiful in conception, and passionate in mood than Shakespeare's', though, she concludes, its remarkable synthesis of speech and spectacle offered 'a version of the narrative more like Shakespeare's sources' than like Shakespeare's play. The treatment of the language, in particular – the cutting, the substitution of the visual for the verbal, the naturalistic mode of speaking, the breaking up of pentameters, the occasional additions and repetitions – 'reduce its qualities as Elizabethan art and increase its correspondences with modern life' (Levenson 1987: 115–16, 123). Shakespeare's language, Zeffirelli remarked much later, looking back on his work with this play, is like the frame of a painting: 'The original poetry was an additional beauty to the painting, but the painting was there, apart from the beauty of the poetry. That was [. . .] why many of the critics attacked me, because I didn't start from the poetry, going down instead to the dramatic values of the piece' (Zeffirelli 1990: 241). He was immensely proud of the enormous popularity of his film, especially with young audiences, and of its emotional accessibility, dismissing critics who sneered at it for aesthetic self-indulgence: 'I don't believe that millions of young people all over the world wept over my film of *Romeo and Juliet* just because the costumes were splendid' (Zeffirelli 1986: 341). And, as the work of many scholars has demonstrated (see, for example, in addition to Levenson, Cartmell 2000, Donaldson 1990, Jackson 2007, Pilkington 1994, Tatspaugh 2000), it occupies an important place in the history of filmed Shakespeare for a great deal more than just its popularity, extraordinary though that was.

Romeo and Juliet was Zeffirelli's third film and his second Shakespeare film. (His impressive documentary record of the disastrous floods in Florence in 1966, *Florence: Days of Destruction*, came between the two.) The first film he directed independently (as well as with Visconti he had worked alongside Pietrangeli, Rossellini, Antonioni, De Sica and many of the other great names in Italian cinema in the 1940s and 1950s) was *The Taming of the Shrew*. This remarkable exercise in popularisation, guaranteed box-office success by the casting of Elizabeth Taylor and Richard Burton as Katharina and Petruccio, unashamedly exploited the notoriously tempestuous off-screen relationship of its stars in the play's depiction of a tempestuous courtship. The film was made in 1966 in Rome; it used less than a third of the text and made more changes to the order of scenes than *Romeo and Juliet* was to do two years later. That a directorial film début should attract such star casting was partly due to Zeffirelli's by then enormous international reputation as an opera director but also to Burton's desire to return, if only temporarily, to classical work. Visually, it had all the Zeffirelli trademarks of lavish attention to period detail in sets and costumes – much of it based, as Graham Holderness (1989: 60–3) has shown, on specific paintings of the Italian Renaissance – and enormous physical energy. The not-inappropriate solution to the latent violence of Petruccio's treatment of Kate was the time-honoured (and sure-fire) filmic device of the chase, with long and exuberantly energetic pursuits (one of them ending in a huge heap of wool) of Taylor by Burton providing the film's most easily remembered sequences. The urgent interest in money exhibited by the Paduans of Shakespeare's text became something of an obsession in the film and one from which Petruccio was by no means immune; it provided, in fact, the sort of realistic explanation for his behaviour that Zeffirelli's work almost always seeks to offer. That Taylor gave Kate's final speech of submission entirely seriously was, Zeffirelli claims (1986: 216), a surprise both to himself and to Burton; that so notoriously problematic a scene had not been the subject of prior discussion may seem incredible, but it is not incompatible with Judi Dench's account of being left to get on with Juliet's language (Dench 1996: 201) or with Zeffirelli's own disparagement of the folly of too much discussion of motivation with those 'simple creators', who do the acting.

Zeffirelli's care to make sure that the first Italian screening of his first film should be in the Florence cinema where he had seen Olivier's *Henry V* twenty years earlier is a clear illustration of the continuity of his attitudes to

Shakespeare, a continuity made the more poignant by the fact that, in the audience for that first showing, were the few survivors from that pre-war group of expatriate English women among whom he had first made the acquaintance of Shakespeare's plays (Zeffirelli 1986: 224). And that Shakespearian link continued when, more than thirty years later, he made his semi-autobiographical film about that same group of women, *Tea with Mussolini*, and cast as its leads Joan Plowright, widow of the actor-director whose Shakespeare films had convinced him that he must seek a career in theatre and who, as founder-director of the NT, had invited him to direct *Much Ado about Nothing* there; Maggie Smith, who had been his Beatrice in that production; and Judi Dench, the Juliet of his first Shakespeare production. The Shakespearian wheel, one might be forgiven for thinking, had come full circle.

That 1965 *Much Ado about Nothing* was Zeffirelli's last Shakespeare theatre production and came the year before his film of *The Taming of the Shrew*. Between the Old Vic *Romeo and Juliet* and the NT *Much Ado about Nothing*, he made his only directorial visit to Stratford-upon-Avon. His *Othello* was the last production to enter the repertoire in the 1961 season, the second under the overall direction of Peter Hall. The production has gone down in theatre history as a legendary failure, a reputation produced partly, at least, by the combination of, on the one hand, the impossibly high expectations of seeing Sir John Gielgud in the only major Shakespeare role he had not yet played and with a director new to Stratford whose international reputation was enormous, and, on the other hand, a first night full of disastrous accidents that included wobbling scenery, an unplanned interval after half an hour when the set went wrong, Gielgud's beard coming unfixed in the 'brothel scene', and actors betraying their under-rehearsed state by missing, paraphrasing and generally fluffing lines. The half-dozen 'preview' performances that were, a decade or so later, to become standard at Stratford (and elsewhere) would surely have allowed a more balanced assessment than the accounts of first-night reviewers who, almost without exception, allude ruefully to the four-and-a-quarter hours they have just spent in the theatre.

According to Sally Beauman, 'the history of the production was simple: Hall wanted Gielgud to play at Stratford; Gielgud wanted to play Othello and [. . .] to work with the newly fashionable Zeffirelli' (Beauman 1982: 247). Zeffirelli himself has another version. He describes his ideas for Othello:

> A Moor by the colour of his skin, but . . . certainly more civilized than most Europeans . . . a Venetian by adoption, a man of the Renaissance . . . highly refined and controlled . . . Uppermost in my mind was the elegance of Africans I had met – the Ashanti, the Nubian peoples . . . I knew we needed a great and cultivated speaker for the part, someone

> scholarly, not the usual brooding hulk. The obvious choice was John Gielgud, who turned out to be very keen to do it.
>
> (Zeffirelli, 1986: 166)

Whether actor chose director or director actor, both were to be disappointed. 'Gielgud and I never seemed to react together. He sailed through the piece, his usual self [. . .] hardly what I had in mind' (Zeffirelli 1986: 166). Gielgud's letters reveal that, though he thought Zeffirelli 'quite brilliant', he was exasperated by his tendency to demonstrate and by his 'irresponsible and irrepressible charm, mixed with his dreadful lack of discipline and punctuality'. But he knew also that 'Franco is excellent for me – won't let me sing or declaim', though he felt strongly that 'the realistic business and pauses, as if playing Chekhov' that Zeffirelli wanted were 'no earthly good in Shakespeare' (Gielgud 2004: 276–7). The fatigue of those involved in creating the production must have contributed to its problems. Between *Romeo and Juliet* in October 1960 and the Stratford *Othello* twelve months later, Zeffirelli had directed (and designed) four operas in four countries. His actors must have been at least as overworked, for the *Othello* was the sixth production to enter the Stratford season and apart from Gielgud himself, and Peggy Ashcroft who played Emilia, both of whom arrived just for the *Othello*, the rest of Zeffirelli's company were heavily involved in the earlier repertoire, and Ian Bannen, in particular, was adding Iago to Hamlet, Mercutio, and Orlando and so carrying something approaching 3,000 lines in his head – plus the one he notoriously invented on the opening night announcing the unexpected death of Cassio (quickly corrected to a near miss). 'Gielgud and Bannen were like oil and water', Zeffirelli reports (1986: 166), and Gielgud's letters reveal a sharp personal dislike of his Iago: 'tricky, a bad study, interfering, inefficient and impertinent' (Gielgud 2004: 276). That an actor of 'modern' style cast as Iago (before this Stratford season most of Bannen's work had been in new plays) should clash with an actor of an older 'grander' style cast as Othello is virtually written into the text of *Othello*, and successful on-stage partnerships have no necessary connection with off-stage relationships. Indeed, many of the reviewers, while chronicling the first-night problems, wrote enthusiastically about the extraordinary power and tension of the temptation scene as the two of them sat working on papers at the general's marble conference table (business that has been repeated in a number of later productions). What seems to have sunk the production – it did not go to the Aldwych in London in the usual RSC way and so played only eighteen performances in that last part of the Stratford season – was a fundamental incompatibility between the performers and the set that Zeffirelli had designed for them.

The most successful revivals of *Othello* have been fast-moving, simply set productions, often in small spaces (those by Trevor Nunn at The Other Place or Sam Mendes' at the Cottesloe, for example), that create a close focus on the terrifying rapidity of Othello's disintegration and on Iago's ratcheting-up of that process. At Stratford in 1961, however, 'the actors were somehow at odds with the setting I had created: the magnificent Venice of Tiepolo and Veronese was meant to emphasize the magnificence of the character [of Othello] and of the poetry' (Zeffirelli 1986: 166). The splendour of the series of pictures that were the sets – the night-time reflections of dappled water shimmering on the pillars of Brabantio's palace; the reddish glow of the light at the midnight meeting of the Senate, the stage picture constantly changing with the comings and goings of messengers and soldiers; the magnificent sweep of steps for Othello's landing in Cyprus and the remarkable number of supers with gold and silver and crimson banners to welcome him; the armoury where the drinking scene took place with many dozens of assorted swords gleaming in racks on the wall; the great four-poster bed with its magnificent silk hangings for the final scene – fatally held up the action. 'The clumsiness of the scene changes is catastrophic' remarked the *Daily Express* (11 October 1961), and Philip Hope-Wallace was ominously reminded of 'opera and ballet at the Bolshoi' (*Guardian*, 11 October 1961). The name of Beerbohm Tree was invoked by many reviewers, and Edmund Gardner (in the *Stratford Herald*, 13 October 1961) pointed out the total dependence of the production's magnificent pictures on the proscenium arch as picture frame, a situation which, ironically, flew directly in the face of the modifications that Peter Hall had, just a few months earlier, made to the Stratford stage – a rake and a 3-metre projection into the auditorium (Beauman 1982: 239) – in order to wean audiences away from expecting a series of pictures. Like many other reviewers, Gardner thought the grandeur of the production had dwarfed the actors, 'leaving Shakespeare buried under a mound of outmoded conventions'.

Ian Bannen had a few articulate defenders among a general chorus of complaint at his supposedly misguided attempt to psychologise Iago, and there was admiration for the strikingly aquiline and tense grandeur that Gielgud brought to the title role and to the highly unusual idea of taking the royal lineage of Othello at least as seriously as his martial history. The consensus, however, was that Gielgud was miscast and when, not long afterwards, he saw Olivier's Othello, Gielgud came to regret his rejection of Zeffirelli's attempt to convince him that 'this man is very vain' (Potter 2002: 147). Peggy Ashcroft had found the 'detailed, naturalistic manner' of the rehearsal period 'one of the most exciting I remember, in that we were preoccupied with truth and reality' and thought that Gielgud was 'about to give one of the performances of his life' (Billington 1988: 192). But the move from rehearsal room to stage destroyed almost all they had created, for the attempt to impose on the fast-moving theatricality of Shakespeare's text, on the 'domestic tragedy' they had been exploring in rehearsal, the realistic pictorial grandeur of the opera house was, inevitably, doomed to failure, even if to a rather magnificent failure. 'In the circumstances', Peggy Ashcroft recalled, Gielgud 'had no choice but to succumb to rhetoric' (Billington 1988: 193), which is no doubt what Zeffirelli meant by 'he sailed through [. . .] his usual self'. The space between theatrical triumph and disaster seems, as so often, to have been rather narrower than might have been supposed from the production's reputation. Zeffirelli's conception of the role of Othello – 'the perfect embodiment of European culture' – and his belief that it needs to be seen against the visual splendour of the Venetian empire he serves as its greatest painters had depicted it, were, finally and splendidly, realised when, in 1985, he directed Plácido Domingo in Verdi's *Otello*, not on stage but on film and 'on the scale of a Hollywood epic', allowing his vision of the story to be realised without the time constraints of theatre (Zeffirelli 1986: 166, 333–4; it is interesting that, in his 2006 *Autobiografia*, all mention of the Stratford *Othello* is expunged).

In 1963, eighteen months before his last Shakespeare stage production in England, and a little before his open-air production of *Romeo and Juliet* was setting off on its tour of the Roman amphitheatres of Italy, Zeffirelli's first production of *Hamlet*, with Giorgio Albertazzi as the prince, was on the road in Italy, in eastern Europe, in Paris (where, as the *Romeo and Juliet* would do the following year, it won the Prix des Théâtres des Nations) and, for two weeks in the autumn of 1964, in London, as part of the world theatre season at the Old Vic. *The Times*, reporting on a performance in Rome, contrasted it with the *Othello* at Stratford, where 'the settings drowned the play' and recorded a single set with locations indicated by lighting changes, a stage projecting well into the auditorium, costumes that alluded both to the Renaissance and to the present day and a continuity of performance and theatrical self-consciousness that 'inevitably recalls Brechtian theatre' (3 February 1964). The total change of style from the Stratford *Othello* is an important reminder of the variousness of Zeffirelli's work and of the rapidity with which he could move from the grandeur of Verdi at Covent Garden or the Met to, for example, the first European production (and one of his greatest successes) of Albee's *Who's Afraid of Virginia Woolf?* in Paris.

He returned to *Hamlet* (the only Shakespeare play he ever directed that lacks an Italian setting) much later, in 1990, for his third and latest Shakespeare film, with Mel Gibson as Hamlet and Glenn Close as Gertrude. And, unsurprisingly, he followed (but went way beyond) Olivier, the Shakespearian idol of his youth, in making theirs an incestuous relationship, the Ghost's entry in the closet scene seemingly only just in time to prevent its sexual consummation. The opening sequence, in the vault of the Danish royal family, sets up a triangle of attraction and anxiety among Claudius (Alan Bates), Hamlet and Gertrude, using lines from the play's second scene (other parts of Claudius's opening speech are deployed in later scenes). Ennio Morricone's score moves into strains reminiscent of Wagner's *Tristan und Isolde* as Gertrude's grief overpowers her – Polonius (Ian Holm) has to support her after she has prostrated herself on the dead king's tomb – and Claudius looks on warily, trying to take the measure of his sullenly antagonistic nephew. Zeffirelli rearranges the text of *Hamlet* with a much freer hand than in his two earlier Shakespeare films and, like Olivier, omits Fortinbras and the political dimension that goes with him. Rosencranz and Guildenstern do appear, however, making valuable foils to the frenetic prince.

The star casting of the title role ensured the film a degree of commercial success as well as a guaranteed appeal to that young audience that seems to be Zeffirelli's target in so many of his films. With the constraints of a contractual limitation to two hours' running time (so that, as usual, almost two-thirds of the text was excised), it is hardly surprising that the film presents the play rather as melodrama than tragedy, with sex and violence its principal ingredients. But its 'return to the roots of Shakespeare's play – the revenge tragedy and *Hamlet* as thriller' (Pilkington 1994: 174) ensures the sort of vitality and energy that are rarely absent from Zeffirelli's work. The presence of experienced Shakespearian actors (Bates, Holm, Helena Bonham-Carter as Ophelia and Paul Scofield as the Ghost) means that the lines are spoken with a clarity sometimes lacking in the two earlier films, and Bonham-Carter's Ophelia in particular, intelligent and feisty, ensures that Gibson's Hamlet does not have everything his own way. By Zeffirelli's own account, Gibson tried, by underhand strategies that would have done credit to Polonius and his 'assays of bias', to take over the direction of the film for himself. Nevertheless, in Gibson he admits that he had found an actor 'perfect for the part' as he had conceived it (Zeffirelli 2006: 391).

Zeffirelli's last theatre production of Shakespeare came, appropriately enough, at the invitation of Laurence Olivier whom he hoped (in vain as it turned out, for Olivier was too busy with administration) would play Don Pedro in the 1965 *Much Ado about Nothing* at the Old Vic, the home of the NT in its early days. (Zeffirelli finally came to direct Olivier in *Saturday, Sunday, Monday* at the NT in 1973.) The company that Olivier had gathered to create the NT included, in addition to a core of well-established actors, many at the beginning of what would prove to be distinguished careers, so that, among the Watchmen, Zeffirelli had Michael York and Ronald Pickup, while the comparatively minor roles of Claudio, Don John and Conrad were played, respectively, by Ian McKellen, Derek Jacobi and Edward Petherbridge. Maggie Smith and Robert Stephens played Beatrice and Benedick, with Albert

Finney as Don Pedro and Frank Finlay as Dogberry. 'I told everyone they were going to have fun', Zeffirelli later reported of his first meeting with this 'wonderful, vivacious team'; the play would be presented in 'Sicilian comic style' and the cast 'let rip as if relieved to be enjoying themselves [. . .] in the only light relief in the National's heavy season' (Zeffirelli 1986: 202). His Benedick felt (retrospectively anyway) rather differently: 'Despite appearances to the contrary, we all hated doing it [. . .] It may have looked all right but it was a misery to do because it was so uncomfortable', with actors 'dressed like Sicilian toy soldiers' and 'pushed around like clockwork oranges'. He adds, however, that while (as Assistant Director) he was rehearsing later cast changes, he 'saw it from the front and wept, it all looked so beautiful' (Stephens 1995: 82–3).

The production is an interesting example of Zeffirelli's working methods. He arrived – for a scheduled six-week rehearsal period of which he used only half, no doubt because he was, at the same time, rehearsing Callas back into *Tosca* in Paris and beginning plans with Anna Magnani in Rome for *La Lupa* (Stephens 1995: 82; Zeffirelli 1986: 198–202) – with a fully fledged vision of exactly what he wanted to do with the play. With a bold literalness apparently hitherto untried, he had taken the play's fictive location in Messina at face value and set it in a small Sicilian town at the end of the nineteenth century – a choice of period, incidentally, since repeated in some dozens of productions of a whole range of Shakespeare's comedies and tragedies. The programme divides the characters into the Army, the Town, the Law, the Church, the Town Band and the Inanimates – the last because (perhaps recalling the problems of his last Shakespeare in England) Zeffirelli more or less dispensed with a set and used instead a series of differently coloured lighting states, playing onto hessian flats, to indicate changes of location, with the proscenium arch lit throughout by hundreds of fairy lights establishing the carnival atmosphere, and the stage furnished with a changing series of statues, presented by actors (the 'Inanimates'), whose freezes were occasionally interrupted by reactions, shared with the audience, to the conversations they were overhearing.

'The moment the play is thus localized', wrote Penelope Gilliatt, 'and all its characters seen as the citizens of a single small town [. . .] it meshes as precisely as a watch'; the greatest beneficiary of such treatment, she thought, was the awkward Hero/Claudio story, which became unprecedentedly believable 'in a Sicily where the same ferocious code of chastity endures to this day' (*Observer*, 21 February 1965). Her enthusiasm was not universally shared. 'On the first night half the audience booed and half cheered', recalled Robert Stephens (1995: 83), and the critics responded similarly, though hardly in so even a division. Among the negative voices, Bernard Levin thought it 'the most excruciating evening this side of hell' (*Daily Express*, 18 February

1965), and Robert Speaight 'the most unintelligent production of Shakespeare' he had ever seen (Speaight 1965: 313). For most reviewers, however, it was impossible to resist the production's energy, even John Trewin, usually so cautiously conservative, admitting that it was 'an exhilarating theatrical exercise' created with 'a blaze of technique' and 'a sense of sheer, uncomplicated fun' (*Birmingham Post*, 27 February 1965). His comparison of its effect with that created by Komisarjevsky's *The Merchant of Venice* at Stratford thirty years earlier – 'the decades between them shrink to nothing' – is not irrelevant to the broader concerns of this book in its linking of the exuberance and panache, the irreverent comedic freedom and energy with which these two overseas directors brought new, and controversial, theatrical life to two of Shakespeare's best-known comedies. The exhilarating freedom of invention that Zeffirelli released in his actors (and which, as the production developed, they exploited with increasing – and some thought excessive – enthusiasm), created a rapport with audiences that gave the production immense vitality in performance. Whatever the anticipatory furore caused by the commissioning of Robert Graves to create a performance script that provided paraphrases for dozens of difficult passages (by no means all of them finally used in performance), or the outrage of many reviewers when Dogberry and his troop of *carabinieri* watchmen broke into a chorus from *La Traviata*, the Old Vic had another Shakespearian box-office hit on its hands, the first since the same director's *Romeo and Juliet* there five years earlier.

And in all of the fun – the cockaded pillbox helmets of the officers, the swaggering, cigar-smoking ham Spaniard of Finney's Don Pedro, the white-suited wide-boy (in his sunglasses) of Stephens's Benedick, the jolly oom-pah-pah town band that began and ended the evening, the small-time Napoleonic self-importance of Finlay's Dogberry and the struggles with his (lady's) bicycle of Michael Rothwell's Verges – for all the 'marvellously prodigal rain of invention', as Penelope Gilliatt called it, some, at least, of the essentials of the play remained intact. The overhearing statues were an astute theatrical realisation of the plot's dependence upon hearsay; all the earlier exuberance, including the comic procession to the altar, made the accusations of the church scene, 'take on all the more unpleasantness in contrast', while Antonio and Leonato, who had earlier seemed just 'silly old pantaloons', suddenly acquired a 'most moving [. . .] pathetic dignity' in their confrontation with Claudio and Don Pedro (B.A. Young, *Financial Times*, 18 February 1965); Beatrice's 'Kill Claudio' had 'a savage force that made laughter unthinkable', and Benedick's delivery of his challenge to Claudio 'a quiet and striking dignity' (*Daily Telegraph*, 18 February 1965; *Spectator*, 26 February 1965). At the production's end, after all the excited bustle of the wedding photographer's magnesium flashes, the dancing of 'the lancers', the protracted final exit, with Beatrice and Benedick's farewell waves to Don Pedro as the fairy lights faded, the Prince was left alone, looking after them, puffing at his cigar before he mimed blowing out the last remaining spotlight that illuminated him and the stage was left in darkness. 'The moment swivels the mood of the play', wrote Penelope Gilliatt, 'a pause full of death set into a gala evening, and it demonstrates the balance of feeling that is the commanding gift of this production' (*Observer*, 21 February 1965). It also, of course, in that final isolation of Don Pedro, anticipated the way that many future productions of the play would end.

Zeffirelli's *Much Ado about Nothing* elicited comparisons with *The Prisoner of Zenda*, *The Chocolate Soldier* and *The White Horse Inn*; and, for B.A. Young, Finney's Don Pedro was 'the direct descendant of the Duke of Plaza Toro' (*Financial Times*, 18 February 1965). Zeffirelli's last stage production of Shakespeare owed much to the conventions of operetta, just as his *Othello* derived from the world of grand opera, and his *Romeo and Juliet* from the opera *verismo* tradition. 'Franco didn't help the actors at all', wrote Robert Stephens; 'he just produced the dressing around it and you had to find a way to fit into it [. . .] He directed the play like an opera' (Stephens 1995: 83).

For, in the final analysis, Zeffirelli's Shakespeare productions are the work of an opera director and, more important, an opera designer. Four-fifths of his work has been in opera, with some scores – *Falstaff, Rigoletto, Don Giovanni, Tosca, Otello* – revisited time and again in opera houses around the world. The composer whose career touched his at various points, Ned Rorem, describes Zeffirelli's productions as displaying 'a sort of sumptuous respect for the tried and true, a vertiginously accurate juggling with expensive toys' (Rorem 2001: 251). Zeffirelli himself puts it very simply: 'You have to offer some kind of total experience to the audience, not only through the ears but also through the eyes [. . .] Sometimes an actor cannot hold the stage alone; he needs [. . .] a beauty around him. It becomes a kind of additional character' (Zeffirelli 1990: 269). The actor (and writer on Shakespearian theatre) Oliver Ford Davies, who was in Zeffirelli's 2003 London production of Pirandello's *Absolutely! (perhaps)*, writes of Zeffirelli's greatest strengths being 'design, bold statement, and theatrical energy' and of the acuteness of his sense 'of what would and wouldn't work in the theatre'. For the Pirandello production he had (as usual) 'worked out a design way ahead which was very beautiful and very meticulous'. He 'blocked the play, apparently off the top of his head, rapidly and dictatorially [. . .] to get to the stage of running whole acts within a week or ten days. Then when he saw them as a whole he might make major changes'. In Davies's opinion – and this rings true of the Shakespeare work too – 'the sanctity of the text was not uppermost in his mind', and he even got his translator/adapter of the Pirandello to write in new jokes during the rehearsal process. Even at the age of eighty he was still demonstrating to actors and giving inflections that 'would work in Italian but not always in English'. Davies felt that 'he liked actors, became excited by their imagination and urged them to go further' – a belief that accords with Zeffirelli's own expressed desire that his work 'should give actors a vehicle in which they can really act, not just recite' (Zeffirelli 1986: 292). 'Our cast started somewhat in awe of him', Davies concludes, 'after two weeks were fed up with his tyrannies (and late arrivals!), and ended up feeling great love for him – he's a great charmer and was obviously so happy to be working in London again' (personal letter to R.S., 18 January 2007, quoted with the writer's permission).

During the rehearsal period for that Pirandello production Zeffirelli gave an interview to the *Observer* (4 May 2003). 'For me, opera is dreams', he there asserts, 'and when I dream I create my own planet'. And that creation has always been abundant, lavish, detailed: 'Yes, it is true, I embellish . . . proliferate. They must always tell me "Stop, is enough, is excessive." But I prefer to go berserk. I will never stop', and he recalls the way he filled the Old Vic with the smell of a Neapolitan ragout simmering on the stove to help create the authentic atmosphere of the family Sunday lunch in his 1973 NT production of De Filippo's *Saturday, Sunday, Monday*. Operatic extravagance, and proliferation and realism of detail (pee stains on the walls, the smell of stew around the auditorium), combined with flamboyant and lavish theatricality and intense emotional energy are characteristics of all Zeffirelli's work, his Shakespeare included, and they are still there in the visually magnificent *Aida* – 'the *Aida* of *Aida*s' as he called it himself (*Guardian* 25 November 2006) – that, in his eighty-third year, he created to open La Scala's 2006–7 season. And with these characteristics goes an unashamed desire for accessibility and popular appeal. His first attempts to film opera were based on the desire to 'make it a living, popular medium again', and a cinema full of people weeping at his film of *La Traviata*, as they had at his film of *Romeo and Juliet*, delights him. He finds it an 'irritating irony' that many who espouse populist views in politics seem to want art to be 'culturally élitist', and he welcomes the charge of populism against his own work and declares a passionate belief in 'a broad culture made accessible to as many as possible' and a desire 'to make the thing really happen for the audience of today – to make the audience understand that the classics are living flesh' (Zeffirelli 1986: 318, 326, 341; 1990: 252).

Zeffirelli's work on Shakespeare may be only a small part of a hugely productive career, but it is a fascinating phenomenon nevertheless, not just because of the immense popular success of most of it, or because one of his productions marked a change in the way Shakespeare's plays would be directed over the next decades, or because his work challenged a language-based British theatrical establishment with the visual traditions of the European opera house, insisting on the physicality of performance and the freedom of actorly invention, or because his films brought an international audience to Shakespeare in previously undreamed-of numbers. His productions of Shakespeare are important above all because they focused the question, sharply, inescapably, for the second half of the twentieth century in which they were created but more generally too, of whether Shakespeare's plays are to be the province of an increasingly élite audience or whether a means of directing them may be found that maintains and reasserts their links with the popular culture of which they were once part, and, if it may, how we are to assess the legitimacy of the directorial methods used to achieve that.

Chronology

Theatre

As Design Assistant

1948 *As You Like It*, directed by Luchino Visconti, designed by Salvador Dali, Teatro Eliseo, Rome

As Designer

1949 *Troilus and Cressida*, directed by Luchino Visconti, Boboli Gardens, Florence

As Director and Designer

1960 *Romeo and Juliet*, Old Vic, London (and international tour)
1961 *Othello*, Royal Shakespeare Theatre, Stratford-upon-Avon
1963 *Hamlet*, Teatro Elisio, Rome (and national and international tour, including Old Vic, London)
1964 *Romeo and Juliet*, Teatro Romano, Verona (and national and international tour)
1965 *Much Ado about Nothing*, National Theatre (at the Old Vic), London (and national tour)

Cinema

1966 *The Taming of the Shrew*, USA/Italy
1968 *Romeo and Juliet*, UK/Italy
1990 *Hamlet*, UK

Bibliography

Beauman, Sally (1982) *The Royal Shakespeare Company: A History of Ten Decades*, Oxford: Oxford University Press.

Billington, Michael (1988) *Peggy Ashcroft*, London: John Murray.

Brown, John Russell (1962) 'S. Franco Zeffirelli's *Romeo and Juliet*', *Shakespeare Survey*, 15: 147–55.

Cartmell, Deborah (2000) 'Franco Zeffirelli and Shakespeare', in Russell Jackson (ed.), *The Cambridge Companion to Shakespeare on Film*, Cambridge: Cambridge University Press, pp. 212–21.

David, Richard (1978) *Shakespeare in the Theatre*, Cambridge: Cambridge University Press.

Dench, Judi (1974) 'Judi Dench Talks to Gareth Lloyd Evans', *Shakespeare Survey*, 27: 137–42

—— (1996) 'A Career in Shakespeare', in Jonathan Bate and Russell Jackson (eds), *Shakespeare: An Illustrated Stage History*, Oxford: Oxford University Press, pp. 197–210.

Donaldson, Peter S. (1990) ' "Let Lips Do What Hands Do": Male Bonding, Eros, and Loss in Zeffirelli's *Romeo and Juliet*', *Shakespearian Films/Shakespearian Directors*, Boston, Mass.: Unwin Hyman, pp. 145–88.

Gielgud, John (2004) *Gielgud's Letters*, ed. Richard Mangan, London: Weidenfeld & Nicolson.

Holderness, Graham (1989) *The Taming of the Shrew*, Shakespeare in Performance, Manchester: Manchester University Press.

Jackson, Russell (2003) *Romeo and Juliet*, Shakespeare at Stratford, London: Arden/Thomson.

—— (2007) 'Shakespeare's "Dream of Italy" and the Generation Gap: Franco Zeffirelli's *Romeo and Juliet*', *Shakespeare Films in the Making: Vision, Production, and Reception*, Cambridge: Cambridge University Press, pp. 191–221.

Kennedy, Dennis (1993) *Looking at Shakespeare: A Visual History of Twentieth-Century Performance*, Cambridge: Cambridge University Press.

Levenson, Jill L. (1987) *Romeo and Juliet*, Shakespeare in Performance, Manchester: Manchester University Press.

Pilkington, Ace G. (1994) 'Zeffirelli's Shakespeare', in Anthony Davies and Stanley Wells (eds), *Shakespeare and the Moving Image*, Cambridge: Cambridge University Press, pp. 163–79.

Potter, Lois (2002) *Othello*, Shakespeare in Performance, Manchester: Manchester University Press.

Praz, Mario (1950) 'Italy' in 'International News', *Shakespeare Survey*, 3: 117–18.

Rorem, Ned (2001) *A Ned Rorem Reader*, ed. J.D. McClatchey, New Haven, Conn.: Yale University Press.

Smallwood, Robert (1996) 'Directors' Shakespeare', in Jonathan Bate and Russell Jackson (eds), *Shakespeare: An Illustrated Stage History*, Oxford: Oxford University Press, pp. 176–96.

Speaight, Robert (1965) 'Shakespeare in Britain', *Shakespeare Quarterly*, 16: 313–24.

Stephens, Robert with Michael Coveney (1995) *Knight Errant: Memoirs of a Vagabond Actor*, London: Hodder & Stoughton.

Tatspaugh, Patricia (2000) 'The Tragedies of Love on Film', in Russell Jackson (ed.), *The Cambridge Companion to Shakespeare on Film*, Cambridge: Cambridge University Press, pp. 135–59.

Trewin, J.C. (1964) *Shakespeare on the English Stage, 1900–1964*, London: Barrie and Rockliffe.

Zeffirelli, Franco (1986) *Zeffirelli: The Autobiography of Franco Zeffirelli*, London: Weidenfeld & Nicolson.

—— (1990) 'Filming Shakespeare', in Glen Loney (ed.), *Staging Shakespeare: Seminars on Production*, London and New York: Garland, pp. 239–70

—— (2006) *Autobiografia*, Milan: Mondadori.

About the author

Tom Matheson (1936–2006) spent almost all his professional life at the Shakespeare Institute of the University of Birmingham, where he was Fellow, Deputy Director, Acting Director and, after retirement, Honorary Fellow. His edition of Robert Greene's coney-catching pamphlets established him as a formidable bibliographical and literary scholar, but his range included some of the briefest, yet most elegantly turned, entries in the *Oxford Companion to Shakespeare* and theatre reviews for the *TLS* that reveal him as an astutely sensitive observer of theatre performance who wrote about it with vividness and wit. These qualities are clearly apparent in the last essay he completed for publication, on productions of *Julius Caesar* at Stratford in the second half of the twentieth century (in *'Julius Caesar': New Critical Essays*, [ed.] Horst Zander: 2005). Although his teaching was mainly of English literature, Shakespeare and his contemporaries above all, his reading was European in its range and remarkable in its breadth; in Italy in particular, through his marriage to Angela Cutrale, he had a profound and lifelong interest. He was fluent in the language and took a keen interest in its politics, its culture (including its football), and especially in its theatre – including, of course, the work of Franco Zeffirelli.

INDEX OF DIRECTORS

INDEX OF PLAYS

GENERAL INDEX

Related titles from Routledge

Inside the Royal Shakespeare Company

Colin Chambers

'This book promises to revolutionise our understanding of what the RSC is. Everyone interested in Shakespeare in performance will need to read it.'– *Peter Holland, McMeel Chair in Shakespeare Studies, University of Notre Dame*

This is the inside story of the Royal Shakespeare Company – a running historical critique of a major national institution and its location within British culture, as related by a writer uniquely placed to tell the tale. It describes what happened to a radical theatrical vision and what happened when that vision turned sour.

Spanning four decades and four artistic directors, *Inside the Royal Shakespeare Company* is a multi-layered chronicle that traces the company's history, offers investigation into its working methods, its repertoire, its people and its politics, and considers what the future holds for this bastion of high culture now in crisis. In a Britain that is increasingly appearing to be incapable of sustaining any artistic vision, this book offers a crucial analysis of the fight for creative expression. It's a must-read for anyone who wishes to explore behind the scenes and consider the changing role of theatre in cultural life today.

ISBN 10: 0–415–21202–2 (hbk)
ISBN 10: 0–203–48868–7 (ebk)

ISBN13: 978–0–415–21202–1 (hbk)
ISBN 13: 978–0–415–48868–3 (ebk)

Related titles from Routledge

Makers of Modern Theatre

Robert Leach

Who were the giants of the twentieth-century stage, and exactly how did they influence modern theatre?

The key theatre-makers who shaped the drama of the last century are Konstantin Stanislavsky, Vsevolod Meyerhold, Bertolt Brecht and Antonin Artaud. Robert Leach's Makers of Modern Theatre is the first detailed introduction to the work of these practitioners. In it, Leach focuses on the major issues which relate to their dominance of theatre history:

- What was significant in their life and times?
- What is their main legacy?
- What were their dramatic philosophies and practices?
- How have their ideas been adapted since their deaths?
- What are the current critical perspectives on their work?

Never before has so much essential information on the making of twentieth-century theatre been compiled in one brilliantly concise, beautifully illustrated book. This is a genuinely insightful volume by one of the foremost theatre historians of our age.

ISBN 10: 0–415–31240–X (hbk)
ISBN 10: 0–415–31241–8 (pbk)
ISBN 10: 0–203–48786–9 (ebk)

ISBN 13: 978–0–415–31240–0 (hbk)
ISBN 13: 978–0–415–31241–7 (pbk)
ISBN 13: 978–0–203–48786–0 (ebk)

Available at all good bookshops
For ordering and further information please visit:

www.routledge.com

Related titles from Routledge

Re: Direction:
A Theoretical and Practical Guide
(Worlds of Performance)

Edited by Rebecca Schneider and Gabriel Cody

Re: Direction is an extraordinary resource for practitioners and students on directing. It provides a collection of ground-breaking interviews, primary sources and essays on 20th century directing theories and practices around the world.

Helpfully organized into four key areas of the subject, the book explores:

- theories of directing
- the boundaries of the director's role
- the limits of categorization
- the history of the theatre and performance art.

Exceptionally useful and thought-provoking introductory essays by editors Schneider and Cody guide you through the wealth of materials included here. Re: Direction is the kind of book anyone interested in theatre history should own, and is an indispensable toolkit for a lifetime of study.

ISBN 10: 0–415–21390–8 (hbk)
ISBN 10: 0–415–21391–6 (pbk)

ISBN 13: 978–0–415–21390–5 (hbk)
ISBN 13: 978–0–415–21391–2 (pbk)

Available at all good bookshops
For ordering and further information please visit:
www.routledge.com